THE BIG BOOK OF ST. LOUIS NOS

By

BILL NUNES

ISBN 9780978799496

WITH LONNIE TETTATON AND DAVE LOSSOS

Thanks to Bill Jacobus whose amazing energy enables me to get my books delivered to various stores and my distributors. A special thanks to my proofreaders, Dave Lossos and Arleigh Jones of Tuscola, Illinois, and to my wife Lorna for hours and hours of working on pictures. I am also grateful to the patient staff of the Glen Carbon library and to Adele Heagney for her meticulous research at the St. Louis Public Library. Kudos to everyone who sent me material for this book.

An index to this book is available from Dave Lossos. Go online at
http://genealogyinstlouis.accessgenealogy.com/SLN.htm

Printed in the USA

Other books by Bill Nunes still available include:

Sixty-Two Nationally Prominent East St. Louisans – 2001 - Seventy-two softbound pages, 45 pictures; also contains the stories of how East St. Louis was founded and the 1896 cyclone. Originally $9.95, sale price $5 plus $2.00 shipping

Illinois in World War II - 2006 - 328 softbound pages, 700 pictures; contains a complete history of World War II, the significant role of Illinois in the war and interviews with Illinois veterans. $19.95 cover price, on sale for $5.00 plus $3.00 shipping

Incredible Illinois: A Year-By-Year Illustrated History – 2004 – 288 softbound pages; stories about famous people, fires, floods, tornadoes, history, geography, geology, politics, sports, KKK, towns, counties, gangsters, coal mines, oil wells, notable women, significant events and much more; $20.95; sale price $5 plus $3.00 shipping

Illinois Trivia Illustrated – 2005 – 288 softbound pages; 50 topics, nearly 4,000 questions and answers covering a wide range of subjects; the only Illinois trivia book still in print; $12.95; sale price $5 plus $3.00 shipping

Illinois in the Roaring Twenties – 2003 – 288 softbound pages, 650 pictures; no state roared more loudly than Illinois during the Roaring Twenties; contains a full-length illustrated novel: *Mike Kriegan and the Capone Wars*, the story of a young man from southern Illinois who becomes a member of The Untouchables; set in Chicago and southern Illinois. $17.95; sale price $5 plus $3.00 shipping

Bill Nunes 3029 Mark Trail, Glen Carbon, IL 62034 bnunesbook@aol.com (618) 288-5185

TABLE OF CONTENTS

Introduction P 1
Lonnie Tettaton Biography P 2
Great Crab Apple War of 1956 P 6
10 Cent Radio Treasures – P 8
Old 78 RPM Records P 10
Reading the Sunday Funnies P 13
Cereal Box Prizes P 15
Big Little Books P 15
The 1950s by Johnny Rabbitt P 16
Songs of the 1950s and 1960s P 17
TV Westerns P 21
Highlands and Chain of Rocks P 22
Barber Shop Days P 29
Route 66 P 30
Dime Store Memories P 36
A St. Louis Christmas P 37
Childhood Memories: Boy-Girl P 40
Mom's Home Remedies P 44
Tribute to the SS Admiral P 48
1960s St. Louis Restaurants P 50
Webster Groves v. Kirkwood P 53
Playing Corkball & Indian Ball P 54
1896 St. Louis Cyclone P 55
Jefferson Barracks P 56
St. Louis Trivia P 57
St. Louis and World War II P 62
1904 St. Louis World's Fair P 66
Kerry Patch Gangsters P 69
Pillow and Cuckoo Gangs P 71
Egan Rats and Dinty Colbeck P 72
Kefauver Committee P 76
"Buster" Wortman Era P 77
Jimmy Michaels and Tony G P 82
John Vitale & David Leisure P 83-84
Strippers and Gun Molls P 85
Great Southwest Bank Robbery P 86
Two Hanged Men P 87
Bobby Greenlease Kidnapping P 90
Harold Gibbons P 91
Brasher's Hoodlum Relatives P 92
Getting Away With Murder P 94
Dogtown/Cheltenham P 96
The Irish in St. Louis P 97
The Hill in St. Louis P 98
St. Louis German Heritage P 100
St. Louis Jewish Community P 102
Gaslight Square P 103
Old North St. Louis/Yeatman P 104
Lafayette Square/Benton Park P 104
Marquette and Cherokee P 105
Kingsbury/Central West End P 105
Compton and Southwest P 106
Shaw and Fairground P 107
Hyde Park and Carondelet P 107
Fairgrounds/Mid-Downtown P 107
Carondelet P 108/Oak Hill 109
Morganford and Baden P 109
Riverview P 109 Arlington P 110
Walnut Park/Cabanne/Oakland P 111
University City/Soulard/ Clifton 112
Webster Groves/Kirkwood P 114
Maplewood/Manchester P 115
Ferguson P115 / Jennings P 117
Normandy/Spanish Lake P 117
Clayton and Ladue P 118
Frontenac and Creve Coeur P 118
Rock Hill and Florissant P 119
Arnold and St. Charles P 120
Veiled Prophet Parade P 122
Hopscotch and jacks P 123
Walter Scott murder P 127
How St. Louis Got its Zoo P 130
Charles Lindbergh P 131
Johnny Londoff Chevrolet P 132
Dave Sinclair Ford P 133
Elijah Lovejoy Murder P 133
The Dred Scott Case P 135
William Tecumseh Sherman P 136
The Metro East P 137
U.S. Grant P 140
The Eads Bridge P 142
The 1896 Cyclone P 144
The Ouija Board P 145
Blondie and Dagwood P 147
More St. Louis and WW 2 P 148
Spooky St. Louis P 151
The Gateway Arch P 155
Subterranean St. Louis P 157
Ralston Purina Co. P 159
McDonnell Douglas Co. P 160
Mayor A.J. Cervantes P 161
Monsanto Chemical Co. P 162
Emerson Electric Co. P 163
St. Louis Wrestling P 164
St. Louis Hawks P 165
Football Cardinals P 167
St. Louis Blues P 169
St. Louis Cardinals P 171
Sportsman's Park P 181
Bowling Hall of Fame P 182
St. Louis Rams P 183
Casa Loma Ballroom P 186
Missouri Coal Mines P 187
Missouri Ozarks Folklore P 190
The Great 1925 Tornado P 191
Dave Lossos St. Louis Memories 192
St. Louis Muny Opera P 195
Colorful Indian Legends p 197
Indian Curse on Kaskaskia P 199
Lost Yokum Silver Mine P 201
Tower Rock Nat. Monument P 202
Missouri Geography/Geology P 202
Missouri's Trail of Tears P 206
African-American Heritage P 207
Missouri Highway Patrol P 209
Amazing Missouri Trivia P 211
St. Louis Taste Buds P 213
Springfield, Missouri P 214
Joplin, Missouri P 215
Kansas City, Missouri P 215
Famous Firsts P 216
Missouri Critters P 217
Route 66/Missouri Roads P 219
Killer Tom Horn P 221
Wild Bill Hickok P 222
Belle Starr P 222
William Quantrill P 222
Bloody Bill Anderson P 223
The James Brothers P 224
Wyatt Earp P 225
1811 New Madrid Quake P 227
Actors and Actresses P 229
Town and Place Names P 231
Branson, Missouri P 236
Mizzou Football/Basketball P 238
Kansas City Chiefs/Royals P 241
Famous Missourians P 243
Missouri History 1600-1821 P 246
Missouri History 1821-1850 P 251
Mormons in Missouri P 255
Missouri History 1850-1860 P 257
Missouri Railroads P 258
The Pony Express P 259
Missouri and the Civil War P 260
Missouri History 1860-1904 P 266
Missouri History 1904-1940 P 270
Kansas City WWI Museum P 274
Kansas City Massacre P 275
The Doolittle Raid P 275
Maxwell Taylor P 276
Omar Bradley P 276
Soldier in Grease Paint P 277
Missouri History 1941-1960 P 278
Missouri History 1961-2008 P 279
You're A Missourian If . . . P 284
Missouri Tourism P 285
Missouri Artists and Writers P 289
Missouri Women P 290
Florence "Candy" Tockstein P 292
Missourian Invents Kewpie Doll 293
James Earl Ray P 293
Missouri Hog Killing Time P 294
Moo, Moo; Oink, Oink: Farming 295
Lewis and Clark Expedition P 302
Greatest Publishing Mistake P 303
Missouri River Lore P 303
The Big Muddy P 308
Rivers and Steamboats P 310
Great Flood of 1993 P 311
Burma Shave Signs P 312
Missouri Trolleys P 312
Making Railroad Ties P 313
Railroad Trivia P 313
Old Missouri Superstitions P 317
Busch Beer Barons P 318
Billie Boykins Affair P 322
Pioneer Remedies/Home Cures P 323
It Looked Like an Oldsmobile
Sucking a Lemon P 323
President Harry Truman – 324
Bibliography/Sources P 326

ST. LOUIS & MISSOURI NOSTALGIA

© 2009 by BILL NUNES

With Lonnie Tettaton and Dave Lossos

INTRODUCTION

WARNING! We traffic in nostalgia, preying on those who ruminate on the past and treasure dusty memories from bygone days. Our books accost people as they stroll merrily down memory lane. The word nostalgia comes from the Greek and it literally means "pain from an old wound." But this kind of hurt is more like a twinge in your heart that wants to take you back to a wonderful era where you ache to go again – those idyllic days of yesteryear.

For the past fifteen years or so, Lonnie, Dave and I have taken advantage of those poor souls susceptible to that longing for an earlier time where neighborhoods were safe, when sodas and candy bars were a nickel instead of a dollar, when kids played sandlot ball (and it wasn't necessary for adults to organize games for them), when there was no need for rating the movies, when the only serial killer you could name was Jack the Ripper, when youngsters used their imaginations, when people didn't bother to lock their doors, and when you never heard children utter those repulsive words - "**I'm bored**."

Betsy Bruce of Fox News interviewing author Bill Nunes

Through narrative and visualization we plan to give readers a personally guided reverie through those long-vanished days which, to some, may seem as remote as ancient Egypt, but which are, in reality, only yesterday.

How in the world can an Illinois native have the audacity to write a nostalgia/history/trivia book about St. Louis, Missouri? Well . . . there are several explanations. First, I'm crazy. Second, I kept waiting for someone else to do it, but it never happened. (Actually, that's a lie. I was hoping no one else would do it before I had a chance.) Third, I'm qualified to do this kind of a book, having published twelve such books about Illinois since 1995. Fourth, I own property in Missouri. Fifth, I have a bit of Missouri DNA - Missouri is my adopted state. I have *de facto* dual citizenship. Finally, I've teamed with Lonnie and Dave who have done numerous St. Louis memory books.

St. Louis Steak N Shake on Rock Road in 1957 (Lonnie Tettaton)

My connections to Missouri are varied. I was born and reared (my mom said you raise corn and rear children) in **East St. Louis**, a sister city to St. Louis. My grandmother, Beulah Stagner, was born in **Cape Girardeau**. My father was born in **St. Louis**. My wife's father was born in **Wesco**. Her mother was born in **Sullivan**. My wife and I had numerous aunts, uncles and cousins who lived in St. Louis. As a kid, my mother took me shopping in St. Louis several times a year, especially at Christmas time to see the Famous & Barr window displays. I remember going to Cardinal baseball games, wrestling at Kiel Auditorium, walkathons on South Broadway, the Zoo, and the Forest Park Highlands. The best carnival ride in history was the Flying Turns at the Highlands. It actually simulated a ride on a bobsled with thrilling twists and scary banked turns.

Every Fourth of July we had family get-togethers at the Chain of Rocks Park. My boyhood chums and I were in attendance at Kiel in the spring of 1958 when Bob Pettit scored 50 points against the mighty Boston Celtics and the St. Louis Hawks became World Champions.

When I was a teenager, my mother worked for **Curlee Clothing** in downtown St. Louis. My first suit, for high school graduation, was a black wool suit from Curlee. I remember riding the electric streetcar to Hodiamont to visit relatives. My sister's first job when she graduated from high school (at age 16) was at the **Bank of St. Louis** on Washington Avenue.

My first real job, after I graduated from East Side High in 1957, was at **Midwest Pipe** on South Second, between **Nooter Corporation** and **Monsanto**. I wonder whatever happened to Marge Nickerson (copy room), Nick Fancuff (metallurgy), Russ Giese, E. Frank Parks and old man A.G. Stoughton. When I married in 1960, I worked for the **Emerson Electric Company** in St. Louis. I attended Washington Park Church of God and we were in a basketball league and played our games in the gym at **First Church of God at Riverview and Broadway**. My first date with my future wife was to see the Ice Capades at the **Arena**. After that our favorite place to go on dates was to the Fabulous Fox Theater with Stan Kann at the Wurlitzer Organ. Don't tell me I'm not a Missourian!

I married Lorna Sanders of **Collinsville** and our wedding and reception were at First Church of God in north St. Louis. We had to get our marriage license from St. Louis City Hall and my wife fainted when they drew blood from her for the mandatory venereal disease test.

In 1962, I worked part-time as a checker at a Kroger Store in north St. Louis that gave out Top Value stamps. The next year, I was "best man" at Ken Hoelker's wedding in north St. Louis County at **St. Pius X Church**. Ken was a CBC graduate who went on to have a fine career with the Missouri Highway Patrol.

When I became a teacher, my first job in social studies (1963) was at **Bayless High School** in South St. Louis. August Ernst was the principal. I've got Bronco blood in me.

When the new I - 270 Chain of Rocks Bridge opened up, I took my family to First Church of God at Riverview and Broadway three times a week from 1966 to 1982. I taught Sunday school and was Youth Minister there for a couple of years. I drove the church bus and took the kids to conventions in **Kansas City**, Blues hockey games and float trips on the Black River. Don't tell me I'm not a Missourian!

When the football Cardinals drafted **Neil Lomax**, I bought season tickets and cheered myself hoarse for the Big Red. Our group of friends would go to Sunday school, then eat brunch at Stouffer's Riverfront Inn (revolving) Restaurant, and then walk over to Busch Stadium for the game.

About eight years ago, I sold my 1965 red Mustang convertible and 1967 black Cougar. My wife and I used the money to buy a timeshare at Stonebridge in **Branson**. Nearly every Saturday my wife and I eat breakfast with our St. Louis friends at Golden Corral in **St. Charles,** off Zumbehl Road.

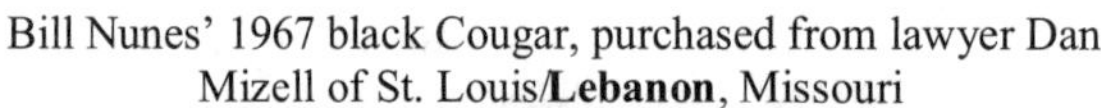

Bill Nunes' 1967 black Cougar, purchased from lawyer Dan Mizell of St. Louis/**Lebanon**, Missouri

Don't tell me I'm not a Missourian!

Where was your St. Louis neighborhood when you grew up? Was it Florissant, Ferguson, Soulard, Dogtown, Webster Groves, Kirkwood, Normandy, Wellston, Crestwood, Clayton, or any other of those great neighborhoods? I may have grown up in East St. Louis, but St. Louis and its environs was my second home. In this book, Lonnie and I have tried to describe the middle-class, blue collar, doings of ourselves and our families and friends. We want to take readers on a journey back in time and help them reconnect with the past and see what it was like growing up in the heartland of America in the fabulous Forties and Fifties. We hope these pages will serve as a mirror that reflects the ordinary lives of most of our readers. We consider ourselves fortunate having made the perilous quest from boyhood to adulthood when growing up might have had its hardships, but out of that crucible came valuable lessons and rock-solid Midwest values, as well as lives that were thankful for the guidance from our parents and the companionship and unconditional love of brothers and sisters.

Lonnie Tettaton (2nd from right) with polo team mates

We believe it's important to ponder the past, because that's where our roots are, and reflecting on the things that shaped our character helps give meaning to life in a larger sense. Your childhood best friend, parents and siblings, schoolyard chums, acquaintances from school activities, your church congregation, social clubs, your neighborhood and the city itself; all combine to give connection to every decade of your life. If you're like us, the St. Louis metro area is ingrained in your soul.

This is our love letter to the city of St. Louis. We were entranced by its sights and sounds, its smells, its parks, its buildings and, most of all, its wonderfully diverse people. This is a city like no other that gives us our unique sense of identity.

Permission is granted to use any of the trivia questions in this book, but please don't bet money on their veracity because they were obtained from a single source with no cross-referencing. Sorry, we can't assume liability for misspelled names, typos, omissions, or factual errors. Some copyrighted logos are used in this book and they remain the domain of the owner(s).

This is not a scholarly work full of polysyllabic words and footnote citations, although we did include a source bibliography at the end. Instead, the three of us cobbled together a patchwork of fascinating bits and pieces – a scrapbook history and fond memories of Missouri. Although a large range of topics are included, it is by no means a definitive work. This book is for fun. Enjoy!

ST. LOUISAN LONNIE TETTATON

I was born in 1937 on a small farm in the **Missouri boot heel** area. When World War II came along, my family of nine left on a train and headed for St. Louis. It was dark when the train backed quietly into Union Station. My older brother and father drove our meager belongings to St. Louis in a borrowed truck. We took a cab to a relative's house at North Market and Hogan. I remember seeing the seven-story steeple of **St. Laboris** Church at the crack of dawn. Our new residence was the second floor of a two-story, two family flat at **2217 Warren**. It had an outdoor toilet, but that was something we were already used to.

I remember when FDR died, a boy in the neighborhood wrote on the sidewalk in big letters, ROOSEVELT DIED TODAY. Everyone was so sad. When the war ended, I remember people celebrating as church bells were ringing, work whistles were blaring and people were dancing and making noise by beating on pots and pans.

My mother wanted to enjoy life and felt tied down with seven kids. She divorced my father and my sister went with her to live. My dad was left with the job of caring for six sons.

There were peddlers of every stripe on the streets where we lived. The milkman, in his horse-drawn wagon, delivered milk bottles on a daily basis. This was before milk was homogenized so there would always be delicious cream on top. There was also the rag man, the scissors grinder, the junk man, the ice man and even a guy who came around selling wooden clothes props for wash lines.

The ice man delivered ice in the summer and coal in the winter. Back then, most folks had wooden three-door ice boxes lined with galvanized metal. The expensive ones were lined with porcelain. You had to empty out the melt water every night before going to bed. In the winter, rather than buy ice, some residents attached an orange crate next to their outside kitchen window to keep perishables cold. There was this cardboard sign that you put in your front window to tell the iceman whether you wanted 25, 50,75, or 100 pounds of ice. The deliveryman had a leather protector on his shoulder and he used huge ice tongs to pick the block up and then lug it up to our 2nd story apartment. I remember thinking that was a tough job.

Hodges Chile Parlor sign (Lonnie Tettaton pic)

I had many childhood adventures. I went swimming with my brothers to **Shady Nook Quarry** on Natural Bridge, which was abandoned in the Thirties and filled up with water. Sometimes we went to Lambert Field to see an air show. On the way back, we stopped at **White Castle** on Natural Bridge and Kingshighway. What a treat. Sometimes we went to **Dee Lange's Carnival** at 6th and Broadway, now Keener Plaza. The place even had a shooting gallery.

At Broadway and Market was the **Diamond Horseshoe**, a strip club that was a favorite with military personnel. Burt Graham operated a tattoo shop on Broadway near the **Greyhound Bus Station**. The **Grand Play House** was between 6th and 7th streets on Market. It had three shows on Saturday – 8 p.m., 11 p.m. and 2 a.m. – the Milkman's Matinee.

Because of our large family, I always worked. I sold newspapers from a push cart. I peddled fruit for 50 cents a day. I sold the *Post, Globe,* and *Star-Times.* The *Star-Times* second edition had a green stripe on the edge. I usually finished around 11 p.m. and then stopped by the **White Palace Grill** (Jefferson & St. Louis) and bought a Coney Island, fries and slaw for 10 cents. Another fifteen cents paid for a malt.

When I was ten, I sold snow cones and cotton candy during events at Walsh Stadium on Oakland Avenue. Called **Oakland Stadium** in my time, the stadium hosted stock car races, soccer matches between Kutis and Joe Simpkins teams, pro football games and dare devil shows. I also sold cotton candy at **Public School Stadium** on Kingshighway. That's where the Shriners held their annual 4th of July weekend event.

During summers, I caddied at the **Triple A Golf Course** at Forest Park. The hardest job I ever had was setting pins at the bowling alley. I worked after school and started at 6 p.m. and finished at 11 p.m. Being on my own, I washed my own clothes with a wringer type machine. When they were dry I ironed them.

I also worked at **Chain of Rocks Park**. It was on a high bluff overlooking the Water Treatment Plant and the Chain of Rocks Bridge on Route 66. Near the entrance to the Park there was a large wooded area called Chain of Rocks Grove. Inside the Park there was the Sky Gardens, an open air pavilion overlooking the river, that served fried chicken dinners. The park had a large swimming pool that straddled the city and county boundaries. They had a sideshow exhibit called **The Petrified Man** which was merely a plaster of

Paris or stone likeness of a human being. The roller coaster there was called "the Comet" as was the one at the Highlands.

After the park went out of business, a subdivision was built on the site of the grove and low-income housing units were built on the park grounds near Glasgow Village.

Stock car races at Oakland Stadium

My older brothers, Al and Louie, rode motorcycles back in the Fifties and brother Jesse was president of the St. Louis Motorcycle Club. They had their clubhouse at the **Riverdale Speedway** on Old Telegraph Road at the Meramec River. **Widman Motorcycle Sales** on South Broadway sponsored them. Of all things, brother Louie went into the heating and air conditioning business on the East Side. In 1973, he installed the air conditioning units on the house in Glen Carbon where Bill Nunes lives. For years he installed furnaces for all the houses built by Bill's father-in-law, Noel Sanders of **Collinsville**. Small world, isn't it?

My brother, Jesse, became part owner of **Lake Hill Speedway** out in **Valley Park**. Such great names as Rusty Wallace and Kenny Schrader got their start racing stock cars there. One year the Meramec River flooded and covered the track with about four feet of water. The entire racing season was lost and that was the end of the Speedway.

I went to high school at **Hadley Tech**, located at North Grand and Bell Avenue. I was on the swim team and did some diving, but my *forté* was swimming. I took courses in commercial art. While riding the streetcar to school, I noticed that every business on Grand Avenue had signs and I figured that would by a good vocation. The Lindell, Northside and Tower theaters were on the way to school. I started doing signs for pay while still in high school.

Crystal Grill at Market and North Broadway (Tettaton picture)

When in high school, I worked during the summer as a lifeguard at the **Fairgrounds Swimming Pool**. It was built for the 1904 World's Fair and back then, it was one of the largest in the nation, holding 300 swimmers and requiring 18 life guards. One day, **on a bet, I dove off the deck of the McKinley Bridge**. It was only a 60 foot fall, but it was still dangerous because there could have been a submerged log floating by. The bridge isn't named for President McKinley. The name is for Illinoisan William McKinley who developed a network of trolley lines in the state. Even more daunting was the time I dove off the 100 foot light tower at the pool into twelve feet of water.

While I was swimming for the **downtown YMCA** in AAU meets, I decided to go for the time record of swimming from the **Alton Dam** to the Eads Bridge, a distance of about 20 miles. I was accompanied by Dennis Breen, a **Soldan High** graduate. We were assisted by a Coast Guard auxiliary boat. Dennis gave up after trying to go through the Chain of Rocks Canal. He got into the boat after he became exhausted trying to swim through the backwash at the mouth of the Canal. When I came within sight of the **Merchants Bridge**, my legs began to cramp. The record was 3 hours and 35 minutes and my time was 3 hours and 42 minutes. My brother, Rich, was waiting for me with his Nash Rambler when I staggered up the bank exhausted, but feeling no pain except a burning sensation in my throat.

I also joined a summer water polo league where the contests were played at **Shaw Park Pool** in **Clayton**. Water polo is a demanding sport because you are swimming continuously. Dennis Breen was on my team and we went to Detroit to play in the national YMCA Tournament. Dennis got suspended for spitting water at a referee, but officials relented and let him play in the championship game, which we won. Our team also competed in Olympic tryouts held in **Chicago**. Our team finished third so we did not get to go to the Olympics.

My high school Prom date was **Gale Wooten**. Gale went on to be crowned "Miss St. Louis" in 1958 and she once posed for the cover of a **Davy "the Nose" Bold** album. I was friends with **Chuck Norman** and we often double dated together. Chuck later became a radio announcer for WIL.

I went to Southern Illinois University in 1957 on a swimming scholarship. I did not return in 1958 because a number of jobs kept me busy.

In the spring of 1958, I was offered an apprentice sign painting job by Dick Newman of **Kim Sign Company**. By the early 1960s, I owned a sign shop at Twentieth and Salisbury near **Hyde Park**, now Breman Park. When I lived at Thirteenth and Monroe, I formed a partnership with Michael Lopez. Our first customer was **Marx Hardware** at North 14th Street and Benton. I once spent a night in jail for writing a check that bounced because it was for two dollars more than what I had in the bank. My dad bailed me out and the case was dismissed because the check was quickly covered and there was no attempt to defraud.

After I got married and had a baby boy, my wife and I lived on Bluff Road (**Edwardsville**) near what was to become the SIUE campus. We lived in a twelve-room farm house rent free as long as we kept up the house and grounds.

I got a job at Rite-Electric Sign in **Granite City** but then got laid off in the fall, and soon my wife and I were flat broke. We moved to a two room efficiency apartment in **Madison** while I went around on the streets trying to get sign work. I opened up a storefront sign shop in **Venice**. One day a big truck crashed into my small truck that was parked in front of my shop. I borrowed $200 from a loan shark with dark glasses to buy a junker replacement truck. I had to pay back $300 and made payments every Friday at Eddie's Market until it was paid off three months later. Like many people in that neighborhood, we were living from paycheck to paycheck. We eventually moved into public housing in Venice.

Bill Nunes' red Chrysler 300 and Lonnie's water tower sign at the Glen Carbon Dairy Queen (photo by Bill Jacobus of Belleville)

One winter night, at 4:00 a.m., I got a call from Venice police telling me that someone had crashed a pickup truck through the front of my sign shop. I was heating the place with an old coal stove with a chimney feeding into a larger chimney for two apartments above. The only thing left in the bottom of the coal bucket was some coal dust. I threw it inside the stove and closed the door. The stove exploded, knocking the stovepipes out of the flue and blowing soot all over the two apartments above.

A year later, we moved to **Madison**, Illinois and bought a two-story building with a store below and apartment on top. Next door was **Ray's Doughnut Shop**. His wife must have been going through the change or something because she seemed to have mental problems. One night, when I was working late, I heard someone running around on my roof. I locked the door, figuring the police were chasing someone. Suddenly, I saw a woman run past my shop stark naked. I thought I was seeing things. I went outside and looked. It was Ray's wife running naked as a jay bird through the street, waving her red panties in the air. She had a nice figure. A short while later, the Madison police brought her back home.

Taylor Pensoneau's best-selling book (Bernie –L, Carl - R)

The largest sign I ever painted was at the old **National Stock Yards** in East St. Louis. I painted the National Stockyards Bank sign on the two-block long, abandoned, Armour Packing Plant. Bank officials wanted a sign large enough so that it could be seen from **Stouffer Hotel**, that round building in St. Louis with a revolving restaurant on the top floor.

Another job done by Tettaton Sign was painting the water level gauge markers on the **Missouri River Bridge** on I-70 that connected St. Louis County with St. Charles. I also did a similar job on a new bridge across the Missouri River at **Kansas City**. A year later, Lonnie Jr. and I did another bridge project on the Mississippi, connecting **Chester**, Illinois with **Perryville**, Missouri. Working from heights on scaffolds and ladders, held in place by rigging ropes and pulleys, can be quite dangerous at times.

One of my most interesting jobs was in **Glen Carbon**, Illinois (where Bill Nunes lives), along Route 157 near Judy Creek. It was an old concrete grain silo 85 feet tall. It was bought by a young man who was going to put a nursery business there. We painted the round Norman tower grain bin so the concrete looked like stone work.

Another Glen Carbon job was painting the water tower next to the local Dairy Queen. The tower is 110 feet tall. It is only five blocks from where Bill lives. We finished the job after working late one Saturday. There was enough light from the intersection and surrounding businesses that we could see well enough to take our rigging down. I threw a cable off the tower and it must have hit a power line because all of a sudden the sky lit up in an orange glow and there was a crackling "bzzt" and sparking flashes of electricity. Then **the whole area suddenly went dark**. People rushed out of Hardees and Dairy Queen wondering what the heck was going on. In a few minutes the lights came back on. For the next few days, every time the phone rang I got nervous. I was afraid it was someone calling to tell me I had screwed something up in a local business there.

Over the years Tettaton Sign Company has hired over 100 different workers on a wide variety of projects. About sixteen years ago, I decided to start producing St. Louis Memories books that are sold at places like **Crown Candy** and **Chuck-A-Burger**.

I first met Bill Nunes around 2000 when **Emmett McAuliffe** had the two of us together on his late night KMOX radio talk show. We were billed as "Mr. East Side" and "Mr. West Side." Bill had written six nostalgia books about southern Illinois and callers asked us questions and shared memories from both sides of the river.

There was another big event we had the next year where four authors got together. In addition to Bill and me, there was Taylor Pensoneau of **Belleville/New Berlin**, author of *Brothers Notorious*, a book about the

Shelton brothers. Gary DeNeal of **Herod**, Illinois was there to talk about his biography of gangster Charlie Birger. From 3-4 p.m. we gave a presentation at the old **Glen Carbon Library**. Then from 7-8:30 p.m. the four of us gave a presentation and signed books for a large crowd in the huge Scottish Rite temple in **West Belleville**. Bill had just written *Southern Illinois: an Illustrated History*, and I had just published the St. Louis gangster book, written by **John Auble**. Then we went back to Bill's house, got about two hours of sleep, and then came over to do Emmett McAuliffe's show in St. Louis from 2-5 a.m. After the show, we went to Krispi Kreme on Lindbergh near I-55 to meet patrons and sell books. What a fun night that was.

GREAT CRABAPPLE WAR OF 1956

By Marilyn Kinsella of **Fairview Heights**

Although this story takes place in the Metro East, if you grew up anywhere in the St. Louis area you can probably identify with it. It's one of those classic stories of pre-teen angst that nearly all of us experienced in one form or another.

Baby Ruth was made in by Curtiss Candy Co. in Chicago

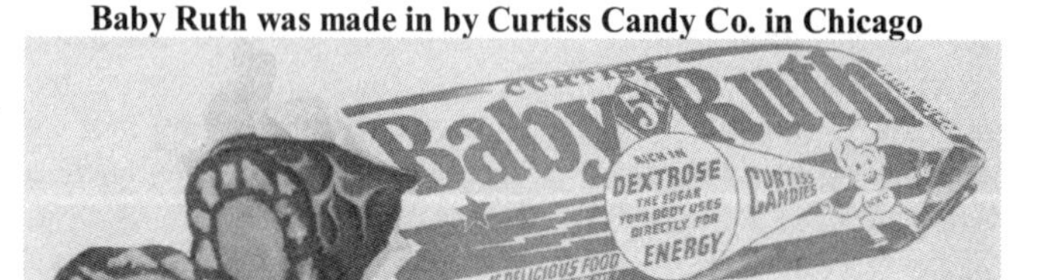

Sometimes I think that I lived in the greatest neighborhood in old Fairview that there ever was. First of all, you have to understand the layout. **Fairview Heights** is between Collinsville and Belleville. The main street, the one I lived on, was called St. Clair Rd. It led back off an old highway called Old Lincoln Trail, purportedly named because Abe Lincoln once stayed in one of the houses along that road. There were many off-shoots on St. Clair Rd. – North Rd., South Rd., Judith Ann Place and Center, Dogwood and Deppe Lanes. These roads always dead ended in the woods that provided a backdrop for my neighborhood. It was the perfect place for me and my wild imagination to soar.

For my 10th birthday I got my first bicycle – a sky blue **Western Flyer**. It was big and bulky, but it was my ticket to freedom. It had such character with white hand grips and colored plastic streamers coming out the end of them. It had a white leather seat and gleaming chrome trim. I called her "Ole Blue." Every evening Ol' Blue and I took a ride up and down the streets of my neighborhood. I knew every house and tree and almost every person. As I sailed by, I waved at my neighbors and they waved back. When I got back home, Ol' Blue shone with the evening dew clinging to her chrome flanks. I always helped her up the front porch and put her away for the night.

Monark brand bicycle

Other times Ol' Blue and I rode up to Grant School that faced Old Lincoln Trail. Even though I went to St. Albert the Great School, a lot of my friends from the neighborhood went to Grant School. Oftentimes, the school had some event going on. So, the kids from St. Albert's from my class in the neighborhood met up with the Grant School kids. We just went along and made ourselves at home. On Saturdays, they showed old black and white movies. We could buy a bag of popcorn and a small soda for ten cents. Our gang sat there in the darkened gym and laughed at the antics of the Our Gang movies.

Close to the school Mr. Randle had a tiny little house where he served root beer in icy mugs. There was a small counter with only four stools with puckered red leather seats. Ol' Blue waited patiently outside while I plopped down fifteen cents. Mr. Randle went to the freezer and took out a frosty mug. Then, he poured the dark brown liquid until a foamy head formed on top. He gave me a wink and slid the root beer down to where I was sitting. On hot summer days with no air-conditioning anywhere, there was nothin' better than to sip that root beer and let those icy crystals slip down my face and hands. After I was refreshed, I hopped back on Ol' Blue and headed for the corner store.

Now, even though it was already the Fifties, we still had a country store called the Fairview IGA. It was unbelievably small, but it had everything you could possibly want. Every inch was taken up with various sundries – seed potatoes, a dairy case, and even a butcher who cut fresh meat right there in the store. One of my favorite places in the store was a chest freezer where they kept their goodies – Popsicles, Fudgesicles, Dreamsicles. They also had malted milk bars, Eskimo pies, ice cream sandwiches and little flavored Dixie Cups with their very own distinctive wooden spoons. Since we didn't have an air conditioner at home, sometimes I opened the glass lid of the freezer and took in huge gulps of frozen air. I breathed in till my nose hairs felt like sharp needles and I thought surely my lungs would burst. Then I closed the case and, since I didn't have enough money, pretended as if nothing in the case really appealed to me. I then walked over to the candy counter and began my perusal of the chocolates. If I do say so myself, I was quite a connoisseur of candy – Milky Ways, Oh Henrys, Baby Ruths, Fifth Avenues and **Clark Bars**. I loved them all equally and with passion. But, sometimes I couldn't cough up even a nickel for a candy bar. So, I had to settle for a piece of gum. Back then you could buy a piece of gum for the pricey sum of one whole penny. I didn't have to think about it either because there was only one brand of kids gum to choose from back then and that was **Double Bubble Gum**. Childhood doesn't get any better than chewing a piece of Double Bubble and blowing massive bubbles while riding Ole Blue down the back roads of my old neighborhood.

It's true. Sometimes I liked to be myself, but other times I liked to be with my gang of friends. When we put our creative minds together, we had very imaginative, if not downright wild, adventures. In the woods we had a clubhouse. It was just a dugout old ditch with a big piece of tarpaper over it. We used that as a home base for our excursions into the vast woods. Other times we played war with our little plastic army men. They were small green men cast in different poses; there was one with his carbine rifle positioned to shoot, another with his bayonet ready to charge, but my favorite was the little green man with a bazooka on his shoulder – boy, what power!

We dug out elaborate catacomb foxhole passages into the sides of our clubhouse for our troops. Eventually, someone would call out, "To arms!" and we delighted in either flooding or destroying the enemy. By *destroying* I mean that every once in a while one of us would come up with an old firecracker left over from the Fourth of July. Now, you have to remember that this was a long time ago when firecrackers were actually legal. I'm surprised we didn't injure a hand or put out an eye in those battles, but we managed to get out of harm's way just in the nick of time. I remember this one time when someone came up with a cherry bomb. Needless to say – there wasn't much left of the catacomb, much less the fort, after that thing went off. But really, there was no finer childhood memory than finding your enemy's little green men making a hasty retreat as they slid down an avalanche of mud and rock after a surprise attack.

Tin can telephones

But, even though we had a good time together, we all quivered and shook in the presence of the true kings of my neighborhood – a group of bigger, older, and stronger boys aptly named "the super cool." You know, I never actually saw the "super cool" play together. They just sort of hung-out . . . looking cool. They actually congregated outside the front of my corner store leaning against the plate glass window, taking swigs of Coke from a bottle. Make no mistake, that storefront was staked out as their territory and they never let anyone pass without dishing out an armload of insults and then laughing uncontrollably.

You can understand why sometimes going to the corner market could be a chore. And, I found myself going to that store almost daily. My family was spoiled by having that store so close. Inevitably, we'd be ready to sit down and eat, when I'd have to run out at the last minute and get a loaf of bread or a bottle of milk. And, of course, I'd run into the super-cool gang. There they'd be . . . sucking on those Coke bottles, lookin' cool.

Tootsie Rolls

I always parked Ol' Blue well away from their bikes. They even had super cool bikes. They all rode an expensive Schwinn bike called "The Phantom" – a jet black bike with a silver racing stripe. I knew better than to leave Ol' Blue anywhere near the Phantoms. After I parked (around back), I tried to act nonchalant as I walked up to the front door, but I was always so intimidated that I usually stumbled all over the place. Even inside I could hear their jeers all the way down the dairy aisle.

And, if the super cool acted as if they owned the store front, they did likewise with the streets. My gang and I were, to cop a term from today's vernacular, referred to as "geeks." And the geeks – I mean our gang – were allowed on the streets anytime, as long as the super cool weren't around. It was as if they feared some of our geekiness would rub off on their royal highnesses, if they should stoop to share the streets. If we were riding down the street and the super-cools came around the corner, it was expected that we would have to move over to the other side to give them all the room they wanted. Some unwritten laws of the streets were just naturally understood by one and all. So, we blindly abided by it.

But, then there was that fateful day in August. I was taking Ol' Blue out for her morning ride, when a whole slew of Phantoms came into view. I politely got over to the other side of the street but that wasn't good enough. Oh, no. There was too many of them and they kept coming closer. Worse, they acted as if they didn't even see me. Like I was some sort of invisible . . . nothing. I knew Ol' Blue and I were going to have to cut our losses so I headed for the ditch. The next thing I knew, Ol' Blue was on top of me and the super cool were having a laughing fit. Now, I don't mind getting a couple of scratches or bruises, but Ol' Blue didn't come out too well. Her handlebars were all twisted around and several spokes were bent. That did it. This could only mean one thing – WAR!

However, when the enemy is bigger and older and stronger, it does pose a problem. But, the line had been drawn in the tar across St. Clair Road and there was no turning back. There was only one way to retaliate for such a breach in neighborhood etiquette, and that was to catch the enemy unaware, to seize the moment, to stage a surprise attack.

First, I gathered my troops. When I told them what had happened they were more than happy to enlist. We scouted around for the perfect natural fort from which to execute our strategic maneuvers. There was only one such site. On the corner of North Road and St. Clair there was an empty lot owned by Aunt Josie and Uncle Blainey. Growing around the corner were large lilac and snowball bushes that had long since lost their blossoms. Now they were just a massive tangle of greenery that would provide us with an impenetrable walled fortress. Growing behind the bushes was our ammo supply – a line of crab apple trees just full of tiny green apples – perfect for flinging with our wooden school rulers.

Being a child with a flair for the dramatic, I ran home and got a handful of coal chips from the coal bin in the basement, and all the old head scarves I could find. When I got back to my troops we streaked our faces with the coal dust and wrapped the scarves around our heads like bandanas. The last scarf we tied to the end of a long stick. It would make the perfect inspirational ensign – a flag to wave as we went into battle. Next, we picked all the crab apples off the trees that we could reach. We virtually denuded the whole bottom half of the trees. We stored our ammo in orange crates requisitioned from our garages. With our powder kegs full we were ready for action. We didn't have to wait long. Through our hand-made periscope we could see the jet black Phantoms coming over the rise. We loaded up our rulers and cocked them. Then we waited. At just the right moment someone shouted, "To arms."

Making radio sound effects

In an instant, crab apples began catapulting across the ramparts and toward our designated targets. Like V-1 rockets our crab apples hit their marks time and again – arms, heads, butts – anything was fair game. Ha-ha-ha! They were caught completely off guard. The Phantoms began to wobble. Soon they went out of control and headed straight for the ditches. The super cool were down . . . but certainly not out. They began scrounging around for stray missiles and counterattacked by throwing them back toward the bushes. Hah! Very few missiles could penetrate our fortress.

According to plan we were ready for phase two of the battle. And, this was crucial. To run now would be to run for the rest of our lives. So with our pockets filled with crab apples, we charged out of our fortress and met the enemy head on.

What happened next went down in the annals of neighborhood lore as stuff from which legends are born. With our ensign flying high, bandanas on our heads, faces menacingly streaked with black war paint, and crab apples in hand, we ambushed 'em! Oh, they tried a feeble counter-attack, but they were actually awestruck and apple struck. They hurriedly retreated to their bikes and rode off with a barrage of crab apples pelting their backs.

We won! We couldn't believe it. We won! The mighty store front gods had Achilles' heels after all.

Well, things changed after that. Oh, not drastically. The cool ones still never talked to me or anything as civil as that. But now when I rode Ol' Blue down the street the Phantoms didn't try to crowd me off the road. And, when I went to the corner store, I parked right up front and nary a word was said. I suppose they could have pounded the daylight out of me or wrecked my bike, but I guess they had a grudging respect for my spunk.

Jack Armstrong Secret Whistle Code Ring

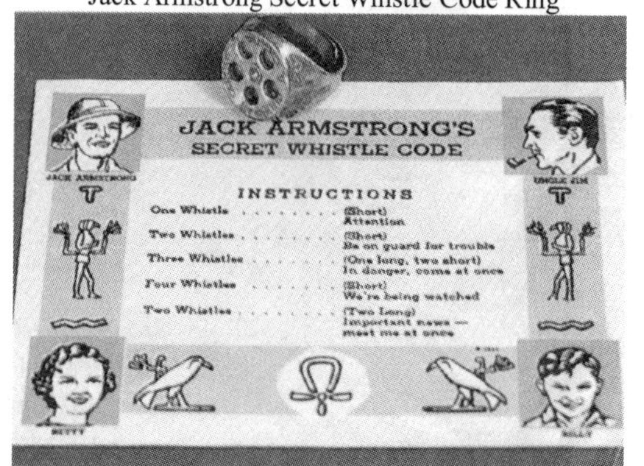

That fall my Aunt Josie and Uncle Blainey began harvesting their fruit trees. Unfortunately, there wouldn't be any of their famous crab apple jelly that year. There just weren't enough to make it worthwhile. They 'sposed the squirrels got to them. Although they did think it a bit odd that the squirrels stopped precisely halfway up the trees. Hmmm.

I never told them what actually happened. After all, they were half right. A squirrelly bunch of kids *did* rob their trees.

A couple of months ago I went for a walk down my old neighborhood streets. The people had changed but I nodded "hello" to the familiar homes and trees. Then, I came to that hallowed ground where the Great Crab Apple War of '56 took place. Gone were the bushes; gone were the crab apple trees. But the memory lingered on like a thick fog. I closed my eyes and I heard once again the echo of a far off, rallying cry, "To arms!" And I thought – childhood memories . . . they just don't get any better than this!

For more of Marilyn's great memories, go to her website at www.marilynkinsella.org.

THOSE TEN CENTS-AND-A-BOX-TOP RADIO TREASURES

This will resonate with anyone in Missouri who came of age in the 1930s, 1940s or 1950s.

The quiet of the front room was broken by the crackle of a paper-coned radio speaker. Most kids back then rushed home after school to turn on the set. A time to open one's ears and mind to a parade of exciting fifteen minute adventure programs. Radio's exhilarating tales offered youth the ideal opportunity to exercise keen imaginations. The sound-stirring action shows held high favor with kids back in the old days. They developed a close relationship with those daily airwaves friends. They were as familiar as the kids on the block that you played games with - marbles, kick the can, cork ball and mumblety peg. These after school friends from the airways included Jack Armstrong, Tom Mix, Captain Midnight, Sky King, Sergeant Preston, Don Winslow, Little Orphan Annie, Henry Aldrich, Dick Tracy and others. Tuning in, kids enjoyed putting faces that they felt went with the voices coming through the speaker cloth. Naturally, most boys had a crush on Betty, the young girl in the Jack Armstrong series.

My dad talked about the time when he was a boy how he did odd jobs to earn enough money to buy a crystal radio set. The total cost was about $5.00 and the parts included a set of earphones, a crystal and a "cat's whisker," some copper wire for an induction coil, and another long piece of antenna wire with insulators and a lightning arrestor. The coil was made by wrapping wire around an empty Quaker Oatmeal box. The antenna wire went out his bedroom window and traveled about 100 feet to a wooden pole on top of the chicken coop.

By moving the end of the cat's whisker to different points on the crystal, he could tune in stations from all over the area.

When I was nine, Dad bought me a one tube radio kit from **Walter Ashe** on 11th and Pine in St. Louis. It was a bit more powerful and slightly more sophisticated than Dad's old oatmeal box radio.

There was yet another reason kids were devoted radio listeners - the attraction to the different serials' enchanting giveaways offered regularly by the show's sponsors. These attractive offers were hawked by a most influential-sounding radio announcer towards his audience of attentive charges. While similar items could be found as "prizes" in cereal boxes, much like the ones in a box of Cracker Jack, the ones offered on radio were generally a step up in quality. Sometimes the offer included something as large as a drinking mug with a picture of the radio star on it. Roy Rogers had an offer for a mug where the handle was a replica of the butt-end of one of his six-shooters.

Popeye

"Well, boys and girls, do I have some great news for you! Have a pencil and paper ready. At the end of today's exciting adventure we have an offer you won't want to miss. I'll give you all the details at the end of today's exciting program. But now . . ."

At the end of the daily cliffhanger the smooth-voiced announcer described in glowing terms the merit and desirability of the offer. "I'll bet every boy and girl would like to own one of these!" You could almost see the words

Little Orphan Annie Ovaltine mug

on our black dial Zenith heterodyne set with the cool lightning bolt dial tuner. Sending in ten cents and a box top would soon put one of those highly desired treasures in my grasp. In summertime, after waiting two weeks from the mailing, kids pestered the mailman every day, looking for that small box that brought a "thank you" and an instant smile on their face.

Often, the giveaways opened the way to other exclusive benefits. They opened the door to becoming a member of a club or society that was working to better America by helping the radio hero fight spies, criminals, or enemy agents. It gave you a feeling of belonging, a sense that you were part of a team – a key member of an elite group that was fighting for decency, truth, fairness and justice. It gave you a sense of community.

You might be too young to vote, but here was a way for young people to promote the ideals of democracy. The sponsors knew that being part of the "in crowd" boosted self-esteem. They played to the ego. "Be the first kid on your block to own this beautiful Straight Shooter's bandana – just like the one worn by Tom Mix. Be the envy of your neighborhood and friends." The announcer's sales pitch included a smorgasbord of descriptive adjectives related to the beauty, performance and desirability of owning one of the prized items.

The variety of "must have" premiums over the years seemed infinite. There were arrowheads that glowed in the dark, skull rings with rubies in the eye sockets, shiny gold detective badges, code books, decoder rings, miniature comic books, and signed pictures of the radio star. At the end of the program, the announcer gave listeners a secret message that provided a clue to the content of the next episode. You needed a ring to decode the special message. Jack Armstrong (that intrepid hero of Hudson High) and Wheaties offered a HIKE-O-METER that was very popular with energetic youth. One show offered a full-color map to enable listeners to follow our hero's thunderous adventures that took him to all sorts of exotic places and remote islands. Through close association with these radio friends, youths became a Straight Shooter, Secret Society regular, Squadron of Peace member, and a full-fledged member of the Lone Wolf Tribe, the Solar Cadets, and the Secret Squadron.

There were many other programs reserved for later in the evening that appealed more to adults. The Golden Age of Radio included programs such as The Shadow, The Fat Man, The Inner Sanctum, Lights Out, I love a Mystery, Gang Busters, Sam Spade, Richard Diamond, Groucho Marx, The Avenger, Sherlock Holmes, Charlie Chan, The Creaking Door, Suspense, Mr. Keene, Tracer of Lost Persons, Perry Mason, Straight Arrow, Fibber McGee and Molly, Boston Blackie, Escape, Deadline For Danger, Mystery is my Hobby, I Cover the

Waterfront, I Deal in Crime, Casey Crime Photographer, The Green Hornet, The Lone Ranger, Hopalong Cassidy, Roy Rogers, Blackstone The Magician, Amos And Andy, Burns And Allen and many, many others.

The music that heightened the dramatic tension was part and parcel of what made the shows great. I was quite surprised to later learn that much of the stirring music heard on the Lone Ranger program was taken from classical music – Rossini's "William Tell Overture" and Franz List's "Symphonic Poems."

Do you remember when you heard a rumor at school that there was an invention coming out that had pictures? It was going to be called tel-e-vision. One day, kids came home from school and found a piece of mahogany furniture in their living room. It contained a round seven inch cathode ray tube in the middle of the set. At the time, kids had no idea that television would kill off their first love . . . **radio**.

Old time record labels

THOSE OLD BRITTLE 78 RPM RECORDS

The sight of a 78 r.p.m. record spinning on a turntable at a dizzying speed would be startling to those who only knew of LPs that revolved at a leisurely pace of a mere 33 and a third revolutions per minute. In the days of my youth, before the advent of television, 78 r.p.m. records and the radio were the principal means of home entertainment. In hundreds of radio stations, thousands of jukeboxes and in millions of homes, records spun at 78 r.p.m.

Those old records inspired figures of speech that have worked their way into our vocabulary. "Groovy" became an expression to describe something that was pleasant. The term "disc jockey" was coined to describe someone who played records on the radio. A St. Louis favorite was Ed Bonner of KXOK. He was introduced by a musical jingle.

"Here's Ed Bonner, tops in pops. He's sure loved by the bobby sox. The older folks, they like him too, 'cause he plays all that's old and new!"

Doris Day

The first records oldsters ever saw were some of those old 10 inch 78s. They were popular songs of the day, the time being the early Forties. My mother bought a few, but the one I remember most was "Near You," a piano piece by Francis Craig. The song eventually became the theme for Milton Berle's television program. He ended each program by singing, "There's just one place for me, near you." Then he closed with "Goodnight everybody. We hope to see you again next week." "Near You" was on a bright yellow Bullet label with black lettering.

One had to be quite careful with these records because they were made from a type of plastic that was very brittle. There were several ways in which these records could be damaged or broken. I remember seeing some records that had small chunks missing. They looked as if a mouse had taken a bite out of them. Some developed cracks that ran through the first one-third of the song. You could still play the records, but an annoying "pop" was heard every few seconds. If you dropped the record on a hard floor, it broke into a dozen of pieces.

The songs back then weren't very long. Disc jockeys and producers developed a theory that listeners grew bored if a song was much longer than three minutes. It wasn't until **Marty Robbins** came out with a song called "El Paso" that things changed. The song had two versions, with the longer four minute one being on the flip side. Amazingly, audiences preferred the longer version. Most songs today are closer to four or five minutes than three minutes.

Some records had flaws and the needle would get stuck in a groove and play the same lyrics over and over until you pushed the tone arm over. Sometimes this could be fixed by taping a dime on top of the tone arm to make it heavier.

Twelve inch 78 r.p.m. records existed back then, but they were usually for longer classical pieces. Just below the title on the label there were often words to describe what type of music was being played. Waltz, jazz, march and two-step are some that I remember. When **Bill Haley and the Comets** came out with "Rock Around the Clock," producers didn't know what to call it because Alan Freed had not yet invented the phrase "rock and roll." So Decca executives labeled the first rock song a fox trot.

For a brief time in the 1940s, needles produced by the Kakti Company were made from prickly cactus thorns. However, the most common type of needle was made of steel. It looked pretty much like a sewing needle. These needles played for only twelve hours before the tip was ground down and a change was needed. One could move up a step with higher quality osmium-tipped needles that lasted about twenty-five hours. When 45 r.p.m. records came out, the grooves were smaller and there were appropriate sapphire needles that were good for forty hours. The best needles were diamond-tipped and lasted 200 hours, but I was never able to afford one of these.

My grandparents listened to records and music that was reproduced mechanically, without amplifiers. These old Brunswick consoles can often be seen in antique shops. They had a crank on the side that wound up a spring that moved the turntable around as it unwound. Because the sound was reproduced mechanically instead of electronically, the sound was amplified with a large metal cone, much like a megaphone. The tone arms on these sets were very heavy and the needles wore out the records after about forty plays.

If this is hard to picture, think about the RCA logo that shows the dog Nippur listening to "his master's voice." RCA called their early sets Victrolas, and the term became a generic name for all similar machines, much in the manner that Kleenex became the generic name for tissues and Band-Aid was the vernacular for all bandages placed over small cuts.

In the late 40s, some manufacturers began pressing records out of "vinylite." It was softer than the old "shellac" records that were so fragile. The softer vinyl records reproduced higher frequencies better and were advertised as "unbreak-able." They cost two dollars, twice as much as the old type. RCA's vinyl records were translucent and cherry red in color. Columbia's were opaque and black.

Then **Columbia invented the long-playing LP** and RCA came along with the 45 r.p.m. I quickly switched over to the smaller and thinner 45s, but some of my friends doggedly clung to the 78s, believing that the faster speed gave better fidelity.

An ensuing "battle of speeds" occurred. The 45s eventually won out much like VHS triumphed over Betamax video tapes. Most new phonograph players that came out had all three speeds. One needle was used for 78s and a flip mechanism gave you a different needle for 45s and LPs. A spindle adaptor was needed to play the 45s.

Frank Sinatra – the Voice

You can't imagine the excitement when monaural records changed to **Hi Fi** in the early 1950s and then stereophonic sound came out in 1958. Record players soon took on the name stereos. In 1962, shortly after I was married and my wife and I were still in college, I went out and bought a magnificent Admiral six foot long stereo console with twelve inch speakers on each end. It was our nicest piece of furniture.

Secret Squadron booklet

In the early days of stereo, some sounds came out of one speaker while others came out of the other speaker. Check out a Ray Conniff record circa 1962. You'll find the higher female voices coming out of your left speaker and the lower male voices wafting through the right speaker. This produced a novel "ping pong" (back and forth) effect that I thoroughly enjoyed, but many found to be annoying. The practice was eventually stopped.

Records were replaced by reel-to-reel tapes, which never caught on and lost out to eight tracks, which were replaced by cassettes, which, in turn, became outdated by the CD, played with a beam of light.

While it is nice to have the quality sound of compact discs, free of pops and scratches, it is kind of sad to see old records being thrown away or given to Goodwill. I kept all of my 45s in their sleeves and, despite their age, they have transferred nicely to CDs in the MP3 format. I have 865 old songs on four MP3 CDs. My wife thinks I'm ready for the men in white coats. She listens to classical music in the kitchen while I, in my study, revel in old nostalgic songs like "Harbor Lights," "Don't be Cruel," "A White Sport Coat," "It's Only Make Believe," "See You Later Alligator" and "Don't Forbid Me" by Pat Boone. Ah, yes, the good old days.

P.S. If you recognize at least four of these

songs, it means you don't have Alzheimer's . . . yet!

REMEMBERING THOSE GREAT CEREAL PRIZES

Think back to your childhood . . . those carefree days of kick-the-can, tag, homemade scooters with skate wheels, cork ball and Kukla, Fran, and Ollie. What kind of cereal did you eat? Was it from a box of Wheaties with Mickey Mantle on the box? Lone Ranger Cheerios? Kellogg's Sugar Corn Pops featuring Guy Madison and Andy Devine? Or did your mother disdain the sugar-coated stuff and make you eat (gulp) CORN SOYA?

Dick Tracy's two-way wrist radio was offered as a "send for" prize

Like so many other good things, the great cereal bonanza began in the early 1950s. That's when the cereal aisle at the grocery store, as we know it today, began. Pre-sweetened cereals such as Sugar Crisp, Frosted Flakes and Cocoa Puffs were developed during the Eisenhower decade as exciting alternatives to boring Cream of Wheat or oatmeal. My early memories of this, which had fallen through the trap doors of my mind, were rescued by *Cereal Goodies*, a recent book by Scott Johns.

Remember the "Free Inside" irresistible bait that reduced all of us who had been on the planet less than thirteen years to a whimpering, fidgety, glob of blubbering need? When Mom took me to the neighborhood grocery store, I usually spent all of my time roving up and down the cereal aisle, with eyes wide as saucers, eagerly scanning for the box with the best toy inside. I had no particular loyalty to Wheaties, Corn Flakes, Pep, or Nabisco Shredded Wheat; it was the prize inside the box that mattered.

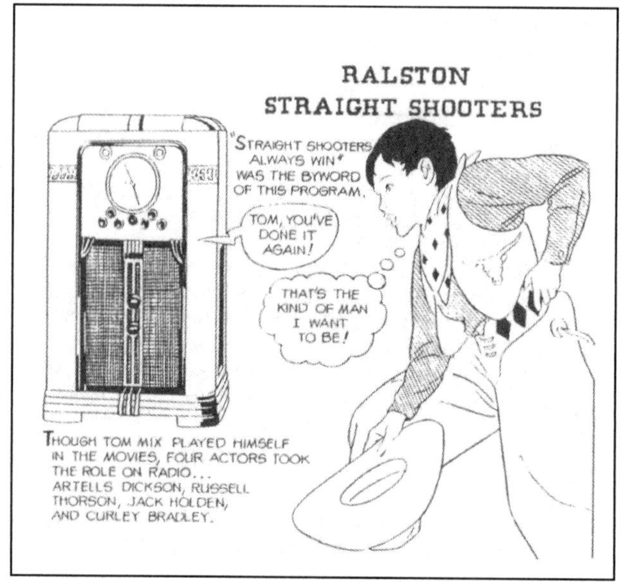

Kellogg's Corn Flakes, with a Chiquita banana on the front dressed like **Carmen Miranda**, offered a toy jet-powered whistle locomotive made out of colorful plastic. The jet effect, created by air escaping from a balloon attached to the smoke stack, gave it plenty of get up and go. A tapered cantilevered cab provided the mouth piece for an eardrum-piercing whistle. I just had to have one so I yanked it off the shelf and ran er, walked, to where Mom was pushing the cart around the store.

Mom wouldn't let me open the precious package until it was time for breakfast the next morning. She didn't want the contents inside to "become stale." When my eye lids fluttered open the next day, I rushed to the kitchen and grabbed the box from the pantry.

"Don't forget to wash your hands and carefully open the box so it will close properly," Mother admonished.

"Sure, Mom," I glibly replied. After the fastest hand wash in history and a quick swipe at the towel, my skinny arm plunged through the crunchy stuff to the bottom of the box. Nothing was there. I frantically went to the other side. It too produced nothing but frustration. Then I laid the box on one side and poked around until my fingers curled around that precious cellophane that enveloped my coveted prize.

After driving everyone in the family nuts with ear-splitting toot! toot! whistle blasts, and watching the jet-propelled engine scoot across the linoleum floor, I tired of the novelty and placed it in a cigar box – depository of my treasured collectibles (baseball cards, colored rocks, marbles, used stamps, Cracker Jack toys and novelties).

The assortment of free cereal box goodies was truly amazing. Kellogg's Pep offered **Tom Corbett** space rings. (My favorite character on the show was a cocky fellow played by Jan Merlin. When he was ticked off he muttered, "Aw, go blow your jets.") Post's Raisin Bran featured Hopalong Cassidy badges. Quaker Puffed Wheat promised one of six different miniature western guns inside. Ranger Joe's Wheat Honeys tossed in a plastic jet plane and a cardboard cut-out hangar. Rice Chex, from the **Ralston Company** of St. Louis, tempted youngsters with Buzz Cory "Space Patrol" rocket ships and Grape Nuts had a plastic model of a Ford car within its contents.

Occasionally, the best part of the cereal wasn't the prize inside, but the promise of childhood bliss proffered through an extra offer detailed on the back panel of the box. The biggest obstacle was having to wait until the box was empty before Mom would let me cut off part of the box top so that I could send for the offer. Sometimes I ate cereal straight out of the box as an afternoon snack to hurry the process along. I would then cut off the box top and Scotch tape the required quarter to the address panel. I eagerly filled out the front of the panel with my address – 4901 Lincoln Avenue, East St. Louis, Illinois. Then I pasted a three cent stamp in the upper right hand corner. Next, I placed everything inside the envelope and licked the glue (ugh!) to seal it shut. Then I placed it on the mailbox on the front porch so the mailman would pick it up that day.

What followed always proved to be an agonizingly "slow as molasses in January" wait. After a week, I would dash home from school to check the mail to see if my package had arrived. Day after day there was nothing. A couple of weeks stretched into an eternity. Did the company run out of stock? Did my letter get lost? Did the post office lose my box? Worse, did they accidentally deliver it to another kid on the block? Was it possible that the mailman decided to keep the prize for one of his kids? There was a frustrating array of possibilities. It was sheer agony. I pestered my mom about the delay, and she said that I was a WORRY WART. "It will get here in God's good time," she reassured, with a condescending pat on my noggin.

Finally, after I had almost completely forgotten about it, there was a taste of Christmas in May for an eager kid. I excitedly tore the package open and admired the shiny treasure – a Roy Rogers plastic drinking mug. For the next few months I drank **Ovaltine**, Cool-Aid, soda - anything that was liquid – through a large hole that was in the top of Roy's head.

There were many, many others: **Jack Armstrong** goggles from Wheaties, Snap, Crackle and Pop hand puppets from Rice Krispies, a **Sergeant Preston** ore detector from Quaker Puffed Rice, a Howdy Doody marionette from Post Krinkles, a Gabby Hayes prospector's map from Post Toasties and an inflatable Tony the Tiger doll from Sugar Frosted Flakes.

Years later, I switched to "adult" cereals such as shredded wheat, Total, and bran flakes. No prizes inside these boxes – merely a claim about how they provided you with a healthy dose of the government's recommended level of vitamins and minerals, gave needed bulk or fiber to your diet or led you to the promised land of "regularity."

When I became a parent, I discovered that part of the fun of taking my son and daughter to the supermarket was pushing them in a cart down the cereal aisle while my wife shopped for lesser things.

A delirium spread across my mind as the fantastic, eye-popping graphics grabbed me by the collar, brought back childhood fantasies and bombarded my senses with promises of breakfast ecstasy. As far as I was concerned, these colorful packages were modern-day Rembrandts, or Van Goghs. The boxes vaguely looked the same as yesteryear, but a new phalanx of morning idols adorned the brightly printed boxes. Instead of **Dick Tracy, Sky King**, **Mandrake the Magician** or Mary Hartline heaping praises on the product's wholesomeness, the new heroes of the Play-Doh set were Marky Maypo, Trix Rabbit and Sonny the cuckoo bird.

The Nunes' progeny must have had good genes because my daughter, Laurie, reached for a box of Frankenberry cereal that promised a mouth watering treat and a blue-colored replica of the loveable cereal monster inside. Son Steven opted for Count Chocula, offering a free set of scary, washable tattoos inside. My chest swelled with fatherly pride and the joy was indescribable. "Great choices," I quipped.

READING THE SUNDAY FUNNIES

The Sunday "funnies" provided a wonderful world of adventure, humor, suspense, and mystery for kids in the 1940s and 1950s. They offered us a glimpse into the lives, loves, adventures, fears, successes and failures of others told

by using pictures and words – something hardcover books didn't do.

On Sundays, Dad got up early and went to the corner confectionary at 49th and Caseyville, across from Beverly's Tavern. He bought a St. Louis *Globe-Democrat* newspaper and a dozen glazed donuts. While he delved into the news and editorial section, my sister and I fought over the comics section. We usually ended up spreading them out on the 9 x 12 rose patterned rug on the living room floor. No matter what the season or weather, I spent Sunday mornings before

church, at Washington Park Church of God, with my pals – the funnies.

I grew up with **Steve Canyon, Terry and the Pirates, Blondie and Dagwood, Prince Valiant, Dick Tracy, Li'l Abner, Nancy and Sluggo, Donald Duck and Ally Oop** – the cave man whose muscles bulged at the lower end of his arms and legs. I also followed the Lone Ranger with a fierce loyalty. Prince Valiant was in narrative form and contained no balloon speech captions over a character's head. A typical Prince Valiant yarn sometimes took nearly a year to complete.

It all started back in 1895 with a character named the Yellow Kid. This yellow, nightgown-clad youth was introduced in a series called Hogan's Alley for the New York World. Richard Outcault's character was the main reason for a newspaper circulation war – giving rise to the term "yellow journalism" – stories that focused on the lurid and sensational. Some say that the spirit of public jingoism, fueled by the outrageous stories and newspaper headlines of competing newspapers, were responsible for getting the U.S. involved in the Spanish-American War in 1898.

Outcault followed up his early smash success by creating **Buster Brown**, a character whose haircut and outfits were emulated by parents who required their kids to dress in a similar manner for church and Sunday school. Buster Brown shoes were even popular into the 1950s. Remember the old television jingle? "Hi, I'm Buster Brown; I live in a shoe. Woof, woof! That's my dog Tige, look for him in there too." Fortunately knickers and Buster Brown haircuts were out of style by the time I attended Manners Elementary School in Washington Park.

I also remember **Mutt and Jeff** and the **Katzenjammer Kids** (Hans and Fritz). They became heroes to young readers by getting away with pranks played on adults.

Dad said that he remembered a one-paneled cartoon called Rube Goldberg. Rube always managed to come up with some elaborate mechanical invention to make life easier. A typical complex mechanism of his included an overly complicated maze of gears, pulleys, levers, springs and belts that led the reader from point A to point Z. The strip became part of our national lexicon as people who came up with complex ideas, thought to be impractical, were referred to as Rube Goldbergs. Sometimes the idea itself was called a Rube Goldberg scheme.

Comic strip character, Henry

Because of East St. Louis horse racing at Fairmount Park and Cahokia Downs, **Barney Google** and his horse Spark Plug were wildly popular in the St. Louis metro area. Since the strip started in 1919, I had already missed out on a number of races won by Spark Plug before I started reading the comic. Barney lived in the hill country in a southern state and was ultimately joined by Lowizie and Snuffy Smith. Over the years the Snuffy character became even more popular than Barney Google. In the 1920s there was a wildly popular song titled *Barney Google* – the character with the "goo – goo – googly eyes."

My sister went ga-ga over Li'l Abner, the character created by Al Capp. She also loved Brenda Starr and Little Orphan Annie with her faithful dog, Sandy. She even had one of Annie's plastic Ovaltine shaker mugs from an offer broadcast on one of Annie's radio programs. I only got excited over that strip when Asp or Punjab were a part of the story. I never could figure out how her creator got away with drawing a female heroine that had no pupils in her blank eyes. Yet that quickly became one of her endearing trademarks.

Naturally I ogled the curvaceous Daisy May in the Li'l Abner strip. She wore a tight-fitting, off the shoulders blouse that accentuated her charms. She also had a fantastic set of gams that were on display since she always wore short shorts. Daisy was always trying to figure out ways of getting that big lummox to marry her. Somehow he always resisted. Cap came up with the novel idea of Sadie Hawkins Day, a time when it was perfectly acceptable for a female to ask a man out on a date. This soon translated into **Sadie Hawkins Day** dances at most high schools. Daisy Mae finally captured Abner on Sadie Hawkins Day, the wedding ceremony officiated by Marryin' Sam. That $1.15 ceremony made the cover of *Life Magazine*.

It would be easy to say that I follow the funnies now as intensely as I did when growing up. But that is not the case. Somehow the modern characters have lost their appeal and charm, and I no longer follow the newspaper comics. But I do have a 1941 Philco radio in my study that still works and has been magnificently refinished to recapture its original character. I also have numerous old radio and commercial anthologies in the MP3 format that places a hundred old shows on one disc.

I lost interest in the comic strips when I went away to Anderson College in Indiana and somehow never reestablished the emotional connection. My wife complains endlessly about my living in the past, yet I have fond memories of my boyhood years when a little imagination and a few colored panels in a newspaper whisked me away to adventure and excitement.

BIG LITTLE BOOKS

For some youngsters the first books they ever read were 3-1/2 x 4-1/2 inch Big Little Books that were enormously popular in the 1930s and early 1940s. They contained about 300 pages and were sold at the five and dime stores in East St. Louis – Newberry's, Woolworths and Kresge's. Half of the pages carried the text and the story, and the other half on the opposite page contained black and white illustrations. Although kids later used the expression "comic books," they weren't really books like these. Comic books were magazine in format.

I honed my rudimentary reading skills on comics and copy from Big Little Books. Although Big Little Books were going out of style as I grew older, giving way to comic books in color, there were still plenty to get my hands on.

Smilin' Jack – Big Little Book

Most of the BLBs were "novelized" from the comic strips and represented the first successful commercial reprinting from the funnies. BLBs were sometimes criticized for merely cannibalizing the strips and substituting unnecessary text to explain the panels. Yet, these books brought joy to millions. In some instances, a BLB such as "Mickey Mouse at Blaggart Castle" was the only present Depression-stricken parents could afford to give their kids. I was positively thrilled one day when my cousin, Del Shinn, gave me some of his old books. This was my first experience with BLBs.

Kids looking for detective, police and G-men tales were not disappointed. There was the **Green Hornet, The Shadow, Charlie Chan, Dick Tracy, Dan Dunn, and Radio Patrol**. Airplanes, pirates and super science were popular. These included **Smilin' Jack, Buck Rogers, Tailspin Tommy, Flash Gordon and Jack Armstrong**. Boys and girls alike played cowboys and Indians. Whitman Publishing Company didn't ignore this fact and featured books starring **Tom Mix, the Lone Ranger, Buck Jones, Ken Maynard and Red Ryder**.

Pogo – first created in 1954 by Walt Kelly

Books that appealed more to girls included: **Ella Cinders, Brenda Starr, Blondie and Dagwood, Little Orphan Annie, Myra North Special Nurse and Little Annie Rooney**.

The first BLB was Dick Tracy, and it came out in December of 1932. Because these books had colorized cardboard covers they survived better than comic books and are not as expensive to collect as old comics. Most are around five dollars apiece, but ones in near mint condition go for twenty-five dollars. The most expensive BLB is "Buck Rogers in the City of Floating Globes," worth around sixty dollars.

Among those doing illustrations for BLBs were Alex Raymond and Henry Vallely. Vallely's work can be seen in "Jack Armstrong and the Ivory Treasure," or "Tom Mix and Montezuma's Horde."

The writing in these books weren't about to win any Pulitzer prizes, but it was exciting fiction for wide-eyed kids. Read this bit of hyperbolic narrative from "The Shadow and the Living Dead."

"The Shadow, cloak flaring, eyes burning beneath the brim of his slouch hat, blazing away at a veritable army of homicidal zombies coming up the stairs to get him, coming . . coming . . . more shots, then – no more ammunition! But from the stygian darkness were thrust twin automatics, forty-fives, fully loaded, more welcome than water on the parched Sahara Desert. The Shadow's faithful, mysterious 'agents' had arrived."

Whitman Publishing did the originals and printed around 500 different titles, but success breeds imitation: Little Big Books from Saalfield, Fast Action Books from Dell, Dime Action Books from Fawcett, Five Star Library, Engel-Van Wiseman and others. Whitman, however, remained the giant in the field. There were movie adaptations with still photos reproduced including, "The Count of Monte Cristo" and "The Three Musketeers."

The death knell for BLBs was struck in 1938 when a caped hero named Superman appeared in Action Comics. The dark and ominous Batman appeared on the scene a year later in Detective Comics #27. This started an avalanche of caped crusaders, masked and unmasked characters in tights that evolved into a craze. In 1944 it was **Captain Marvel** who was the superhero of choice. Big Little Books never recovered from the shock. They quickly lost out to the spectacular color and gloss of comic books. A few new titles came out, and there were variations in format, but they never sold as well as in previous years.

Efforts to include superheroes just didn't quite work out. They never cut the mustard in the confined black and white world of BLBs. For all practical purposes, Whitman gave up on BLBs in 1950. The BLBs permanently belong to the Thirties and war-rationed Forties, when times were hard, people scrimped and saved practically everything (even pieces of string) and when small pleasures in a small format were a big thing.

THE 1950s: A TIME TO REMEMBER

By Ron Elz (Johnny Rabbitt) (Johnny B. Goode)

So you're too young to have first hand Fifties memories? Then parts of this book are just what you need to get a glimpse of how it was way back then. And if you were there, this stuff will open many doors in your mind to allow that really not so long ago time to tumble into today.

St. Louis in the Forties and Fifties meant getting there on Public Service Company buses and streetcars; reading the green stripe edition of *Star Times*; if you were in high school, not letting a week go by without thumbing through the latest edition of *Prom* magazine; shopping downtown at Skruggs-Vandervoort & Barney; spending coupons at **Katz Drug Store**; buying a pretzel from Gus on Arsenal Street near the brewery; riding the respective roller coasters at Westlake (Old Natural Bridge/Rock Road), Chain of Rocks and Forest Park Highlands.

Bill Nunes and Johnny Rabbit at WRTH Radio 2004

There was dancing at **Tune Town**, Westminster Ballroom, Casa-Loma and George Edick's Club Imperial; getting your milk delivered by "Pinky" Pevely; having a phosphate at the neighborhood drug store soda fountain; crusin' Steak and Shake at the Circle; barbecue at Vic's on Skinker or Taystee at Kingshighway and Delmar; having a "Like Hell it's Yours" card inside your Levine's hat; getting a Mr. B (Billy Eckstein) shirt at Kenner's; catching the train at the Wabash Delmar Station, on either the Frisco or MoPac lines at Tower Grove and Vandeventer.

In the Fifties radio was with us everywhere. In the early part of the decade we had Transit Radio on buses and streetcars. It was actually KXOK-FM broadcasting from the Commercial Building and piped in on small round beige speakers spotted in the ceilings of the vehicles. Ted Manger, Skeets Yaney, Roy Queen and Johnny Rion were familiar names to country western music fans. Spyder Burks, George Logan, Dave Dixon, Robert B.Q. and Lou Thimes spun rhythm & blues music. The "tops in pops" were played by the likes of **Ed Bonner, Gil Newsome, Ed Wilson, Peter Martin, Bruce Hayward, King Richard, Chuck Norman and Ray Manning**. Mid-day found shows such as "Queen for a Day," "Ma Perkins," "The Romance of Helen Trent," and young "Dr. Malone." After school, kids ran to their radios to listen in on Mark Trail, The Lone Ranger, Bobby Benson, Straight Arrow and Tom Mix. Among the top local newscasters were Sterling Harkness, John Roedel, Lindley Hines and Frank Eschen. Network newsmen such as Gabriel Heater, Walter Winchell, H.V. Kaltenborn and Lowell Thomas were household names. Until TV finally killed off nighttime network radio in the mid-Fifties, there were such shows as: "The FBI in Peace and War," "Dimension K," "The Inner Sanctum," "The Fat Man," "Duffy's Tavern," "The Great Gildersleeve" and "Baby Snooks."

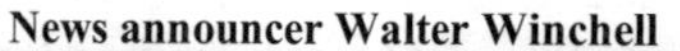

News announcer Walter Winchell

St. Louis television in the Fifties was loaded with local talent - people like Russ Carter, Russ Severin, Charlotte Peters, Ernie Heldmann, Wilma Sims, Bob Ingham, Pat Fontaine, Stan Kann and Texas Bruce (Harry Gibb) . Stan Kann, a collector of old vacuum cleaners, holds the record for most appearances (77) on Johnny Carson's *Tonight Show*. In the early part of the Fifties Channel 4 was KWK-TV and KTVI was WTVI, located on Signal Hill between **Belleville** and East St. Louis.

As far as theaters were concerned, the neighborhood theater, which started off OK in '50, was pretty much dead by 1959. Remember going to see a double feature, complete with a cartoon and a newsreel and previews of coming attractions at places like the Ivanhoe, Grenada, Fairy, Will Rogers, Victory, Lindell, Michigan, Melba, Cinderella, O'Fallon, Bremen, Compton, Lafayette, Kirkwood, and about a hundred more? The American was still in its original location in the white brick American Hotel building at 7th and Market. The Grand was our principal burlesque house on Market next to the York Hotel and both the Garrick and World were in competition with "adult" shows. The Empress, on Olive near Grand, ran legit stage presentations for a time and the Ambassador was converted so it could show "*This is Cinerama.*"

For night life you couldn't beat the DeBalieviere Strip with attractions ranging from Evelyn West, K.O. Koverty's Mural Room, Sorrento's and great eats at Joe Garavelli's. Around town were hot spots like The Chase Club, the Town and Country in the Congress Hotel, the Merry-go-Round at the Park Plaza, old time melodramas at the Goldenrod Showboat on the riverfront, Harry Fender broadcasting live from the Steeplechase Room at the Chase, the Coal Hole in the Coronado, the Boulevard Room at the Jefferson, the Crown Room of the Kings-Way, Mike D'Amico's Chi Chi Room, the Carasal, Buster Wortman's Paddock . . . the names could more than fill this book.

Dining out meant dropping in at such notable eateries as Edmond's, Pagliaccis on Kingshighway and Manchester, La Casa de los Toros, Mrs. Yoest's Hitching Post, Salas, Odorizzi's

Spaghetti House, Amadeo Fiore's Melrose Pizza, Parente's, The Orient, the Rock Grill, Eddy's cafeterias, The Pelican, Ruggeri's, Oldani's, Belevedere Joe's, Johnny Molina's, the Golden Lion, Van Horn's and Buckingham's.

There were no Japanese cars on the road then, but plenty of American cars. There were Studebakers, Kaisers, Henry Js, Edsels, Packards, Mercurys, Desotos, the Jeepster, Nash, Ramblers, Oldsmobiles and Plymouths. For a time we had the St. Louis Browns at Sportsman's Park, the Saints playing football at Public School Stadium and the Hawks basketball team at Kiel. Dizzy Dean, Gus Mancuso, Gabby Street, Harry Caray, France Laux, Joe Garagiola and Stretch Miller were as well known to sports fans as Griesedieck Brothers, Hyde Park and Alpen Brau were to drinkers.

5900 Natural Bridge

In the Fifties we saw the start of channels 9 and 11, the demise of Vandeventer Place, the beginning of Gaslight Square, the demolition derby at the Coliseum, the creation of Busch Bavarian Beer, the tornado of 1959, a movie with Steve McQueen based on a robbery at Southwest Bank, Pookie Snackenberg, Mayor Raymond Tucker, "Hot Rod" Moore, Jules Blattner and the Teen Tones, Sumner High's Chuck Berry, Ike and Tina Turner, the Greenlease case, shopping in the Wellston Loop, Blue Ridge soda, Tip-Top Bread, Korea, poodle skirts, D.A. haircuts, 3-D movies, rock 'n' roll and a simpler way of life . . . that's gone forever.

Here's to the Fifties, they were fabulous!

SONGS OF THE FIFTIES

My older sister Jackie said she grew up in a house where my mother had radio music on all the time while she did household chores. Jackie listened to the music and learned how to sing before she could talk. We never had a very good record player when I was young because my father fixed radios and television sets as a hobby in his spare time. He put together an old clunker changer and figured why spend the money on something else. The up side was that we had television before anyone else in my neighborhood.

Bill Nunes' license plate

The first record my sister ever bought was an old 78 with the purple Capitol label. The hit side had the song "**Sixteen Tons**" by Tennessee Ernie Ford. My sister quickly discovered that she liked the B side and nearly wore our needle out playing it. The title was "You Don't Have to be a Baby to Cry" (All you need is for love to go wrong.) She had just broken up with her boyfriend in a puppy love romance and she moped around for a month, playing that song to death.

DJ Spyder Burks

My first record was "**Mule Train**" by Frankie Laine. I talked my mom into buying it for me when I was in the 6th grade. I memorized the lyrics and played the song over and over. When I was in the 9th grade I talked my mother into buying me an Artone record player from Stix, Baer & Fuller in St. Louis. It cost about a hundred bucks and they gave you one free record with it. My first 45 was "If You Can Dream" by the Four Aces.

I learned that a distributor in East St. Louis sold used records that were taken off juke boxes and charged customers $1.00 for five records. A new record cost 99 cents at the time. I went with my neighborhood pals once a week to make purchases and soon had an extensive collection.

The early Fifties were dominated by singers such as Rosemary Clooney, Perry Como, Les Baxter, Eddie Fisher, Doris Day, Frankie Laine, Mel Tormé, Jo Stafford, Nat "King" Cole, Tony Bennett, Johnny Ray, Patti Page, Theresa Brewer, Dinah Shore, the Ames Brothers and Vic Damone.

Then along came **rock 'n' roll**. Bill Haley and the Comets sang "Rock Around the Clock" in the 1954 Glen Ford movie, *Blackboard Jungle*. I remember seeing the 78 rpm record once and it was labeled a fox trot by bewildered producers. It was Cleveland disc jockey Alan Freed who coined the "rock 'n' roll" phrase. Few knew at the time that it was a euphemism from the black community to describe sexual activity. Another thing that contributed to the music revolution was the fact that teens, for the first time in history – thanks to post-war prosperity – had money to spend. The final component was the **invention of the electric guitar** by Les Paul of Les Paul and Mary Ford fame.

The airwaves went from playing songs like "Doggie in the Window," "This Old House" and "If I knew You Were Coming I'da Baked a Cake" to raucous finger snappin', foot-stomping songs like "See You Later, Alligator," "Roll Over, Beethoven," "Ka Ding Dong" and "Long, Tall Sally." The new music was characterized by songs with teen lyrics, a strong boogie woogie blues rhythm with an accent on the offbeat, electronically amplified instrumentation and a steady beat accentuated by drums.

African-American singers like the Ink Spots, Mills Brothers and Billy Eckstein were quickly replaced by Chuck Berry, Bo Diddley and Little Richard. Blacks dominated the market so completely that record executives frantically searched for the Great White Hope – an Anglo who had moves and could sing like a black person. That persona was found in a hip wiggling, droopy lipped, Mississippi hillbilly by the unlikely name of **Elvis Presley**. Sam Phillips, of Sun Records, immediately signed him to a contract. He was quickly followed by the likes of Carl Perkins, Jerry Lee Lewis and Roy Orbison. The influence of Elvis on the adult population was shocking. The first time "the Pelvis" appeared live on the Ed Sullivan Show the cameras showed him only from the waist up so audiences wouldn't be offended by his gyrating hips.

Yet there was room enough for traditional male crooners like Frank Sinatra ("French Foreign Legion," "Mr. Success") and Tony Bennett ("Stranger in Paradise") to survive, but females such as Rosemary Clooney, Jo Stafford and Patti Page disappeared from the scene. Doris Day survived with songs from her popular formulaic movies with Rock Hudson. She scored with "Teacher's Pet," "Don't Eat the Daisies," "Pillow Talk," "Move Over, Darling" and others.

Groups were still popular, as illustrated by the success of the Crew Cuts, the Four Coins, Four Aces, the Hilltoppers, the Platters and the Four Lads. The music landscape was littered with "one-hit wonders" such as Jimmy Bowen, Russ Hamilton, George Hamilton IV, Royal Teens, Cathy Carr and Bonnie Guitar. There were also "two-hit wonders" such as the Four Preps, Gene Vincent, and Linda Scott. There were also fresh faces that had staying power such as Steve Lawrence, Connie Francis, Andy Williams and Johnny Mathis.

KWK's DJ King Richard

Pat Boone was another hugely successful newcomer. Interestingly, Little Richard and Fats Domino accused him of stealing their hit songs. Pat scored big with white audiences with "Long Tall Sally," "Ain't That a Shame" and "Tutti Frutti." This was possible because, unlike today, singers didn't write their own songs. It was fun back then to see two different artists come out with the same song and you would root for your favorite to triumph over the other on the sales chart. I pulled for Vince Martin and the Tarriers to beat out Eddie Fisher with the song, "Cindy, oh Cindy." I rooted for Frankie Laine's version of "A Woman in Love" to outsell the same song by the Four Aces. I preferred the Hilltoppers' version of "Only You" to the one by the Platters. I also thought Carl Perkins' version of "Blue Suede Shoes" was superior to the one put out by Elvis.

Here is an unprecedented trip down memory lane – a list of Fifties and early Sixties songs that I listen to nearly every day on my MP3 CD player. These are the songs that you hummed along with, listened to, sang in the shower and watched others dance to on American Bandstand. These were the gems that expressed how we felt and how we loved. When you started going steady with that special guy or gal you probably picked out "our song." – a melody that magically said all the words you wanted to say to each other. For me and my gal the song that said it all was, "If Dreams Came True" by Pat Boone.

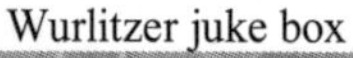

Wurlitzer juke box

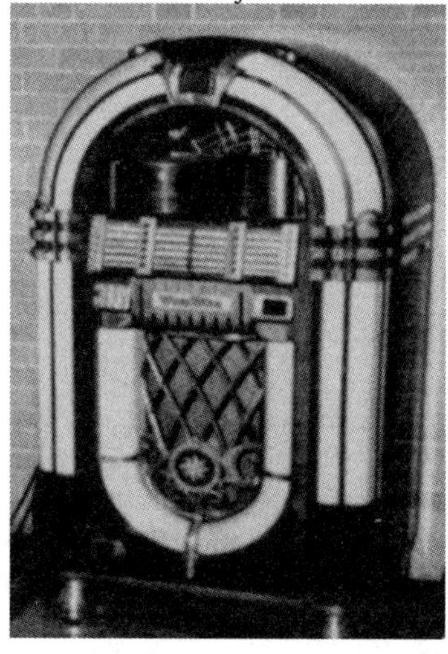

If you were paying close attention back then, you'll probably recognize songs on this list you haven't heard in over 40 years.

Peggy Sue - Buddy Holly, Since I Don't Have You – Skyliners, At the Hop – Danny and Juniors, Blueberry Hill – Fats Domino, Sorry: I ran all the Way Home – Impalas, Lisbon Antigua – Les Baxter, Let Me Go, Lover – Joan Weber, It's Only Make Believe – Conway Twitty, For Your Love – Ed Townsend, Sea of Love - Phil Phillips, Chances Are – Johnny Mathis, Smoke Gets in Your Eyes – Platters, This I Swear – Skyliners, Pledging My Love – Johnny Ace, Chapel Bells – Fascinators, Bye, Bye Love – Everly Brothers, Whole Lotta Shaking Going On– Jerry Lee Lewis, Hush a Bye – Mystics, Shangri La – 4 Coins, Unchained Melody – Les Baxter, Cry Me a River – Julie London, Band of Gold – Kit Carson, Poetry in Motion – Johnny Tillotson, Autumn – The Vogues, Rock Around the Clock – Bill Haley, Summer Holiday – Cliff Richard, Ronnie – 4 Seasons, Dream – Everly Brothers, I Wonder Why – Dion & Belmonts, Venus – Frankie Avalon, You Cheated, You Lied – The Shields, 16 Candles – The Crests, Poor People of Paris – Les Baxter, Be Bop Baby – Rick Nelson, Shake, Rattle and Roll – Bill Haley, The Worrying Kind – Tommy Sands, My Blue Heaven – Fats Domino, Street Where You Live – Vic Damone, Ivory Tower – Cathy Carr, With all my Heart – Jody Sands, When I Fall in Love – Lettermen, Sunday Kind of Love – 4 Seasons, To Know Him is to Love Him–Teddy Bears, Just a Matter of Time – Brook Benton, One Summer Night – Danleers, Where the Boys Are – Connie Francis, You Were Mine – The Crests, Angel Baby – Marcy Blaine, Till – Jill Fontaine, Young Love – Tab Hunter, This Time – Del Ray, Keeps on Hurting – Johnny Tillotson, The World Outside – 4 Coins, Moments to Remember – Vogues, Return to Sender – Elvis, Dancing Shoes – Cliff Richard, To the Aisle – 5 Satins, Goodnight Sweetheart – Spaniels, I'm Available – Margie Rayburn, 16 Reasons – Connie Stevens, He'll Have to Stay – Jeanie Black, Angel on My Shoulder – Shelby Flint, Twilight Time – Platters, Your Precious Love – Stylistics, In the Still of the Night – Satins, ABC Boogie – Bill Haley & Comets, Ain't That a Shame – Fats Domino, Band of Gold – Don Cherry, Stood Up – Rick Nelson, Only You – Hilltoppers, Blue Suede Shoes – Carl Perkins, Tonight Josephine – Johnny Ray, Love Me Tender – Elvis, There's a Moon Out Tonight– Students, Earth Angel – The Penguins, Where or When – Dion and Belmonts, Love Letters in the Sand – Pat Boone, I Only Have Eyes for You – Satins, Moments to Remember – 4 Lads, All the Things You Are – Les Baxter, Memories of You – 4 Coins, Rag Doll – 4 Seasons, Canadian Sunset – Andy Williams, The Book of Love – Monotones, Six Nights a Week – Crests, Just to be with You – Passions, Turn Me Loose – Fabian, Triangle – Janie Grant, Love Letters – Ketty Lester, Johnny Get Angry – Joanie Sommers, Are You Sincere – Andy Williams, Happy, Happy Baby – Bill Haley, I'm in Love Again – Fats Domino, Waiting in School – Rick Nelson, Loving You – Elvis, Gidget – James Darren, Diana – Paul Anka, Ring My Phone – Tommy Sands, Wake the Town – Les Baxter, Only the Lonely – Roy Orbison, Love You in Many Ways–Brook Benton, Blue Velvet – Bobby Vinton, A Love Affair to Remember – Vic Damone, Turn Around Look at Me – Vogues, Lucky Lips - Cliff Richard, Silence is Golden – 4 Seasons, 3 Coins in a Fountain – 4 Aces, Pretty Blue Eyes – Steve Lawrence, I Only Have Eyes for You – Lettermen, Without You – Johnny Tillotson, Two Hearts – Pat Boone, The Way You Did Before – Cliff Richard Lonely Street – Andy Williams, White on White – Danny Williams, Unchained Melody – Righteous Brothers, Hearts of Stone – Fontaine Sisters, Teach Me Tonight – DeCastro Sisters, Butterfly – Charlie Gracie, All in the Game – Cliff Richard, I'm Into Something Good– Pacemakers, 100 Pounds of Clay – Gene

McDaniels, A Rose and a Baby Ruth – George Hamilton IV, Since You've Gone – Ferlin Husky, Standing on the Corner – 4 Lads, Born to be With You – Chordettes, I'm Stickin' With You – Jimmy Bowen, So Sad – Everly Brothers, The Great Pretender – Platters, Party Doll – Buddy Knox, Twinkle Little Star – Stylistics, Come Softly to Me – Fleetwoods, Rhythm of the Rain – Drifters, When – Kalin Twins, I will Follow Him – Peggy March, Susie Darling – Robin Luke, Mr. Blue – Fleetwoods, The Twelfth of Never – Cliff Richard, Donna – Ritchie Valens, 1000 Stars in the Sky – Linda Scott, Hey Paula – Paul and Paula, Close to Cathy – Ted Mark, Johnny Angel - Shelly Fabares, My True Love – Jack Scott, Great Balls of Fire – Jerry Lee Lewis, Wake up Little Susie – Everly Brothers, Stormy Weather – Spaniels, Angels Listened In – Crests,

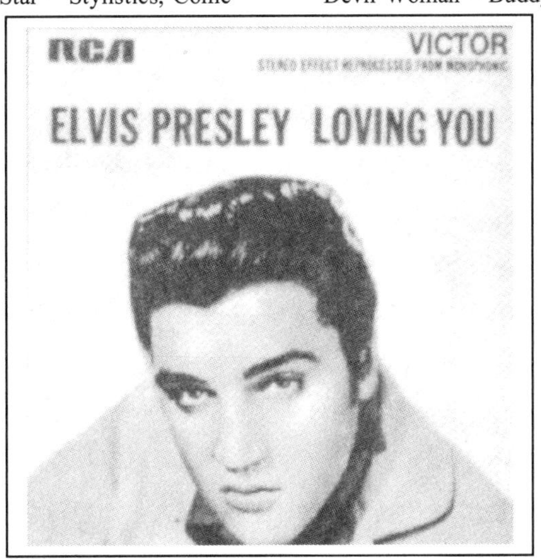

Susie Q – Dale Hawkins, Short Shorts – Royal Teens, Bobby's Girl – Marcy Blaine, My Coloring Book – Sandy Stewart, Just One Look – Doris Troy, Don't Talk to the Lifeguard – Diane Rey, Loving is a Way of Living– Steve Lawrence, Dim the Lights – Bill Haley, Too Young – Nat Cole, Walking in the Rain – Johnny Ray, Stranger in Paradise – 4 Aces, When My Dreamboat Comes Home – Fats Domino, Believe What You Say – Rick Nelson, I Need Your Lovin' Tonight – Elvis, Goodbye Cruel World – James Darren, The Diary – Neil Sedaka, Roses are Red – Bobby Vinton, Big Man in Town – 4 Seasons, Forever isn't Long Enough - McGuire Sisters, Unchained Melody – Lettermen, Ain't That a Shame – Pat Boone, Dreamy Eyes – Johnny Tillotson, Wild Cherry – Don Cherry, Oh, Lonesome Me – Don Gibson, Sh-Boom – Crew Cuts, A White Sport Coat – Marty Robbins, Summertime Blues – Eddy Cochran, Eddie My Love – Fontaine Sisters, A Teenager in Love – Dion & Belmonts, Tonight, Tonight – Mello Kings, Because They're Young – James Darren, Sealed With a Kiss – Bryan Hyland, Poor Little Fool, Rick Nelson, Razzle Dazzle – Bill Haley, Dreaming – Johnny Burnette, Don't Just Stand There – Patty Duke, You're the Reason – Bobby Darin, Midnight Mary – Joey Powers, Please Mr. Sun – The Vogues, I'll Be Home – Pat Boone, Unforgettable – Nat Cole, Why do I Love You So? – Johnny Tillotson, I'm Still a King to You – Don Cherry, Things We Did Last Summer-Lettermen, You're my World – Celia Black, Into Somethin Good – Earl Jean, The Wedding – Julie Rogers, Angel of the Morning – Marilee Rush, R-O-C-K – Bill Haley, A Fallen Star – Hilltoppers, Look Homeward Angel – Johnnie Ray, Why – Frankie Avalon, Honey Don't – Carl Perkins, My Prayer – Platters, Why - Steve Lawrence, I Spoke too Soon – Crew Cuts, Blue, Blue Day – Don Gibson, Heartache Street – 4 Coins, Bye, Bye Baby – 4 Seasons,

Ghost Town – Don Cherry, Love is a Many Splendored Thing – 4 Aces, Our Winter Love – Lettermen, Born too Late – Ponytails, Where Did We Go Wrong? – Vogues, Blue Ribbon Baby – Tommy Sands, Put Your Head on My Shoulder – Paul Anka, Happy Birthday Sweet 16 – Sedaka, Her Royal Majesty – James Darren, Don't Forbid Me – Pat Boone, Endlessly – Brook Benton, Pretend – Nat King Cole, Because They're Young – Duane Eddy, There's Only One of You – 4 Lads, Moonlight Gambler – Frankie Laine, Green Door – Jim Lowe, The Wayward Wind – Gogi Grant, Plaything – Ted Newman, Battle of New Orleans – Johnny Horton, Devil Woman – Buddy Knox, Crazy With Love – Guy Mitchell, I'm Never Gonna Tell – Jimmy Rogers, Rock and Roll Waltz – Kay Starr, Yellow Rose of Texas–Johnny Desmond, Help Me Rhonda – Beach Boys, Till I Kissed Ya – Everly Brothers, All the Way – Frank Sinatra, Alphabet Song – Tommy Sands, Hey, Little Girl – Techniques, No Regrets – Hilltoppers, How Can You Tell Me - Buddy Knox, Wasting Your Time – Hilltoppers, New World - 4 Coins, Go Away Little Girl – Bobby Rydell, No Not Much – 4 Lads, It Doesn't Matter Anymore–Buddy Holly, More – Ray Conniff, Let Me Try Again – Frank Sinatra, He – Al Hibbler, Splish Splash – Bobby Darrin, Stupid Cupid – Connie Francis, Rags to Riches – Tony Bennett, Tiger – Fabian, Goodbye Baby – Jack Scott, Be My Baby – Crystals, Don't get Around Much Anymore –Tab Hunter, French Foreign Legion-Frank Sinatra, Little Darlin' – Diamonds, I Can See Clearly Now – J. Nash, Send Me the Pillow You Dream On – Dean Martin, Younger Girl – Critters, Then He Kissed Me – Crystals, You're 16 – Johnny Burnette, Only Sixteen – Sam Cooke, Dream Lover – Bobby Darin, What a Difference a Day Makes - Dinah Washington, Ooby Dooby – Roy Orbison, Magic Touch – Platters, Sea Cruise – Frankie Ford, Queen of the Hop – Bobby Darin, Cupid – Sam Cooke, Knock on Your Door – Eddie Hodges, Rubber Ball – Bobby Vee, Strangers - Everly Brothers, How Happy I'd Be – Sam Cooke, You Were Mine – Mark Dinning, It Isn't Fair – Platters, Now That We're in Love –Steve Lawrence, Shiela – Tommy Roe, Trouble in Paradise – Rays, Under the Boardwalk – Drifters, Gotta Girl – 4 Preps, Cherish – Blue Boys, Bahama Mama – 4 Aces, I'm in the Mood for Love – 4 Aces, Guess What the Neighbors Will Say–4 Lads, Gee, But It's Lonely – Pat Boone, You Don't Have to Love Me – Eddie Fisher, Wonderful, Wonderful – Tymes, Surfer Girl – Beach Boys, Save the Last Dance for Me – Drifters, All in the Game – Tommy Edwards, All Summer Long – Beach Boys, Melody D'Amour – Ames Brothers, If I Could Only Go Back – Andy Williams, One Boy – Ann Margret/Bobby Rydell, Unchained Melody – Cliff Richard, Sittin' By the Phone – Cliff Richard, Footsteps – Steve Lawrence, I Live for You – Cliff Richard, The 12th of Never – Ray Conniff, Lonely Mixed up Kid – Vogues, Lonely Boy – Paul Anka, Sea of Heartbreak – Don Gibson, Love Letters in the Sand – Pat Boone, Since I Met You Baby – Ivory Joe Hunter, Johnny Angel – Shelly Fabares, Graduation Day – 4 Freshmen, Soldier Boy – Shirelles, I Love How You Love Me – Paris Sisters, You Don't Owe Me – Johnny Ray, Breaking up is Hard – 4 Seasons, Bobby Sox to Stockings – Frankie Avalon, Mambo Rock – Bill Haley, Blue Monday – Fats Domino, Never Be Anyone Else – Rick Nelson, I Need Your Love Tonight – Elvis, Time to Cry – Paul Anka, Ring a Ting Ting – Tommy Sands, It's Over – Roy Orbison, Think Twice – Brook Benton, Gigi – Vic

Damone, Do You Wanna Dance – Cliff Richard, Calendar Girl – Neal Sedaka, End of a Rainbow – Earl Grant, Endless Sleep – Jody Reynolds, You Are My Special Angel, Vogues, Don't Be Afraid – Steve Lawrence, Everybody's Got a Home – Eddie Fisher, Love of my Life – Everly Brothers, No Wedding Today – Johnny Ray, You're Breaking My Heart–4 Coins, Boppin the Blues – Carl Perkins, It's a Woman's World – 4 Aces, Why Baby, Why? – Pat Boone, I Only Have Eyes for You – Platters, I'll Be Around – Don Cherry, Tonight – 4 Lads, Gum Drop – Crew Cuts, I'm Gonna Love You – Frank Sinatra, The Young Ones – Cliff Richard , Everybody Loves a Lover – Doris Day, Little Things Mean a Lot – McGuire Sisters, White Silver Sand – Don Rhondo, Lessons in Love – Cliff Richard, Red Sails in the Sunset – Tab Hunter, Forget Him – Bobby Rydell, Lonesome Town – Rick Nelson, Tin Soldier – Cliff Richard, Falling in Love Again – Jimmy Rogers, Drive in Show – Eddy Cochran, California Dreaming – Beach Boys, Outsider, That's Me – Cliff Richard, Seattle – Perry Como, Love, Love Go Away – Bobby Rydell, Pledging My Love – Johnny Tillotson, Blueberry Hill – Andy Williams, I Cried a Tear – Chordettes, Devoted to You – Everly Brothers, Earth Angel – Johnny Tillotson, Sugartime – McGuire Sisters, I Like Your Kind of Love – Andy Williams, To Know Him is to Love Him – Chordettes, I Got a Feeling – Johnny Tillotson,

St. Louis broadcaster Ray Quinlan

Keep a Knocking – Everly Brothers, Tall Paul – Chordettes, Are You Sincere – Andy Williams, A Woman in Love – 4 Aces , Who Needs You – 4 Lads, Remember You're Mine – Pat Boone, Hold You in My Heart – Eddie Fisher, Let's Hang On – 4 Seasons, Lollipop – Chordettes, Build Your Love – Johnny Ray, Breathless – Jerry Lee Lewis, This Life – 4 Coins, Mr. Teardrop – Don Cherry, Sing Boy Sing – Tommy Sands, See You Later Alligator – Bill Haley, I'm Walkin' – Fats Domino, Puppy Love – Paul Anka, Children Want to Rock – Carl Perkins, Next Door to an Angel – Neil Sedaka, Too Young – Nat King Cole, A Boy Without a Girl – Frankie Avalon, Lips of Wine – Andy Williams, I Only Have Eyes for You – Lettermen, That Same One – Brook Benton, Harbor Lights – Platters, It's Late – Rick Nelson, Crying Over You – Roy Orbison, OOHEEE – Johnny Tillotson, You Don't Know – Steve Lawrence, Moon River – Henry Mancini, Hot Diggety – Perry Como , Juke Box Baby – Perry Como, Got a Funny Feeling – Cliff Richard, Mr. Sandman – 4 Aces, Cindy – Eddie Fisher, Girl Come Running – 4 Seasons, Street of Memories – Johnny Ray, Boppin' at the Hop – J. Lee Lewis, New World – 4 Coins, 14 Karat Gold, Don Cherry, Teenage Crush – Tommy Sands, Don't Knock the Rock – Bill Haley, Uh, Huh, Oh Yeah – Fats Domino, Destiny – Paul Anka, True Love – Carl Perkins, Let's Go Steady Again – Neil Sedaka, Answer Me My Love – Nat Cole, Just Ask Your Heart – Frankie Avalon, Can't Get Used to Losing You - Andy Williams, In the Still of the Night – Lettermen, Fools Rush In – Brook Benton, Ebb Tide – Platters, A Little too Much – Rick Nelson, Pretty Woman – Roy Orbison, Princess – Johnny Tillotson – Loving is Way of Living – Steve Lawrence, Boots – Nancy Sinatra, Then He Kissed Me – Crystals, Hawaii 5-0 – Ventures, I Hear you Knocking – Gale Storm, Seventeen – Fontaine Sisters, Short Shorts – Royal Teens, Eddy my Love – Shepard Sisters, Sink the Bismarck – Johnny Horton, Hearts of Stone – Fontaine Sisters, Don't be Cruel – Elvis, Can't Help Falling in Love – Lettermen, Portrait of my Love – Steve Lawrence, Queen of the Hop – Bobby Darin, Rock & Roll is Here to Stay – Danny & Juniors, Baubles, Bangles & Beads–Kirby Stone 4, Love is a Golden Ring – Frankie Laine,

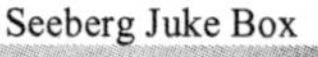

Seeberg Juke Box

Friendly Persuasion – Lettermen, Magic Moments – Perry Como, Runaround Sue – Dion, Big Man – Four Preps, Sugartown – Nancy Sinatra, Wildwood Days – Bobby Rydell, Young Love – Sonny James, Looking for Someone – Buddy Holly, Come Back Silly Girl – Lettermen, He – McGuire Sisters, Dark Moon – Bonnie Guitar 26 Miles – 4 Preps, Secretly – Jimmy Rogers, Around the World – Victor Young, Wishing – Buddy Holly, The Girl on Page 44 – 4 Lads, Julie – Sammy Salvo, Singing the Blues – Guy Mitchell, Be Bop a Lula – Gene Vincent, See You in September – Tempos, Hawkeye – Frankie Laine, As Long as I'm With You– Dean Martin, – Fabulous – Charlie Gracie, Tallahassee Lassie – Freddy Cannon, Sittin' in the Balcony – Eddie Cochran, Lotta Lovin – Gene Vincent, Pillow That You Dream On – D. Martin, Crazy Love – Paul Anka, My One Sin – 4 Coins, Miss Me Just a Little – Johnny Ray, The Tip of my Fingers – Don Cherry, I'll Wait For You – Frankie Avalon, Mona Lisa – Nat "King" Cole, Earth Angel – Johnny Tillotson, Come Back Silly Girl – Steve Lawrence, April Love – Pat Boone, Hot Dog, Buddy Buddy – Bill Haley, Whole Lotta Lovin – Fats Domino, A Guy is a Guy – Doris Day, I'm Sorry – The Platters, Sherry – 4 Seasons, Doesn't Matter Anymore – Paul Anka, The World Outside – 4 Coins, Little White Cloud That Cried – Johnny Ray, They're Not Teardrops – Don Cherry, Togetherness – Frankie Avalon, Smile – Nat King Cole, The Sparrow That Cried – Tillotson, Let's Rip it Up – Bill Haley, Walk Like a Man – 4 Seasons, Walk You Home – Fats Domino, Let It Be Me – The Lettermen, Matchbox Blues – Carl Perkins, Don't Break up With Me – Jerry Lee Lewis, Tina Marie – Perry Como, I'm Not Afraid – Rick Nelson, Till – Vogues, Good Luck Charm – Elvis,

The Way You Did Before – Cliff Richard, Still in Love With You – Tillotson, Woman Helping Man – Vogues, Cry – Johnny Ray, Message to Mary – Don Cherry, Don't Talk to Him – Cliff Richard, That Empty Feeling – Tillotson, Moments to Remember – Vogues, Born to be Your Baby – Perry Como, Love of my Life – Everly Brothers, No Not Much – Vogues, Don't Knock the Rock – Bill Haley, I'm Sorry – Brenda Lee, Dawn – 4 Seasons, Hound Dog – Elvis, Judy – Johnny Tillotson, Statue Of A Fool – Don Cherry, Burn That Candle – Bill Haley, Be My Guest Tonight – Fats Domino, Cinderella – Paul Anka, It'll Be Me – Cliff Richard, My Dream – Platters, Hi Lilly Hi Lo – McGuire Sisters, I Want You, Need, Love You – Elvis, Tears On My Pillow – Little Anthony, Candy Girl – 4 Seasons, Earth Angel – Vogues, A Blossom Fell – Nat King Cole, Street Where You Live – Eddie Fisher, When I Fall In Love – Doris Day, Let's Talk About Us – Jerry L. Lewis, Promise Me Love – Andy Williams, All Shook Up – Elvis, Big Girls Don't Cry – 4 Seasons, Lonely Street – Andy Williams, What In The World – Jack Scott, Can't Get Used to Losing You – Andy Williams, End of the World – Skeeter Davis, Can't Help Falling in Love – Elvis, Secret Love – Doris Day, Happy Heart – Andy Williams, You Belong To Me – Stylistics, Only Love Can Break a Heart – Gene Pitney, Last Dance – Floyd Cramer, If I Give my Heart to You – Doris Day, The Big Beat – Fats Domino, Stars Get in Your Eyes – Perry Como, When I Fall in Love – Nat Cole, Lucky Lips – Cliff Richard, A Fool Never Learns – Andy Williams, Running Scared – Roy Orbison, Stay – 4 Seasons, You Can Make it Happen – Don Cherry, Music To Watch Girls By – A. Williams, I'll Be Seeing You – McGuire Sisters, When I Fall in Love – Nat Cole, Too Much – Elvis, Never Stop Loving You – Doris Day, Devil or Angel – Bobby Vee, Sealed With a Kiss – Brian Hyland, Silhouettes – The

Rays, Patches – Dickie Lee, Make me a Miracle – Jimmy Rogers, Half of My Heart – 4 Aces, Big Man – 4 Preps, Long Hot Summer – Jimmy Rogers, Youngblood Hawke Theme–M. Steiner, Looking Back – Nat "King" Cole, Dancing Shoes – Cliff Richard, A Fool Never Learns – Andy Williams, I Will – Vogues, You Can't Run Away From It – 4 Aces, A House With Love in It – 4 Lads, Jenny, Jenny, Jenny – Eddie Cochran, Things – Bobby Darin, Thirteen Going on 14 – Crew Cuts, Every Day of My Life – McGuire Sisters, Since You've Gone – Joey Heatherton, Treat Me Nice – Elvis, One Last Kiss – Bobby Vee, You'll Never Know – Platters, Difference A Day Made – Dinah Washington, Devoted to You – Everly Brothers, I Have Dreamed – Frank Sinatra, Because of You – 4 Lads, My Heart Belongs to You – 4 Lads, Toy Soldier – 4 Seasons, – All in the Game – Tommy Edwards, Never Walk Alone – Frank Sinatra, Mr. Sandman – Chordettes, Kisses Sweeter Than Wine – Jimmy Rogers, Good Time Baby – Bobby Rydell, Unforgettable – Natalie & Nat Cole, My Girl – Temptations, Love and Marriage– Sinatra, What is Love? – Playmates, Autumn Leaves – F. Sinatra, Wonderland by Night – Bert Kampfert, People – Barbara Streisand, Little Things Mean a Lot – Platters, Don't go Home – Playmates, The Next Time – Cliff Richard, Twelfth of Never – Johnny Mathis, Tender Trap – Sinatra, Non Dimentecar – Nat Cole, – Wait for Me – Playmates, Lonely One – Paul Anka, Strangers in the Night – Bert Kampfert, Wonderful, Wonderful – Mathis, Bewitched – Doris Day, Star Love – Playmates, Small World – Johnny Mathis, Only You – Platters, Hey, Little Girl – Techniques, Love me to Pieces – Jill Corey, Jo Ann – Playmates, Stardust – Nat Cole, She's Not You – Elvis, Don't Bet Money, Honey – Linda Scott, Blue, Navy Blue – Diane Renay, Lawdy, Miss Clawdy – Elvis, This Nearly Was Mine – F. Sinatra, Make Me Forget Her – Bobby Rydell, I'm Hurting – Roy Orbison, That's My Desire – Frankie Laine, More – Ray Conniff, Priscilla – Eddy Cooley, Saturday's Kisses – Charley Applewhite, Mr. Success – F. Sinatra, Angry – Frank Pizzani, Wandering Eyes – Charlie Gracie, – Here Comes Summer – Jerry Keller, Tallahassie Lassie – Freddy Cannon, I Hear You Knocking – Fats Domino, Rock-A-Billy – Guy Mitchell, I Love My Girl – Cozy Cole, I Need Your Lovin' – Conway Twitty, Runaway – Del Shannon, I'll Remember You – Elvis, Wind and Rain in Your Hair – Pat Boone, East Virginia – George Hamilton 4, Young and Foolish – Ray Conniff, Pretty World – Blue Boys, People Like You – Eddie Fisher, Too Young to Go Steady–Tommy Sands , There She Goes – Jerry Wallace,

St. Louisan Chuck Berry (L. Tettaton)

White bucks from Zerensky Bros. in Maplewood popularized by Pat Boone

Walk Right Back – Everly Brothers, One Boy – Joanie Summers, I Think We're Alone Now – Shondells, Younger Girl – Critters, Sugar, Sugar – Archies, Our Day Will Come–Ruby & Romantics, Why Baby, Why? – Pat Boone, You Send Me – Sam Cooke, I Dreamed – Betty Johnson, First Date – Sonny James, My Promise – Patty Page, I'll be Home – Pat Boone, I Will Follow Him – Peggy March, That's All – Rick Nelson, Take Care of my Baby – Bobby Vee, You'd be Surprised – Kathy Linden, Rosie – Chubby Checker, After School – Joy Lane, The Secret – Gene McDaniels, Living Doll – Cliff Richard, He's So Married – Doris Day, What do You Want? - Craig Douglas, Rainbow – Russ Hamilton, Wind in the Willow – Jo Stafford, Happy Together – Turtles, Blue on Blue – Bobby Vinton, Teddy Bear – Elvis, Volare – Bobby Rydell, Love is a Many Splendored Thing – Ray Conniff, Lover Come Back – Ray Conniff, Jamaica Farewell – Harry Belafonte, Round and Round – Perry Como, Autumn Leaves – Roger Williams, Sincerely – McGuire Sisters, Tammy – Debbie Reynolds, Catch a Falling Star – Perry Como, Put Away Teardrops – Steve Lawrence, Sweet Little– Chuck Berry, Walking to New Orleans – Fats Domino, Rocking Through the Rye – Bill Haley, True Lovers – Vogues, School Days – Chuck Berry, Trying to Lose the Blues – Hilltoppers, My Love – Blue Boys, Twixt Twelve and Twenty – Pat Boone, Are You Beautiful Because? – Mel Torme, Dungaree Doll – Eddie Fisher, Got You Under my Skin – Mel Torme, Games That Lovers Play – Eddie Fisher, Cindy, Oh Cindy – Eddie Fisher, You're the One – Vogues, Stay Here and Love You – Steve Lawrence, Does Your Heart Beat For Me? - McGuire Sisters, Teen Angel – Mark Dinning, Love me Tender – Elvis, The Way You Look Tonight - Lettermen, Splish Splash – Bobby Darin, Rockin' Robin – Bobby Day, Dream – Roy Orbison , Together – 4 Lads, A Woman in Love – Frankie Laine, I'll Never Love Again – 4 Coins, Carnival Time – Cliff Richard, It's Up to You – Rick Nelson, Ka Ding Dong – Hilltoppers, Old Enough to Love – Rick Nelson, Summertime – Rick Nelson, Such a Shame – Crew Cuts, Dream World – 4 Coins, That's All She Wrote – Rick Nelson, Be True to Me – Rick Nelson, Don't Take Advantage of Me – Rick Nelson, You Tear Me Up – Rick Nelson, Uptown – Roy Orbison, My Little Corner of the World – Osmond, Most Beautiful Girl – Ray Conniff, Ko Ko Mo – Crew Cuts, Light in the Window – 4 Lads, When the Swallows Come Back to Capistrano – Pat Boone, Cry Softly – Andy Williams, My Love Loves Me – 4 Coins, to Know You is to Love You – Vinton, Written on the Wind – 4 Aces, Singing in the Rain – Doris Day, P.S. I Love You – Vogues , No Sun Today – Vogues, Give Her Love – F. Sinatra, Moulin Rouge Theme – Percy Faith, We Say Yeah – Cliff Richard, Please Don't Leave – Fats Domino, Good Time Baby – Bobby Rydell, Lewis Boogie – J. Lee Lewis, She's Something Else – Eddie Cochran, Kissing Time – Bobby Rydell, Baby the Rain Must Fall - Glen Yarborough, Once in a While – Chimes, Don't Know What You've Got – Ral Donner, Football Season's Over – Shelly Fabares, Around the World – McGuire Sisters, Forget Him – Bobby Rydell, Rock Your Baby to Sleep– Buddy Knox, Next Stop, Paradise – Teddy Rendazzo, Apple Blossom Time – Tab Hunter, Palisades Park – Freddy Cannon, Cindy - Vince Martin & Tarriers, Ko Ko Mo – Beach Boys, Party Doll – Buddy Knox, Kiss and Make Up – Bobby Vinton, Oh, Carol – Neil Sedaka, What I've Been Looking For – Vogues, Walking Proud – Steve Lawrence, Take Good Care of my Baby – Lettermen, Hawaiian Wedding Song – Andy Williams, Bernadine – Pat Boone, Heart – 4 Aces, This Life – 4 Coins, Don't Be Afraid – Steve Lawrence, Two Hearts – Crew Cuts, Sentimental Over You – Frank Sinatra, Please Mr. Sun – Vogues, Without You – Tillotson, Tell me When – Nat King Cole, Embraceable You – Nat King Cole.

If you have an MP3 player and would like information about owning this collection, call Bill Nunes at 618-288-5185.

WESTERN TV PROGRAMS OF THE 1950s & '60s

Remember how westerns used to dominate television? Ride back with me through the mists of time. At one point in 1959 there were twenty-eight different television westerns on every week. These cowpokes and sheriffs were the heroes of our youth as they looked evil straight in the eye and never flinched. As the Encore Western Channel puts it, these gunslingers made towns back then safe places for decent folks to live. To them, right and wrong was as simple as black and white and they were always on this side of the law. No such thing as the anti-hero in the good old days. What follows is a list of what author Bill Nunes watched.

.

Lawman – John Russell and Peter Brown
Gunsmoke – James Arness, Amanda Blake and Dennis Weaver
Rawhide – Clint Eastwood, Eric Fleming, John Ireland
Wyatt Earp – Hugh O'Brian (brave, courageous and bold)
Wild Bill Hickok – Guy Madison and Andy Devine
Roy Rogers – Dale Evans and Pat Brady, Trigger, Bullet
Gene Autry – Pat Buttram and horse Champion
Wanted: Dead or Alive – Missourian Steve McQueen (he carried a sawed off Winchester shotgun instead of a .45 revolver)
Johnny Yuma The Rebel – Nick Adams, Johnny Cash song
Laredo – Peter Brown, Neville Brand
Bat Masterson – Gene Barry
Sugarfoot – Will Hutchins
Cheyenne – Clint Walker
Maverick – James Garner (Bret), Jack Kelly (Bart), Roger Moore (Beau Maverick)
Bonanza – L. Greene, D. Blocker, M. Landon, Pernell Roberts
Champion the Wonder Horse – Barry Curtis, song by Frankie Laine
Have Gun Will Travel – Richard Boone
Wild, Wild West – Robert Conrad, Ross Martin
Cade's County – Glen Ford, Edgar Buchanan – modern western
Yancy Derringer – Jock Mahoney
The Lone Ranger – Clayton Moore, John Hart, Jay Silverheels
The Cisco Kid – Duncan Renaldo, Leo Carillo, Diablo, Loco
Wagon Train – Ward Bond, John McIntyre, Robert Horton
Hopalong Cassidy – William Boyd, Edgar Buchanan, Topper
The Virginian – James Drury, Doug McClure, Clu Gulager, Lee Cobb, Shiloh Ranch at Medicine Bow, Wyoming
The Guns of Will Sonnett – Walter Brennan, Dack Rambo
Death Valley Days – Hosted by Ronald Reagan, Dale Robertson
Tales of Wells Fargo – Dale Robertson as agent Jim Hardie
The Big Valley – Barbara Stanwyck, Lee Majors, Linda Evans
Cimarron Strip – Stuart Whitman, Jill Townsend 90 minute show
The Gabby Hayes Show – George "Gabby" Hayes host
Trackdown – Robert Culp as Texas Ranger Hobie Gilman
The Deputy – Henry Fonda
High Chaparral – Leif Erickson, Cameron Mitchell
The Iron Horse – Dale Robertson, Gary Collins, Ellen Burstyn
Johnny Ringo - Don Durant and Karen Sharpe
Broken Arrow – John Lupton & Michael Ansara

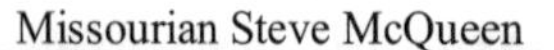
Missourian Steve McQueen

John Russell & Peter Brown

FOREST PARK HIGHLANDS

Opened in 1896 and burned in a July 19, 1963 electrical fire
260 firefighters battled the flames in 97 degree heat that day
Located on Oakland Avenue, just east of the Arena
Octagon entrance with ticket booths and concession stand
The Comet – roller coaster ride that lasted two minutes
Flying Turns – Bobsled ride inside a barrel-like track – only seven in entire U.S. were ever built
The swimming pool was at the west end of the park
Dance Hall where the likes of Duke Ellington performed
Snow Cone concession stand
Fun House with curved mirrors that made you fat or skinny
Kiddie Land with an assortment of rides for toddlers
Shooting gallery
Tilt-A- Whirl and Ferris wheel left undamaged by the fire
Tall tower with a metal flag that had only 48 stars
Little Toot train ride that went under Comet superstructure
Dodge-'em Cars – head on collisions were a no no
Circle Swing airplane ride
Circle Swing rocket ship ride
Aero Jet ride with a hand operated joystick for up or down
Grazing sheep that kept the grass trimmed by the Comet
Arcade section with skee ball and coin operated games
Red and black Japanese pagoda bought after 1904 Fair
The refurbished Carousel is now in Faust Park in **Chesterfield** where they have that great display of live butterflies
Forest Park Community College is on the old Highlands site

TAKING A DATE TO THE CHAIN OF ROCKS AMUSEMENT PARK

What follows is an excerpt from ***Illinoistown***, Bill Nunes' 2005 novel set in East St. Louis/St. Louis during the summer of 1950. Our hero, Brad Logan, is head-over-heels in love with Lorna Sanders, but she is not yet smitten. Lorna is hesitant about a serious relationship, fearing it will interfere with her pursuit of a budding journalism career.

Chain of Rocks Amusement Park: a thrill-a-minute carnival with an assortment of rides that promised plenty of "chills and spills." Located in rural north St. Louis on bypass Route 66, it sat high on the bluff overlooking the Mississippi River. Not as big as its city counterpart, the Forest Park Highlands, it, nevertheless, had plenty of its own charm and appeal.

"How about some cotton candy, Lorna?"

"That sounds fine."

Lorna and Brad watched in fascination as the vendor took a long cone of paper and held it down in the spinning metal bowl. It magically converted sugar and food coloring into spider-like strands that were adeptly wound into a fluffy ball. Pink angel hair.

"Here, try some," Brad said, after

paying the man a dime. They were finally on their first real date.

"I haven't had one of these in a coon's age." She held the cone to her mouth and closed her lips around the sweet fleecy fibers. "Ummm . . . good stuff; it literally melts in your mouth."

"And, unfortunately, on your face. You have some in the left corner of your mouth."

She flicked her tongue sideways then frowned in puzzlement. "I mean your other left," he corrected. Because he was facing her, he had told her the wrong side. "Here, it works better when you pick it off the cone with your fingers." He plucked a sticky morsel and playfully dangled it close to her mouth. She leaned her face forward and took it with her tongue.

"Over the lips and past the gums, look out stomach, here it comes!" she puckishly rhymed.

Brad smiled while licking his fingers. "Are you up to riding the Comet?"

"What?"

"The roller coaster?"

"Oh, of course," she said. "I love exciting challenges. Why is it called the Comet?"

"Pure psychology. If you close your eyes it seems as if you are zooming through outer space."

"Let's do it," she said with an impish smile.

They finished the cotton candy then headed toward the ride.

Chain of Rocks Park on the Mississippi – Wikipedia

"I just love the clinking sound of the chain as it tows the string of cars up the incline," he said.

A rush of adrenaline pulsed in their ears in fearful anticipation of plummeting down the back of an ancient writhing sea monster. The cars nearly came to a complete stop as they reached the apex of the wood and steel labyrinth, slowly negotiating the turn at the top.

"The brink of impending doom," she said, placing her hands over her eyes.

Then they began to fall, like a car going over a cliff—headlong into the abyss. Faster. Faster. Hands moved quickly to the steel safety bar and maintained a vise-like grip as they held on for their lives, looking straight ahead, too terrorized to glance at each other. A gale force wind from the breakneck speed pulled Lorna's ponytail backwards. The harsh sounds of cast alloyed wheels, groaning on metal rails, and the whoosh of rushing air were nearly drowned out in a rising crescendo of screams and yells from passengers.

They hit bottom, caught their breaths, and zoomed up the next hill. As the train of cars careened around the first turn, passengers mouthed "oohs" and "aahs" of excitement. The centrifugal force threw Lorna's body against Brad; she squealed and clamped her hand on top of his. The metal monster squirmed and thrashed as if it were trying to dislodge its offending tormentors. Brad and Lorna trembled through the harrowing final stretch, their limp bodies slumping forward as the brake mechanism brought the ride to a screeching halt. The terror was over. They had survived.

"We're still alive. Thank God," she said.

Two exhausted bodies were gasping for air after the ninety-second exhilarating adventure. Lorna modestly slipped her hand away from his. He had been surprised that the casual, incidental touch of their bodies caused his nerve endings to jangle. Her touch left him feeling uneasy, as if his heart was wandering into uncharted territory.

"Let's go again," she said, with excitement in her eyes. "I felt like we were riding a blazing comet, zooming through the cosmos in frenzied search of a distant galaxy."

"Spoken like a true writer. That's very poetic," he chided.

They rode the roller coaster four more times before moving on to other pleasures.

"Have some hot roasted peanuts," he said, offering the newly purchased bag.

She daintily selected a few shell-covered morsels.

"See the swimming pool over there?" he pointed. "It's sitting smack dab in the middle of the boundary line between St. Louis and St. Louis County."

"How do you know?" Lorna challenged, as if he had made it up to impress her.

"A good friend of mine, **Ed Wood**, a St. Louis policeman, told me."

Their next stop was the Ferris wheel—a giant Erector set circle with swinging gondolas. It sat near the edge of the bluff, perpendicular to the river.

"When we get to the top look out over the Mississippi," he said. "It's a breathtaking sight—almost as good as the view from an airplane."

Lorna surveyed the picture-perfect view below. "It's absolutely magnificent," she gasped, as the air rushed from her lungs.

Brad loved everything about the amusement park—its carnival atmosphere, the happy sounds, the mixture of smells—Cracker Jack, popcorn, sawdust, crackling electricity—the revelry, the crowds, the energy of it all. They took in as much as they could. A derby-topped barker in a red-checkered vest was persuasive as he described fantastic human anomalies. Side shows—a man completely covered with tattoos, a female contortionist, a sword swallower, the alligator boy, the petrified body of a male dredged from the Ohio River. Brad figured it must have been plaster of Paris.

His marksmanship earned a small fuzzy Teddy bear at the shooting gallery. Lorna jumped up and down and squealed with excitement whenever his small caliber bullet knocked down one of the moving animal targets. A brass casing plopped down on the counter each time he squeezed off a shot.

"Are those real bullets?" Lorna asked.

"Yes, and no."

"Meaning?"

St. Louisan Caroline Charlwood on Chain-of-Rocks-Bluff 1938

"It's what they call a .22 B-B. Twenty-two caliber bullets are made in regular, long, and short lengths. This shell fires a B-B pellet similar to an air rifle. The pellets are strong enough to knock over the targets without damaging them. Most .22 rifles throw their shells off to the right, but the ejection port on these is on the bottom so they won't hit anyone standing nearby. The gun is mounted on a swivel for reasons of safety."

"Could I try it? I've never shot a gun before."

"Sure—there's practically no kick to these things. You know what Raymond Chandler says?"

"What?"

"There's nothing more dangerous than a beautiful dame with a gun."

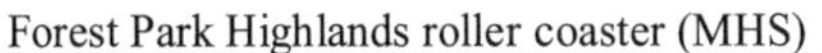

Forest Park Highlands roller coaster (MHS)

"Yeah, that's probably why they fasten them down." Lorna gave him a sly smile and then cradled the weapon against her right shoulder.

He leaned over from behind and showed her the proper grip. The intoxicating smell of her hair momentarily caused him to lose concentration.

"Don't squint like you see it done in Western movies. When both eyes stay open you have better depth perception. Keep your breathing controlled. Line up the target in your sights and squeeze off a round."

Lorna excitedly began pulling the trigger. She let out little joyous squeals each time her B-B found its mark. She kept pulling until the gun made only a metallic clicking sound.

"You're a natural," he said. "One more bull's-eye and you would have won a prize. A regular Annie Oakley, that's what you are."

The Tilt-A-Whirl spun them dizzy; then they rode side-by-side on spirited merry-go-round horses while the machine's happy calliope cranked out several peppy tunes. Lorna won a Kewpie doll at a ring toss game. They gorged themselves on plump roasted hot dogs smothered with mustard and pickle relish.

"You have a yellow glob on your chin," she teased.

He playfully thrust his angled feature toward her and she dabbed it with a paper napkin.

"There, that's better. You need someone to take care of you."

"Thank you, Miss," he playfully mocked. "That's exactly what my mother says."

They screamed and hollered on the Whip, an oblong-shaped seated ride that hurled its occupants around the ends with the same cracking motion made by the snap of Lash La-Rue's bull whip. They scampered their way through the fun house—a winding maze of slanted floors. Distorting mirrors brought smiles of mirth. Goofy images—thin, fat, spindly legs, squished body, misshapen faces. Harmless obstacles mixed with unexpected sounds and noises. They recoiled at a clown face when it popped out. The floor below began rocking as if the entire building were about to be consumed by a massive earth-quake spawned by the New Madrid fault. Lorna grabbed his shoulder in a futile effort to maintain her balance. She couldn't help but notice the firmness of his muscle tone. ***Masculine yet gentle in spirit***, she thought. One final surprise at the exit—a sudden blast of air went up her dress, eliciting a startled, indignant yell.

Brad mildly protested when Lorna grabbed his arm and dragged him past a tall man wearing a painted sandwich board. The advertising promised bedazzlement from dark-eyed dancing beauties clad in veils and flimsy Turkish pantaloons.

Later, they stood in amazement and listened in fascination as a mustachioed organ grinder, dressed like a gypsy in old-world clothes, turned the crank on his hurdy-gurdy. There was a patch on the sleeve of his shirt. His clothes were worn but clean. They were transfixed by the playful antics of his small monkey, dressed in a red and yellow bellhop uniform, ceaselessly chattering. It darted back and forth on the wooden top of the music machine. A few coins were dropped in his tin cup at the end of the entertaining routine.

"***Hvala lijepo***" (Thank you nicely), the man said in perfect Croatian.

"Hey, there's a gypsy lady. Let's go in and have her read your fortune." Brad dragged Lorna into the small booth before she could answer.

"Have a seat and show me your hand," the old world woman said to her.

"But, this is silly – I don't believe in palmistry."

"Please, give me your hand—it's a spiritual roadmap."

Reluctantly, Lorna let the gypsy woman take her hand.

She studied the lines. "You're a Cancer, aren't you?"

Lorna nodded. ***Lucky guess.***

"And you're an only child."

A soft *yes* escaped Lorna's lips. ***Next she'll be telling me that I'm going to inherit a very large sum of money.***

"You should treasure that which you have recently found."

More mumbo-jumbo.

A difficult period of great sorrow will soon come into your life, and if you have the strength and will to survive, a long spell of much happiness will follow."

Flying Turns/Bobsled ride at the Highlands (MHS)

"I don't suppose you'd care to elaborate?"

The gypsy lady shrugged. "I'm sorry, that is all your hand tells me; I can say no more."

Lorna gave Brad a skeptical look as they left the fortune teller's booth. He smiled. "I thought the old woman's predictions were very interesting."

Lorna rolled her eyes.

Brad changed the subject. "Let's go through the Tunnel of Love." They neared the end of a perfect day and Brad saved the best for last.

Lorna was caught off guard. She hadn't expected such a request and a look of confusion spread across her face.

"I'll behave," he promised. "I'll be a perfect gentleman." He had carefully watched her body language all day long, and even though she was clearly having the time of her life, she had offered no romantic encouragement. They hadn't even progressed to the hand holding stage of a male-female relationship.

Bird's eye view of the Forest Park Highlands (MHS)

"Okay . . . but only if you swear."

"Scout's honor," he said, giving a two-fingers over his heart mock salute.

"Isn't it supposed to be three fingers against your brow?" she skeptically asked.

"Oops, sorry. You found me out. I was never a Scout."

"Gee! A poet and doesn't know it. Do you know their motto?"

"Sure. 'Be Prepared.' "

"Very good. How about the Girl Scouts credo?"

"Uh, no."

"Look Out For The Boys!"

He enjoyed her sense of humor. They gingerly climbed into a boat in front of a darkened entrance that featured a big flashing red heart at the top. An attendant held the ride steady to keep it from rocking back and forth. All of the couples in front were sitting close together. The guy directly ahead had a friendly arm around his girl. They pretended not to notice. A moving current slowly pulled the boat through a meandering stream of shallow water, artificially colored by a blue dye. The murky interior was decorated in the style of a lush tropical paradise with soft Hawaiian music playing in the background. Electronically reproduced sounds of assorted exotic birds occasionally interrupted.

"That's a toucan calling to his mate," he whispered, hoping she would at least give him a peck on the cheek. An invisible bundling board separated them.

"Yes . . . well, don't let that get you all hot and bothered. I'd hate to see you come down with jungle fever."

She spoke in a manner that was defensively mild, a libido-deflating device. His ego had sent up a trial balloon, and her pointed words pricked it and made it go "pop."

They sat for the rest of the ride in uncomfortable stillness. The enormity of what had just transpired hit her. She had in-tended to make him keep his distance—not to wound or emasculate. But it ended the date on a sour note.

They drove home in stilted silence. As the car crossed the seven-piered Chain of Rocks Bridge, Lorna finally spoke. "I've had a wonderful time today," she said as she leaned over and tenderly allowed her lips to brush his cheek. "I'm sorry if I bruised your enthusiasm. I like you a lot, but . . ."

"But what?" he frowned.

"It's just . . . I'm not ready for a steady relationship with a man. I'm only going on twenty and I want to experience what life has to offer before I get serious with anyone."

"What about the fellow at your office I hear you're dating—Lance . . . Mackerel?"

"It's Troutman, and that better have been a

Freudian slip. He's taken me to lunch a few times, but I feel the same way about him. I don't want an exclusive relationship. I'm not ready for courtship. At this point I'd like to continue going out with both of you. And, who knows, someone else could come along I might want to date."

"You do want to eventually get married and have children?"

"Of course, some day. But how will I know what kind of a man I want as a life-long companion, and what personality traits to look for, unless I have a variety of first-hand experiences with men of all makes and models. Er, excuse the car-buying metaphor."

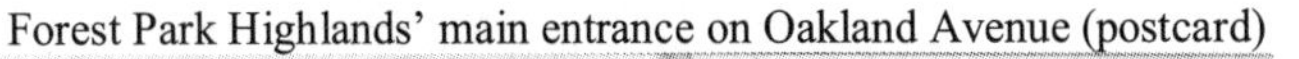

Forest Park Highlands' main entrance on Oakland Avenue (postcard)

"It makes sense, I guess—quite logical. But the process doesn't seem to allow for the unknown part of the equation that brings most men and women together in marriage. Two hearts beating as one in three-quarter time."

"And what exactly is that, pray tell?"

"I don't know if I can explain."

"Please try."

"Uh, did you see the movie ***Pinocchio***? "

"Yes."

"Remember the scene where Pinocchio has drowned after his encounter with Monstro, the whale? Then an angel comes down from a bright star in the heavens and brings him back to life. Before you kissed me on the cheek back there, I felt like that dead little wooden puppet. I probably shouldn't be telling you this, but I find you magical, a lovely person who has the power to make me truly feel alive."

Duke Ellington entertains a Highlands ballroom crowd of 1,700 (UMSL)

"I wish I could tell you I tingle all over when I am with you, but I don't. And I don't feel it with Lance either. I have seen other women follow the dictates of their hearts. Sometimes it works, and sometimes it doesn't," she explained. "I am not sure I'm ready to entrust my heart to a man. That's a very scary proposition for me. And I've got my career to think about. A serious relationship would only complicate my life."

"I think I grasp what you're saying," he said. "I wish you felt otherwise, but I'm willing to follow your ground rules if that's what it takes to continue seeing you."

"Thanks for understanding. You're not upset, are you?"

"Totally crushed, but I'm resilient—I'll bounce back... You know what?"

Lorna shook her head. "Tell me."

"Maybe your heart is so filled with the other things life has to offer, they're crowding out the trust needed to make any kind of commitment to a relationship. You have to keep your heart soft, you know."

"Why?"

"Cupid's arrow will never penetrate if you build a hard shell around his target."

"I don't think I'm ready to feel the sting of his barb just yet."

"I'm not sure it's something you plan for—it just happens."

"You sound like an incurable romantic."

He turned his head toward her. "I'm sor–"

She pushed her hand softly against his lips and covered them with her fingers. "Hush! It's okay—probably what I like about you the most - that, and your wonderful offbeat sense of humor." She looked him straight in the eyes. "I honestly don't know what my problem is." Her hand moved to his cheek and lingered there. "And I don't know how long it will take to find out. I'm happy with our relationship, just the way it is. Please be patient with me; don't become possessive. And don't rush it." She retreated to the far side of the seat.

"I'll try," he said. "Thanks for being square with me. All I know is I like being with you, and at this point I'm willing to accept you on those terms."

They parked by the curb at the Beulah Club, the boarding house in East St. Louis where Lorna lived.

"Say, don't we have this dating routine backwards?" he asked.

"What do you mean?"

"Isn't it the woman who is supposed to push things to a serious state of affairs while the man dawdles and hesitates? I'm a bit confused by this modern woman-in-pursuit-of-a-career thing. Do you think perhaps I was born in the wrong century? Maybe I should have been a dashing knight in King Arthur's court."

"You know, I really do have fun when I'm with you." She sat there looking down at her lap as her face broke out in a pretty smile. "I hope you stick around awhile."

He got out of the car, went to her side, and opened the door.

"Thank you, Sir Lancelot."

"The pleasure was mine, my Lady... "

"... Guinevere," she reminded.

"Ah, yes—Guinevere."

Lorna glanced up. "Look," she said as he closed the door. "A shooting star—quick, make a wish!"

Brad looked up at infinity. “Okay, I wish—”

“No.” She was waving her hand in front of his face. “If you say it out loud it won’t come true.”

“It already has.”

“What?”

The Parkmoor Drive-in Restaurant on Clayton Rd. (Tettaton picture)

“We’re here, together, aren’t we?”

“That’s very sweet.” She leaned forward and gave him a quick kiss on his lips. When they reached the front door, he gently took her hand and said, “I cheated and made two wishes.”

“And what was the second one?”

“Can I have a hug?”

“A hug? I’ve never had a guy ask me for a ***hug*** at the end of a date.”

Brad gave her a boyish smile. “Well, get used to it because I come from a long line of great huggers. In my family, it’s tradition. Think of it as a safe way to start becoming involved with someone emotionally.”

“You’re a real schemer, aren’t you? I think—”

Brad stopped her in mid-sentence and pulled her toward him. As he lightly kissed her hair she melted in his arms and took comfort in his reassuring strength. She loved his smell, a manly scent of body oils, soap and aftershave.

He released her as she pushed away. “What’s wrong, don’t you like it?”

“Au contraire. I ***loved*** it; that’s the problem. Goodnight, sweet prince,” she whispered, as she turned and disappeared inside.

Brad blew her a kiss that she did not see, then turned and loped back to his car. Whistling a happy tune, he playfully leap-frogged over a fireplug in his path.

She likes me.

“We Will Kill the Old Red Rooster When She Comes”

I talked with a number of St. Louisans who told me they grew up in rural areas that are now completely urbanized. Aleeta Verman Urbahns (of **Florissant)** said that when she was a little girl the congested intersection of New Halls Ferry Road and Lindbergh (Cross Keys) was all farm land.

The 49th Street Washington Park house I grew up in had a nice back yard that was about 50’ deep by 75’ wide. It had once been part of a farm, and when my parents bought the property (in 1945) it had a 10’ x 12’ chicken coop with one bantam rooster and about nine laying hens. A wire fence confined the feathered fowl to an area about 20’ x 20’. Our deed restriction said we were not allowed to sell to a Negro, nor could we convert it to a saloon or keep pigs, horses, or cows on the property. But it didn’t say anything about chickens. The coop had a large window in front, a door on the right side and an incline that led to a small opening for comings and goings. The incline was necessary because the coop rested on six strategically placed cinder blocks that served as piers. Inside there were several horizontal poles for “roosting” at night, plus some wooden cubicles with straw to serve as nesting sites for egg laying. On the outside, the coop was weatherized with a medium brown asphalt siding marked off to look like bricks. It was topped with a roof that sloped from front to rear to shed water.

I was only six at the time and never quite understood why we had so many hens and only one rooster. I later found out in a science class why he was such a cocky little devil. Every once in a while, on “special” Sundays, we had chicken and dumplings for dinner.

It was silly, of course, but it was my job to change the water and feed the chickens and I grew attached to them. I gave them all names from either female radio personalities or widows who lived in the neighborhood. One was named Mary, after Mary Kent. She had this incredible tangle of auburn hair that looked a bit like a Brillo pad. Mary suffered from bad kidneys and neighborhood gossip had it that one night she was miraculously healed by **Little David**, that phenomenal 12 year old kid minister. Mary had gone to doctors, chiropractors and people who mixed roots and mumbled incantations to cure illnesses, but she was unable to obtain relief.

KMOX Radio’s Emmett McAuliffe – both Nunes and Tettaton have been frequent guests (Tettaton picture)

One night she went to the Ainad Temple to hear Little David at a revival. At the conclusion of the service he held a faith healing session and she climbed the stairs to the stage where he could lay hands on her. He anointed her with oil, whispered a prayer and then said, “Praise God, you’re healed!” Mary felt the spirit inside her and began to dance around in celebration. While in the throes of ecstatic joy she tripped over a microphone wire and fractured her arm. Several men rushed to her aid and one suggested that an ambulance be called. Another said, however, that all that was needed was for Little David to say another prayer. The young Bible-thumping evangelist demurred and replied, "I think you had better call an ambulance. I don't do broken bones, just migraine headaches, rheumatism and insomnia."

Ruby Paugh was another hen named for a neighbor. She lived a few houses down the street between the Fritsch and Forquer families. Nony Fritsch was the captain of our 1955 undefeated East Side High football team. I trained Ruby to peck corn out of my hand and she learned to respond to her name in less than a week. When I called, "Come here, Ruby," the chicken that responded was the one with that name . . . I think. Sometimes it was hard to tell them apart.

Cruise night at Chuck – A – Burger (Tettaton picture)

I don't think Mom or Dad or sis ever got attached to the chickens as I did. One day when it came time for one of those special chicken and dumpling dinners, my mother went out to the pen and caught Ruby. Ruby was squawking furiously, the way chickens do when their mortal lives are in danger. I watched aghast as my sweet mother wrung Ruby's neck with a quick twist and circular motion. What really scared the bejeebies out of me is how the headless chicken flapped its wings and flopped around for almost a minute while blood squirted all over the place and was strewn helter skelter. Mom then made my older sister dip the lifeless body in scalding water, then pluck the bird naked. The stench from that pot of hot water and feathers almost made me throw up. I was very quiet as I ate my chicken and dumplings that day. Mom didn't notice that all the meat on my plate was pushed to one side.

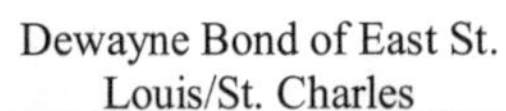
Dewayne Bond of East St. Louis/St. Charles

I wondered about human beheadings after that. I knew the bloodthirsty French mob had executed hundreds in this manner during the French Revolution. Sometimes I had nightmares about people who lost their head in the Tower of London or to the French guillotine.

Our chicken farm experiment came to a screeching halt one day after my St. Louis cousin Sandy came to visit my sister. The two of them went inside the fenced area to watch the chickens' impulsive scratching and pecking behavior. Suddenly, our bantam rooster, perhaps thinking that the stranger was a threat to his brood, flew into a rage and began clawing at Sandy's face. Frantically, she batted him away with her hand and ran back to the house with tears and blood streaming down her cheeks. Luckily, she didn't lose an eye that day, but she still has small scars from the incident. The next day, Mom went out to the enclosure, caught the rooster and wrung his neck. One by one we ate the rest of the chickens and Dad took down the chicken wire fencing. My buddies and I used the old coop for a clubhouse for a few years. Then Dad tore it down to make room to have a new garage that he was going to convert to a radio-TV workshop. Dad spent most of his spare time fixing other people's sets.

For a period of several months, after the death of the rooster, my eyes would inexplicably fly open at the crack of dawn. Strangely, I had the eerie feeling that it was a loud cock-a-doodle-do rooster reveille that awoke me from my sleep.

WINTER PLAYGROUND GAMES

Author Bill Nunes attended Charles Manners Grade School in Washington Park/East St. Louis. Recess was eagerly looked forward to as a time for letting off steam. In good weather the boys shot hoops, played catch, climbed the monkey bars competed at marbles, or spun dizzily on the playground favorite that we called "the tub." If you fell and scraped your chin or sprained your arm, you chalked it up to your carelessness. Nobody ever sued.

Sometimes we taunted a tall awkward kid whose ears stuck out a bit. We teased him and he would chase us. (Yes, kids haven't changed much. They could occasionally be cruel, even back in 1950.) If you were unlucky enough to get caught, he would pound your shoulder with his fist and make it sore for three days. Dwayne moved away and he didn't go to my junior high or high school. I was reading the *Globe-Democrat* sports page in March of 1958 and was astonished to see that a tall center by the name of Dwayne Bond had led the **St. Charles Pirates** to the Class L (1,000 students or more) high school basketball championship. *Good for him*, I thought.

Mark Twain once said that the weather in the upper Mississippi Valley does about 101 different things. It was late March but it might as well have been mid-January. In this blustery part of America, winter is nature's way of weeding out the faint of heart. A strong wind whipped in frigidly from Canada. When it collided with moist air coming up from the Gulf of Mexico, tons of snow was the inevitable result. And when it snowed, the fun really started on the playground. The stage was set for epic snow battles. These games of "war" usually started out on a small scale, with a few guys pelting each other. And if girls occasionally wandered by, we'd pelt them, too.

Sometimes things escalated into all-out war. We'd make

sure our galoshes were firmly buckled, then we'd pull down the earflaps on our caps and fasten them under our chin. This was standard warrior dress and the only time it was considered okay to lower those flaps without being called a sissy. Jack Frost, that playful sprite who blew his breath on window panes and sent his icy breath howling around the corners of buildings, was nipping at our noses.

Normally, the older and bigger kids ganged up on us smaller kids. This was also a time when Dewayne Bond got a measure of revenge.

Ritenour High 1950s extreme flat top

The first thing each side did was roll enough snowballs on the ground so they became big enough to serve as "stones" in the wall of our redoubt. These rude snow forts, about waist high on a kid, offered a measure of protection from incoming white missiles.

In one particular memorable instance, the battle was hotly contested, but slowly and inexorably my group was retreating to a fall-back position with the school building at our backs. Memories of Custer's Last Stand at the Little Big Horn (in Montana) began to haunt us. We needed a miracle!

I spied a young phys ed specialist who was at school that day and saw what was going on from a second floor window. He was our only chance. I dispatched Freddie Durham to break through enemy lines to bring back an inspirational leader with a strong right arm.

I could see him in my mind's eye, hurrying down the steps while pulling on a warm coat. His arrival caused a cheer to rise from our pathetic remnant of sore-armed survivors. Under murderous fire, he reorganized our fighting formation and offered words of encouragement. I don't think General Patton could have done better.

Barber shop

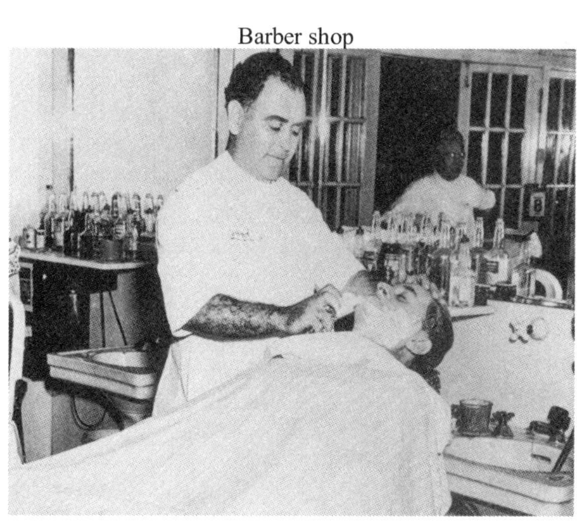

Some kids became ammunition carriers . . . others were "loaders," supplying snowballs as fast as our relief man could throw them. He took the point and slowly we began advancing.

He was like a snowball throwing cannon, firing away with deadly accuracy. Occasionally, we sent someone on a suicide mission to attack the other side's redoubt, landing on the wall feet first in an effort to destroy part of it. They usually came back with a fat lip and only partial success. Yet it was a morale booster.

Our intrepid leader yelled "charge" and we all rushed forward, lobbing snowballs for all we were worth. The enemy retreated as we smashed their breastworks to smithereens. Some turned and ran. Others pulled coats over their heads and ran inside the building. Some sought safety by hiding among the girls. Yes – victory was ours!

Just then the bell rang, signaling the end of recess. We trooped into the building giving "hurrahs" to our fearless leader who accepted our praise with a modest grin. Then we hurried to our classrooms hoping we'd make it before any of the girls complained to our teacher about snowballs we'd thrown at them earlier.

BARBER SHOP DAYS

I remember those days in the late 1950s when I was in high school and got my ears lowered (hair cut) every two weeks at that bastion of male territory – the barber shop. It's all different now. Men and women get their hair "trimmed" or "styled" at the same place in what are usually called hair salons. These unisex places charge sixteen bucks instead of six bits and have fancy names such as Mane Tamers, Scissor Shack, or Great Clips. When a guy goes into one of these places his olfactory senses are usually assaulted with the smell of styling gel and permanent wave solutions. In the good ol' days, men went to barber shops and women went to beauty parlors. And ne'er the twain should meet.

I was just your average Joe back then with a bit of an inferiority complex. But I took smug satisfaction in knowing that my particular barber was more skilled than the others and gave me a superior flat top that other boys couldn't match, unless they went to him.

Barber shops in those times had an aura and mystique about them. The first time I saw the chair it looked a bit scary since it resembled a dentist's chair. I was in awe of the man who wielded that deadly looking straight razor with such aplomb. For men who wanted a shave, the lather came from a special mug that contained a brush and a special soap. No such thing as Barbasol out of an aerosol can. The barber ran a little hot water into the mug and then whipped up a foamy lather with the brush. I only sported a modicum of peach fuzz in 1957, but the barber still used the razor to trim the back of my neck and around my ears. I'll never forget the pungent, manly smell of that mixture of oils and soap. I looked forward to the day when I would be man enough to have whiskers and the barber would tug on the lever that took the chair back to a near horizontal position. I would remain calm and serene as the barber stropped the razor back and forth on that leather strap. My face, hopefully free of pimples by then, would be the beneficiary of a steaming-hot towel (to soften the whiskers) and warm foamy lather. I wouldn't blink an eye when the barber finished by rubbing my face with a towel and then applying witch hazel, a substance that stung like crazy.

The conversation was always lively at the shop as the barber and the customer usually talked politics and sports. Those waiting their turn occasionally looked up from their copy of *Sport Magazine*, *Field and Stream* or *True Crime* to throw in their two cents worth. When grown men sat in the chair, John (the barber) handed them a copy of some girly magazine. I supposed it was either *Playboy* or *Stag*, or something similar. These magazines were never on the table next to the waiting seats. John kept them on a shelf underneath the top one that sported a vast array of clippers, scissors, combs, brushes, powders and lotions.

Gerald Mizell, of South St. Louis County, remembers that most St. Louis barber shops had a checkers set where two could play while they were waiting. Next in line was done on the honor system. When you came into the shop you were supposed to look around and see who was there so you would know when it was your turn. I don't ever remember any arguments between customers over whose turn it was.

One day I mentioned to John that I had just turned seventeen and, to my surprise, he handed me one of those magazines. I guess he figured that was the age when a boy was on the verge of manhood. Now I had attended a conservative church ever since the fifth grade and should have politely refused. But I didn't muster the courage and so I began leafing through it, feigning mild interest in those glorious pin up shots and spending most of the time reading the mundane articles.

My particular barber had a partner who cut hair and there were two chairs in the shop. There was also a radio in the shop, but the only time they turned it on was when there was a Cardinal ballgame. Some shops had shoeshine boys, but these were pretty much on the wane in my coming of age years. Shoeshine boys would use a carnauba paste wax and had a special rag that they used to buff your shoes to a mirror-like shine. I polished my own shoes at home every Saturday night with Kiwi brand wax and kept wax, buffing cloth, and polish rags in a special wooden box that I had made in junior high shop class. My cousin Del Shinn, who lived in St. Louis on Pepper Lane, and had been in the Korean War, taught me how to get a military gloss with the spit shine technique.

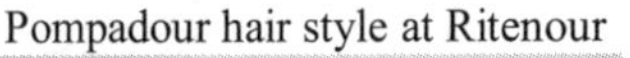
Pompadour hair style at Ritenour

When I first started going to the barber shop, there were red and white striped poles outside – the traditional sign for that craft. This was sort of similar to pawn shops which you recognized instantly when you saw those three round brass balls. The distinctive candy cane was motorized and I was nearly hypnotized by watching the spiraling red stripe that snaked eternally upward. Where did it come from? Where did it go when it reached the top?

The red and white dated back to the early days when barbers performed another function – bloodletting. In George Washington's era little was known about germs or illness or disease. If you were sick, it was thought to be caused by bad blood. A barber would be called in and he would cut a vein and drain off about a pint of blood. For those who couldn't handle the sight of so much blood, leeches were sometimes used. The red and white on the barber pole symbolized the blood and the bandages. When the 1960s came along, someone must have thought this was too gruesome and a blue stripe was added so the red, white, and blue spiral is what most people remember.

Incidentally, in case you're wondering about that "six bits" reference, that's seventy-five cents in today's vernacular. Back in colonial days a common coin in use was the Spanish Pieces of Eight. It was scored into eight parts so that smaller amounts could be broken off. When the New York Stock Exchange was started in 1790, they decided to use these "bits" in reference to a dollar. Market fluctuations were figured in eights of a dollar with one eighth equal to 12 ½ cents. If a stock went up one and two-eighths, that meant one share increased in value a dollar and twenty-five cents. Thus my haircut that cost six bits was actually seventy-five cents. It is only recently that the stock market switched from eighths to tenths.

Men have only themselves to blame for the demise of that venerable institution, the barber shop. Nobody wore shaggy hair in the Fifties. If the principal saw a guy with long locks walking the halls in high school, he would take him by the ear (or hair), drag him into the office, and give him an instant haircut. Long hair started becoming popular shortly after the Beatles arrived on the scene from Liverpool. Kids got crew cuts in the Fifties because they wanted to emulate GI Joe. Pompadours were popular with some kids because Paul Anka or Bobby Rydell had one. Kids of the Sixties let their hair become a mess to emulate rock stars. Long hair was also an easy way to protest the traditional values of the older folks – it drove them nuts. Most of the barbers went out of business when the new generation limited haircuts to graduations or weddings.

ROUTE 66

An old Missouri Department of Transportation study once concluded: "Rarely is the social and cultural impact of transportation engineering on society as evident as it is with the first paved highways created by state governments."

U.S. Route 66, although a federal highway winding its way gloriously for more than 2,000 miles from Lake Michigan to the Pacific Ocean, may be the single most outstanding example of this legacy in the United States. Over the years Route 66 has acquired an almost spiritual meaning through its billboards, Burma Shave signs, restaurants, motels, service stations and entertainment spots. Part and parcel of that experience is the natural landscape, geological character and topography of Missouri that is on display. Today it is possible to travel much (about 300 miles) of the Missouri roads that were once designated Route 66. Some pieces are located under parts of other highways such as I-44. Others are missing, dug up and seeded, or have become frontage roads.

To travel Missouri Route 66 from St. Louis to the Kansas border enables you to capture the spirit of the land and understand why Missouri is one of the most scenic states in America and why agriculture and mining is such a major part of its economy. During much of the trip through the heartland a traveler is presented with a view of various hybrid strains of corn, soybeans, oats, wheat or other crops. Evidence of large-scale animal husbandry is plentiful. However, a trip from one end of the corridor to the other is also an encounter with a major urban metropolis, county seats and counties filled with urban sprawl, as well as small town America.

By 1900, road building had not improved much since colonial times. There was nothing in America that even remotely resembled Rome's Appian Way, paved magnificently with stones. The earliest roads used by the Jamestown settlers of Virginia were merely Indian trails that had been cleared and widened. The first big improvement was corduroy roads – so named because they resembled ribbed corduroy cloth – *cor du roi*, cloth fit for a king. These roads consisted of trees that were felled, stripped of their branches and placed side by side. This took care of the quagmire problem when it rained, but the roads were hard on wheels and axles, and the ride was bone jarring.

The next improvement came with the introduction of plank roads – constructed of smooth wooden boards. These worked fine but were expensive to build and fell victim to decay, rot and termites. To help pay for their cost and upkeep, the turnpike was invented. A turnpike was simply a toll road with a gatekeeper and removable barrier across the road. Once the required fee was paid, the long pole or pike, with a counterbalance on one end, was turned to allow passage, hence "turnpike." These toll roads were universally hated. Officials even had the gall to charge fees for velocipedes (bicycles) when that invention came along.

Bicycle enthusiasts were the first to call for improved roads, but the need for hard roads was not deemed a necessity until large numbers of Americans began buying the "horseless carriage," after World War I. When alternate paths of Route 66 were built during the Depression, they were often bricked instead of concreted. The brick process was used because it was labor intensive and WPA projects like this put more men to work during the Depression.

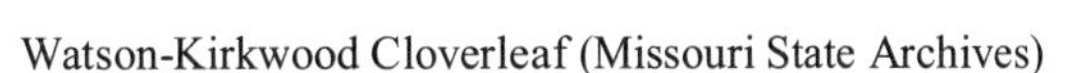
Watson-Kirkwood Cloverleaf (Missouri State Archives)

During the 1920s and '30s, Missouri roads were a mish-mash of assorted character. This jumbled variety consisted of graded earth, gravel, oiled gravel, brick, macadam (crushed stone mixed with tar; named for the Scottish inventor), asphalt, asphalt over a concrete base and Portland cement. The Show Me State was in need of improved roads to enable it to wrest the title "**Crossroads of America**" from neighboring Illinois - roads that would sail past verdant fields of winter wheat in the spring and tawny rows of corn in the fall. These roads could criss-cross the state and connect its pulsating cities with the hinterland and beat the economic drums of trade and commerce.

Before the fabled Route 66 artery existed, there was a dirt road that went from **Chicago** to **East St. Louis**. Dirt roads back then were improved by what came to be known as a split-log drag process. Invented in Missouri, the device used several teams of horses or mules that dragged logs over a dampened roadbed to dramatically improve its utility.

Route 66 started out in 1926 as a patchwork of mixed road surfaces that linked Chicago with St. Louis and St. Louis with Santa Monica, California. This was the Age of Ballyhoo and showman/entrepreneur C.C. ("Cash and Carry") Pyle drew national attention to the new road in 1928 by organizing an international **Bunion Derby** – a footrace from LA to New York, with the first two thirds to follow Route 66 and go through Chicago. To this day it remains the **single most important event** known to Route 66 in terms of exposure and publicity. A first place prize of $25,000 was offered, drawing 275 contestants. Runners covered a predetermined distance each day. **Red Grange**, the former U of I star and Chicago Bears' football player, was hired to fire the gun each morning to begin the race anew. His celebrity status was used to promote interest in the race at various stops along the way. To help draw crowds, Pyle assembled a circus sideshow that arrived at each leg's destination a day in advance. The show included carnival rides, sideshow attractions (**including a mummified dead outlaw**), games of chance and concession stands. Grange acted as master of ceremonies in some of the featured attractions. When the exhausted runners reached St. Louis, a Brit of Italian ancestry by the name of Peter "Iron Man" Gavuzzi clung to a tenuous lead. After a grueling 84 days and a distance of 3,423 miles, with numerous contestants dropping out from exhaustion and raw feet, Andy Payne, a young Oklahoman of Native American extraction, claimed the prize at New York's Madison Square Garden. There were only 55 finishers.

Originally labeled Route 60, this proposed road, which would become so revered, was planned by the "**Father of Route 66**," Cyrus Avery, President of the Associated Highways Association of America (what a mouthful). The name change was forced by North Carolina, Virginia, and Kentucky, whose governors whined that a Route 60 should logically start on the East coast - not Chicago - and go through *their* states. At a special meeting in **Springfield**, Missouri, an Oklahoma engineer named John Page suggested the number 66 be used as a compromise. Many historians thus consider this **Missouri meeting as the birth of Route 66**. This intervention by fate, causing a signage change, turned out to be an amazing stroke of luck. It is significant because "Route 60" simply lacks the charisma and magnetic appeal of those incredible double sixes emblazoned on a black and white shield. A Route 60 designation would have been roughly equivalent to Adolph Hitler adopting a yellow flag with an acorn on it instead of the mesmerizing twisted cross, a black swastika within a white circle on a blood red field. Furthermore, can you imagine songwriter Bobby Troupe struggling to pen catchy and rhyming lyrics for Route 60?

Edmond's Restaurant in St. Louis (author's postcard collection)

Missourians were a practical, pragmatic breed in those jaunty days of "tin lizzies" and hardly gave the new highway thought except for the fact that they could now get from point A to point B much quicker. It was a boon to traveling salesmen and a convenient venue for St. Louis bootleggers to keep in touch with their counterparts in southwest Missouri and Chicago.

Gasoline back then came as simply regular and ethyl instead of the three octane ratings used today. When Route 66 was completed in Missouri, regular cost about 15 cents a gallon; Ethyl was a penny more. Only Ethyl was leaded because it was introduced in 1923 by Dupont Ethyl Company that made tetraethyl lead. Lead raises the octane rating of gasoline. The higher the compression ratio of a car's engine, the greater the need for a higher octane rating to eliminate "engine knock." Both Ethyl and regular gas in the Twenties was clear, like water, as the natural end product of the refining process. Housewives began using leaded gas as a cleaning agent to remove grease spots on clothes. Since tetraethyl lead was soluble, it penetrated the skin, causing lead poisoning. To discourage this practice, the company added a red dye to the gasoline giving it a pinkish cast. The dye caused a permanent stain on clothing and housewives quickly stopped using Ethyl gas as a cleaning agent.

In the 1920s and 1930s, **gasoline was dispensed mechanically**. The attendant pushed a long pump handle back and forth, which brought the gasoline from a storage tank below into a large glass container at the top with markings to show the number of desired gallons. Anything between even gallons was a guesstimate. The nozzle was then placed into the gas tank and the gasoline went into the car by gravity. Quarts of oil (an ugly, thick greenish brown color) at filling stations were stored in glass containers that looked like a pop bottle with a long tapered metal spout for pouring oil into the crankcase. It had the viscosity of sorghum molasses and was not nearly as efficient as modern oil, necessitating frequent "ring jobs."

Patching an inner tube

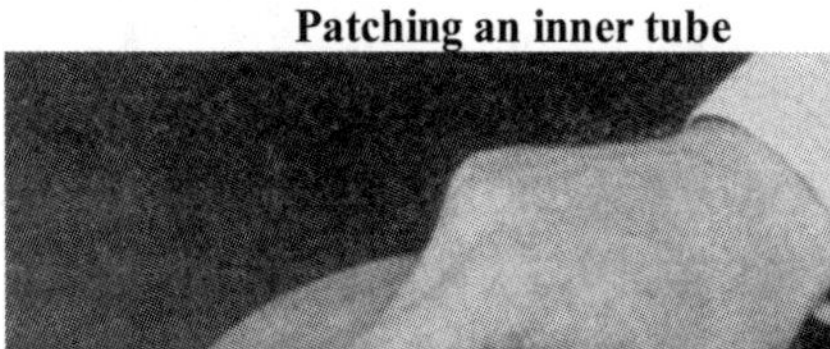

During World War II, drivers were limited to about 3 gallons of gas a week and were encouraged to either use public transportation or carpool. No cars were produced from 1942-45 because auto factories were converted to wartime production. There was a shortage of rubber and car owners were asked to contribute the spare tire in their trunk to the war effort. Punctured inner tubes, instead of being replaced, were fixed with "hot patches." Some patriotic Americans jacked their cars up, removed all of the tires, and left their vehicles on cinder blocks for the duration of the war. And all Americans were expected to strictly obey the **nationally imposed speed limit of 35 miles per hour**.

What kind of autos used Route 66 when it was first completed? Originally called a horseless carriage, the term motorcar was now very much in vogue. Tin Lizzie or "flivver" was the vernacular for cheaper models such as the Chevrolet, Ford and Plymouth. Classic autos of this age of driving by the seat of one's pants included the Packard, Essex, Durant, Nash, Olds, Dodge, Reo, Studebaker, Buick, Auburn, Chrysler, Hudson, Stutz, DuPont, McFarland, Franklin, Peerless, Hupmobile, Cadillac, Dorris, Pierce-Arrow, Willys-Knight, Lincoln, Daniels, Dusenberg, Maxwell, Rolls Royce, Rickenbacker, Stanley Steamer and Locomobile.

Cars of this happy-go-lucky era, when the journey was almost as important as the destination, generally lacked radios and black box heaters (recycled hot air from the manifold), were optional. Windshield wipers were often found only on the driver's side and were originally operated by hand. Some old models were started with a hand crank. Brakes were mechanical, not hydraulic. Two-seaters with open cockpits were dubbed "roadsters." Some smaller coupes had fold out seats in the rear known as "rumble seats." The larger square-roofed sedans made for long-distance travel were called "touring cars." Vehicles that took people from hotels to train stations were known as "station wagons." Rear side doors were often hinged in the back. If you stepped out of the car and the driver absentmindedly pulled forward with the rear gate open, you could be knocked down and run over, hence the term "**suicide doors**."

Back at the turn of the century there was so much prejudice against motorcars that numerous towns passed ordinances requiring a man holding a red flag to walk ahead of the vehicle. These restrictions often prohibited the use of offensive horns, bells or whistles. Missouri even passed a 1905 law regulating the top speed of automobiles at fifteen miles per hour.

It can be argued that Route 66 gave birth to a national network of highways, giving rise to the trucking industry. Trucks made it possible for smaller regional stockyards to spring up. This ultimately eliminated the need for huge terminal stockyard facilities, ergo it spelled doom for Missouri's large stock yards. The trucking industry also put many railroads out of business.

There was a lot of politics involved back then when determining exactly which route the road would take and what towns would be visited or bypassed. There was so much at stake - just as when the railroads were built back in the 1850s. Towns that had trunk lines grew and prospered. The American Automobile Association predicted in 1927 that tourist travel along Route 66 towns would amount to an astounding $3.3 billion annually. Places that were bypassed shriveled and died on the economic vine; some became ghost towns or, at the very most, irrelevant. Some towns had big parades to celebrate the opening of a stretch of the road through their boundaries. The new road quickly became a boon to mom and pop stores, motels, filling stations, restaurants, refreshment stands, repair shops, sign painters and virtually all of the building trades.

St. Francis de Sales Church (1895) on 2653 Ohio in St. Louis – 300 ft.

I was born on September 1, 1939, and am known as a "Tweener." My generation is neither Depression-era nor Baby Boomer. We were sandwiched between those two groups during the years that Europe and America were at war, almost too young to remember blackouts, scrap metal drives, war bond rallies and rationing. I grew up listening to exciting heroes like Jack Armstrong and Tom Mix and the crazy antics of Fibber McGee and Molly. America still had a large rural population, and Norman Rockwell waxed nostalgic with folksy covers on the "Saturday Evening Post."

I first became vaguely aware of Route 66 when **Nat King Cole**, in his rich velvety voice, sang Bobby Troupe's song about having fun on the open road and getting "your kicks on Route 66." That song tugged at the wanderlust in a great many of us.

Jasper County stone courthouse at Carthage on Route 66

There were numerous cousins, aunts and uncles on my mother's side and many of them lived in St. Louis. Every Fourth of July we had a family get together and picnic at the Chain of Rocks Amusement Park. It was accessed from my house in Washington Park by traveling north on Route 111 and turning west on Route 66 at the Bel-Air Drive-in at **Mitchell**. From there it was a short trek to the Chain of Rocks Bridge - that long trussed structure that had a crick (dogleg) in the middle of it, ostensibly to counter a quirky part of the river's current. I remember wondering why its steel girders looked so different from the camelback trusses of the McArthur Bridge in **East St. Louis**, and why it sat on so many piers when the Eads Bridge, built 50 years earlier, required only two. And like most pubescent teenagers blissfully living in the present, I was barely aware that Route 66 traversed East St. Louis and went across the St. Louis-owned MacArthur Bridge. But I did know that in Missouri it headed down a cultural corridor for Illinoisans that included Ted Drewes Frozen Custard on Chippewa, the 66 Park-In Theater (Crestwood) and those notorious art deco/glass block Coral Court (no tell) motel units (1953 Bobby Greenlease kidnapping) out on 7775 Watson Rd. in the Marlborough part of south St. Louis County. Furthermore, I had no way of knowing that one day a seemingly ordinary road that went through my hometown would embody a certain magic, a kind of mystical quality that would stir men's blood and capture their imaginations.

Route 66 took on new meaning for me in the early 1960s when Stirling Silliphant began writing screenplays for a four year CBS television series about a couple of nomadic adventurers. It starred freckle-faced Martin Milner as **Tod Stiles**, who usually drove the fawn beige 1960 Corvette, and the brooding, mercurial George Maharis (**Buz Murdoch**). When Maharis (Buz) became ill with hepatitis, actor Glenn Corbett filled in for him. It was one of my favorite programs, and I watched it regularly. And no one has ever written a better road theme than Nelson Riddle's bouncy score for the show's opening credits. Never mind that most of the stories themselves had nothing to do with the highway.

I fell in love, married a pretty Collinsville girl, taught high school at **Collinsville** and **Edwardsville** and raised a family. I taught social studies but naively came to the conclusion that local and state history were dullsville and focused on the national and international scene. Only since I started writing books (back in 1995) did I come to realize that state and local history was the American past firsthand - and it was never boring. I read history – not literature – and didn't know that John Steinbeck had forever embedded the Dust Bowl, Oakies and the highway into our national psyche by terming it "**the Mother Road**" in *The Grapes of Wrath*.

Despite my newfound appreciation of things that are state and local, I am still not a Route 66 "junkie" or a "Rootie." I leave that to the keepers of the highway – the Bob Waldmires, Dan Oberles, and **Skip Curtisses** of the world. No book about Missouri would be complete without a cursory look at this national phenomenon, and at groups of people who go gaga over "the most magical road in the world" and haunt the annual Route 66 road tours and festivals. My hat is off to them for helping to preserve this important part of Missouri history.

Route 66 originally went from **Chicago** to **Edwardsville**, Illinois, along a diagonal route. From there Route 66 took **three separate paths to St. Louis**. The earliest went down Chain of Rocks Road where it turned left near the Luna Café in **Mitchell**. Next, it jogged south along Route 203 (Nameoki Road) and then west along Madison Avenue in **Granite City**. It continued through **Madison** into **Venice** where Madison Ave. becomes Broadwalk. This took you directly to the McKinley Bridge and crossed into north St. Louis. The McKinley Bridge was owned by the city of Venice (named for Venice, Italy, because it flooded so often). The bridge, originally a people traffic and streetcar bridge crossing into north St. Louis, was named for Illinois congressman William B. McKinley, not president William McKinley. McKinley, a **Danville** native, was responsible for building a large number of streetcar lines in central and Southern Illinois. The bridge has been closed for several years because it has fallen into disrepair, but work progressed and it reopened in late fall of 2007.

MacArthur Bridge with its deadly curve (Harry Fiebig postcard)

Around 1940, a **second route** was created that entered St. Louis through **East St. Louis** and the Municipal Bridge (later renamed McArthur Bridge). It connected with East St. Louis by splitting off at **Hamel**, bypassing **Edwardsville** and **Glen Carbon**, crossing Route 143 before brushing the edge of **Troy** and **Maryville**. Linking up with **Collinsville** on Vandalia Street, 66 turned west on the Beltline (U.S. 40) and then went to the base of the bluffs at the current Moto Station. It followed 157 for a spell before heading west on Collinsville Road past Evergreen Gardens, Fairmount Park, Cahokia Mounds, **Fairmont City** and Horseshoe Lake. (Note the slight difference in spelling of Fairmount Park and Fairmont City. Many books erroneously spell them the same). Route 66 went past the Y Café and then sunk beneath a railroad underpass with a set of double tracks used by the Pennsy and B&O and crossed St. Clair Avenue in **East St. Louis** at 9th Street. Then it moved into south St. Louis via the Municipal Bridge at Choteau Avenue. A 1957 alignment went across the Veteran's Bridge, but Route 66 never went across the Eads Bridge.

Coral Court Motel in St. Louis County - Wikipedia

A **third route**, known as a bypass, was established around 1939 across the Chain of Rocks Bridge. As Route 66 dropped below the bluffs from **Edwardsville**, it followed the old Chain of Rocks Road, which today parallels Interstate 270, then went north of **Granite City**, and passed through **Mitchell**. Now, the road crossed over into north St. Louis at the Chain of Rocks Bridge.

The trussed toll bridge, arguably the most famous on all of Route 66, is named for a stretch of rocks in the river, placed there by ancient glaciers moving down from Canada. They were a hazard to river traffic, and their rapids can still be readily seen. The Chain of Rocks toll bridge (spanning 5,353 feet) was built in 1929 by the Scott brothers. They started construction on the Missouri side *before* they found bedrock on the Illinois side. When they did find bedrock, it necessitated a sharp dogleg in the middle of the bridge to reach it. The bend was so severe that two large trucks coming in opposite directions on the 24-foot wide roadway could not meet each other at this point on the two-lane girder bridge.

Unfortunately, highway officials in Illinois and Missouri failed to place the bridge on their maps, jeopardizing the Scott brothers' $2 million dollar investment. The brothers extended the bridge route, and it eventually linked up with Lindbergh Boulevard and this became the bypass around St. Louis. The brothers, discouraged by financial hardship, finally sold the bridge to the city of Madison in 1939 and, as luck would have it, the girdered structure soon became a cash cow.

The old Chain of Rocks Bridge was closed two years after the 4-lane Interstate 270 Bridge opened in 1966. Today the bridge is used as an eagle watch site and a path for cyclists. It is now considered the **World's Longest Pedestrian Bridge**, well over a mile in length. The Kurt Russell movie, *Escape From New York,*, was partially filmed at the Chain of Rocks Bridge.

Because of the dangerous stretch of river past the chain of rocks, it was deemed necessary to build a canal with a bridge (completed in 1949) to skirt that part of the Mississippi. Up on the bluffs, overlooking the bridge, was the popular Chain of Rocks Amusement Park that featured an arcade, Ferris wheel, swimming pool, skating rink, dodge-em cars, roller coaster and picnic area. It closed in the mid-1970s. The two cute little stone castles in the middle of the river near the bridge are pumping stations to send Mississippi water to large settling pools on Riverview Drive in St. Louis for the waterworks department. They are still in operation for this very purpose. Just south of the bridge on the Illinois side is Granite City's Choteau Island. The famed **Lewis and Clark** expedition camped here overnight as they made plans to go up the Missouri River to explore the newly acquired Louisiana Territory. They didn't stay at St. Louis because it was still under control of the Spanish.

Devil's Elbow Café on Route 66 (author's postcard collection)

All three of these St. Louis access corridors of Route 66 traveled along a geographically unique area of Illinois known as the **American Bottom**. The Bottom stretches from **Alton** to **Chester** and varies from four to twelve miles in width. The flat floodplain was carved out by glacial meltwater and a meandering Mississippi River.

Madison and St. Clair counties have long led the nation in the production of a certain crop. That part of Southern Illinois is referred to as the **Horseradish Capital of America**, and the city of **Collinsville** holds an annual Horseradish Festival. First introduced to Illinois by German settlers, it grows robustly in the rich black soil of the American Bottom. Horseradish is used as a condiment on roast beef and is blended with catsup to make cocktail sauce for eating with fish.

Route 66 took three main exit routes through St. Louis. The oldest one came off the McKinley Bridge then went south on Broadway and headed west on Chippewa. Chippewa became Watson Road shortly after it passed Ted Drewes. Then it went through or near Shrewsbury, Marlborough, Webster Groves, Crestwood, Sunset Hills, Fenton, Valley Park, Eureka (**Route 66 Visitor's Center**), Times Beach, Pacific (**Beacon Motel** & **Red Cedar Inn**), Pond, Hollow (**Monroe's 66 Diner**), Gray Summit (**Shaw Nature Preserve**), Valley Ridge, Union, Moselle, St. Clair, Stanton (**Antique Toy**, **Jesse James Museums**), Oak Grove, Sullivan, St. Cloud, Bourbon, Hofflins, Cuba (**Wagon Wheel Motel, Mid-way Restaurant**), Fanning, Rosati, St. James (**Ruby's Ice Cream**), Rolla (**Mule Trading Post, Totem Pole Trading Post, Zeno's Motel**), Martin Springs, Doolittle (**Vernelle Motel, Stony Dell Resort**), Hooker, through the famed Hookers Cut to the Devil's Elbow (**Grandview Court, Elbow Inn**), St. Robert, Waynesville, Hanna, Laquey, Hazelgreen, Lebanon (**Stave/barrel Company, Munger Moss Motel, Wrink's Market, Route 66 Museum**), Phillipsburg, Conway, Niangua, Marshfield, Northview, Holman, Strafford, Mulroy, Springfield (**Skyline Motel**, **Gillioz Theater**), Elwood, Halltown (**White Hall Store**), Paris Springs, Spencer, Heatonville, Albatross, Phelps, Rescue, Plew, Log City, Stone City, Avilla, Forest Mills, Maxville, Carthage (**Boots Motel, Route 66 Drive-In**), Brooklyn Heights, Carterville, Webb City and then Joplin (**Dale's Route 66 Barber Shop**).

Hooker Cut on Route 66 (Missouri State Archives)

There was the Chain of Rocks/Lindbergh bypass route that was previously mentioned. The third path through the city was the one that came across the MacArthur Bridge and exited onto Chouteau (**Eat-Rite Diner** at 622). Chouteau became Manchester near Vandeventer. It followed Manchester Road (Route 100) and went through Maplewood, Brentwood, Rock Hill, Warson Woods, Glendale, Kirkwood, Des Peres, Manchester, Winchester, Ballwin, Ellisville, Wildwood, Grover, Pond, and Gray Summit (**Diamonds Restaurant & Greyhound Bus Station**), just past where 100 joined the original 66.

It was said that the whole world traveled down Route 66. Not anymore. Route 66 was decertified (decommissioned in official jargon) as a bona fide highway in January of 1977. This meant that the famed conduit would no longer appear on any official highway maps. The new interstates were billed as a triumph over time and space, but in a sense it was a Pyrrhic victory. Travelers would now be forced to drive on dull, mind numbing stretches of boring, homogenized concrete that bypassed practically everything. We sold our souls to the devil in return for the ability to arrive at our destination ten minutes sooner. We gave up a road that was like a gift from God – textured by hills, dips and bumps, girdered bridges, parallel railroad tracks, S curves, classic billboards with catchy slogans, oddball logos, roadhouses, dancehalls, souvenir stands, truck stops and gaudy neon signs. And for what? It was for nothing more than mind-boggling blandness, bleak as a Dorothea Lange Dust Bowl photo that flim-flamers sold to us as *progress*.

Any other decertified road would have fallen into the dustbin of history and been quickly forgotten. Not so Route 66. Memories of Route 66 soon exerted a powerful grip on our collective imagination. For many of us, that road personified freedom, the wide-open spaces, and postwar prosperity that enabled Americans to buy a car and head to Chicago or go out West for an annual family vacation. Disparate images of roadway advertising, courthouses, barbed wire, train tracks and grain silos along the road helped to amplify that perception.

America's love affair with the automobile is as strong as ever. For tourist nirvana while traveling Interstate 44, pull off at one of those quaint towns along the way to get a true feel for history. Better yet, take a blood oath and don't use I-44 in the first place! Take the road less traveled with those old-fashioned sweeping curves for a slice of Americana and a treasure chest of memories. Sit down with a few old timers on an old porch swing and soak up some local color. Marvel at some of the vintage architecture. Make a trip down memory lane, back to America's glory years of the 1940s and 1950s when commercial buildings had substance and character because they were not cookie cutter images of some franchise in another town. Visit one of the classic family-owned eateries. Talk to a long time resident and discover what it was like back when things were at a slower pace and when we had a greater sense of community. Let them take you back to an era when people took on life's challenges one at a time and had to figure things out with just their common sense. Drive a bit on an old frontage road that was once part and parcel of the original Route 66. Stop, look and listen. You'll discover through its trappings and ambience that Route 66 was much more than just a highway. It's a shibboleth from the past, a touchstone that tells us what we are about.

Shriners' Mosque in Springfield on Route 66 -author's collection

President Ronald Reagan once said, "If we don't know who we are and where we came from, how will we know where we are going?" If you close your eyes and conjure up a bit of childhood imagination, you might be able to hear some of the sounds from the road's storied past – the whispers of countless ghosts that made the **Colossus of Roads** the most famous and nostalgic in all of our history. Then, with the words of guru Bob Waldmire, you can say, "I still get my kicks on old Route 66!"

See any Skip Curtiss book or www.missouri66.org for more information.

DIME STORE DAYS

Do you ever get the urge to wax nostalgic? I have several antiques in my home to serve as reminders of that bygone era of childhood memories. A bright red 1940 Lionel engine and tender sit on top of a restored Zenith console radio in my foyer. I have the seven inch round picture tube from my parent's first television set perched on a shelf in my study. And there's a Gone With the Wind **hurricane lamp** sitting on the dresser in our bedroom.

Let me take you back to a magical time when the simple pleasures of life helped build the Great American Dream, offering temporary escape from an otherwise ordinary and humdrum existence. Remember when you were young and your mother took you shopping at those wonderful Five and Dime Stores such as Newberry's, W.T. Grant, Kresge's, and **Woolworths**. And occasionally you got to sit at the marble-topped lunch counters to eat a hot dog and gulp a fountain coke while your mother had a club sandwich and a cup of coffee.

Wasn't it fun wandering the aisles, mouth agape, and looking at comics, Big Little Books, art deco salt and pepper shakers, Roy Rogers lunchboxes or a **Kewpie doll** that in my young brain could be instantly transformed into a living breathing Rita Hayworth?

The five-and-dimes were part of that amazing culture back then that forever impacted our lives. Somehow, those colorful aisles lined with gobs of toys, candy, notions, bobby pins, lipstick, mascara, button cards, nail polish and magazines, had an amazing capability of evoking an adoration so intense from little boys and girls that it almost sent up sparks. Looking back on that period of breezy ironies and stylish fun conjures up images of the "stuff that dreams were made of" in a time when we could afford the luxury of dreaming.

The fun and fancy free that youngsters sought and found without limit in the dime stores began the second the doors swung open. Once past the red and yellow enameled scale (Your Weight & Fate 1¢), the perfume of a thousand and one mysteries engulfed us. In those unair-conditioned days the smells of every five-and-ten were far more pungent with character and substance; the oiled bare wood floors, peanuts roasting, potato chips in glass bins warmed to fragrance by the meager heat of a 100 watt light bulb, the synthetic dextrose of the candy counters (especially the candy corn and the pastilles inside miniature glass cars or telephones), the heavy musk of Blue Waltz perfume, oriental incense cones, hamburgers frying on griddles, cherry phosphates, Skippy Cups, Animal Crackers, banana splits . . . all these combined in one stupendous smell that made my senses reel.

In the summertime, when the giant fans blew, the ambrosial air would be sent in billows of steamy fragrance, cyclones that gusted from one end of the store and back again, creating the 1940s and 1950s equivalent of "nose candy."

Dime store salt and pepper shakers

Dime stores hawked the seasons, and they sold the holidays of those seasons. I will forever remember the distinct smells of Christmas with those peppermint striped candy canes, plastic ornaments and strands of **Noma bubble lights**. Wandering the aisles during this time of hope and optimism was cause for rejoicing in all the tender and joyous qualities of humanity. Usually spelled Xmas at the dime stores, it was also a welcome opportunity to revel in a carnival of unparalleled brilliance, mirrored by tinsel and the hypnotic radiance of bubbling tree lights.

During Easter the stores sold chocolate bunny rabbits and live baby chicks chirping away in their dyed pastel colors. At Halloween orange and black crepe streamers dominated the stores and there were pomegranates, false faces and black and orange jelly beans. Halloween, with its witches, fiends, phantoms, hags and demons, fed our perpetual desire to be terrified by spooks, monsters and apparitions. The make-believe world of our childhoods found no greater source of raw material than the dime-store effigies and disguises of a prankster's holiday.

Typical dime store lunch counter, circa 1952

The glorious trash of those stores often reflected what was popular at the movies. There might be ceramic or plastic miniatures of Bambi, Dumbo, or one of the Seven Dwarfs. Perhaps a marionette replica of Pinocchio, a Donald Duck windup doll, Carmen Miranda earrings, Bette Davis paper dolls, a Modern Screen magazine with Tyrone Power on the cover, Joan Crawford "rat" hair rolls, Betty Grable sunglasses, Three Little Pigs playing cards, Charlie McCarthy souvenir spoons, Little Black Sambo Parcheesi games and so forth.

In my early teens, I took up **collecting cigar bands** – El Producto, Roi Tan, White Owl, Prince Edward, Dutch Masters – a whole cornucopia of treasures that could be found on sidewalks or lying next to the curb. I frequently took the bus on Saturdays and went to downtown St. Louis by myself, searching for these freebie collectables. After I tired of that, I usually went to the closest dime store and had a cherry coke. Then I would peruse those magical aisles before walking back to the bus station on Broadway at Washington Avenue for my return trip. I now was a little older and a little wiser, but those displays still mirrored my childhood dream of the universe perfectly, with a kaleidoscope of color and whimsy. It was still an endless parade of phosphorescence, of giddy illusions made especially to seduce and satiate the appetites of a youngster hungry for caprice and escape. It was still a world in which I knew positively that I would never be cheated – a place of significant joys, a bewitching playground that kept my life a constant celebration.

Noma bubble lights

Currently, as I inch toward old age, those dime store days are a small but terribly significant part of my life's history, a past that slipped by when I wasn't looking. . . . It's just over there, that second star from the right.

A ST. LOUIS CHRISTMAS

Aren't you glad you live in the St. Louis area where there are four distinct seasons and we get beautiful white snow during the winter? I would hate living in southern California or Florida while listening to Bing Crosby sing "I'm dreaming of a white Christmas," or Mel Torme waxing nostalgic about "Chestnuts roasting on an open fire" and that puckish sprite "Jack Frost nipping at your nose."

Yes, St. Louis Christmases were special. If you lived in South St. Louis perhaps you bundled up and went with your dad to pick out a tree on Ted Drewes lot or from a Lions Club lot if you lived north or west. Wasn't it neat that each family had their own Christmas tradition? For some it was hanging garlands on the tree made of popcorn and red berries. Other families put the Star of Bethlehem on the top of their tree, while at my home we always topped ours with an angel. In some families Mom or Dad might read the story of Christmas from the King James Version of the Bible. For others part of the joy of the season was joining a carolers group from church and going around the neighborhood singing songs of good cheer. If you were Catholic, perhaps you attended a midnight mass at your local parish cathedral. If you were Jewish, you probably didn't celebrate the birth of Jesus, yet there was still the happy season of Hanukah.

At our house Dad had the responsibility of picking out the tree while Mom would get out the strands of lights. Dad usually waited until a week before Christmas before going to get a tree. The name Nunes is Portuguese, but Dad must have been part Scottish because he always looked for the best bargain. It usually ended up being a scrawny tree with limbs bent or missing. But my sister and I didn't care. We had a tree.

When we got home we put the tree in a metal stand that held water. You didn't want the needles to dry out because the lights back then weren't those little twinkle things you buy today. They were six watts and burned quite hot. Too dry a tree was a fire hazard. We usually had a strand or two of Noma bubble lights, one of the greatest inventions of all time. I was literally mesmerized by those happy, bubbling lights that sang an effervescent tune as they wended their way to the top of the tube. It usually took several minutes for the Noma lights to get hot enough. Finally, those little pockets of air started rising to the top and everyone watched in fascination as that unending stream of bubbles churned its way to the tip of the elongated bulb.

The strands were wired back then in series - if one bulb burned out the whole string went dark. You had to replace the bulbs one by one to find the bad one. Everyone gave a joyous shout of "Hooray!" when the burned out bulb was found.

Some of our ornaments were plastic and this was partially due to a glass shortage during World War Two. My sister and I pitched in, hanging strands of tinsel one by one until most of the bad spots on the tree were hidden. When we finished, Mom had us go outside and gather up some snow to make home made ice cream. According to custom, you never made ice cream from the first snowfall because it collected most of the contaminants in the air.

Christmas window display at Famous and Barr (Tettaton picture)

Everyone in the family had a favorite ornament that they personally hung on the tree. The ornaments seemed like old friends and we carefully took them from their newspaper wrapping. Mom's was an old silver one handed down from the Holmes side of the family. Dad had a gold one that belonged to his mother. My sister had a blue one that looked like there was a tad bit of snow on its top. Mine was not an ornament and it was placed at the bottom of the tree next to our small manger scene. It was a heavy cardboard cutout of Rudolph the red-nosed reindeer. Rudolph was in sections that were slotted but they fit together with ease. The Rudolph character was invented back in the 1930s by a Montgomery Ward employee for a Christmas promotion. Cowboy Gene Autry sang the hit tune that became a million seller. This was about the same time that the song "All I Want for Christmas is my Two Front Teeth" became popular.

The other big treat for kids back then was when mom took us to Stix and Famous to see Santa and to look at the fantastic window displays for wide-eyed boys and girls. Riding the escalators was always a thrill and the hustle and bustle of Christmas shoppers lent further excitement to the air. It's probably hard for anyone in the modern world to believe that when children back then wrote a letter to Santa, placed a three cent stamp on it, and addressed it to the North Pole, sans Zip Code, there were only one or two items requested at most. Sister Jackie might ask for a doll or a new dress and I would ask for a sled or ball glove.

One day the time came when my wife and I had children of our own and it was time for me to go out and buy a tree and start another family tradition. Money was no object – the affluent society. I selected a beautiful Canadian balsam and proudly brought it home to my wife and two kids. My family looked at it horror which I mistook for awe. "Hey, Dad, how much did the guy on the lot pay you to haul this thing away," my seven-year-old son, Steven, said. After turning the tree just so and after hours of meticulous decorating, the glaring holes and crooked branches were masked, transforming the tree into a thing of beauty.

ON THE STREET WHERE I LIVED

Close your eyes and see if you can conjure up visions of your old St. Louis neighborhood stomping grounds. I can still picture my old Washington Park environs in my mind's eye. Our house at 4901 Lincoln Avenue was two blocks north of Caseyville Avenue and the houses across the alley behind us fronted North Park Drive. Neighborhoods were significant in those days because they gave you a sense of identity, determined what schools you would attend (Charles Manners), who your friends would be, what church you would likely attend (Church of God) and, sometimes, what girl you would marry (Lorna Sanders, from church). Most of the fathers on the block were regular working stiffs at places like Hunter Packing, Monsanto, Obear-Nester or Aluminum Ore on Missouri Avenue in East St. Louis. My father was a foreman in charge of the second shift at the Mepham Paint Company on 20th and Lynch. Most of the houses were frame four or five room structures with a chat driveway and detached single car garage. Nothing fancy. The Fritsch family owned a blue 1947 Plymouth, the Hallets had a 1951 Studebaker Champion in their garage, the Griffins had a Pontiac with an

amber Indian head that lit up and the Thompsons, with only one child, could afford a new Desoto with gobs of chrome. My parents owned an unpretentious maroon Chevrolet with Power Glide.

The neighborhood flock of 6th and 7th graders often played by eagerly pushing along their box scooters (a wooden crate nailed on its end to a four-foot board mounted on old roller skate wheels). I embellished mine by nailing bottle caps to the outside of the crate to display logos such as 7-Up, Dr. Pepper, Orange Crush, Nehi Grape, Hires Root Beer, Royal Crown Cola, Vess Cream soda and Double Cola. Smaller tykes would pedal their kiddie cars along the side of the street. Sometimes we made rubber band guns from inner tubes and played *Gangbusters*.

I spent most Saturday mornings playing with my Lincoln Logs or Erector set. I frequently played a game of corkball with my neighborhood buddies, the Rudd brothers. Sometimes my mom and the three of us would ride the bus downtown to the Avenue Theater for a Saturday matinee. Arriving before the theater opened, we ducked into the adjoining shoe store to peer at the bones in our feet through the nickelodeon-like viewers of the shoe **fluoroscope**. One by one we stuck our feet into the base of the machine to get a gander at the X-ray images of our bony appendages. Going to the shoe store in those days was a little like going to the doctor or dentist, without the pain or anxiety, complete with free lollipops and balloons. You could pick out the kids who tuned in *Andy's Gang* for they were the ones peeking inside the display Saddle Oxfords looking for Buster Brown and his canine pal, Tige. Still others harassed their moms to buy them Red Goose or Poll Parrot shoes to get them the free giveaways they offered. My only concern when it came to footwear was that my PF Flyers not wear too thin on their rubber-winged soles. After all, they gave me the speed and balance to play tag or kick the can with the best of 'em. We paid our ten cents and entered the theater, then scooted over to the refreshments counter to get some goodies. My favorites were **Black Crows** and Jujubes. Sometimes I selected a nickel box of **Good and Plenty** pink and white sugar coated licorice. Mmm, yummy!

The maroon suited usher had epaulets on his shoulders and enough gold braid on his uniform to make him look like an admiral. He showed us inside and poked his flashlight around in darkened aisles until he found four seats abreast. We stuffed ourselves full of dinner-spoiling sweets during an afternoon laughfest which included a Porky Pig cartoon, Little Rascals comedy short, Abbott and Costello feature, and Chapter 9 of the serialized cliff hanger, *Flash Gordon*, starring Buster Crabbe. We loved every minute of the show and, when I peeked at mom out of the corner of my eye every now and then, she was laughing and enjoying herself. For her, anything had to be an improvement over last month's three hours of animated madness in the Looney Tunes Cartoon Marathon.

We were thrilled to see a large ad in the lobby that advertised next Saturday's funfest. It was a Monster Movie Marathon. Out of the bowels of dormant volcanoes, down from the uncharted galaxies of outer space, and up from slimy dark lagoon waters they came to wreak havoc upon a defenseless American public – blood sucking spiders . . . radioactive monster ants . . . a fire breathing tyrannosaurus . . . giant sized robots . . . brain eaters. Best of all, Abbott and Costello were going to meet some of the classic monsters from the 1930s in a laugh-filled thriller.

I didn't get to see too much of my dad in those days. Oh, he was usually around the house in the mornings, but he left at 2:30 P.M. for his 3-11 shift at the mill. In his spare time, he frequently was in his workshop out back, staring at an oscilloscope trying to fix someone's radio or TV. Whenever he did take my sister and me somewhere it was usually an unforgettable experience. Once we went to the Police Circus in St. Louis to catch the afternoon performance of Ringling Brothers Barnum and Bailey circus in the **Arena**. Perched high above the floor, we roared with delight at the sad-eyed hobo clown, Emmett Kelly, hopelessly trying to sweep up the elusive Big Top spotlight. Clutching our souvenir circus pennants, my sister and I thrilled to a three-ring, star-studded extravaganza of death defying, steel-nerved tightrope walkers, bareback-riding beauties clad in dazzling sequined outfits, and nimble, high flying trapeze acrobats. With my stomach packed tight with Cracker Jack, hot dogs, roasted peanuts, and Chock-ola chocolate drink, I fell asleep in the back seat on the way home thoroughly convinced that daredevil lion-tamer **Clyde Beatty** had to be just about the bravest man in the whole wide world.

Although Dad was a Browns fan, he acquiesced to my diehard patronage of the St. Louis Cardinals. They never won the pennant in those halcyon days of the Fifties, but with players like Terry Moore, Stan Musial, Enos Slaughter, Red Schoendienst, Lindy and Von McDaniel, **Vinegar Bend Mizell**, Wally Moon, Bill Virdon, Rip Repulski and Marty Marion, they sure made Cardinal baseball exciting. Dad took me to Sportsman's Park on a couple of occasions to see my baseball card heroes in action. Those were the days when you could see the Reds, Pirates, Phillies, Giants, Braves and Dodgers compete with stars such as Duke Snider, Pee Wee Reese, Carl Erskine, Jackie Robinson, Ralph Kiner, Willie Mays, Sal Maglie, Bobby Thompson, Ted Kluszewski, Warren Spahn, Hank Aaron and Robin Roberts. We left the game with a tinge of sadness, for the Giants had edged my beloved Cards by a score of 6-5. Disappointment over my team's narrow defeat quickly faded as I anxiously sat on pins and needles all the rest of the way home thinking about how I would tell my friends what it was like seeing a big league game in person.

The Bootery at 2515 Watson Road in St. Louis

I didn't know much about politics except what I heard my parents say. Normally, they voted Democratic but when General Eisenhower ran against former Illinois governor Adlai Stevenson, they decided the man with the infectious smile would receive their vote. When the President suffered a heart attack, I remember Miss Schuetze asking my class at school to pray for a speedy recovery.

There was a kid a couple of blocks over on 51st Street who suffered from polio. I remember feeling sad every time I rode my bicycle past his wan-looking house.

There will always be a special place in my heart for that time of innocence when patriotism was in full bloom, when most families went to church, when children could grow up with a loving set of parents in a safe neighborhood and do all those things which evoke great memories as I grow older. Those were happy, glorious days.

Cardinal outfielder, Bill Virdon

CHILDHOOD MEMORIES

Just about every red-blooded boy in my neighborhood had either a Marx or Lionel train set in his basement. Mine sat on a ¾ inch plywood board supported by saw horses. The Marx set was a bit inferior to the Lionel, and I was glad that in my letter to Santa I emphasized that I wanted a Lionel . . . if at all possible. My setup couldn't compare to the ones in the window display at **Famous and Barr** at Christmas time, but it still gave me many hours of pleasure. The interlocking tracks wound through paper maché hills and tunnels and around a miniature city and industrial complex. The city consisted of snap together houses, a church, a fire department, a library, a drug store and a school. The streets were dotted with miniature hand-painted people who owned plastic cars with metal wheels. Manning the controls of my silver and black transformer, I pushed the orange handle to sound the lusty steam whistle as my lumbering 4-4-2 came to a crossing. Then I gently eased my ten car freight train into the automatic cattle loader, around the bend to drop off the silver-leaded milk containers and headed back to the depot to put another smoke pellet into the engine's stack.

The only way I could be lured away from my railroad empire was by the soft tinkling bells of the Good Humor truck making its afternoon rounds. It seemed as if all the kids on our block would converge at the same time upon the bright white truck with the partially eaten ice cream bar painted on its sides. Out of its smokey, dry ice freezer came a delectable assortment of mouth-watering treats, including my favorite coconut ice cream bar and jumbo half-sherbet, half-vanilla ice cream Dixie cups (not with the movie star's picture on the lids – that was a different brand). M-m-m, boy! They just don't make ice cream the way they used to.

I have been addicted to television ever since I was old enough to finger paint along with Miss Frances on *Ding Dong School*. I would normally make a habit of rising early on Saturday morning, suiting up in my all black Hopalong Cassidy cowboy outfit, and clicking on our postage stamp sized **Capehart** television with a round 7 inch screen. Now I was all set to watch my silver-haired western hero lock horns with outlaw desperadoes. Instead of killing the outlaws, Cassidy usually either shot the gun out of their hand or winged them in the shoulder. And you never saw any blood. Mom usually served up Saturday breakfast in my favorite bowl, emblazoned with a color graphic of Tom Mix nuzzled up to his faithful wonder horse, Tony. Hoppy had a horse named Topper, but I thought that was a rather uncool name for a horse. After Hopalong had deposited the crooks in the local hoosegow, and rode off into the sunset back to his Bar–20 ranch. I quickly scarfed down my toasted Wonder Bread, gobbled up the rest of my

Nabisco shredded wheat, and then looked over the Straight Arrow Indian village cutouts that came printed on the cardboard used to separate the different layers of biscuits. Finally, I finished off my glass of **Sealtest** chocolate milk, courtesy of Bosco Syrup.

Good Humor ice cream vehicle

Calling out a quick goodbye to Mom, I rushed across the street to watch television with the Rudd brothers, my neighborhood buddies. We sat on the 9 x 12 rose-patterned carpet in front of the television set. Surrounding us was a half-finished Popsicle stick fort that Gordon was working on. There was also an empty Silly Putty eggshell, a cloth tobacco pouch with drawstrings that contained cat's eye marbles, a **Kid Colt Outlaw** comic, a Plastic Man comic and several Classics Illustrated. Being knee-deep in debris never seemed to bother us as we sat mesmerized through a three-hour marathon of kiddie mayhem and adventure. We tacked up our magic plastic screen over the ten-inch Admiral set to use a crayon and draw Winky Dink out of one of his weekly jams. Space Patrol then soared through the galaxies on an exciting interplanetary mission before returning to home base. Next, Captain Midnight and his crew outthought, outwitted and outfought the bad guys before sending out a secret message at the end of the program. We easily figured it out because we had all sent in the top seal from a jar of Ovaltine to get one of those rings with a round-shaped dial. Roy Rogers and Dale Evans closed their action-packed western adventure series singing "Happy Trails to You." They were brought to the screen courtesy of Post cereals and Jell-O pudding. Roy Rogers was King of the Cowboys, Dale Evans was Queen of the West and the smartest horse in existence was Trigger, that golden palomino. Their goofy sidekick, Pat Brady, was lame, but that cool German shepherd named Bullet made up for that. My favorite sidekicks were Al St. John (paired with either Lash LaRue or Buster Crabbe) and Gabby Hayes.

Kukla, Burt Tilstrom, Ollie, and Fran

Rolly poly, squeaky-voiced Andy Devine squared off against mischievous Froggy the invisible gremlin each week in his role as storyteller-host of *Andy's Gang*. Midnight the cat and Squeaky the mouse gave us additional laughs. We got our biggest kick out of the zany show when **Froggy plunked his magic twanger** and surfaced from behind a puff of smoke and said, "Hi ya, kids, hi ya!" Then the show went on to tell a jungle story set in mysterious India. When we became so bleary eyed we couldn't tell the difference between Rin Tin Tin and Rootie Kazootie, we headed out the door and went outside for a game of bicycle tag.

I'll never forget the time in the fourth grade when it was announced that the nurse was going to give us polio shots. Polio was a dreaded disease back then. President Roosevelt had contracted polio back in the 1920s and was a cripple the rest of his life. Johnny Weissmuller, the guy who portrayed Tarzan, contracted polio and overcame it with a vigorous regimen of daily swimming. My mother nurtured the fear of polio and warned me never to let my lips touch the spout on public drinking fountains or to play in the ditch when it was filled to the brim with water after a thunder storm. As a youngster, every spring I went out knocking on doors to collect for the **March of Dimes**. I'll never forget during one drive there was an iron lung on display downtown. People with severe cases of polio were enclosed in a metal tube that pretty much looked like a water heater. The only thing that stuck out was your head and neck. The tube was pressurized to expand and contract the chest to help with breathing.

Fortunately, it was announced, **gamma globulin** had been invented to save the day. Our mothers dragged us off to the family physician for shots (my mother leading the charge, of course). The amount that you received was proportional to your size and weight. As luck would have it, they later announced that gamma globulin was ineffective. A few months later, officials announced another scientific breakthrough. **Dr. Jonas Salk** had devised an effective vaccine. This time the public school served as the scientific laboratory for testing Salk's experimental vaccine. Amidst a chorus of whimpers, my class lined up for the shots. With shirt sleeves rolled up to the indelible smallpox imprint on our arms, we trudged reluctantly to the nurse's makeshift station. How I fought back the tears when that huge hypodermic needle plunged into my arm. The aftereffects of this trauma left me light headed and weak kneed. After a nerve-wracking series of three injections, with my arm left looking like a pin cushion, Dr. Salk's serum was hailed as a success. Four months later, my teacher informed the class that some of us had been injected with a placebo. Yep, you guessed it. I had to take that series of painful shots all over again!

A YOUNG GIRL'S CHILDHOOD MEMORIES

By Jacqueline Rogier nee Nunes of **Highland**, Illinois – Bill's older and smarter sister

Shortly after my parents bought a house (1946) in the Washington Park section of **East St. Louis**, there was a flood. Unfortunately, we bought in a flat section of town that was at the bottom of a two block long, gently sloping street. My brother and I were evacuated by neighbors in a Jon boat as Mom and Dad stayed behind and put some valuables in the attic and piled furniture on top of tables. It rained steadily for four days in a row and the water got up as high as the switch plates on the wall. We didn't own a car yet so at least my parents were spared that disaster. We went everywhere on public buses that were only two blocks away and came by the stop every twelve minutes.

When the waters receded and Mom and Dad had to clean up the mess and repaint, they sent me to stay with my aunt who lived in an upstairs duplex in the **Wellston** part of St. Louis. Aunt Colleen and Uncle Solly Maltzman didn't have any children at the time.

Frozen cream popping out at the top of milk bottles

Every other day the milkman left two quart bottles of milk for them on the front porch. I guess homogenized milk had not yet been invented because the milk and the cream would separate and the cream would rise to the top. We would wake up in the morning and go out to the porch to get it. She shook one bottle while I shook the other to mix the cream with the milk. "During the winter," she explained, "the milk would freeze and expand, forcing the cream to pop off the cardboard cap on top." To show what she meant, one time she put a bottle in the ice box and encased it in ice. Four hours later she took it out and the cream had popped out of the narrow neck of the bottle by two inches. She cut it off with a knife, placed it in a bowl, and sprinkled granulated sugar on it. We each grabbed a spoon. "Dig in," she said with a mischievous wink.

The cap had the Pevely name on it, stated that the milk was pasteurized (to kill germs), and that it contained 3.5 percent butterfat. The cap had a small tab on one side which enabled you to grab hold of something when you wanted to take off the top and pour some milk from the bottle. This is what people referred to as whole milk as opposed to skim milk. Now Uncle Solly worked for Veteran's Linoleum on the east side of the river. Not long after that they moved right next door to us in Washington Park. Their house sat higher up by two rows of cinder blocks more than ours. I guess they figured the chances of another flood were slim because after the flood the city built a huge drainage ditch (a block behind us) that emptied into the Mississippi River near the stock yards.

The iceman

I was born in 1935 – smack dab in the middle of the Depression - the same year Elvis was born. Most of the toys my friends and I played with did not come from stores. They were products of my imagination and creativity. Dolls were made from hollyhocks and clothespins. We painted faces on round wooden clothespins and attached hair made of yarn. Cradles for rocking our dolls were made by cutting an opening on one side of a round Quaker oatmeal box. My playmates and I made clothes and quilts for our dolls from scraps of material our mothers gave us. Nearly all mothers back then knew how to sew and make dresses for themselves and their daughters. Mom's machine was one of those seven-drawer black and gold Singers with a foot operated treadle. There were three ornate wooden drawers on each side and a long narrow one in the middle. Mother was quite a seamstress and taught me how to sew. These homemaking skills were reinforced at school where cooking and sewing classes were offered.

My friends and I made a beanbag toss game by saving misshapen navy beans that otherwise would have been discarded. The bag came from scrap material. Then we drew hopscotch-like squares on the sidewalks and put numbers on them that equaled points. Any bag that landed on a line resulted in no points. We had a variation on that. We took a large piece of cardboard and reinforced it with wood strips from old orange crates. Then we painted a clown's face on the front and propped it up at a slight reclining angle. We cut out the eyes and mouth and the object was to toss the homemade bean bags through the holes.

Dads back then frequently made toys for their children. My dad once made me a pair of stilts from some old scrap lumber. They were merely two by twos that were six foot long with two wedge-shaped blocks fastened to them for platforms to stand on. At first, Dad had them only six inches off the ground until I became adept at walking on them. Later, he raised them to twelve inches. They gave my friends and me many hours of pleasure.

Some toys came from our garden. Cucumbers too large to eat became boats when hollowed out. Lollipop sticks and thin cardboard worked nicely for the mast and sails. A hollowed out acorn and a matchstick became a pipe. We even blew soap bubbles with dandelion stems.

Sometimes we prepared play meals that were actually edible. Dandelion leaves provided the salad and Mom allowed us to fix our own Kool-Aid. We found apples from a neighbor's tree that were lying on the ground. We cut out the bad spots and cooked the apples in tin foil that was placed on top of a 75 watt light bulb.

On rainy days, when we had to play indoors and entertain ourselves, we devised a game called Shooting Star. One person would lie on his back and draw the knees to his chest while making a platform to sit on with the bottom of his feet. The other person would sit on the platform and then the person on the floor would push his legs straight, catapulting the other person several feet into the air and tossing them about five or six feet away from the launcher.

One early summer day, when my cousin Barbara Jean was visiting, we put on a neighborhood carnival show in Jo Ann Griffin's big garage. We charged a couple of cents for admission and lemonade, made with fresh lemons, of course.

We had a ring toss game. A wooden crate of empty soda bottles worked nicely. I forced, uh, talked my brother into putting on a pair of swimming trunks and acting like a strong man. We could hardly keep from laughing at his knobby knees. We told fortunes, dressed like gypsies in our mothers' old house dresses for gowns, with long silk scarves over our heads. An overturned fishbowl served nicely as a crystal ball.

We had fun, and so did everyone who attended.

Another thing we did indoors was to make little samplers of buttonholes and fancy embroidery stitches, again taught by our seamstress mothers.

Empty spool and yarn

Mother also gave us her empty wooden **thread spools**. We'd pound four small brads around the center of the spool then loop yarn over the nails. We pulled the yarn through the hole in the spool and formed it into a knitted rope. When the rope was long enough we placed it on a metal jig especially formed to make pot holders.

My parents may not have been able to buy me many store bought toys, but we never lacked for entertainment. When the war came along and Dad got a good job at Mepham Paint Company, my parents bought me a shiny new J.C. Higgins bicycle, with shock absorbers called knee action, to make up for the lean years. I thought I was in kid heaven.

Author's note: My sister taught me how to ride a bike on her fancy new J.C. Higgins from Sears. She would sit on the seat, put her hands on my waist, and dangle her feet while I stood on the pedals and pumped and steered.

A BUZZ FROM THE GOOD OL' DAYS

Not long ago my wife and I were eating breakfast with a group of friends at the **Golden Corral** on Zumbehl Road in **St. Charles**. A pesky fly was flitting about and every once in a while it would be necessary to shoo him away from our food. It made me think back to the days of my youth when restaurants had a quick solution for the problem – fly paper.

10 inch 1949 Zenith television

Fly paper hung from ceilings in barns, kitchens, restaurants, ice cream parlors, porches – just about anywhere flies gathered in squadrons for strafing missions against humans. They would bump into the strip, become hopelessly stuck and eventually die from starvation. Now fly paper looked pretty much like someone took a roll of Ansco film, let it uncoil, then hung it from the ceiling. One side of the roll was coated with a sweet smelling sticky substance that attracted flies and held them fast when they landed. Coated with dead flies and squirming lives ones, it wasn't pretty, but it was effective. You don't see them in restaurants anymore. I guess the health department considers them unsightly and unsanitary.

Before fly paper was invented our ingenious forefathers came up with a solution for dealing with flies at mealtime – **shoo fly pie**. This rich dessert was first concocted by the Amish, sometimes referred to as the Pennsylvania Dutch. It consists of a gooey mixture of molasses beneath a crumb topping. During mealtime, a small portion of this would be set in a corner of the room. The flies wouldn't bother the goings on at the meal because they were preoccupied with a different and more irresistible food. Incidentally, Dinah Shore's first top ten hit was "Shoo Fly Pie and Apple Pan Dowdy."

In the 1920s, there was a product called Flit. "Quick, Henry - the Flit," was a well known advertising phrase at the time. Magazine ads featured a cartoon "Henry" character busily killing the critters wherever he went by shooting them with poisonous clouds from a small garden sprayer.

To my young adolescent brain the Nobel Prize should have been given to the man who invented window screens and screen doors. What a boon to mankind. Since almost no one had air conditioning in 1950, everyone left windows and doors open for summertime ventilation. Had it not been for screens, flies would have been a huge problem. Mothers, of course, were far more vigilant about this than youngsters. Many a time our household would reverberate with a thunderous, "Sonny, close that front screen door, you weren't reared in a barn!"

My childhood friends and I devised an ingenious way of killing flies with rubber bands. Yes, rubber bands. Sometimes we sat near a porch railing and waited for a fly to land. Then we took a rubber band that had been cut and pulled one end back, much as you would a sling shot. After taking dead aim at the fly, we let one end go and quick as lightning its zooming tip would cut the fly in two. The rubber band was a bit messy, but about 95 percent effective. It was also considered more civilized than pulling wings off butterflies, which some young boys were known, on occasion, to do.

Around 1900, the fly problem in the St. Louis area was so bad that **public schools offered youngsters a penny for every 100 dead flies that they brought to class**. I suspect that these children probably used old-fashioned fly swatters to collect their bounty.

When we visited our farm relatives in Kentucky, I noticed that one of my uncles had fashioned a fly trap in the barn. It was a 2-foot tall cone of screen wire mounted on stubby legs. Inside was a saucer of sugar water for a bait trap. The greedy flies would enter the bottom, munch on the bait, then fly up, only to discover that they were hopelessly trapped inside the screen cylinder. (Yes, they could have escaped down through the hole where they entered . . . but flies have very small brains.)

Over in the dairy stall the milk cow was perpetually annoyed by flies. Bossie's only line of defense was her tail which she swished in near perpetual motion. This made milking often hazardous since you could be squeezing and tugging on a spigot and suddenly get smacked in the face by the cow's tail. Now this wasn't like getting hit with a feather duster. The texture of a bovine's tail in no way resembles a feather duster. Think more like one of those lashes administered to seaman Alan Ladd in *Two Years Before the Mast*.

My dad was quite adept at killing flies with a rolled up newspaper. However, even a good newspaper like the *St. Louis Star* was reduced to shreds after about 22-25 swats. Our local paper, the *East St. Louis Journal*, became tattered more quickly.

Flies were also an annoyance for picnickers, horses, cats and dogs. An outdoor meal attracted flies for miles around. Some of them even came from different ZIP codes.

It seems as if flies aren't as big a nuisance anymore. My wife and I have solved the problem by keeping several cats as pets. They're pretty good at trapping the flies against the window and then eating them. I try not to think about that when one of them occasionally saunters over to me and gives me a lick on my face.

Did you ever give much thought to the businesses that donated money for ads to help sponsor school yearbooks? Here is a list of some that were in the **Riverview Rams** *Echoes* yearbooks of the mid 1950s.

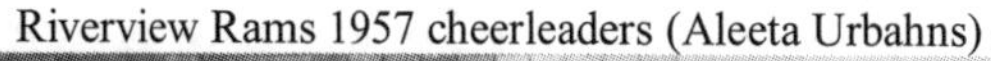

Riverview Rams 1957 cheerleaders (Aleeta Urbahns)

Teich Drugs on Bellefontaine Rd; Diedrich Groceries at 591 Scranton; Adams Wrecker Service on Chambers Rd; Louis Ernst Barber Shop at Diamond and Chambers; Troy and Duke's Barber Shop on Chambers Rd; Baden Melody Mart; Meyer Chevrolet; Lloyd's Hunting and Fishing Supplies; Dellwood Beauty Shop; Bradford Jewelers in Jennings; Hathaway Pharmacy on Chambers Rd; Narsh's Super Market; Mueller's Service Station on Riverview Dr; Wiegand Pharmacy on Diamond Dr; Moline Hardware on Chambers; Steinmann's Sinclair Service; Wolfe Bow and Arrow Shop; Economy Chevrolet in Wellston; Vorhof-Duenke Realtors

OH, NO! PLEASE, NOT THAT! MOM'S HOME REMEDIES

When I was just a youth, back in the 1940s, I remember my mother giving me all kinds of home remedies and patent medicines that were so dreadful that they still haunt my memory. I almost get sick today just thinking about some of them. Many of these cure-alls were merely "old wives" tales that had been passed along, due to someone supposing that a particular remedy had been successful. If fact, many treatments fitted into the same category as throwing salt over your shoulder to ward off bad luck.

Medicine cabinet

One of my earliest memories is when I became ill with spasmodic croup when I was about four years old. My mother treated me at night with a Cresolene lamp that burned alcohol and heated a coal tar substance that gave off healing vapors – or so it was thought. The Food and Drug Administration took the lamps off the market because they were found to be ineffective.

Cod liver oil was all the rage then and moms across America forced spoonfuls of this awful tasting stuff down kids' reluctant gullets. It was even worse for the previous generation. Children in the 1920s had to endure doses of skunk oil. I was always skeptical of these concoctions, but perhaps Mom did know best. After all, thanks to her watchful guidance, I've made it to adulthood and retirement.

Moms were doubly important in that era because few people went to the doctor. In fact, I was thirteen years old before I made my first visit to the dentist. My sister, born in 1935, was born at home – not in a hospital. After all, a week's stay in the hospital back then cost $35.00. Moms were forced to play the role of home healer. Whenever I got a very bad cough Mom administered a dose of sugar and coal oil (kerosene).

I can still picture our medicine cabinet that was filled with products like Prid salve (to draw out infections) Father John's Tonic (fortified your body with vitamins), Vicks Vapo Rub, Epsom salts, Listerine, Watkins Liniment (for sore muscles) and various other nostrums. There was also a glass eye-washing cup for sties.

If you got a sore throat, your mother would paint your tonsils with tincture of merthiolate. Nowadays merthiolate is used as a surgical antiseptic. If you cut your finger, she painted it with mercurochrome. If you got a canker sore, she gave you alum to put on it. You were given Ex Lax, Fletcher's Castoria or mineral oil for constipation. The cabinet also was stocked with Doan's pills, Carter's Liver Pills, carbolic acid and a host of other items. If I remember right, my mother cleaned the bathroom wash basin with carbolic acid to kill germs. My older sister Jackie remembers something called 666. It was some kind of cold remedy, and she says it was the most bitter stuff ever invented by mankind. Your mouth would still be puckered for two hours after taking it, she said. My cousin Del Shinn told me that his mother's cure for a sore throat was a tablespoon of mineral oil spiced with a drop of turpentine. Yes, turpentine!

When we whined about our treatment mother would tell us she had it much tougher because she had to go to school in wintertime wearing an asafetida bag around her neck. Her mother told her it was for warding off germs. "What it did was ward off friends," she told us. This bag had garlic and onions and asafetida, a pungent resin from plants related to the carrot family. I just figured Mom grew up in the Stone Age because she used such old-fashioned terms as carbuncle (bacterial skin infection with pus), apoplexy (stroke), sepsis (blood poisoning), apothecary (drug store), consumption (tuberculosis) and grippe (flu).

No youngster faked an illness to get to stay home from school in my generation because the treatment was far worse than suffering through the three Rs. My mother didn't use asafetida bags to ward off germs. She knew that colds and germs were transmitted by contact and she was always on my case to wash my hands frequently. That made sense, but I never could figure out why it was so important to wash behind my ears.

Old health department quarantine sign

WHOOPING COUGH

KEEP OUT

At the first hint of sniffles, some mothers began boiling onions to make one of those folksy miracle cures. Sometimes kids were administered sassafras tea, which had a rather interesting taste. If you got a chest cold, your mom would rub Vicks salve all over your chest at bedtime. I'll have to admit, inhaling the vapors from that icky stuff made me breathe better at night. A cousin of mine, who lived in Mayfield, Kentucky, said his mother frequently used a mustard plaster. He said if a mustard plaster was left on too long it would dry tight to your skin and was hard to peel off. It, like the asafetida bag, had the ability to clear congestion all right – it cleared congestion in school hallways due to its unpleasant odor. I was glad I didn't grow up on a farm because I also heard stories about well-meaning parents using cow manure poultices to draw out the infection from a boil.

You prayed for winter to end so you wouldn't have to endure any more home remedies. But, much to our chagrin, we discovered kids weren't out of the woods yet. When spring came along, that was when you were most likely to get regular doses of castor oil or sulphur and black strap molasses if you lived in the country. Mothers claimed sulphur and molasses cleared your body of "winter germs." Castor oil ostensibly "built up your blood." It had iron in it so there might have been a bit of truth to that homily. Cod liver oil was another one of those preventative springtime medicines. My sister and I would line up nightly, reluctantly waiting for Mom to force that fishy-tasting stuff past our clenched teeth.

Front of *S.S. Admiral* (note old elevated railroad tracks)

Some of these concoctions had multiple uses. Listerene could cure halitosis (bad breath), but it was also said to be an effective treatment for dandruff. Mom used castor oil to polish my sister's patent leather Sunday shoes.

I would sometimes lie awake at night and think about the foul substances forced on me by my mother. I thought about the times when I had been disobedient and had been given a spanking. Perhaps these remedies weren't remedies at all but instead were thinly disguised efforts at killing off an unruly child who gave her constant grief. She would get away with it, too, because it was quite common for kids to die from childhood diseases; penicillin was still in its infancy. I could get a blister and die from blood poisoning. That's what happened to Calvin Coolidge's son. He died from a tennis blister that got infected. After each of these soul-searching sessions I'd make a promise that I was going to try to behave and not cause my mother so much grief. She'd get fewer migraines and I'd live longer, I reasoned. I lost track of the number of times I inadvertently broke that promise and had to make a new one all over again. Kids will be kids.

Maybe I did improve my behavior. Either that or God made mothers with near unlimited patience because here I am, 68 years old, with no criminal record. Perhaps my mother knew something I didn't about childhood illnesses. Who's to say I'm not still reaping the benefits of those long-ago remedies today? Maybe regular doses of castor oil and a few good spankings helped straighten me out.

A TRIBUTE TO THE S.S. ADMIRAL

For anyone who grew up in the St. Louis metro-area, going on an *Admiral* excursion in bygone days was a special treat. This fine boat drew tradition right out of the river and one could almost imagine meeting Mark Twain on the Mississippi as the ship followed a bend in the river. This author still has a scar on his forehead from tripping as a youth on the last step descending to the *Admiral's* second deck. Such an accident would probably be worth thousands today, but in those times a Band-Aid took care of it and the matter was quickly forgotten.

Whenever the *Admiral* turned around and headed downstream to begin its journey, I was always on the top deck. As the boat passed under the MacArthur Bridge, I ran as fast as I could from fore to aft, trying to keep the bridge directly above my head. I could never quite keep up.

While the adults spent most of the cruise on the air-conditioned ballroom level, my cousins and I found a young teen's paradise on the first floor arcade level that was filled with a wide assortment of games. It was always very noisy down there because the engine room and drive pistons were located just below. It's too bad that recent generations have missed out on the wonderful experience of going on an *Admiral* cruise, one of those legendary experiences reserved exclusively for old time St. Louisans and visitors.

Marilyn Kinsella (of **Fairview Heights**) also has fond memories of this grand dame of the river.

"We went on an annual trip to the *Admiral* with a Mothers' Club from church. As we crossed the Veterans

Bridge I looked down and could see the Mighty Mistress of the Mississippi – her stainless steel hull gleaming in the sunlight with the word ADMIRAL emblazoned in bright red letters along her side. We parked our car at Laclede's Landing and stumbled our way across the cobblestones until we reached the large wooden gang plank that led to the inner sanctum of the ship.

"A blast of hot, dry air swept our faces and our ears were

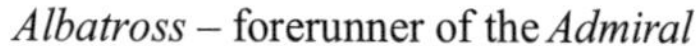

Albatross – forerunner of the *Admiral*

filled with the mechanical sound of five huge engines revving up. On the first deck was the penny arcade, but we bypassed that to quickly get to our favorite table on the dance floor. We walked up a sweeping staircase that led to blue leather padded doors with round windows. When those doors opened we were met by a blast of arctic air that kept the second and third levels cool. Nobody I knew lived in an air conditioned house in the Fifties. This main deck was also art deco giving the place a New York glitzy atmosphere. There were rounded pillars and pink and blue streamlined pipe lighting. There was a large wooden dance floor and a big stage where **Russ David** and his orchestra played.

"And the ladies rest rooms . . . what a hoot! Not only decorated in art deco, but they also had names . . . like "Greta Garbo" and "Sonja Heine." We made our way up to the third floor balcony that overlooked the dance floor and found our Holy Grail - a table next to a large window that allowed us to view the passing scenery outside. Oftentimes, a local TV personality such as **Charlotte Peters** hosted the entertainment. Once we found our table our mothers gave us a handful of change to go to kid heaven.

We ran back down to the first level and took in the sounds of pings, whistles, and pops coming from every direction. There was every kind of pinball, Skee Ball and electronic game imaginable. One game had a Ray–o-Light gun. A bear made its way across the screen and **when you shot the bear he rose up on his hind legs and gave a terrible growl**. There was a novelty stand with salt and pepper shakers, snow globes, giant pencils with the word Admiral printed on it. Then there was a machine that stamped out a metal coin about the size of a half-dollar. You could print your name and date on one side and the words *SS Admiral* were stamped on the other. There were vending machines that dispensed 4 x 6 black and white photos of movie stars and baseball players. These pictures came out at random and you swapped to get the one you wanted.

Admiral: the world's most beautiful river boat

"There was one booth that had a figure of a seated mystical **Gypsy woman**. You inserted a coin in the machine and she would nod and turn her head, then out popped a card with your fortune on it. Before we knew it we were out of money and the girls had to run back to the ladies' tables and beg for more. After our cash cows finally gave out we went up to the top deck to amuse ourselves. It was filled with multi-colored umbrella tables and Adirondack chairs to sit on and watch the scenery go by. We nearly jumped out of our skins when the captain pulled the chain and there was an earsplitting HOOONNNNKKKK! from the deep-throated steam whistle. Sometimes we ran to the bow of the ship, closed our eyes, and held out our arms to pretend that we were flying.

"One year, when I was in the 7th grade, I went on the *Admiral* with my best friend, Rosemary. We were beginning to think we were too big for Kiddie Land, having just discovered boys. Unfortunately, the boys were too engrossed in racking up big scores on pinball machines to pay us much attention. Then we found something new. There was a booth where you could have your picture taken and get the results instantly. What would they think of next? We sat inside the booth and put a quarter in the slot. We posed . . . smiling our prettiest. FLASH, FLASH, FLASH, FLASH. There was just enough time between shots to change your look or position. We always wanted one shot where we were looking a bit goofy, just to unnerve our parents. After about a minute it would spit out a small strip with four pictures. Somewhere in my house today . . . somewhere . . . are those pictures.

"But that wasn't all. That year there was another booth called the **Voice-o-Graph** where we could actually have a small vinyl record made. My friend and I looked at each other. After all, our music teacher had complimented us on our voices. This was just too cool. Now, this wasn't Karaoke so there were no lyrics or background music. No, we had to sing *a capella* and whatever words came out of our mouths. We argued back and forth and finally settled on Doris Day's hit, "Que Sera, Sera." We had to pool our money because it cost a whole dollar. When we got home we played the record over and over and thought we gave that perky freckle-faced singer a run for her money.

"In the Sixties the *Admiral* had Teen Night and that was great fun. Sometimes the band would be **Bob Kuban** and the In-men and other nights it would be **Jules Blattner** and the Teen Tones. We got out on the floor to twist and shout, do the mash potato, and the jump up and down to the Watusi."

The *Admiral* was built on the framework of an Iowa boat named the *Albatross*. It was originally used to haul 16 railroad cars. Streckfus Steamers Service Company bought the boat and spent $30 million refurbishing it. The boat was designed by a woman named Maizie Krebs, a fashion illustrator for Famous-Barr. The vessel had a streamlined Art Deco style that separated it visually from any other boat on the Mississippi. At 374 feet long and 92 feet wide, the Admiral was longer than a city block. At the time of its construction, **the *Admiral* was the largest passenger steamboat on inland waters in the world**. The magnificent boat had five decks, two of which were air-conditioned, an unheard of luxury at the time. It had a capacity of 4,400 passengers, and departed for its first cruise from the St. Louis waterfront in June of 1940. Most members of the Streckfus family worked on the boat in some capacity or another.

In 1979, the boat was converted into the President Casino featuring 1,230 slot machines, 59 gaming tables, 18 restrooms and a restaurant.

The St. Louis band Pavlov's Dog played their farewell concert on the Admiral in May of 1977. In 1998, the *Admiral* was rammed by three barges causing eight of its ten mooring lines to break. Fifty people had minor injuries and the boat sustained $11 million in damages. The city has had to bail out the boat financially in recent years so the future of the boat is in doubt and it could very well end up on the scrap heap. But no matter what happens, that fine old boat will be forever emblazoned in the memories of St. Louisans.

Cracker Jack and Bingo

ST. LOUIS MEMORIES FROM LONNIE TETTATON

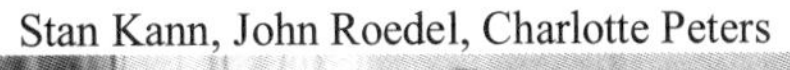

Stan Kann, John Roedel, Charlotte Peters

THE PETRIFIED MAN AT CHAIN OF ROCKS AMUSEMENT PARK, WALLY MOON, WORLD THEATER, POODLE SKIRTS, DUCKTAILS, RAG MAN, PAGLIACCI'S, MAYOR TUCKER, CLIFF HAGEN, SCISSORS GRINDERS, LOMBARDO'S, WALK-A-THONS, HODGES CHILI PARLOR, HYDE PARK BEER, VESS BILLION BUBBLE BEVERAGES, MOON PIES, ASHPITS, SWITZERS LICORICE, OLD JUDGE COFFEE, FORD WOODIE STATION WAGONS, CRYSTAL GRILL, SKRUGGS, VANDERVOORT & BARNEY, HARDY'S SHOES, BOYDS, BLUE SUEDE SHOES, MR. B SHIRTS, GIL NEWSOME, ED BONNER, CORAL COURTS, CLARION BALLROOM, MR. SANDMAN BY THE CHORDETTES, BURGER CHEF, CHUCK-A-BURGER, EVELYN WEST, MAUREEN THE SPIDER WOMAN, DRAG RACES AT SMARTT FIELD, THE ARENA, CHUCK BERRY, WALTER SCOTT, MUSIAL AND BIGGIES, MARTY BRONSON, CHARLOTTE PETERS, RAY JABLONSKI, ROARING TWENTIES CLUB, CASA LOMA, TUNE TOWN, GARAVELLI'S, IMPERIAL BALLROOM, JOE GARAGIOLA, MELROSE PIZZERIA, STAN KANN, LOEWS STATE THEATER, AMBASSADOR THEATER, WELLSTON LOOP, RAY QUINLAN DANCE STUDIO, WRESTLING AT THE CHASE, RUSS DAVID, JACK MURDOCH, CHUCK NORMAN, SPYDER BURKS, ED WILSON OF KWK, RUSS HUGHES OF KXOK, HARRY FENDER, KATZ DRUG STORE, VEILED PROPHET PARADE, GRAND FOLLIES, KAISER/FRAZIER, HENRY J, FAMOUS BARR CHRISTMAS WINDOW DISPLAY, CRINOLINES, AMBASSADOR THEATER, CINERAMA, 3-D, BWANA DEVIL, UNION STATION, THE KEFAUVER COMMISSION, LOEW'S STATE, ST. LOUIS THEATER, LOEW'S ORPHEUM, GREISEDIECK BROS. BEER, CHOCK-OLA, PROM MAGAZINE, PINKY PEVELY, CRANK WALL TELEPHONES

SEALTEST ICE CREAM, COONSKIN HATS, TEXAS BRUCE, THE ORIENT, PACKARD AND DESOTO, MEL TORME, PUBLIC SCHOOLS STADIUM, GUS MANCUSO, TIP-TOP BREAD, HARRY CARAY, BUSCH BAVARIAN BEER, LEMP MANSION, SPORTSMAN'S PARK, ST. LOUIS BROWNS, DEBALIVIERE STRIP, PAGE-ANT THEATER, BUCKHOLTZ MORTUARY, COAL HOLE, SACK DRESSES, ST. LOUIS ORANGE THREAD-NEEDLES, KWIK-WAY GRILL, CONELRAD, SUTTON FORD, INK WELLS, BLACKBOARD ERASERS, LOU THESZ, PANDA PAINT, STUDEBAKER LARK, WOOLWORTH'S, CROWN CANDY COMPANY, 1954 HEAT WAVE, BIG SNOW OF 1958, BANK NITE, DISH NITE, RAY MANNING OF WIL, GOLDENROD SHOWBOAT, BUSH'S STEAK HOUSE, RACING AT FAIRMOUNT PARK, TERRY MOORE'S PLAYDIUM, BUSTER WORTMAN, DINAH SHORE AND PATTI PAGE, THE ICE MAN, JACK CARNEY, THE PAD-DOCK, RAY BLUTH, RED SCHOENDIENST, FLOOD OF 1973, PRINCESS PHONES, KRIEGSHAUSER MORTUARY
RABBIT EARS, FEARLESS FOSDICK, HOLY COW, POLICE CIRCUS, FIREMAN'S RODEO, PAPER BOYS, BLUE DOT TAIL LIGHTS, CURB FEELERS, WHITEWASHED TREES, FENDER SKIRTS, BERMUDA BELLS, BUSTER BROWN HAIRCUTS, STEERING WHEEL SPINNERS, TAIL FINS, PENNY LOAFERS, TONI HOME PERMS, HADACOL, CHO CHOS, BOB PETTIT, STREET-CARS, BOTTLE CAP BALL, CORK BALL, INDIAN BALL, RUBBER GUN FIGHTS, SPEAR FIGHTS, SNOW FORTS, BAZOOKA JOE, HEY MABEL, BLACK LABEL, EASY ED MCCAULAY, MOVIE SERIALS, DOUBLE FEATURES, WILD'S PALACE OF POISON, STAG BEER, THE EDSEL, BONNIE BUTTERED BEEFSTEAKS, PENCIL THIN BELTS, PEGGED LEVIS, CREW CUTS, PETER PAN COLLARS, TEEN TOWN, PONTICELLO'S, GLAS PAC MUFFLERS, WESTMINSTER BALLROOM, PHOSPHATES, QUEEN FOR A DAY, FATHER KNOWS BEST, RED RYDER, LITTLE LULU, THE GREEN HORNET, SKY KING, STRAIGHT ARROW, MARK TRAIL, HENRY ALDRICH, JACK ARMSTRONG, SPACE PATROL, TOM CORBETT, AW, GO BLOW YOUR JETS, LOWELL THOMAS, IPANA, THE HITCHING POST, ROUTE 66, RUGGERI'S, BUCKINGHAM'S, THE TORNADO OF '59, FATS DOMINO, RICK NELSON, DINAH SHORE, PERRY COMO, EDDIE FISHER, OAKLAND STADIUM, ST. LOUIS KNIGHTS, ST. LOUIS FLYERS, THE CISCO KID, GUY MADISON, DICK WEBER, VITALIS HAIR TONIC, GILETTE BLUE BLADES, DON CARTER, RAY BLUTH, STAR TIMES, THE ADMIRAL, PARENTE'S, SPUTNIK, MUNY OPERA, ROI TAN CIGARS, LAWRENCE

WELK, AREN'T YOU GLAD YOU USE DIAL? BETTER BUY BIRDSEYE, ART LINKLETTER, EVENING IN PARIS PERFUME, WALTER ASHE RADIO, EADS BRIDGE TICKETS, BUS TOKENS, SALES TAX MILLS, SHAW'S GARDEN, THE JEWEL BOX, PHIL THE GORILLA, VAN HORN'S, WHITE BUCKS, ARGYLE SOCKS, BOBBY RYDELL, FABIAN, SENOR WENCES, GLEEM TOOTHPASTE GONE WITH THE WIND HURRICANE OIL LAMPS, CALIFORNIA DO-NUTS, WALTER WINCHELL, SKELLY GASOLINE, TCP, IRONING MANGLES, CAPTAIN 11, THREE STOOGES, OVALTINE SHAKER MUGS, JIM BOLEN, COOKIE AND THE CAPTAIN, BUSTER BROWN SHOES, SHINOLA, PLAYTEX GIRDLES, SIMONIZE YOUR CAR, BOBBY SOX, SADDLE OXFORDS, CLEAR-ASIL, CHARLES ATLAS, FOUR ACES, GRAND LEADER, TAPS ON SHOES, JAMES DEAN, ELVIS, MARILYN MONROE, JOHN CAMERON SWAYZE, RECAP TIRES, INNER TUBES, HOT PATCHES, PARTY LINES, WILDROOT HAIR TONIC, MACARTHUR BRIDGE, MONSANTO, EMERSON ELECTRIC, MCDONNELL AIRCRAFT, INTERNATIONAL SHOE, CURLEE CLOTHING, MISSOURI ATHLETIC CLUB, 1958 WORLD CHAMPION HAWKS, KIEL AUDITORIUM, OX BLOOD SHOE POLISH, TOM MCCANN SHOES, SWITZER'S LICORICE, OLD JUDGE COFFEE, WASHING MACHINE WRINGERS, WASHBOARDS, CLOTHES PROPS, STOKER COAL, CROSLEY RADIOS, CONELRAD, RED GOOSE SHOES, THURSDAY DOLLAR DAY AT STIX AND FAMOUS FRENCH ONION SOUP ON 6TH FLOOR AT FAMOUS, CORKY THE CLOWN, BOWLING ALLEY PIN-SETTERS, CREAM AT THE TOP OF A BOTTLE OF MILK, WHIZZER MOTOR BIKES, INDIAN MOTORCYCLES, RINSO SOAP POWDER, RALSTON STRAIGHT SHOOTERS, NIPPUR THE RCA DOG, SOAP OPERAS, WHITE BUCKS, SADIE HAWKINS DANCES, SOCK HOPS, ISINGLASS, KILROY WAS HERE, VERMICULITE INSULATION, MISS HULLINGS, THE SEARCH FOR BRIDEY MURPHY, SPUTNIK, YELLOW AND RED CITY SERVICE ICE MACHINES, HALLOWEEN MASKS THAT WERE CALLED FALSE FACES, WOODEN ESCALATORS ON THE TOP FLOORS AT STIX, GETTING ONE PRESENT AT CHRISTMAS TIME, RIDING BIKES EVERYWHERE, ROUND SEVEN INCH TV PICTURE TUBES, GREEN, FLESH, AND BLUE ACETATE SHEETS TO TAPE OVER YOUR TV TO ACHIEVE COLOR, WHITE SHMOOS, JACCARDS STUDENT BUS PASSES SKATES WITH KEYS, JUNE BUG STRINGS, POLICE PADDY WAGONS, BOY SCOUT EXPOSITIONS AT THE ARENA, U.S. KEDS, SNOW CONE MAN ON A MOTOR SCOOTER, THE SPOOK HOUSE AT THE HIGHLANDS, WATCHING PLANES TAKE OFF AT LAMBERT FROM THE ROOF OF THE OLD TERMINAL, RED FIRE BOXES ON STREET CORNERS, MR. MOKE AT THE ZOO CHIMP SHOW, DAD GETTING UP IN THE MIDDLE OF THE NIGHT TO STOKE THE FURNACE, GET THE BEST, GET THE BEST, GET SEALTEST, STORM WINDOWS THAT YOU PUT UP IN THE FALL AND TOOK DOWN IN THE SPRING, PLAYING OUTSIDE ALL DAY IN SUMMER UNTIL THE STREET LIGHTS CAME ON, DISH NITE AT THE NEIGHBORHOOD THEATER, CAPTAIN MIDNIGHT DECODER RINGS, CHRISTMAS TRAIN DISPLAYS AT FAMOUS, LITTLE ORPHAN ANNIE OVALTINE MUGS, SANKA COFFEE, POSTUM, COMET STICK MODEL AIRPLANES, ETHER AS AN ANESTHETIC WHEN YOUR TONSILLS WERE REMOVED, KELLOGG'S CORN SOYA, HADACOL, ASK, ASK, ASK FOR KAS POTATO CHIPS, CAPTAIN GALLANT, YOU CAN BE SURE IF IT'S WESTINGHOUSE, TOOTSIE ROLLS, YO–YO COMPETITIONS AT HOBBY SHOPS, POWERHOUSE CANDY BARS, LOG CABIN MAPLE SYRUP IN A TIN, HOLIDAY HILL IN ST. ANN, THE HOT TAMALE MAN, THE RECORD DEPARTMENT ON THE 3RD FLOOR AT FAMOUS, SAM THE WATERMELON MAN, HOBBY HORSES, BOUFFANT CRINOLINE SLIPS, CANDLESTICK TELEPHONES, SEARCHING FOR DISCARDED EAGLE STAMP STUBS AT FAMOUS, MOSQUITO TRUCKS THAT FOGGED UP THE BLOCK ON SUMMER NIGHTS, NIGHT TRIPS ON THE ADMIRAL THAT TURNED AROUND AT THE JEFFERSON BARRACKS BRIDGE, POULTRY SHOPS WHERE THEY BUTCHERED LIVE CHICKENS ON THE SPOT, ICE SKATING AT THE WINTER GARDENS, STOPPING WHAT YOU WERE DOING AND COMING TO ATTENTION WHEN THEY RAISED THE FLAG AT SCHOOL, ADAMS DAIRY, SO-GOOD POTATO CHIPS, THE ST. LOUIS HOP, OLD VIENNA POTATO CHIPS, TRADEWINDS RESTAURANT ON CHOUTEAU, VELVET FREEZE, SAULK VACCINE POLIO SHOTS, THE IRON LUNG, COLLECTING FOR THE MARCH OF DIMES, RED TIPPED CANDY CIGARETTES, DOG AND SUDS, ERNIE HELMAN THE TV MAGICIAN, PEOPLE SLEEPING ON BLANKETS IN THEIR YARDS ON HOT NIGHTS, HAVING YOUR PICTURE TAKEN AS A KID ON ONE OF THOSE PONIES, HOWDY DOODIE, WOOLWORTH'S AND KRESGEE'S LUNCH COUNTERS, THE PHOTOGRAPHER TAKING YOUR PICTURE ON THE SIDEWALK IN FRONT OF THE FOX THEATER, NURSES AT SCHOOL CHECKING YOUR SCALP FOR COOTIES, SEVEN HILLS OF HELL NEAR ST. CHARLES, MORON JOKES, KNOCK KNOCK JOKES, BADENFEST, BUYING SERVICE FOR 12 NORITAKE CHINA FOR $50 AT THE GEM STORE IN N. ST. LOUIS ON 244 (1960), THE PLANTATION DINNER THEATER ON 244, SKYWRITING AIRPLANES, HOBOS KNOCKING ON YOUR BACK DOOR, DOUBLE DECKER BUSES THAT WENT TO THE ZOO, STORES THAT DELIVERED GROCERIES TO YOUR HOUSE, PAPERBOYS BUILDING FIRES IN 55 GALLON DRUMS, LISTENING TO A RECORD IN A BOOTH AT THE STORE BEFORE YOU BOUGHT IT, THE FORTUNE TELLER LADY ON THE ADMIRAL, GUYS SWIMMING NAKED DURING PE AT SCHOOLS THAT HAD POOLS, KNUCKS DOWN WHEN

Kilroy and his inventor

Rinso wash powder commercial

SHOOTING MARBLES, HOMEMADE STILTS, CRUSHED TIN CANS FOR HOMEMADE HORSE SHOES, JAW BREAKERS CANDY, BUSY BEE CANDY, BIEDERMAN'S, FREUND'S

SWIMMING NAKED AT THE DOWNTOWN YMCA, PINKIE LEE, PEDAL PUSHER PANTS, SHOTGUN HOUSES, BEE'S KNEES, BERT GRIMM'S TATTOO PARLOR ON NORTH BROADWAY, ABSORENE WALLPAPER CLEANER (FORERUNNER OF PLAY DOH), BEVO FRANCIS OF RIO GRANDE, AEOLIAN HI FI SHOP, MARX, LIONEL, HEALTH DEPARTMENT QUARANTINES FOR SCARLET FEVER, BORAXO, WELCOMING NEWLYWEDS WITH A SHIVAREE, DUCK AND COVER DRILLS AT SCHOOL, AND AMERICAN FLYER TRAIN SETS, GILBERT CHEMISTRY SETS, MACHINES AT SHOE STORES THAT X-RAYED YOUR FEET TO INSURE PROPER FIT, SHEENA, QUEEN OF THE JUNGLE, TINKERTOWN HOBBY SHOP, GREGG SHORTHAND, PLEATED PLAID SKIRTS, A BALD-HEADED COMIC STRIP KID NAMED HENRY, PENNY LOAFERS, CAR HEAT GAUGES THAT SAT ON TOP OF THE RADIATOR, HODGES ROLLER RINK, BOKAR COFFEE AT A&P, OXYDOL, ARENA ROLLER RINK, HOPE CHESTS, OILCLOTH, CARNATION MILK – FROM CONTENTED COWS, GOING DOWN THE WOODEN SLIDE AT WESTLAKE ON A GUNNY SACK, QUICK MEAL STOVES WITH THE OVEN ON TOP AND TO THE RIGHT OF THE BURNERS, MUMBLETY PEG, FLOUR SIFTERS, TOP VALUE STAMPS, EAGLE STAMPS, LANE CEDAR CHESTS, THE HARDY BOYS, NANCY DREW, PILLBOX HAT, BEEHIVE HAIRDOS, RALEIGH CIGARETTE COUPONS, RUMBLE SEATS, COLORING WHITE MARGARINE AND TURNING IT YELLOW WITH PACKETS OF RED POWDER, STREETCAR TOKENS AND TRANSFER SLIPS, YOUTH FOR CHRIST AT THE LYN THEATER ON GRAND, SHATTINGER MUSIC, MYLES STANDISH, TOMBSTONE RADIOS, MONKEY BARS, MAYONAISE SANDWICHES, WATER PIPES THAT RATTLED BECAUSE OF AIR IN THEM, MOHAWK TIRES, STANLEY HOME PARTIES, FRICK AND FRACK, HARVEY GIRLS, TOOTHPASTE TUBES THAT YOU COULD ROLL UP BECAUSE THEY WERE MADE OF SHEET LEAD, STEINBERG RINK, A-BOMB BASEMENT SHELTERS, BOATMEN'S BANK, HIS MASTER'S VOICE, GAS WARS, SATURDAY NIGHT BATHS IN A GALVANIZED TUB, 8 O'CLOCK COFFEE, WALKATHONS, I'D WALK A MILE FOR A CAMEL, A & P GROCERIES, FOOTBALL GOALPOSTS ON THE FRONT OF THE END ZONE INSTEAD OF THE REAR, STOUFFER'S RIVERFRONT INN WITH A REVOLVING RESTAURANT ON TOP (IT TOOK AN HOUR FOR ONE COMPLETE REVOLUTION), JEWEL TEA TRUCKS, ST. LOUISAN BERT CONVY AND THE CHEERS SINGING "BLACK DENIM TROUSERS AND MOTORCYCLE BOOTS" IN 1955, PRINCESS PHONES, PHELAN FAUST PAINT, HILLBEHAN LUMBER, GETZ GETS 'EM, MUNTZ TVs, TIPTON APPLIANCES, BURMA SHAVE SIGNS, HALITOSIS, BOBBI BROOKS BLOUSES, DOT CANDY ON ADDING MACHINE PAPER, J. C. HIGGINS BIKES, MAXWELL HOUSE . . . GOOD TO THE LAST DROP, DREAMSICKLES, NOMA BUBBLE LIGHTS, LEATHER STROPS AT THE BARBER SHOP TO SHARPEN A STRAIGHT RAZOR, PANDA PAINT . . . IT WEARS LIKE A BEAR, STEVE MIZZERANEY, RADIO FLYER WAGONS, CEREAL PRIZES, LADY CIGARS FROM CATALPA TREES, BAZOOKA JOE, KNICKERS AND MACKINAWS, BRINGING GARDEN SNAKES TO SCHOOL, PF FLYERS GYM SHOES, $1 CHRISTMAS ALBUMS AT GOODYEAR, DRINKING CITRATE OF MAGNESIA FOR CONSTIPATION, HEALTH QUARANTINES, HOLSOM BAKERY ON KINGSHIGHWAY, ZOOT SUITS, METAL FIRE ESCAPE TUBES AT SCHOOLS, PRANG METAL PAINT BOXES FOR ELEMENTARY ART, GUS' PRETZELS ON ARSENAL ST., CHRISTMAS SEALS TO FIGHT TUBERCULOSIS.

Kellogg's Pep – this author's favorite Breakfast cereal as a kid

O'Fallon Tech Commercial Art class
George Vawter, Dave Hagler, Ray Wallace, Lonnie Tettaton

TYPICAL RULES IN 1955 HIGH SCHOOLS

No running in the halls
No chewing gum in class
No cursing
Sun glasses cannot be worn in the classroom
Boys cannot wear hats in class
Girls must wear uniforms in PE class
No wearing tennis shoes to school
Girls are not permitted to wear slacks to school
Boys are not permitted to have shaggy hair
Girl's dresses and skirts must be well below the knee
Boys are not permitted to wear T – shirts to class

At St. Louis Catholic high schools, such as CBC, if you misbehaved in class, one of the brothers took you out in the hall and punched you hard. In many public high schools, if two boys got in a fight, they were taken down to the gym, donned boxing gloves, went a few rounds, and then shook hands.

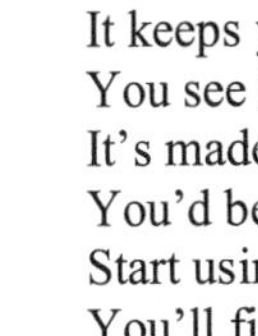

Get Wildroot Cream oil, Charlie,
It keeps your hair in trim.
You see it's non alcoholic, Charlie,
It's made with soothing lanolin.
You'd better get Wild Root Cream Oil, Charlie,
Start using it today.
You'll find that you will have a tough time, Charlie,
Keepin' all the gals away!

"Old Spice means quality," said the Captain to the boson,
So look for the bottle with the ship that sails the ocean!

Shredded Ralston for your breakfast

Starts the day off shining bright
Gives you lots of cowboy energy
With a flavor that's just right
It's delicious and nutritious
Bite size and ready to eat
Take a tip from Tom
Go and tell your mom
Shredded Ralston can't be beat.

Star light, star bright
First star I see tonight
I wish I may, I wish I might
Have the wish I make tonight.

Kellogg's Sugar Corn Pops,
Sugar Pops are tops!

Try Wheaties – they're whole bits of nutritious bran
Won't you try Wheaties, for wheat is the best food of man
They're crispy, they're crunchy, the whole year through
Millions can't resist them and neither will you
So just buy Wheaties – the best breakfast food in the land!

To look sharp, every time you shave
To feel sharp, and be on the ball
Just be sharp, use Gillette blue blades
For the quickest, slickest shave of all

Ivory Soap, 99 and 44/100 % pure – it floats

Whiz . . . best candy bar there is!
Packard – Ask the man who owns one!
Sooner or later you'll own Generals (tires)
I'd walk a mile for a Camel!
See the USA in your Chevrolet
Duz does everything
Bon Ami – hasn't scratched yet
Is there a Ford in your future?
Folgers coffee . . . it's mountain grown

N-A-B-I-S-C-O, Nabisco is the name to know
For a breakfast you can't beat,
Eat Nabisco Shredded Wheat

You go in the snow or we pay the tow – Firestone
Everything from scoop to nuts, including the kitchen sink – Central Hardware
You'll wonder where the yellow went, when you brush your teeth with Pepsodent.
Ovaltine: the heart of a hearty breakfast!

What a thrill to take the wheel, of a merry Oldsmobile
Down the road of life we'll fly, Automobilling, you and I
To the church we'll swiftly steal,
And the church bells they will peal
You can go as far as you like with me in my merry Oldsmobile.

Woof! Woof! That's my dog Tige
He lives in a shoe
I'm Buster Brown
Look for me in there too!

Lemonade, lemonade!
Made in the shade, and stirred with a spade,
Good enough for any old maid!

Prank phone calls – Hello, can you tell me how many fleas there are in a dog pound? Hello, is your refrigerator running? Well, you'd better go catch it. Hello, do you have Prince Albert in a can? We'll, you'd better let him out before he suffocates!

Rinso white, Rinso white,
Happy little washday song!

Step on a crack, break your mom's back
Step in a hole, break your mom's sugar bowl!

1960s ST. LOUIS RESTAURANTS

Bag of Chicken – 951 S. Kirkwood Rd.
Bama's Café – Highway 30
The Barn Restaurant – Route 66
Bartolino's – Hampton Avenue
Bellistri's Steak House – Route 66
Belvedere Joe's Restaurant – 1414 Brentwood
Big Bend Grill - 836 E. Big Bend
Biltmore Restaurant – 8407 Olive Street Rd.
Bippen's Estate – 11420 Gravois Road
Blu Top Restaurant – 9800 Page
Bo-Haven Inn – Route 2 Hillsboro
Bolego's Restaurant – 6725 Chippewa

Steve Mizeraney

Bonnie Boys' Restaurant – 102 Glashop
Brass Bell – 124 S. Kirkwood
Buckingham's Chicken Dinners–8945 Manchester
Busch's Grove - 9160 Clayton
Caruso's Pizza 8804 Manchester
Castle Point Café – 10018 Halls Ferry
Causey's Steak House – Highway 30
Chalet de Normandie - 9748 Manchester
Chu Wah Restaurant – 9628 Olive Street Road
Chuck-A-Burger – Route 66
Chuck-A-Burger – 9025 St. Charles Rock Road
The Chuck Wagon - 9233 Manchester Road
Cool Valley Restaurant – 1613 S. Florissant
Cornucopia Restaurant – 790 St. Francis
Crest House – Broadway near Market St.
Cristo's Restaurant – North Broadway

Culpeppers 12316 Olive & 300 N. Euclid
Cumpari's Pizza on 6240 Natural Bridge
Cyranos – Clayton Road near Skinker
Dellwood Restaurant – 1448 Chambers
Desert In – 12870 Manchester Rd.
Favazza's 5201 Southwest
The Flame – Highway 66 & Lindbergh
Flying Saucer Restaurant – Natural Bridge Rd.
Garavaglia's Restaurant – 7895 Watson Rd.
Garavelli's - Baliviere and De Giverville
Gia's – The Hill
Goody Goody's – Natural Bridge
Green Parrot Inn – 12120 Big Bend
Hamburger Heaven - 1919 Woodson Rd.
Heidelberg Inn – 11035 Bellfountain Rd.
Herbst Brothers Restaurant – 10262 Gravois
Howard Johnson's Restaurant – 3501 Kingshighway
Il Vesuvio Restaurant – 9942 Route 66
Kennedy's Happy Landing – 9311 Watson Rd.
Kraft's Miracle Bar – 10523 St. Chas Rock Road
Le Chateau – 10405 Clayton Road
Robert E. Lee Drive-in – 9000 Page
Lombardo's – Natural Bridge
Mammy's Inn – 12562 St. Chas Rock Rd.
McDonalds Hamburgers – 8320 Airport Road
Melrose Pizza – Easton at Kingshighway
Milo's Restaurant – 219 N. Florissant
Mittino's Inn – 2119 S. Brentwood
Old Barn Inn – St. Albans
Old English Lodge – 2747 Telegraph
Oldani's Restaurant – 2132 Edwards
Pagliacci's Restaurant – 4592 Manchester
Parente's – 6600 Chippewa
The Pines – 12950 St. Charles Rock Rd.
Ponticello's Restaurant – 1218 Chambers
Quonset Café – Highway 66
Rigazzi's – The Hill
Rizzo's – 1839 Dunn Road
Roads End Inn – New Halls Ferry Rd.
Romano's Ferguson Lounge–North of Airport Rd.
Romine's Restaurant – 9053 Riverview
Roncaros – 9815 Manchester
Ruggeri's Restaurant – 2300 Edwards
Schneithorst's Restaurant 1618 S. Lindbergh
Sea Isle – 627 N. Grand
Shanghai Café – 6314 Delmar
Steak 'N' Shake – 9009 Riverview
Steiny's Inn – Highway 66
Talanya's – Skinker & Forest Park Expressway

Parente's PIZZERIA

California Do Nut (Lonnie Tettaton)

The Chip Room – 1401 Hampton
Tony's Spaghetti – 826 N. Broadway
Wagon Wheel Restaurant – 8787 N. Broadway
Whirl A Way Café – 6105 N. Lindbergh
Wishing Well Restaurant – 8435 Airport Rd.
Yacovelli's Restaurant – 717 E. Big Bend

End of year Schoolyard ditties

School's out, school's out
Teachers let the mules out!

No more homework, no more books,
No more teacher's dirty looks!

"Playmate" song

Playmate, come out and play with me
And bring your dollies three,
Climb up my apple tree,
Holler in my rain barrel,
Slide down on my cellar door,
And we'll be jolly friends, forevermore!

But she couldn't come out to play.
It was a rainy day.
With tearful eyes she heaved a sigh,
And I could hear her say:

Playmate, I cannot play with you,
My dolly has the flu,
Boo hoo hoo hoo hoo hoo
Ain't got no rain barrel,
Don't have a cellar door
But we can still be friends, forevermore.

The Hand Pat Song

I am a happy little Dutch girl
As happy as can be
And all the boys in my hometown
Go chasing after me.

My boy friend's name is Sambo
He came from Alabambo
With a pickle on his nose
And a pumpkin on his nose
That's the way my story goes.

SCHOOL DAYS SONG

School days, school days,
Good old golden rule days,
Readin' and writin' and 'rithmetic,
Taught to the tune of a hickory stick,
I was your queen in calico,
You were my bashful barefoot beau,
You wrote on my slate, "I love you so,"
When we were a couple of kids.

CHOOSING SIDES

Eeney, meeney, miney mo,
Catch a tiger by his toe
If he hollers,
Make him pay,
Fifty dollars every day.
My mother told me to pick this very best one.

Lettermen sweaters at Normandy High - 1957

CHILDHOOD MEMORIES

Marbles, horseshoes, washers and ping pong
Tag, Kick the can, capture the flag, Bicycle tag
Rover, red rover, Mother, may I?
Jacks, Kite flying, croquet, tug of war
Badminton, Hop Scotch, Picture puzzles
Hangman, Ledge ball, Rubber guns
Jump rope - double Dutch, double Irish
Snowball fights, Snow sledding – belly flop
Tire swings, Cushman Eagle motor scooters
Snipe hunts, Slinky, Pick up Stix, 3-D comics
Lincoln Logs, American bricks, Tinker toys
Erector sets, chemistry sets, Pea shooters
Hula Hoop, Whiffle ball, Bottle cap ball
Stamp, butterfly, and coin collecting
Canasta, Rook, Slap Jack, coloring books
Battleship, War – with a deck of cards
Red Ryder B-B guns, Cowboys and Indians
Treehouses, Paper, scissors, rock
Comet and Guillows stick model airplanes
Playing house and dress up, Lemonade stands
Paper dolls, dollhouses, spin the bottle, post office
Ducking for apples at Halloween, riding a hobby horse
Delivering newspapers, playing grocery store
Patrol boys – sponsored by the Travelers Protective Association, 4 H Clubs, play doctor and nurse
Jumping in fall leaf piles, making snow angels in winter
Statue – swinging a playmate around and letting go; then he or she has to freeze in that position
jumping on a Pogo stick
Searching for 4-leaf clovers - He loves me, he loves me not
Making clover chains, saving string to make a string ball
Saving tin foil from gum wrappers to make a ball
Little looms for girls to make potholders, making things out of popsicle sticks, Eating an all-day sucker (Sugar Daddies) lard and sugar sandwiches, fried bologna, eating a Brown Cow, Carom boards

Ed Bonner of KXOK

Dohacks on Lemay Ferry and Lindbergh

JUMP ROPE DITTIES

Down in the valley where the green grass grows,
Bob and Donna were in love I suppose,
They went to a preacher and they got married,
Across the threshold she got carried.
They learned about the birds and bees, I'm told,
How many kids were born before they got old?
One, two, three, four, five . . .

Down in the valley where the green grass grows.
There sat Shirley as sweet as a rose,
Along came Jerry and kissed her on the cheek,
How many kisses did she get last week?
One, two, three, four . . .

Glenda and Larry sitting by a tree,
Doing things that come naturally,
First comes love, then comes marriage,
And after that comes the baby carriage.
How many kids were born in their family?
Now we're gonna count so let us see,
One, two, three, four, five . . .

Sittin on a tree limb looking below,
Watching Don and Shirley put on a show,
What I saw next was hard to believe,
How many kisses did Shirley receive? One, two, three, four . . .

OLD TELEPHONE EXCHANGES

How many of these old St. Louis telephone exchanges do you remember? Answers are at the end.

AC – AT – BU – CA – CO - CR – DA – ES – FI – HA – HE – IV – JA – JU – KE – LA – LE – PE – SH – TA – TE – TH – TI – TR – TU – TW – UL – UN – VA – VI – WA – WO – WY – YO – HU – MI – MA – BR – CE – PR – FL – CH – EN – JE – EV – OL – FO – PA – LO – GA

Academy, Atlas, Butler, Capitol, Colfax, Crestview, Davis, Essex, Fireside, Harrison, Hempstead, Ivanhoe, Jackson, Justice, Keystone, Lafayette, Lehigh, Pershing, Sherwood, Taylor, Temple, Thornwall, Tilden, Tremont, Turner, Twinbrook, Ulrick, Underhill, Valley, Victor, Walnut, Woodland, Wydown, Yorktown, Hudson, Mission, Main, Bridge, Central, Prospect, Flanders, Chestnut, Enterprise, Jefferson, Evergreen, Olive, Forest, Parkview, Logan, Garfield

How did you call a person who was on your party line in 1960? You dialed the operator, gave her the number, and told her the person was on your party line.

ST. LOUIS MOVIE THEATERS

Airway Drive-in
Ambassador
American
Apollo

Arsenal
Baden
Brentwood
Esquire
Fox
Grandview
Hi Point
Ivanhoe
Lafayette
Loews Orpheum
Manchester Drive-in
Martin Cinerama
Michigan
North Drive-in
Ozark Theater
Park Theater
Ritz
Saint Ann 4 Screen
Savoy Theater
66 Drive-in
Tivoli
Varsity
Will Rogers

Avalon
Bremen
Compton
Fairy
Gem
Grenada
Holiday Drive-in
Kirkwood
Lindell
Loews State
Maplewood
Melba
Missouri
Osage Theater
Pageant
Rio
Ronnie's Drive-in
St. Louis Theater
Shenandoah
South Twin Drive-in
270 Drive-in
Victory

NORMANDY HIGH 1958 FOOTBALL

Calvin Wilson, Ron Schmidt, Paul Fraser, Rich Meyer, Dan Overman, William Straub, Bob Moutrie, Gary Niedfeldt, Darrel Corse, James Meador, Gordon Alexander, John Vallina, Vince Giardino, James Bodin, Charles Zinser, Wes Faser, Rusty Williamson, R.H. Autz, Gary Johnson, James Terrall, Nate Hall, Robert Lee, John Lettman, Carl Bayer, Ronald Riggs, Richard Ward, Bob Allendorf, Carson McKinney, Jerry Van Mill, Jerry Seaton, Ray Evans, Gary Bridell, Dale Prange, John Krieger, Joe Taormina, Roger Boschen, Robert Balk, Dennis Sisson, James Christian.

PAROCHIAL PREP HIGH SCHOOLS

Assumption Pioneers
Cardinal Ritter Lions
CBC Cadets
DeSmet Spartans
Lutheran High Crusaders
Rosary High Rebels
St. Elizabeth Seahawks
St. Joseph Angels
St. Louis U High Billikens
St. Thomas Aquinas Falcons
Villa Duchesne Saints

Bishop DuBourg Cavaliers
Chaminade Red Devils
Cor Jesu Chargers
Duchesne Pioneers
Notre Dame Rebels
Rosati Cougars
St. John Lions
St. John Griffins
St. Mary Dragons
Ursuline Bears
Visitation Academy Vivettes

WEBSTER GROVES V. KIRKWOOD TURKEY DAY GAME

By David Lanius of Kirkwood

The year 2007 marked the 100th anniversary of the annual Thanksgiving Day football game between Webster Groves and Kirkwood. Kirkwood smothered Webster Groves in the 2007 contest 49-7.

The competition between the two schools became so fierce that officials had to devise a means of restoring a friendly rivalry with emphasis on good sportsmanship. This was done by holding a Friendship Dance the previous weekend with both schools participating and the event being held alternately at each school. The week prior to the game, both schools hold a hall decorating contest based on a specific theme. The day before the game each school has a spirited pep rally followed by a huge bonfire that evening. The game usually draws national media attention and crowds of up to 8,000 on Thanksgiving morning. The game has been mentioned on ESPN and *Sports Illustrated* even did a featured article about the rivalry. At the end of the game, both teams meet in the middle of the field and shake hands.

In the 1970s, the football Cardinals and the Detroit Lions played games on Thanksgiving Day. Because of this traditional prep rivalry, the city resisted the move and after two years the game was taken from the Cardinals and given to the Dallas Cowboys who still play on that holiday.

In the early years of the competition, the losing coach was given a little brown jug that was to set on his desk to remind

Ritenour High School (courtesy Carol Charlwood Block)

him that his team had lost the game. That tradition has been replaced by a bell that was taken from a retired engine that belonged to the Frisco Railroad. The winning team gets to keep the bell. Not only does the winning team ring the bell furiously in the end zone at the end of the game, it is then put on a truck and driven through town with its clanging ringing in the ears of joyful residents.

Although the tradition has lasted 100 years, there have not been 100 games played. There was one spell where a few years passed without the game being played. Kirkwood lost one particular game and was upset due to what it perceived as biased officiating. It had several touchdowns in the game called back due to dubious penalties and they boycotted the game until cooler heads prevailed. In 1988, Webster Groves was unable to play the game because it was in the state playoffs. **There was such a public outcry** that officials decided after that to go ahead and play the game regardless if one of the teams was in the playoffs. In 1980 the game had to be played on Saturday because of thirteen inches of snow on the field. In 1971 and 1972, the game was played at Wash U's Francis Field because of highway construction.

Orange and black Webster leads the red and white Kirkwood teams in the series 48-37, with five games ending in ties.

1959 CBC HIGH BASKETBALL TEAM

Jim Butler, Phil Naser, John Butler, Buddy Prow, Jim Pelchman, Bill Eigel, Mike McCotter, Jerry Strange, Jerry England, Joe Mimlitz, John Archer, John Berra, Ron Jaudes, Garry Garrison, Jim Redd, Bart Freihaut, Coach D.C. Wilcutt

RITENOUR HIGH 1958 FOOTBALL

Mickey McIntyre, Mike Yaeger, Gene Meyer, Jerry Maxey, Clem Buschmann, Cliff Land, Glen Zoll, Dominic Orlando, Bill Twitt, Jack Yaeger, Leonard Wiggins, Leonard Lumar, Ron Hunt, Ron McIlvain, Ted Kulongoski, Bill Menkus, Ollney Mueller, Gene Petty, Mike Gorman, Ron Burch, Larry Wagner, Matt Petty, Steve Pursley, Doug Collins, Joel Langston, Luther Davis, Rich Manley, Larry Hesskamp, Bob Heberer, Dave Dale, Gary Powell, Terry Straeter, Ron Hawkins, Don Williams, Calvin Boze, Bill Hurt, Mel Caldwell, Jerry Hart, Bob Jansen, Jim Reuss

1958 ST. CHARLES STATE "L" CHAMPIONSHIP BASKETBALL TEAM

Forwards Ken Clark and Frank Williams, Center DeWayne Bond, Frank Williams, John Lloyd, Henry Dueringer, John Bruere, Ed Johnson, Wayne Hallrah, Kenny Clark, Harold Oetting, Wayne Hoffman, Paul Ell, Gerard LeDaux, Kenny Kemp, manager Tom Sandfort, coach Bartow.

Author Bill Nunes went to grade school with **DeWayne Bond** in the Washington Park section of East St. Louis. By the time I went to junior high his family had moved away and I never saw him again. What a thrill it was to discover he was a member of St. Charles' 1958 championship team where they won the title at the Washington University Field House. If anyone knows his whereabouts, please contact me at (618) 288-5185

This author also went to Lansdowne Jr. High with a girl named **Judy Finkeldey**. When I reached high school her family had moved away. As a result of researching this book, I discovered that her family had moved to **Riverview Gardens** in North St. Louis. Aleeta Verman Urbahns told me she attended their 50th class (2007) reunion. She was able to get her phone number from the directory and we reconnected after 54 years. I have included her senior picture as a member of the Queen's Court.

Judy Finkeldey of E. St. Louis, a 1957 Riverview High grad (Nunes' classmate)

ADVERTISERS IN 1959 NORMANDY HIGH YEARBOOK

Moog Industries, Bernetta's Dance Studio, Gaines Heating, Stone Rexall Drugs, Vogt Sporting Goods, The Chicken Cottage, Pine Lawn Florist, Fran's Shell Service, Bob Hostkoetter Studio, Steven's Drug Store, Pollard's Market, Stanley Hanks Painting, Beverly Hills Barber Shop, Mallory Buick, Pasadena Cleaners, Art Gaines Baseball Camp, Jones Ice Cream, Lenz Market, Cumpari's Pizza, Jewel Beauty Shop, Woodson Hills Hardware, McKinney Bros. Café, Floyd Heckel Florist, Pagano Super Market, Nabb's Market, Carsonville Cleaners, Youth For Christ, McKelvey Oldsmobile, Bel-Nor Pharmacy, Godat Drugs, Anderson Music, Perry Television, Nash Music Corp., Hillmann's Camera, Schmidt Bakery, Edith's Beauty Salon

PLAYING CORK BALL AND INDIAN BALL

Although I grew up on the East Side, as a kid I played two games that were common only to the St. Louis area. I have seen movies or TV shows that depict stickball, but I have yet to see one that showed or mentioned cork ball or Indian ball.

There was a large vacant field across the street from where I lived in Washington Park. Two brothers lived next to the lot, Gordon and Jerry Rudd. Gordon was my age and Jerry was a year older. You only needed three people to play cork ball. One guy batted while another one pitched and the third one caught. Each player kept track of his own score and when the person batting made two outs everyone rotated positions.

I have heard it said that the hardest thing to do in sports is to hit a baseball. Wrong! It's hitting a corkball. A corkball is thrown hard, exactly like a baseball, yet it is only slightly larger than a golf ball. And you don't get three strikes in corkball; you get just one. The ball itself, made by the **Rawlings Company** of St. Louis, is a miniature baseball complete with leather covering and seams with stitches. The bat, slightly thicker than a broomstick, was a Louisville Slugger made of ash.

You don't run the bases in corkball and there are only two outs to an inning. If you swing and miss, and the ball is caught by the catcher, you're out. If he drops it, the batter is still alive at the plate. Any foul tip also constitutes an out.

There are only singles and homers in field corkball. Any ball hit fair is a single. If it is caught by the pitcher or catcher on the fly it's an out. Our sandlot rules said that if you hit a fly ball that went all the way out into the street, it was a home run. I think it becomes obvious that you really had to have quick reflexes and a good batting eye to successfully compete. There was no such thing as balls or strikes. If you didn't like a pitch you let it go by.

High school cafeteria scene with pint milk bottles

The game originated at St. Louis taverns and was played either in the back of the lot or in an alley. It was called corkball because the first object used for a ball was the cork from the bunghole of a large keg of beer. In later years corkball cages were built and leagues were formed. Balls and strikes are called by an umpire in competitive com-petition.

When we were the batter we usually chose one of our favorite Cardinal players and imagined that he was our alter ego at the plate. "Wally Moon steps into the batter's box with a look of steely determination. As the ball comes to the plate he uncoils like a cat with lightning-fast reflexes. Swung on . . . there's a drive . . . way back . . . it might be, it could be, it . . . is, another home run for the Texan who looks to be a sure bet for rookie of the year honors!"

Owner of Dad's Cookies (Lorna Nunes photo)

Another favorite diversion was Indian ball, but you needed a minimum of four to play this game. Once again, we didn't run the bases but in this game you fielded the ball. We played the game in the street and only occasionally had to call a temporary halt to let a car pass. It could also be played in a vacant lot or on a diamond.

Our asphalt street had ditches on each side and residential houses all along the block. We used two pieces of shingles as first and third base markers. Any ball hit foul that went past these markers was an out. The opposition had an infielder and an outfielder. Any ground ball caught by an infielder was an out. If he fumbled it or it got past him it was a single. Any fly ball caught by either fielder was an out. A fly ball that went over the outfielder's head was a homer. Unlike corkball, there were three outs to an inning.

1896 tornado damage on Eads Bridge

A regulation softball was used in this game on the streets. If we went to a more spacious park to play the game we used a regulation baseball. Everyone used a Rawlings glove and such brands as Wilson were disdained. People back then didn't have a lot of extra money so sometimes only two of us had gloves and we shared them with our buddies.

When you batted, your teammate pitched the ball to you underhanded, standing off to one side. If it was where you wanted it, you swung. If it was in a bad spot you bunted the ball back to your pitcher because there was no catcher behind the plate. Any fly ball that went fair past the infielder and was not caught on the fly by the outfielder was a single. As in corkball, there was no such thing as a double or triple.

DADS COOKIES

Dad's original Scotch oatmeal cookies arrived in San Francisco from Scotland around the time of the 1904 Worlds Fair. A traveling salesman paid a visit to Carpenter's Ice Cream on Goodfellow Ave. After sampling the cookies, Mr. Carpenter realized that the unique taste of the cookies would be a good compliment to his ice cream. He obtained a franchise for the St. Louis area, making Dad's Cookie Company one of the country's first franchise companies.

In 1938, Henry Renz Sr., a South St. Louis baker, acquired Dad's Cookies from Mr. Carpenter. The Renz Bakery at Keokuk and Louisiana became the new home of Dad's Cookie Co. where it remains to this day. Hank Renz Jr. took over the family operation in 1949 and continued the time honored tradition.

In 1988, Dad's passed to yet another generation of the Renz family, the Hastey brothers. A visit to the store is a step back into the past with the antique wood and glass display cases. The marble counters have not changed since 1938. They still weigh the cookies on the original bakery scale and wrap them in a brown paper bag tied with a white string.

THE 1896 ST. LOUIS CYCLONE

Do you think living in California near the San Andreas Fault is dangerous? Hah! That's nothing compared to being a resident of southern Missouri and Illinois. **Our dangerous area ranks number one in**

the U.S. due to numerous deadly tornadoes that have hit the region. Missouri averages 27 tornadoes a year and is smack dab in the middle of Tornado Alley. Additionally, the 1925 tornado that hit Missouri, Illinois, and Indiana, is ranked number one in U.S. history in terms of death and destruction. Add to that the danger imposed to denizens from the nearby **New Madrid fault**, which is said to be three times as dangerous as the one in California. Pretty scary, isn't it?

Path of 1896 tornado as it damaged the Eads Bridge

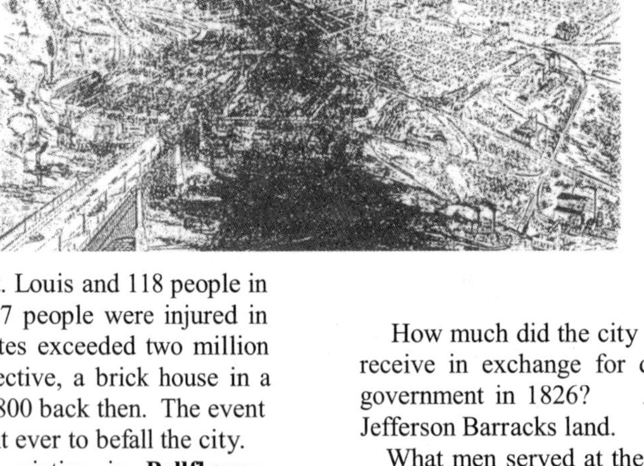

The tornado of 1896, which occurred around 5:15 PM, on Wednesday, May 27, tore through the two Mississippi sister cities killing 137 people in St. Louis and 118 people in East St. Louis. Approximately 367 people were injured in East St. Louis and damage estimates exceeded two million dollars. To put this loss in perspective, a brick house in a nice neighborhood sold for about $800 back then. The event remains the single deadliest incident ever to befall the city.

The tornado claimed its first victim in **Bellflower**, Missouri, killing a woman there. The tornado did all its damage in about 29 minutes. Lafayette Park, (**the oldest park west of the Mississippi**) was hit hard, with large trees felled like so many match sticks. The bandstand, built in 1876, was completely wrecked. At 6th and Chestnut, the gale-force winds threw a four-horse truck 100 feet down the street without overturning it. The storm cut a ten-mile path through St. Louis, roughly along the route of present I-44, then crossed the Mississippi (destroying seven steamboats), and went into the rail yards and commercial district of East St. Louis.

Ralston Purina, in St. Louis and East St. Louis, was damaged

The cyclone curved just south of downtown St. Louis and severely damaged boats and grain elevators on both sides of the river. Wiggins Ferry Company lost five of its six boats to the storm. The devastating winds struck the city around 5:30 p.m., knocking away part of the approach to the Eads Bridge and blasting through the commercial district of East St. Louis. It crushed three locomotive roundhouses, the main grain elevator and four freight stations.

At the height of the storm, the wind velocity reached seventy-five miles per hour. Rain fell in ceaseless torrents. The first to fall victim were the telegraph poles which became flashing monoliths of blue flame. While the storm was at its fullest, the air was full of deadly beams, iron rods, girders, planks and wreckage of every conceivable description.

Chief Black Hawk (ISHL)

On the Eads Bridge (The MacArthur Bridge was yet to be built), the whole top abutment of the first pier, as well as the big rocks and iron girders of the Illinois approach, were torn loose and thrown upon the exposed deck, just behind a passenger train of the Chicago & Alton line. The upper roadway was torn down and thrown onto the train and four wagons loaded with merchandise. It also knocked over two streetcars on the upper deck.

This killer tornado was so severe, **it ranks number three on the all-time USA list for devastating storms**. In all, 255 people were killed in the bi-state area.

JEFFERSON BARRACKS

How much did the city of Carondelet, in South St. Louis, receive in exchange for deeding 1,702 acres to the U.S. government in 1826? A five dollar gold piece paid for Jefferson Barracks land.

What men served at the Barracks and went on to become U.S. presidents? U.S. Grant and Dwight Eisenhower

What historical distinction does Jefferson Barracks possess? It is the **oldest permanent military installation west of the Mississippi.**

What unique "first" was achieved with the establishment of Jefferson Barracks? It was the nation's first infantry school.

How far away from St. Louis was Jefferson Barracks when it was built? Ten miles

What fort was it intended to replace? Fort Bellefontaine in North St. Louis

Who was in charge of laying out the first parade ground and constructing the first barracks? Major Stephen Kearney

By 1846, what claim to fame did Jefferson Barracks have? **It was the nation's largest military establishment.**

What famous sports broadcaster is buried at Jefferson Barracks? Jack Buck

What did Robert E. Lee do while he was stationed at Jefferson Barracks? His corps of engineers built a series of dykes to attach Bloody Island to the Illinois shore and redirect the main channel of the Mississippi River to the port of St. Louis.

What happened to most of his project? It was washed downstream in the devastating 1844 flood.

Was the project rebuilt? Yes, but St. Louisans had to foot the bill this time and complete the project themselves.

What life changing event happened to U.S. Grant while stationed at Jefferson

Barracks? He met and married Julia Dent of St. Louis.

How did Dred Scott, the famous slave, come to live at Jefferson Barracks? His master, Dr. John Emerson, was stationed there as post surgeon.

How did Chief Black Hawk of the Sauk Indians find himself imprisoned at Jefferson Barracks? After his defeat in 1831, he was brought to Jefferson Barracks in chains, escorted by Robert E. Lee.

What famous author interviewed Chief Black Hawk while he was at the barracks? Washington Irving

What famous western artist painted Black Hawk's portrait during his confinement? George Catlin

Are any Confederates buried at the Barracks? Yes - 470 victims of smallpox, while imprisoned on Arsenal Island, were re-interred here.

What famed African-American unit, that distinguished itself in the Plains Indian Wars of the 1870s, received its training at Jefferson Barracks? Buffalo Soldiers

What was Suds Row? It was the housing location near the Barracks of women (mostly Irish) who did laundry for the men at the post. There was one laundress for every 19 men at the Barracks and they were paid for their services and given housing and rations.

What was the first railroad to run tracks to Jefferson Barracks? Iron Mountain Railroad, which became the Missouri Pacific

Is the original brick railroad depot still there? No. Built in 1904, it was eventually torn down.

Where were hundreds of wounded Civil War soldiers taken to at Jefferson Barracks? A hospital steamship anchored in the river, next to Jefferson Barracks

Why were female WAACs brought to the Barracks in 1942? To perform clerical and other duties so that more men could be released for combat

What was the largest building at Jefferson Barracks? Atkinson Hall – the mess hall; its nickname was the White Elephant.

When was Jefferson Barracks named a National Cemetery? 1866

When was Jefferson Barracks decommissioned as a major military installation? 1946

What amazing event took place at the Barracks on March 1, 1912? The **nation's first successful parachute jump** was performed by Thomas Benoist who owned an aviation school in Kinloch Park, St. Louis. In 1913, Benoist built a flying boat of spruce, wire and fabric and **it was used in the world's first airline that went from St. Petersburg to Tampa**.

How big is the cemetery at Jefferson Barracks? 331 acres

How many bodies are interred there? About 159,000

Who was responsible for building hard surfaced roads and walkways at Jefferson Barracks in 1836? The WPA

Are there any unknowns buried in the cemetery? Yes – over 3,000

Who was the first person buried at Jefferson Barracks? Elizabeth Lash, daughter of an army officer stationed at the barracks

Jefferson Davis of Mississippi was once stationed at Jefferson Barracks. What is his claim to fame? He later was the president of the Confederacy.

Philip Sheridan was stationed at the Barracks. What is his best known quote? It was Sheridan who said, "The only good Indian is a dead one."

Jeb Stuart was stationed at the Barracks. What is his claim to fame? He was one of the South's ablest cavalry commanders and was killed during the war at Yellow Tavern.

B. Nunes' aunt and uncle, Vi and Joe Rafferty, are buried at Jefferson Barracks

James Longstreet was once stationed at the Barracks. What was his chief claim to fame? He was one of Lee's ablest generals in the Civil War.

Henry Dodge was stationed at the Barracks. What is his chief claim to fame? He fought in the War of 1812, participated in the Black Hawk War of 1831, and then became the first governor of Wisconsin Territory.

ST. LOUIS TRIVIA

When the Japanese attacked Pearl Harbor, how did Professor Roland Usher of Washington University think they pulled it off? A German authority and head of the History Department, he speculated that Hitler's Luftwaffe may have helped them out.

What is considered **Missouri's first all-black town**? Kinloch

Where is the beginning point of the annual St. Patrick's Day parade in St. Louis? Downtown in front of the Old Courthouse, ending at 20th Street near Union Station

St. Louis broadcaster Buddy Blattner was a notable player in what sport? Table tennis

What big time event was held at Bellerive Country Club in 1965? The U.S. Open in golf

What nickname was given to cheerleaders for the St. Louis steamers? Steam Heat

How did the Crossing Restaurant in **Clayton** get its name? It serves a blend (crossing) of the finest French and Italian cuisine in the city.

According to this author's cousin, Connie Jeter, "Mesh" Rothman is Becky Rothman's **Queen of Carpets**) father. They used to live in East St. Louis in the 1400 block of Cleveland Avenue. Connie's future wife, Hermadine Young, lived on the same block. My maternal grandmother, Beulah Jeter, used to baby sit Becky. Connie grew up in a house in St. Louis at 3945 Market, about 9 blocks from Sportsman's Park. He once was a batboy there and remembers seeing Pete Gray, the one-armed outfielder. About ten of my relatives – aunts, uncles and cousins – lived in that house. My aunt Luda married Morris Maltzman who owned Economy Linoleum and was a friendly competitor of Mesh Rothman who owned Veterans Linoleum on Collinsville Road, not far from Fairmount Park racetrack. Becky got her start with her friend Wanda at the Collinsville Road store. As a youngster, I can remember seeing Mesh at several social get-togethers at Aunt Luda's house, when she lived on Hall Street in East St. Louis.

Original Frederick Roofing on Natural Bridge

Connie and Hermadine now live in **High Ridge**, Missouri where he runs C & H Western clothing store.

When KSD television first came on the air in St. Louis, how many homes had television sets? Four

What writer once bragged that in his early years he could have bought the whole town of St. Louis for $6 million dollars? Mark Twain

Doodling was in the daily newspaper in the 1950s

HOW ARE YOU AT DOODLING?

POLAR BEARS EATING POPCORN IN A SNOW STORM

TWO CATS FIGHTING ON A TIN ROOF

A SOLDIER AND HIS DOG

USED LOLLY POP

Who drew the famous *Post-Dispatch* Weather Bird for about 60 years? Amadee Wohlschlaeger, who also drew sports caricatures

What is unusual about the Edison/JC Penney Building at 14th and Spruce? For a long time it was a distribution warehouse owned by the Edison brothers who owned Just Jeans, the 5-7-9 Store, Chandler's Shoes, Baker's Shoes, Joan Barry and Leeds. The entire building became a work of art when it was repainted by NY artist Richard Haas and the brick was made to look like stones. There are obelisks, statue-like figures and St. Louis World's Fair mural scenes. Since the building is adjacent to elevated Route 40, it can easily be seen near the approach to the Poplar Street Bridge. Now the Sheraton City Center Hotel (and condominiums), it features **the largest atrium in Missouri**. The Edison Brothers went out of business around 1989.

Winterowd Florist 6969 St. Charles Rd. 1957

What television sports news announcer featured sports bloopers and unusual plays on Friday nights? Christopher "Zip" Rzeppa; viewers loved his hyperbolic exuberance and his **Zippo Awards** for sports bloopers were just hilarious. After working with KTVI from 1984-1988 and then at KMOV, Zip finally quit the business because the long hours were too demanding. Now a **Barnhart** resident, he decided to quit TV in 2001 and become more involved in community service. He is now executive director for the St. Vincent DePaul Society. **Dan Buck**, who once hosted *Show Me St. Louis*, is also into serving the needy and is a fellow parishioner of Zip's at St. Joseph's in **Imperial**, Missouri. (Thanks to *Post-Dispatch* writer Pat Gauen of **Collinsville/ Highland**).

What St. Louisan, who grew up in the Normandy area of St. Louis, **later founded Churchill Downs and the Kentucky Derby**? Meriwether L. Clark Jr.

What Class 1 school has the most undefeated state wrestling champions? Oak Grove with 18. Francis Howell has 15

Who was the *Post-Dispatch* "swimmer of the year" for 2006? Scott Jostes of Chaminade

What St. Louis school won its 11th prep state basketball title in 2006? Vashon

Who was the first person of Asian descent to edit a major metropolitan newspaper? William Woo – *St. Louis Post-Dispatch*

What former St. Louis sports news announcer is now featured as a regular on ESPN? Trey Wingo

What happened at a 2006 March Missouri Valley title game that caused the American Association of Cheerleading Coaches to recommend against dangerous stunts? A Southern Illinois University cheerleader fell from a pyramid at the Savvis Center and suffered a concussion and a cracked vertebra.

Missouri is the only state with two Federal Reserve Districts out of a total of twelve. One Federal Reserve Bank is in St. Louis and another is in Kansas City.

The first skyscraper in Missouri was the Wainwright Building in St. Louis, designed by the famed Chicago architect, Louis Sullivan. Sullivan was commissioned to do the building by Catherine Wainwright, widow of brew master Sam Wainwright. She wanted the building as a tribute to her husband.

What statue is in front of Kiel Auditorium? Johan Schiller, a German dramatist

Sappington Road was named for Dr. John Sappington, one of the discoverers of the drug known as quinine. Sappington also published the first medical book west of the Mississippi. **Sappington's great, great, great granddaughter was actress Ginger Rogers**.

What is the record in St. Louis for the latest date to have a snowfall? On May 22, 1924, it snowed four inches.

Ted Drewes on Chippewa (Lorna Nunes photo)

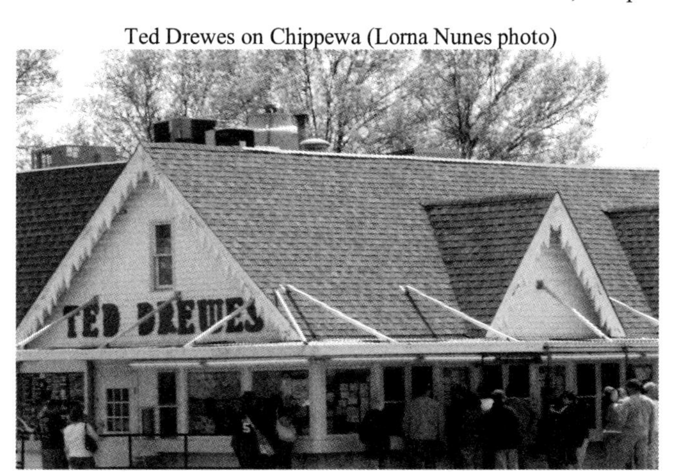

Where can one find a replica of Michelangelo's ceiling in Florence's Laurentian Library? At the public library on 1301 Olive Street which was built in 1913 with nearly half of the funds borne by Andrew Carnegie.

What 1974 television program starred David Hartman as a suburban St. Louis high school teacher? *Lucas Tanner*

What was Mallinckrodt Chemical's role in developing the atomic bomb? Mallinckrodt Chemical of St Louis participated in the Manhattan Project by processing the uranium ore and ridding it of contaminants before shipping it on to the Oak Ridge facility.

What 1990 movie, starring James Spader of *Boston Legal,* and Susan Sarandon, was partially filmed in St. Louis? *White Palace*

What was the original purpose of Shaw's Botanical Garden? First opened in 1940, it was designed to show the public what typical Missouri Ozark country looked like

Where was Cinerama first shown in St. Louis? Ambassador Theater

What famous radio newsman in Chicago spent a few early years working for radio stations in St. Louis? Paul Harvey

What St. Louis native wrote a coming-of-age book called *King of the Hill* that was later made into a movie? A.E. Hotchner in 1972

What product did the Laister Kauffman Company make during World War II in the Arena near Route 40? Gliders

What St. Louis airplane company secured a government contract and hired Charles Lindbergh to fly the mail from St. Louis to Chicago in the 1920s? Robertson Aircraft

What was the name of the theater, on Lindell Boulevard, built especially for Cinerama Martin Cinerama

On what street was the Playboy Club located in St. Louis? Lindell Boulevard, not far from Martin Cinerama

Palace of Poison official certificate

PALACE OF POISON

Death Certificate

THIS IS TO CERTIFY THAT

CORPSE SINE HERE (IN BLOOD) RALPH STILLE

— having so foolishly et at Wild's Palace of Poison, 1500 Lemay, St. Louis 23, Mo. is hereby declared null, void and all shook up-

Cause of kicking Bucket ARSENIC FIZZ Date 5-15-

WILD'S PALACE of POISON ASSUMES NO RESPONSIBILITY FOR DEMISE OF CORPSE SINCE CORPSE WAS DEAD FROM NECK UP FOR HAVING ET HERE IN THE FIRST PLACE

THIS CORPSE ENETERED IN COUNTY MORGUE AS

WITNESS Ann Wild

ATTESTED BY Arthur J. Stille

ARSENIC SUNDAE

№ 58629

SIGNED By the cold + clammy hand of ART WILD • Palace Poisoner

In what year did the city of St. Louis ban the use of high sulfur coal from Southern Illinois in an effort to cut back pollution? 1951

Knights of the Round Table, starring Robert Taylor, was made in Cinemascope. What St. Louis theater had the exclusive engagement for this movie? Loews State Theater on Washington Avenue

What was the name of the theater, on Lindell Boulevard, built especially for Cinerama? Martin Cinerama

What was the **Palace of Poison**? It was a big teen hangout located on Lemay Ferry near Telegraph.

How tall is the St. Louis Gateway Arch? 630 feet; the nation's tallest man-made monument The Washington Monument in D.C. would fit under the Arch. The Arch is also 630 feet wide at the base and is the **third most visited attraction in the world.**

For tourists, what is one of the most attractive things about visiting St. Louis? **It has more free attractions than any other city in America after Washington D.C.**, including the Mercantile Money Museum (7th and Washington) that features rare old coins and notes.

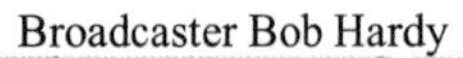

Broadcaster Bob Hardy

The oldest circulating library west of the Mississippi is the St. Louis Mercantile Library at 510 Locust. It features paintings by George Caleb Bingham, George Catlin and Sarah Peale.

The St. Louis Museum of Westward Expansion is located beneath the Arch, tucked away underground.

The St. Louis Wax Museum, featuring about 150 effigies, can be found on Laclede's Landing at 720 North Second St. (314-241-1155). Also at Laclede's Landing is the Spaghetti Factory, Planet Hollywood (recently closed) and the Royal Dumpe restaurant (recently closed)..

Ambassador Theater (Lonnie Tettaton)

The oldest stone Catholic Church west of the Mississippi is the Old Cathedral, located on Memorial Drive just west of the Arch. The cathedral was built in 1834 and is of Greek Revival architecture. At one time **this was the mother church for nearly half of the Catholics living in the U.S**. The Old Cathedral Museum is at 209 Walnut (314-231-3250).

McDonalds built a floating restaurant on the St. Louis riverfront and it was the first of its kind in the nation. It was removed from the riverfront after the novelty wore off.

What was the name of that great cafeteria across the street from Famous-Barr? The Forum on 7th Street

Where was China Town in St. Louis? It was only four square blocks between 6th and 7th and between Market and Walnut; it was called Hop Alley.

The Poplar Street Bridge is the more common name for the Bernard Dickman Bridge. Dickman was a St. Louis mayor in the 1930s.

Where is the St. Louis Walk of Fame where prominent citizens are enshrined? On Delmar in "The Loop"

Why have hundreds of St. Louisans (since 1925) trekked nightly across the river to Fairmount Park in Illinois, near **Collinsville**? Because horse racing has not been legalized in Missouri since 1905

Where was the original Musial and Biggies Restaurant in St. Louis? On the north side of Chippewa near Ted Drewes; they later moved over to Oakland Avenue off Route 40.

What St. Louis/St. Charles firm built the **World's Tallest Fountain** on the East St. Louis riverfront? The Sverdrup Corp. - the fountain shoots almost 630 feet high. It is so expensive to operate city officials turn it on for about 15 minutes each day 12 noon to 12:15.

What was the original name of Martin Luther King Drive? It took over Franklin and parts of Easton at Grand Avenue.

Since 1963, what has been the number for St. Louisans to call for time and temperature? FAirview 1-2522 or 321-2522

The Sappington House, built in 1808, is believed to be the oldest brick house in St. Louis County (**Crestwood**)

What public building is a replica of the tomb of King Mausolus of Asia Minor? The Civil Courts Building, constructed in 1930. The original building is famous because it gave us the word *mausoleum* and it was one of the Seven Wonders of the ancient world.

How much money does the annual spring Famous-Barr book fair raise for a west county day care center? Back in 2005 the net was $280,000 for the 57th annual event.

How long has the County Parks

department been hosting World War II reenactments at Jefferson Barracks? Twenty-one years, usually in early May 314-544-5714

What are the plans for the failed shopping mall at the downtown St. Louis Centre? It is being converted into condominiums.

When did the Express Highway, forerunner of Route 40, open along the south edge of Forest Park? 1934.

When did Forest Park Parkway, on the northeast corner of Forest Park open? 1962

Where do St. Louis post card collectors have to go for conventions? They are held across the river in **Collinsville**, IL, due to cheaper rent of facilities.

What fancy restaurant on Broadway was connected to the stock yards in East St. Louis? The Crest House

What St. Louis firms had plants across the river in East St. Louis? Among others, Cotton Compress, Ralston Purina, Missouri Malleable Iron, Emerson Electric and St. Louis Structural Steel

How large geographically is the city of St. Louis? 64 sq miles

Did this author ever work at Emerson Electric in St. Louis? I worked there in 1961-62 in the Receiving Department.

Where do the St. Louis Aces World Team Tennis play their matches? At the Dwight Davis Center in Forest Park Davis was park commissioner around 1913 and made improvements (tennis courts and golf course) that improved the quality of life in St. Louis.

What personality on KMOX radio was known as "Mr. Trivia?" David Strauss

What shop is home to a large glass factory where classes are offered in glass art and glass blowing? The Third Degree on Delmar at the U. City Loop – 314-367-4527

What St. Louis native died in a car crash while in warm-ups for the IRL race at Homestead, FL, in March of 2006? Paul Dana, who was with the Rahal-Letterman team

What controversial Lambert Airport project made its debut in April 13, 2006? A new $1.1 billion airstrip Dozens and dozens of families with homes in **Bridgeton** were forced to relocate. Opponents of the new runway adopted a theme song, sung to the tune of "Home on the Range:" "Oh there are no homes where the concrete now roams, and a plane may occasionally land"

The project's *raison d'être* evaporated. Due to the 9-11 scare and after TWA went out of business the airport was no longer a hub and volume dropped off dramatically.

How did the first report of the sinking of the *Titanic* first get into print? A reporter from the St. Louis *Post-Dispatch* was vacationing aboard the *Carpathia* and that was the first ship to reach the survivors. He threw his dispatch to someone in a smaller boat that was headed back to New York. It was delivered to the *New York Herald*, owned by Pulitzer who also owned the **Post-Dispatch**.

Where is the Shaw Nature Preserve? 35 miles west of St. Louis at the intersection of Interstate 44 and Highway 100 636-451-3512

Phyllis Diller, a nationally known comedienne of the 1960s, started out in St. Louis playing at places like Gaslight Square and referred to her husband as Fang.

Lambert International Airport – Tettaton drawing

Who was Steve Fossett? He was an eccentric millionaire aviator who obtained an MBA from Washington University in St. Louis. His plane went missing out west on September 4, 2007. He was legally declared dead in February of 2008. In July of 2002, he became **the first person to fly solo around the world in a balloon**, the *Bud Light Spirit of Freedom*. Fossett previously had competed in Iditarod, LeMans, and triathlon endurance races.

How long was Ford's plant at **Hazelwood** (Lindbergh and I -270) in production before it closed in 2006? 58 years For many years **St. Louis was second only to Detroit** in automobile production. The General Motors plant was at Union and Natural Bridge and had three separate buildings that made the Corvette, the Impala and trucks, and housed the Fischer Body works. The Corvette plant moved to Bowling Green, KY in the early 1980s. Buick and Cadillac eventually moved out to **Wentzville**.

State Bank of Wellston (Saga Yearbook)

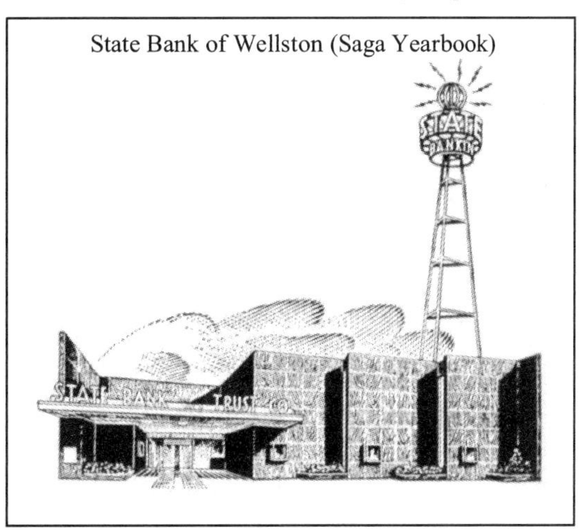

Chrysler had two plants in Fenton, Building One and Building Two.

What **University City** native participated in the 2006 Olympics at Turino, Italy? C. Kepka competed on the men's speed skating team.

What modern era NCAA record was set by the St. Louis University basketball team in a 2008 January 10 conference game? **They scored only 20 points in the whole game, a modern record for futility, dating back to 1942**.

Dodge-em cars at Holiday Hill at Brown & Natural Bridge

What former Desmet star made a goal and recorded two assists in leading the U.S. Soccer Team to a 4-0 win over Guatemala in February of 2006? Chris Klein

What St. Louisan starred in the *Beverly Hillbillies* television series? Buddy Ebsen

What well-known music bar in south St. Louis closed in February of 2006? Frederick's Music Lounge at 4454 Chippewa

Where were the three Parkmoor drive-in restaurants in St. Louis? One was in Clayton on Big Bend, near the Esquire Theater; the one in South St, Louis was at Kingshighway at Chippewa and the one north was near Public School Stadium (across from McBride High School) on Kingshighway near Natural Bridge.

What was the original name of Oakland Stadium? Walsh Stadium with a 10,000 seat capacity

Where was Oakland Stadium located? Just east of the Forest Park Highlands on Oakland Avenue

What were some major uses of Oakland Stadium? It was home to the St. Louis Knights football team and there were auto races there as well.

What replaced the Forest Park Highlands after the place was destroyed by a fire in July of 1963? Forest Park Community College was built on the site in 1966.

Where was the **first University in America to be established solely for women**? It was the Anna Sneed Carins Kirkwood Seminary, chartered in 1861.

Where was the seminary located? It was torn down in 1927 and replaced by the St. Louis Arena.

When was St. Louis University High School on Oakland Avenue constructed? Archbishop John Glennon laid the cornerstone in 1924.

What was on the site before the new high school was built in 1924? It was the location of the university's sports stadium and athletic field.

What happened to St. Louis University High in 1927? It was hit by a tornado, sustaining $150,000 in damages. Fortunately, there was no loss of life.

What sports expansion plans were announced by officials at St. Louis University in February of 2006? A new basketball arena will be built with groundbreaking due in September of 2006.

Where do the Billikens currently play their home games? At the Savvis Center, but they will shortly move into a new facility

What kind of swim trunks were required at the YMCA on Grand Avenue, across from Sportsman's Park? Due to worries about keeping the pool clean, the men swam naked. The same thing was true for the YWCA.

What chemical company in St. Louis participated in the making of the atomic bomb by processing uranium ore and ridding it of contaminants before sending it on to the Oak Ridge facility? Mallinckrodt Chemical

Why were three University of Missouri at St. Louis baseball players arrested in February of 2006? They were charged with stealing large quantities of merchandise from Dick's Sporting Goods Store.

What happened to the ugly concrete wall surrounding the St. Louis Arch for security reasons? It was replaced in February of 2006 with equally ugly four ft. high steel posts called bollards.

What is the St. Louis connection to legendary jazz great, **Miles Davis**? Davis grew up in East St. Louis, but in 1944 he was filling in on trumpet behind Billy Eckstein at **Club Riviera** in St. Louis. Davis was impressed with the band's alto saxophonist, Charlie "Bird" Parker. After Davis left for New York, he quickly became a member of Parker's quintet.

During World War II, where was the dance hall known as **Tunetown** in St. Louis? Grand and Olive – 2nd floor above Garavelli's

ST. LOUIS HOUSEWIVES

SOCK 'EM WITH YOUR SKILLET"

JOIN THE "KITCHEN COMMANDOES"

Help the war effort by saving fat, recycling tin cans, and serving high nutrition meals. Pick up a free badge at Laclede Gas Co.

What unique plan was unveiled by St. Louisan Gary Long to lose weight in 2006? The **Fenton** man planned to lose weight (about 160 pounds) and restore his health by walking from St. Louis to New York, then flying out to Los Angeles, and walking back to his starting point at the Gateway Arch.

What school reform measure was enacted by St. Louis city schools in 2006 to help improve the learning environment? Uniforms for students - popular with parents, hated by students

What bottled gas company made the national news as fire and explosions at its southwest St. Louis plant made spectacular fireworks during the summer of 2005? Praxair

What national organization in December of 2005 handed out video cameras to "responsible persons of color" to videotape St. Louis police and capture any acts of racism on film? The ACLU

ST. LOUIS AND WORLD WAR II

(For further info see Betty Burnett's marvelous book, *St. Louis and World War II*)

ST. LOUIS AREA COMPANIES CONTRIBUTE TO THE WAR EFFORT

AMP Corp. – aircraft products
Absorbent Cotton – surgical dressings
S. G. Adams – metal mess kits
Alco Valve – airplane control valves
Alcoa – sheet metal for airplanes
Alton Box Board – crates for large bombs
Aluminum Ore of **East St. Louis** – world's largest processor of bauxite
American Car & Foundry – hospital cars
American Optical – aviator sunglasses
American Steel at **Granite City** – navy guns, steel for tanks
American Stove – casings for 500 pound bombs
American Can on N. Broadway – torpedoes
Angelica Corp. – uniforms
Anheuser Busch – subassemblies for gliders, beer for GIs
Bemis Bag – burlap bags
Benwood-Linz – signal corps equipment
Bray Company – leggings for military
Brown Shoe – military shoes and combat boots
Bussmann Company – fuses for planes and ships
Carter Carburetor – parts for jeeps and trucks
Century Electric – hydraulic brakes
GM Chevrolet Plant – DUKWs
Crunden-Martin – helmets
Curtiss-Wright – trainers, fighter aircraft (Helldiver)
Diagraph-Bradley – gears for gun turrets
Duke Manufacturing – LST equipment
Ehrhardt Tool – precision gauges
Emerson Electric – gun turrets for B-17 and B-24
Empire Stove of **Belleville** – jelly bomb containers
Forest City Mfg. – nurse's uniforms
Foster Brothers – Steel cots for ship and LST berths
General Electric – military lights for vehicles
General Steel – hulls for Sherman tanks
Guth Lighting – Signal Corps equipment
Hyde Park Beer – 15 % of its production went overseas
Krey Packing – canned meat for the military

War cartoon: "I'm conserving wool – this bathing suit is painted on."

Laister-Kauffmann – made gliders inside the Arena
Lambert Pharmaceutical – medical drugs
McDonnell Aircraft – parts for B-29
McQuay-Norris – piston rings for aircraft
Mayrose Meat – C and K ration packs
Mallinckrodt Chemical – ointment, processed uranium ore
Midwest Pipe – fabricated pipes for destroyers and cruisers
Mississippi Valley Structural Steel – portable railroad bridges
Monsanto – sulfuric acid for TNT
National Stamping of **Granite City** – containers for gas, oil
Nooter Corp. – 20,000 gallon tanks for penicillin production
Olin Corporation of **East Alton** – brass cartridges
Orchard Paper – stencils to mark military equipment
Owens Glass of **Alton** – bombsights
Pet and Pevely dairies – powdered milk
Ralston-Purina – K rations
Rawlings Sporting Goods – tank personnel leather helmets
Robertson Aircraft – gliders
St. Louis Aircraft Corp. – P-19 and P-23 training planes
Schlueter Company – Military helmets
Scullin Steel – Railroad car wheels
Shell Oil at **Wood River** – 100 octane aviation fuel
Socony-Vacuum – high octane aviation fuel
Southwestern Bell – signal corps equipment
G.S. Suppiger of **Belleville** – canned stew and meat products
Stupp Brothers – portable Bailey bridges
U.S. Cartridge - .30 and .50 caliber machine gun cartridges
Universal Match – signal flares
Wagner Electric – brakes for military vehicles
Walworth Valve of **East St. Louis** – ship valves
Western Cartridge of **East Alton** – ammunition
Wiles-Chipman Lumber – shipping crates

Curtiss-Wright factory near Lambert Field

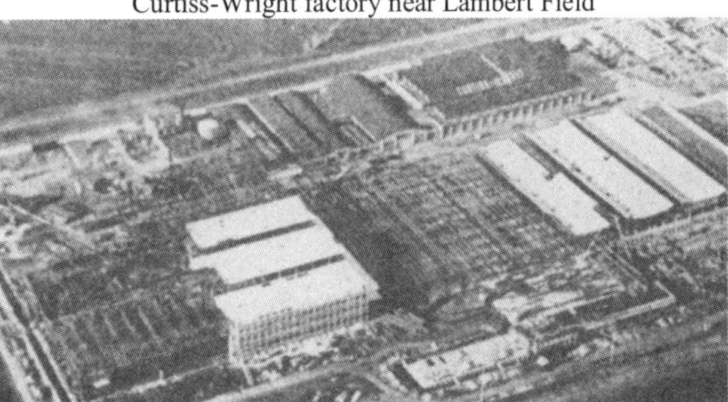

World War II children's outfits in Montgomery Ward of Chicago catalog

Due to fear of sabotage, police were sent to watch the Daniel Boone, Eads and Chain of Rocks Bridges.

All property owned by Japanese and Koreans was seized and their assets were frozen.

Tetsu Uyeda, manager of the Bridle Spur Hunt Club, was arrested and jailed as a possible spy.

Almost all private planes were sent east or west to patrol the coastal areas.

Republican Mayor William Becker ordered all city employees to be fingerprinted to help curb saboteurs.

Thousands attended a giant war rally at Municipal/Kiel Auditorium to hear speeches. World War I hero Alvin York was a featured speaker.

Civil Defense volunteers were taught how to smell the difference between mustard, tear, lewisite, phosgene and chlorine gas.

Radio announcers were not allowed to describe weather conditions at baseball or football games. Weather forecasts on radio were cancelled.

Small Arms plant on Natural Bridge – largest in the USA

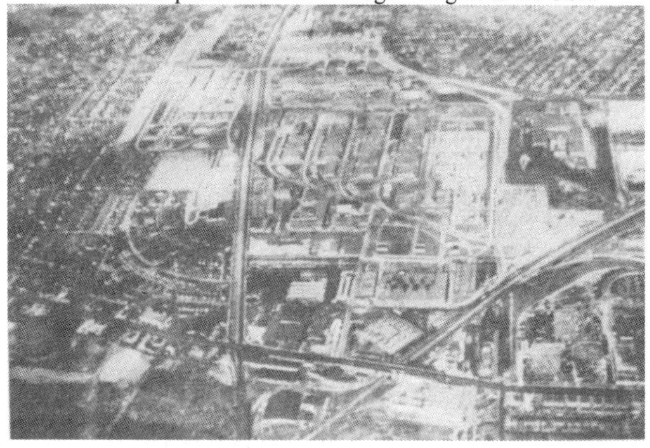

Archbishop John J. Glennon spoke on the radio and urged all members of the St. Louis Archdiocese to support the war effort.

Another pageant was held at Municipal (Kiel) Auditorium in February of 1942 with the theme, "St. Louis Prepares." Actress Helen Hayes gave a dramatic reading of "America" while surrounded by soldiers from Scott Field.

By mid-January of 1942 18,741 St. Louisans were enrolled in Red Cross first aid classes.

The first blackout of the city was held on March 7, at 7:21 P.M. All the city street lights went out after a switch was thrown. At a blackout in **East St. Louis**, airplanes flew overhead and swooped down to warn drivers who were in violation. Either black tape or metal inserts were used on car headlights so that only narrow horizontal slits beamed out a light. There were numerous civilian injuries as a result so bumpers were painted white as were curbs and light posts. Most blackouts lasted about a half an hour.

Civilian pilots who accidentally flew over Western Cartridge in East Alton and the small arms plant on Goodfellow were fired upon by watch towers.

Two hundred places were designated as air raid shelters which could only protect a total of about 40,000 people. They were designated with a luminescent red, white and blue paint forming the letter S.

Training for members of the Coast Guard was done at a facility located at the foot of Washington Avenue. Radio and Signal Corps training was done at nearby Scott Field, near **Belleville**. Pilot training was conducted at Curtiss Field in **Cahokia**. Draftees were processed at Jefferson Barracks and basic training was given at Fort Leonard Wood at **Rolla**, Camp Crowder at **Neosho**, and at Jefferson Barracks. One-third of the entire Navy was trained at the Great Lakes facility in **Chicago**.

Over 80,000 St. Louisans between the ages of 21 and 40 registered for the first draft. Married men with children were exempted. The age would later be lowered to 18 and the marriage exemption would be eventually dropped.

Union Station became a throbbing mass of humanity as trains became filled with servicemen and citizens who flocked to the city from the hinterlands looking for work in war factories.

"A" Gas Ration Sticker

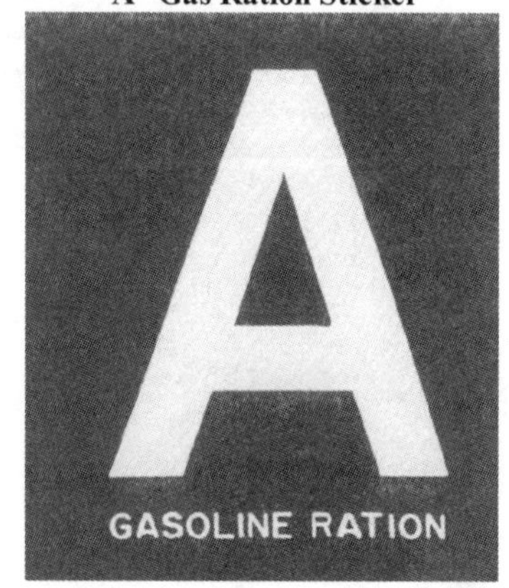

Red Cross Poster

The war brought on a marriage boom, a baby boom and a divorce boom. Women married the boyfriends who might be going away for an indeterminate number of years. **Quickie marriages** in Arkansas and **Waterloo**, Illinois became common. The divorce rate soared as women who found jobs in factories became more independent.

St. Louis had a head start on most other cities since its Chamber of Commerce produced a census booklet in 1940 that gave detailed information on the manufacturing capability of its many industries. The fact that St. Louis was a transportation hub also greatly helped as about 27 railroads converged here. Thanks to Charles Lindbergh and civic leaders with foresight, the city was seen nationwide as a leader in aviation. And the adjacent Mississippi River still saw tons and tons of high bulk items such as coal, salt, gravel, grain, aluminum ore and coal moving up and down the river on barges. St. Louis firms were receiving large amounts of money from government contracts well before Pearl Harbor. By December 7, 1942, U.S. Cartridge/St. Louis Ordnance (on Natural Bridge) had produced one billion rounds of ammunition. The nearby McQuay-Norris plant made the bullet's steel core.

By the time the war ended, over 75 percent of St. Louis firms were involved in war production. The national average was closer to fifty percent.

There was some unrest in St. Louis because most Blacks lived in substandard segregated housing and unemployment was high. No downtown restaurant would serve them. The Red Cross did not give black blood to whites. Things got worse when it was learned that in January of 1942 a Negro accused of accosting a white woman had been lynched in **Sikeston**, Missouri. A huge protest rally was held outside Kiel Auditorium in August. Most large companies began training Blacks for skilled war jobs, but black unemployment remained high throughout the war years. President Truman did not desegregate the military until war's end.

Because of rubber shortages the sale of new auto tires was frozen and strict rationing was enforced. Tire theft became a new problem in St. Louis. The use of rubber was forbidden in the manufacture of girdles, suspenders, corsets and bras. When gasoline rationing came along, many people parked their cars in their garages and used public transportation for the duration of the war.

"Butch" O'Hare (L) & John Thatch

After sugar was rationed downtown restaurants such as the Senate put its sugar bowls away and handed out cubes only when customers asked for them.

When Reverend Fred Kalkbrenner, of the Chesterfield St. John's Evangelical church, began collecting money for conscientious objectors and objected to singing patriotic songs in church, he was fired from his job and run out of town.

Most foreign nationals that were jailed at the start of the war were eventually released. The vast majority of Italians, Japanese, Romanians and Italians in St. Louis remained loyal and joined the military and bought war bonds in large numbers. Italians on the Hill even formed an Anti-Fascist League.

Defense savings stamps were sold at Boyd's, Famous, Stix, Scruggs, Garlands, Sonnenfeld's and Kline's.

OPA Ration Stamps

St Louisans had an early hero in the war. Edward "Butch" O'Hare grew up in south St. Louis. His mother still lived on Bates Street. He attended Western Military Academy in **Alton** the same time as Paul Tebbets of **Quincy**, Illinois, the man who flew the atomic bomb-equipped *Enola Gay* over Hiroshima.

Butch was a fighter pilot assigned to the aircraft carrier *Lexington* in the South Pacific. One day his entire squadron was sent on a mission. After he was airborne, he looked at the fuel gauge on his F-4-F Wildcat and realized that someone had forgotten to top off his fuel tank after his last mission. He would not have enough fuel to complete his new mission and get back to his ship. His flight leader told him to return to the carrier. Reluctantly, he dropped out of formation and headed back to the fleet.

As he was returning to the mother ship, he spotted something that turned his blood cold – a squadron of Japanese bombers was speeding its way toward the American fleet. The American fighters were gone on a sortie and the fleet was all but defenseless. He couldn't reach the squadron and bring them back in time to save the fleet. Nor was there time to warn the fleet of the impending danger. There was only one thing to do. He must somehow divert the enemy from the fleet. Laying aside all thoughts of personal safety, he dove into the formation of Japanese planes. Wing-mounted .50 calibers blazed as he charged in, attacking one surprised enemy plane and then another. Butch weaved in and out of the now broken formation and fired at as many planes as possible until finally all his ammunition was spent. Undaunted, he continued the assault. He dove at the planes trying to clip off a wing or a tail, in hopes of damaging as many of the planes possible and rendering them unfit to fly. He was desperate to do anything he could to keep them from reaching the American ships.

Finally, the exasperated Japanese squadron took off in another direction. Deeply relieved, Butch O'Hare and his tattered fighter limped back to the carrier. Upon arrival he reported in and related the event surrounding his return. The film from the camera mounted on his plane told the tale. It showed the extent of Butch's daring attempt to protect the fleet. He had become an ace in a single day, destroying five enemy bombers. This made him the **first American pilot to shoot down five enemy aircraft in a single day**.

That was in February of 1942 and for that action he became the Navy's first Ace of the war and the **first naval aviator to be awarded the Congressional Medal of Honor**. He was given a huge welcome home parade in St. Louis. A year later the "Savior of the Lexington" was killed in aerial combat at age 29, shot down by "friendly" fire. Today, O'Hare Airport in **Chicago** is named in tribute to the courage of this great man. So the next time you're in O'Hare visit the memorial with his statue and Medal of Honor. It is located between terminals 1 and 2.

St. Louisans line up for ration books at Eugene Field School on Olive Street

Captain Elliot Vandeventer was another St. Louis hero. He was awarded the Distinguished Flying Cross when

he sunk a Japanese transport and damaged three others near the Philippines.

Sgt. Russell Dunham was awarded the Congressional Medal of Honor. During fighting near Kayserberg, France, he armed himself to the hilt and attacked three German machine gun nests. He single-handedly killed nine, captured two, and wounded seven.

Nurse LT. Beulah Greenwalt, stationed in the Philippines, was the heroine Peggy in the book, *They Were Expendable*. She returned to her childhood home in **Licking**, Missouri, in March of 1945. After John Ford's film version came out, starring Robert Montgomery, John Wayne, and Donna Reed, Peggy sued MGM and won a settlement of about $4,000 because the film inaccurately showed her character (Donna Reed) romantically linked with John Wayne.

Old Bremen Bank at Broadway and Malinckrodt (L. Tettaton)

TURN OF THE CENTURY ST. LOUIS

When was the first car made in St. Louis? J.D. Lewis made an electric car in 1893 that ran at 8 mph.

What St. Louisan invented the 2nd commercial motor car ever made in America in 1898? George Dorris (born in **Nashville**, Missouri) who made the St. Louis brand motorcar at 1211 Vandeventer

How many cylinders and how many horsepower did it have? It had one cylinder and one horsepower.

How was the St. Louis steered and how fast did it go? It was steered with a tiller and attained a top speed of 8 mph. It could climb a 35 percent grade.

What carmaker made the steering wheel popular? Thank Missourian George Dorris for your steering wheel; his 1901 model started a trend away from tillers.

Before Dorris invented the carburetor float, what did motorists have to constantly adjust? A gas-metering valve

What car was built by St. Louis-based Gardener Company? The Ruxton

What motivated Joseph Moon of St. Louis to go into the car making business? He rode in a car owned by his friend, Richard Sears of Sears and Roebuck.

What bakery device was invented by a St. Louisan in 1900? The bread slicer

What caused the infamous 1900 streetcar strike in St. Louis? Workers, numbering 200, demanded a ten hour day and pay at a rate of 25 cents an hour. United Railway balked at the demands.

What caused the first streetcar strike riot? Streetcar workers had piled timbers on tracks to keep the cars grounded. The company began clearing the tracks and threatened to bring in strikebreakers from **Mexico**, Missouri.

How many people were killed in the riot? Twelve - in subsequent riots hundreds of people were injured before the company finally gave in to worker demands.

How many different brands of cars were made in St. Louis between 1898 and 1930? Twenty-three

On what street was "Motorcar Row" located in St. Louis? Lindell Boulevard was home to numerous auto showrooms.

What St. Louisan opened the **first auto supply house in America**? A.L. Dyke

What was the **first police squad car in America**? It was the Dorris "Skidoo," made in St. Louis.

Farmers hated cars on rural Missouri roads because they were noisy and scared their horses. How did they get revenge? When the cars got stuck in muddy roads, farmers charged exorbitant amounts for hitching up a team of horses to pull the car free.

Where were motorcar races held in St. Louis after the 1904 World's Fair ended? On the old fairgrounds site in Forest Park. Climbing Art Hill in the park was deemed a good test for the car's pulling efficiency.

Boatman's Bank on Broadway– upper floors housed Olympians

As St. Louisans took motorcar jaunts out into the country, what became a popular stopping place? The Meramec Highlands Hotel, about 15 miles west of the city near the road that one day would become Route 66.

In what year did St. Louis celebrate its 100th year of incorporation? 1909, with four torpedo boats coming up from New Orleans and firing a 21 gun salute

What was unusual about the celebration parade that was held? It was the last parade where the mayor went down the streets in a horse drawn buggy instead of a motorcar.

By 1916 Chevrolet was operating two plants in St. Louis. One was at Main and First on the riverfront; the other was at Bulwer and Broadway.

WORLD'S FAIR OF 1904

Temple of Mirth at the 1904 Fair

The 400th anniversary of the discovery of America by Columbus was going to be a huge event and several U.S. cities competed vigorously to host the event. In the end, Congress chose Chicago over St. Louis for the Columbian Exposition, much to the chagrin of David Francis and dignitaries who raised over $4 million in subscriptions to pay for the event.

In 1896, Pierre Chouteau proposed the construction of a

Jefferson Memorial near Lindell to house documents and artifacts related to the Louisiana Purchase and the Louis and Clark expedition. In 1899, St. Louis beat out New Orleans as the site to hold an international exposition commemorating the purchase. A special tax levy was authorized and bonds were sold to pay the costs. The U.S. Congress appropriated $5 million to help defray the costs. St. Louis citizens raised another $5 million and corporate St. Louis kicked in another $5 million, matching the $15 million originally paid to France for the swindle, er, deal. This event was going to showcase St. Louis to the rest of the world. The city was now a thriving metropolis with a population of 575,000, ranking it after New York, Chicago and Philadelphia – the Fourth City.

Battle Abbey castle reproduction at the 1904 Fair

Carondelet Park and O'Fallon Park were considered as sites, but the western half of Forest Park was chosen as the fair location. Additional acreage adjacent to the park was also purchased. The Wabash Rail-road already served the site and the construction of spur lines by MoPac, Iron Mountain, Cotton Belt and Frisco assuaged con-cerns about access to the fair. The Terminal Railroad built a Belt Line to the northwest edge of the grounds to expedite the movement of construction materials. There were thoughts given to building a subway, but the prospect of cutting a gap through solid rock seemed daunting.

New hotels were built. The Kingsway and Jefferson were prime examples. The Statlers built their first-ever hotel, a temporary structure on the fair grounds. New streetcars were added by the transit authority. Parts of the Washington University campus were also rented for the fair. The water system at Chain of Rocks was improved by treating river water with ferrous sulfate and milk of lime. Fairgoers were treated to refreshing drinks of crystal clear water. A wooden bridge was built over Kingshighway to give attendees access to Shaw's Botanical Garden. In early days, the king's royal road was used to separate the village's common pastures from the King's domain. Lindell Boulevard, which was merely a gravel road, was paved with stone. More stringent smoke abatement measures were put in place so that visitors would have fresh air instead of smog and fumes.

Dumbbell competition at 1904 Fair

Carpenters earned about 55 cents an hour while common laborers sweated away at twenty-five cents an hour. Meanwhile, roughly one-hundred millionaires lived within twenty blocks of the construction site. Nearly 100 painters needed to apply 3,000 gallons of paint to make ready for the fair.

Getting everything ready proved to be daunting, so the date for the fair was bumped up to 1904. D.R. Francis went on a tour of Europe to convince nations to build pavilions. Edward VII loaned him Queen Victoria's Diamond Jubilee presents for display purposes.

The third modern Olympic Games were held at Francis Field (Washington University). They proved to be the last to adhere to the premise of individuals against individuals. Thereafter, nations sent "teams" to the events; they marched under patriotic flags, accom-panied by stirring national anthems.

What was the **Battle Abbey** Building? It was a castle reproduction and on the inside were cyclorama reproductions of the battles of Gettysburg and Manassas.

Due to slowness and expense of trans-oceanic travel, only twelve countries were repre-sented in the events. Little wonder that the Americans racked up 238 medals – 223 more than the second place Germans. Cynthia Crossen, of the *Wall Street Journal*, writes that an American gymnast named **George Eyser won six medals despite having a wooden leg**. Fred Lorz ran the marathon, dropped out after nine miles and hitched a ride back to the stadium. When the car overheated, a revived Lorz ran the rest of the way and was the first to lope into the stadium. He admitted the fraud just as officials were about to give him the gold medal.

The St. Louis roads were unpaved and one runner was hospitalized for dust inhalation. A Black South African was chased off the course by some large dogs. Another runner named Hicks, close to the finish line, begged his sponsors to let him quit. Instead, they fed him small doses of sulfate of strychnine, mixed with raw egg, to stimulate his central nervous system. He won the race but lost ten pounds in the process. Only 14 of the 32 starters made it to the finish line.

Facilities back then were crude. In the 400 meter race there was chaos because the course had no lanes.

The most unusual aspect of the games was an "Anthropology Day" where "uncivilized" tribes of pygmies, Sioux, and Patagonians competed against each other in running, throwing, pole climbing, and in **an exciting mud fight**.

George Poage, from Milwaukee, became the first African-American to win a medal in the Olympics.

Forty-four states were represented at the fair with only Delaware and South Carolina absent. Arizona, Alaska, and Hawaii had not yet achieved statehood.

Missouri had the largest state building, constructed at a cost of a million dollars.

Virginia built a replica of Jefferson's home, Monticello. Tennessee rebuilt a full-scale model of Andrew Jackson's Hermitage. Alabama replicated an ante bellum mansion and had a huge statue of Vulcan. (Birmingham was the "Pittsburgh of the South.") Pennsylvania brought the Liberty Bell. North Dakota built a full-size model of Teddy's Roosevelt's ranch cabin.

India built a huge model of the Taj Mahal.

For many fairgoers, the scariest exhibit was a mechanical recreation of the Galveston Flood which was a frighteningly **realistic simulation of the tidal wave that killed five thousand people in 1900**. Raging waters and mournful winds convinced many that they were in real danger.

The 1944 film ***Meet Me in St. Louis*** was based on a 1942 novel by St. Louisan Sally Benson. It was based on her real-life experiences at the time of the 1904 fair. The character of Tootie (Margaret O'Brien) came from her childhood nickname. Director Vincent Minnelli worked closely with Sally to make sure sets of the period were accurate. Sears catalogues were consulted for the fashions of the day.

Meet Me in St. Louis movie poster

TOMORROW NIGHT'S THE NIGHT...
AND ALL ST. LOUIS
WILL BE THERE!
M-G-M PROUDLY PRESENTS
Judy Garland
Margaret O'Brien
TECHNICOLOR
THRILLS!
MEET ME IN ST. LOUIS
MARY ASTOR · LUCILLE BREMER · TOM DRAKE · MARJORIE MAIN
LOEW'S STATE

In real life, Benson's father took the family to NYC and they never returned to St. Louis for the Fair. Many of the events in the story were also based on the real life experiences of Sally's sister, Agnes.

Judy Garland balked at first when MGM told her she was going to portray yet another teenager. She was 21 at the time. Vincent Minnelli convinced her to do the film and she eventually considered it one of her favorite roles. She fell in love with Minnelli and they married soon afterward.

The "Trolley Song" (#26) and "Have Yourself a Merry Little Christmas" (#72) made the Film Institute's All-Time 100 Movie Songs list.

Esther Smith's home on 5135 Kensington was replicated on a period street at MGM Studio lot #3. It was dubbed "St. Louis Street" and was used for 27 more years in various movies and television shows. In St. Louis, Kensington Avenue is located in the Cabanne neighborhood near the northeast corner of Forest Park.

Who came up with the idea of having a fair to commemorate the 1803 Louisiana Purchase? Pierre Chouteau, the great, great grandson of Madam Chouteau, the "Mother of St. Louis"

How did St. Louis get a bit of sweet revenge on Chicago after it lost the 1893 Fair? The Olympic Committee, which had already awarded the 1904 Olympics to Chicago, took the event away and gave it, instead, to St. Louis to coincide with the Fair. **Chicago is the only city to ever be victimized in this manner by Olympic officials**.

The Pike penny arcade at the 1904 Fair

How much were plasterers and plumbers paid for their work on the fair? About 80 cents an hour

About how many people visited the Fair? 20 million

How many foreign nations participated in the fair? 62

What was the Fair's average daily attendance? 100,000

When was the Fair open? From April to November, 1904

What president officially opened the Fair by pressing a telegraph key? Teddy Roosevelt

What inventor had an exhibit of his personal inventions on display? Thomas Edison

What young man entertained crowds by doing rope tricks at the "Early St. Louis" Exhibition? Will Rogers

What 228 ft. long exhibit still exists, donated by the Smithsonian Institute? The birdcage at the zoo

How many train boxcars were required to haul in all of the exhibits? 12,000

What kind of unusual fountain was in front of the Palace of Liberal Arts? A bubble fountain, producing 176,000 bubbles per minute

What did the state of North Carolina bring to the Fair? An 800 year old tree

About how many buildings were at the Fair? 900

How big was the gigantic Ferris wheel? Twenty-five stories tall

How big were the cars on the Ferris wheel? Each of its 36 cars held about 40 people

How was the 5 acre map of the USA composed? It was made up of flowers native to the states depicted.

How was it possible to get an aerial view of the Fair? Hot air balloon rides were available.

What mechanized transportation was available on the fairgrounds? There was a streetcar line with 15 stations.

Who was the famous band leader at the Fair? John Philip Sousa

What kind of ride was available in the Grand Basin? Gondola rides were brought over from Venice, Italy.

What was the admission price to the Fair? Twenty cents

What personalized Chinese transportation was available to Fair goers? Jinrikishas

What sat on top of Art Hill? It was topped by the majestic Festival Hall, with a dome larger than St. Peters cathedral in Rome.

What "world's largest" item was inside? The world's largest pipe organ

What was the largest building on the fairgrounds? The Agriculture Building – 1/3 mile long

What unusual exhibit was sent by the Philippines? They recreated an entire native village with 65 tribes covering 40 acres.

What building was donated to the city of St. Louis by the Exposition Company that planned and ran the Fair? The Art Museum on top of

Art Hill with the statue of Louis IX in front; during the Fair it was called the Art Palace. It was the only building made of stone and steel.

How did the equestrian statue of Louis IX in front of the Art Museum, come into existence? It is the bronze version of a plaster statue that stood near the entrance to the Fair.

What was The Pike? The penny arcade section of the Fair

What was the Temple of Mirth? An old fashioned fun house, complete with mirrors

Did the Fair have a roller coaster? It was called the Scenic Railway and the ride had three dips.

What was **Kansas City's** chief contribution to the Fair? Their fire department gave fire fighting demonstrations and pitched in to help the Exposition Fire Department fight real fires at the Fair.

Where was the Fair's administration center located? At Washington University (Brookings Hall), located on the northwest end of the fairgrounds

Who was president of the Fair? St. Louis mayor and (later) Missouri governor, David R. Francis, a graduate of Washington University

Igorot tribe of Philippine natives

What was named in his honor? Francis Field, the athletic complex at Washington University where numerous events of the 1904 Olympics were held.

What equestrian event was held at the Fair? The greatest horse show in the world took place there.

Of what material was most buildings and statues at the Fair made? Staff – plaster-of-Paris and fiber, cheaply made and designed to last only about three years

How did **St. Charles** residents get to the Fair? The rich had automobiles, but a streetcar bridge was built spanning the Missouri River just in time for the Fair.

How many cars were displayed at the popular Palace of Transportation at the Fair? 152 American, French and German

What drink was introduced at the Fair? Iced tea

What was done with the small houses especially built for Fair construction workers when the Fair was over? They were sold to an Illinois coal company in Macoupin County, painted white, and moved to provide housing for their workers. The town is still called **White City.**

What was done with the statues of Abe Lincoln and Stephen Douglas, in the Illinois exhibit, after the Fair was over? They were moved to **East St. Louis** and placed in front of Rock High School on 9th Street.

What famous St. Louisan, later a movie star, helped his father sell candy at the Fair? Vincent Price who became known as "the candy kid"

1940s photo of World's Fair birdcage (Lonnie Tettaton)

What is the special significance of these Olympic Games They were the first ever held in the United States

What fast food was invented for the Fair? **Hot dogs**

What other fast food, already invented, was popularized by the Fair? Hamburgers – invented by the Hamburg Steamship Line in the 1890s and served to immigrants coming to America from Germany

Where did St. Louis obtain its Ferris wheel for the Fair? It was left over from Chicago's Columbian Exposition of 1893.

What was eventually done with the Ferris wheel? It was dynamited and sold for scrap.

How big was the axel on the Ferris wheel? Six feet in diameter

Did St. Louis lose money on the Fair? No, when expenses and receipts were totaled there was a balance left of $600,000.

THE KERRY PATCH GANGSTERS

By Lonnie Tettaton

It was Prohibition that gave rise to organized crime and nowhere is that better illustrated than in the predominantly "wet" Irish ghetto of St. Louis known as the Kerry Patch, named for a county in Ireland.

The Irish, as a people, had suffered through years of hardship and humiliation back in their native homeland. Their patron was St. Patrick, the religious man who had converted the island to Catholicism and drove out all the snakes. Centuries ago, the British imposed their rule to make sure no enemy used that emerald island as a staging area for invasion. The Irish hated Protestant England and loathed their empire. They fought back by forming the Irish Republican Army, a surreptitious guerrilla force that killed the hated oppressors.

The Irish first started coming to America in large numbers after the devastating Irish Potato Famine of the 1840s. Their numbers increased as they were recruited to build roads, bridges, canals and railroads in America. A stereotype soon developed as most of them seemingly became either politicians, priests or policemen.

Yet, because they were Roman Catholic and generally voted en masse with the Democrats, they were derided as the people of Rum, Romanism and Rebellion. "No Irish Need Apply" was a common sign in storefront windows.

The Kerry Patch section in St. Louis adjoined a Little Italy section of north St. Louis near Eighth and Carr, just a bit north and west of the current Edward R. Jones Dome. The Kerry Patch area spawned a rough breed of

Irish gangsters. One of them, William T. Egan, a Fifth Ward committeeman, started the **Egan Rats** gang. Another was **Edward "Jellyroll" Hogan**, who was business agent for the Brewers and Soft Drink Workers Union. Jellyroll was one of six sons born to St. Louis policeman Edward Hogan. Humbert Costello was the "muscle" for the Hogan gang. He was probably involved in numerous shootings before he was sent away for 25 years following a jewelry store robbery. After his release, he was deported by the feds in 1937.

Many of the colorful names that are associated with St. Louis gangsters were dreamed up by members of the press in order to make their subjects seem more Runyonesque and colorful. This would also sell more newspapers.

Kerry Patch neighborhood with litter on streetcar tracks during 1901 strike

After Prohibition was ended, the Irish Mafia moved on to other lucrative pursuits such as labor racketeering and "protection." Restaurants, the produce business, laundry establishments and garbage collection also seemed to fit the bill.

A rivalry soon developed between the two factions. "Big Max" Greenberg, an Egan Rat, was serving a five year stretch at Leavenworth. In 1920, his boss somehow greased the right palms and got him released after serving only six months. Max repaid the act of kindness by gypping Egan out of $2,000 in a liquor deal and, then, switching allegiance by going over to the Hogans. In March of 1921, Max was wounded at Sixth and Chestnut in a drive-by shoot-ing. There would be payback. In September, **William Egan was shot and killed** outside a saloon at 14th and Franklin. He died in the City Hospital # 1 on 13th and Lafayette, refusing to indicate who might have shot him. It was rumored that $30,000 was paid for the hit. Meanwhile, Greenberg went to the police station with the Hogan Gang lawyer, Jacob Mackler, and produced an "airtight" alibi.

William **"Dinty" Colbeck**, a World War I veteran, became the new leader of the Rats. He was born in 1891 in the Kerry Patch ghetto of St. Louis. His nickname came from the fact that he had worked as a pipe fitter and his wrench often dented the pipes. Denty evolved into "Dinty."

Dinty Colbeck

Dinty figured out that Greenberg and his associates had been responsible for William Egan's murder. He swore vengeance. Mackler, thought to be the payoff man in the Egan hit, was gunned down in his automobile on February 21, 1922.

According to researcher Walter Fontane, Dinty Colbeck believed that James Hogan, Jellyroll's brother, was one of the shooters. In May of 1922, one of the perceived perpe-trators, Luke Kennedy, was murdered. Three days later, Hogan's men shot up Colbeck's plumbing establishment at 2215 Washington Ave. Despite extensive damage to some lead pipes and cast iron tubs, no one was injured. In a tit for tat retaliation, Hogan's home at 3035 Cass was blasted with gunfire, but no one was hurt. Shades of gangland Chicago!

Colbeck and his Rats, pressured by Humphrey Bogart-like police lieutenant Duley McDonald, moved their base of operations to St. Louis County. They remodeled an old 11 room Victorian home into a clubhouse that they dubbed the Maxwelton Club. It was near the Maxwelton Racetrack on St. Charles Rock Road in the wilderness of St. Louis County.

Roughly a year later, the Hogans dynamited the place and blew it to smithereens. There's not much there anymore except a cemetery – Laurel Hill Memorial Gardens.

For the next two years the bitter rivalry resulted in more trigger-happy forays and the violent deaths of about twenty assorted gang members a la Capone v. Bugs Moran in Chicago. It got so bad that church leaders, police, and an irritated public called for a truce between the two factions. In typical gangland fashion, it lasted a mere two months.

In one infamous incident, State Representative William McGee was slain when Col-beck's men, trying to kill James Hogan, fired irresponsibly into a crowd. For a spell, the gangs turned to the lucrative mail robbery business. In April of 1923, a mail truck was held up at gunpoint near Fourth and Locust. The take was over $2 million in negotiable bonds. A similar robbery of the post-master in **Staunton**, Illinois netted a cool $55,000.

Finally, one of the Rat hooligans had a twinge of conscience and decided to make a deal with the police and tell everything he knew. Ray Renard "spilled his guts" to police and gave them names and details. Dinty Colbeck, David "Chippy" Robinson, "Red" Smith and six other Rats were rounded up and charged. Colbeck was sent to the federal prison in Atlanta, the same one that would later host Al Capone before he was sent to Alcatraz. The Rats, as a gang, pretty much fell apart after those arrests.

Max Greenberg fled the city and went back east. In April of 1933, he was found shot to death in a New Jersey hotel room.

Monsignor Joseph O'Toole of **Webster Groves**, at the behest of Colbeck's wife, visited Dinty in prison. He tried to talk him into giving up a life of crime and going straight. After serving sixteen months Colbeck was released and he immediately returned to his life of crime. On February 17, 1943, Colbeck crossed the **McKinley Bridge**, coming home from some nefarious gambling activity on the East Side. He was followed by a dark sedan, and at Ninth and Destrehan its occupants opened fire with their .45 machine guns. The funeral for the 58 year-old gangster was held at St. Catherine's.

Fred "Killer" Burke, a former Eagan Rat, gained notoriety by being one of the shooters in Chicago's **St. Valentine's Day Massacre** in 1929.

Leo Brothers, another ex-Rat, was hired to make a hit on Chicago reporter Jake Lingle. Lingle was friendly with the Capone mob but, apparently, either knew too much or did something to anger "Scarface" Al. Brothers traveled from St. Louis to Chicago via Route 66 (in 1930) and shot the "**World's Richest Reporter,**" from behind, while in an underground pedestrian walkway. He was caught and sentenced to 16 years in prison. "I can do that time standing on my head," a defiant Lingle told the judge. Brothers was released after serving eight years and died of natural causes in 1951.

Hogan remained active in state politics (he served four terms in the state senate) until he was defeated in 1960 by Theodore McNeil, **the first black to be elected to Missouri's senate**. Hogan died a natural death (age 77) in 1963.

Chippy Robinson

THE PILLOW GANG

By Lonnie Tettaton

The **Pillow Gang** was one of the earliest Italian criminal groups in St. Louis, dating back to 1910. Its name was derived from the fact that their leader, **Carmelo Fresina, was once shot in the derriere, and carried a pillow with him for ease of comfort**. This was reminiscent of Nathan Bedford Forrest, the Confederate Civil War cavalry officer who led his charges while riding in a buckboard and sitting on a pillow.

The extortionist and bootlegger was mentioned by Senator Estes Kefauver in his 1952 book about his investigation into organized crime. Fresina was eventually dispatched with a couple of bullets in his head and he no longer needed his pillow.

THE CUCKOO GANG

By Lonnie Tettaton

When Prohibition arrived on the scene in St. Louis there were five different groups that staked out territory and indulged in criminal activity. They were the Sicilian Green Ones (Green Dagoes), the Pillow Gang, the Egan Rats, the Hogan Gang and the Cuckoo Gang.

According to Allan May, the **Green Ones** ostensibly received their name in the Sicilian farming community from whence they came. Some say the name came from the fact that they were "greenhorns" when they first arrived in America. In St. Louis they were led by brothers John and Vito Giannola and Alphonse Palizzola. The trio quickly levied an extortion tax on the city's Italian community, placing a levy on all goods sold. Next they moved into the rackets and by 1923 gained a stranglehold on the wholesale meat industry. When one brave and recalcitrant distributor balked at the idea, his body was found under the Kingshighway viaduct September 16, 1923.

The Green Ones soon decided that liquor sales afforded more of an opportunity. When they tried that venue they found it to be dominated by the Irish Egan Rats Gang. When the Greens challenged the Rats, one of their gang members, a cousin, was found murdered. After most of the Rat gang's leaders were imprisoned in 1925, the Greens next found their path to be blocked by the Cuckoo gang.

Two Greens, Tony "Shorty" Russo and Vincent Spicuzza, were slain in Chicago while trying to collect a $50,000 bounty put on Capone by rival Joe Aiello. Each dead man had a nickel in his hand, the well known signature of "Machine Gun" McGurn.

Warfare between the two groups ensued with destruction and death following in the wake of events, culminating in the murder of Al Palizzola in 1927. Vito Giannola was killed a few months later when his body was found riddled with 37 bullets. John Giannola was smart enough to quit the business and he died peacefully in his sleep in 1955. A recount of the statistical mayhem from this rivalry shows 30 dead and 18 wounded.

The Cuckoos were headed by the Tipton brothers, Herman, Ray and Roy. Like most gangs, they were into murder, mayhem, pistol whippings, extortion, bootlegging, robbery and kidnapping. They received their unusual moniker when Al Capone decided to muscle in on the St. Louis territory. He sent a couple of his men to St. Louis to lay the groundwork and they came back in pine boxes. Capone sent some more men and they were also bumped off. After a third futile attempt, with the same result, Capone threw up his hands in exasperation. "That's it. I've had it. I'm not messing with those guys anymore. They're crazy . . . nuts, cuckoo!"

Hanging of Charlie Birger, 1928 (Franklin County Hist. Museum) – Mitchell photo

In the mid-1920s the Cuckoos survived a gang war with the dangerous Green Ones. Thirteen men were killed in the ensuing mayhem.

Two of its gang members, Oliver Hamilton and "Dizzy" Daniels, were given life sentences for killing St. Louis police officers Ed Griffin and John Surgant during a robbery. The Cuckoos received a boost when **Tommy Hayes** (born in **Wellston**) got out of prison (1925) and joined their forces. He had served three years for committing a mail robbery in **Wood River**, Illinois.

As the war between the Greens and the Cuckoos continued, Tommy **Hayes killed two more Greens, Mike "the Chink" Longo and James Russo**. The war came to an end on July 9, 1928 after St. Louis police escorted the surviving Russo brothers – William, Tom and Lawrence – to Union Station so they could get out of town alive.

The Cuckoos also sided with the Shelton Gang in East St. Louis to fight their chief rival, the Charlie Birger gang. **After Birger was hanged in 1928**, Carl Shelton banished the Cuckoos back to Missouri. Herman Tipton enjoyed his new found wealth on the East Side and balked. A dozen men were killed in the ensuing warfare. In February of 1931, three Shelton men were killed in an attack on one of their roadhouses in southern Illinois. Tommy Hayes, a Cuckoo member who had originally split from the gang to side with the Sheltons, pulled a double-cross and was responsible for the killings. Carl Shelton, the savvy leader of the gang from **Fairfield**, Illinois, suspected the double-cross. On April 15, 1932, **Hayes was found in Madison, Illinois with 12 slugs in him**. With his death, the Cuckoos steadily declined as a criminal force, although some merely teamed with the Egan Rats.

Handsome Carl Shelton (Both Shelton pics courtesy SIUE)

The Sheltons had an amazing criminal run lasting 25 years. Few gangs had that kind of longevity. Carl and brother Roy were killed in 1950 on their farms in Fairfield, Illinois, while Bernie was shot in **Peoria**, Illinois in 1952. The remaining Shelton brother, "Big" Earl, surreptitiously fled to Florida and died a quiet natural death when he was in his nineties. The Sheltons made the mistake of refusing to share their southern Illinois empire with the St. Louis/Capone Outfit syndicate. **Charles "Blackie" Harris**, an old Egan Rats member, was thought to have been Carl Shelton's killer. Shortly after the killing, Harris was arrested in Tulsa, but was never successfully prosecuted for the crime. All three Shelton brother murders went unsolved.

Taylor Pensoneau, with whom author Bill Nunes attended **Belleville** Junior College in 1959-60, wrote the definitive biography on the Sheltons – *Brothers Notorious.*

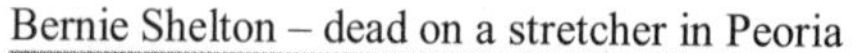

Bernie Shelton – dead on a stretcher in Peoria

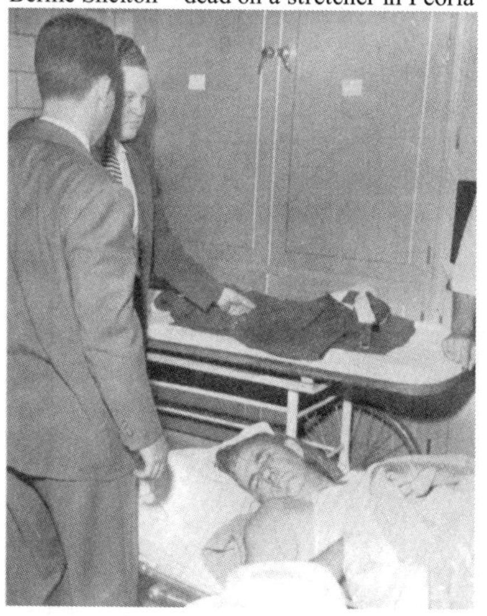

THE EGAN RATS AND DINTY COLBECK

by Lonnie Tettaton

Around 1902, city politics fell under the control of a triumvirate: Thomas Kinney, Frank Hussey and Cornelius McGillcuddy a.k.a. "Cuddy Mack." All three ruled various wards of the city through the House of Delegates and were supported by vicious gangs of cutthroats. After a swift gang war and a bloody election, Cuddy Mack lost power to Thomas Kinney. By 1910, Hussey had also been neutralized and Kinney dominated city politics. Now that he was firmly in control over city politics (Kinney had since become one of the state's most popular senators), Kinney began to distance himself from gang affairs. Leadership over his gang of psychopathic hooligans was relinquished to **Tom Egan**. Egan had all of the qualities of the ideal crime boss. He was quiet, powerful, patient, resourceful, connected, popular with the troops and public, imaginative, and often thoughtful about the future. When Tom Kinney died in 1912, Egan assumed control over city politics and crime. Unlike his predecessor, Egan had no qualms about connecting politics and crime. In fact, he almost seemed to flaunt his position. In an interview to a reporter for the *St. Louis Post-Dispatch*, Egan said that his gang numbered over 400 men. This was more than enough to tip any election in the city during those turbulent days. Undoubtedly **William Colbeck** was among the 400 gang members. The headquarters for the city's crime and politics was Egan's saloon. Whenever there was a gang murder, it was a police ritual to raid the saloon. The gangsters that infested the place were hauled off to jail with much fanfare, only to be quietly released shortly afterwards. One police officer that was bored with the routine **simply called them Egan's Rats when hauling them off to the city jail instead of listing their names**. The moniker stuck.

St. Louis had been regulating the liquor industry since the 1890s. The number of regulations had increased coincidental with the rise of the temperance movement. Expecting Prohibition to become the law, Tom Egan took steps to insure the tranquility of the St. Louis underworld. Most of the other city gangs made deals with Egan to maintain the peace. Even his primary political rival, **Edward "Jellyroll" Hogan**, agreed to Egan's peace proposals. The relationship between Egan and Hogan was similar to that between Tom Pendergast and Joe Shannon in **Kansas City**, albeit on a smaller scale. At the time, Hogan was not a real threat to the Egan political faction, but he would become the archrival of "Dinty" Colbeck. When arrangements had been made to establish gang territories, Egan focused on building his liquor supply base. He sent henchmen to cities like **East St. Louis**, Terre Haute, Cincinnati, Detroit and New Orleans. These places were to arrange for liquor to be sent to St. Louis and supply security for the shipments. At the outset of Prohibition, liquor poured into St. Louis, so much so that there was hardly a decrease in the supply of booze. Unfortunately, Tom Egan never saw how smoothly his plan operated. He died in April 1918.

Tom Egan was probably the most capable gang leader ever produced by St. Louis. With one eye on politics and another on the public, Egan tried to limit gangland activity by using the police to pursue rival, less powerful gangs. The incarceration of lesser gangs made the police look good to both the media and the public, and in return the police often let the Egan Rats carry on their activities without molestation. Using these tactics, Egan steadily increased his underworld power and influence. William Colbeck had been privy to the rise of Tom Egan. However, the spectator was a minor player in the underworld at that time. Colbeck was a man of action and did not favor the slow and steady methodology used by Tommy Egan and Tom Kinney. Whether out of national pride or a thirst for adventure, Colbeck joined the American Expeditionary Force in World War I and was sent to France, allegedly serving in the Battle of the Marne. Upon his return to St. Louis, he was regarded as a full-fledged member of the gang.

Reporter John Auble wrote *A History of St. Louis Gangsters*

William Egan, brother of the late Tom Egan, took over the gang. Willie Egan kept the booze flowing to the city and generally kept the peace. An upstart Italian gang was causing trouble. Another gang had degenerated into civil war. Although he was efficient and clever, he was not as strong as his brother was. He continued to keep the law enforcement community from interfering with the Egan's Rats as well as maintaining Egan Gang supremacy over the underworld. In an ironic twist of fate, the city's top crime boss was also a constable, commissioned to fight crime! The power structure of the gang remained much like that created by Tom Egan. All of the top figures in the gang were primarily involved in the liquor business. However, there was a small faction of the gang that preferred to engage in high-risk crimes such as holdups and robbery. Willie Egan was able to keep the "red hots" under control as long as he was aware of their activities.

The **red hots** were often the soldiers who were paid by Egan and his lieutenants to protect liquor shipments. In an effort to increase their pocket money, they often resorted to more violent crimes. A similar situation existed within the Hogan Gang. A small Southside gang, the Cuckoos, was more devoted to robbery than bootlegging, but active in both rackets. In consequence, the Egan red hots, the Hogans, and the Cuckoos found camaraderie as they united in violent crime. Among the Egan red hots was William Colbeck. As a cover for his illegal activities, he became a plumber. Colbeck was imaginative and successful. Many young toughs including Thomas Hayes, Frank Wortman and Peter and "Yonnie" Licavoli looked up to Colbeck as a role model. Despite his influence over the Egan Gang's chief gunmen and enforcers, Colbeck remained firmly loyal to Willie Egan. Colbeck probably was not one of Egan's lieutenants. Egan's gang was structured for liquor trafficking and Colbeck was unsuccessful in his liquor dealings. However, Colbeck was a perfect liaison to the troops, and therefore found a place at Egan's inner circle of consultants.

John Doherty

The history of the St. Louis underworld would have been very different if Willie Egan had not been murdered in 1921. Based on the confessions of Ray Renard, the murder of Willie Egan was engineered by his chief lieutenant, Max Greenberg. According to Renard, Egan blamed Greenberg for swindling him out of $50,000 worth of booze. When it became clear to Egan that Greenberg would not pay him back the money, Egan tried to have Greenberg murdered. The assassination went awry and Greenberg escaped. Greenberg went to Jacob Mackler, "the mouthpiece of the Hogan Gang." In return for an alleged $15,000, three Hogan gunmen, James Hogan, Luke Kennedy and John Doyle, murdered Egan on November 1, 1921. Colbeck was one of the first Egan gangsters on the scene and supposedly with his last breath, Egan told Colbeck the identities of the gunmen.

Renard would later blame the Egan's Rats for most of the gang murders (1920-1924), but he did not blame them for the Egan murder. It is unusual that Colbeck was present at the murder scene. More interesting is that the next gangland victim was George Ruloff. Ruloff was Egan's shadow and bodyguard. He was at Egan's side before Colbeck, and underworld gossip ran that Ruloff was killed "so that he couldn't identify the slayers of Willie Egan."

Although circumstantial evidence would suggest that Colbeck had been privy to what would happen to Egan on that fateful night, it is unlikely that Colbeck was behind the murder or even encouraged it. It is more plausible that he heard rumors of the murder plot, but he did not take them seriously. He did pursue a vendetta against the three Hogan gunmen, a vendetta that would become a full-fledged gang war.

Colbeck assumed control of the Egan Rats as an avenging angel. The old Egan lieutenants thought that Colbeck would crush the Hogan Gang, thereby allowing them to expand their liquor operations and generally increase the power and prestige of the gang. John Doyle was murdered in January 1922 and Luke Kennedy was slain shortly afterwards. "Jellyroll" Hogan was furious and scared. He was outgunned by a powerful and expansionistic new rival who had targeted some of his closest gang associates, including his brother, for death. After the Kennedy murder, Hogan reluctantly went to war. The two gangs followed very different strategies. The Egan Rats sought revenge, but their bloodlust had subsided slightly when Kennedy was slain. After the Kennedy murder, the Egan Gang pursued the gang war as either a pastime or an immediate retaliation after a Hogan attack. The Hogan Gang sought survival. Their energy was devoted to the defensive. Rarely did they venture from their territory along Cass Avenue to attack their foes.

The war was at its peak in 1922 when **the two gangs waged vicious gun battles from speeding automobiles along St. Louis streets**. Bystanders were run down and injured more often than the feudists. Several children were hit by cars and public outrage grew with every confrontation. In March 1922, Hogan gunmen ambushed Colbeck in his plumbing shop. They riddled the storefront with bullets and shotgun slugs, but no one was injured. Greatly perturbed, the Egan chief struck back violently. A cavalcade of at least four touring cars full of gunmen slowly drove past the Hogan residence and poured a fusillade into the house. Again, no one was injured.

After the plumbing shop incident, **Colbeck moved his gang to the Maxwelton Club and Racetrack on St. Charles Rock Road in the wilderness of St. Louis County**. From this location, the gangsters could easily be alerted to the presence of Hogan gangsters. Egan gunmen also practiced their marksmanship at the club. Cans and bottles were placed in the center of the track. Gunmen from the grandstands or in cars racing around the track fired at the targets. The Egan gangsters also terrorized local residents. One time they waylaid a farmer and his family. Evicting them from their car, the gangsters cartwheeled it into a ditch. The farmer called Colbeck at the club and demanded reparations. Colbeck was not only a gangster, he was also a politician. Previously he had been a committeeman in the fifth ward. At the height of his power, he was the Sergeant-at-arms of the St. Louis Democratic Committee. Despite the public outrage at the gang war, he knew it was in his best interests to keep the people happy. **Colbeck sent the farmer enough money to purchase two cars**.

Tony "the Pip" Lopiparo

During the early phases of the war (1922), Colbeck became increasingly distracted from the gang's bootlegging activities. He began to rely on young gunmen and thieves for advice about gang matters. Although such men were in abundance in the gang, few of them had any lengthy expertise, especially in the alcohol industry. David **"Chippy" Robinson**, Eddie Linham, and James "Sticky" Hennessey were fearsome gunmen, but poor lieutenants. Slowly the liquor interests of the Egan Gang were usurped by the **Italian crime boss, Vito Giannola**. The Egan gangsters outside of St. Louis (in Terre Haute, Cincinnati, Detroit, etc.) operated their own rackets and ceased to obey the Egan hierarchy. The old lieutenants of the era of the Egan brothers faded away. The money that had financed Colbeck and his vendetta against the Hogan Gang was quickly dwindling. The new gang chief and his lieutenants needed to find a new means by which to support themselves. Once they had to work for a living, the gang war began to subside.

Paul J. Leisure

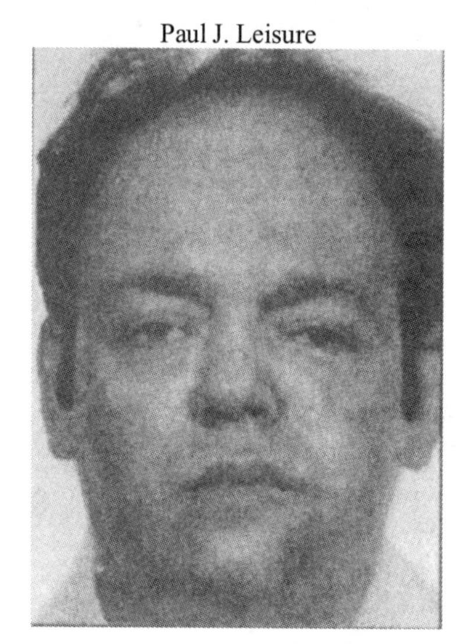

According to the True Crime Library, **Ray Renard** joined the gang in 1920 by becoming acquainted with one of the red hots, Gus Dietmeyer. Renard demonstrated his skill as a get-away driver for the gang during the glory days under Willie Egan. Renard became increasingly valuable to Colbeck when, around 1923, the crime lord had to resort to robbery as the gang's chief source of money. At first the gangsters held up banks, jewelry stores, and anything that had a large bankroll. Then, almost suddenly, Colbeck learned that company payrolls were sent by cash through the mail. The gang could get $50,000 cash by simply holding up a few postal inspectors.

St. Louis firms often employed policemen to guard their payrolls when transferring from a bank to an institution. These transactions had become speedy, efficient and routine. It would have been dangerous to try to rob the St. Louis post-office, especially when similar prizes were awaiting the gang in Illinois at far less risk. During the first half of the twentieth century, Illinois possessed some large mining communities in places like **Glen Carbon, Collinsville** and **Belleville**. Colbeck and his gang had to learn when the mining companies would deliver their payrolls. This was easily learned by bribing miners or lounging around taverns frequented by miners. Ray Renard, in his confessions, goes into elaborate detail on how the gangsters planned and rehearsed a crime before they went through with it.

It will never be known how many crimes Colbeck and his gang committed. Since the fall of the Egan Gang in 1925, the popular press mentioned that the gang collected "at least $2.4 million from robbery;" but in just one crime alone, they escaped with $2.1 million. The Egan Gang became increasingly disorganized as Colbeck isolated himself within a core group of gunmen. The vast rings of lesser members and associates, including Tommy Hayes, Pete Licavoli and Frank Wortman, began to associate with the Cuckoos, Italians and Eastsiders respectively and drifted away from Colbeck and his criminal empire.

Distrust ruptured the Egan Rats. During the years of the Egan-Hogan feud, around twenty-three feudists were slain. Well over half of those were Egan gangsters killed by their own comrades. Some were minor members of no importance. Others were at the top of the gang. In 1922, "Chippy" Robinson and Eddie Linham were vying for the position of the gang's premier gunman. If we are to believe Ray Renard, Robinson killed Linham so that he could become Colbeck's chief lieutenant and enforcer. It should be noted that although "Chippy" Robinson was regarded by many as the city's most fearsome gangster after the Linham murder, he was not as bloodthirsty as Sammy "the Bull." According to Ray Renard, Colbeck had poor control over his henchmen and used Robinson to kill them for questionable motives.

The beginning of the end for the Egan Rats began in south St. Louis with the Cuckoo Gang. **Roy Tipton**, the leader of the gang, walked a fine line between bootlegging and robbery. Sometime in early 1923 an associate of the Cuckoos, Max Simmonson, approached Tipton with a proposition. As a dealer in stolen bonds, he had learned through his connections that, on a given date, an armored car carrying over $2 million in negotiable bonds and cash would be traveling between various businesses in downtown St. Louis. Tipton did not believe that the Cuckoos could pull off such a crime by themselves so Tipton took the information to Colbeck. On April 2, 1923, the gangsters held up the armored car at the intersection of Fourth and Locust in downtown St. Louis.

The gangsters split about $260,000 in cash and awaited Simmonson and other fences to sell the stolen bonds. However, many of the stolen bonds were seized in several police raids. Quickly identifying the Egan Gang with the crime, the police and the postal inspectors began to increase their harassment of the gang. Despite increased police pressure and public outrage at the gang war and blatant crimes, Colbeck was at the height of his power. Unbeknown to Colbeck, the Egan Gang was on the verge of ruin. Father Timothy Dempsey was able to arrange for the two gang chiefs (Colbeck and Hogan) to meet and sign pledges that the gang war was over. The truce lasted only a few months when James Hogan was spotted by a group of intoxicated Egan red hots. Remembering orders to kill Hogan in revenge for Willie Egan, the red hots opened fire. Hogan escaped unharmed, but William McGee, a member of the state legislature was critically wounded and John P. Sweeney, a lawyer loosely affiliated with the Hogan political faction, was slain. After the Sweeney murder, the gang's political protection turned its back on Colbeck causing many Egan gunmen to flee the city.

St. Louis

Tired of continual police harassment and fearful of his associates, Ray Renard, the gang's wheelman, fled the city to avoid prosecution for robbery. Renard was just one of many Egan gangsters in the growing exodus from the crumbling empire of the Egan's Rats. Hunted by the authorities, Renard was captured in Los Angeles. On the train ride back to St. Louis, Renard was accompanied by Harry Brundidge who managed to elicit a confession from Renard. Renard said that the reason he was breaking the gang code of silence was that he was tired of constantly being broke. "I spent everything I got." He said that he wanted to start a new life. Renard would be sentenced to five years for robbery. He obtained leniency for testifying against his former comrades in the robbery trials.

Anthony J. Leisure

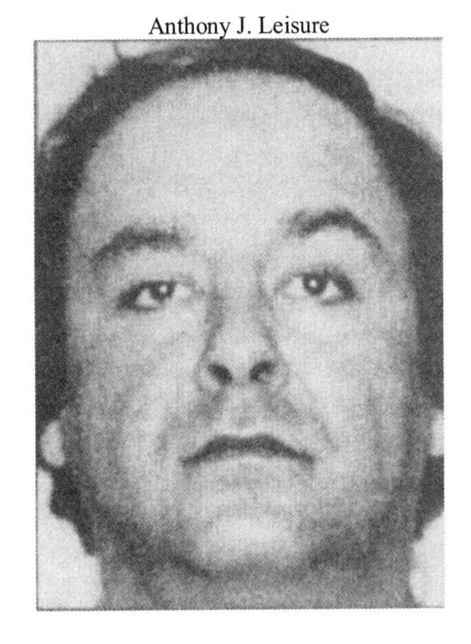

In November 1924, Colbeck, Robinson, Gus Dietmeyer, Louis Smith, Stephen Ryan and Oliver Dougherty were convicted of a mail robbery in **Staunton**, Illinois. Colbeck received fifteen years. It had been a victory for postal inspectors. However, their most notable victory against the underworld would come the following year. In January, a motley assortment of Egan and Cuckoo gangsters were brought to trial for the armored car robbery. Most of the gangsters received a sentence of twenty-five years. Another batch of Egan gangsters was convicted of a mail robbery in **Pocahontas**, Illinois, in which they made their escape by airplane.

Within the winter of 1924-1925 the core membership of the Egan Gang had collapsed. Colbeck and most of his lieutenants were incarcerated in Leavenworth Federal Penitentiary. **The lone exception was Fred Burke, destined to become infamous as one of the gunmen in the St. Valentine's Day Massacre**. The destruction of the Egan Gang was complete. After the convictions, there were few Egan gangsters who could fill the power vacuum. Most of the Egan gangsters still alive and free were leaving the city or joining other gangs. A small shadow of the gang remained active for a few months, but was quickly crushed by the police.

Even after his incarceration, Colbeck remained a media sensation. In 1926, there were close to twenty Egan gangsters incarcerated in Leavenworth. Colbeck's lawyers were busy appealing the convictions and made headlines when they found new evidence in favor of their clients. Eventually Colbeck hit on the idea that his henchmen should write confessions absolving him of the crimes. This did not sit well with his followers, and two distinct camps existed among the gangster clique. Hostilities became so bad that several of the combatants (including Colbeck) were transferred to Atlanta Federal Penitentiary. According to researcher **James Brasher**, Colbeck ended up being a **cellmate with Al Capone**. Colbeck and the other gangsters convicted with him would make headlines whenever they came up for parole.

Beginning in 1940, those convicted of the armored car robbery were slowly released one by one from prison. All were at liberty by mid-1944. "Dinty" Colbeck was released late in 1940. He immediately resumed his former role as a plumber and opened a shop. He was soon involved in election fraud and petty racketeering. As a former rackets boss, he had little difficulty in finding employment in the underworld. Within a few years, however, he was trying to reassert his control over the underworld. Unfortunately for him, things had radically changed since he was a big shot. The **East St. Louis** gambling halls, run by Frank Wortman, not the St. Louis political clubs, governed the underworld. When Colbeck learned that some of his old henchmen were running some of the gambling clubs, he began to demand a cut of the profits. This did not sit well with any of the established underworld groups operating on the East side.

On February 17, 1943 "Dinty" Colbeck was coming home from some East Side activity and crossed the McKinley Bridge. **Another car pulled along side of him and a man with a machine gun strafed Colbeck's car**. The notorious crime chief was dead.

Scores of hoodlums were arrested for questioning. Among these were former Egan gangsters affiliated with a gang that had the support of the Chicago mob. Others arrested were members of the Shelton and Italian gangs. There were no substantial leads and there were no prime suspects. Some historians blame the embryonic Wortman Gang, but they did not gain full power until after World War II. The Italians were too engrossed in their own internal power struggles to exert any great control over the Eastside gambling community. The most likely perpetrators were members of the Shelton Gang. According to historian Walter Fontane, the Sheltons were the real masters of the Illinois underworld until Wortman successfully challenged them. The Shelton Gang had the most to lose from Colbeck's latest activities.

This time, the Egan gangsters did not rally around a concept of revenge. Instead they did nothing. Fontane maintains that Chippy Robinson, Stephen Ryan, Gus Dietmeyer and other former Egan gangsters offered their loyalty to the new crime syndicate being organized by Frank Wortman and Elmer Dowling, both formerly associates of the Egan Gang during its heyday under Colbeck and Willie Egan. The flashy bravado of this hoodlum was visible in the powerful Wortman Gang. Colbeck's former associates formed the backbone of the organization and remained fixed on using blatant gangster tactics to achieve their desires. Their high profile served as a beacon to law enforcement members and especially the IRS who devastated the Wortman Gang. Wortman hoodlums who had not been influenced by the Egan Rats and Dinty Colbeck remained more elusive to prosecution. Instability plagued the Wortman Gang, as it was a huge assortment of poorly organized thugs, much like the Egan Rats. It was hard to control and internal rivalries split it apart.

THE KEFAUVER COMMITTEE

By Lonnie Tettaton

According to Pat Huck, of south St. Louis, the letters KGPC were the 1940s call letters on their AM band broadcasts for St. Louis police calls. She says the letters stood for "Keep Going, Police Coming." Pat, who now lives in **Troy,** Illinois, said there was so little crime back then you would go for long spells before you heard anything interesting.

The Kefauver Senate Committee came to St. Louis in late February of 1951, one of 14 cities they eventually visited. The hearings in St. Louis were held downtown in the Federal Building. Their purpose was to investigate organized crime and its negative influence on the business community and politics. Some citizens thought that tall and bespectacled Kefauver was performing a valuable public service, while others thought he was simply posturing for a national television audience for political gain.

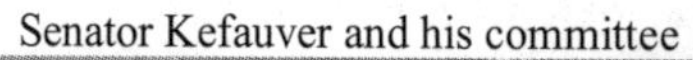
Senator Kefauver and his committee

Many officials and mobsters who were called to testify came down with bad cases of "Kefauveritis" – a strange kind of temporary amnesia. Mobsters, counseled by their attorneys, stood for hours in front of a mirror practicing their mantra: "Yer Honor, I hereby invoke my Fifth Amendment rights and decline to answer that particular question."

Colonel **William Holzhausen**, Chairman of the St. Louis Board of Police Commissioners, was one of the first called to the stand. What did the committee want to know in reference to gangsters by the name of Binaggio and Gargotta from Kansas City?

American Mafia.com asserts that the Committee wanted to know what attempts, if any, were made by the Kansas City mob to influence St. Louis authorities by payoffs. The answer was negative. Holzhausen confirmed that organized gambling, facilitated by race wire services (through Western Union and Southwestern Bell) was a big law enforcement problem. Pioneer News, located in the Fullerton Building at 11 N. Jefferson, was the race track gambling news service in St. Louis that the committee was concerned about. **Paul "Bev." Brown** and **Clarence "Gully" Owen** were the two St. Louisans who started the racing news service in St. Louis in 1927.

When the Missouri Attorney General told of his efforts in 1938 to cut off St. Louis-based Pioneer News, he said his efforts were thwarted by legal action. East St. Louis businessman Frank "Buster" Wortman gained control of Pioneer News and moved its location to **Fairmont City** near the race track in **Collinsville**. He later changed the name to Reliable News. It was firmly believed that Wortman had ties to the Chicago Syndicate. He was known to make several trips to Chicago a year. Notable St. Louis attorney Morris Shenker represented Pioneer News and Reliable News in legal matters.

According to Mr. Taylor, the Attorney General of Missouri, Simon Partnoy of Harmony Publishing Co. was the main bookmaker in the Kansas City area.

The Kefauver Committee surmised Western Union's reluctance to react was due, in part, to **William Molasky**, a well-known St. Louis gambler, being a major stockholder in the company. When service was finally cut off, around June of 1950, Pioneer News found other illegal means to supply racing results to local handbooks.

What follows next are excerpts from a fictionalized, but fact-based, account of the St. Louis hearings that appeared in Bill Nunes' 2002 book, *Illinois Crime.*

On returning to the courtroom, Brad and Harry spotted **St. Louis Mayor Darst** and **Paul Simon**, crusading editor of the *Troy Tribune*. Simon was sporting his trademark bow tie. The courtroom grew quiet as one of the committee members gaveled the afternoon session to order.

"The committee calls **James J. Carroll** to the stand."

Carroll and his lawyer made their way from the back of the room to the small table in front of the committee. A dark shirt and a light gray tie made Carroll look like a caricature of the hoodlum species. Carroll was the top banana among the bookies. He was known as the area betting commissioner—a bookie's bookie. He had flown to Lambert Field in St. Louis from Miami. He cupped his hand over his eyes, trying to peer through the bright glare of television lights. Then he flailed his arms and hands at the cameras, like a movie director signaling a technician to douse the lights.

"Mr. Carroll, the committee would like to ask you a few questions regarding gambling operations in St. Louis and East St. Louis."

"I ain't gonna tell this group nothin' unless those d—n lights an' cameras are turned off." Carroll reinforced his stereotype with a peculiar vernacular that resembled Pidgin English.

"Please watch your language, Mr. Carroll," the man in the horn-rimmed glasses warned.

"Those cameras are an invasion of my privacy. Unless they are turned off, I'm gonna follow the advice of my lawyer an' claim the Fifth Commandment, which says I don't have to testify if my rights are being violated."

Even Brad softly chuckled out loud at that one. The crowd, knowing any outburst would draw the ire of the chairman, tried unsuccessfully to control its amusement. Broad smiles led to audible laughs, which in turn evolved into raucous, hysterical laughter, echoing around the room. Several committee members placed their hands over their brows and stared down in a futile effort to conceal their mirth at the unintended malapropism.

The unflustered Chairman allowed some time to pass so everyone could regain their composure. Then wood met wood, three successive times. Meanwhile, Jimmy Carroll was hunched over in a conference with his St. Louis attorney, **Morris Shenker.**

"That is the Fifth Amendment, not the Fifth Commandment, Mr. Carroll," Kefauver said. The former is in the Constitution, and the latter in the Good Book."

"I know that, Your Honor, I misspoke," Carroll angrily answered.

The senator with the determined jaw decided to overlook Carroll's second gaffe of calling him "Your Honor."

"In any event, Mr. Carroll, we can't turn the cameras off because of the need for the viewing audience to be informed on this subject. The public interest supersedes your right to privacy."

"That's a lot of malarkey, an' you know it." Carroll once again conferred with his attorney.

"I'll bet he's explaining what supersede means," Brad said.

"I won't take that bet," Harry replied. "At least not in ***this*** courtroom."

"Well, even if you are a lawyer, I say you're wrong, an' if you don't turn them cameras off, I'm gonna walk outta here in about ten seconds. You can take the matter up with my attorney."

The crowd, stunned by Carroll's audacity, sat glued to their seats, and waited to see who would be wounded in the next verbal volley.

"Mr. Carroll, I warn you to think long and hard about your proposed course of action. It could incur dire consequences."

"I'm outta here." Carroll stood up, the vein on his right temple puffed out and appeared to be ready to burst. He shook his fist at the committee and began using his hands to punctuate sentences. "If you think the whole country is gonna see me perform like a trained monkey, you've got another think comin'. An' you can take those ***dear*** consequences you were threatening me with an' stick 'em. . . well, you know what you can do with 'em."

A collective gasp of disbelief escaped from the onlookers' lungs as Carroll slammed his fist on the table, turned around, and stormed out of the room.

"That is the most surprising turn of events I have ever witnessed in a courtroom," Harry said.

"Not bad for free entertainment," Brad said.

Morris Shenker, of course, was the mob's lawyer who also doubled as an attorney for labor leader, **Jimmy Hoffa**.

Frank "Buster" Wortman"
(Mercantile Library St. Louis)

THE "BUSTER" WORTMAN ERA

(Compiled from area newspapers, articles by Paul Simon, *Brothers Notorious*, by Taylor Pensoneau, and *St. Louis Gangsters* by John Auble)

Funeral services will be held Wednesday, August 5, 1968, for Frank Wortman, 63, rackets boss who outlived eras of prohibition, gang war and post-World War II gangland power struggles. Wortman died at **Alexian Brothers** Hospital, St. Louis, after surgery Thursday for a lesion on the larynx. He also had suffered from liver and heart ailments.

Wortman's internship in gangland was during the prohibition period that brought Al Capone to his peak of power. After 1946 he was referred to as the representative of the Capone gang (now led by Accardo-Guzik-Fischetti) for the area between **Springfield**, Illinois, and **Jefferson City,** Missouri, with his main activities in the East St. Louis area.

Wortman was **born in St. Louis** of Irish and German parentage on December 4, 1904, the year the **Worlds Fair** was held in St. Louis. When his parents separated, he was reared in the McKinley Bridge area of North St. Louis by grandparents. Later, he moved to **East St. Louis** with his father, Edward Wortmann, who lived at 1835 St. Louis Ave. where he originally worked as a molder for a steel casting plant. Ed Wortmann, who later moved to 724 Pershing Dr., first came to East St. Louis in 1899. His father, John Worthmann, was a proofreader on the *St. Louis Globe-Democrat.* He was killed by a streetcar in 1894.

Edward became an East St. Louis fire captain at Engine House # 3 and was active in the politics of his time. He died in 1954 and was survived by his wife, Inez Foster Wortmann and three sons, Frank, John and Ted. There was also a stepson, Foster Courtney, and a stepdaughter, Juanita Houseman, of San Fernando, Calif. The father dropped the "h" from the family name and the younger grandsons dropped the extra "n" from the end of their name.

Police mug shot of "Buster" Wortman

As a youth, Frank Wortman is supposed to have held various jobs involving hard labor and little pay. However, by the middle 1920s he had become a hanger-on with the old Shelton gang. By the time he was twenty-one, he was running errands for the crew and learning the ropes.

Wortman's schooling ended when he finished the eighth grade. Those who knew him in the early years considered him above average in intelligence and shrewd in making his way to the top. That, coupled with his willingness to do the lesser jobs when needed and a two-fisted toughness, enabled Wortman to climb to a position of more importance with the Sheltons, a gang that terrorized Southern Illinois during the 1920s and early 1930s.

Wortman's first arrest is not noted, but it was thought to be when he was about 22 years old. During the years he was to be arrested between 35 and 40 times (mostly when he was in his twenties) - 20 times as a robbery suspect, twice for carrying concealed weapons, once for auto theft, and again for transporting bootleg liquor, and several simply for investigation.

His time in a federal prison resulted from an assault on a federal officer when he was guarding a still, and his most contentious trouble with the law grew from another assault on a federal agent who was checking records at the Paddock tavern.

In 1933, Wortman, a Shelton employee, made the first of his two most serious mistakes. The Sheltons and other gangs hijacked their liquor, bought the quality stuff from sources in Canada and made the inferior spirits in their own stills. In any case trucks moved the liquor from sources of supply to the market and drivers of such trucks received high salaries.

Wortman at the mike conferring with Shenker
(Lamont Irons of **Cahokia** ink drawing)

Whether Wortman was picking up a delivery at a still **near Collinsville** one day in 1933 or was in charge of production was never clear. However, federal agents raided the still, and Wortman resisted. A federal agent was injured in the ensuing fight and Wortman was charged with the assault.

Wortman was sentenced to ten years, and he served seven at Fort Leavenworth Penitentiary. Wortman was released in 1941, just before World War II. He was amazed to discover that Sheriff Jerome Munie had run the Sheltons out of town and it was there for the picking. He returned to find the old style gangs and their warfare diminishing as leaders of lawlessness took on a veneer of quieter activity and increasingly were known not as gangland lords but as rackets bosses. The way Buster saw it, he simply was running a business and defending his territory.

Wortman worked for a time as a steamfitter. That experience and associations with former gang figures, who became prominent in some union ranks, gave him clout with labor. Old-timers who had no other work haven and young men who had connections were known to be admitted to the ranks of some construction unions through the influence of Wortman.

While Wortman was in prison, gang wars and the legalization of liquor had cut down the ranks of the Sheltons. The slot machines had always been a big money maker for gangland elements. During the 1940s two other types of coin-operated machines became more and more lucrative. They were the juke box and the pinball machines. Underworld members with their slot machine distribution systems and choice spots for such machines had the edge over legitimate operators of coin-machine businesses.

There was, however, no really powerful figure at the head of the machines' distribution. Wortman formed an uneasy alliance with the crumbling **Egan Rats** gang and won over several Sheltons. They used their muscle to take over the **Hyde Park Club in Venice,** which would eventually gross as much as $8 million annually. Then they strong-armed the racing wire service from **Bev Brown** and **Gully Owen**. Wortman quickly extended his territory as far south as **Cairo, Illinois,** and as far north as **Peoria**. When dynamite was found at the **Spur Inn**, high rollers in **Pulaski** and **Alexander Counties** knew that things had changed.

There had been speculations, which never materialized, that younger men returning from the war, would be taking over leadership of the rackets. By the time they returned, Wortman's **Plaza Amusement** Co. had a tight hold on machine distribution. In the middle 1940s, there was no single gang figure more important than another. Most of the old boys still alive had faded into the background. While most underworld activities in the area could be attributed to Wortman or his henchmen, it soon became the thing to attribute almost anything to him. Wortman quickly gained a near monopoly on gambling, slot machines, pinball machines, horse parlors, crap games and card games. At various times, Wortman and his associates owned or controlled taverns, Reliable News (a racing news service), handbook or policy operations, race horses, real estate companies, nightclubs and a trucking line. Numbers runners went virtually unmolested, thanks to police who supplemented their salaries with payoffs, and city officials who looked the other way in return for campaign contributions.

Then, too, the younger element seemed hard put to work peacefully among themselves. For one reason or another, the 1950s saw a number of murders, woundings and mysterious disappearances of the younger hoodlum element, who were hangers-on to the Wortman crowd, or wanted to be known as such. By the late 1940s, almost any illegal activity of a major nature was attributed to the Wortman gang, an organization that never did really emerge in the gory colorfulness of the prohibition era but, rather, took on a more subdued, backroom, big business cloak of attempted respectability. Wortman liked to work things out peaceably whenever he could.

Rare photo of Buster Wortman (SIUE)

At Wortman's side, as he started his post-war rise, was his brother **Edward "Ted" Wortman**. Usually farther in the background, Ted was reported as a calming influence on his elder brother until more recent years. Wortman also worked closely with **Elmer "Dutch" Dowling** and **Louis "Red" Smith**.

It was said that the Wortman influence was felt in all segments of the underworld. He angered quickly if there was a hint he had any connection with narcotics, prostitution or kidnapping. Those who knew him well, including law officers, said those were three fields he never entered. It was believed that post-war younger hoodlums' activities in prostitution led to conflict with Buster.

Along with their underworld activities, the Wortman brothers became involved in a number of legitimate businesses, a trucking firm, taverns and others. **Sam Magin**, a **Collinsville** resident, managed the Paddock in the 1950s. Ted Wortman also managed the rather unpretentious tavern for a while. In 1948, the bar was turned into a night club/ restaurant. The tavern name came from the paddocks of the horse race tracks. The Wortmans had special box seats at both area tracks and vested interests in race horses.

Bugsy Siegel – the man who built Las Vegas and was gunned down by the Mob in Virginia Hill's house

There were several East Side establishments popular with the St. Louis crowd. Bush's Steak House on West Broadway – near the Eads Bridge – was one. Another was former Cardinal center fielder **Terry Moore's Playdium** on Collinsville Avenue. The third was the Terrace Lounge on Collinsville Avenue. Finally, there was Wortman's Paddock Lounge on 6th Street.

These places were frequented by St. Louisans because of blue laws that forbade St. Louis restaurants to serve alcohol on Sundays. The other reason is that St. Louis closed night clubs at 1 a.m. and rolled up the sidewalks. East Side establishments did not close until 5 a.m.

It was reported that old timers, once high in the rackets, always stopped at the Paddock when in the area. When needed, they received orientation and often a financial assist. As Wortman's name became synonymous with big crime, efforts were increasingly made to pinpoint his activities. He avoided most attempts by grand juries and by the famous **Kefauver Crime Committee** to subpoena him. The latter did, however, delve into some of his holdings.

With the years, Wortman's temper grew worse. Time and again, incidents were reported at the Paddock. The clientele outside of the rackets began to drop off and with it the prestige of the night club. Wortman might not have been considering what resulted from that 1933 still raid when, in 1956, an Internal Revenue agent went to the Paddock. The agent was checking to determine if the tavern was paying a cabaret tax. Buster was there and angrily called him a "stool pigeon." Before the smoke cleared, he had cursed the agent and slugged him. The incident led the Internal Revenue Service into six years of investigation of Wortman's finances at a cost reputed, at one time, to run into millions of dollars.

In 1962, Wortman and two associates, **Elmer "Dutch" Dowling** (Wortman's chief lieutenant) and **Gregory "Red" Moore**, were convicted in the United States District Court in East St. Louis of conspiracy to evade federal income taxes. The jury could reach no verdict on Ted Wortman, who was charged with conspiracy. Before sentence would be passed, Dowling and his bodyguard **Melvin J. Beckman** were shot to death. Their bodies were found near **Belleville**. The murders were never solved, but a 1968 article by *Post* reporter **Ted Link** speculated that Wortman later avenged Dowling's death. It was believed that there was an argument over $20,000 that **Virgil Summers** was supposed to use to bribe the jury. When convictions were handed down, Wortman and his associates believed that Summers had pocketed the money. Speculation holds that Dowling and Beckman's deaths were due to arguments about the money.

"Doc" Summers was killed by three blasts from a shotgun in front of his apartment at

707 Pennsylvania Ave. in East St. Louis. Summers had been a member of the old Shelton Gang. After Summers' death, Wortman reportedly took a vacation on Mackinac Island in Michigan.

A napkin was found in Dowling's pocket. It contained scrawled notes concerning discussions the jury had behind closed doors. This touched off an investigation of alleged jury tampering in the tax case. It came to no conclusive end.

Later in the year, Wortman and Moore were sentenced to five years in prison and each fined $10,000. Both convictions were overturned two years later with an appeals court holding that immaterial, incompetent and prejudicial evidence had been admitted wrongfully into the trial by Judge William Juergens. New trials were ordered and Wortman was acquitted.

One of the longest stretches Wortman spent in jail was in 1954. His refusal to tell a federal grand jury his address resulted in forty-one days in jail for contempt of court. He was released when he finally answered the question.

A 1956 **Carl Baldwin** story in the *Post-Dispatch* announced that newly elected State's Attorney, **Dick Mudge Jr**. of **Edwardsville**, elected on a reform-minded anti-gambling platform, had chased Wortman's operations out of Madison County. Wortman suffered another blow in 1957 when federal agents smashed his numbers empire in St. Clair County.

Wortman's nemesis in East St. Louis was a tough cop named Robert "Tree" Sweeney. Sweeney had a reputation for he had **killed twelve men in the line of duty**. He once spotted **Bugsy Siegel** in a bar. Siegel was in town trying to get mob money to finance the beginning of that gambler's paradise known as Las Vegas. Siegel was later gunned down in Virginia Hill's Beverly Hills home in 1947 because he was thought to be skimming profits.

When Sweeney spotted Siegel, he walked over to him and grabbed him by the lapels on his suit. "You've got five minutes to get back to St. Louis and get outta my town, you punk," Sweeney hissed. Sweeney took early retirement in 1965 when city officials told him to go easy on local hoodlums.

As Wortman's influence began to wane, there were some elements in the city who decided it was time to contest him for a piece of the action. In the early-to-mid 1960s there was an incident where someone tossed a hand grenade into **McCoy's Tavern** on 13th and State. The device rolled under a bowling machine which bore the brunt of the blast. Four or five people were taken to the hospital with shrapnel in their legs, but nobody was killed. Witnesses at the scene said that the grenade had been thrown by a couple of black men. About four or five days later, the mob paid a surprise visit to a meeting of the **Warlords**, a leading black gang. According to sources, one of Wortman's top henchmen was there, accompanied by a couple of lieutenants from a faction of the **St. Louis Mafia**. They were armed with machine guns and reportedly lined the whole gang up against a wall and threatened to gun them down, in a manner similar to the St. Valentine's Day Massacre in Chicago. They were told that they had crossed the line between competing areas of interest, and that if they did it again, they'd be "swimming to Cairo wearing a pair of cement shoes." The Warlords decided that discretion was the better part of valor and bided their time before making another move.

For a number of years Wortman had lived on the bluffs along Route 157 in a brick ranch-style home at 2 Summit Drive in the Morris Hills Subdivision in west Collinsville, not far from brother Ted's house on Route 157. Because several other Wortman associates lived nearby the area was tabbed "**Hoodlum Haven**" by a local newspaper. After his first wife divorced him, he began living in the Broadview Hotel on East Broadway until he married his second wife, Sylvia.

St. Louisan Morris Shenker, representing Jimmy Hoffa

He built a fortress **moat house** southeast of Collinsville. Wortman's steamfitter buddies installed an elaborate piping system in the moat-surrounded house, which featured an elaborate steam bath room and steel plate on the roof to protect from aerial attacks. At the time of his death, the hospital listed his address at the Paddock.

In 1965, Wortman was taken to an East St. Louis hospital with a gunshot wound of the buttock. He said he accidentally shot himself, but versions of the shooting varied. One account said that Harry Kelly, owner of the Gypsy Inn, on Route 3, shot Buster. Others said that Buster was shot by his wife when she saw him eyeing another woman.

Wortman had four children by his first wife. His second wife filed for separate maintenance in 1963. Legal battles and the loss of coin machine territories, along with several other reverses, diminished Wortman financially in his later years.

Wortman was occasionally represented in court proceedings by **Morris Shenker**, a St. Louis attorney who worked out of offices in **St. Louis** and the **Dunes Hotel** in Las Vegas. Shenker was a Russian Jew who fled the pogroms in the Ukraine at the age of 13 and migrated to this country. With a Jesuit education at **St. Louis University** and a law degree from **Washington University**, it was said that he was a mouthpiece for the mob, and that he kept more hoodlums out of the slammer than any other attorney in the area. Some speculated that representing people from all walks of life became his obsession, and that it was due to his personal experiences of persecution and oppression from the days of his youth. Because of his Mob connections, he was heavily investigated by the FBI and was once indicted by a Federal Grand Jury in Las Vegas, having been suspected of concealing funds from the IRS. **U.S. Senator Ed Dowd** once called Shenker "the most investigated man in the country." **Thomas Guilfoil**, a noted St. Louis attorney, once estimated that the Justice Department spent $50 million dollars trying to pin something on Shenker. Shenker would die of cancer in 1989 at the age of 82. Authorities discovered that he left behind a staggering debt of about $55 million and some 71,000 case files, enough to fill nine garages.

Shenker was married to **Lillian Koplar Shenker**, also a lawyer, whose father, Sam Koplar, was the founder of the **Chase Park Plaza** and **Forest Park hotels**. Both Shenker and his wife were noted civic leaders and were heavily involved in fund raisers for the Democratic Party and charitable organizations. Shenker's most notable work was his efforts on behalf of the **Dismas House**, a half-way house facility for convicts just released from prison. Shenker worked with St. Louis teamster boss **Harold Gibbons** to bring **Frank Sinatra** and his "Rat Pack" buddies (**Dean Martin, Joey Bishop and Sammy Davis Jr**.) to do a fund-raiser at the **Kiel Opera House** on Market Street in the 1960s.

Wortman died at age 63 in 1968. Present at his funeral was Edward J. Hare, sometimes known as **"Baldy" O'Hare,** also known as "Hairless O'Hare." O'Hare had been Wortman's friend through most of their lives, serving as Wortman's chief lieutenant and was constantly at his side during Wortman's post-World War II rise to power. Hare was known to be tough and never hesitated to prove it. He was to go from a Wortman night club manager to operating a popcorn machine as fortunes of his boss dropped.

There were flowers, flowers and more flowers at Buster's funeral. They banked his casket, surrounded it, filling two rooms and a hallway. The night before, about two truckloads of flowers had to be turned away, and that many more again on the day of the funeral. Those not accepted went to nursing homes and other institutions. A traffic jam was created the day of the funeral due to the large crowd in front of Kassly's funeral home on Vandalia in Collinsville. The lot on the side and in back was jammed with cars. Others had to be parked in the surrounding residential area. Wortman counted friends not only in the underworld but in the sporting world and the world of entertainers, night club operators, bartenders, waitresses and cab drivers.

Truth is sometimes stranger than fiction. Frank Wortman and Robert Sweeney, mortal enemies in life, are buried next to each other in plots at Mount Carmel Cemetery in West **Belleville**.

Buster was a colorful character and those who knew him have interesting stories to tell. It is a little known fact that Wortman did not pay cash for his new cars. According to **Harry Cruncleton,** of First National Bank in East St. Louis and later president of Westpointe Bank in Belleville, Buster got loans for all his cars. After the papers were signed, some of the bank officials were talking about it. They wondered who would be the person to go knocking on Buster's door if he missed a payment or defaulted. According to Harry, Buster never missed a payment.

Buster Wortman also had an interesting way of dealing with competition. Harry Cruncleton says that in the bank's basement there were vending machines that were used by

Rathskeller in Wortman's moat home (photo by Harry Fiebig)

employees. One day somebody he knew came in and told him that he was just starting his own vending machine company. He asked if it was okay to place his machines in the basement of the bank. Harry said that as far as he knew, that would be okay. The man delivered his machines and placed them along a wall opposite the machines that were already there. He and his men turned those machines around so they faced the wall. The next day, one of the custodians told Harry that he needed to come downstairs to see something. When Harry went downstairs he saw that the new machines were full of bullet holes and the old machines had been turned around.

Adam Wondoloski of Belleville, who worked in Buster's juke box business, had this to say.

"I used to work for Buster and Ted Wortman (from about 1948-1970) servicing pinball and juke box machines. Buster ran Plaza Amusement Company, which was located at 1818 **Washington Avenue in St. Louis**. Buster was part owner along with brother Ted, **Red Smith** and **Elmer "Dutch" Dowling**. They bought it from **Abbie Lauman**, whose father was an East St. Louis police commissioner. Plaza Amusement headquarters were later moved to **Fairmont City** in Illinois.

"Buster could be kind and generous, and he was usually a soft touch for anyone who came to him with a down-on-his-luck story and needed money for his kids. He also donated money to numerous local charities. Guys who sponsored youth organizations sometimes brought the kids to the Paddock for burgers and sodas, and Buster always said there was no tab for this. At his moat house in Collinsville, he had a bar on the first floor and another on the second floor. His kids weren't allowed to use the one upstairs because that's where he kept his liquor. The one downstairs was available to his kids and their friends and was stocked with soda and snacks.

"One day the nuns at **Holy Rosary School,** in Fairmont City, called Buster and asked for a pinball machine for the kids to use. He sent one over, free of course. When it needed fixing, they would call and ask me to come over. 'By the way,' they always said, 'tell Mr. Wortman we are praying for him.' Buster would send me over and tell me not to charge them anything. 'Tell them to quit praying for me,' he said. 'Every time they pray for me, it costs me money.' "

JIMMY MICHAELS SR.

By Lonnie Tettaton

Jimmy Michaels started his career back in the 1920s when he was known as "Horseshoe Jimmy" and belonged to the Cuckoo Gang. He rose to become the godfather of the St. Louis Syrian community. At the tender age of 19 he was arrested for robbing the Illinois Central freight yards on the **East St. Louis** riverfront. He posted bail and then skipped out, but about a year later he was recaptured, convicted and sent to prison for 13 years. He was finally paroled in 1944.

Jimmy Michaels

Michaels quickly went into the gambling business and in 1959 he was arrested again, this time for operating a gambling joint on Hampton Avenue. Michaels was also owner of the **Trade Winds Lounge** over on Chouteau, directly across the street from the Clinton-Peabody housing projects. Not far from there was the **Merry Widow Theater**.

Historian Rick Porrello says that Michaels secured a Missouri insurance broker's license in 1959, but then it was taken away due to his felony conviction. In 1963, Michaels and Tony Giordano were arrested and charged with disorderly conduct in a hotel room where Michaels had registered under the name Frank Wortman. These charges were eventually dismissed. It is believed that Michaels was being groomed to take over Wortman's empire.

In the late 1970s and early 1980s, there was a vicious struggle to gain control of the Laborer's Local #42 in St. Louis. The bloody struggle dated back to 1965 when Louis Shoulders Jr., George "Stormy" Harvill and William "Shotgun" Sanders gained control of the local. **In 1966, Harvill was gunned down, and in 1973 Shoulders was blown to pieces in a car bombing**. Jimmy Michaels now backed **John P. Spica** to take control of the leadership position. Spica had served 10 years in the Missouri State Penitentiary for murdering a real estate agent. Spica was opposed by **Ray H. Flynn** who sought permission from **Joey Aiuppa** and the Chicago Outfit to support him in this struggle. Chicagoans reassured Spica that the St. Louis Family would not oppose the move so long as nothing happened to Jimmy Michaels. In November of 1979, Spica was found murdered by a car bomb at his Richmond Heights home. Meanwhile, Tony Giordano died of cancer in August of 1980.

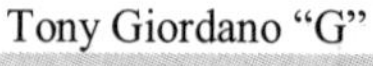

Tony Giordano "G"

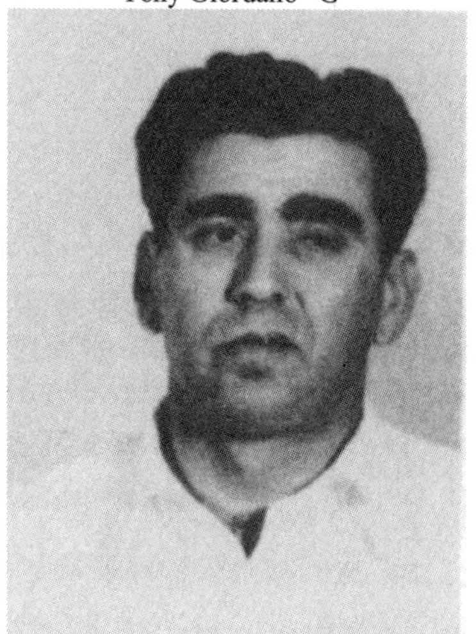

Flynn lured away Anthony and Paul Leisure (members of Michaels' Syrian faction) by offering them good paying jobs within the union. Shortly after Giordano's demise, **David Leisure planted a bomb** under the seat of Michaels' black Chrysler Cordoba. Shortly after Michaels left St. Raymond's Maronite Church, the remote controlled bomb was detonated. The blast, on Interstate 55 near Reavis Barracks Road, raised the car three feet off the highway and tore off Michaels' legs. The force of the explosion hurled part of Michaels torso against a passing car. Michaels was the last of the old Cuckoo gang.

Police authorities believed that with the death of Giordano and Michaels, John Vitale became acting boss of the St. Louis Family.

TONY GIORDANO

By Lonnie Tettaton

Anthony Giordano was a native St. Louisan, born June 2, 1914. His police record began in 1938 and never seemed to stop as he accumulated over fifty arrests in his lifetime. Among the charges were carrying a concealed weapon, armed robbery, holdups, tax evasion and counterfeiting tax stamps. Giordano's mentor for his rise to the top was Tony Lopiparo.

In 1942, Giordano was sentenced to five years for holding up a Hollywood insurance office.

In 1950, Giordano was a drug courier for the St. Louis mob. He made various trips to Italy for this purpose.

Giordano liked to dress up and he rarely was seen without his expensive pearl-gray hat, tailored suit, Italian shoes and diamond rings. In the 1960s, he decided that this ostentatious apparel was dangerous so he changed his wardrobe to look a bit more blue-collar. During this time, he and his wife lived in a rather conservative home in southwest St. Louis.

In 1956, Giordano and a couple of others were given four year prison sentences on tax evasion charges connected with their vending machine business. By 1963, the loud, hot-tempered, and boisterous Giordano was head of the St. Louis mob.

In 1964, Giordano's left eye became diseased. It had to be removed and replaced with a glass (actually porcelain) eye.

In May of 1965, a government agent walked into Giordano's **Marie's Restaurant on 2622 North Broadway**. When confronted at the counter, Giordano flew into a rage and asked the man if he had a warrant. He shook his fist and threatened to "break the agent's head." Giordano was calmed by his nephew, William Trupiano, and an employee named Sal Lopiparo.

He had ties with Metropolitan Towing Company, which contracted with St. Louis police to remove vehicles from crash sites. A warrant was issued for his arrest in 1970 after he threatened a priest from St. Teresa of Avila who came with a couple of other men to retrieve a church van that had been stolen. Giordano allegedly grabbed the priest by his shirt and screamed, "I'm Catholic too. You run your church and I'll take care of my business." He threatened to blow the man's head off with a sawed-off shotgun.

In January of 1971, the *Globe-Democrat* reported on a study by a Missouri task force on organized crime. They identified three groups controlling St. Louis crime. First was the group headed by Giordano and John Vitale, with strong ties to the Detroit syndicate. Second was the group headed by the aging Jimmy Michaels. The last group was identified as remnants of the late Buster Wortman's East Side gang.

The report said that the Giordano faction depended heavily on gambling for income and that they had infiltrated legitimate businesses such as Banana Distributing and Metropolitan Towing. The task force accused Giordano of using these fronts to launder illegal income and to provide an outlet for stolen auto parts.

John Vitale

What seemed to upset the task force the most was that mobsters were into labor racketeering with about 30 of their associates working as business agents for local unions.

Giordano was indicted in the mid-1970s after he tried to elbow his way into hidden ownership in the Frontier Casino in Las Vegas. A couple of Detroit mobsters were convicted with him and all three served almost two years in prison from 1975 to 1977.

By 1980, Giordano was in ill health and there was much speculation about who would replace him. Giordano, who was survived by a wife and adopted son, died from cancer in August of 1980.

JOHN VITALE

By Lonnie Tettaton

After Giordano's death, John Vitale assumed leadership as the Mafia chieftain in St. Louis. This was actually his second go at running thugdom in St. Louis.

Johnny V. was born in 1909 and was one of eight immigrant Italian children in the family. In school he loved athletics and excelled at soccer and baseball. During the 1930s, he worked as an usher at the **Ambassador Theater** in downtown St. Louis, earning three dollars a week. He loved to brag about the fact that while working there, he met actress **Ginger Rogers**. They struck up a friendship of sorts and he tried to impress her with his expensive clothes and stories about his amateur baseball days with the Mound City Brews.

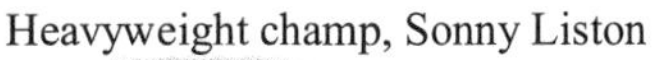
Heavyweight champ, Sonny Liston

In 1934, Vitale was arrested in connection with the death of a young man named Mike Palazzolo. His lifeless form was found on **Florissant Avenue at Chambers Road**. The whole thing stemmed from a quarrel after Palazzolo's girl friend was slapped by a certain **Walter Mushenick** in a tavern at 19th and Cass. Palazzolo confronted Mushenick and when he arrived back at his house, Vitale was there waiting for him. The two left together with Vitale being the last person to see him alive. A murder warrant was issued against Vitale but a grand jury issued a "No True" bill and failed to indict.

Over the years Vitale managed to stay out of prison most of the time. One exception was in the early 1940s when he spent two years at Leavenworth for violating federal narcotics laws.

In 1952, a 39-year-old trucking company operator named **John Randazzo** was given a vicious beating (broken jaw) outside of **Genovese's Steak House** at 8th and Lucas. Vitale was present, but so were four policemen including Barney Mundt and detective John Doherty, who went on to have a distinguished police career.

Vitale claimed it was John Doherty who beat up Randazzo. Vitale was quoted as saying. "I have no love for Doherty, but I tried to hush it up because we wanted to avoid trouble since we had people in the place after the 1:30 a. m. closing." Vitale allegedly told Doherty that he had nothing to worry about. Vitale said he would make sure the bloody victim received medical attention and he would also see to it that matters would be squared with Randazzo.

When the matter was brought before a grand jury, Vitale refused to sign a waiver of immunity that would have allowed him to testify without fear of prosecution. Vitale shrewdly knew that "you don't have to explain silence."

Doherty and Mundt probably had no business going to the steak house. Inside were such shady characters as Gregory Moore, former part owner of the Hyde Park gambling casino, David Creely and Rolla "Blackie" Dean (both ex-cons) , former Eagan Rat **Louis "Red" Smith** and a former police sergeant. This was another instance where the long arm of the law fell just short of nabbing Vitale.

In 1958, Vitale was dragged before the McClellan Congressional Committee which was investigating organized crime. **Bobby Kennedy** had a keen interest in this and questioned Vitale on the witness stand. The quiet and introspective Vitale was reluctant to give the Committee anything of substance. An exasperated McClellan told him, "You will help us a little, I believe . . . if you take that gum out of your mouth." **Victor Riesel**, the investigative journalist who was later blinded by acid for asking too many pointed questions, had this to say. "Vitale was a valuable witness." "It," Vitale mumbled slowly, "is not gum. It's peppermint." When Bobby bluntly asked Vitale if he had any men on his payroll where murder was necessary from time to time, Vitale quickly invoked his Fifth Amendment rights to remain mum.

Another time (1959) Vitale received nine months in the City Workhouse. He pleaded guilty to assault after an argument over a parking space. In 1981, he was arrested, but not charged, after an incident at Lambert Field. He was coming home from a trip to Las Vegas where it is believed he was receiving kickbacks for arranging gambling junkets. The **police found him with $30,000 in his pockets**.

In 1971, Vitale was believed to have been connected to the murder of Primo Caudera. Caudera was involved with the Las Vegas junket gambling trip business. He went to authorities and complained that Vitale, Giordano and Paul Leisure were shaking him down for part of the money involved in this business. Not long after that **Caudera was found shot to death** in the trunk of his Cadillac at 3100 South Broadway. The feds never solved the case.

A federal grand jury began looking into the gambling scene and possible mob ties to four Las Vegas casinos – the Dunes, the Riviera, the Stardust and Caesar's Palace. They discovered that two prominent St. Louisans had vested interests in the Dunes through M & R Investment Company. One was attorney **Morris Shenker** and the other was **James Nangle**, the son of a prominent Circuit judge with the same name. Shenker, who was chairman of **Mayor A.J. Cervantes'** Crime Committee, also represented Vitale from time to time. Nangle, who shared an office with Shenker at 408 Olive Street, was an attorney for the Steamfitter's Union.

Cervantes was embarrassed by a 1967 *Life* magazine article titled "The Mayor and the Mob." The article alleged that Cervantes was involved in a two-faced fight against local crime. One of the mayor's associates, **Tony Sansone**, even married Jimmy Michaels' daughter, Mary Ann.

David Leisure

Vitale was also mixed up with the St. Louis boxer, **Sonny Liston**, who went on to become world champion. Liston first got into trouble with the law in 1949 after he robbed a store clerk in an Italian section of north St. Louis that was slowly turning black. Not long after, Liston robbed the **Wedge Service Station** at O'Fallon and North Broadway. He was given five years in the state penitentiary at Jeff City. It was in prison where Liston learned to box. Liston was paroled in late October of 1952 and rose to the top of the amateur ranks in just four months by winning the Golden Gloves heavyweight division. Frank W. Mitchell, owner of the ***St. Louis Argus,*** paid Liston's expenses in exchange for half of the purse. It turned out that Mitchell, a pillar of the black community, was a front man for Vitale's interests. Another thug in Liston's corner was mobster **Frank "Blinky" Palermo**. Liston was being controlled by the mob.

Liston was called to testify before another Kefauver Committee, this time investigating monopolies. Liston admitted knowing that a lot of bad actors were involved with his career, but protested that he had no choice if he wanted to go somewhere in the world of professional boxing. When Vitale refused to answer questions about underworld ties to St. Louis boxing, Kefauver threatened to draw up contempt charges.

Champion Floyd Patterson's handlers were reluctant to give Liston a title shot because of his mob ties. The fight was finally held in Chicago in 1962 and **Liston knocked out Patterson in one round**. Liston again knocked Patterson out in the first round in a 1963 rematch. In 1964, Liston faced contender Cassius Clay and surprised everyone in the seventh round when he declined to continue the fight, saying his shoulder was injured. In a rematch the following year, Clay (now Ali) knocked out Liston with the famous "**phantom punch**." Many came to the conclusion that both controversial fights had been fixed.

In January of 1971, Liston was found dead in his Las Vegas home by his wife. Although police ruled out foul play, many believe his mysterious death was a mob hit.

Chief of detectives John Doherty had little use for Sonny Liston and his kind. It was **Doherty who eventually received credit for getting the Mafia out of St. Louis**.

THE DAVID LEISURE EXECUTION

By Lonnie Tettaton

Back in 1977, Ray Massoud, business manager for Local 110 of the Laborers Union in St. Louis, promised Anthony Leisure that he would succeed him in that position. While in the hospital, terminally ill, Massoud changed his mind asked Anthony to accept the position of assistant business manager so that his son John could take over. Leisure reluctantly agreed to the change.

After Massoud's death, in June of that year, his son expanded his power by hiring Mike Trupiano as president of the union. Leisure was ticked off because he was supposed to be in charge of hiring and firing union officials. Anthony secretly met with his brother Paul and cousin David and discussed the possibility of killing Massoud. At that point they decided it was too risky because Massoud was connected with the Giordano family. They decided instead to **kill Jimmy Michaels Sr.** figuring it would strengthen their position in the union among the Syrian faction, headed by Michaels.

David Leisure and John Ramo stole a car similar to Michaels' and practiced planting a bomb. They began to carefully study Michaels' movements and habits. On September 17, 1980, they parked a van next to Michaels' car in the parking lot of **St. Raymond's Church** in St. Louis. With the van shielding their actions, they slid under the car and planted the bomb. They followed Michaels after he left the church, trying unsuccessfully on several occasions to get a garage door opener to detonate the bomb. Finally, after Michaels was on Interstate 55, the bomb detonated.

About a week later, Paul Leisure met with Vitale, the leader of the Italian faction. He agreed to Syrian control of Local 110. After an intensive investigation by authorities, David Leisure was arrested and charged with murder. His trial began on April 2, 1987. The jury found him guilty and recommended the death penalty. In April of 1988, the Missouri Supreme Court upheld the conviction. His lawyer argued that Leisure should not be put to death because of mental retardation. The appeal went to Governor Carnahan, but he denied a stay of execution. David Leisure was put to death on September 1, 1999, by lethal injection. Reverend **Larry Rice** held a candle light vigil outside the prison to protest the execution.

Leisure had married a girl that he knew since grade school. He fathered two children with his wife and one with a girl friend. He and his wife later divorced and he remarried while in prison.

Paul and Anthony Leisure, the purported leaders of the "Leisure gang," were convicted in separate trials and were sentenced to 50 years in prison without the possibility of parole.

In January of 1985, **Jimmy Michaels III** was convicted of conspiracy to commit capital murder by car bombing Paul Leisure, who lost a leg and a foot. He was sentenced to eight years for the act of revenge.

AMAZING FACT: Drehmann-Harral Funeral Home on Natural Bridge (later owned by the John Stygar family) became the funeral home of choice for many St. Louis mob figures.

GANGSTERS, STRIPPERS, AND GUN MOLLS

By Lonnie Tettaton

Evelyn West was born Amy Coomer in 1922 in Kentucky. She died in 2004 of natural causes in Florida. She started out during World War II posing for provocative 2.5 x 3.5 inch pictures that GIs could carry in their wallets. The buxom West was billed as the original "Hubba, Hubba Girl." Male Life, in 1957, ran a spread and named her (along with Lili St. Cyr, Candy Barr, and Bettie Page) one of the "Ten Best" undressed women in the USA. Evelyn even did a series of nude pictures in Miami for famed photographer, Bunny Yeager.

Evelyn West (Lonnie Tettaton)

Evelyn ran a strip club called the **Stardust** over on the DeBaliviere Strip, near Lindell. It was a few doors south of the fashionable **Terrace**, owned by one of the town's premier restaurateurs, Al Baker. Her place became a favorite hangout for St. Louis area gangsters. The one thing most people remember her for was her **$50,000 Treasure Chest**. It stemmed from an incident in Miami Beach where **Evelyn was arrested and booked for throwing a tomato** at blonde bombshell, Anita Eckberg, who was performing. Fearing retaliation, Evelyn had her breasts **insured by Lloyds of London for $50,000**. It proved to be a great advertising gimmick, even though few knew the insurance coverage was for only twenty minutes of one day.

There were other places in St. Louis that had strippers, including the Grand, the Windemere, the Top Hat, the Melanie Club and the Barrel. The World Theater, just a stone's throw from the bus station at Washington and Broadway, showed nudie "art films" such as *The Immoral Mr. Teas* and *Kipling's Women*.

Maureen the Spider Woman

Harry Wahl, one of the Grand's owners, had an interesting gimmick. Between acts little boxes of candy with taffy in them were sold. Members of the audience were told that one of the boxes had an expensive diamond ring in it. Occasionally someone in the audience would yell out that he had found a ring. He was either a plant or Harry's brother.

Another popular stripper in the area was **Maureen the Spider Woman**. There was a rope net in her act that looked like a spider's web. She was married to Fred "Skinny" Straub who provided comic relief between striptease acts. After he died she married to a local trumpet player named Tommy Battreal.

Maureen was 26 when she first started working as a waitress for T. J. Harvel, the gangster who ran the Windemere for Eddie Hotchecker. T. J was married to a stripper named Bonnie Bails. Ted Tillman, a local booking agent for a number of strippers, talked Maureen into making the easy money. She got her first big break working at a club called Becky's in **Cairo**, Illinois. **Buster Wortman**, of course, had most of what was going on in Southern Illinois.

In those days burlesque was big-time entertainment and was often financed with mob money. Maureen once worked at Jimmy's Gay Inn in **East St. Louis** with novice comic Jackie Vernon. She also worked the White Swan in **Granite City** with Billy "Zoot" Reed. Maureen made about $550 a week in the 1950s, which went a long way toward helping her raise her daughter.

Her husband at the time was Fred Stroud, a ventriloquist who also worked in burlesque houses. Fred was frequently seen at Buster Wortman's Paddock Lounge, in downtown **East St. Louis**, playing the piano. A number of St. Louis strippers like to go to Wortman's place after their performances in St. Louis. It was a good place to go to relax and unwind and Wortman's associates made sure they were not bothered by eager young men trying to hit on them.

When actor Don Murray was in St. Louis, making the film, *The Hoodlum Priest*, Maureen was offered a part in the movie. She turned it down because she didn't think it would do well at the box office. It turned out to be a blockbuster.

Maureen, age 76 and living in North St. Louis, was interviewed by **John Auble** for the 2001 book, *A History of St. Louis Gangsters*.

MOB LAWYER MORRIS SHENKER

Morris Shenker, whom Life Magazine once called "Lawyer to the Mob," died in 1989 while owing the IRS $55 million. During the 1960s, Shenker represented Jimmy Hoffa, was on a first name basis with Bobby Kennedy, and owned the Dunes Hotel in Las Vegas. Shenker, though not a member of the mob, represented many of them in court. He was also on a first name basis with Harry Truman, who in 1940 was often called the "Senator From Pendergast," a reference to his connection to the corrupt political machine in Kansas City. Shenker was very active in local Democratic politics.

Former *Post-Dispatch* writer Ronal Lawrence once reported that it was Shenker who took money from the Teamster's Union pension fund to help the mob penetrate Las Vegas. Shenker's influence extended far beyond the underworld, enabling him to get two federal indictments against him dismissed.

THE GREAT SOUTHWEST BANK HOLD-UP

By Lonnie Tettaton

St. Louis gained national notoriety in April of 1953 when a group of thugs from **Chicago** tried to rob Southwest Bank, located at Kingshighway and Southwest. A few days before, a sister of one of the robbers wrote cryptically with lipstick on an outside wall, "going to be rob . . ." The robbery was such a dramatic event that United Artists signed actor **Steve McQueen** to star in one of his early movies (1959), *The Great St. Louis Bank Robbery*. McQueen struck gold the next year when he starred with Yul Brynner in *The Magnificent Seven.*

At 10:15 a.m., on April 24, several armed gunmen walked into the bank and shouted, "This is a holdup." All the men had some kind of cloth hiding their lower face and they wore "Kroger hats," those flat, round hats with a small bill worn by all Kroger store employees.

Fortunately, as soon as the men walked in, they were spotted by tellers Betty Valenti and Blasé Mugavero who pressed their treadle foot alarms. The alarm went to Potter Electric Signal Company where employee Theodore Klix telephoned the police on a direct line. A police dispatcher put in a call to Corporal **Robert Heitz** and Patrolman **Melbourne Stein** who were only a few blocks away in their cruiser at Kingshighway and Shaw. The nearest police station was at Hampton and Chippewa, less than a dozen blocks away. The policemen arrived six minutes after the first alarm was sounded.

Current procedure would call for police to surround the place and begin hostage negotiations with the robbers. Back then they went in with guns blazing and when it was over, one gunman was dead (suicide) and another was killed by police bullets. Two others were wounded and a fifth managed to escape.

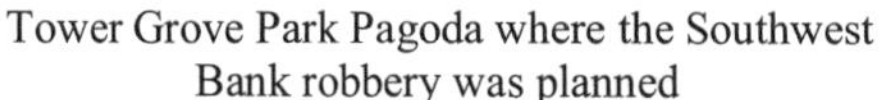
Tower Grove Park Pagoda where the Southwest Bank robbery was planned

When the bandits walked into the bank, they ordered everyone onto the floor and then began scooping up the cash and placing it in a cloth bag. The bank's directors were in an executive meeting, not far from the main lobby, at the time of the holdup. Executive Vice President **Carman Smith** heard the commotion and opened the door. When he saw what was going on, he quietly closed the door and bank president, **Dillon Ross**, phoned the switchboard operator in the basement (Marilyn Miller) and told her to phone the police.

It wasn't long until 100 police officers surrounded the building. Employees and customers hugged the floor as bullets flew overhead. Many of them fled to the basement when tear gas canisters were lobbed inside by the police.

Bandit leader John Frederick grabbed Eve Hamilton, stuck his shotgun in her back, and headed for the front door. "Don't shoot or I'll kill her," he shouted. **Officer Stein** ignored the warning and fired at Frederick, hitting him in the side, the bullet piercing his lung. Frederick threw Hamilton to the sidewalk, fracturing both of her wrists. As Frederick reached for a handgun in his waistband, Stein leaped on top of him and took the gun away. Stein played himself in the movie version of the robbery.

Southwest Bank

Frank Vito, the gunman with the moneybag, grabbed bank Vice President **Wilmer Lee** and used him as a shield in his attempt to escape. He fired at the police over the hostage's shoulder. After he reloaded his gun, he killed himself rather than allowing capture. Gunman William Scholl grabbed customer Gloria Cantino and tried to use her as a shield. It didn't work as he was gunned down by Heitz. Officer Heitz then passed out and was rushed to **City Hospital** on Lafayette. He had been wounded in the ear and neck, leaving him hearing impaired.

The fourth gunman inside, Fred Bowerman, was killed by police rounds. The driver, Glen Chernick, managed to escape and flee back to **Chicago**. Fortunately, authorities were able to write down his Illinois license plate number. He was arrested and brought back to St. Louis to stand trial where a jury found him guilty.

When police opened the money sack they discovered that the robbers had nearly made off with about $141,000 of loot.

The film version opens with the gangsters crossing the Veterans Bridge. It includes a great shot of the Eads Bridge and the *Admiral*. The gangsters plan their strategy in the gazebo in **Tower Grove Park**. The fact that five streets converged at the site, making a getaway easier, was one of the main reasons Southwest Bank was chosen. Actor Steve McQueen, the King of Cool, grew up on a small farm in **Fowler**, Missouri. McQueen is designated as the driver of the getaway car. He steals a license plate from a car in the **Southtown Famous and Barr** parking lot at Kingshighway and Chippewa. You get a glimpse of **Placke Chevrolet**, catty-cornered across the street from the lot. There are two other notable scenes. McQueen has a nostalgic flashback at Public School Stadium, where he was a high school halfback, and there is another scene at **Tom's Grill**.

City Hospital – where those injured in Southwest bank robbery were taken (Missouri Historical Society)

McQueen meets an ex-girl friend who suspects that he is up to no good. She writes a warning on the outside of the bank; *going to be robbed*. Her warning was largely ignored by bank officials.

Southwest Bank still sits proudly on its corner. The bank is recognized by economists as a national leader in helping to establish the prime interest rate.

TWO HANGED ILLINOIS MEN BURIED IN ST. LOUIS

There is a tombstone in St. Matthew Cemetery in St. Louis that bears the inscription, "THE VICTIM OF A MOB." The man buried there was named Robert Praeger, and he was hanged April 5, 1917. It happened in the southern Illinois burg of **Collinsville**, a mining town with a population of 4,000.

Robert Praeger was a German national who had come to America to find work and make a better life for himself. He hoped to find a wife, settle down and raise a family. He worked for a while as a baker in St. Louis, but then crossed the river and became a coal miner in Collinsville. He began attending socialist meetings and soon fell under the spell of that radical doctrine.

Unfortunately for Praeger, there were three forces working in America that made his political stance dangerous. One was the doctrine of nativism. Those who had already immigrated to America began to resent newcomers who brought with them unusual ideas, old world culture and strange languages. In response, the U.S. government passed laws severely restricting the flow of newcomers. Also, the national press, back then, was not sympathetic to unions, socialism, communism or anarchists. Violence was often associated with their unpopular causes, best exemplified by the Haymarket Square Chicago riot in 1886. Finally, America was at war with Germany and those with Teutonic heritage were already under a cloud of suspicion, especially Germans who were born in the old country. A similar thing happened to Japanese-Americans in World War II.

Robert Praeger began to speak out against the capitalist ruling class and espoused Marxist doctrine. Then he began criticizing the war, saying things that could be interpreted as being disloyal. Even the U.S. Supreme Court ruled that "things said in times of peace could not be said in times of war." Socialist leader Eugene Debs was jailed for his utterances during the war. Patriotism ran high in America back then, fueled by wartime slogans and popular songs.

Most likely, Praeger was not a disloyal citizen. He was simply speaking his mind. He had registered for the draft when in St. Louis and even tried to join the navy but was rejected because he was nearly blind in one eye. He even kept American flags in his room. As he went about making speeches and posting propaganda handbills, the ire of many in the community was aroused. After making one particularly damning speech, he was called a spy.

Things came to a head in a Collinsville saloon where inflammatory words about Praeger flowed as freely as the liquor. The word was that Praeger had attended a socialist meeting in **Maryville** (earlier that night) and had said some nasty things against President Wilson. As the men inside, mostly miners, became more sodden, Praeger's remarks of criticism were turned into words of treason. Around 9:00 p.m. the angry miners went outside and marched to Praeger's apartment at 208-A Vandalia Avenue, near the heart of the downtown. The mob broke inside, dragged him out, draped an American flag on him, and marched him down Main Street barefoot. The police arrived on the scene and took Praeger into protective custody.

Robert Praeger tombstone – Collinsville mob victim

Instead of the crowd of about 300 people going home, they remained and milled about, grumbling about what alternatives remained. The mayor of Collinsville, J.H. Siegel, arrived on the scene and implored the unruly mob to disperse. "We don't want a stigma marking Collinsville," said Mayor Siegel. He then ordered that all saloons be closed. But instead of returning to their homes, as the mayor had suggested, the mob remained nearby on the streets. Around 10:00 p.m. the mob began to regroup in front of the jail, shouting angry threats. The mayor tried another strategy that didn't work. He told the group that Praeger had been spirited away to safety in nearby **East St. Louis**. Joseph Riegel, a twenty-eight year old man who had just returned from the army, emerged as the crowd's leader. He demanded that Praeger be sent out to face vigilante justice. When officials refused, the mob forced its way into the jail and found Praeger squirreled away in the basement beneath a pile of tiling.

To their discredit, the police, only four in number, merely stood by and made no attempt to interfere. Praeger was carried down the street with the mass of humanity waving flags and cheering themselves hoarse. The policemen were placed under guard so they couldn't follow and try to interfere. On the outskirts of town the mob halted. They were at the intersection of Collinsville Road and Casey-ville Road, near Mauer Heights. For about twenty minutes they questioned and taunted Praeger. One man accused him of plotting to blow up the mine in Maryville. Praeger vehemently denied the accusation. Others questioned his loyalty. He said that he was a patriot. Finally, some in the crowd suggested that he be tarred and feathered and run out of town. A young lad of fifteen was sent for supplies, but he came back with a rope.

Bob Rea photo of the rope used to hang Charlie Birger

Praeger begged for mercy, but his plea fell on deaf ears. He was allowed to make a final request. He asked that his body be wrapped in the flag when he was buried. He was also given time to write a letter to his mother and to pray. Then the noose was placed over his head and the other end thrown over the branch of a sturdy elm tree. Dozens of people pulled on the rope and hoisted him up. But Praeger's hands were not bound and he managed to pull himself up and support his weight. He was lowered to the ground and his hands secured. Then he was pulled back up in the air. By the time he expired from strangulation it was near midnight. After the hanging, two men remained behind to guard the body and make sure it was not cut down before dawn. Anyone who approached was warned against removing it lest they meet the same fate that befell Praeger. A man from Herr Funeral Home cut the body down at 8:00 the next morning.

Building Birger's gallows (Bob Rea – of Benton, Illinois - collection)

Newspapers and politicians around the state quickly condemned the evil act. Governor Lowden said the act was repulsive and inhuman. Arrests quickly followed. Riegel confessed, even bragged, that he had been the one to tie Praeger's hands. A grand jury was called into session and they handed down indictments, with eleven men being brought to trial.

The sensational three week trial was held a month later. Riegel renounced his earlier confession and claimed that he tried to have a calming influence on the crowd. Naturally, the proceedings, covered by dozens of reporters, took on a circus-like atmosphere. The sympathetic jury took only forty-five minutes to come back with a verdict of *not guilty* on all counts. There was wild applauding and cheers from most everyone present. The first vote taken resulted in an 11-1 outcome in favor of acquittal. After more deliberation a second ballot was taken and the all-male jury reached its verdict. Governor Frank Lowden said the sad verdict was "a lamentable failure of justice." Two years later Wesley Beaver, one of the mob's main agitators, was so haunted by the incident that he committed suicide.

This was the first killing for "disloyalty" in United States history. Prior to this incident, men were merely tarred and feathered and run out of town.

Charlie Birger's heyday was the 1920's—a time of booming coal mining activity in southern Illinois and occasional economic relapse. Birger was one of those bigger than life characters who grabbed headlines in the downstate area while Al Capone was rubbing people out in Chicago. Bill Nunes' friend, Gary DeNeal, wrote *A Knight of Another Sort*, the definitive biography of Birger. In it, he tells about how **Birger grew up in north St. Louis** in the 22-hundred block of Biddle Street. Charlie Birger was no ordinary bootlegger. He had a penchant for telling tall tales about serving in the cavalry part of the military, true to the dime novel traditions of the Old West.

The press gave him the Robin Hood label due to his habit of tossing coins to children in the school yards. To those down-and-outers who occasionally were on the receiving end of a bag of free groceries, he was a charitable man. He won people's admiration despite the fact that he was a modern-day Jesse James who substituted a machine gun and armored car for a revolver and a horse.

The "Scourge of Egypt" was born in Russia (now Lithuania), probably around 1883. He was married three times, first to **East St. Louisan** Edna May Hastey (around 1909) and then to Beatrice Bainbridge (1921-25). He married Bernice Davis in February of 1926, but they, too, were later divorced. Charlie spent his early years with his mother and father and three siblings in places like **St. Louis** and **Glen Carbon**. His was one of those unusual lives enshrouded with fascinating folklore. He had a deep hatred for manual labor and quickly gravitated to the likes of others who cut corners and tried to make a fast buck in gambling and bootlegging. He shielded his wife and two daughters as best as he could from his shady activities. Birger also owned a couple of entertainment spots in the colored section of **East St. Louis** where gambling, bootlegging and prostitution were the chief sources of income.

After living a while in **St. Louis**, the family moved to **Glen Carbon** where older brother Sam Birger ran a general store and became a prominent druggist.

Birger moved to a house in **Marion**, Illinois and went into the lucrative bootleg business. He became a bitter rival with the Shelton brothers from **Fairfield**, Illinois.

Birger built a gang hangout near Marion that was called Shady Rest. According to Ripley's *Believe-it-or-Not*, **the first aerial bombing attack on U.S. soil occurred in 1924** when the Shelton brothers hired a barnstormer to fly one of them over Shady Rest. Home made bombs were tossed from the open cockpit of the Curtiss Jenny, but inexperience resulted in little damage to the place. Each side in the rivalry built home made tanks and armored cars and engaged in serio-comic battles on local roads.

Although Birger had killed half a dozen men, he was always able to claim self defense. He made a huge mistake in 1927 when he had two of his gang members gun down the mayor of West City, a Shelton ally. When confronted by authorities, the brothers confessed to the killing and said that they were acting under Birger's orders.

Birger gang in front of Shady Rest (Mitchell photo courtesy Bob Rea)

On February 24, 1928, the State Supreme Court denied Birger's final appeal and set his execution date for Friday, April 13. While in his cell, Birger was visited by the famous baseball player turned evangelist, **Billy Sunday**. On April 12 Birger heard the disheartening news that the Illinois Board of Pardons declined to intercede in the case. Further last minute appeals delayed the execution until April 19. A few days before his execution, Birger nearly successfully hanged himself with strips of cloth torn from his sheet.

"Buster" Wortman's moat home in rural Collinsville (Bill Jacobus)

Thousands of people came to **Benton**, Illinois, the night before in the hope that they might secure a good place to watch the execution. That same evening, Birger allowed a reporter (**Roy Alexander**) from the **St. Louis** *Post Dispatch* to interview him about his final thoughts. To the very end Birger denied his responsibility for the Adams murder, but he admitted that he had done a lot of things he had never been punished for, so he called it even. He prayed with **St. Louis** Rabbi Mazur to make his peace with God for the sake of his family. He was in a jovial mood that night and joked and bantered with various people. But his hands shook badly.

Early the next morning Birger was led from his cell to the gallows. Rabbi Mazur was with him as he walked the thirteen steps to the platform to meet his rendezvous with destiny – that hangman's noose with 13 knots. Photographers were busy snapping pictures. Armed guards stood on top of nearby buildings keeping a watchful eye on the crowd. A good number of people had climbed up in trees to get a better view of the execution. Even Birger's first wife Edna was at the gala affair.

Birger refused to take a shot of morphine tranquilizer that was traditionally offered to the condemned. He was wearing a gray suit and a dark tie. His last words were that he had forgiven everybody and, thanks to the wisdom of the Rabbi, he was not bitter. Straps were firmly tightened around his arms and legs. Charlie smiled and surveyed the crowd of about 500 people one last time before a black hood was placed over his face. Charlie was offered his choice of white or black and said he didn't want white because he was no KKK Klucker. Entrepreneurs were selling cookies, popcorn and soft drinks to the festive crowd. Several young kids were perched on their fathers' shoulders.

The hangman was **Phil Hanna**. He had executed about seventy men in the course of his work in Illinois and Indiana, and he always refused to take payment for the job. He said that the first hanging he ever witnessed was botched, and the poor man slowly strangled to death. No man deserved that, he said. Hanna also supervised the carpenter's construction of the gallows. The hangman slipped the noose around Charlie's neck, and Sheriff Pritchard pulled the lever that sprang the steel trap doors. Charlie's neck snapped at 9:43 a.m. and his limp body went into a large wicker basket below the trap doors. Several minutes later a doctor checked for a pulse and a heartbeat, then pronounced him dead.

Birger became the last man to be *publicly* hanged by the State of Illinois. His body was buried near his father in a small Jewish cemetery in **University City** a suburb of St. Louis. His headstone bears the inscription, Shachna Itzik Birger.

THE 1953 BOBBY GREENLEASE KIDNAPPING

By Lonnie Tettaton

Who was responsible for the murder of George Dowling, East St. Louis businessman Frank Wortman's associate? According to Jeanne Humphreys (in *Mafia Princess*), Frank "Buster" Wortman had connections to the Chicago Outfit. She says that her husband Murray "the Camel" Humphreys was frequently visited in **Chicago** by **St. Louis** handbook operator Tony Giardano and "racketeer" Frank "Buster" Wortman of East St. Louis. Ms. Humphreys says that Wortman's association dated back to about 1941 after he was released from prison, having done time for an altercation with a prohibition agent (near **Collinsville)** while working for the Shelton Gang. When the Sheltons failed to take care of him in prison, he turned to the Outfit for help. Jeanne maintains that Capone's heirs gave Wortman help in his protracted gang war with the rival Sheltons.

Carl Austin Hall

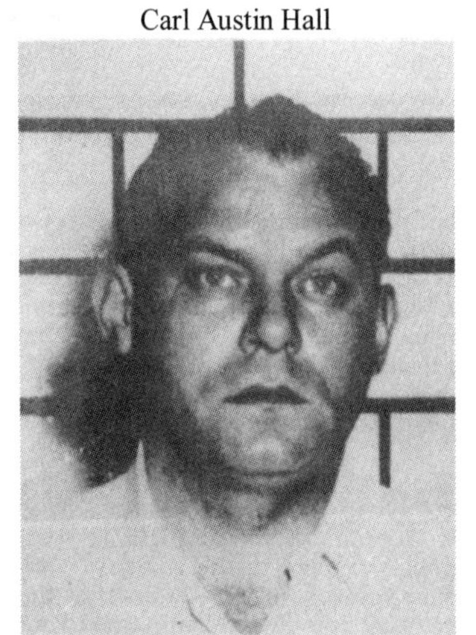

James Deakin, in his book about the Greenlease kidnapping, says that Wortman spent time at Leavenworth in the 1930s due to the altercation with a federal officer. After the Sheltons were eliminated as a threat, Wortman sold his ranch home on the west **Collinsville** bluffs and built a new place on the rural east side of Collinsville – the place with the famed moat around it.

Jeanne Humphreys remembers that Wortman and his St. Louis associate, Elmer "Dutch" Dowling, came to see Murray at least twice, begging him for an audience with Joe Batters (Accardo). Murray said that there was nothing he could do for them – Dowling had broken the rules and would have to pay the price. When Dowling was executed after leaving the Bel-Air bowling alley in **Belleville,** three years later (1962), Jeanne concluded it all must have been connected to the Bobby Greenlease kidnapping back in 1953.

Bonnie Heady

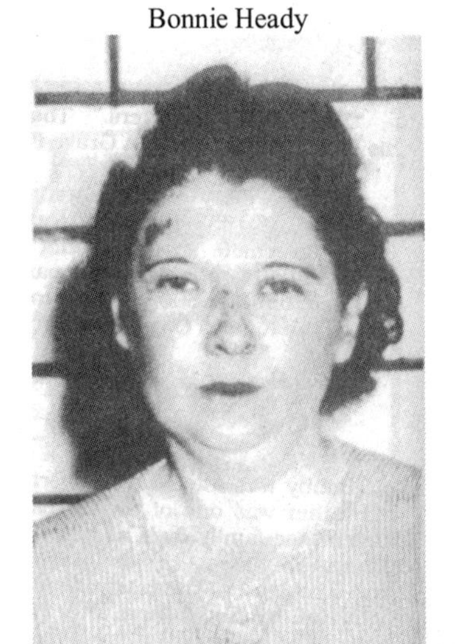

Bonnie Heady and her ex-con partner, Carl Hall, kidnapped the Greenlease boy from his Catholic school in **Kansas City**, Missouri. They killed the boy, buried his body in the back yard of Bonnie's home at **St. Joe**, Missouri, and sent a ransom note (demanding $600,000) to his wealthy father, a Cadillac dealer. The ransom was paid at the **Coral Courts Motel** in South **St. Louis** on Watson Road. The kidnappers had the unfortunate luck of taking a cab from a fleet owned by Joe Costello, a local gangster in the Wortman sphere. Interestingly, Costello was a business partner with Leo Brothers in 1945, co-owners of the Clover Club on Delmar. Brothers had served 14 years in prison for killing Chicago reporter Jake Lingle. The two also became co-owners of Ace Cab Company in **St. Louis**.

Hall and Heady paid the Ace Cab Co. driver Ollie Johnson with big bills, and he took them to Coral Court Motel run by John Carr, another Wortman hood. Cabbie Ollie Johnson informed Costello about the pair and Costello, in turn, was thought to have tipped St. Louis police lieutenant Louis Shoulders, a friend of both Costello's and Wortman. Years later, Shoulders was given a position of power in Wortman's St. Louis Steamfitter's Union.

Heady and Hall were quickly arrested, and less than three months later, were **executed with potassium cyanide** while sitting next to each other in the gas chamber. Heady has the distinction of being the **only woman in the U.S. executed in the gas chamber**.

At the time of Hall's arrest, at an apartment, only $298,000 was recovered, stashed in a suitcase and footlocker. Bonnie was arrested later at a rear town house apartment on Arsenal Street. Hall told police he thought maybe he had buried half of the money near a bottom road by the Meramec River near **Fenton**, Missouri. He said he was too drunk to remember. A search of the area proved fruitless. The FBI concluded that the missing money was taken to **Chicago** for laundering when some of the bills began surfacing. About half of the bills recovered surfaced in Chi Town.

One police officer later claimed that he saw Shoulders and Joe Costello take part of the money, and said it was given to Chicagoan Barney Baker, an associate of the Outfit.

When Hall left Bonnie at the apartment on Arsenal, he had his cabbie secure a prostitute for him (Sandy O'Day), and they spent time together at the Coral Court Motel on Watson Road. Hall gave her an astounding $1,200. Sandy O'Day said Hall had a huge stash of cash with him and tried to figure out how she could steal part of it. She drove to Wortman's Paddock Lounge in **East St. Louis** and told Dutch Dowling about the money, thinking he could help her. He, in turn, (many assume) later informed Wortman, who was not there at the time. Then she went back to the Coral Court. Sandy never told the FBI or St. Louis police about her search for Wortman. She only told this part of the story many years later.

It was also theorized that O'Day slipped Hall a Mickey Finn, and while he was out, Dowling stole half of the loot. There is the possibility that she actually succeed in stealing the other half of the money. Shoulders told ***St. Louis Post-Dispatch*** reporters he thought that the money was stolen by gangsters from the Coral Court Motel.

St. Louis investigative reporter Ted Link said there was a possibility that Shoulders did not bring the money into the Newstead police station until an hour after Hall was brought there and booked. Seven other police officials in the station at the time do not remember seeing it when Hall was brought in. Shoulders later changed his story and said the money was brought in ten minutes later, and that's why the seven police officials didn't see it at first.

Shoulders and his partner (Elmer Dolan) were indicted by a grand jury for lying about what happened to the money and both served a few years of jail time.

The hunt for the missing money continued for years. Ostensibly, the dough was laundered in Chicago without Humphrey's knowledge through a Mafia-linked bank, the Southmoor Bank of Chicago.

When Humphreys and Accardo learned of the role played by Dowling in the affair, his fate was sealed. Unlike Capone, the Outfit had long ago decided to keep a low profile and avoid having its name bantered about in the newspapers. Author Gus Russo says that despite Wortman's long and trusted friendship with Humphreys, he could not save Dowling. The hit was made long after the Greenlease affair for two reasons. First, it gave Dowling time to worry and stew over his fate. Second, the long interval between the Greenlease incident and the executions made it less likely that authorities would connect it to the Chicago outfit. It apparently worked. When Dowling's body was found on a rural road near **Swansea**, Illinois, local authorities were totally flummoxed about the possible motive.

Louis Shoulders Sr.

The mystery of the missing $300,000 ransom money in the Greenlease kidnapping has **never been solved.**

TEAMSTER BOSS HAROLD GIBBONS

Harold Gibbons, who led the St. Louis Teamster's Union for 30 years, was the city's most interesting labor leader.

Gibbons was born (the youngest of 23 children) in a coal camp near Scranton, Pennsylvania, in 1910, the son of parents who had come to this country from Ireland. The family moved to **Chicago** when Harold was young, and he dropped out of school to work in a factory. Despite his lack of education, he became a leader in Chicago's teachers' union in the early 1930s.

Harold Gibbons (Dave Lossos picture)

In 1941, Gibbons was sent to **St. Louis** to direct a new union of warehouse workers. In those days, the area where Busch Stadium is now located was crammed with warehouses. The thousands of men and women who worked in them were poorly paid. Under Gibbons' leadership, the standard of living of warehouse workers greatly improved.

Gibbons was a lifelong socialist who brought a bit of socialism to St. Louis. The Labor Health Institute he created in 1945 gave warehouse workers and their families full medical care, all paid for by their employers. Later he established a 300-acre camp at **Pevely**, Missouri, where union members could swim, fish, play golf and so forth. "Rich people have country clubs," Gibbons said. "Now our members have one too."

In 1948, Gibbons' warehouse union became local 688 of the Teamsters Union. In the early 1950s, a group of gangsters associated with **Collinsville's "Buster" Wortman** took over several Teamster locals in St. Louis. They sent word to Gibbons that they would kill him unless he turned over his local as well.

Gibbons defeated Wortman's gang with the help of the rising young Teamsters' new president, Jimmy Hoffa. Then, in 1957, when Hoffa went to Washington as the Teamsters' new president, Gibbons went along as his right hand man.

In 1958, Gibbons appeared before the **John McClellan Committee** that was investigating labor racketeering. A *Time Magazine* article, the next week, castigated him as a "blood brother to the hoods and goons who have filed before the committee for two weeks." The article continued: "Far from abhorring violence, as Gibbons piously testified, during a **1953 St. Louis cab strike** he used a crew of enforcers that included an enforcer, a stickup man, a pimp and . . . a Teamster arrested for shooting his mother." The article noted that while Gibbons was head of the union in St. Louis, he called 250 strikes in "an established pattern of violence. He is pretty good as an engineer of violence – which previous testimony clearly shows."

Nearly all of Gibbons' union officers carried guns. He charged their holsters to the "office supplies" account. Robert Kennedy wrote about the alleged corruption in Gibbons' empire in *The Enemy Within*.

It might be noted that Bobby Kennedy's motives in all this might have been less than pure. The Kennedys rode the publicity of this sensationalism all the way to the White House, much as Kefauver secured the second spot on the Adlai Stevenson ticket as a result of his hearings in 1951.

Gibbons and Hoffa were partners until November 22, 1963, when President Kennedy was assassinated in Dallas. Gibbons, who was in charge of the Teamsters' headquarters in Washington, lowered the flag to half mast and sent all the employees home. Hoffa, who hated the Kennedys because Attorney General Bobby Kennedy hounded him, flew into a rage when he heard what Gibbons had done. After a bitter encounter, Gibbons quit his job and came home to St. Louis.

He continued to be Hoffa's ally in the union, however. In 1967, when Hoffa went to prison after being convicted of jury tampering, most of his former Teamster friends deserted him for the union's new president, Frank Fitzsimmons. Gibbons was the one Teamster vice president who remained loyal to Hoffa.

In 1972, he hatched a plan with his friend Henry Kissinger, then President Nixon's foreign policy advisor, whereby Gibbons and Hoffa would fly to Hanoi and arrange the release of U.S. prisoners of war. This, they hoped, would accomplish three things: free POWs, help end the war and help Hoffa reclaim the union presidency from Fitzsimmons. Unfortunately, Chuck Colson, a Fitzsimmons ally in the White House, managed to sabotage the plan.

Later that year, Gibbons further incurred Fitzsimmons' wrath when he became the only Teamster vice president to refuse to endorse Nixon for reelection. Gibbons backed the Democrat George McGovern.

In the spring of 1973, Fitzsimmons plotted successfully with Gibbons' enemies in St. Louis to take Local 688 away from him. Gibbons himself had helped make this possible. In the 1960s and '70s, he was increasingly away from St. Louis, involved in national and international politics and spending time with show business friends like Frank Sinatra.

Mabel Vie McQuillen

Gibbons, a member of the NAACP and the ACLU, died in 1982, all but forgotten in St. Louis. In some ways, Gibbons was responsible for jump starting the civil rights movement in St. Louis. In the 1940's, his people protested the Jim Crowism that existed in all the major department stores in St. Louis. He was a complex man of many accomplishments and deserves to be remembered.

The site of old Sportsmans Park in St. Louis, now a playground, was named to honor him. In 2001 Labor's International Hall of Fame elected Gibbons to that select group.

MY ST. LOUIS HOODLUM RELATIVES

By James Brasher

I grew up in the Clinton-Peabody complex in the Forties and Fifties. The projects were built for the families of servicemen who were stationed overseas during World War II. My family was lucky to qualify for an apartment in 1944 when my dad was inducted into the army.

Schneithorst's Restaurant at Bevo Mill (David Lossos collection)

What young St. Louis boy at the time didn't get on a streetcar and travel to the end of the line in **Kirkwood**, or **Lemay** or **Baden**. Or get a transfer ticket and end up in some unknown neighborhood that was almost as exotic as traveling to the Swiss Alps. The Mississippi River; who could resist it? The elevators and the escalators at the downtown department stores were also a special delight to a bunch of adventurous boys. Then, when you throw in the camaraderie of always being able to find at least one friend when you were ready to travel, you have a fun-filed adventurous life. Sure, sometimes there were petty tiffs, but no one really had time to be mad for any length of time. There were just too many things to get done. Movies, bowling, skating, dancing at the Casa Loma, shows at the Fox theater when Ray Anthony came to town, and convincing the doorman at the Garrick Burlesque Theater, at 16-years-old that, "oh, yes, we are 18." All very important things to accomplish! Who had time to get into any real trouble? But, being half Irish, I somehow managed to have my share of misadventures, too.

I am James Brasher, born in St. Louis in 1935 (same year as Elvis) when my parents were living on 1815 N. Market Street, smack dab in the middle of the Irish Kerry Patch. The Irish part of me comes from the McQuillens and the Brashers supplied the English part. While researching the "shanty" Irish twig of the family tree I couldn't find a single thing I could brag about.

My grandmother, Mabel Vie, was married to Henry James McQuillen, a mean, drunken lout of an Irishman. He was a brother to one of St. Louis's biggest gangsters, William Patrick "Bow Wow" McQuillen. **Patrick was into bank robbing, dope peddling, gambling, kidnapping and bootlegging**, just to name a few of his extra-curricular nefarious activities. Henry came to an untimely death in 1932 when he was found in an alley shotgunned to death. That rascal, Henry McQuillen, was my maternal grandfather.

Just how did Patrick get the nickname "Bow Wow?" One version has it that as a youngster he liked to sing a song about a dog named Bow Wow. But I think it's connected to the time when the Sheltons tried to kill rival Charlie Birger at his hangout in **Marion**, Illinois, a place he called Shady Rest. Bow Wow owned several airplanes and I think he was in the Curtiss Jenny that did the aerial bombing. The homemade bombs missed Shady Rest, but Birger's favorite dog ended up being a casualty – hence Bow Wow.

There was this one time when Henry had been drinking heavily and he came home (on 11th Street near Cass) in a mean and confrontational manner. When Mabel had the audacity to back talk him, he grabbed her by the arm and hauled her down to the railroad tracks that ran along the banks of the Mississippi. **He proceeded to tie her to the tracks and then took off**. When Mabel saw that he wasn't coming back, she started to scream and struggle, in fear for her mortal life. It was no use. Then she became terrified as she felt the tracks vibrate and realized there was a train approaching. This sent her into more violent screams and struggles, but it became apparent that she was a doomed woman. All of a sudden, a hobo appeared from out of nowhere and began untying her, but the thundering train was coming closer and closer. Finally, just as the train was about to run over her, the bedraggled man reached down and pulled her to safety. Mabel went to stay with a relative and filed for divorce, which was granted in 1919.

My grandparents, on the McQuillen side, lived at 1511 Ridgley, under the Fourteenth Street viaduct, directly behind Kiel Auditorium – not exactly the most exclusive of neighborhoods.

My mother, Margaret Florence Brasher nee McQuillen, never talked about the McQuillen side of the family when I was growing up. I guess she was afraid my brother (Gary) and I might somehow get tangled up in a life of crime, due to the lower end of the gene pool represented by the wild and woolly McQuillens. She finally told me about the skeletons in our closet shortly before she died in 1995.

James "Bow Wow" McQuillen

Bow Wow McQuillen died in September of 1969 while living in **Valley Park**. His funeral was at St. Patrick's and he was buried at Calvary Cemetery. His house had been a resort on the Meramec River that Bow Wow built back in the 1930s. That was his sanctuary when things got too hot for him in St. Louis. His city address was 1304 Cass Avenue, not far from the current Greyhound Bus Station.

Bow Wow's rap sheet is long and it started as a youth around 1909 when he was sent, on two separate occasions, to the **State Reform School at Boonville**. Apparently, he was caught pilfering things after hours in someone else's business establishment long after the doors had been locked for the night.

Bow Wow, during the late 1920s and 1930s, was part owner of the Mounds Club on **Collinsville Road**, not far from the great Indian mound and Fairmount Park racetrack. By the early 1960s, it had been closed and converted into one of Grandpa Pigeon's stores, frequented by author Bill Nunes. Harry Murdock, a convicted bootlegger, was also part owner with the final third being owned by Frank Woller, an **East St. Louis** bookmaker. I tried to find old records of Bow Wow being convicted of bootlegging, but to no avail. I spent hours and hours searching through old police records. Finally, one older officer spoke up. "Everyone knows how corrupt the St. Louis police were in the old days," he said. It took me a while to figure out what he meant. Bow Wow had a cousin on the police force who saw to it that some of his convictions were expunged.

James Brasher

While Bow Wow was busy with other underworld activities, brother Henry ran a speakeasy from the property they owned on Cass Avenue. They both ultimately became members of the Cuckoo Gang.

Once Prohibition was in full swing, Al Capone decided to try and muscle his way into the St. Louis area. The only problem was that the Cuckoos were running things in the city and southern Illinois was controlled by the Birger and Shelton gangs. It wasn't until Capone was dying of a social disease that the Chicago Outfit made an inroads. They looked after Buster Wortman when he was sent to Leavenworth in the early 1930s. When he got out, in 1941, and rose to the top of the heap, they had a faithful ally. By 1952, the Sheltons were no longer a factor after three of the brothers were shot and killed. Their murders were never solved.

As you might suspect, **John Dillinger** had his eye on **East St. Louis** banks as possible targets for holdups. East St. Louis was out because its 13 square miles were criss-crossed by 550 miles of railroad tracks. He did not want a train to block his escape route. He also feared the Sheltons in the 1930s. He once reportedly had this to say about them. "The Sheltons would have given me a hotter welcome than the FBI. I ain't going to East St. Louis."

The old Kerry Patch, where the McQuillens lived, was long known for its unsavory reputation. Before the turn of the century, fighting was so frequent there that the police named it the "**Bloody Third District**." There was many a time when a policeman there could do nothing to stop a fight but shed his coat, roll up his sleeves and join in the brawl himself.

Fire companies were often the cause of riots. The Irish-dominated fire fighting companies formed rivalries that compared with those of the street thugs. With their "fighting Irish" competitive spirit, there was keen rivalry as to which company could get there first to put out a fire. Many a time there were two rival fire companies that arrived on the scene simultaneously and let the fire rage out of control while they kicked, gouged and battled with fists to determine which company got the honor of putting the fire out. Sometimes, two rival companies set fires themselves in order to provoke a good rollicking fight.

The gang rivalries of the Twenties and Thirties may have been brutal, but they were also colorful and exciting. One relative told me that she and other Kerry Patch neighborhood ladies loved their second story windows. It seemed there was always something going on near the neighborhood tavern. The gangs would start shooting up and down the street and all the women would be hanging onto the window sill to watch while holding on tightly, without any fear of being shot. They didn't want to miss a thing. They knew bootlegging was afoot and they could always count on the Hogan gang for a very lively and interesting afternoon or evening. Why, what the heck, this was better than watching a Rudolph Valentino movie at the neighborhood theater.

In 1944, my dad, Ralph W. Brasher, was working nights at the small arms plant on Natural Bridge and Goodfellow.

We lived at 4478 Vista near Kingshighway and Manchester. This was just before he went into the army.

In 1943, after having numerous shouting matches with my mother Florence, Dad drifted into an affair with a young married woman who drove a truck. As a cover, Dad frequently took me on Tuesday evenings on an outing, usually at Forest Park where his girl friend joined us. We went to places like the Jefferson Memorial, the Jewel Box, the Art Museum, and we always had this nice lady with us. I thought it was great because Dad let me smoke his pipe on Art Hill, above the boat lake. In return, I had to give an "honest Injun" Cub Scout promise never to mention Lois to my mother. Gee, nine years old and there I was all grown up smoking that pipe. Before long I wasn't even turning midnight green anymore and I had stopped puking shortly after that.

"Easy Eddie" O'Hare

My mother grew suspicious and started wondering where Dad was spending all that time away from home. She finally wore me down. After all, she was my mom. To comfort her, I finally spoke up. "Don't worry, Mom. Dad's probably over at Lois's house. She is a very nice young lady." It was the only time in my life I was able to compare silence to thunder and I can verify that Mom's silence was much louder than thunder.

Right there, late at night, my sister and I got to sleep over at a friend's house. The next morning, when Sharon and I got home, Dad was sporting a very bright shiner under his left eye. I figured it was a good thing I had spilled the beans because Mom must have gone out and saved Dad from some terrible fate. Maybe she rescued him before he got struck by lightning and he was lucky that, whatever it was, all he got out of it was a black eye!

For more derring-do and exciting further details about crime in St. Louis, log onto James Brasher's website at http://genealogyinstlouis.accessgenealogy.com/Brasher.htm........................

MAN WHO MARKETED MECHANICAL RABBIT FOUND MURDERED

The man who invented the mechanical rabbit (that led to dog racing becoming a popular activity) was a promoter and greyhound lover from **St. Louis** by the name of Oliver P. Smith. He invented the device around 1909 and spent several years testing and perfecting it. He then formed a partnership with an astute lawyer from St. Louis named **Edward J. O'Hare**. O'Hare is an Irish name and the Gaelic translation means *bitter* or *angry*.

Thirsty, just Whistle! (Vess Whistle Orange soda)

O'Hare soon realized dog racing was so profitable that he decided to open a track of his own. It was known as the **Madison** Kennel Club, and it was located just north of East St. Louis. Race tracks in Missouri were forbidden under the Blue Laws.

O'Hare married Selma Lauth (German) at a young age and fathered three children, including a lad named Edward who became known as "Butch." They started their family while living in an apartment above Selma's father's **Soulard** grocery store. As a result of dog racing profits, O'Hare moved his family into a new house – with a swimming pool and a skating rink – in **Holly Hills**.

O'Hare, known colloquially as "Easy Eddie," loved flying and once hitched a ride with Lindbergh on one of his mail flights to Chicago. He also built tracks in Chicago and went into partnership with **Al Capone**. When dog racing was declared illegal in Illinois, the track was converted into Sportsman's Park for racing thoroughbreds.

O'Hare moved his family there and had fancy cars and a spacious home, but his conscience began to bother him. What kind of legacy was he leaving to his son? O'Hare went to the feds and offered to give them material on Capone's finances in return for an appointment for Butch to the U.S. Naval Academy at Annapolis. Using O'Hare's information, the feds successfully built a case against Capone for tax evasion.

When Capone was released from Alcatraz in 1939, **O'Hare was gunned down** November 8 while driving his car on Ogden Avenue in Chicago. This was Capone's homecoming present and payback for O'Hare being a snitch.

"Butch" O'Hare was sent by his father to Western Military Academy in **Alton** because his father thought he was getting lazy. After his appointment, Butch graduated from Annapolis and became a navy pilot. Early in World War II he became the first ace in the conflict when he shot down five Japanese airplanes in one day, earning him the Medal of Honor. Butch O'Hare was later killed in the war.

GETTING AWAY WITH MURDER
by David A. Lossos

The name of the accused is hidden to protect the guilty. I've been "working" a murder case that took place in April of 1928, just outside of the city limits of St. Louis. Since the victim actually died in St. Anthony's Hospital at Grand and Chippewa, the death officially took place in the City.

My mother did not have much of a relationship with her father, Conrad Tappeiner. It's ironic that in 1928, when this crime took place, she was a boarding senior at St. Elizabeth's Academy, not far from the hospital were her father died. There is certainly evidence that the relationship she never had might well have been developed at that time had it not been for this murder. I might have come to know this man that I never got a chance to meet.

This St. Louis *Globe-Democrat* morning newspaper account appeared Monday, April 16, 1928, the day after the shooting, and gives a small glimpse as to what took place...

"REFUSED ADMITTANCE, MAN SHOOTS 2 OTHERS"

"Conrad Tappeiner, 50, who operates what is known as "Connie's" at Grant and Pardee roads, St. Louis County, and George Michaeli, 24, of 5109 Dresden Avenue, were shot and seriously wounded shortly before midnight last night by one of four men, who with two girls, drove up to Tappeiner's home and sought admission.

Tappeiner, with nine slugs in this right side and hip, and Michaeli, with two slugs in his right arm, were rushed to St. Anthony's Hospital where physicians said their condition is serious.

Tappeiner told county authorities he refused to admit the men and women, and when he went outside one of the men produced a sawed-off shotgun from beneath his coat and began firing. The men and women made their escape."

Webster Groves High School (courtesy Judy Bach Hrasky)

The next day, April 19, 1928, testimonies took place in the St. Louis City Coroner's office.

From Officer John J. Fitzgerald (2nd District, St. Louis Police Dept.): "Well, we got a call to go down to St. Anthony's Hospital on South Grand Avenue that there were two men shot, and when we got there we found Tappeiner and Michaeli, they were both shot, Tappeiner in the side and the other fellow in the right arm. I asked them how it happened and they said they were at Vergere's home and that they were coming up out of the cellar, these two men, and some fellow stepped from the roadway into the yard and walked up to about 20 feet of them and pointed a shotgun at them and told then to throw up their hands and fired either two or three shots. They named Dietz as the man that did the shooting."

From Constable Jacob Pfeiffer (St. Louis County - **Carondelet**.): "I was called to the Vergere home and when I got there he had been taken to **St. Anthony' Hospital**. Got a statement from one witness, O'Toole. He says he was in the yard when this fellow come back and he said it was a man by the name of Dietz."

From witness Oliver O'Toole: "Well we had a party out at Vegere's house and about 11 o'clock I was down in the basement and I heard some noise upstairs and I run upstairs to see that there were three fellows. Dietz and three other unknown men and two women came into Tappeiner's home and later left in an angry mood as Tappeiner refused to sell any drinks. Cooney wanted to put them out of the yard. One of them got away and the other one jumped in the Chevrolet sedan with these two women and he wasn't going to drive out of the yard at all, and so finally Michaeli made him get out, and when he did he jumped out of the car and made a pass at Michaeli and Michaeli hit him, and when he did I pulled him off, and so this one fellow says "Well, we're going to get our gang and come back and get you all," and so they drove out of the yard."

From witness George Michaeli: "I was standing there talking to this man and a man come there on the sidewalk on the side of the house and said "Holdup" had a handkerchief over this face and he was about 10 feet away from us and after he took a couple of steps I guess he was about five feet away, and he just started shooting, and he was right on top of us."

From accused murderer Lawrence "XXXXXXXXX" - No statement.

After the shooting Tappeiner and Michaeli were conveyed by the above named Allen Vergere in Tappeiner's automobile to St. Anthony's Hospital. Ten other witnesses accompanied Tappeiner and Marchaeli to the hospital in several automobiles. Once there, everyone was arrested by the officers and brought to the City of St. Louis Police Station where they were held for St. Louis County authorities, suspected of an affray and later turned over to Constable Jacob Pfeiffer of Carondelet Township. Tappeiner and Michaeli were not held prisoners at St. Anthony's Hospital as they stated to Constable Pfeiffer that they would not prosecute the man known as "Dietz" who is supposed to have fired the shots at the time.

The Coroner's Office issued the following statement: "Deceased came to his death at 2:20 p.m. on the 18th of April 1928 at St. Anthony's hospital from general sepsis (blood poisoning), following multiple gunshot wounds caused by bullets fired from a gun in the hands of one Lawrence "XXXXXXXXX", at Grant and Rock Hill roads, St. Louis County on 16th of April about 1:00 a.m. - homicide."

At that time an order for Dietz's arrest was given.

I had hoped to get additional information about what happened next from the Police Department of **Webster Groves**, but they had absolutely nothing.

Based on the testimonies given by the numerous witnesses, this appeared to be an "open and shut" case. However, I was unable to discern the outcome of a trial, if indeed the case had ever gone to trial.

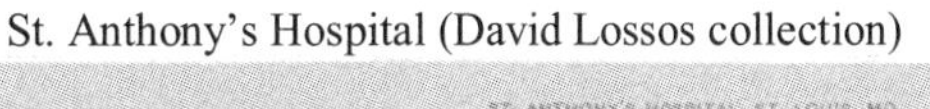

St. Anthony's Hospital (David Lossos collection)

In 1982, I was finally able to make contact with someone that was actually at the scene of the crime.

It turns out that after my grandparents divorced in December of 1909, Conrad remarried Anna B. Mueller (nee Klein). Although they did not have any children of their own, they did adopt Anna's sister's son, Oscar, after his parents died in 1922.

Although Oscar was only nine years old at the time of the murder, he remembers that night. He was asleep in the house at the time. He was also able to explain why the case never went to trial. Apparently Lawrence "Dietz" "XXXXXXXXX" was able to threaten the witnesses into not testifying against him, and his lawyer, Sigmund Bass, was able to have the case dismissed for lack of evidence.

More detail is provided in the news story that appeared in the St. Louis Daily *Globe-Democrat* on Tuesday morning, March 12, 1929:

"STAR WITNESS GONE, MURDER CASE ENDS" Charge Against Lawrence "XXXXXXXX", 22, Dismissed at **Clayton**.

A first degree murder charge was dismissed by Judge Mulloy in the Circuit Court at Clayton yesterday because the state lacked its star witness. The case dismissed was that of Lawrence "XXXXXXXXX", 22, of 5115 West Popping Street who was charged with slaying Conrad Tappeiner, a carpenter at Grant and Rock Hill roads, St. Louis County, on the night of April 16, 1928. It was announced the chief witness for the prosecution, Oliver O'Toole, had left the state and that it would be useless to carry the case further. Tappeiner was visiting at a neighbor's house when some men and women drove up and demanded entrance, which was refused. An hour later the car re-appeared and one of the number fired upon Tappeiner with a shotgun. He died at a hospital shortly after."

Sculin Steel (Missouri Historical Society)

And that is where the case ends - Almost.

Tracing Lawrence "XXXXXXXXX"'s genealogy was relatively easy. I had detail on him and his family. I even knew when each of his three sons were born. His first was born less than three years after the murder. It suddenly dawned on me that it wouldn't be too much longer and there wouldn't be a soul alive that had any knowledge of the murder.

Davey at the Claridge Lounge

According to published reports and verbal interviews I was able to determine that Dietz's brother was a Lieutenant on the St. Louis Police Department and Dietz himself was, for a time, also a policeman. In 2005, using appropriate channels, I officially asked from the St. Louis Police Department for confirmation of the two brothers service. They had no record of either.

I guess you could say this is still an ongoing investigation.

ST. LOUIS NEIGHBRHOODS

Bill Nunes grew up in **Washington Park**, a suburb located on the northeast edge of East St. Louis. Dave Lossos was a climber of birch trees in South St. Louis. Lonnie Tettaton was a Northsider. If you think about it, the Missouri neighborhood you grew up in was the setting for your home, your school, and the church you attended. Most likely you have fond memories of going to the neighborhood movie theater and the bakery, drug store, confectionary and service stations located there. Your neighborhood determined who your school chums would be; it was the setting for church social events. For many, it is quite likely that they met their future spouse at that church, high school, or neighborhood grill and malt shop. That neighborhood is likely where you got your first job at babysitting, mowing grass, working at a filling station or bagging groceries.

For St. Louisans, perhaps you lived far north in the Riverview area. Some grew up around Tower Grove. If you lived in the extreme south you probably remember the bear pits in Carondelet Park. If you were Irish, most probably you lived in the Kerry Patch neighborhood, although a good number lived in Dogtown and attended **St. James**. If you were Italian, the Hill was your stomping grounds. If your ethnicity was French, perhaps you lived in the Soulard District.

In *King of the Hill*, A. E. Hotchner writes poignantly about growing up impoverished in a run down St. Louis Hotel during the Depression. The young boy learns to cope with living alone much of the time because his father is a traveling salesman and his mother is in the hospital.

DOGTOWN/ CHELTENHAM

If you lived in Dogtown you probably have memories of businesses shutting down for three hours on Good Friday, thanks to the influence of St. James Church. You also likely remember places such as the clay mines behind the Arena, **Scullin Steel**, Lungstraus Cleaners, Howard Fire Brick, Winkle Terra Cotta, Tamm Pharmacy, The Bottle Inn, Schmid's Bar, John Dolan Real Estate, Schweikert's Dry Goods, Gratiot and Dewey schools, High Pointe Theater, Deaconess Hospital, Clayton and Tamm business district, Koeneke Drug Store, Placke's Service Station and the White House Bar. You might also remember the Poor House and the Insane Asylum, just south of Manchester Road.

The **Dogtown** neighborhood is directly south of Route 40 (Red Feather Express) and bounded on the other side by the Frisco Railroad tracks. Dogtown includes such neighborhoods as Hi Pointe, Oakland Terrace, Cheltenham, Franz Park, Justin Place, Sulphur Spring, Benton, Ellendale, Gratiot Place and Victoria Place. No one knows for sure how the neighborhood received its name but there are several good theories put forth by amateur historian Bob Corbett. The most colorful is that, during the 1904 World's Fair, the Philippine government sent a whole tribe of aboriginal Igorot natives, village and all. These wild men didn't particularly like the iced tea, hot dogs, ice cream and Cracker Jack being served at the Fair. So, they went on a hunting expedition in the nearby woods looking for wild dogs to kill – hence Dogtown.

Another! When the city purchased the acreage for what became Forest Park there were a number of poor Irish squatters living there. They were thrown off the land so they moved to another mostly uninhabited area to the south. There were small deposits of coal in the area and the squatters dug lots of small holes to get just enough surface coal to build fires and keep warm. Soon the area was pockmarked with numerous holes that looked as if they had been made by a pack of dogs. A variation on that holds that these impoverished men built a shantytown of sorts out of materials left over from the Fair. To outsiders, it looked as if it was the shabby sort of place that dogs might inhabit.

Yet another version holds that farmers used to come to a favorite watering hole at Clayton and Graham to imbibe in the spirits. Every time they drove their wagons along the dirt road there seemed to be a spate of dogs that came along and barked and nipped at the legs of the horses. The area seemed to have more dogs than people – hence Dogtown.

It has been said that the Irish were treated better in St. Louis than in most other large American cities. Their ethnic neighborhood was the **Kerry Patch**, named for a southwest county in Ireland. Most merely called it "the Patch." Researcher **Jim Brasher** says the Kerry Patch boundaries were 18th Street to the west and the Mississippi on the East. Market Street was the southern boundary and St. Louis Avenue marked its northern limits.

Irishman John Mullanphy, a real estate developer, was the city's first millionaire and quite a philanthropist. Jeremiah Connor was St. Louis' first Sheriff.

St. Louis Mark Twain Hotel (David Lossos collection)

The Kerry Patch area centered around St. Patrick's Church, located at Sixth and Biddle. The old church was torn down around 1973 and the new St. Patrick's is located at 1000 North 7th Street. So many Irish flocked to the city that, by 1850, roughly 43 percent of the St. Louis population was Irish. John Mullanphy donated a tract of land for the Irish to settle on. It was located north of Carr Square. The heart of Kerry Patch was said to be N. 18th and O'Fallon streets, but the neighborhood kept expanding north and west. When the clay mines opened around the Hampton area, many Irish found work there and moved to Dogtown. By the turn of the century, many Irish found work in one of the 70 breweries that existed in St. Louis.

Well known Irish Catholic churches included St. Patrick, St. Michael, St. Bridget, St. John, St. Malachy, St. Kevin, St. Leo, St. Liborius, St. Theresa, St. Matthew, Holy Rosary and St. Cronan.

After World War II many of the Irish had moved away from the Patch to other neighborhoods and the government began building public housing for African-Americans, who began to dominate the area. Carr Square and Pruitt-Igoe were built to improve the neighborhood and reduce crime. Just the opposite happened and Pruitt-Igoe, built in 1956, met the wrecking ball and bulldozer in 1972.

THE IRISH INFLUENCE IN ST. LOUIS

By David Lossos

Post-Dispatch writer Carl Baldwin stated that the Irish have long been a force in St. Louis and East St. Louis. Unlike the Germans, most of them came to Missouri with few resources. They lacked the money to buy land, so they often settled in urban areas. They first came to the area in large numbers in the 1840s due to a potato crop blight and to escape repressive British rule. They came to St. Louis and

St. James Church (MHS)

settled around **St. Patrick's** on the near north side. The ensuing famine caused nearly a million deaths in the Emerald Isle. The potato, originally grown on the Andean Plateau in South America, was brought to Europe by the Spaniards. The crop normally prospered in the damp Irish soil, but a fungus destroyed nearly all the crops, starting in 1843. Many more Irish died from typhus and cholera. Thousands of Irish fled to America seeking a better life for themselves and their children. It was due to circumstances of famine that caused John F. Kennedy's grandparents to migrate to America and settle in Boston.

Do not confuse the Irish with a group known as the **Scots-Irish**. People from Scotland migrated to Northern Ireland (Ulster) in the 1600s to escape the tyranny of the Church of England. They were followers of John Knox and were staunch Presbyterians.

The **Black Irish** had darker hair and skin color than most fair-skinned Irish. It is thought, by many, that fleeing ships of the Spanish Armada (1588) foundered on the Irish shore. The Spaniards intermarried with the native population producing progeny with darker features.

The Irish, a gnarled muscular lot, helped build the railroads that ended, in the 1850s, in **East St. Louis** on the riverfront. Many eventually settled in St. Louis.

When Illinoistown incorporated as **East St. Louis**, many opposed the name change. The railroads were already using East St. Louis on their letterheads and warehouses and favored the switch. They rounded up Irish railroad gandy dancers and bribed them to vote for the change with either money or whiskey.

Irish women brought their domestic skills and folklore with them. Irish mothers often made potato pancakes topped with caraway seeds. Myrna Adams Blue, of **Belleville,** remembers her grandmother telling her that if you started telling a friend something and then forgot what you were going to say, you were better off because it probably was untrue.

Because the Irish, more than any other group, were responsible for bringing Catholicism to America, they often bore the brunt of early prejudice and discrimination. The Know-Nothings of the 1850s were an anti-Irish group. Businesses often hung a sign in their windows that said, "No Irish Need Apply." Yet, as a whole, Protestants and Catholics generally got along fairly well in the greater St. Louis area.

It was St. Patrick who went to Ireland as a missionary and converted the people there to Catholicism. According to lore, it was **St. Patrick who drove all the snakes from Ireland** which explains why none currently exist on the island.

Italian Anti-Fascist League meeting on the Hill – circa 1942 (Missouri Historical Society)

Researcher **James Brasher** notes that Irish kids were frequently told by their parents and grandparents that God was an Irishman. He cites an 1878 guide book that describes the Kerry Patch Irish. "Poor but independent folk, whose chief amusement amounts to punching each others eyes. Though they spend a wretched existence within their miserable abodes, the people still talk as cheerfully and laugh as though they were dwellers in marble halls."

It has been said that the Irish Trinity in the local area consisted of priests, police and politicians. These were the popular vocational choices made by many Irish. Tennis star **Jimmy Connors** grandfather, John Connors, served as Mayor of East St. Louis. As a youngster, Jimmy played tennis in winter time at the St. Louis Armory.

The National Order of Hibernians was founded in America in 1836. The group was established to promote Irish interests in this country. In many cases they collected money to bring relatives and friends over from Ireland. In more recent years many Irish-Americans sent money to the Irish Republican Army to help them in their efforts to drive out the British.

The Climatron at Shaw's Garden (Lorna Nunes photo)

The Celts are **credited with originating the holiday that became Halloween**. For them it was a celebration of the harvest. It also marked a day when they believed souls could return to Earth to find a new body to inhabit. Believers dressed in frightening costumes and made lots of noise, hoping to be less attractive to those wandering spirits. When Christianity arrived, the celebration shifted to the night before All Saints Day, a Catholic feast honoring all saints.

Trick or treating began when early Christians went from door to door promising to say prayers for the deceased on behalf of those who donated "soul cakes."

The Irish brought the tradition to America where the jack-o-lantern was adapted from Irish folklore, although it was a lit pumpkin instead of a turnip. Over the years, candy and other treats replaced the soul cakes.

Centuries ago, the British occupied Ireland to prevent countries such as France or Spain from using it as a staging area for invasion. Numerous people from Great Britain eventually settled in Northern Ireland. When the Irish were finally granted their independence, in the 1920s, Northern Ireland remained in British control. This led to the formation of the IRA, seen by some as freedom fighters and thought by others to be terrorists. During World War II, Ireland remained neutral. After decades of conflict, President Clinton was able to secure a truce between the two sides.

The St. Patrick's Day Parade in St. Louis has been a long standing tradition. It is seen as the fifth largest such gathering in the U.S.

St. Louis Irishman **Tom Dooley** gained fame in the 1950s working as a physician in refugee camps in Vietnam and Laos. He also reportedly collected intelligence for the CIA. He was a staunch anti-Communist who died in 1961 from cancer. Before he died he wrote the best-selling book, *Deliver Us From Evil.*

Some of the more popular Irish establishments in St. Louis are Mike Shannon's Steak House at 620 Market, Maggie O'Brien's at 2000 Market, and John McGurk's Pub at 1200 Russell. St. Louisan **Diane Shaw** has an Irish website. She knows of no restaurants that are noted for Irish cuisine, but a number of Irish establishments serve Guinness beer on tap.

The Irish sport of "hurling" has remained popular in St. Louis and a club team has been formed to play teams in other nearby cities. 314-422-2268

McBride High School was a popular place for Irish families to send their sons to get a good education.

Some prominent Irish surnames include: O'Brien, Price, Hennessey, Donahue, O'Malley, Dooley, O'Toole, Kennedy, Monahan, Canty, Connors, Fields, McGlynn, McMahon, Dougherty, Foley, Keeley, Borders, Ganey, Conatay, Driscoll, Higgins, McDaniels, McConnell, Tierny, Hilley, Nash, Walsh, Hoertel, Brennan, O'Reilly, Madigan,

Flannigan, Cavanaugh, O'Leary, Murphy, Conner, Brennan, Forhan, Downey, O'Neill, Brady, Kelly, Halloran, Noonan, Kerry, Dempsey, Macelwane, Ryan and O'Connell.

This writer did a book titled *St. Louis Irish* in 2004. Although I have no Irish blood in me I have three grandchildren who can proudly claim their Irish heritage. One granddaughter is a descendant of arguably the first Irish Kelly to settle in New England in the mid-1650s.

One of my main sources was Fr. William B. Faherty (a St. Louis University Jesuit) who wrote the 2001 book, *The St. Louis Irish – An Unmatched Celtic Community*. His book became my bible. If you want to learn about the historical facts of the Irish in St. Louis, buy Father Faherty's book. If you want to learn about Father Faherty as well as some other local Irishmen (such as Helen Gannon and Joe McGlynn), buy my book. It was McGlynn, a lawyer, who helped found the St. Patrick's Day parade over three decades ago.

Incidentally, my genealogy web site has a great deal of Irish data on it. "Genealogy in St. Louis" http:/genealogyinstlouis.accessgenealogy.com

Bob Corbett, of the Dogtown Historical Society, has found 26 soccer players from Dogtown who were prominent in the sport. You can contact him at corbetre@webster.edu.

THE HILL

On high ground south of the River des Peres and I-44, the Hill is mostly an Italian-American neighborhood in St. Louis south of Forest Park. Hampton Avenue is generally considered its western boundary. Kingshighway is the eastern boundary and Manchester and Southwest are the north and south boundaries. Non-Italians sometimes called it Dago Hill.

Spielberg Furniture on the Hill (Lonnie Tettaton)

Male immigrants from Lombardy and Sicily, according to writer Eleanor Berra Marfisi, earned about 15 cents an hour loading clay or carrying wheelbarrow loads of bricks at the mine and factory. When work was over, they trudged up the hill (Arsenal and Sublette) to their shotgun house, thus giving the neighborhood its moniker. The intersection at Arsenal and Sublette borders Sublette Park, the former site of the **Social Evil Hospital** built there in 1873. The "social evil" refers to prostitution. City fathers decided that they were unable to abolish prostitution so they decided to regulate it. The hospital was built for the purpose of examining prostitutes who were required, by law, to have regular check-ups. In 1873, $134,000 was collected by the hospital in examination fees. The hospital was razed in 1914 and its 13.5 acres became Sublette Park. The Missouri State Hospital, at 5400 Arsenal, was four stories high with a huge cast iron dome.

Italian Immigrant Statue on the Hill

The Columbia Theater and Family Theater were the prominent movie houses. Club Casino was a popular night spot in the 1940s and 1950s. Bocce Ball, long a traditional pastime, is still played at **Milo's Bocce Garden**. The Big Club became a community center for all Italians. Southwest Bank opened in 1920. Quick Meal Stove, Banner Iron, Blue Ridge Bottling and R & F (Ravarino & Freschi) Spaghetti, Viviano Retail Groceries, Missouri Baking Company, McQuay-Norris Piston Ring, Volpi Foods, Chemetron and Liggett & Meyer Tobacco (on Tower Grove Avenue) were major businesses. Because of the Hill's proximity to the clay mines, many of the homes are made of durable brick. Visitors can almost feel the traditional work ethic, pride and heritage steeped in the neighborhood. Columbus Day parades were a prominent tradition of the Hill area.

The only railroad traversing the area was the Oak Hill and Carondelet branch of the Missouri Pacific. There were two streetcar lines – one on Arsenal and Southwest and the other was the Southampton Line on Kingshighway.

Its subdivisions included Garden Place, Fairmont, St. Louis Heights, Submoor, Reber Place, Jasper Park, Regal Place, Macklind Heights, Porta and Cheltenham.

Churches in the area included St. Aloysius Gonzaga (German), St. Ambrose (Catholic), Italian Evangelical Church (Protestant) Mount Tabor Church and Pattison Avenue Baptist. Southwest High and St. Ambrose Parochial were prominent schools.

Italians from northern Italy began settling in the area in the late 19th century. They were mainly attracted by jobs available in the nearby clay mines and brickyards, notably St. Louis Smelting and Refining. The **Italians were so poor that railroad officials often let them sleep in empty boxcars**. They frugally saved their money and sent for their families as soon as they could afford it.

When the Worlds Fair closed, building materials were offered free to anyone who would haul them away. The Italians used the material to build "shotgun" houses that were similar in shape to the boxcars they had called home. The Viviano family obtained equipment from the Italian Pavilion, and this is how their pasta business started. Viviano's Grocery is currently at 5139 Shaw.

The National Origins Act of 1924 closed the door on immigration to America from areas of Eastern Europe.

The Parish of St. Ambrose was founded in 1903 to serve the needs of the immigrants. The existing St. Ambrose Church was built in 1926.

The area has been able to retain its Italian flavor with nearly ¾ of the current population living there being Italian-Americans. They do this by refusing to sell their homes on the open market, using word of mouth instead. Fire hydrants in the Hill area are proudly painted white, red and green. Some existing businesses are Amighetti's, J. Viviano and Sons Grocery, Di Gregorio's grocery, Rigazzi's Restaurant and Missouri Baking Company. This author and his wife have a bedroom suite that was bought from Fair Mercantile Furniture in 1964. Their name brand furniture was cheaper because they did not advertise or have fancy showrooms.

Lilly Pond at Tower Grove Park (David Lossos collection)

Baseball greats **Yogi Berra** and **Joe Garagiola** grew up on the Hill; their boyhood homes are across the street from each other on Elizabeth Avenue. Jack Buck bought his first home here. Four of the five St. Louisans on the U.S. soccer team that defeated England in the 1950 World Cup came from here. A movie of this was made and is available on DVD as *The Miracle Match.* The Soccer Hall of Fame is on Daggett Avenue between Shaw's Coffee and St. Ambrose Catholic Church.

According to Joe Garagiola in his book, *Baseball is a Funny Game*, his neighborhood was derisively called Dago Hill by outsiders. Yogi Berra invented another Yogism when he said, "**Ruggeri's Restaurant is so crowded nobody goes there anymore**." Yogi and Joe once worked there as waiters.

Amighetti's Café and Bakery at 5141 Wilson is a current lunch favorite for many St. Louisans.

If a person's surname ends with a vowel such as an o, a, or i, as in Dimaggio, there's a good chance they're Italian.

THE STRONG GERMAN HERITAGE

People of German descent came to Missouri for a variety of reasons – war, religious persecution, economic opportunity. Martin Luther created religious and political instability in Germany when he nailed his "95 theses" to the church door at Wittenburg. By fomenting rebellion he was responsible for creating the revolution against the Catholic Church and establishing Lutheranism and other Protestant sects by other reformers. Northern Germany became mostly Lutheran, while southern Germany remained Catholic. This led to violence and discrimination to whatever group happened to be in the minority.

In advertisements, Missouri was depicted as the New Fatherland. Independent and thrifty, many Germans came to places like **Hermann** and brought their businesses and crafts with them. They used their secrets to grow grapes and produce wine in the fertile hill country near rivers.

Large numbers of Germans originally settled in and near St. Louis, Missouri, but then Missouri entered the Union as a "slave" state in 1821. Most Germans disliked slavery and some of them migrated to Illinois where slavery was forbidden. **Columbia, Waterloo, Germantown, Red Bud, New Baden, Belleville, Lenzburg** and **Millstadt** are all southern Illinois towns with large Teutonic populations.

Those who stayed in the city tended to live either in the Baden area or in South St. Louis.

In 1816, after the Napoleonic Wars in Europe ended, the farmers and industrial workers in Germany were hit with hard times. German soil was poor due to having been tilled for centuries. Crop failures, high taxes, constant warfare and revolution were the norm. Primogeniture laws were still in effect. When a landholding father died, if there were four sons in the family, only the oldest inherited the estate. This was done to keep family farms intact. Letters from those who had migrated to Missouri told others back home of limitless opportunity – a place where land could be bought for a dollar an acre. Many of the young German males came here with visions of once again becoming part of the landed gentry.

Europe was hit by a number of revolutions in 1848 and Germany was not an exception. Political refugees streamed to America and to Missouri. An item from an old newspaper said that a number of Germans had arrived in this country at the port of New Orleans. They often knew so little English that they had notes pinned to their coats telling authorities who they were and where they wanted to go. The article said that 228 of them traveled up the Mississippi and settled in **St. Louis**.

Before 1870, there was no such country called Germany. Germany was merely a loose collection of states such as Prussia, Saxony, and Bavaria. Otto Von Bismarck, known as the "Iron Chancellor," united the various regions by precipitating a war with France. Numerous Germans fled to escape the draft then, again during World War I, and yet again to flee Hitler's Nazi regime.

Another thing that attracted Germans to Missouri is that they were told the land and climate was similar to the Fatherland. This geographical factor is why Swedes and Norwegians often settled in northern Missouri while Italians preferred southern Missouri.

The Germans were often referred to as Latin Farmers because they were generally better educated than most other immigrants. Unlike most immigrants, the Germans came to St. Louis with significant financial resources. By 1860, there were nine German newspapers operating in St. Louis. Although the Germans in St. Louis were the largest minority, they did not elect their first mayor, Henry Overstolz, until 1876.

One of the crops they brought with them was horseradish. The crop prospered and did so well on that alluvial floodplain stretching from **Alton** to **Chester,** Illinois (the American Bottom), that the area became known as the **Horseradish Capital of America**. Two-thirds of those who currently raise this labor-intensive crop are descendants of the original German settlers.

The Germans were the first to teach the science of agriculture in their universities. They practiced crop rotation and used manure as a fertilizer. They studied plant and animal diseases and developed methods to combat them. They learned how to test the soil to determine what minerals and nutrients it lacked. America benefited because the arriving immigrants brought this knowledge with them.

The Germans were the first to introduce the concept of early childhood education known as ***kindergarten***. The idea did not take hold in this country until after the turn of the century.

It was the Deutschlanders who introduced the custom of the **Easter bunny** to America, although it was originally called the Easter Hare. According to an old Norse legend, one of the gods turned a bird into a rabbit. The rabbit thought it was still a bird and continued to build nests and lay colorful eggs. It was believed that children who found these eggs during the Easter season would have good fortune and longevity. The Germans also introduced the concept of the **Christmas tree** – the *tannenbaum*.

German Turnverein acrobatic group (MHS)

Perhaps the most lucrative skill the Germans brought with them was the art of brewing beer. Numerous breweries flourished in **East St. Louis** and **Belleville, Kansas City and St. Louis**.

As the story goes, around 1939 there was a German baker in St. Louis who mixed the wrong proportion of ingredients and **accidentally invented "gooey butter coffeecake**."

Around the turn of the century a steamship company of the Hamburg Line began serving sandwich bread with a meat patty. This was the **origin of the *hamburger***. German families who made the long voyage by boat were required to bring with them a fifty day supply of food. This hoard usually consisted of such items as bread, ham, beans, molasses, rice, sugar and potatoes. Immigrants frequently took one boat down the Rhine River to Rotterdam, Holland, and then took another boat across the ocean.

Benton Park (David Lossos collection)

Germans in Missouri had to suffer through World War I. Before America entered the war, their loyalty was with Germany in the fight against traditional enemies, the French and English. Though many by now were native-born Americans, their loyalty was doubted just as Japanese-Americans were distrusted in World War II. The teaching of German as a language was dropped in Missouri high schools and colleges. The St. Louis Symphony dropped works by German composers from its concerts. Berlin Avenue was renamed (John) Pershing and Van Verson became Enright (to honor the first American killed in the war). August A. Busch bought many Liberty Bonds, but he was criticized for portraits of Germans which were hanging in the Anheuser-Busch Brewery. The fact that Germans were steadfastly loyal to the Union in the Civil War seemed to count for nothing.

Sauerkraut became "liberty cabbage," cute wiener dogs were now called "liberty pups," German chocolate cake became Dutch chocolate cake. In **Collinsville**, Illinois, a German coal miner named Praeger was lynched because he spoke out against the war.

Germans are also known for their love of Leiderkranz music and festivals. In the fall of the year Missouri is filled with Oktoberfests. Most German communities in Missouri built halls where dances, meetings and wedding receptions were held. The Germans celebrated with cultural Strassenfests, dressed in ethnic costumes, danced Polkas, ate bratwurst and sauerbraten, drank beer and finished things off with a piece of apple strudel. They listened to bands that featured tubas and accordions. They were among the first to get into exercise and fitness and organized Turnverein societies that were later Anglicized to Turner Halls.

Germans became the largest ethnic group in St. Louis, but they never formed a closed homogeneous community. They tended to live in neighborhoods interspersed with other immigrants and native Missourians. St. Louis public schools taught one class a day in German. The rest were taught in English which encouraged rapid assimilation of the second generation Germans. In 1887, St. Louis schools did away with German in the elementary school curriculum. Germans held on to their mother tongue through their newspapers (*Anzeiger, Westliche Post*) and through sermons in their churches.

German immigrants had a certain stubbornness and toughness that helped them adapt to Missouri climate. There was an old saying about German temperament that went something like this: "You can always tell who's a German, but you can't tell a German anything."

People of German descent currently live throughout the state of Missouri. They carry on the tradition with names such as Bauer, Mollman, Lohmueller, Melhauser, Hinkle, Jacobus, Hackman, Wortmann, Volz, Turnwart, Krughoff, Hoffman, Leibrock, Buhrmann, Boucher, Bieser, Reither, Kurrus, Abt, Gallenbeck, Sternberger, Hauss, Schultz,

Bauman, Trendley, Schwartzenbach, Schmelzel, Hornback, Siegmann, Krieger, Spiesbach, Biehl, Giesing, Belz, Greisedieck, Schoendienst, Dietrich, Boekenkroeger, Schmidt, Schneider (one who is a tailor), Westerheide, Schwartz, Walther, Eisele, Rothe, Schuette, Block, Detchemendy, Koch, Von Brock, Brichler, Fuchs, Harmon, Beyersdorfer, Gruber, Kriegen, Then, Hoelker, Becker, Bischoff, Goeddeker, Fiebig, Koenig (the German word for king), Brandt, Braun, Schuetze, Busch, Henning, Jaeger, Sauer, Schulze, Vogt, Wolf, Kohnleier, Weber, Winkler, Guenther, Reinhardt, Wiedeman, Deppe, Spiller, Boeker, Schneider, Herr, Sandefur, Metzger and many, many others. And how about those classic Christian names such as Eva, Marie, Franz, Fritz, Gunter, Otto, Kermit, Gottfried, Karl, Gustav, Wilhelm, Max, Ludwig, Ignatz, Adolph, Anton, Hermann, Gerhard, Konrad, Emil, Friedrich, Wolfgang, Engelbert, Henerfauth (tax collector), Kohlmeier and Horst.

JEWISH COMMUNITY IN ST. LOUIS

The earliest evidence of a Jew settling in St. Louis is that of Joseph Philipson, a Pennsylvanian who arrived here in 1807. Wolf Bloch, a native of Bohemia, arrived in St. Louis in 1816 and is considered the Jewish Pioneer of St. Louis. Two other brothers followed and they became the first Americans to establish a permanent store in St. Louis.

The early settlers were non-practicing Jews. Not until 1836 was the first Jewish religious service held when ten men rented a small room over Max's Grocery at the corner of Second and Spruce (now the Arch grounds). The next year these men organized the United Hebrew Congregation, which is still in existence. The first building used as a synagogue was located on Fifth Street between Green and Washington avenues. In 1855, this organization erected its own temple on 6th Street between Locust and St. Charles streets. The B'nai El congregation moved into its own house of worship at 6th and Cerre streets in 1855. Shaare Emeth congregation was organized in 1866 and Temple Israel was organized in 1886 by a dissatisfied faction of that group. There are also six regularly organized Orthodox congregations in the city. Mount Olive Jewish Cemetery was established in 1856. Mt. Sinai Cemetery was chartered in 1873.

Due to Czar Alexander III's persecution, many Russian Jews came to St. Louis and settled along Easton Avenue, gradually moving into the northern part of the Central West End near Soldan High.

The main Jewish social organization in early St. Louis was the Harmonie Club on Market Street. By 1905, the Columbian Club was the only Jewish organization in the city.

The Chicago Fire of 1871 left many Jews homeless so they relocated to St. Louis. The United Hebrew Relief Association was organized for this purpose.

Realizing the need of a hospital for the poor, the Jews of St. Louis donated $100,000 and the Jewish Hospital of St. Louis was incorporated in 1900. The hospital located on the eastern edge of Forest Park in 1927. In 1996, it merged with Barnes Hospital, which was two blocks away, and Barnes-Jewish Hospital is the largest in Missouri. Barnes-Jewish is known throughout the world as one of the finest hospitals in existence.

By 1905 there were two Jewish newspapers in St. Louis, the *Jewish Voice* and the *Modern View*.

Another wave of St. Louis Jews arrived here in the 1840s and 1850s, fleeing Germany because of social and political revolution.

There was a yellow fever epidemic in the Southern States (1878) and a good number of Jews left and came to St. Louis to escape the conflagration.

Another wave of Jewish immigrants came along in 1880 due to a new round of anti-Semitism that was sweeping Europe.

At the turn of the century, Russian riots against Jews, called pogroms, were so bad that yet another new group of Jewish immigrants came to America.

A fourth wave occurred during the 1930s due to persecution by Nazi Germany. Unfortunately, many of the Jews who tried to flee to America were turned away due to strict immigration laws that were passed in 1924.

Beginning in the 1930s, many Jews began moving to **University City** and by 1946 it had become the center of Jewish culture in St. Louis.

A final large group of Jews came to America, and cities like St. Louis, after the collapse of the Soviet Union in 1989.

The Jews of St. Louis were prominent in the efforts to bring the World's Fair to the city. Isaac Schwab, Jonathin

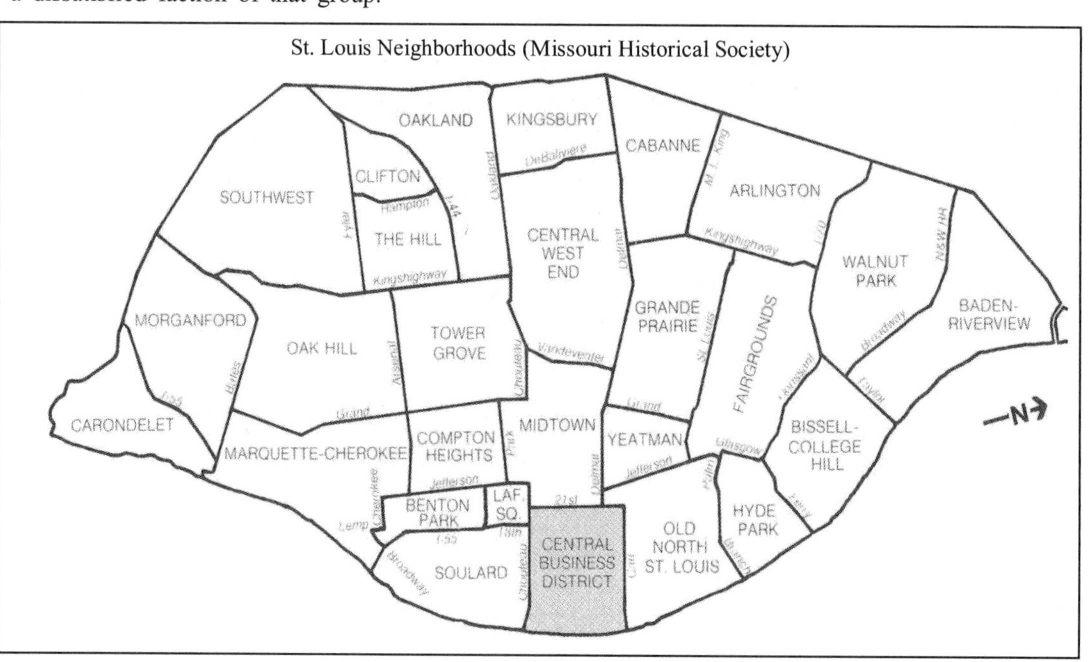

St. Louis Neighborhoods (Missouri Historical Society)

Rice, Jacob Wertheimer, Elias Michaels, Nathan Frank and Charles Stix were members of the Exposition's board of directors. Frank was owner of the *St. Louis Star* newspaper. Other Jews of prominence were Elias Michaels, president of the Mercantile Club; Marcus Bernheimer, a president of the Merchants' Exchange; Jacob Goldman, who was president of the Cotton Exchange; Meyer Rosenblatt, who served as a city revenue collector; Moses Sale, a judge of the Circuit Court and Jacob Lampert who was a wealthy cigar manufacturer. In 1912, he was Grand Master of the Masons in St. Louis. At the time of his death (1921) he had the largest estate in the history of Missouri.

Jews currently constitute only 1.1 percent of the state's entire population. Typical Jewish names include Lipsutz, Grodsky, Lieberstein, Rothman, Goldberg, Goldman, Silverman, Pearlman, Hochdoffer, Tenenbaum, Spritz, Copilevitz, Goldenhersh, Arenstein, Weiss, Weissman, Zuke, Frankel, Cohn, Waghalter, Wallman, Novack, Schneider, Shankman, Baum, Routman, Shaftal, Silver, Korein, Greenberg, Khoufax, Covitz, Eisenstein, Folberg, Katz, Siegel, Keyser, Goodman, Kaplan, Shenker, Maltzman, Margolies, Gallop, Schneiderman, Chackes, Rosenberg, Hurwitz, Shectman, Altman, Fitter, Plattner, Shaftal, Tzinberg, Fleishman, Ravad, Keyser, Hirz, Hartstein, Arnstein, Bromberg, Schwartz, Sussman, Shapiro, Prywitch, Rochman, Folberg, Spelker, Ofstein, Tuvil, Spirtas, and Janklow.

Gaslight Square

For those who are wondering why Morris is such a popular Jewish first name, it is a modern variation of the Old Testament name Moses.

Despite a rich heritage chronicled in the Old Testament, Jews in modern times did not have a homeland until the nation of Israel was created by the U.N. after World War II. In 72 A.D., the Romans threw them out of their homeland in Palestine after they rebelled. This scattering of the Jews throughout Europe is called the **Diaspora**. Known for their resourcefulness and tenacity, Jews managed to prosper despite persecution by the Roman Catholic and Eastern Orthodox Church. Many blamed the Jews for the crucifixion of Christ. Medieval Knights who went on the Crusades killed hundreds of Jews along the way as they went on their mission to free the Holy Land from the Moslems. Hitler blamed Jewish bankers and merchants for Germany's defeat in World War I and ended up killing 6 million of them in the Holocaust.

Compton Reservoir Tower

The **Jewish Sabbath is on Saturday**, actually starting on Friday after sunset. In the old days, Hebrew children were sent to public schools in St. Louis and religious and language training was conducted Monday through Thursday at the Synagogue after schools were dismissed in the afternoon. Jewish families celebrated Hanukkah, the High Holidays of Rosh Hashanah (Jewish New Year) Yom Kippur (Day of Atonement) and Succor the Feast of the Tabernacles.

Jewish families were close knit and children were expected to marry within the faith. Some parents felt so strongly about this that when their children married Gentiles they went through a **Shiva ceremony, rent their clothes, and disowned their progeny, considering them to be dead**. If you have seen Neil Diamond in *The Jazz Singer*, this is what his father (Lawrence Olivier) did in that movie when he divorced his wife.

GASLIGHT SQUARE

It's hard to believe, but one of the most popular and famous places in America in the 1960s was Gaslight Square, a thriving entertainment district that became far more notorious than Bourbon Street in New Orleans. That two block section of Olive Street, between Boyle and Sarah, in the Central West End, was like a magical state of mind.

The area previously had been a haven of antique shops, but it was hit by a devastating tornado in 1959. The Mill Creek Valley neighborhoods at the time were meeting the wrecking ball and undergoing wholesale urban renewal. Many fixtures, appliances and decorative ornamentations from Mill Creek found new homes in the Square.

In the tornado's wake rose an effervescent spirit that hasn't been matched anywhere since. An influx of insurance money allowed the place to be transformed into a mecca for beatniks, artists, musicians, singers, poets, comedians and other performers. Original music was everywhere and the streets were lined with packed clubs, bars, theaters, restaurants and coffee houses with discussions that carried into the wee hours of the morning. The area also boasted live jazz, Irish dancing, street mimes and a street car. Old timers swear that it sometimes took a half an hour to go two blocks by car.

It was truly a unique hot spot of entertainment. Like New York's Greenwich Village, Gaslight Square became one of the main hubs of the Beat Generation. This nexus of Bohemian nightlife helped construct an important alternative American scene. The Bohemian's church was St. John Nepomuk at 12th and Russell. Writers Jack Kerouac, Alan Ginsberg and others traveling coast to coast would make Gaslight a deliberate stop to witness hipster nirvana.

The names of people who performed at **"Camelot in St. Louis"** sound like a veritable *Who's Who*. The list included Judy Collins, Lenny Bruce, Woody Allen, Mike Nichols, Elaine

May, Barbara Streisand, Miles Davis, Jackie Mason, Davy "the Nose" Bold, Gypsy Rose Lee, Phyllis Diller, the Smothers Brothers, Chris King, Bob Dylan, Clea Bradford, Marty Bronson, Bob Kuban, Joanne Cameron, the Russ David Trio, Quartette Tres Bien, Singleton Palmer, Jeanne Trevor and Dick Gregory.

Webster Groves resident Phyllis Diller went on to national fame and Tommy Smothers, in an interview, said the first joint he ever smoked was at Gaslight Square.

Popular current restaurants such as Dressel's and O'Connell's had their origins at Gaslight Square. Jack Parker, proprietor of O'Connell's, left in 1972 and relocated to the corner of Shaw and Kingshighway. Other joints and eateries at Gaslight included the Crystal Palace, Richard Mutrux's Three Fountains Restaurant, Golden Eagle Saloon, Gaslight Bar, Whiskey A Go Go, the Laughing Buddha Coffeehouse, Smokey Joe's Grecian Terrace and the Dark Side. Jimmy Massucci had an opera house at Gaslight and when things declined he left and started Café Louie's and tried to reinvent Gaslight Square on Laclede's Landing.

In the later 1960s, the crowds turned younger and rowdier and the entertainment became racier. Surrounding residents fled to the suburbs as crime escalated and newspaper reports of drugs and fights bred fear. White flight and urban decay set in during the 1970's and the place, noted for its decorative sidewalk gas lights, quickly fell into oblivion. It looked as desolate as a landscape on a Salvador Dali painting. Not a trace of Gaslight Square remains today.

This once lively hot spot appears to be on the rise again. Starting in 2004, the Home Builders Association sponsored a redevelopment project called CitiRama that featured new homes and condos built by ten different developers.

Sometimes history can be found in the heart and mind in addition to books. For many St. Louisans, the "happening scene" was in the Central West End in the 4200 block of Olive Street. (Some info provided by **Patrick Schneider** of Dogtown)

Fairground Park 1880 (Missouri Historical Society)

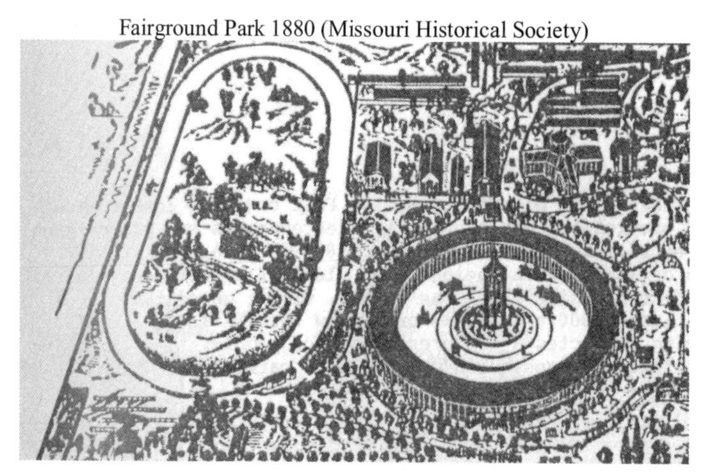

Central High School

White Corinthian Grand Water Tower (MHS)

OLD NORTH ST. LOUIS & YEATMAN

This neighborhood was adjacent to the downtown business district and had the Mississippi to the east and Jefferson Avenue on its west. There was a thirty foot high and 150 foot long Indian mound at the Great Trail (Broadway) and Mound streets. The mound was demolished in 1869. Natural Bridge was laid out in the 1840s as an extension of Mound Street. The early settlers in the area were predominantly English. Next came the Kerry Patch Irish and the "Little Paderborn" Germans.

The Neighborhood Garden Apartments were built in 1936, Carr Square Village in 1942 and Cochran Garden Apartments in 1952.

By the 1920s the neighborhood was a polyglot of ethnicity with immigrants from the Balkans and Russia moving in. Gang warfare, brought on by Prohibition liquor profits, became common.

The **Yeatman** area, directly west of the Old North neighborhood, extends to Grand Avenue. The name comes from James Yeatman, who made his fortune in ironworks and later founded the Mercantile Library. **Central High**, the first west of the Mississippi (1853), was at 15th and Olive. Hadley Tech started in 1929 and in 1931 moved into a larger building on Bell Street. When Hadley Tech was superseded by O'Fallon Tech, its old building became the new home for Vashon High. The Odeon Theater, Central YMCA, Pruitt-Igoe and Mullanphy Hospital were significant structures. By 1929, Mullanphy was renamed DePaul and it moved to 2415 North Kingshighway. The YMCA later moved to Grand and Franklin. The Odeon, at 1038 North Grand, was home to the St. Louis Symphony for many years.

LAFAYETTE SQUARE & BENTON PARK

Lafayette Park, the city's first, was created in 1836. This area is sandwiched between

Compton Heights to the west and Soulard to the east. Benton Park, also known as City Park, was platted in 1866 by Montgomery Blair. Both areas evolved into nice residential neighborhoods. The De-Menil Mansion is the most outstanding existing structure in Benton Park. It was barely saved by preservationists when I-55 came through the area. The Lemp Brewery was its biggest industry, although there were also brickyards and ropewalks. Benton Park has an obelisk monument dedicated to Friedrich Hecker, a German-American brigade commander in the Civil War. **Hecker**, Illinois is named for him.

Lafayette Park was severely damaged by the tornado of 1896. The area started going commercial in the 1930s. The German House, later known as the Gateway Temple, was built in 1928 at Lafayette and Jefferson.

MARQUETTE-CHEROKEE DISTRICT

This part of south St. Louis is sandwiched between Soulard to the north and Carondelet on the south. Much of the area slopes toward the River des Peres. Sugar Loaf Indian mound, at the foot of Wyandotte Street, was razed a long time ago. Roosevelt High School, built in 1927, was located at 3230 Hartford. Holy Cross Church inspired many with its beautiful tall spire. Bellerive Park, at Bates Street, was purchased in 1908. Concordia Lutheran Seminary was on Jefferson at Winnebago, until it moved to **Clayton** in 1926. Concordia Publishing House remained in the area.

Cleveland High was at 4352 Louisiana. The old Marine Hospital, at Marine Avenue and Winnebago, was razed during World War II. The government built the federal records center on the site in 1959 and it later moved to Page Avenue.

KINGSBURY

Kingsbury is due west of the Central West End and the city limits mark its western boundary. DeBaliviere is on its eastern boundary. Oakland Avenue marked its southern limits. It took its name from James Kingsbury, son-in-law to John Cabanne who was a large landholder. The part of Kingsbury north of Forest Park was slow to be developed due to frequent flooding by the River des Peres. Robert Forsyth and Daniel Catlin were later large landholders. Early subdivisions included High Pointe, Parkview Place, Washington Heights, Tesson's Subdivision, Arundel Place and DeMun Park. Thomas Skinker's estate was developed as Ellenwood in 1922.

Garavelli's Restaurant (now on Chippewa) was a landmark place on DeBalieviere from 1920 to 1950. DeGiverville and Cafferatas were other early eating establishments. The **Winter Garden** on DeBalieviere was built in 1903 as a jai alai stadium. It was later converted into an ice skating rink that gave hours of pleasure to many St. Louisans. It was torn down in 1964.

Donut Drive-in at 6525 Chippewa (Lorna Nunes photo)

Winter Garden rink prior to demolition

Shaw's Garden (David Lossos collection)

Delmar was a word coined by property owners from DELaware and MARyland. **Steve "the watermelon man"** had a place at Pershing and DeBalieviere and Parkmoor had a fast food restaurant on DeBalieviere. The DeBalieviere neighborhood declined rapidly after the closing of the Wabash Railroad's Delmar Station in the 1960s.

CENTRAL WEST END

The Central West End, largely a residential area, is bounded on the north by Delmar, the south by Oakland, the east by Vandeventer and the west by DeBalieviere. It was once an enclave created for the wealthy and social elite. Its prominent subdivisions consisted of Dorris Place, Oakland Place, Lenox Place, Hortense Place, Vandeventer Place, Portland Place, Kingsbury Place, Pershing Place, Washington Terrace, Westmoreland Place and a string of magnificent mansions along Lindell.

This was a wealthy district created by men and women of property who wanted to escape the noise and pollution of downtown St. Louis. Real estate ads in the late 1880s said this was a magical place where "property never depreciates."

For years the annual **Easter Parade** was held at Kingshighway and Lindell. Union Boulevard was named by northern sympathizers during the Civil War. The Central

West End also includes Forest Park, Barnes Jewish Hospital and the St. Louis Cathedral. St. John's Methodist, Temple Israel and Second Baptist Church were at the "Holy Corners" of Washington and Kingshighway. Trinity Episcopal and Second Presbyterian were other important churches. The Chase Hotel was built in 1922 and the Park Plaza in 1931. Movie houses included the Congress and the Lyric. The industrial focus was along the Wabash Railroad right-of-way that went through the area.

A 1948 Supreme Court decision held that racially restrictive covenants in local neighborhoods were unconstitutional. African Americans began moving into areas that had previously been closed to them. Newspapers began running stories about "creeping blight" and many whites in the Central West End fled to the county or across the river to St. Charles.

COMPTON HILL

This neighborhood is directly east of the Tower Grove area. It is bounded by Grand Avenue on the west, Jefferson on the east, Arsenal on the south and Park Avenue to the north. It is noted for its huge 56,000,000 gallon water reservoir (1871) that is surrounded by a decorative wall. The large Romanesque water tower was erected in 1896. It features a statue that was controversial in its time (due to nudity), "the Naked Truth."

Beaumont High in Fairground

Churches in the area include St. Francis de Sales (1908), with its lofty spire, Church of the Immaculate Conception (1908), St. Wenceslaus (1925), Compton Heights Baptist, Compton Hill Congregational, St. Luke's German Evangelical, Emmaus Lutheran, Messiah Lutheran, Peter's Memorial Presbyterian, Berea Temple, Memorial Methodist and Church of Christ Scientist.

Incarnate Word Hospital is located at 3545 Lafayette. James B. Eads resided on Compton Hill in the 1870s. The first branch of the St. Louis Public Library was the Barr facility at Jefferson and Lafayette.

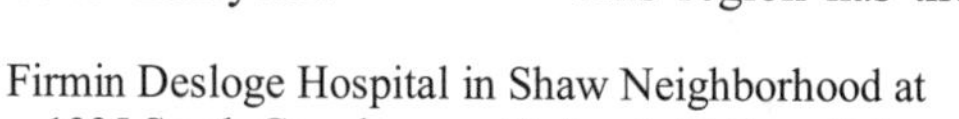

Firmin Desloge Hospital in Shaw Neighborhood at 1325 South Grand – now St. Louis U. Hospital

THE SHAW NEIGHBORHOOD

This area was sandwiched between the Hill to the west and Compton Heights to the east. It was bounded by Grand on the east, Tower Grove Park and Arsenal on the south, Kingshighway to the west, and Chouteau and Manchester on the north. Under the French, this was called Prairie des Noyers. By the 1850s, Henry Shaw had acquired large tracts of land in the region. Shaw platted his Grand Avenue subdivision in 1878. Some of these houses had one window bricked up, following an old custom due to the English tradition of taxing based on the number of windows in a house. Other subdivisions were Tyler Place, Flora Place, Dundee Place and Magnolia Place. Mary Tyler, an early resident, sold her property holdings to Western Improvement Co.

Henry Shaw, a rich man at age forty due to investments in the hardware business, visited his native England. He was so impressed with the Royal Botanical Garden that he was determined that St. Louis should have one. The Missouri Botanical Garden (314-577-9400) was laid out next to his estate, which he named Tower Grove. After his death, in 1889, Shaw's will bequeathed Tower Grove Park to the city and he was entombed in a mausoleum on the garden grounds. The spectacular Plexiglas geodesic dome greenhouse, known as the **Climatron**, was designed in 1959 by Buckminster Fuller of Southern Illinois University. Shaw's money paid for three statues in the park – Columbus, Von Humboldt and Shakespeare.

Churches in the neighborhood include St. Margaret of Scotland, Tower Grove Baptist, Compton Heights Baptist, B'Nai El Temple (converted to apartments in 1982), St. Peter's Lutheran, Reen English Lutheran, Mount Olive Lutheran, Shaw Avenue M.E. Church, Tyler Place Presbyterian, Gibson Heights Presbyterian. Other buildings include **Firmin Desloge** Hospital (1933), St. Louis University Hospital and medical schools, Cardinal Glennon Hospital, Bethesda General Hospital, Missouri Pacific Hospital and the Missouri School for the Blind.

The Missouri Pacific and Frisco lines came through the Shaw neighborhood.

SOUTHWEST

This region has the city limits on its southern boundary, Oak Hill and Kingshighway to the east and Cliffton and the Hill area on its north. It has the distinction of being the largest neighborhood in the city. The Frisco Railroad operated commuter trains to St. Louis from the Lindenwood and Gratiot stations until 1920. Early subdivisions included Gartside Estate, Lindenwood Addition, Harlem Heights, Tilles Park, Crawford Place, Morningside Park, Gardenville Terrace, Jameston Place, Woodland Park, Princeton Place, Hadley Park, Lynna Park and Nottingham.

Francis Park was acquired in 1916. It was the farm of David Francis and was considered as a possible site for the 1904 Fair. **Southwest High School**, at

Kingshighway and Arsenal, was completed in 1936. Kemper College was formerly on the site. Bishop DuBourg High was completed in 1951. Former 1970s student Bob Stretch says that because of its relatively plain exterior, students called it "the Factory." Hampton Village Market was one of the earliest "supermarkets" in St. Louis. A shopping center grew around it at Hampton and Chippewa.

FAIRGROUND NEIGHBORHOOD

Streetcar lines at Grand and Olive

This neighborhood takes its name from a huge fairgrounds park that existed there. It is bisected by Natural Bridge Road, so named because a natural stone formation arched over a local creek. It covers a broad section in north St. Louis and is bounded by Interstate 70 on the north, St. Louis Avenue to the south, Kingshighway on the west and Glasgow on the east. The site of the fairgrounds was once owned by railroad baron John O'Fallon.

Around 1855, Colonel Richard Barrett led a movement to establish a permanent annual agricultural and mechanical fair. Fifty acres were purchased from John O'Fallon at the corner of Grand Avenue and Natural Bridge Plank Road. This site was chosen due to its proximity to the Grand Tower, insuring an adequate water supply. The fair opened in October of 1856. In 1860, over 150,000 people came to see the Prince of Wales (Edward VII) who attended the fair. A large amphitheater was constructed in the 1870s for horse shows and sulky racing. There was also a monkey house, a clubhouse, a large oval track and a grandstand to view horse racing events. By 1883, the site had expanded to 83 acres and included an Art Gallery, Textile Hall, Bandstand, Machinery Hall, cattle pens, swine pens, Zoological Gardens, Natural History Museum and bear pits. **No other city in America could boast of such an annual spectacle.** The fair was discontinued after 1902. Around 1912, the circular amphitheater was torn down and the **world's largest swimming pool** took its place. The park was renovated by a 1955 bond issue that resulted in lighted ball diamonds and tennis courts.

Bevo Mill (Tettaton picture)

Penrose Park (50 acres) is located on the area's western edge and there is also a W.C. Handy Park and a Union Marcus Quarry Park.

The old Sportsman's Park was in the Fairground neighborhood. It was torn down and replaced by the Herbert Hoover Boy's Club in 1967.

Subdivisions in the area include Cote Brilliant, White Place, San Francisco Court, Penrose Park and Lindell Park. Penrose Park was 90 percent African American by 1970. Steamboat man Henry Shreve lived in the Fairground neighborhood as did James Clay, son of Kentuckian Henry Clay. Ashland Street is named for his boyhood home.

Churches include St. Engelbert's, Holy Rosary Catholic, Memorial Boulevard Christian, St. John's United Church of Christ, Salem Evangelical, Lee Avenue Presbyterian, Emanuel Lutheran, Pilgrim Lutheran, Bethlehem Lutheran, Bowman United Methodist, Church of Christ Scientist, Cote Brilliant Presbyterian.

Beaumont High, built in 1926, was named for a St. Louis surgeon. Northside YMCA, located directly across from the ballpark on Grand and Sullivan, is now closed.

Carter Carburetor, near Grand and St. Louis, and Schorr-Kolkschneider Brewery were major employers.

HYDE PARK

Bounded on the east by the Mississippi River, on the west by 23rd Street, on the north by East Grand, and the south by Natural Bridge Rd. In its early years, it was called Bremen, for the town in northern Germany that was home to many of the early immigrants. They were enticed to the area by Emil Malinckrodt, one of the early founders. The clatter of wooden shoes in the streets marked it as an early German settlement.

A horse-drawn trolley connected the place to the city of St. Louis in 1845. From Hyde Park, it continued north to the ferry at Bissell's Point. St. Louis annexed Bremen in 1855.

Hyde Park and Windsor Park are the two islands of green and serenity in the neighborhood.

The riverfront area, east of Broadway, thrived with lumbering, barrel and furniture making. After the Civil War, Hyde Park Brewery, Malinckrodt Chemical and Union Stockyards employed the most workers.

The McKinley Bridge (1910), one block north of Salisbury, connected the area to the east side towns of **Venice, Madison** and **Granite City**. Salisbury Street was long the business center of Hyde Park.

Other places of note included Grand Water Tower, Bissell Street water tower, Henry Clay School, Bethlehem Lutheran Church, Friedens United Church of Christ, North St. Louis Turnverein, Hyde Park Congregational Church, Holy Trinity Catholic Church, Bremen Bank and Krey Packing.

Salisbury and Hyde Park are British names derived from English settlers who also came to the area.

MID DOWNTOWN

This lively area thrived in the days of this author's youth as a theater and commercial district. There were so many times when my wife and I drove over from Illinois to dine at fine restaurants or see movies such as *Move Over, Darling, Psycho, The Sons of Katie Elder* and *Kings of the Sun*. We would park free on Washington Avenue, about three blocks from the Fox, then walk to the theater and try to avoid the street side photographer who took pictures and sold them to couples. We had one of the few auto wrecks in our lifetime at 9th and Washington. We were on our way to the Fox (1961) when another car, its view blocked by a bus picking up passengers, pulled out from the side street and hit us on the passenger fender. Fortunately, it wasn't serious and we made it to the show on time.

Tradition said that everyone in St. Louis passed by the bustling corner of Grand and Olive at some time in their life. The Grand-Olive intersection was proclaimed "fifteen minutes from anywhere."

Highway 40 marks the southern edge, Compton was to the east, Cook Avenue was the northern extremity and Midtown extended as far west as Spring Avenue.

Boating on Carondelet Park Lake (MHS)

Notable places include Daniel Boone Expressway (Highway 40), Grand Avenue Viaduct (over Mill Creek Valley) St. Louis University (Grand & Lindell), Scottish-Rite Cathedral, 22-story Continental Building, Vaughn Cultural Center, Fox Theater, Sheldon Concert Hall, Grandel Square Theater, St. Louis Theater/Powell Symphony Hall, Vandeventer Place, St. Alphonsus (Irish) Church and the Princess Theater on Grand near Olive.

CARONDELET

Carondelet stretches from the Mississippi on the east to Morganford Road in the west, with River des Peres marking its southern boundary and Meramec Street defining its northern limits. Carondelet is in the extreme southeast section of St. Louis. It was founded in 1767 by Clement DeLore de Treget on a trip upriver from **Ste. Genevieve**. He built a home on Elwood Street and was soon joined by other families from places like **Cahokia** and **Kaskaskia**. French Creole was the preferred language. It was named Carondelet in 1794 for the Spanish Governor (who was a Frenchman) of the territory. After Carondelet was annexed by St. Louis (1870), the north-south streets that previously had numbers were given names of states.

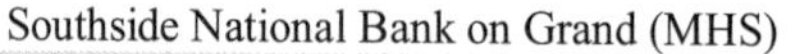

Southside National Bank on Grand (MHS)

A German immigrant named Jacob Stein acquired a lot and was so impressed with Carondelet that he persuaded other Germans to settle there. That part of the settlement became known as Stein's Town. At the time of the Louisiana Purchase, in 1803, Carondelet had a population of about 250. In 1826, the town sold the land that eventually became the site of Jefferson Barracks for a meager $5.00 to the U.S. government. Jefferson Barracks became the military nerve center for the western half of the U.S.

Around 1855, U.S. Grant, soldier turned farmer, earned money by delivering firewood to wealthy residents of Carondelet. In 1859, the Carondelet Common, which surrounded the town on three sides, was subdivided. Early prominent citizens were Henry Blow and Wilson Primm. Christian **Hoffmeister** began a livery stable business in 1858 but later went into the undertaking business. In 1862, City Hall was located at Broadway and Loughborough. Henry Blow was the leader of the pro-Unionists during the Civil War. **Carondelet Park** was created in 1876.

Carondelet Presbyterian was organized in 1850. St. Boniface German Catholic Church, on Michigan Avenue, was founded in 1860. St. Columbkille's Church, on Michigan Avenue, was organized in 1872 to serve the Irish laborers at nearby Vulcan Iron Works. The parish was discontinued shortly after the iron works closed in 1952. The Irish neighborhood was originally known as "**the Kelly Patch**." The Carondelet Baptist Church was organized in 1867. Carondelet United Church of Christ dates back to 1869. The Methodist Church on Virginia Avenue dates back to 1857. Other churches included St. Paul's Episcopal and Kingshighway Methodist.

The main commercial part of town was, and is, along South Broadway. Klaussmann's Brewery was located on South Broadway near the River des Peres. Marine Ways, at the foot of Davis Street (near the mouth of River des Peres), was the site where James Eads built his ironclads during the Civil War. The Edgar Zinc Company employed a large number of Spanish immigrant workers. Their parish was Our Lady of Covadonga. St. Louis Ship-Federal Barge was one of the nation's largest makers of barges. By 1906, National Lead had a plant that covered 80 acres. Carondelet Packing Company on Ivory Avenue was another important business. Franz Sheet Metal, founded in 1887, is still in business on South Broadway.

John Scullin almost convinced the World's Fair Committee to hold the 1904 extravaganza in Carondelet, but the place lost out to Forest Park.

Carondelet Park, consisting of 180 acres, is the third largest park in St. Louis.

Carondelet students attended Cleveland High, the city's southernmost high school.

Harry Keough and **Raymond Tucker** were Carondelet natives. Keough captained the extraordinary American soccer team that knocked the favored British out of the World Cup in 1950. Tucker was elected mayor of St. Louis.

Railroads, such as the Iron Mountain, were constructed from St. Louis and went through Carondelet to reach the mining areas in southern Missouri. Electric streetcars ran to downtown St. Louis from 1891 until the 1950s, when they were replaced by busses.

The Des Peres School, at 6307 Michigan Avenue, was where Susan Blow opened the **nation's first kindergarten.** This historic building is now home to the Carondelet Historical Society.

Sugar Loaf, on Ohio Avenue, is a large Indian mound that can still be seen from I-55.

In the 1960s, the construction of Interstate 55 took away customers from the business district by routing traffic past the town. In 1991, the Borden Pasta Group opened the largest plant in North America on the riverfront.

The United States Coast Guard has a base in Carondelet with about 50 employees. Reservations for tours can be made by calling 314-832-5941.

Standard/Amoco sign at Skinker & Clayton

OAK HILL AND MORGANFORD

These two adjacent areas are in southeast St. Louis with Morganford being due west of Carondelet and Oak Hill is located on the northern side of Morganford. Arsenal Street is the northern boundary and Kingshighway is the western boundary. Grand Ave. forms the eastern boundary. Oak Hill was annexed by the city in 1876.

William and James Russell were early landowners who gave it the name Oak Hill. They discovered coal deposits at the intersection of Tholozan and Morganford (Gravois coal diggin's) and shipped coal into the city by oxen drawn carts starting in 1820. James Russell's grandson was **Charles M. Russell**, the famed "Cowboy Artist."

William Christy was another early landowner. He made a fortune from an extensive underground clay mine.

Various early subdivisions included Tower Grove Heights, Oak Hill Heights, Newport Heights, Ellenwood Park, Chester Heights, Beckville, Bevo Mill, Humboldt Heights, Rosa Park, Grand Boulevard Park, South End Park and Brandon Place. There was a wooded area west of Grand was called Bamberger's Grove.

Gravois Avenue began as a road that led to a salt spring and a ferry, near present-day **Fenton**, in 1804. It was known as "the road to Fenton:" The road was paved with a macadam surface in 1840. In 1914, it became **the first concrete highway in the state**.

Early churches included Holy Family, St. John Catholic Church, Resurrection of Our Lord Catholic Church, St. John's Episcopal, Holy Innocents Episcopal, St. John's Lutheran, Trinity United Church of Christ and Christy United Methodist.

The four corners at the convergence of Grand and Gravois became one of the most important commercial centers in St. Louis. Kingshighway and Chippewa became an important commerce center when Southtown Sears opened a store there in 1951 (demolished 1994).

An Oak Hill-Carondelet branch of the Missouri Pacific Railroad came through the area in 1886. Important industries were Knapp Monarch and Brown Shoe Company. In 1942, **American Can** moved from North St. Louis to 3200 South Kingshighway on the site formerly occupied by Superior Brick. During the war the plant made torpedoes. In the 1970s, the place employed over a thousand people as it made beer cans for Anheuser-Busch. By 1995, there were only 450 employees, mainly making coffee cans.

For decades, the six-story art deco Dickmann (real estate) Building (1929) has been a landmark at 3115 South Grand. The most compelling landmark, however, was the ten story **Southside National Bank**, at Grand and Gravois.

Early landowners in the **Morganford** area were Roswell Field, Chris Koeln and James Bowlin. Prominent subdivisions were Dover Place, Holly Hills, Helena Place, Dixie Place, Austria Heights, Wayne Place, Carondelet Parkview, Morganford Park, Upton Place, Tesson Court and Morganford Gardens.

Early churches included St. Stephen Protomartyr, St. Lucas Lutheran, Epiphany Lutheran, Grace United Church of Christ, Brandt Presbyterian and Four Square Gospel Church.

BADEN-RIVERVIEW

The origin of this neighborhood goes back to the early days when a road was established that connected St. Louis to the Spanish Fort Don Carlos Del Rey, at the mouth of the Missouri River. This fort was superseded by Fort Bellefontaine, which was established on higher ground by that scoundrel James Wilkinson, Governor of Louisiana Territory. There was a large spring at the foot of the bluff below the fort. The fort was occupied until 1827 when the troops were moved to Jefferson Barracks.

Chevrolet plant at Natural Bridge and Union in Arlington

Bellefontaine Road was later renamed North Broadway. Baden developed at the intersection of this road with the road to Hall's Ferry. Old Hall's Ferry Road was built in 1815. It ran north to the Missouri River, near Portage des Sioux, where Edward Hall began operating a ferry around 1836. As the road from St. Louis approached Baden, it pretty much followed the path of present-day Hall Street, across bottom land, before it turned northwest and crossed Bellefontaine Road at the Baden wedge. Before the Civil War, Old Halls Ferry was a plank road.

Columbia Bottom Road, now Riverview Drive, was laid out around 1830. These roads were important for early farmers in northern St. Louis County to get their crops and produce to market.

Octagon Building on Delmar in University City (MHS)

Both Calvary and Bellefontaine cemeteries were established before the Civil War. Calvary was once the estate of James Clay, son of the Kentuckian who ran unsuccessfully for president on three occasions. Clay was induced to move there by his schoolmate friend, **James Bissell**. Early notable settlers included William Carr Lane, first St. Louis mayor, **Samuel Wiggins**, who operated the ferry monopoly in **East St. Louis**, and Amadee Valle.

Baden was annexed by St. Louis in 1876. At the time it was noted for its many vineyards. It was served by the Wabash Railroad and a horse-drawn streetcar that went to St. Louis. The Bissell Point waterworks plant was built in 1871. The huge Chain of Rocks waterworks and settling pools were built in 1915. They were the **largest in the world at the time**. The Bissell Point plant was phased out around 1960.

Prominent churches included Holy Cross Catholic, Our Lady of Mt. Carmel, Ebenezer Lutheran, Winsor Methodist, Prince of Peace Episcopal, Baden Baptist and First Church of God.

Sporting News on Washington Avenue (Lorna Nunes photo)

Chain of Rocks Amusement Park overlooked the Mississippi River at the bridge. Just north of the park was the **North Shore Country Club** and golf course, which began as a boat club in 1916. A swimming pool was built in 1919. Frequent flooding has caused it to be abandoned.

St. Louis Car occupied 52 acres in south Baden. **Paulus Gast** opened his brewery on Hornsby Avenue in 1899. **Charter Oak Stove** was located at Hall and Antelope streets in 1921. In more recent years, Hall Street became a huge complex for trucking companies. In order for this author to get his books to the distributor, he had to deliver them from **Glen Carbon** to Holland Express on Hall Street. About four years ago, Holland and a number of other companies moved from Hall Street to a new complex in south **Edwardsville,** off I-270.

ARLINGTON AND WALNUT PARK

Arlington is in northwest St. Louis and is bounded on the east by Kingshighway and on the west by the city limits. Martin Luther King Drive (formerly Easton Avenue) is on the south and the Mark Twain Expressway (I-70) is on the north. The earliest travel through this area was on the road from St. Louis to St. Charles, known as the Rock Road. A ferry, established in 1805, afforded a river crossing to St. Charles. It became a turnpike in 1837 with a 24 foot wide roadway. It was converted to a plank road in 1851. The road was spread with crushed rock in 1865, hence the title Rock Road.

Early subdivisions were Arlington Grove, Mount Auburn, Motor Heights, Mars Place, Hedgleigh Park and Norwood Square.

Erastus Wells, an early railroad mogul, built a narrow gauge railroad line from St. Louis to give access to his 65 acre estate. The line began near Grand and Olive and followed what later became the right-of-way for the Hodiamont streetcar line. It ended at his estate and this became the basis for the Wellston Loop and shopping district.

Dr. Rudolph Bircher's estate was on the site where the small arms plant was built during World War II. Another heavily traveled road led to the Goodfellow estate. This road was later named Goodfellow Boulevard.

Early churches included Blessed Sacrament Catholic Church, St. Edward the King Catholic Church, Our Savior Lutheran Church, Third United Presbyterian and All Saint's Episcopal.

Christian Brothers College was a huge four-story complex on Kingshighway and Easton. It burned in 1916 in one of the city's worst fires. Ten people lost their lives. The college moved to its present location on Clayton Road in 1922. Public Schools Stadium, completed in 1928, was on Kingshighway, north of St. Louis Avenue. It later became the site for the Mathews-Dickey Boys Club. De Paul Hospital, on North Kingshighway (1828), was the oldest existing Catholic Hospital in the nation. It relocated to the County in 1977.

The main industrial plants included General Motors on Natural Bridge, the Pullman Company, Rexall Drugs and Maloney Electric.

The Terminal Railroad had a belt line that ran from Hall Street to the western city limits.

The **Walnut Park** area is bounded on the north by the Calvary and Bellefontaine cemeteries, on the west by the city limits and on the south and east by the Mark Twain Expressway. Prominent early landowners were Octavia

Boyce, Brian Mullanphy, Ann Biddle, Charles Chambers, Richard Graham, Mary Switzer, William Jennings and Mary Harney. West Florissant, Bircher Road, Kingshighway, Goodfellow, Euclid and Geraldine were the major roads that penetrated into the area.

Walnut Park, Jennings Heights, Harney Heights, Elmwood Park, Acme Heights, Florissant Hills, Strodtman Heights, Westfield, Durant Park, Coshocton Heights, North Pointe, Electra Park, Norwich Place and Lillian Heights were prominent early subdivisions.

Dwight Davis Park is the main recreational and picnic site in Walnut Park.

Notables buried at Calvary Cemetery include Auguste Chouteau, General William T. Sherman, members of the Lucas, Mullanphy and DeMenil families and Dr. Tom Dooley.

Early churches included St. Philip Neri Catholic, St. Matthew Lutheran, Catholic Church of the Nativity, Sunny Mount Baptist, Bethel Temple Church of Christ, Salvator United Church of Christ and Walnut Park Baptist.

Sumner High School

Before 1900, the children of Walnut Park had to walk to schools in Baden. Then Mark Twain School was built and **Northwest High** (5100 Riverview) was constructed in 1964, due to overcrowding at Beaumont. Laboure High (5421 Thelka), an all-girl's school, was opened in 1942.

Most of the area's industry was located along the Terminal Railroad Belt Line. Companies included were Alton Box Board, Pillsbury Mills, the Chevrolet Plant, Combustion Engineering, Barry-Wehmiller Machinery and Quality Dairy (on West Florissant).

CABANNE

This neighborhood is sandwiched between the Central West End (south) and Arlington (north). It is bounded on the west by the city limits.

Jean Cabanne came to St. Louis in 1806 and married Julie Gratiot, a descendant of the Chouteau family. His estate was north of Delmar between Kingshighway and Union.

Curlee Clothing near 10th & Washington where Bill Nunes' mother worked in 1956

Some of the early subdivisions were Clemens Place, Rosedale, Cabanne Place, Rosedale, Hamilton Place, Maryville Addition, Chamberlain Park, Arcade Addition, Amherst Place, Savoy Court, Beverly Place, Windermere Place, Mount Gamble and Horton Place.

Visitation Academy was located on Belt Avenue between Clemens and Cabanne. It was a huge three-story complex built by nuns who first came to St. Louis from **Kaskaskia**, Illinois after the 1844 flood. It relocated to the County in the early 1960s.

Prominent churches included St. Rose of Lima Catholic, St. Mark the Evangelist Catholic, West Presbyterian, Maple Avenue Methodist, Episcopal Church of the Ascension, Union Avenue Christian, Church of the Holy Apostles, West Park Baptist, Pilgrim Congregational, Hamilton Avenue Christian, Eden-Immanuel United Church of Christ, B'Nai Amoona (moved to University City in 1950), Cabanne Methodist, Mount Calvary Lutheran, Unitarian Church of the Messiah and Church of Christ Scientist.

F. Louis **Soldan High** School was completed at 918 Union Boulevard in 1909. It was named for a well-known St. Louis educator.

A group of Episcopalians established **St. Luke's Hospital** in 1866. It moved to the site at 5535 Delmar in 1904. St. Luke's West, located in the County, was opened in the 1970s.

A narrow gauge steam railroad line went from St. Louis to Florissant in 1878, was electrified in the 1890s and came to be known as the Hodiamont Streetcar Line.

Easton Avenue was once the eastern terminus of the Santa Fe and Oregon trails.

GRAND PRAIRIE

This neighborhood is sandwiched between the Central West End on the south and Fairgrounds to the north. Grand Avenue marks its eastern boundary and Kingshighway borders the west end. Early landholders included John Lay, Daniel Page, David Evans, Nathaniel Taylor and Thornton Murphy. Early subdivisions included Vandeventer Place, Evans Place, Taylor Place, Elleardsville (known as "the Ville), Delmar Place, Lewis Place and the Chouteau Addition. William T. Sherman lived in Cote Brilliante. David Francis and oil magnate H. Clay Pierce lived in Vandeventer Place. Pierce's house was said to have cost an astounding $800,000 in the late 1880s.

The area's prominent streets include Delmar, Martin Luther King Dr., St. Louis Avenue, Taylor, Sarah and Vandeventer. Carter Carburetor and Killark Electric were its major employers.

Prominent churches in Grand Prairie included St. Theresa of Avila Catholic, Holy Ghost Catholic (for Germans), Our Lady of Visitation, St. Matthew the Apostle, Antioch Baptist, Memorial Boulevard Church, Plymouth Congregational, First Christian Church, St. Peter's German

Evangelical, Faith United Lutheran, Shaare Zedek Jewish, Grace Lutheran Church, Mt. Calvary Lutheran, Third United Presbyterian, Protestant Episcopal and Wagoner Place Methodist Church.

Charles **Sumner High School**, at 4248 Cottage, was the first high school for African Americans west of the Mississippi. Annie Malone, who lived in the Ville, established Poro College at Pendleton and St. Ferdinand to train students to sell her line of Poro Beauty Products. A generous woman, she also established the Annie Malone Children's Home in 1822.

Homer G. Phillips Hospital, at 2601 North Whittier, was built in 1937 and named for its benefactor, a black lawyer.

Tivoli Theater on Delmar (Lorna Nunes photo)

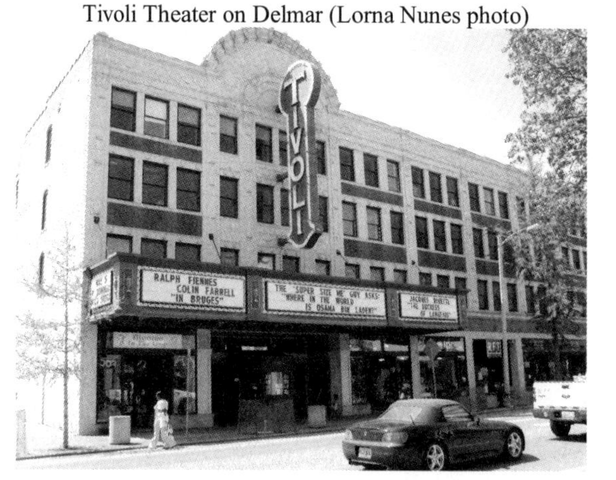

OAKLAND AND CLIFTON

These two areas are west of the Hill. Hampton Avenue is Clifton's eastern boundary. The two regions are separated by I-44. The city limits form the western boundary of Oakland. Both places were originally part of Gratiot League Square, so designated because it was supposed to be a league (three miles) square. Charles Gratiot originally settled in Cahokia and then moved to St. Louis and married Victoire Chouteau, sister to Auguste Chouteau. Subdivisions in Oakland included Victoria Place, Oakland Terrace, Dillenberger Place, Justin Place. Macklind Avenue was named for a surveyor who laid out subdivisions in the area. The building of the Pacific Railroad brought many Irish immigrants to what was called the Cheltenham area. The Arsenal Street Viaduct, over the River des Peres, was built in 1929. Part of the Scullin Steel plant was used by Gateway Ammunition Plant in World War II.

Other places of note include Walsh Stadium, the Arena, Musial and Biggies, St. Louis University High, Dogtown, Forest Park Highlands, Booksource, St. Louis Community College, Deaconess Hospital, O'Fallon Tech, Humane Society of Missouri.

Soulard Market Building (MHS)

SOULARD

Soulard is sandwiched between Broadway, Interstate 44 (north) and on the west by Interstate 55. It extends a far south as Lyon Park on Utah St.

The area, once part of the St. Louis Common, was given to Antoine Soulard, Surveyor General of Upper Louisiana, as payment for his services. His widow, Julia, donated two blocks for use as a public market. Germans, Irish and Eastern Europeans later settled in the neighborhood. The Czechs lived on what was called **Bohemian Hill**. Many of the four family dwellings, sitting flush with the street, still exist. Trinity Lutheran, St. Vincent de Paul and Saints Peter and Paul are significant area churches. There was also Gravois Church of God, St. Agatha Catholic, and St. Joseph Croatian. Czech Sokol and German Turnverein societies performed social and benevolent functions. **Smile Soft Drink** Company later occupied the Sokol Building on 9th Street.

Soulard suffered significant damage by the 1896 tornado.

As early immigrant groups moved out, they were replaced by rural people from Kentucky, Arkansas, Tennessee and Missouri, who came to St. Louis looking for jobs. Many found employment at nearby Busch brewery.

A weekly trip to **Soulard Market** was an experience in the memories of many St. Louisans. Dating back to about 1779, it is the only municipally operated market operated in greater St. Louis. Early produce was sold from carts and wagons, but the Soulard Market Building was constructed in 1929 and town officials currently rent out stalls to vendors.

Soulard, of course, is well known for its Mardi Gras and St. Patrick's Day celebrations.

UNIVERSITY CITY

This town of 40,000, on the western edge of St. Louis, was a cosmopolitan mixture of specialty shops, businesses, bookstores, cafes restaurants and houses of worship. It was founded in 1902 by flim flam entrepreneur Edward Lewis. Lewis made quite a bit of money selling Wonderful Bug Chalk, Anti-Skeet and Anti-Fly repellant. He had a publishing plant on Delmar for his prominent *Woman's Magazine*. Lewis was responsible for planning the University Heights subdivision. He attracted visitors from the 1904 Fair by installing a powerful searchlight on top of his octagonal publishing building. Lewis also built a bank building that resembled the Egyptian Temple at Karnak. It was razed in 1930 to make way for the Shaare Emeth Temple.

University City is bounded on the west by I-170, the east by Skinker Blvd., Page Blvd. to the north and Millbrook on the south. Delmar, Olive and Hanley are other prominent streets.

The beautiful old, octagonal Magazine Building is now home to City Hall. Inside is a model of Lewis' never completed Civic Plaza, which was to contain replicas of the Parthenon and the Taj Mahal.

Noted for its beautiful parks (such as Ruth and Heman), by 1945 its thirteen scenic areas made up one-third of all park acreage in St. Louis County. Around 1915, U City was one of the first in the nation to develop a junior high school system.

Blueberry Hill Restaurant, Streetside Records, Paul's Books and the renovated **Tivoli Theater** are prominent businesses. The St. Louis Walk of Fame, with bronze plaques on the Delmar sidewalk, pays tribute to prominent locals such as Betty Grable, Shelly Winters and Vincent Price. The famed Delmar Loop (a streetcar turnaround) is one of the most recognized areas in all of St. Louis.

In the early days the Delmar Gardens Amusement Park and the Delmar Racetrack drew large crowds.

The famous **Lion Sculptures**, stand magnificently on Delmar at Trinity to mark the entrance to U City's magnificent subdivisions. Edward Lewis called them "the gates of opportunity." It is now thought that one of the creatures is actually a tiger. Prominent subdivisions include University Hills, Walton Terrace and University Heights.

WEBSTER GROVES

Interstate 44 cuts through the southern part of Webster Groves (St. Louis County) and its approximate eastern and western boundaries are Summit Avenue and Rock Hill Road, respectively. The community dates back to 1892 when developers began to tout its numerous single family residences and beautiful tree-lines streets, calling it "the **Queen of the Suburbs**." Its location on the Pacific Railroad was largely responsible for its development. St. Louisans flocked to this bucolic neighborhood and commuted to and from work by train.

Tuxedo Park, Selma, Webster, Old Orchard and Webster Park were its 1890s communities that merged and incorporated as Webster Groves. . The Frisco Railroad also came through this picture perfect community, giving it a total of five stops between the two railroads.

North Webster is an African American community that dates back to the Civil War. In 1918, Missouri's highest court ruled on a case in a suit brought by residents. The ruling said that white communities had to educate their black students. North Webster was annexed by Webster Groves in 1960.

Webster College for boys was built in 1852. It was named for statesman Daniel Webster. For years it was an orphanage and later it served as a center for children with behavioral disorders.

In 1896, a city ordinance was passed outlawing all saloons. Webster Groves Rotary Club was founded in 1924 and the Lions Club organized in 1925. A blue law that forbade the Sunday showing of movies in theaters was repealed in 1937. Webster YMCA held its first teen town dance in 1959. Commuter train service from Webster Groves to St. Louis ended in 1961. The 1960-61 Statesmen girls' field hockey team went undefeated. The Webster Groves Cinema closed in 1979.

When Interstate 44 was built in the 1960s, two hundred homes in Webster Groves were lost. The Webster Groves Boy Scouts, circa 1911, was one of the earliest scouting groups in America.

The Central Webster Historic District is a fourteen block long area in the geographic heart of Webster Groves. Most of the homes there were built between the 1860s and 1920s.

Old Delmar Air Dome open movie theater

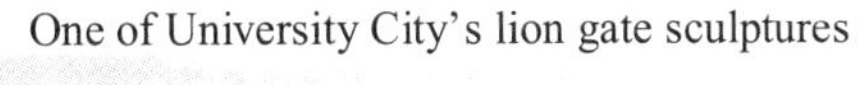

One of University City's lion gate sculptures

Old Meramec Highlands Hotel (MHS)

The Rolling Ridge Nursery is a garden center run by descendants of Henry Schulz, who started a large grain and feed business in 1893. The venture was so successful that MoPac built a spur line to accommodate his business.

Some of the oldest religious institutions in the town are the Emmanuel Episcopal Church (1866) and Eden Theological Seminary (1924). Across the street from the seminary is Webster University. Conrad Hilton gave the college $1 million to build a Center for the Performing Arts. It is also the home of the **Repertory Theater** (paid professionals) of St. Louis.

Webster Groves is a close-knit community known for its annual 4th of July parade/picnic and Turkey Day prep football game against **Kirkwood**.

Webster Groves is the former home of novelist Jonathan Franzen, whose settings are often St. Louis and his hometown. Other notables include Gordon Jenkins, who arranged music for several Frank Sinatra albums, William Webster (FBI and CIA director), Ivory Crockett (100 yard dash record holder),

Phyllis Diller, Charlotte Peters, Harry and Skip Caray, novelist Jane Smiley and actress Marsha Mason.

A RECOLLECTION: BY SHERYL PRATER: When my husband and I went shopping for a house, it didn't take long for us to choose one in Webster Groves. We had considered several subdivision houses in nearby areas – uniform houses on uniform streets with the sun baking down on the uniform trees. I feared that our six year old daughter would grow up stunted in such places; that we would feel our creative juices drained.

When Nella Hoyer showed us the little house on Newport Avenue, we knew at once that we were home. Tall trees rustling in the wind, nearby houses each unique in size and design, gardens blooming, children skipping ahead of their parents and dogs on old fashioned sidewalks . . .

Daniel Brown's Kirkwood Gardens

We moved in on July 4, 1975. Neighbors welcomed us and we immediately felt the warmth of the community. Within four years we were walking our newborn son in a buggy down those same sidewalks. Our children have skipped down those sidewalks to schools filled with intelligent, caring teachers.

Twenty years have passed since we moved here – our children blooming like those perennials in the surrounding gardens. I feel that we are part of a beautiful patchwork quilt, each unique piece adding its texture and color.

When we moved to Webster Groves, we didn't just move into a house, but into a vibrant and genuine jewel of a neighborhood.

Webster Groves High ECHO yearbook sponsors, 1960-61: Smith Sporting Goods, Big Bend Bikes, Old Orchard Cleaners, Webster Record Shop, Shattgen's Bake Shop, Webster Groves Trust, Husmann and Roper Freight, Jean's Motor Service, Stanley Gore Jeweler, Wichman's Flowers, Knudsen Manufacturing, Spicer's 5 & 10, Yorkshire Hardware, Flora Sinclair Service, Farotto's Pizza, Thiemeyer Hardware, Wendel's Shell, Leone Cooper Art Classes, Webb's Greeting Cards, Carson Pontiac, Mac Hardware, Yorkshire Barber Shop, George Grant Photography, Bond Cleaners, John's Dairy Swirl, Anderson Plumbing, Forest Cadillac in Clayton, Ozark Theater, Knight Shell Service, Charlie's Barber Shop, Howard Johnson's, Barker's Beauty Salon, Koenig Chevrolet, Faulkner's Gulf Service, Warson Village Shopping Center, Leonard Hughes Optician, Jansen's IGA, Chapman Insurance, Petrolite Chemical, Mittleberg Funeral Home, Lemcke TV, Wood Drug, Tompkins Shell, Kaegel Shell, Jordan's Cafeteria. Lacey Real Estate, Ann's Hair Fashions, Lee Wood Standard Service Eagan's Mobile Station, Straub's Lunch Counter. (Courtesy of Judy Bach Hrasky, Webster Groves High Class of 1961.) Her father owned a garage and had **the first tow truck in the state of Missouri** Judy remembers Webster Groves High choir teacher Esther Replogle who once said **she'd rather be the Webster Groves choir teacher than the Queen of England**.

KIRKWOOD

This suburb (26,936), which developed largely after World War II, is bounded by Interstate 270 on the south Berry Road on the north, I-44 on the south and Manchester Road on the north. Like Webster Groves, it began as one of the stops on the Pacific Railroad. James P. Kirkwood was responsible for building the railroad through the town. The place was also serviced by the Frisco Railroad.

Richard Elliot and Hiram Leffingwell were early landowners. Planners laid out the city on a rectangular grid with large lots and reserved space for a depot and a hotel.

Brownhurst, at 1201 South Kirkwood Road, is a Romanesque wood and stone home that belonged to Daniel Brown and sat on 140 splendid acres. He was a horticulturalist who had many exotic plants in his greenhouse. When a coal shortage threatened his greenhouse during World War I, he donated many of his specimens to Shaw's Garden, which became the basis for the garden's famous orchid collection.

Kirkwood is noted for streets that are named for U.S. presidents.

In 1895, it was possible to take a streetcar from Kirkwood to Forest Park, get a transfer ticket to the Lindell Line, and go to downtown St. Louis – all for ten cents.

Kirkwood train Depot

Kirkwood went through a downtown revitalization program in 1989 with supplemental funds from the Missouri Main Street Program.

Other places of note in idyllic Kirkwood, past and present include the Kirkwood Theater (now loft apartments), Kirkwood Hobby Shop (now closed), Vianney High School, St. Joseph's Hospital, Meramec Community College, Eliot Unitarian Church, the Wisconsin House (brought over from the 1904 Fair), Kirkwood Train Depot on Argonne Drive, Russell Kraus House (designed by Frank Lloyd Wright),

Olive African Methodist Episcopal Church, the Meramec Highlands Historic district (on bluffs overlooking the Meramec River) that once had a hotel, a swimming complex, a dance pavilion, a boathouse and a bath house.

Notable former residents include Rams quarterback Trent Green, actor **Scott Bakula**, Wimbledon doubles champion Ken Flach (attended SIU at **Edwardsville**), novelist Ridley Pearson (now lives in West County) and actor Lyle Waggoner (*Carol Burnett Show*).

The very popular **Magic House** and Children's Museum, at 516 S. Kirkwood, is a major St. Louis attraction. (314-822-8900)

Scott Bakula of Kirkwood

MAPLEWOOD & RICHMOND HEIGHTS

Maplewood is just outside the city limits of St. Louis, south of Manchester Road and north of Interstate 44. It was once part of the historic nine mile square Gratiot League Square. James Sutton, an ironmonger and a blacksmith, was one of its earliest residents. Maplewood incorporated as a city in 1908. By the 1920s, Maplewood had about 250 retail stores, mostly along Manchester Road. The city's main industries were Sunnen, Mississippi Valley Structural Steel and Cupples Products. Maplewood shares a school district with neighboring Richmond Heights. Maplewood High School was built in the early 1930s. In 1958, this author went on a date with his future wife to the Maplewood Theater (opened in 1926 at 7170 Manchester Road) to see Marlon Brando in *Sayonara*. I was wearing white bucks shoes, made popular by singer Pat Boone.

Richmond Heights (pop. 9,602) was also part of Gratiot League Square land grant. Route 40 cuts through it going east to west and the southern terminus of I-170 is near the **University Club Tower**. It incorporated in 1913. Its busiest intersection is at Big Bend and Lindbergh. The city reached its zenith of population in 1960 with 15,622 residents. **Westroads** Shopping Center opened in 1955. It has been replaced by the **Galleria** Shopping Mall. The 23-story University Club Tower is the city's only skyscraper. For years this author went to Dr. Koetting in the Club Tower to get his contact lenses. Brentwood Square features a large new Borders Bookstore. Back in 1997, when I was doing books about Illinois, this author drove from Glen Carbon to the Kinkos Store near Brentwood Square because there was no equivalent store on the east side. I always made a stop at **Donut King** before coming home. The old **Esquire Theater,** where my wife and I saw *Spartacus***,** was on the northern edge of Richmond Heights.

According to an old legend, Robert E. Lee, when he was stationed in St. Louis with the Army Corps of Engineers, gave the name Richmond Heights to the area to honor the capital of his native state of Virginia.

MANCHESTER

This West County suburb is on Manchester Road (Highway 100) and it was a stage stop on the way from St. Louis to **Jefferson City**. This road was originally an old Indian trail. It owes its existence to a sulphur spring that was located near the modern-day traffic nightmare at Manchester and Woods Mill (Route 141). (One study, in the 1990s, reported that 97,000 cars passed through the intersection over a 24 hour period.) Much of the congestion problem was solved with the recent widening of Highway 141.

In 1835, the state legislature declared Manchester Road to be the first official state road in St. Louis County, because of its connection to **Jefferson City**.

Bryson O'Hara, an early settler, made ox yokes and axe handles. Early settlers made a living by farming and selling their crops and produce to St. Louis. Thus the early name for Manchester Road was Market Street Road. The Missouri Pacific Railroad went just south of Manchester through the Valley Park area. The train gave weather forecasts from the telegraph office by blowing its whistle with long and short blasts in Morse Code.

Elijah P. Lovejoy, the famous abolitionist editor, once wrote that **Manchester was "noted for its wickedness**."

Manchester retained its rural atmosphere until 1950 when St. Louisans started moving to the county in droves.

Points of interest and notable buildings include the Lyceum Building (built in 1894 by Jacob Straszer), which now houses City Hall, Manchester United Methodist Church, the Jarville House (home of the American Kennel Club **Museum of the Dog** 314-821-3647) in Queeny Park. The St. Louis Symphony summer concerts are held on the other side of Queeny Park at the Weidman Road access.

There is also the Bacon log house, Paul Schroeder Park, Parkway South High School, St. Joseph Catholic Church, Mandalay Subdivision and the Meramec Railway station in Valley Park. Stoecker Soda Water Company was around from 1882-1967.

Goedeker's Super Store, serving the St. Louis area for 55 years, moved from its South County location to Manchester Road several years ago. This author remodeled his kitchen in 2005 and bought all of his appliances from Goedeker's.

FERGUSON

This town takes its name from William Ferguson who deeded part of his property (1855) to the Wabash, St. Louis and Pacific Railroad. He stipulated that the company had to build a depot on his property and name the town after him. In 1876, the Wabash built a spur line linking Ferguson directly with St. Louis, 13 miles away. The town incorporated in 1894 and a streetcar line to St. Louis was built in 1900. The Ferguson line joined up with the Florissant line at Kinloch and it went all the way to an alley on Grand, next to the Fox Theater. When it was built, it was **the longest streetcar line in the nation**. It was discontinued after World War II.

Ferguson (pop. 22,406) is located in St. Louis County with Pershall Road (paralleling Interstate 270) to the north, West Florissant Avenue on the east, Cool Valley is adjacent on the south and Berkeley is on the west boundary.

A two-story brick and stone Masonic Lodge was built in 1926 on South Clark. Its lower level had a large dining room and an elevated stage which doubled as a movie theater.

As more and more people chose the convenience of automobiles, the streetcar lines shut down in 1950. When Northland Shopping District opened in 1955, many of the businesses in downtown Ferguson went out of business. Universal Match and McDonnell Aircraft were popular places of employment.

Famous former residents include General Jimmy Doolittle, Louis Maull (barbeque sauce) and Michael McDonald, the "blue-eyed soul performer" who was lead singer for the Doobie Brothers. Jimmy and (wife) Mae Haizlip set a new airplane transcontinental U.S. speed record in the early 1930s.

Notable businesses include Florissant Valley Jr. College (built in 1970), Emerson Electric and Negwer Materials, a building supply place that has about 200 employees. Kienstra Concrete started out in Ferguson, off Florissant Road. There was a Teen Town for high school students on Airport Road.

Ferguson High (courtesy Don McNab)

Places of interest include January-Wabash Park and Ferguson Depot. The Bindbeutel buildings, dating back to 1895, have been rehabbed and are now a vital part of Ferguson's commercial district. There is also Caboose Park (Great Northern caboose) and the Tiffin residence.

Places in Ferguson readers might recall: Thyme Table Restaurant, Bank of Ferguson, King Drug Store, Ferguson Hardware, Lammert's Department Store. Mannino's Market, Olie's Barber Shop, Gasen Drug Store, Shear's Department Store, Hilker's Floral Shop, Orr's Service Station, Stiver's Auto Sales, Town Pastries, Bolin's Service Station, Ben Franklin Store, Savoy Record Mart, Wells Shoe Store, Tally's Grill, Golden Greeks Café, Heady Cleaners, Stabenow Brothers Service Station, South-western Bell Office, Ferguson Printing and Paul Crump's Market.

Don McNab remembers seeing 3-D movies

Churches included St. John and James Catholic, United Methodist, Immanuel United Church of Christ, Zion Lutheran, St. Stephen's Episcopal, First Baptist, First Christian Church, Church of the Nazarene, First Church of Christ Scientist, Our Lady of Guadalupe, St. Peter's Evangelical, North Hills Methodist and Memorial Missionary Baptist.

Emerson Electric Plant in Ferguson

Interview with Don McNab, a longtime resident of Ferguson: "I graduated from Ferguson High in 1956. The school was on January Avenue and their sports teams were called the Comets. Their main rivals were schools like Jennings, Normandy, Ritenour, Riverview, Webster Groves and Kirkwood. Back then, kids who lived in **Black Jack, Florissant, Hazelwood** and **Dellwood** attended Ferguson High.

"Enos Slaughter and Wally Moon lived in Ferguson when they played for the Cardinals. Slaughter lived on Nancy Place and Moon lived on Marguerite. My family lived several blocks away from them on Forest Avenue. I collect autographs and have dozens including Slaughter's autograph as well as Steve Stipanovich's and Ed Macauley's. Macauley told me how he got the name 'Easy Ed.' He played for St. Louis U. and one time he came out of the dressing room and dribbled the ball on the court. 'Take it easy, Ed,' one of his teammates cautioned. 'They're playing the National Anthem.' A reporter heard the remark and started calling him 'Easy Ed.'

"As kids, we played sandlot ball at Robert Field, now called Jeske Park. The theater was the Savoy and it was on Florissant Road, next to Ferguson Bowling Lanes, owned by Kenny Wasser. The Savoy is now the Savoy Banquet Center. January-Wabash Park and Lake, on the north end of town, named for the old January family that lived there, was built by the railroad for their steam engines. They transferred water from the spring-fed lake (by pipes) to their train station. A concrete swimming pool was built there in 1950.

"The teen hangout in those days was an ice cream parlor called Green Leas. Steve Milo bought the place and everyone started calling it Milo's.

"Neighborhoods were safe in those days and we never locked our doors. In fact, when we sold our house, we had to have a lock installed on our front door because we didn't have one.

"Helen Stephens lived in Ferguson on Henquin Drive when she was in her thirties. She was a track star and won medals at the 1936 Olympics. She was called the "**Fulton Flash**" and I have an autographed picture of her and Jesse Owens. She died about six years ago.

Eddie's Snack Bar in Ferguson

"I once met Buster Wortman at the Ferguson Lounge, owned by Ken Haveland. It was on Blackburn, off Florissant Road. Buster's bodyguard was from Ferguson. He was killed in **East St. Louis** and his body was dumped in **Wellston**.

"Back around 1942 or 1943, a B-17 bomber (training flight) crashed near our back yard, not far from Chambers Road, killing all on board. I guess it was trying to land at Lambert Field. My older brother was the first to arrive on the scene.

"My wife, the former Ida Tiepelman, was a 1957 graduate of **Riverview High**."

NORMANDY

This town, incorporated in 1945, is on land once owned by Charles Lucas. He purchased the land from victims of the 1811 New Madrid earthquake. After he was killed in the duel with Thomas Hart Benton (1817), part of his land was left to his sister Anne who married explorer Wilson Price Hunt. This is the origin for the name given to Lucas and Hunt Road.

Normandy's boundaries are long and narrow. It is south of the city of Ferguson and Lucas and Hunt Road is on its eastern border. Interstate 70 passes through the northern tier of the district. Normandy's population in 2000 was 5,153. In 1960, the Normandy School District bought the **Bellerive Country Club** (relocated to Creve Coeur) to form a junior college, but it never materialized. Bellerive was named for the last French governor of North America. In 1965, Bellerive hosted the U.S. Open, won by Gary Player. In 1963, the old Normandy Residence Center became the University of Missouri-St. Louis. The old site of St. Vincent's Hospital is now occupied by Castle Park Apartments.

Levine's Hats on Washington Ave.

St. Peter's Cemetery is the final resting place of Billy Lyons, who was murdered in 1895. **The murder became the basis for the song, "Stagger Lee."**

Glen Echo and Normandy are well known golf courses in the area. The Norwood course was built in 1922, and the U.S. Open was played here in 1948 (won by Ben Hogan) It is located in Country Club Hills, adjacent to Normandy.

JENNINGS

Jennings, a historically significant African-American community of 15,469, occupies less than four square miles and is nearly 80 percent black. The town was named for early Virginia settler James Jennings, who came to the area with his family and forty slaves. The town incorporated in 1946.

River Roads shopping mall (torn down in 2006) and **Northland** shopping mall went out of business due to creeping blight and is currently being replaced with Buzz Westfall Plaza. Merollis Chevrolet started out in **Baden**, moved next to River Roads, and is now at Parker Road and Highway 367 on the **Spanish Lake/Black Jack** border. Flordell Hills is a small incorporated city, completely surrounded by Jennings.

The approximate eastern boundaries of Jennings are I – 70 on the north, Riverview Blvd. on the southeast and Pine Lawn is on its southern border. Lewis and Clark Blvd (367) runs through it as well.

The old North Drive-in (on Route 367) has been replaced with Alexander Place housing development. One of the first McDonald's hamburger places in the area was across from the drive-in.

SPANISH LAKE

Spanish Lake was named after the Spanish troops who stayed there while building a Spanish fort for Spain in 1768. It is a well defined area with the Mississippi River on the east, the Missouri River on the north, Highway 367 and **Black Jack** on the west, and I-270 on the south. Much of the area was once the property of James de St. Vrain, a brother of the last Spanish governor of Upper Louisiana.

Farmers in the area took their crops, animals and produce to St. Louis via Bellefontaine Road. However, Spanish Lake did not become a well-defined area until the German immigrants moved there. The Catholic parish of St. Aloysius was founded by a group from Baden. The

Bank of Baden played a significant role in financing homesteaders who bought property in Spanish Lake.

The median income for a family in Spanish Lake is $44,139 and the place is about 42 percent white and 55 percent African American.

CLAYTON

Approximate boundaries of Clayton: Skinker is on its eastern boundary, Ladue is adjacent on the west, Clayton Road is on the south and Forest Blvd. is on part of its northeastern border.

Clayton is the seat of St. Louis County and it has a population of 12,825. It is 83.7 percent white. The city was organized in 1877 and was named for Ralph Clayton who donated land for the courthouse. Martin Hanley also donated land for the same purpose and those 104 acres donated by the two Virginians are covered by the city's central business District. Hanley's two-story house still stands on the north end of town. Clayton formally incorporated in 1813 to prevent neighboring University City from annexing it. Mayor Charles Shaw, a banker and real estate mogul, served as mayor from 1933 to 1940 and was responsible for initiating WPA projects the widened the streets, built the existing library and created a public park named in his honor. In 1957, zoning laws were changed and this led to the construction of some of the high rise office towers. All of the spaces were quickly leased before construction was completed.

Clayton, sometimes referred to as the "**Jewel of St. Louis**," is home to **Fontbonne University** and Concordia Seminary of the Lutheran Church – Missouri Synod. Washington University is located in an unincorporated area of St. Louis County, on the eastern edge of Clayton. Clayton is an important secondary business district for the St. Louis Metropolitan Area.

Clayton High was ranked 230th in the nation by *Newsweek* as one of the better schools in America. Clayton High won the Class 4 football championship in 2004. CBC High is located at 6501 Clayton Rd.

In 1920, Clayton had a Gretna Green reputation – a place where couples could get quickie marriages by a justice of the peace. **Waterloo**, Illinois had this same reputation in the 1930s.

Famous-Barr opened a Clayton store in 1948. Other prominent retailers there were Vandervoort's, Lammert's and Boyd's. Clayton is noted for its many Colonial Williamsburg architectural-style buildings.

LADUE AND FRONTENAC

Ladue, in St. Louis County, has a population of 8,645. It is directly west of Clayton. An old hunter's trail, a mile north of Clayton Road, became known as Ladue Road in 1853. Ladue incorporated around 1929 to avoid annexation. Ladue boasts of being the **best educated city in Missouri** with 74.5 percent of adults holding an associate degree or higher. It also has one of the highest median incomes for any city in the U.S. Its prestigious private schools include **Mary Institute, Country Day and John Burroughs**. The city is 96.8 percent white.

Famous residents, past and present, include: Joe Buck and Jack Buck, William B. Bush, brother to former president George H.W. Bush, John Danforth, John F. McDonnell and actor Scott Foley of *Dawson's Creek* and *Scrubs* fame.

In the early 1990s, a Ladue woman placed an anti-war (Desert Storm) sign in her front yard. City officials said it violated an ordinance against yard signs. The city made national headlines when it lost the case of Ladue v. Gilleo in the U.S. Supreme Court, based on First Amendment free speech rights.

Horton Watkins High and Ladue's other public schools rank in the top two percent in the nation, according to *Newsweek.*

Downtown Clayton: circa 1990

Busch's Grove, a famous restaurant, was immortalized in the popular *Official Preppy Handbook*. Built in the 1850s, it was known as the Ten Mile House on the St. Louis stage route. Babe Ruth and Vice-president Alben Barkley have dinned there.

Bogey Golf Club was organized in 1945. Warson Country Club, on old Warson Road, was organized in 1954.

St. Louis Walk of Fame on Delmar (Lorna Nunes photo)

Frontenac is immediately west of Ladue and is named for Louis Frontenac, governor of New France. Des Peres Presbyterian Church on Geyer Road was a church where Elijah Lovejoy rode on horseback from St. Louis to preach there. It was also a station on the "underground railroad." Until the 1950s, the Bridlespur Hunt Club conducted fox hunts in the Frontenac area. Frontenac incorporated in 1948 to avoid being annexed by Ladue. Plaza Frontenac, a high end shopping mall with an art theater on the inside, opened in 1974. The parking garage is filled with cars such as Jaguar, Lexus, Volvo, BMW, Cadillac and Mercedes.

CREVE COEUR

The city's name comes from the French for "broken heart." According to local lore, an Indian maiden was broken hearted because she loved a French fur trapper who left her with a broken heart and never returned. She then leapt from a ledge overlooking the lake which then reformed itself into a heart shape.

Paul Anka visits St. Louis in 1960

It shares a border with neighboring Town and Country. Occupying about 10 square miles of land, it has a population of 16,500. The median income for a Creve Coeur family is $99,100. In 2003 the FBI reported that there was not a single homicide or murder in Creve Coeur. Creve Coeur incorporated in December of 1849.

Some of its more historic buildings include a one room facility called Lake School House and the Tappmeyer farmhouse, built in the late 1800s.

Creve Coeur started out as a farming community with Olive Street Road, now Olive Boulevard. It followed an old Indian trail that went from the Mississippi River to the Missouri River.

Creve Coeur Airport (3127 Creve Coeur Mill Road), formerly known as Dauster Field, has a museum with about **60 antique or restored light aircraft**. The airport hosts the annual Waco Owners Fly-in. The fly-in is held on Fathers Day weekend. They fly in on Thursday and leave on Sunday. The airport is just outside the city limits. (314-878-6400)

Students in the western part of Creve Coeur attend Parkway North High. Private schools include St. Louis Priory, DeSmet, Chaminade and Westminster Christian Academy.

Interestingly, when non-residents are asked what they think of when they hear the city's name, a majority respond "Creve Coeur Camera."

ROCK HILL

Rock Hill, population 4,765, is a St. Louis County entity that is about 68 percent white.

This author's first pastor, Reverend R. Ruthven Neff (Washington Park Church of God), left around 1954 to become the first pastor of the Rock Hill Church of God.

Rock Hill is said by Internet sources to be notorious for its "speed trap" on Manchester Road.

Rock Hill's first library was voluntary – not tax supported but established with the help of the public school system, the Lions Club and local churches. The library opened in the Fairfax House with 1600 books in 1944. Donations came from a wide variety of sources, including gifts from people in nearby towns. Two years later, the issue was put on the ballot and the library became tax supported. In 1957, the library moved into the old Lions Club facility on Manchester Road. The old building was razed and in 1965 a new library and city hall were erected on the site. In 2005, the library moved to a new facility, the **Colonial Square** Shopping Center on Manchester Road.

Trainwreck is a current popular sports bar in Rock Hill on 9243 Manchester Road. There is a train car on the premises and, inside, a model train runs around the perimeter of the dining area on elevated tracks.

Living in Florissant and Webster Groves by Dr. Andrew Theising

My family moved to Florissant in 1957, several years before I was born. We lived in the Rolling Meadows subdivision built by the Frasier Construction Company. My parents previously lived in Vinita Park and the University City areas. My mother was a nurse at St. Mary's Hospital in Richmond Heights and my father was an industrial engineer for Olin Corporation in **East Alton**, Illinois. Both were graduates of St. Louis University and founding members of St. Dismas Parish in Florissant. My dad was in the occupation forces from 1946 to 1948 in Japan, and went through SLU on the GI Bill.

My mom's sister and her husband, Rosemary and Leslie Davison, were already living in Florissant. Uncle Les was a retired U.S. Marshal and had worked on the Greenlease kidnapping case. He tended bar at his own place, called Davison's in Florissant, located on New Florissant Road at St. Anthony Lane across from the Fischers of Florissant store. Aunt Rosemary was active in the charter reform movement of 1963 and went on to be Florissant's longtime City Clerk. James J. Eagan was the longtime mayor of Florissant under the new charter. He was a parishioner at St. Dismas, where my family attended.

Pageant Theater on Delmar where Bill Nunes saw *Ben Hur*

When our house was built, it was adjacent to the Florissant Country Club. However, the golf course disappeared and was purchased by the Calvary Baptist Church congregation. The man who led that flock was John Stormer. I knew him as the pastor who let us play on the church grounds, but I came to learn later that he was a radical conservative thinker of the 1960s, writing best-selling books like ***None Dare Call it Treason*** and *None Dare Call it Education*.

The other famous name in the neighborhood was Dick Weber, the Hall of Fame bowler. His home was at the corner of Arlington Drive and Parker Road—across from the old country club entrance. I could see his house from our back yard. I had always heard rumor that he had a bowling lane installed in his basement. I never met him or his family, but could see the comings-and-goings of the house.

My family was active in historic preservation, and I lived for a time as caretaker of the Taille de Noyer House on the **McCluer High School** campus and also the Old St. Ferdinand Shrine, where the annual Valley of Flowers Festival was held. I was active in the Florissant bicentennial celebration in 1986 and belonged to the Jaycees for many years.

When I married in 1991, I moved to Webster Groves. Webster Groves, established in 1896 and called "Queen of the Suburbs," is a beautiful community with old Victorian homes, large lawns, and trees that touched over the middle of the street. It was and remains a delightful community, rich in history. The land on which my home stood was owned once by Pierre Chouteau Jr., grandson of Pierre Laclede, and was later sold to Missouri's first senator, Thomas Hart Benton. Many familiar faces lived around me—not people I knew personally, but people I would see in the newspaper and on television. I would see *Post-Dispatch* editor **William Woo** out on his morning jog often. Veteran journalist **Don Marsh** also could be seen around town. Of course, the whole town turned out for the annual Turkey Day game between Webster High School and its arch rival, Kirkwood High.

"Trial by Jury" – 1960-61 Webster High School play

There was considerable change going on as the city neared its 100th birthday. The new mayor shortly after we moved there was Terri Williams. Her husband is comedian Craig Hawksley, star of comedy clubs and TV commercials. Her ideas for change in the city ran against the grain of many traditionalists, and a recall petition was launched. Though there were enough signatures to put her removal on the ballot, I remember feeling good for her that she won more votes to stay in office than had put her there in the first place.

New development started creeping in to Webster in the 1990s, and old storefronts started closing up. Rudolf's clothing store on North Gore disappeared, so did Webster Hardware on Big Bend, and the Two Nice Guys Restaurant. New buildings popped up and gave new space for old names—Straub's grocery renovated its storefront, Wichman's Florist moved from its home on Gray Avenue, and much later **Cyrano's** restaurant moved down Big Bend into the Old Orchard neighborhood. Other institutions stayed in place. The venerable Webster Groves Bookshop remained at the corner of South Gore and Lockwood. Webster University expanded, building its own library and moving out of the one it shared with Eden Seminary across the street.

It was all relatively new to me, but I know that some of the old timers in Webster didn't like the change. Webster Groves was the first place I lived where I encountered trains with any frequency. I had grown up near the airport and was used to that noise as a child, but the trains had both a noise and a feel—the chugging of the engines and the rumbling vibrations beneath my feet. I later served on the board of the Webster Groves Public Library until I moved out of the city after my wife passed away. (Author's note: Dr. Theising is a professor of political science at SIUE and is the author of *Made in USA: East St. Louis.*)

FLORISSANT

Florissant, in North County (11.7 square miles), extends north past Howdershell to the Missouri River and is bounded on the south by Interstate 270. Its eastern boundary is adjacent to the Black Jack neighborhood, just on the other side of New Halls Ferry Road. Lindbergh Boulevard cuts diagonally through the town of about 51,387. New Halls Ferry runs north and south through Florissant but Old Halls Ferry is outside the city limits on the eastern side.

Florissant is the largest and oldest county community. Its name means "flowering valley" and the early French were attracted to its fertile land. The Old Town District centers around the old Spanish community of St. Ferdinand. For years the community was known as St. Ferdinand but the name was officially changed to Florissant in 1939.

For decades Florissant remained a farming community with its only link to St. Louis being a narrow gauge rail line built in the 1870s. In 1892, the route converted to electricity and became a streetcar line which lasted until 1931. Florissant began to grow rapidly during World War II as families moved there due to employment opportunities afforded by McDonnell Aircraft. After the war, the Ford plant opened up in **Hazelwood** and real estate developers Joseph Vatterott and Alfred Mayer bought up farm land and converted it into subdivisions. Vatterott's Duchesne subdivision's streets are all named for

St. Stanislaus Seminary (MHS)

Catholic saints. In 1960, the city hired the firm of Harland Bartholomew to plan for new growth. By 1980, the FBI reported that the city had the second lowest crime rate of any city in the U.S. of comparable size.

The historic John B. Myers House, on Dunn Road, built in the 1860s, barely escaped destruction when the I-170 inner belt highway was constructed.

Sacred Heart Church, at 753 Jefferson, was built for German Catholics so they wouldn't have to travel 14 miles to St. Louis for confession.

St. Stanislaus Jesuit Seminary, on 700 Howdershell Road, was established in 1823. Pierre DeSmet received his training there. A vineyard was maintained there until 1950, producing a white DeSmet wine.

The Florissant Civic Center, on Parker Road, was built in 1972 and includes a swimming pool, a gym, a theater, an ice rink, an exercise room, and meeting rooms. The John F. Kennedy Civic Center is on Howdershell Roads.

Cross Keys, Grandview and Village Square are the main shopping districts. Grandview Theater and I-270 Drive-in are no longer in business.

Florissant's Shandi Finnessey was Miss USA in 2004, and Neil Rackers, kicker for the Phoenix Cardinals, also hails from the town. Google **Scott K. Williams** for further info.

ARNOLD

Arnold (pop. 19,965) is south of Jefferson Barracks in Jefferson County. Its northern boundary is the Meramec River. In 1776, Jean Baptiste Gamache was granted 1050 arpents of land by the Spanish authorities in return for establishing a ferry service across the Meramec. He built his ferry about a mile from where the Meramec empties into the Mississippi, close to where the Missouri Pacific would later build its railroad bridge. The Meramec River was too shallow for steamboat travel.

There was an early road that came through the area from southern Missouri that was used by cowboys driving their herds to St. Louis. The trail was often referred to as Cow Dung Alley. The road that came through Arnold, from Cape Girardeau to St. Louis, was known as the Camino Real – Royal Road. It was renamed Telegraph Road just before the Civil War when the first telegraph lines in the state were erected along it. The road that went from Arnold to Fenton became Highway 141. In 1834, Francois Lemais (Lemay) began operating a Ferry on the road that went to Carondelet, thus the name Lemay Ferry Road. Lemay Ferry became an 18 foot wide concrete road in 1924.

By the time of Missouri statehood, land in the area was owned by the Soulards and Lacledes for purposes of speculation.

The first people to settle the land were eastern Americans migrating west and European immigrants – some Swiss and English – but mostly German due to the German-Dutch

1970 Arnold Fire Department (Arnold Historical Society)

nature of St. Louis. Since most Germans were either Catholic or Lutheran, it is not surprising that the first churches were the Immaculate Conception Church and St. John's Lutheran.

Other Arnold churches are New Hope United Methodist, First Baptist Church, Latter Day Saints, St. Mark's United Church of Christ, Grace Free Will Baptist, Church of Christ, Saint David Catholic, First Assembly of God, Starling Road Baptist, Arnold Nazarene Church, Disciples of Christ, Rockport Baptist, Good Shepherd Lutheran, Parkview Baptist, Baptist Tabernacle, Assembly of God and First United Pentecostal.

By the mid-1970s Arnold had seven elementary schools, three junior highs, and Fox High School (Warriors).

Most of the original town of Arnold was on land once owned by Mr. and Mrs. George Arnold, hence the German town name.

The early settlers were self-sufficient. Their sugar came from maple trees. They grew fruit trees for jams and jellies. Wild animals were hunted or trapped and their furs were used for clothing. They fished from ponds and streams. Some cotton and flax were grown for clothing. Domesticated cows were a source of milk and butter. Hogs gave them bacon, ham and sausage. They grew corn, pumpkins, wheat, cucumbers, squash, cabbage and potatoes for food.

Sacred Heart Academy – St. Charles

Arnold incorporated in 1972 and today is a thriving town with banks, shops, businesses, a library, restaurants and other amenities. The construction of Interstate 55 gave Arnold residents easy access to jobs in St. Louis.

The Defense Mapping Agency, which used to be near

Pine Lawn, at 4300 Goodfellow, then it moved to South Broadway and recently relocated to Arnold, off Vogel Road, with help from Congressman Richard Gebhart.

ST. CHARLES

St. Charles (French) / San Carlos (Spanish) is the county seat of St. Charles County, located on Interstate 70 overlooking the Missouri River. St. Charles was the first capital of Missouri, 1821-1826). It was founded in 1765 by Louis Blanchette who called it Les Petites Cotes – the Little Hills." St. Charles was also the last "civilized" stop for the Lewis and Clark expedition as they headed west.

American Foundry in St. Charles

It is the site for the Saint Rose Philippine Duchesne Shrine. It is also the home base for the St. Louis National Weather Service Forecasting Office. The population, as of 2000, was 62,304.

St. Charles has two high schools, the newest being built in the late 1970s. The Lewis and Clark Tech Building is located on Zumbehl Road. Many students who live on the southern edge of town attend Francis Howell North High. **Lindenwood University** was founded by George and Mary Sibley in 1827. It was the first institution of higher learning west of the Mississippi. For a number of years the St. Louis Football Cardinals used their facilities for summer training camp.

St. Charles is at the eastern end of the 225 mile long Katy Bike Trail. St. Charles has enjoyed a building boom since the 1980 in what is referred to as the Golden Triangle region bordered by highways 70,40 and 94. About the only thing lacking in St. Charles is a golf course.

Historic Main Street in downtown Old St. Charles is known for its cobblestone streets, specialty shops and dining places. A convention center along Interstate 70 hosts conferences, trade shows and business meetings.

St. Charles is known for its festivals. At Christmas, about 30 costumed Legends of Christmas stroll the streets and interact with visitors. There is a Fourth of July Riverfest, complete with fireworks. The Festival of the Little Hills is a craft fair that happens every August. The annual Octoberfest celebrates the German influence on the town. Finally, Tartan Days, celebrating local Scottish heritage, is an event that features a parade, complete with bagpipes.

Alice Busch – Veiled Prophet Queen 1922

Ameristar Casino is on the riverfront at St. Charles as is the old **Heart of St. Charles** (overlooking the river). It is a popular banquet center (with large, scenic windows) that frequently features Bob Kuban and his band. It was built back in the 1950s. Just north of I-70 is a **Bass Pro** sports shop & Schultz Harley Davidson. **Noah's Ark Restaurant**, on 5th Street, was torn down about a year ago. The restaurant was shaped like the Ark with Noah standing on the top of it. The animals were getting ready to board from the parking lot.

This author and his wife regularly visit **Golden Corral** (Zumbehl Road) on Saturday mornings to be with our friends, including Gene and Doris Moore, Gerald and Shirley Mizell, Bob and Donna Bullock, Ken and Judy Hoelker, Aleeta Urbahns, Gloria Von Brock, Wes Bokal, Geneva Carroll, Larry and Glenda Williamson, Carla and Jewel Cawthon and Don, Shirley DeWitt and Gary Tesson.

THE VEILED PROPHET

The tradition of the Veiled Prophet started in St. Louis in 1878 when Charles and Alonzo Slayback bought all the floats and costumes from the New Orleans Mardi Gras. The Veiled Prophet organization became a vital institution in St. Louis for well over a century. The organization was modeled after the New Orleans Carnival Society, the Mystick Krewe of Comus. The parade was meant to revive lagging interest in the annual Agricultural and Mechanical Fair held in St. Louis. The Agriculture and Mechanical Fair, first begun in 1856 at Fairgrounds Park, ceased in 1894.

The annual parade and ball, and the selection of a queen and her maids of honor, marked the beginning of the new social season for the rich and elite in St. Louis. Bankers, judges, prominent politicians and lawyers dominated its membership. The Veiled Prophet of Khorassan presided over the crowning of the Queen of Love and Beauty. **Suzanne Slayback** was chosen as the first queen.

The gala event was so notable that President Cleveland and his wife attended the elite event in 1887.

Historian Thomas Spencer asserts that the celebration originated as the power structure's response to the St. Louis general strike of 1877, a year of nationwide labor unrest. Taking back control of the streets was a symbolic gesture by the elite. The parade was intended to "awe the masses" with a show of power and elegance. The Veiled Prophet, wearing a white sheet and a pointed white hat, bore a remarkable resemblance to that old iconic figure – a **Klansman**. The fact that the Prophet carried a pistol and a shotgun further reinforced that threatening image. Spencer asserts that since many of the workers involved in the rail strike of 1877 were black, the purpose of the Prophet was to intimidate.

As late as 1907 the Eads Bridge was closed by fair organizers to prevent East St. Louis street gangs from coming across to rob and pickpocket.

Organizers believed they were helping the city's economy by putting on a cultural display that would draw visitors from the entire metro area. It was also intended for the parade to set an example for the middle and lower classes, showing them the social graces and providing alternatives to undesirable behavior such as drunkenness and carousing.

Queens of the Fair were **forbidden to marry** for one year. Around 1965, African-Americans began to protest the white exclusivity of the event. To gain public sympathy they tried to get others to view the parade and ball as a waste of taxpayer money. As media coverage lessened and pa-rades were interrupted by protest groups, membership began to decline. The leadership decided to inject new life into the event by integrating the parade and holding it on the Fourth of July and having a VP Fair on the riverfront. It became a weekend extravaganza attended by the hundreds of thou-sands as crowds were attracted by an air show, fireworks displays, a carnival atmosphere, food and merchandise booths and live stage shows. The event is now seen as a unifying event and a celebration of diversity. Fair St. Louis has added untold millions of dollars to the city's economy.

The fair is currently held on the grounds of the Jefferson National Expansion Memorial surrounding the Arch. Over 50,000 people line the city's streets to see the parade and floats. **Over 2.5 million people attend the three or four day event. It is billed as the nation's largest 4th of July celebration**.

Dad's Cookies, 3854 Louisiana (Lorna Nunes photo)

HOPSCOTCH AND JACKS

By Ida Tiepelman McNab
of Ferguson

These wonderful games were played all over the St. Louis area, mostly by little girls. If the playing surface were asphalt or concrete, a hopscotch pattern would be drawn on the ground with chalk. Usually, there were eight numbered sections. Each player had a marker such as a coin, rock or beanbag.

The first player stood behind the starting line to toss her marker in square one. She would hop over square one to square two and then continue hopping to square eight, turn around, and hop back again. She would pause in square two to pick up her marker, hop in square one, and then out. She then continued by tossing her marker in square two. All the hopping was done on one foot until she reached sections six and seven which were side by side. Then two feet could be placed down with one foot on each square. Players always had to hop over any square where their marker had been placed. If a player stepped on a line or their marker did not land in the proper square, they lost their turn to the next person. A square with a domed top was added on to the top of the hopscotch pattern. The player could rest here a few seconds with both feet on the ground before hopping back to the starting point.

Voice-O-Graph machine on the Admiral

Eggs in the basket, Toad in the Hole, Onesies. Who knew? When I was a kid it was just jacks. Never questioned it, just did it. I played jacks at home, at my cousin's house, with girls in my neighborhood and at camp. I competed with kids who played jacks for a living, or would have, if you could make a living at jacks.

Jacks are a very old game that was once played by kids who used knucklebones instead of the six pronged modern metal jacks with bobbles on the end of each prong. Think of a jack as a kind of three dimensional cross.

The game, as we played it, was usually competed on the front porch or on a wooden or linoleum covered floor. Two to six could play. Equipment consisted of fifteen jacks and one red rubber ball, slightly smaller than a ping pong ball. Two players would sit face-to-face; more than two sat in a circle. Deciding who went first was either eeney-meeney-miney-moe or throwing the jacks up in the air and trying to catch as many as possible with both hands together, thumb to thumb, palms down. Then you would toss them again and this time catch them palms up. This process was called **Flipping**. Whoever caught the most jacks went first.

The player going first gathered all the jacks in one hand, gave them a gentle toss to scatter them inside the space encircled by her opponents. Following that, she would toss the ball in the air. The object of the game was to pick up the designated number of jacks with one hand and catch the ball after the first bounce with the same hand. It started with one jack and went up to ten.

If a player threw the jacks and two of them were touching, it was called **Kissies**, you had the option of picking them up and throwing them again.

At onsies, you would pick up one jack at a time. On twosies, you would pick up the jacks two at a time. When that player would miss, she would continue with the number she had reached on her next turn. The first player to reach tensies won the game.

Fancies were specialty rounds that were agreed upon in advance. At the start of the game, the players decided how many and what kind of fancies would be included. Some fancies included a specific chant with lyrics while others consisted of a certain, trickier way of picking up the jacks.

Another fun thing to do with jacks: Spin them like little tops.

COMING OF AGE IN NORTH ST. LOUIS

In the early 1930s, my mother (Edith) worked at International Shoe and my father at Century Electric, both in St. Louis. They were laid off when the Depression hit and decided to move to a farm in **Washington**, Missouri so they wouldn't starve. I was born there in 1940. When the war started, they moved to Elm Grove Lane on

Highway 141 (Lindbergh) in north St. Louis (near Village Square). Dad (Louis Verman) found war work at the Atlas Powder Company, located in what is now the Busch Wildlife Reserve. After the war, Dad borrowed money from his brother to become trained as a barber, which became his life's vocation.

3 Chuck-A-Burgers: Pagedale, St. John, Crestwood

It would probably be difficult for younger St. Louisans to believe that the area near present Lindbergh and I-270 back in 1946 was completely rural. I went to a one room schoolhouse that has been preserved and is still there. One year they taught grades 1-3-5-7 and the next year they taught grades 2-4-6-8. When I started school, I could already read so they bumped me up a grade and gave me a double promotion.

Our rural house did not have indoor plumbing. Our toilet was an outhouse. Our kitchen sink had a hand operated pump that drew water from the well. I took baths in a galvanized tub with water heated on a kitchen stove fueled by coal and wood. We had chamber pots in our bedrooms for night use. There was a well in the yard but the water was brackish so we drank and cooked with bottled water that came in ten gallon glass jugs.

We had a chicken coop out back and I quickly learned not to walk barefoot in their fenced in area. Sometimes I pretended to be a rancher and rounded up the chickens/cattle on my hobby horse. One named Penny was spared from the stewing pot because she was my pet.

Kids were never bored back then because we had active imaginations. When my cousins, Glenda and Carla Cawthon, came over, we played out dramas from one of my favorite radio programs, Sergeant Preston of the Yukon. We got out my red Sears wagon. I was magically transformed into Blackie the horse and I pulled the wagon. Glenda was Sergeant Preston and she sat in the wagon. Carla was King, the dog, and we pushed and pulled the wagon throughout the imagined snowy north woods wilderness. We were supposed to trade places periodically, but somehow Glenda always managed to come up with another game when it was her turn to pull or push the wagon.

We also had three 55 gallon drums out back with fuel oil. One was silver colored, the other painted black, and the third was suffering from rustitis. The three of us mounted the drums and pretended they were our bold and majestic steeds. The black one was Blackie, the silver one became Silver, and the tawny one was dubbed Rusty. We used pieces of old rope as bridles. We galloped along the Santa Fe Trail, roped maverick cattle, and chased after rustlers. Sometimes I pretended to be Roy Rogers or the Lone Ranger. Hi yo, Silver, Awwaayyy!

On several occasions we decided to be bad little girls and we went down to the basement to try our hand at smoking. We cut newspapers into the size of a Big Chief school writing tablet and rolled them into cigars. We coughed and hacked our way through the process, thinking we were quite grown up and sophisticated. We were lucky we didn't burn the house down.

If it was cold outside, or raining, we stayed indoors. We would get out boxes and canned goods from the pantry and became entrepreneurs by playing store. Sometimes we got out old pillows and rode them down the second floor wooden steps – bumpety bump, bump, bump! On Saturday nights we gathered around the radio and listened to the Grand Old Opery.

Of course I also listened to the traditional after school programs. My favorite was Bobby Benson of the B-Bar-B Ranch. "Here they come! They're riding fast and they're riding hard. It's time for action and adventure!"

Bobby was a teenage orphan who inherited a ranch in

Molls (since 1858) at 8th and Spruce in St. Louis (Tettaton)

Texas. Other members of the cast included a young girl named Polly, Harka the Indian, Wong Lee the Oriental cook and Buck Mason was the ranch foreman.

Bobby Benson Big Little Book

When I was by myself, sometimes my mother let me play "grown-up." I'd get out an old pair of her high heeled shoes, some toilet water (cologne), glitzy costume jewelry, and ruby red lipstick.

When I was ten we moved to Jacobi Drive in **Dellwood**. I attended Moline Acres Elementary School on Chambers Road. My family became members of the old First Church of God on Newstead and Penrose. I graduated in 1957 from Riverview High. Like just about every other St. Louisan, I have fond memories of taking trips down the river on the ***Admiral***.

MORE ST. LOUIS TRIVIA

What natural disaster hit St. Louis in 1959? The city was hit by a tornado. It took part of the roof off of the Arena, killed over a dozen people along the way, and crossed into Illinois near the McKinley Bridge. The winds also blew down the TV broadcasting tower of Channel 2 News.

What unusual weather hit St. Louis in the winter of 1982? About 13 inches of snow fell on the city over a 24 hour period. This author was living in **Glen Carbon**, Illinois, at the time and remembers snow drifts in his driveway that were as high as the roof of his car.

Wagner Electric complex in Wellston

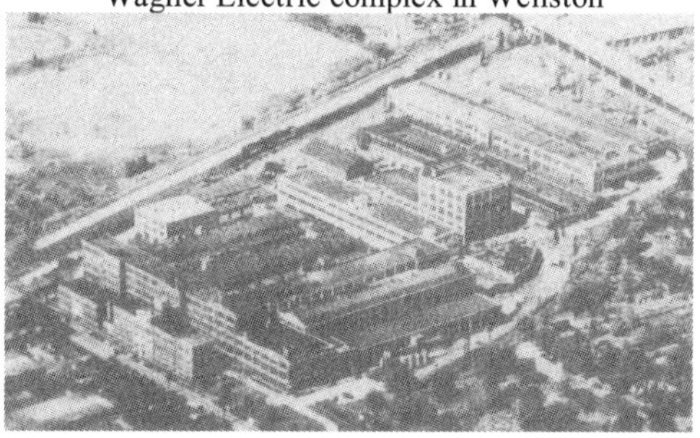

What unusual weather phenomenon hit St. Louis in April of 2001? The city was hit by what came to be known as the Billion Dollar Hailstorm with stones as large as golf balls. Estimates were as large as two billion in damages overall to cars, windows, house siding, etc.

What organ transplant first was performed at Barnes Hospital in St. Louis? Lung transplant

What type of cancer operation was first performed at Barnes in St. Louis? Lung cancer

Sportswriter Bob Burnes

What Yankee baseball manager dissed New York doctors and came to Barnes for his prostate surgery? Joe Torre

What true event in St. Louis inspired a book and a very scary movie about demonic possession? The rite of exorcism performed by a priest from the St. Louis University School of Theology – *The Exorcist*

What article of apparel did St. Louis once lead the world in production? Shoes

Where did all the leather come from for those shoes? Mostly from the East St. Louis stockyards, just across the Mississippi

What were the two biggest makers? International Shoe and Brown Shoe

What was Brown Shoe Company's best-selling brand? Buster Brown shoes

What logo was inside the shoe? There was a picture of Buster Brown and his dog inside.

What was their slogan/jingle? "Hi, I'm Buster Brown/ I live in a shoe . . ." Next, his dog would bark 'Aarrf' . . . "That's my dog Tige/ Look for him in there too!"

What haircut was popularized by Buster? The Buster Brown pageboy look

Where can one find **the largest mosaic wall and ceiling art in the world**? Inside the Cathedral Basilica of St. Louis in the Central West End

Washington Ave. looking west in 1930s (Tettaton picture)

What is the oldest institution of higher learning west of the Mississippi? St. Louis University

What essential items used by pioneers going West were made in St. Louis? The Hawkins Rifle and the Murphy wagon . . . Hmm, I wonder if it's the same guy who made that crazy bed?

What cocktails were invented by the Planter's House Hotel in St. Louis? **The Martini, Tom Collins, Bloody Mary** and Planter's Punch; the first **Southern Comfort** was served at the Southern Hotel's bar.

What famous guests stayed at the Planter's House? Henry Clay, Charles Dickens, Daniel Webster and Louis Kossuth

What bad news did St. Louisans receive in 2007? According to government statistics, St. Louis was once again the homicide capital of America.

If you are underage in a St. Louis bar and order a Mississippi Highball, what will you be served? A glass of water

Why were St. Louisans outraged when the Windy City reversed the flow of the Chicago River in Illinois? Because Chicago's wastes were now literally being flushed down the Illinois River which empties into the Mississippi about 20 miles north of St. Louis.

What action did St. Louis take to counter the measure? First they sued, and when that failed they built more water treatment plants.

How was the practice of placing a chocolate treat on a hotel room pillow started? Actor Cary Grant was staying at the Mayfair Hotel in St. Louis and he placed a chocolate treat on his girl friend's pillow.

What is the third-ranking botanical garden in the world? Missouri Botanical Gardens in St. Louis

Where was the first Jewish synagogue west of the Mississippi? St. Louis

Where was America's first ironclad ship built? At Carondelet, in South St. Louis, by Captain James B. Eads

What other invention did Eads make? The diving bell so he could salvage wrecks from the bottom of the Mississippi

What Missouri city has more free major tourist attractions than any other city in America except Washington, D.C.? St. Louis – The Zoo, Museum of Westward Expansion, Art Museum, Grant's Farm, Science Center, Missouri History Museum, Anheuser-Busch Brewery, the Planetarium and Busch Stadium . . . if you can sneak inside

The name of the daily column written by sports writer Bob Burnes for the *Globe-Democrat* was "The Bench Warmer."

Why did Charles Lindbergh name his airplane the "Spirit of St. Louis?" To thank St. Louis business firms that backed his effort

Where is Lindbergh's plane now? It was donated to the Smithsonian in Washington, D.C. in 1928.

What is the longest river in the U.S? St. Louisans, who have a long standing feud with National

Geographic, claim it's the **Missourisippi** – the Mississippi is actually a tributary of the Missouri

Are you making up any of these questions? Nope – Scout's honor. (When I was a kid we said "Honest Injun," but that is now politically incorrect.)

Who is depicted on the statue in front of City Hall? U.S. Grant

What KTRS radio announcer was fired immediately, in March of 2006, for making a racial slur about Condoleezza Rice becoming commissioner of the NFL? Dave Lenihan, who used the word "coon"

What could have easily saved him had he been a quick thinker? The station has a seven second delay button to eliminate bloopers, but no one thought to use it

Who built and operated Union Station? The Terminal Railroad Association; Union Station was built in 1897.

Where is Grant's Farm? It's at 10501 Gravois Road (314-843-1700). General Grant once farmed part of the property. The 281 acre estate is owned by August Busch Jr. and is used as a Clydesdale breeding farm. Grant's 1856 log home is there as well as a petting zoo.

What has been the cause of the holdup on building the new bridge connecting St. Louis to Illinois? Illinois wants to pay for it with taxes and St. Louis Mayor Francis Slay wants to charge a $2.00 toll.

Where would the new bridge across the Mississippi be located? It would be north of the 1950s Martin Luther King/Veterans Bridge.

Quality Dairy Billboard (Lonnie Tettaton)

Critics say the city earnings tax in St. Louis keeps new businesses from locating here. How much annual revenue does the city receive from the earnings tax? $130 million

What practice over the last two decades has hurt city income? Nearly every new project built in the city has received either a tax abatement (sweetheart deal) or tax-incremental financing.

How do St. Louis and Kansas City rank when it comes to having female partners in law firms? Both are slightly below the national average of 17 percent. St. Louis has 16 percent and Kansas City has 14 percent.

What criticisms do architects like Bill Burke of **Glen Carbon** make of the St. Louis riverfront? Now that the riverboats and railroads are gone, the city should recapture it with housing developments, they assert.

When did St. Louis receive its first telegraph office? 1848 – wires were stretched across the Mississippi from East St. Louis.

What park at Natural Bridge and Grand once had a zoo? Fairgrounds Park

What was/is the famous dance hall at 3354 Iowa? Casa Loma

What was the nightclub on DeBaliviere that Evelyn West called home? The Stardust

Evelyn had a certain part of her upper torso anatomy insured. What was the amount? Fifty thousand dollars

According to the U.S. Geological survey, how many feet above sea level is St. Louis? 413 feet

Where is the city directrix bronze datum plaque located, used by engineers and surveyors for shooting elevation? On the east face of the westernmost pier of the Eads Bridge

Where did the Playboy Club move to when it left its location on Lindell Blvd? Holiday Inn at Lindbergh and Route 55

How did Kingshighway get its name? Kingshighway was the old royal road that separated the old common fields (of French settlers) from the king's domain.

What TV station started out on Signal Hill in **Belleville** as a UHF station called WTVI? KTVI

St. Louis City Hall is modeled after what other famous building? The City Hall in Paris

What church has the **tallest steeple in the city**? St. Francis de Sales – 300 ft

What newspaper tried, and failed, to replace the *Globe-Democrat*? *St. Louis Sun*

What St. Louis woman wrote a weekly column about St. Louis (packed with humor and nostalgia) for the *Post-Dispatch* before moving to Washington D.C? Elaine Viets

What St. Louis Catholic high school announced plans in 2006 to start drug testing its students? CBC

Who won the Final Four NCAA tournament hosted in St. Louis in March of 2005? North Carolina defeated Illinois, 75-70

What St. Louis-based firm posted record profits in the first quarter of 2006? Emerson Electric, this writer's employer back in 1960 and 1961; it posted profits of 96 cents per share.

West End Motors at 276 DeBaliviere (Lonnie Tettaton)

What St. Louis-based firm had three out of the top five viewer's choices for 2006 Super Bowl ads? Anheuser Busch - with the number one spot going to guys worshiping a magic revolving beer refrigerator packed with Bud Light. The number two spot went to a young Clydesdale colt trying to pull a beer wagon.

What two starters for Brad Soderberg's 2005-06 St. Louis Billikens came from nearby **East St. Louis** and **Belleville**? Tommy Lidell and Kevin Lisch

What connection does Lisch's father (Rusty) have with St. Louis pro sports? He was once a third string quarterback for the Big Red.

Who became the new coach for the Rams in 2006 after Mike Martz was eased out of the picture? Scott Linehan

What new job did Mike Martz accept? Offensive coordinator for the Detroit Lions

Chuck Norman interviewing Natalie Wood

What former Saints head coach became Linehan's defensive coordinator? Jim Haslett

What three St. Louisans were on the U.S. World Cup soccer team in 2006? Chris Klein, Pat Noonan and Taylor Twellman

What new state conservation area (in Jefferson County) opened in 2006? LaBarque Creek Conservation Area – 500 acres

What Fox TV news reporter wrote a best-selling book about St. Louis gangsters several years ago? John Auble

Why was the St. Louis deputy police chief forced to resign in April of 2006? After 36 years on the job, Greg Hawkins could not pass the annual physical due to a bad back.

What **St. Charles** native is an avid collector of George Washington memorabilia? Dennis Hahn

Each year, at Christmas time, the St. Louis planetarium in Forest Park places a red bow completely around the top. How was this tradition started? Pranksters, in 1966, tied a bow around the hyperboloid building, and the reaction was so positive, the tradition was continued.

How did Kiener Plaza in front of the historic Old Courthouse in downtown St. Louis get its name? St. Louisan Harry Kiener represented the United States on the track team in the 1904 Olympics at St. Louis.

How many stories tall is the postmodern building at 211 N. Broadway called Metropolitan Square? At 42 stories the building is the tallest in St. Louis.

When was this building completed? 1989

In most towns Division Street is the dividing line, but not in St. Louis. What is the dividing line between north and south in St. Louis? Downtown, it's Market Street, and from Grand on its Lindell and in the county it's Ladue Road.

Van Sickle's Service Station at 6731 Page

Where does Missouri rank nationwide in tort reform, according to the U.S. Chamber of Commerce. It was one of the ten worst but it now ranks number 35 due to recent reforms that limit civil lawsuits.

Where is the largest court-house in the nation? It's the 29 story Thomas F. Eagleton building, named for the former Missouri Senator.

How big is the Eagleton Building? It has more than a million square feet of space. Apparently every inch of space is needed because St. Louis consistently ranks high (top five) among U.S. cities when it comes to violent crime.

What was the upside benefit to St. Louis as a result of Hurricane Katrina at New Orleans? About ten conventions that were scheduled to be held in New Orleans changed their location to St. Louis. A number of people also came to the St. Louis Mardi Gras in the Soulard area (on South Broadway) instead of going to New Orleans.

What Princeton Heights resident gives walking tours of downtown St. Louis nine months out of the year? Maureen Kavanaugh, a substitute teacher – 314-368-8818

What was Missouri's first skyscraper? It was the Wainwright building at 101 N. Seventh St. in St. Louis. The building was designed by Louis Sullivan in the early 1890s and laid the groundwork for future soaring towers around the world.

What is located on **the only piece of land in St. Louis never to be bought or sold**? The basilica of St. Louis on the riverfront by the Gateway Arch

When was the existing stone structure built? 1834 – It is the fourth church structure to stand on the spot; the previous churches were built of wood.

What famous woman had her son christened at the church in 1809? **Sacajawea**, who proved so invaluable to the Lewis and Clark expedition, witnessed the christening of her son, Jean Baptiste Charbonneau, to whom she gave birth on the trail.

What was the original nickname for the city of St. Louis? Mound City – the same native tribes that built Monk's Mound, across the river in Collinsville, built hundreds of mounds in the St. Louis area.

BIZARRE MURDER OF WALTER SCOTT

This writer heard Walter Scott perform live only one time, back around 1978. My wife Lorna was teaching in **Troy**, Illinois with a married colleague who was his second cousin. The four of us went to hear him perform at a small lounge in St. Louis. My wife and I absolutely loved it. Walter (born Walter Notheis in 1943 at Booth Memorial H.) had great stage presence as he went through an amazing repertoire of songs, including some popularized by Elvis. His silk shirt was unbuttoned to his waist, revealing a smooth, hairless chest. He entertained the gals by demonstrating his ability to make his stomach muscles undulate in rhythmic fashion. Then he commented on his body. "As you can see," he said with a wink, I have no hair on my chest. That's because grass doesn't grow on a busy street."

When there was a break, he came over and chatted with us. Walter said that he was going to be featured as a singer in an upcoming Walter Matthau movie. He was hoping that could be his big break. Unfortunately, Matthau underwent triple bypass heart surgery and the whole movie project was cancelled.

In 1983, Walter and Bob Kuban were planning to appear at the Fox for a reunion and anniversary of the In-Men. Walter disappeared and the much anticipated reunion never took place. Their only hit song, *The Cheater*, was released in 1966, reaching the number two spot on the charts. It was recorded at Technisonic Studio on Brentwood Blvd. They even had an appearance on Dick Clark's *American Bandstand*. Bob Kuban grew weary of being on the road all the time and decided he could be content just making a good living in Metro St. Louis. But Walter wanted to continue this track and make it big nationally. The two then mutually agreed to go their separate ways.

Walter disappeared after leaving his home (in **St. Peters)** to go on an evening errand December 27, 1983.

It seemed as if life was imitating art. The hit song was about a "fool-hearted clown" who went around breaking ladies' hearts by cheating on them. Only this time the cheater was Walter's wife. Authorities suspected his wife, but there was no proof until Walter's body was found in a cistern in 1987.

Walter Scott's yearbook picture

James H. Williams, with whom Walter's second wife (JoAnn Calceterra) was having an affair, was charged with the crime. An ironic ending for a singer whose only hit song was about infidelity. Williams was found guilty of capital murder and JoAnn was given five years for hindering the investigation. William's first wife, from **Marion**, Illinois, was thought to have been killed in an auto accident. Her body was exhumed and this time her death was ruled a homicide with her husband the lead suspect. More irony: it was Bob Kuban who introduced Walter, his lead vocalist, to JoAnn. Kuban told this author he still has regrets about that. Walter was introduced to JoAnn at the **Imperial Club** when she was only nineteen.

Attorney/radio personality, Don Wolff

Walter, whose grandmother lived in **Cairo**, Illinois, started singing almost as soon as he learned to talk. He was weaned on "How Much is That Doggie in the Window." Walter's family was Catholic so he attended St. Mary's High, located south of Gravois on Grand. He was already a meticulous dresser and was in a band called the Royaltones. He married Doris, his high school sweetheart, in 1963. A son, Walter III, was born less than a year later. Then a second son was born. Walter became Bob Kuban's lead singer in the summer of 1963. The band changed its name from the Rhythm Masters to the In-Men and Walter adopted Scott as his stage name. Walter spent most evenings with the band at various night clubs. He was ia crane operator at American Car Foundry for his day job.

Jim Williams (courtesy Scottie Priesmeyer)

The band quickly became a favorite in the St. Louis area. They did proms, teen dances, the Playboy Club, wedding receptions and Cardinal baseball games.

Women simply couldn't resist Walter's piercing blue eyes, neatly manicured hair and cleft chin. It wasn't long before he was regularly cheating on his wife with JoAnn. He and his wife separated and Walter and JoAnn Calceterra leased a Cypress Gardens apartment in **Florissant**. Walter and Doris were divorced in October of 1969. He married JoAnn in December. In 1972, JoAnn gave birth to twins. Walter was on the road much of the time doing his shows and being unfaithful to his new wife. She became lonely and bored. They eventually moved to **St. Charles** and the children went to Francis Howell School District. JoAnn met Jim Williams one day when he came to do some electrical work at her house. They soon became lovers.

A friend of mine, **Harry Spiller**, was the sheriff of Williamson County, Illinois, and personally knew Williams and his first wife. Williams spent his later teen years with his biological father in **Marion**, Illinois. He married Sharon, his high school sweetheart, in 1958. They had a baby boy in 1960. In 1963, the couple moved to a trailer park in St. Charles and Jim got a job at McDonnell Douglas. Jim eventually went into the electrical contracting business and Sharon became a reservation agent with TWA.

Sharon began attending the **Harvester Baptist Church** on Route 94. One night Sharon was found in her car, at the bottom of a steep ditch, on Central School Road (off 94), severely injured. **Cottleville** Fire Department paramedics rushed her to St. Joseph's Hospital where she later died. Authorities were perplexed that she had suffered such severe injuries in what appeared to be a minor accident. No autopsy was performed on her body and she was buried in Marion.

Nine days later, Jim and JoAnn were seeing each other regularly. When Jim told JoAnn to get a divorce, she told him Walter would never agree to a second divorce. After Walter disappeared, his parents grew suspicious when JoAnn started canceling all of his bookings after being missing only two days. This fear was quickly reinforced when they realized that every time they saw or talked to JoAnn, Jim Williams was with her.

Walter's car was found at the airport. Police later surmised this was to make authorities think that somehow Walter decided to disappear on his own. When Bob Kuban was questioned, he told them JoAnn had suggested that he and Walter take out $100,000 life insurance policies and make the other the beneficiary. Police surmised it was an effort to make Kuban look guilty if something happened to Walter. Yet there was no proof of anything because there was no body.

Walter Scott

In January of 1984, in sub-zero weather, Jim contracted to have a concrete planter built on top of a cistern in his back yard at 5647 Gutermuth Rd. JoAnn divorced Walter in October of 1985, charging him with unfaithfulness and abandonment. JoAnn and Jim were married in April of 1986. The wedding reception was held at **Yacovelli's** in **Florissant**. Since Williams was the prime suspect in Walter's disappearance, officials decided to take a closer look at what happened to his first wife. **Mary Case** performed an autopsy on Sharon Williams in April of 1987 and concluded that the two traumas to the back of her head were inconsistent with the accident. She surmised that the blows came from either a lead pipe or a crowbar and the death was ruled a homicide.

When police questioned one of Jim's sons, he surmised that the body might be in the cistern in his dad's back yard. At the time of the murder there had been a long cold spell. Lakes and ponds were filled with ice and the ground was too frozen to dig a grave. Jim was arrested when Walter's badly decomposed body was found in the cistern in April of 1987. Mary Case examined the body and determined that Walter had been shot in the back. JoAnn surrendered to authorities a few days later with Don Wolff (a KMOX jazz aficionado) as her attorney. This author met Don Wolff a couple of years ago at WSIE, in **Edwardsville**, where he was doing a jazz broadcast.

St. Louis Zoo Director Marlin Perkins

Due to legal wrangling, it took nearly six years for the trial to begin. Walter's frustrated parents lost faith in an American justice system that seemed to favor the rights of the accused more than those of the victim. Jim was given a life sentence without the possibility of parole. He was sent to the correctional facility in **Potosi**.

The prosecution was wary about taking JoAnn to trial because the evidence against her was less compelling. Yet Wolff told her that if she went to trial she risked a life sentence. She also knew most everyone in the area thought she was guilty. And, in the press, JoAnn was known as the "**Black Widow**" Wolff talked her into accepting the prosecution's deal. JoAnn got off with a five year sentence. She was released from the Missouri correctional facility for women after serving only eighteen months. Once again, Walter's parents felt they had been betrayed by the justice system.

Scottie Priesmeyer, who teaches creative writing at St. Charles Community College in **St. Peters**, wrote the definitive book about the murder – *The Cheaters*. She grew up near Delmar and Goodfellow and later moved to Audubon Park in **Brentwood**. She is also the author of *Silent Justice*, a novel set in the St. Louis area. Some of her information was obtained from Dr. Mary Case, forensic pathologist and Medical Examiner for St. Louis, St. Charles and Jefferson counties. See Harry Spiller's *Murder in the Heartland Vol. 2* for more information.

ST. LOUIS TRIVIA

An NHL team came to St. Louis (1935) from Ottawa and was renamed the Eagles, but they lasted only one season. The St. Louis Arena at this time was home to the Flyers of the American Hockey Association, and they lasted until the league folded in 1942.

The city of St. Louis built the Art Deco **Jewel Box** in Forest Park in 1936. It sits on a 17 acre site and is listed on the National Historic Register. The fountain and floral displays inside make it a favorite site for St. Louis weddings. This huge greenhouse was built at a cost of $117,000 with about 45 percent coming from WPA funds. (314) 531-0080.

The **Soldiers Military Museum** is at 1315 Chestnut. The names of 1,075 men who gave their lives in World War I are etched in granite. Across the street is a park that honors veterans from World War II, Korea and Vietnam. Two large rooms display uniforms, weapons and memorabilia from the Civil War to the present. The building is a popular destination for school field trips. The building was dedicated in 1936 and was another of those Depression-era WPA projects. Critics said WPA stood for We Piddle Around.

The **Missouri Civil War Museum** is located in the old PX and gymnasium building at Jefferson Barracks in south St. Louis at the end of Broadway. The building was finished in 1905 and abandoned and boarded up in 1953. Mark Trout and Jim Hubbard, a couple of Union Civil War buffs, came up with the idea for a museum a few years ago. About 220 Civil War generals saw duty at Jefferson Barracks early in their careers, including U.S. Grant and Robert E. Lee. Much of the restoration is being done with donated labor. During the Great Depression there was a large Civilian Conservation Corps facility at Jefferson Barracks. It is hoped that part of the museum will open sometime late in 2008. Visitors Center 314-544-5714

Who sculpted the "Wedding of the Rivers" statues across from Union Station in St. Louis? Carl Milles completed the project in 1940. There was a huge controversy surrounding the statue and fountains. The nude male figure of the "Mississippi" looks as if he is about to ravish his "Missouri" bride. Some civic leaders demanded that the figures be clothed. A tepid compromise was struck and the name was changed to "The Meeting of the Rivers."

In November of 1940, John Carr bought 29 lots in the largely undeveloped Marlborough Manor, just outside the city limits of St. Louis. He built an Art Deco motel complex on the site (7755 Watson Road) and called it **Coral Court**. Demolition was started in the spring of 1995.

HOW ST. LOUIS GOT ITS ZOO

In the 1870s, a zoological gardens was established by Julius Walsh at the Fairgrounds. When the collection was sold in 1891, some of the animals were purchased by private citizens and kept at Forest Park. After the 1904 World's Fair, the city of St. Louis bought "the birdcage" from the Smithsonian Institution for $6,000. Unfortunately, city parks director Dwight Davis was more interested in having a golf course on the park grounds and had little interest in a Zoo. Davis was the U.S. tennis doubles champion three years in a row (1899-1901) and it was he who designed and donated the cup for international tennis competition, known as the **Davis Cup**. **At Forest Park, Davis built the first municipal tennis courts in America**.

In 1910, a St. Louis Zoological Society was organized through the efforts of Cortlandt Harris, James Abbott and taxidermist Frank Schwartz. Broker George Dieckman became involved and spent his own money to buy animals, hoping that this would prod the city into constructing a zoo. Davis finally came to the belief that a municipal zoo was a good idea; he just didn't want it located in a big city park. A few years later, when Republican Henry Kiel became mayor, he supported the idea of a zoo located near the birdcage.

In 1913, the city authorized a 77 acre zoo plus buildings to house the animals, much to the chagrin of Davis who thought buildings would clutter the serenity of the park. By 1914, there was a veritable menagerie that included bison, elk, llamas, zebras, bears, a kangaroo, monkeys and a few dozen birds. Unfortunately, the critters were ill housed and ill fed and many grew sick and died.

In 1915, the state legislature authorized St. Louis to levy a mill sales tax to support the zoo. The main proviso was that the zoo was to be perpetually free of admission. School children collected pennies and nickels so that an elephant might be bought. They raised $2,385 to buy a female pachyderm.

Anne Keefe of KMOX

The widely admired and emulated bear pits were finished by 1919. Under the four decade leadership of Director George Vierheller, the St. Louis Zoo became recognized as one of the best in the world.

Carthage-born Marlin Perkins further enhanced the Zoo's reputation when he was director in the 1960s. Perkins once got into trouble at Wentworth Military Academy for keeping snakes in his room. He attended the University of Missouri, but dropped out to become a common laborer on the zoo grounds in St. Louis. He went on to become reptile curator and eventually director. In 1960, he went on a Himalaya expedition with Sir Edmund Hillary (first to climb Mt. Everest) **to search for the legendary Yeti (Abominable Snowman)**. Perkins became nationally famous with the television program, *Wild Kingdom*. By October of 1974, his program was drawing higher ratings than *Hee Haw* and The *Lawrence Welk Show*.

KMOX RADIO PERSONALITIES

John McCormack

KMOX radio, "the Voice of St. Louis," started in 1926, the year the Cardinals won their first World Series. The station broadcast the Series play-by-play, but did not do regular season games until 1927. For years the station was located on Hampton Avenue.

Some of the personalities over the years include Bob Anthony, Jim Baer, Ron Barber, Gary Bender, Joan Beuckman, Buddy Blattner, Bill Bradley, Charles Brennan, Bob Broeg, Carole Buck, Jack Buck, Joe Buck, Joel Buchsbaum, Burnes, Jim Butler, Harry Caray, Skip Caray, Jack Carney (Saturday morning comedy show), John Carney, Bob Chase, Mike Claiborne, Larry Conners, J.C. Corcoran, Bob Costas (hired by Bob Hyland as a result of a tape he submitted to the station), Frank Cusamano (a Desmet grad), Carol Daniel, Rex Davis (liked to dine at Bogey Hills Country Club), Bing Devine, Dan Dierdorf (*Sports Open Line*), Nancy Drew (locker room interviews with football Cardinals; she married safety Larry Wilson), Richard Evans (*Thought For the Day*), Harry Fender (Captain 11 on KPLR TV), Art Fleming (the original host of TV's *Jeopardy*), Pat Fontaine (weather announcer), Jan Fox (director of The Big Red Line cheerleaders, owned by KMOX – not the team), Joe Garagiola, Walt Glatthaar (motor sports), Bob Goddard (columnist for the *Globe-Democrat*), Ed Griesedieck (*Ask the Lawyer*), Bob Hamilton, Harry Hamm (entertainment critic), Bob Hardy (his home was in **Marine** and his daughter went to school in **Highland**, Illinois), Bruce Hayward (easy listening music), Jim Holder (sports - teamed with Gene McNary in the Meramec

Mr. Mokes the chimp

River Raft Race), Kevin Horrigan (got into a shouting match with guest, Robert Schuler), Rick Horton (baseball analyst) Dr. David Hoy (ESP expert) Julius Hunter (embarrassed by frank talk when he interviewed sex expert, Sherri Hite), Robert Hyland (general manager from 1955-1992) Charles Jaco (CNN Gulf War correspondent), Ron Jacober (Blues games), Randy Karraker (*Sports Open Line*) Ann Keefe (came over from **Kansas City** - Grand Dame of KMOX; featured on TV's *Donnybrook*), Dan Kelly (finest hockey announcer who ever lived), Gus Kyle (hockey analyst), France Laux (baseball announcer 1930s), Megan Lynch (traffic helicopter), Ed Macauley (sports), Margie Manning (covered the Tony Daniele-Police Commissioner John Frank hostage crisis), Don Marsh, Emmett McAuliffe (started out meeting listeners at The Donut House on Morganford) Kevin McCarthy, John McCormick (the man who walks and talks at midnight, Dan McLaughlin (sports), Charlie Menees (big band sound), Donna Michaels (Schnucks commercials), Don Miller ("gaper block" helicopter traffic reports), Mike Miller (gardening expert), Scott Mosby (home improvement), Miss Nanette (fashion expert), Juli Newman (financial reports), Bob Osborne (disc jockey and *Trading Station*), Mike Owens (city hall politics), Mary Phelan (news), Bob Ramsey (Billiken broadcasts), Jay Randolph (sports), Mike Shannon (baseball color analyst), Uncle Dick Slack (furniture store owner in **East St. Louis**; country music show in 1940s), Bob Starr (football Cardinals), David Strauss (trivia expert), Gabby Street, Elaine Viets, Jim White (Dave Lossos South County neighbor, talk show; Halloween night show), Wendy Wiese (*Morning Show*), Bill Wilkerson (sports and *Morning Show*);Wilkerson and Wiese were part of the group that left KMOX to work for KTRS; Ken Wilson (sports; started River City Rascals baseball in **O'Fallon**, Missouri), Don Wolff (St. Louis attorney (jazz music).

Dr. Tom Dooley and Rex Davis

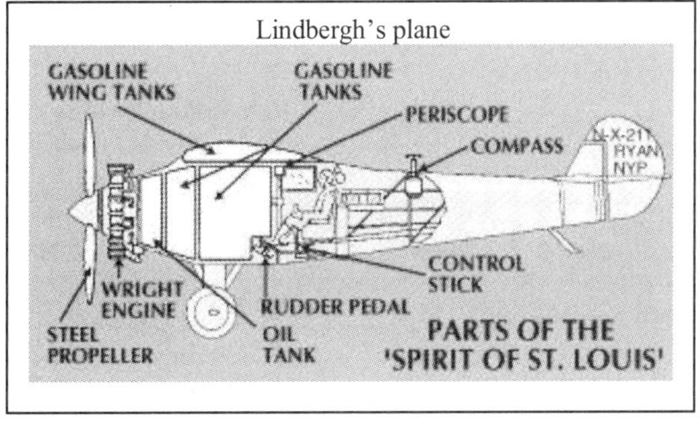

Lindbergh's plane

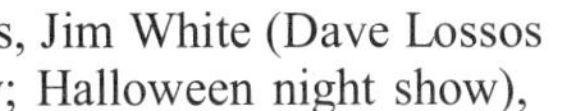

CHARLES LINDBERGH'S ST. LOUIS CONNECTION

Charles Lindbergh was an early aviation pilot who sometimes did barnstorming and worked for Robertson Aircraft of St. Louis as a mail pilot. He flew the mail route from St. Louis to Chicago, often following Chicago & Alton Railroad tracks to keep from getting lost.

A New York man offered a $25,000 prize for the first man to fly solo from New York to Paris. In 1925, the twenty-five year-old Minnesotan sought financial backing for his endeavor. After failing to interest New Yorkers in the venture, he sought help from a fellow St. Louis aviator, A. B. Lambert - the pioneer for whom Lambert Airport is named. **Lindbergh's dare-devil reputation** preceded him. He had barely survived four crashes already and was remembered notoriously for the dangerous stunt of flying under the Eads and Municipal bridges at an air show. The St. Louis Flying Club, the *Post-Dispatch*, and the *Globe-Democrat* all refused to have anything to do with an inexperienced long distance pilot flying an underpowered single engined plane. Finally, the fledgling Ryan Aircraft Company of San Diego agreed to build Lindbergh's plane for about $10,000. The plane had an oversized wingspan for added lift to counteract the weight of the extra fuel needed to cross the Atlantic. Since the huge fuel tank was directly in front of the pilot, there was no windshield. **To see where he was going, Lindbergh used a periscope**.

All of the other pilots who planned to compete for the prize were more experienced and had co-pilots with them. Richard Byrd was one such entrant, having already accomplished the feat of flying over the North Pole. Charles Nungesser and Francois Coli, two flying veterans from the Great War, took off from Paris on May 8, were spotted over Ireland, and were never seen again.

Lindbergh and "Spirit of St. Louis"

While flying his 5,250 pound plane from San Diego to New York, "Slim" Lindbergh broke the coast-to-coast record in his pewter-colored plane by 5 ½ hours. Lindbergh dubbed his 28 foot-long bird the *Spirit of St. Louis* to honor his adopted city. Meanwhile, another contestant (Noel Davis) was killed during a practice run.

While Richard Byrd and Clarence Chamberlin hesitated because of a slight drizzle, Lindbergh took off (May 20, 1927) in his monoplane at Roosevelt Field, his plane barely clearing obstacles at the end of the runway. For the next 33 ½ hours, Lindbergh flew the Great Circle Route by dead reckoning, an incredible feat, landing at Le Bourget Airfield in Paris, France.

The entire world went crazy over "Lucky Lindy." In an age of ballyhoo and cynicism, the masses had a real hero who didn't drink anything stronger than coffee. President Coolidge sent a cruiser to bring him back home. Most thought it should have been a battleship. He was given a ticker-tape parade in NYC and a special banquet in St. Louis to honor his achievement. They even named a dance for him – the Lindy Hop. St. Louis was bursting with a pride that hadn't been seen since 1904. Foreign nations issued stamps in his honor. He became a goodwill ambassador to Nicaragua and Mexico. In Mexico, he met his future wife, Ann Morrow, the daughter of the U.S. Ambassador to that country.

Unfortunately, Lindbergh and his wife were to suffer through the personal heartbreaking tragedy of having their baby kidnapped and murdered. A German immigrant, Bruno Hauptmann, was executed for that crime. Subsequently, the Lindbergh Kidnap Law was enacted which allowed for the feds to intervene when state lines were crossed. Further, the death penalty was invoked if the kidnap victim was harmed in any way.

Lindbergh's reputation suffered when he became an isolationist in the 1930s and opposed war preparedness measures by President Roosevelt.

JOHNNY LONDOFF CHEVROLET

Remember all those great car dealerships in St. Louis in the 1950s? How about those classic cars of the era with big tail fins and massive chrome bumpers? Many of you either bought a car from them, remember their radio and TV ads or drove past their establishments on countless occasions.

Joe Simkins Ford was in **Wellston**. On South Grand there was Andy Berger Ford, on South Jefferson was Big 4 Chevrolet, on North Grand you had Weber-Diebel Ford, Bilgier Chevrolet, Kuhs Buick, Northside Motors Studebaker and a Kaiser Frazer dealer. Mindenhall Ford was at Jefferson and Washington, Vincel Pontiac was on South Kingshighway as was Grebe Olds, King Dodge and Beyer Motors. Gilbert Buick was perched on Gravois (east of Grand), Ackerman Buick, was located out in the sticks on New Halls Ferry and Dunn. Yates sold Oldsmobiles on Natural Bridge.

Out in the county there was Nolting Olds at Manchester and Sappington, Sunset Ford at 11860 Gravois, Riesmeyer Ford in **Webster Groves**, Barton Pontiac on S. Florissant Rd., Castles-Wilson Buick on North Kingshighway, Stivers Ford on Florissant Rd., Tom Smith Rambler on South Broadway, Carlson Olds on Forsyth, Ben Lindenbusch Studebaker on S. Kingshighway, Reuther Jeep on Olive, **Kirkwood** Plymouth at Manchester and Lindbergh, McKelvey Olds on Florissant, Lou Fusz on Brentwood, Forest Cadillac at 7700 Carondelet and Mallory Buick on Natural Bridge.

Johnny Londoff Chevrolet 1961 yellow pages

Johnny Londoff's father had a Chevrolet dealership in **Wellston**. His uncle Harry had a Chrysler dealership on 25th street in North St. Louis. The familiar Johnny Londoff Chevrolet jingle which encourages car buyers to "*buy the low overhead way*" is based upon a 62- year tradition of superior sales, service and "*low overhead*" prices on new and used cars and trucks. The man who did that commercial just recently passed away. After 15 years experience as a dealer, Londoff Sr. founded Johnny Londoff Chevrolet in **Florissant** (1960) on Dunn Road which, through the years has maintained a reputation as one of the top dealerships in the area. In 1983, he was recognized by Time Magazine as **one of the top ten automobile dealers in the United States** and in January, 2007 received GMAC's prestigious Champion of Life Award for lifetime achievement and commitment to the community. The national GMAC award was based upon Johnny Londoff's record of raising millions for children's charities including the Sammy Davis Jr. Variety Telethon and St Louis Children's Hospital.

Johnny Londoff Jr. who, as president of Johnny Londoff Chevrolet and Johnny Londoff Chevrolet in **Pacific**, Missouri, continues the family tradition of business growth and community leadership. He has expanded the Florissant dealership to enlarge the selection of new and used cars, trucks and SUV's and extended service department hours to 7:30 a.m. to 7:00 p.m. on Monday, Wednesday and Friday.

Johnny Londoff Jr. plays a major role in the Johnny Londoff Chevrolet Foundation Scholarship program, now in its 45th year, which awards financial grants to graduates of area high schools who are chosen by principals and guidance counselors. He is a leader in the annual Old Newsboys campaign and in the annual GM Dealers Charity Golf Benefit for St. Louis Children's Hospital.

What makes it all worthwhile? When a customer comes up to him, shakes his hand and says, "It's been a pleasure buying at Johnny Londoff Chevrolet, THANK YOU!"

Aerial view of downtown St. Louis, circa 1930 (D. Lossos Collection)

DAVE SINCLAIR FORD

"If something isn't right, we'll fix it for free." Dave became noted for this customer friendly motto. His many decades of dedication to service, customers and employees have made his business a landmark for many St. Louisans. During this time he has sold over 250,000 cars and trucks. His name became a household fixture after he began offering free undercoats to prospective customers. “We’ll meet or beat any other deal or you get a free undercoat,” he advertised.

Sinclair started out as a hod carrier lugging plaster in a triangle shaped container on his back while waiting for his chance for a spot at the police academy. Four years later, he was in a patrol car. Seven years into his police career his eldest son became ill. Dave had to borrow money from his brother to pay the doctor. His brother urged him to leave the police force and sell cars so he could better feed and clothe his 7 children. He began selling cars for **Vincel Pontiac** on South Kingshighway and later took an offer to be sales manager for a north St. Louis Ford dealership, **Costello-Kunze**. In 1966, Ford agreed to lend him $244,000 to set up his own dealership on South Kingshighway. He recalls having only two parking spaces for his customers; the rest were on the street.

In the early days Sinclair suffered a brain hemorrhage. He didn’t have the money to pay the surgeon, but it so happened that the surgeon had recently wrecked his sports car. He fixed the doctor’s car in exchange for the operation.

Sinclair moved his establishment in 1972 to Lemay Ferry and Lindbergh Boulevard, not far from the Jefferson Barracks Bridge. The strategy was to establish a high volume of sales with moderately priced vehicles.

From 1984 through 1966 **Sinclair was the number one selling Ford dealer in the nation**. Since that time, his family has added four more dealership; three Mercury and a Buick-GM. The Ford dealership still ranks consistently among the top fifty in the nation. All four of his sons are in the family business. Several of his 37 grandchildren are also on the payroll.

SENATOR THOMAS HART BENTON

Benton was born in North Carolina, but moved to Tennessee where he once owned a large plantation. He was admitted to the Tennessee bar in 1805. With the outbreak of the war of 1812, he became fellow Tennessean Andrew Jackson’s aide-de-camp, whereby he represented Jackson’s military interests in Washington, D.C. He chafed under the position which denied him combat experience.

Thomas Hart Benton (Wikipedia)

When, in 1813, he heard of insults Jackson had made against his brother Jesse, Benton physically assaulted Jackson in a Nashville hotel. The entourages of the two men began fighting and Jackson narrowly escaped death from being shot in the shoulder. Jackson and Benton became bitter enemies. After the war, in 1815, Benton moved to Missouri Territory and practiced law in St. Louis.

In 1817, Charles Lucas accused Benton of being delinquent on his taxes and ineligible to vote. They dueled on Bloody Island, in the middle of the Mississippi River. Both men were only slightly wounded so they agreed to meet for a second duel. This time Lucas was killed and

Original Dave Sinclair Ford on 3600 South Kingshighway

Courtesy Dave Sinclair

Benton escaped unharmed. In the 1828 election, Benton and Jackson set aside their personal differences and joined forces. Benton became an ardent supporter of Jacksonian Democracy, championing the cause of the common man and extending the suffrage. Benton supported Jackson’s war on the National Bank and the Specie Circular, which required payment of land purchases in hard money. This earned Benton the nickname, “Old Bullion.” Benton was an expansionist and championed the cause of Manifest Destiny.

Benton was the author of the first Homestead Acts which gave free land to those willing to settle on it. Like Jackson, Benton favored replacing Native-Americans with European settlers. He advocated the annexation of Texas, but opposed the extension of slavery in territory acquired in the Mexican War. His free soil stance was not popular with the rest of his party.

In 1844, he escaped serious injury - and possible death - when a cannon misfired on board the *U.S.S. Princeton*. The incident killed eight and wounded twenty.

During heated remarks during the debate over the Compromise of 1850, a Mississippi senator advanced on Benton wielding a pistol, but was wrestled to the floor where he was disarmed.

When Benton declared himself against slavery in 1849, the Missouri Legislature replaced him in 1851, ending his reign of thirty years. He then served two years in the U.S. House of Representatives.

He remained loyal to the party. So much so that when his son-in-law, John C. Fremont ran for the presidency in 1856, as a Republican, Benton voted for Buchanan the Democrat.

Benton, one of the most influential men of his era, wrote his memoirs in 1854 and died in 1858.

ELIJAH LOVEJOY AMERICA’S # 1 MARTYR FOR FREEDOM OF THE PRESS

In 1836, **St. Louis** enhanced its reputation for violence in the Francis McIntosh Affair. McIntosh, a mulatto steward on a steamboat, was arrested after a skirmish down on the river levee. He was charged with interfering with the duties of law enforcement officials. McIntosh broke free as he was being taken to jail. He killed George Hammond by cutting his throat and then seriously wounded the other officer, William Mull.

Historian James N. Primm says McIntosh was captured and sent to jail where an angry crowd of about 2,000 people gathered. They rushed the jail, overpowered the sheriff and took the prisoner out to hang him. When someone in the crowd suggested that hanging was too good for him, they took him to a tree at 10th and Market and bound him to it. A fire was lit, and **he was slowly roasted alive**. One eyewitness to the event said the flames caused his bowels to fall out of his body. Someone in the crowd asked if he "felt any pain," and he replied with an anguished *yes*. He expired after about eighteen minutes of torture. None of the newspaper accounts of the incident ever identified any specific persons as the ringleaders, and no one was prosecuted for the crime.

Alton mob attacking Lovejoy warehouse (ISHS)

The **Alton *Telegraph*** was highly critical of the lack of government initiative in stopping the mob. And Elijah Lovejoy, editor of a St. Louis religious weekly, incurred the wrath of locals by keeping the issue alive week after week. Judge Luke Lawless (actual name, no kidding) held a grand jury probe that, to no one's surprise, indicted no one.

Lovejoy stepped up his attacks and lambasted Judge Lawless and the jury. He inferred that Judge Lawless's faulty logic was attributable to his Irish birth and Catholic upbringing. After Lovejoy's editorial attacks, his office was twice broken into and damaged. He opted to move to a *safer* location in **Alton**, Illinois, 20 miles north of St. Louis and located in a "free" state.

Lovejoy was a Yankee New Englander who grew up in a religious home where the precocious youth learned to read from the Bible at age four. He graduated from college, taught school for a spell and then his restless bones compelled him to head west. He arrived in St. Louis at age 27. St. Louis was a rough and tumble city in a state where slavery had been extended by the Missouri Compromise of 1820.

At this point in time, Lovejoy was no abolitionist. He personally hated slavery but thought abolitionism was too extreme and divisive. More than anything else, he was interested in spreading the gospel to the "godless" frontier. In 1833, backed by a coalition of St. Louis businessmen, Lovejoy printed his first issue of the *St. Louis Observer*. Lovejoy was an ardent Presbyterian, and he frequently attacked Baptists with his scathing pen for their unorthodox views. Like so many other Protestants, he thought Catholics were destined for hell.

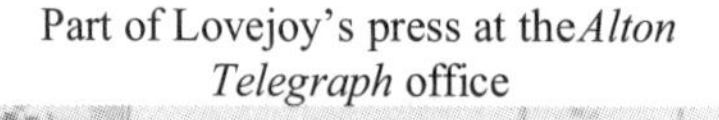

Part of Lovejoy's press at the *Alton Telegraph* office

The McIntosh affair and memories of degrading slave auctions hardened his views toward slavery. He increasingly began to preach against and publish articles denouncing slavery. Missourians, who would later run the Mormons out of their state, did not take kindly to these acerbic criticisms. St. Louisans, in particular, did not take kindly to being called sinners because they supported slavery. After a particularly inflammatory article, a large mob gathered and wrecked his print shop in 1836. Dismayed, Lovejoy left for Alton where he thought his views would be more acceptable.

These high expectations were quickly dashed, for as soon as his printing press arrived from St. Louis, another mob smashed it and threw it into the Mississippi. A new press was ordered and, for about a year, Lovejoy was able to continue his divine mission. He further enraged the locals and St. Louisans when he broached the subject of sex, a hitherto unprintable subject for the press. He castigated slave owners for immorality by having sex with their female slaves and producing mulatto children. The subject of miscegenation (mixing of races) was a touchy subject with southerners.

Alton, the largest city in the state, was on the northern fringe of downstate Illinois that was referred to as Egypt. Pro-slavery sentiment was so strong in southern Illinois that they came very close to amending the state constitution to allow slavery back in 1824. Lovejoy further angered people when he said the Depression of 1837 might be God's way of punishing the people of **Alton**.

One hot August night in 1837, another mob, filled with agitators from St. Louis, destroyed Lovejoy's press. When a new one arrived a month later it, too, was pitched into the river and destroyed. A fourth press arrived on November 7 and this time a group of armed supporters moved the equipment to a stone warehouse near the riverfront. But tempers festered and flared when opponents gathered in local taverns and, aided by "Demon Rum," worked themselves into a frenzy. An armed mob of about 150 men gathered and, bearing torches, marched on the ware-house. At first the crowd was content to shout epithets and hurl paving stones. Son nearly every window in the place was broken.

Lovejoy was inside with fifteen of his loyal and armed supporters. Lovejoy refused to surrender the press and soon shots rang out. Supporters at Alton's First Presbyterian Church rang the bell to alert law enforcement officials, but no help was forthcoming. Alton's mayor, **John Krum**, tried to stop the violence, but no one heeded him.

The mob then raised a ladder to the roof so they could set it on fire, but Lovejoy and a few others ran outside to push it aside. A number of shots rang out and Lovejoy was mortally wounded. He managed to struggle back inside where he died from his wounds. He had been shot five times. Lovejoy's supporters fled the warehouse and the mob finished the dastardly deed by destroying the press and throwing it into the river.

No one was ever convicted of Lovejoy's murder. His friends buried him the next day on, what would have been, his 35th birthday. Owen Lovejoy, his brother, took up the cause and became a leading abolitionist. Alton paid a heavy price for Lovejoy's murder. Once the largest city in the state, its growth now stagnated. A dark pall hung over the once bustling metropolis. Prominent townspeople, who had been supporters of Lovejoy, moved away and the economic and population boom which had marked previous decades was reversed.

Dred Scott: St. Louis slave who spent time in Illinois (Lib. of Congress)

In 1915, a piece of Lovejoy's press was salvaged from the river. It is now proudly on display in the office of the *Alton Telegraph.* Alton since has erected a beautiful monument in his honor. When the SIUE campus was built in Edwardsville, the university library was named for him.

The Lovejoy incident illustrated just how much the country was becoming divided over slavery. His murderers intended to silence him, but their heinous crime had the opposite effect. His death played a significant role in pricking the conscience of a nation and awakened it to the evils of slavery. History's most outstanding example of martyrdom, for the cause of freedom of the press, happened right here in St. Louis and southern Illinois.

THE DRED SCOTT CASE

Dred Scott was born into a Virginia slave family owned by Peter Blow. In 1830, Blow brought his family to St. Louis. When Peter died the family sold Scott to an Army surgeon by the name of John Emerson. When Dr. Emerson was assigned to a post in northwestern Illinois, a free state, he took his servant slave with him. They also resided for a spell in Wisconsin Territory, where slavery was forbidden by the Northwest Ordinance. It was during these travels that Scott met and married Harriet Robinson.

After Emerson's death in 1843, Scott began to seek freedom for himself and his wife. While living in St. Louis, the illiterate Scott offered to buy his freedom from Emerson's widow for the price of $300. When she refused the offer, Scott sought freedom through the court system. His case went to trial in 1847 at St. Louis, financed by the Taylor Blow family of **Carondelet**. Scott lost his first trial but the judge allowed a second trial because hearsay evidence had been allowed in the first one. In 1850, a jury decided that Scott should go free under the doctrine of "once free, always free." Emerson's widow, Irene, appealed and in 1852 the Missouri Supreme Court struck down the lower court's ruling. Now it was Scott's turn to appeal. Aided by lawyer Montgomery Blair, they sued in federal court and lost. Now they appealed to the U.S. Supreme Court.

Absorene wallpaper cleaner

In 1857, Chief Justice Roger Taney of Maryland delivered the majority opinion. The court ruled that Africans were chattel property and, as such, were not U.S. citizens. It also said that the Northwest Ordinance could not confer citizenship or freedom on Black people. Finally, the Court held that the Missouri Compromise was null and void because Congress had exceeded its authority in excluding slavery from northern portions of the Louisiana Purchase.

Scott's wife was now in an insane asylum and Mrs. Emerson had remarried, this time to Calvin Chaffee, an abolitionist. Chaffee was elected to Congress and he persuaded his wife to return Scott to the Blow family. They, in turn, granted Scott his freedom. He then worked as a porter in St. Louis for about nine months before he died from consumption (tuberculosis).

The decision angered many northerners who thought it was the most outrageous decision ever handed down by the court. It became one of the most influential events that led the nation down the path of civil war. Last year was the 150th anniversary of the Dred Scott decision.

If you visit the Old Courthouse you'll see four murals on the dome. One shows the discovery of the Mississippi by DeSoto, another depicts the founding of St. Louis by Laclede, another illustrates the Indian attack on the city in 1780, and the last shows a buffalo hunt.

There were slave pens in St. Louis that belonged to a slave trader named B.M. Lynch. He supplied domestic slaves to affluent St. Louisans. During the Civil War his pens were used to house Confederate prisoners. These pens still existed in the warehouse basement of Meyer Brothers Drug Company until the building was razed in the early 1960s to make room for Busch Stadium.

The Old Courthouse, preserved as a St. Louis landmark, is just west of the Arch on Broadway and Chestnut (314-425-6017). The original courtroom where the Dred Scott case was argued was destroyed during remodeling.

A marker said Harriet Scott was buried next to her husband in Calvary Cemetery off West Florissant. Researchers in 2006 discovered her body in an unmarked grave in the Greenwood Cemetery near Lucas and Hunt. Some think she was the driving force behind her husband's decision to sue for his freedom.

The Dred Scott case was of national importance because, among many other things, it resurrected the career of Abraham Lincoln who was a political nobody until he and Stephen Douglas debated the merits of the case in 1858.

WILLIAM T. SHERMAN OF ST. LOUIS

How did Sherman come to be a resident of St. Louis? He was superintendent of a military academy in Louisiana, but when that state seceded from the Union he resigned and came to St. Louis to head a streetcar company.

Where did William T. Sherman live in St. Louis? 912 N. Garrison St.

Was Sherman ever in Missouri during the Civil War? Yes – he was given command by Henry Halleck. While inspecting troops in central Missouri he let his overactive imagination hinder his better judgment. He was then transferred to Paducah, Kentucky, where he helped Grant capture forts Henry and Donnelson.

Josephine Baker - living in East St. Louis at the time of 1917 race riot

Where was Sherman stationed in St. Louis? Jefferson Barracks

What is his best known quote? The general who burned Atlanta once said, "War is hell!"

When did Sherman take control of the Union Army in the West? After Grant was promoted to top command in Virginia

What nickname was given to Sherman's undisciplined army? "Bummers"

The burning of what city by Sherman is featured in *Gone With the Wind*? (released the year of this author's birth in 1939) Atlanta

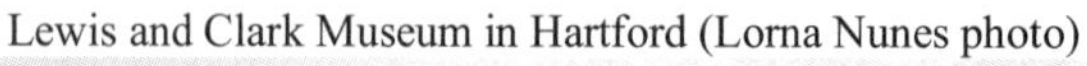

Lewis and Clark Museum in Hartford (Lorna Nunes photo)

Sherman's "march to the sea" saw widespread destruction between what two cities? Atlanta and Savanna

What is Sherman's 2nd most famous quote? Paraphrased: "If a crow flies between Atlanta and Savanna he'll have to carry his own provisions with him or he'll starve to death."

What were "**Sherman neckties**?" Southern railroad rails heated and bent around a tree to make them useless

Sherman died in New York. Where is he buried? Calvary Cemetery in North St. Louis at West Florissant and Calvary, next to Bellefontaine Cemetery

In what sense has history mistreated Sherman? Because he burned Atlanta, and due to the "march to the sea," Sherman is often remembered as a Southern nemesis. He was not a Confederate hater. His surrender terms to southern generals were so generous they were rejected by Secretary of War Stanton. Sherman, who was our greatest Civil War general, hated all politics

A RIVER RUNS THROUGH IT – ST. LOUIS AND THE METRO EAST

Sadly, most St. Louisans are unaware of the significant historic and economic ties the community has to its shirt-tail relatives across the river. Sure, they vaguely know that thousands of Illinoisans cross the bridges every morning to supplement the work force in Missouri, and that there is a fantastic "border war" basketball rivalry between Mizzou's Tigers and the Fighting Illini. They also occasionally come over for a bite at Fast Eddie's in **Alton**, to pick peaches at Eckert's in **Belleville**, or to Fairmount Park at **Collinsville** to bet the ponies, but that's about it. Over the years, there has been much more.

Back around 1794, the city of East St. Louis was founded by Captain James Piggott for the purpose of operating a ferry business from the Illinois side of the river to St. Louis. The first railroad in the state (1837) was the Illinois & St. Louis, built for the purpose of hauling coal from the bluffs at Belleville to St. Louis homes and businesses. By 1855, it was the richest dollar-per-mile railroad in America.

Bloody Island in the Mississippi River, which was eventually attached to the Illinois shore by a series of dykes built by Robert E. Lee (of future Civil War fame), was a favorite dueling site for prominent St. Louisans. Thomas Hart Benton, who later became a notable Missouri senator, killed a man in a duel there in 1817. Benton, Illinois, by the way, was named to honor "Old Bullion."

In 1830, Illinoisans were known by the epithet "suckers." Missourians who worked at the lead mines at Galena (the nation's first mining boom town) gave their cousins that nickname for a fish found in the rivers and streams up there. Illinoisans reciprocated and tagged Missourians as "pukes," for they allegedly consumed so many of the fish it made them ill. If you read narrative material written between 1820 and 1860, you'll discover these terms were quite common back then – Illinois suckers and Missouri pukes.

Inhospitable Missourians chased abolitionist editor Elijah P. Lovejoy to Alton and sent Joseph Smith and his Mormon brotherhood packing to Nauvoo, and mayhem minded Illinoisans murdered both Lovejoy and Smith.

The neighborhood in **Edwardsville** known as Leclaire was founded by St. Louisan, N. O. Nelsen who owned a large plumbing and building supply business. Leclaire was an experiment in co-operative living – a model company town where workers enjoyed a nice park, decent housing and profit sharing. Nelson boasted that the place had no crime, no paupers and had an "extraordinarily low death rate." World-famous reporter Nellie Bly even visited the amazing town to report on its success.

George Mepham, who operated a paint pigment mill in St. Louis, got into his buggy one day in 1890 and drove it across the Eads Bridge looking for a site in rural East St. Louis. Finding an acceptable location, he moved his factory across the river. My father was a foreman at that plant all the days of my youth, and it is one of few factories still operating in that town.

The Niedringhaus brothers of St. Louis operated a metal stamping factory and grew tired of the high tolls charged by the Terminal Railroad/Eads Bridge monopoly for raw materials they needed. They relocated and established the town of Granite City, so named for the durable pots and pans they produced known as Graniteware. For years the town was known as Six Mile Prairie because it was six miles from St. Louis.

In 1900, Windy City denizens reversed the flow of the Chicago River so the city's wastes no longer polluted Lake Michigan. Instead the sludge now flowed down the Illinois River which empties into the Mississippi north of Alton. St. Louisans, fearing their drinking water might be polluted, protested to no avail. They quickly built another treatment plant and added purification steps to the existing one.

Casino Queen, Arch and Old Courthouse

In 1917, there were labor problems in East St. Louis. Strikes by workers at Aluminum Ore and the packing houses caused management to import Negroes from the South as strikebreakers. The city was a tinder box and a case of mistaken identity that resulted in the death of two city policemen (at the hands of a nervous black mob) lit the fire. On July 2-3 there was a two day riot that saw thirty-nine African-Americans and nine whites lose their lives in the **worst race riot in the nation's history**. St. Louisan Josephine Baker wrote in her biography that she was living in Boxcar City (Illinois) near the riverfront at the time of the riot and was in great fear for her life. Hundreds of "coloreds" fled for their lives across the Eads and Municipal bridges to St. Louis and took up residence there permanently. Numerous African-Americans in St. Louis can trace their roots to this tragic episode.

In the 1920s, Chicagoan Al Capone decided to extend his empire to St. Louis. But every time he sent his thugs to Missouri they came back in a pine box. Exasperated, he threw up his hands and said: "Forget about St. Louis, the gang that runs the town is nuts, out of control, cuckoo – hence the famed Cuckoo gang. Another link between the two areas was forged in 1926 with the creation of Route 66.

The future destiny of St. Louis is inexorably linked to the MetroEast. That became readily apparent when MetroLink crossed the river in 1990. There are plans afoot to build another bridge linking the two just north of the M.L. King/Veteran's Bridge.

The *Post-Dispatch* prints a special Illinois Edition every day; talk radio receives numerous calls from southern Illinoisans and St. Louis television stations have special reporters to cover significant news on the East Side.

New Clark Bridge at Alton (Bill Jacobus photo)

Illinoisans are schizophrenic due to the geographic division between the north and south. The northern half roots for the Cubs, while the southern half roots for the Cardinals. Ditto Missouri. Its western section is devoted to the Kansas City Chiefs and Royals, while the eastern segment cheers for the Cardinals and Rams.

Out of a total population of 13,000 plus at SIU in Edwardsville, nearly a thousand of those students hail from Missouri. If you work for a St. Louis company that has twenty or more employees, chances are you rub elbows with someone who lives in O'Fallon, Greenville, Highland, Waterloo, Granite City or another similar Illinois town. My son, daughter and son-in-law all work in St. Louis. East Siders furnish St. Louis with as much as twenty percent of its work force. A huge boost to the St. Louis economy is given annually by Illinoisans who buy tickets to see the Cardinals, Rams and Blues, spend advertising dollars in the *Post-Dispatch*, dine at St. Louis restaurants, attend concerts by the Symphony and flock to see performances at the Fox Theater and Muny Opera. Check it out, folks. You can also see Illinois suckers frequently standing in line at Ted Drewes!

What three Metro-East prep teams have garnered nearly half of all the Illinois soccer titles? **Granite City**, **Collinsville** and **Edwardsville**

What Metro East prep basketball program led the nation in total victories about 10 years ago? **Collinsville** and **Centralia** had exactly the same number of victories and in a head-to-head confrontation Collinsville won the game. By the end of the year, however, Centralia regained the national title.

Where is the downtown St. Louis airport located? In Cahokia; highway signs there claim it's only five minutes away from downtown St. Louis. Businessmen who land here in private planes can get downtown quicker than if they landed at Lambert.

When Don Coryell was coach of the Football Cardinals, where was their training camp? At Normal, Illinois; until a few years ago, the Rams trained at Western Illinois University at **Macomb**.

Where did St. Louisans go in 1974 to see stock car races? At Tri-City Speedway in **Granite City**

Buckminster Fuller (of SIUC) – inventor of the geodesic dome – once proposed placing a Plexiglas dome over what city? East St. Louis

What Metro-East city has a bronze statue of the world's tallest man? Alton

What outstanding Cardinal center fielder of the 1940s owned a night club in East St. Louis called the Playdium? Terry Moore

Why was this place frequented so much by St. Louisans? St. Louisans had "blue laws" for many years that prevented restaurants from serving liquor. When the Yankees came to town to play the Browns, they came to the Playdium because Hank Bauer was an East St. Louisan. Guys like Musial and Slaughter came there because they were former teammates of Moore's. St. Louisans came there because it gave them a chance to see sports heroes up close.

What eating establishment on the east side was a favorite place for Red Schoendinst? The Stoplight Café on Kingshighway in East St. Louis

Dupo High School (David Lossos collection)

What Illinois town has the largest cathedral in the state? Belleville – St. Peter's

What is considered the most significant Native American painting in North America? The famed black, green and red Piasa monster on the **Alton** bluffs. The existing painting is a replica. The original was destroyed long ago for railroad track ballast.

What **Belleville** landmark is the world's largest outdoor Catholic shrine? Our Lady of the Snows on Route 15

Where is the world's tallest fountain? On the East St. Louis riverfront, just south of the Casino Queen. It was built by the Sverdrup Company of **St. Charles.**

What area town publishes the Midwest version of the Wall Street Journal? Highland

What **Highland** man invented condensed milk and started Pet Milk in St Louis? Louis Latzer

What town was home to Hank Bauer, Jimmy Connors, Miles Davis, Kellen Winslow, Jackie Joyner-Kersee, Lillian Gish, Bob Turley and Tina Turner? East St. Louis

What southwestern Illinois town has a spelunking cave that is open to the public? **Waterloo**

What Illinois town was considered as a site for auxiliary expansion of Lambert Field? **Columbia**

What town across the river was the first European settlement in Illinois? **Cahokia**

What nearby town was once called the "Stove Capital of America?" Belleville

What metro town was once called the "Cowbell Capital of America?" Collinsville

What city across the river was the 2nd largest rail center in America and had the nation's 2nd largest packing house complex? East St. Louis

What nearby city once led the nation in processed bauxite, roofing materials and baking powder? East St. Louis

What Illinois town has a huge Lewis and Clark museum complex on Route 3? **Hartford**

What famous TV western star was born in Hartford? Clint Walker – "Cheyenne"

What metro city boasts the most significant archaeological site in the USA? Collinsville has Cahokia Mound – larger in volume than the great pyramid of Egypt.

What Illinois town has been home to five governors – the most of any in Illinois? **Edwardsville**

What is the translation of **Glen Carbon**, where this author resides? Coal Valley

Early corduroy road made of logs

What East St. Louis high graduate was a football star at the University of Missouri, played tight end for the San Diego Chargers, and is a member of the Hall of Fame? **Kellen Winslow**

What East Side High baseball player graduated from Lincoln University in Missouri and played outfield for the Cardinals and Phillies in the 1960s? Ted Savage

What East St. Louisan was named the "Most Outstanding Fighter" in the 1948 St. Louis Golden Gloves tournament and went on to fight Ezzard Charles and Floyd Patterson? Wes Bascomb

What East St. Louisan launched his 30 year teaching career at Bayless High School in South St. Louis in 1963-64? This book's co-author – Bill Nunes

What 1969 East St. Louis High graduate played football for Washington University and went on to play 13 years in the NFL as a lineman, mostly with the Patriots? Shelby Jordan

What University of Illinois football star linebacker, who won the Butkus Award as the best linebacker in the nation, played the 1995-96 season for the St. Louis Rams? Dana Howard

What East St. Louisan attended the University of Missouri from 1977-1980 and earned four Super Bowl rings playing defensive back for the San Francisco 49ers Eric Wright

What East St. Louisan, was the starting pitcher in the 1935 All-Star baseball game, representing the St. Louis Cardinals? Bill Walker, who owned the Straw Hat Tavern near this author's house where he grew up.

What happened in 1929 when the vaunted East St. Louis High football team played a team of St. Louis All-Stars in a game at the Arena? Ten thousand fans sat in stunned silence as the east side team, despite losing their starting quarterback to an ankle injury, won by a score of 6-0.

When baseball Cardinal ownership had difficulty getting the city of St. Louis to help them tear down Busch Stadium and build a new one, where did they threaten to build a new stadium? Across the river in Illinois

What did Illinoisans think of the plan to tear down Busch Stadium and build a new ballpark? Despite the fact that a new stadium wasn't going to cost them a dime in new taxes, Illinoisans overwhelmingly voted in an informal newspaper poll to keep Busch Stadium with its beautiful lighted concrete arches rimming the top of the stadium.

Where and what was the largest bridge in the world built to carry electric streetcars? Across the

Mississippi River connecting north St. Louis with Madison and Granite City (1910) – the McKinley Bridge

What St. Louis actress was the great, great, great granddaughter of the founder of East St. Louis, James Piggott? Virginia Mayo

What was done with the dirt and rock excavated when the Gateway Arch was built? It was sent to East St. Louis and used for fill in low spots near the downtown area.

What St. Louis Company built the world's tallest fountain, located in East St. Louis directly across from the arch? **Sverdrup Corporation**

What economic problem was posed to St. Louis by Bloody Island, which began to form in 1800? It grew so big that it diverted the main channel of the Mississippi River to the Illinois side, threatening to leave the port of St. Louis high and dry.

Remember those mouth-watering refreshment ads at the local drive-ins?

What famous men fixed the island problem? **Henry Shreve**, an experienced riverboat captain was selected to get rid of Bloody Island. He was ably assisted by **Robert E. Lee** and the Army engineers who constructed a series of dikes that attached the island to the Illinois shore and forced the main channel of the river back to St. Louis.

Shreve Street in St. Louis is named for the captain as is Shreveport, Louisiana. Shreve named all the cabins on his steamboats for states. To this day passenger cabins are referred to as staterooms.

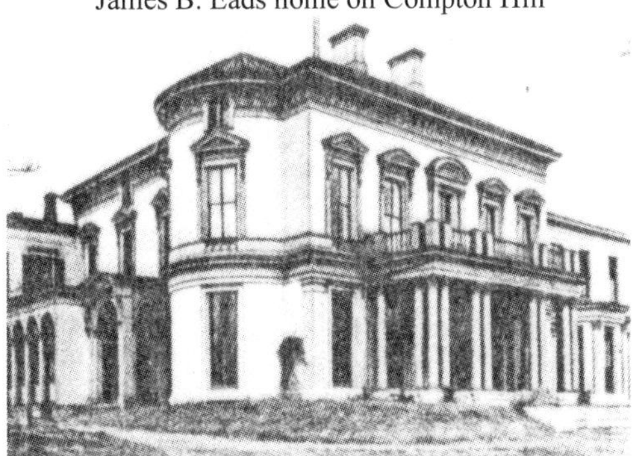
James B. Eads home on Compton Hill

What happened when St. Louisans tried to fix the island problem themselves? Residents in Illinoistown (East St. Louis) armed themselves and drove the workers from the island. If the main channel of the river flowed on the Illinois side they figured it would benefit them.

How was the matter finally resolved? The dispute was mediated (with a little bribing by rich St. Louisans) by the Illinois legislature. St. Louis would be allowed to finish attaching the island to the Illinois shore and, in return, they would build a road (Broadway) from the edge of the river to the far side of the island, connecting it with the city of East St. Louis.

How big was Bloody Island and where was it located? It was nearly a mile long and a half a mile wide. It would be between the M.L. King and Poplar Street bridges had they existed back then.

Did this real estate addition benefit the city of East St. Louis at the expense of St. Louis? Greatly! When the railroads first came to the area in the 1850s there was no bridge so they stopped at the water's edge. Bloody Island became the locus of twenty-seven railroads with a terminus in East St. Louis with numerous repair shops, warehouses and roundhouses as well. Thus East St. Louis, not St. Louis, became the second largest railroad complex in the world.

Were you one of those women in the 1950s that wore hats with face veils?

Are there any visible signs that this area was once an island? No. One might think that there would be a bulge in the river that would be noticeable from an airplane, but even a birds-eye view shows nothing.

Who owned Bloody Island once it was attached to the Illinois side? It was bought by the powerful Wiggins Ferry monopoly.

Before there were bridges, how did people from Illinois cross to St. Louis? There were two ferries – one at **Cahokia** and another at East St. Louis.

Where was the East St. Louis ferry located? It landed at St. Louis almost in line with Washington Avenue.

Was the ferry profitable? The Wiggins Ferry was the most profitable business in East St. Louis and constituted a powerful lobby for the legislators in Missouri and Illinois.

Didn't the Eads Bridge put the ferry company out of business? No! The ferry company built special barges to take train cars across the river to St. Louis. It lasted until around 1914 and still exists today in the form of the St. Louis Terminal Railroad.

How did this ferry monopoly affect St. Louis businesses? If, let's say, you owned a company that bought metal goods shipped from Pittsburgh, you had to pay more for them because the cost of the toll was passed along to the buyer. If, then, your company made pots and pans from this metal and then shipped the goods back East to be sold to consumers there, yet another toll had to be paid.

How did the Niedringhouse brothers of St. Louis solve this problem? They were in the business of making pots and pans and grew tired of paying the tolls. They paid a surveyor to plat a new town on the Illinois side of the river and moved their business there to avoid the tolls. This is how the town of **Granite City** was founded.

What was the original name of Granite City? Six Mile Prairie because it was exactly six miles from St. Louis

Why was the name changed to Granite City? There is no granite in the St. Louis Metro area. The pots and pans made by the Niedringhouse brothers were coated with enamel paint that contained flakes of granite. This made the coating durable and the products were labeled Graniteware.

What did St. Louis do in an effort to get around the Wiggins Ferry/Eads Bridge monopoly? It built the Municipal Bridge (1917), which later became known as the MacArthur Bridge.

What problem was there in the design of the MacArthur Bridge? The Illinois end has an S curve in it that was necessary because of the rail approaches on the lower deck. When the bridge was open to car traffic, about three drunk drivers a year missed the curve, crashed through the railing, and plunged to their deaths.

What "Best Man" actor at Ronald Reagan's wedding hailed from **O'Fallon**, Illinois? William Holden

What star of the *Beverly Hillbillies* hailed from **Belleville**? **Buddy Ebsen**

Buddy Ebsen

What St. Louis singing duo lived in the Alta Sita section of East St. Louis in 1959? Ike and Tina Turner

U.S. GRANT – OUR 18TH PRESIDENT

NOTABLE EVENTS DURING GRANT'S PRESIDENCY 1869-1877

1869 – Elizabeth Cady Stanton and Susan B. Anthony form the National Woman's Suffrage Association.
1869 – The transcontinental railroad is completed.
1869 – President Grant, by proclamation, makes Thanksgiving a national holiday.
1870 – The 15th Amendment gives the vote to Negro males, but not to white or Negro women.
1871 – Grant appoints the nation's first civil service commission.
1871 – The Apache wars (Geronimo) in the southwest begin.
1871 – Illinois passes the first Grange (farmers) laws
1874 – Public anger forces repeal of the Salary Grab Act.
1875 – The Black Hills Gold Rush
1876 - The nation's centennial is celebrated in Philadelphia.
1876 – General Custer loses his life at the battle of the Little Bighorn in Montana.
1876 – Alexander Graham Bell invents the telephone.

U.S. Grant (Wikipedia)

AMAZING FACTS: While Grant was president, he tried to annex Santo Domingo in the Caribbean, but northerners and Liberal Republicans opposed the addition of a black state to the union.

Both Grant and Dwight Eisenhower began their careers at Jefferson Barracks, both commanded great armies, and both were elected president.

What was Grant's first name? Hiram – the papers for Grant's appointment to the U.S. Military Academy were improperly filled out as U.S. Grant and that name stuck.

Were Abe Lincoln and U.S. Grant good dancers? No!

What was the reason for most of Grant's demerits at West Point? Sloppiness of dress – none for disobedience

How did Grant meet his future wife, Julia Dent? She was Grant's roommate's sister when he was stationed at Jefferson Barracks, south of St. Louis. The family lived in nearby St. Louis and it was love at first sight.

When did they get married? August of 1848 in St. Louis

What was the low point in Grant's career? In 1855 Grant was cashiered from the military for drunkenness and went back to his fiancée in St. Louis jobless, penniless and in disgrace.

What did Grant name the home he built in St. Louis on his farm? Hardscrabble – the land on which it was built was a wedding gift from Julia's father.

What was Grant's main source of income on his farm? He cut timber and sold it for firewood.

Did Grant own any slaves? Yes, three of them given to his wife by her father

Did he have any children at this point in his life? Yes – two sons, Ulysses Jr. and Freddie; a daughter named Nellie was born later at Hardscrabble.

When Grant could not make a go of it on his farm in St. Louis, when did he move to **Galena** to work in his father's tanning business? 1860

When did Grant go back into the military? After the fall of Fort Sumter, he attended a meeting in **Galena** and was impressed with a pro Union speech given by attorney John A. Rawlins.

What was Grant's first job in the Civil War? He formed a company in **Galena** and went with them to **Springfield** where he trained and drilled them at Camp Yates; they became the 21st Illinois Volunteers.

After arriving at **Cairo**, what nearby town did Grant take without firing a shot? Strategic Paducah, Kentucky, on the Tennessee and Cumberland rivers, barely arriving there before Confederates took the city

In what **Cairo** building did Grant have his headquarters? The famous Halliday Hotel – now a landmark

How did Grant earn the nickname "Unconditional Surrender" Grant? When he captured Fort Donnelson, the Confederate commander asked him what were the terms? Grant replied, "No terms except immediate and unconditional surrender can be accepted."

What was ironic about this incident in Grant's life? The commander at Fort Donnelson was Simon Bolivar Buckner, a West Point classmate and one of his best friends during the Mexican War.

What commander was with Grant at Fort Donnelson?
General Lew Wallace, who later wrote the novel *Ben Hur*

Where were Grant's headquarters in **Cape Girardeau**? Port Cape Girardeau at 19 North Water Street

What Confederate cavalry leader escaped Grant's clutches before the surrender at Fort Donnelson? Nathan Bedford Forrest – the man who (after the Civil War) **helped form the KKK**; Forrest was a demon and the one Confederate commander Grant truly dreaded.

What was Forrest's famous dictum? "Victory goes to him that gets there the firstest with the mostest."

Grant had always smoked a clay pipe. How did he become a cigar smoker? The newspapers reported him having an unlit cigar in his mouth during the campaign against Fort Donnelson. After that, admirers kept sending him boxes of cigars as gifts.

What did Lincoln say when critics wanted him to fire U.S. Grant because of his drinking? "I can't spare this man, he fights."

When Lincoln began receiving false reports that Grant was drinking again, what was his famous reply? To paraphrase: "Find out what brand he is drinking and send a case of it to each of my generals."

What close friend and commander was referred to as "Grant's right arm?" William T. Sherman

General Lee's favorite horse was "Traveler." What was Grant's favorite horse? "Cincinnati"

Did Grant ever cross swords with **Jesse James**? No

What was Grant's most brilliant campaign of the entire war? Vicksburg – in campaigns against Donnelson and Shiloh, he had made mistakes, but Vicksburg was flawless.

Why was Vicksburg such a strategic stronghold? The city commanded a high bluff overlooking a hairpin curve in the Mississippi River, controlling all river traffic that went past it.

What message did Grant send to Lincoln after the fall of Vicksburg, July 4, 1863? To paraphrase: "Once again the Father of Waters goes unvexed to the sea."

Was Grant at the battle of Gettysburg? No – Gettysburg was being fought at the same time as the Vicksburg campaign.

When was Grant promoted to General-in-Chief? After the capture of Chattanooga (1864), Southern general James Longstreet, who was with Grant at West Point, the Mexican War, and was present at his wedding, warned Robert E. Lee to be wary of Grant. Longstreet was the man who failed Lee at Gettysburg.

In MacKinley Kantor's novel, *If The South Had Won The Civil War*, something unusual happens to Grant. In this "what if?" book, the author has Grant falling from his horse and being killed when his head strikes a rock. Stonewall Jackson survives his accidental shooting and lives to "save the day" at Gettysburg and the South wins the war. The Grant incident is based on an actual event where his horse threw him at Chattanooga, badly bruising his leg.

When U.S. Grant took command of the Army of the Potomac in the East, his troops badly outnumbered Lee's. Lee's strength was about 50,000 while Grant had 100,000. In fairness to Grant, it should be remembered that other Union commanders had greatly outnumbered Lee and didn't get the job done.

Toward war's end, Grant was involved in battles against Robert E. Lee including the Wilderness, Petersburg, Cold Harbor, Spotsylvania Court House and Richmond.

Grant did something that impressed Robert E. Lee when he surrendered to Grant at Appomattox. Grant was kind, generous, and would not let his men celebrate the triumph over their southern brethren. Grant also ordered that Lee's men be given food.

Trying to be polite, he reminisced with Lee about their time together in the Mexican War.

A brick two-story house worth $16,000 was presented to Grant when he came back to **Galena,** Illinois. He didn't live there long because in 1870 he was elected president.

A friend of Grant's, from **Murphysboro**, Illinois, is considered America's greatest "political general" in the Civil War. John Logan – a brilliant orator, capable politician, efficient and brave officer, started out as a pro-slave Democrat. When the Civil War broke out there was a shortage of soldiers and officers. Politicians who gave speeches and formed a company of volunteers were given leadership positions, despite not having any military training from West Point. These men were called "political generals."

Grant first drew attention as a possible Republican candidate when he broke ranks with President Andrew Johnson in 1868, disagreeing with his lenient reconstruction policies.

When Grant became president (1870), he lacked knowledge about governmental affairs, was politically naïve, and made the mistake of appointing his military friends to cabinet positions.

Fortuitous circumstances **saved Grant's son from being killed at the Custer massacre in 1876**. He was attached to Custer's 7th Cavalry, but was granted leave to go to Washington, D.C. for the birth of his daughter.

When delegations of Native-Americans came to visit Grant at the White House, they called him the Great White Father.

Grant gave consideration to running for a third term, but then said no and went on a tour of Europe instead. Nevertheless, he led on the first 35 ballots but could not gain a majority and lost out to Garfield as a compromise candidate. After his European trip he moved to New York City to be near his son, Ulysses Jr., thus the site of his famous tomb. Grant's tomb, overlooking the Hudson River, faces south – toward Appomattox.

Grant's friend Mark Twain paid him to write his memoirs.

Partially completed Eads Bridge (Missouri Historical Society)

The family earned $450,000 in advance royalties and sales the first two years. Grant died a week after they were finished. His memoirs are considered among the best of any written by an ex-president.

Grant had a slave that he owned in 1859 at his hardscrabble farm in St. Louis, but he later granted him his freedom.

The Whiskey Ring scandal occurred during Grant's administration. Between 1873 and 1875 the U.S. Treasury was cheated out of more than $2 million in revenue. A huge bribery conspiracy among officials enabled distillers to sell whiskey without paying the required federal tax.

Grant Comes East, a novel by Newt Gingrich, is a fairly recent book out about U.S. Grant.

James B. Eads

Because there were so many political scandals in his administration, historians consider Grant one of our worst presidents.

BUILDING THE FAMED EADS BRIDGE

The Mississippi River: discovered by Desoto, explored by Marquette and Jolliet, navigated by Mark Twain, spanned by James B. Eads. In 1795, Captain James Piggott built the first ferry service to operate between St. Louis and Illinoistown (East St. Louis). He died in 1799 and his widow eventually sold out to other interests. By 1820, Samuel Wiggins had gained control of the company and made a fortune after being granted a monopoly of the transport business by the Illinois legislature.

The first railroad from the East (B&O) made its way into Illinoistown in 1857. As more and more railroads arrived, they were all forced to terminate at Illinoistown for lack of a bridge. The Wiggins Company charged exorbitant rates to transfer goods from boxcars and ferry them across the Mississippi to St. Louis. In 1870, responding to the threat of a bridge being built, Wiggins installed inclines at Choteau Avenue to enable railroad cars to be run onto barges equipped with rails.

St. Louis merchants were so frustrated by the expenses incurred in the movement of goods across the river that they formed a corporation with the intent of building a bridge to circumvent the Wiggins ferry monopoly. Washington Avenue was chosen as the site for the foot of the bridge because it was wider than most other St. Louis east-west streets. Washington Avenue is the second oldest street in St. Louis.

Another source of growing pressure for a bridge came from the cotton trade. St. Louis was ranked third, behind New Orleans and Savanna, in the cotton business. The St. Louis Cotton Compress Company was founded by J.W. Paramore and had a plant on the St. Louis levee that was the **largest of its kind in the world**. (Paramore and several others were responsible for founding the Cotton Belt Railroad.) Cotton Compress occupied fifteen acres and had another large warehouse across the river in East St. Louis. It took southern cotton bales that weighed five hundred pounds and squeezed them with hydraulic presses down to a thickness of nine inches. The smaller cotton bales were then shipped by rail to New York and cotton mills in New England.

Another disadvantage to the ferry monopoly is that there were times, during the months of January and February, **when the river froze over** and the eight boats that belonged to Wiggins couldn't operate.

The St. Louis and Illinois Bridge Company was formed in 1867 by Edgar Ames, Charles Dickson, et al, with James B. Eads as its chief engineer. A rival group formed the Illinois and St. Louis Company, headed by the noted Chicago architect and bridge builder, Lucius Boomer. It was referred to in documents as the Boomer Company. The Boomer design called for a span farther north supported by five piers while the Eads plan called for only two with an unheard of distance of 515 feet between the piers.

The powerful Wiggins Ferry monopoly saw both bridges as a threat to its future growth and used its considerable influence to undermine efforts to build them.

A considerable rivalry existed between Chicago and St. Louis back then. There is evidence to suggest that Boomer had no immediate plans for building a bridge at St. Louis and the company's proposal was merely a smoke screen. Many in the Illinois state legislature wanted such a bridge to be built at **Alton**, not East St. Louis.

After months of legal wrangling, the two companies merged with Eads as the principal stockholder. The bridge was financed with three-fifths of the bonds being sold to Europeans and eastern U.S. investors, while the remainder were sold to local investors. The finished cost of the bridge was around ten million dollars.

According to historian James Neal Primm, James Buchanan Eads built ironclads for the North during the Civil War and, before that, ran salvage operations on the Mississippi. Eads was also a cousin to President Buchanan.

A self-taught engineer, he developed a diving bell for the salvage operations. His fifteen years in this business gave him thorough knowledge of the river and its tricky currents. Eads personally made about 500 trips below the water. What a thrill it must have been, in 1869 to **actually walk on the bottom of the Mississippi River**.

Salvage profits were good since ship owners offered 50 percent of the take on salvaged goods. Eads (1820-1887) was the perfect person to build the bridge because of his knowledge and talent.

By 1867, work had begun on the bridge and Eads reached bedrock, laying the first 3,000-pound Grafton limestone for the western pier. By 1869, excavation had begun on the east pier of the bridge. By 1870, both piers were protruding above the water line. The west pier was 70 feet deep and the east pier was 110 feet deep. In 1871, both piers were completed and work was started on the superstructure. A tornado that year caused some damage to the bridge work.

Anybody remember getting a dose of castor oil from your loving mother?

The piers caused new currents in the river, forcing the Wiggins Ferry Company to move its riverfront operations in St. Louis/East St. Louis farther south.

Eads and his assistant, Colonel Henry Flad, used carbon steel and a new chrome steel for some of the bridgework and the arched-tube sections. Unfortunately, American steel companies were unable to meet Eads' requirement and he was forced to use wrought iron on much of the bridge.

Of the roughly 600 men who worked on the bridge, fourteen died as a result of the bends. About 118 suffered severely from the mysterious disease caused by going below water level in caissons with compressed air, and then coming back to the surface too quickly. Caisson disease, as it was called, was caused by nitrogen forming in the bloodstream during decompression. **Many of the workers began wearing copper bracelets to ward off the mysterious illness**.

The bridge had three spans of 497, 515 and 497 feet respectively. The roadway was 34 feet wide and there were two footways each eight feet wide for pedestrians.

Andrew Carnegie, a substantial investor in the Bridge Company, provided much of the iron and steel with his own company.

In 1873, a group of steamboat men from Keokuk, Iowa registered a complaint that the arches on the bridge would not be high enough for some of the newer boats with tall smokestacks. William Belknap, Secretary of War, convened a meeting of the Army Corps of Engineers to recommend modifications. Instead, they recommend razing the "monster" and starting over with a bridge of safer design that called for a drawbridge. However, President Grant remembered how he was impressed with Eads' ironclad ships during the Civil War. He ordered Belknap and the engineers to disband and cease their nitpicking.

Completed Arch on Eads Bridge (Library of Congress)

In early 1874, St. Louisan Grant made a personal inspection of the bridge and fearlessly walked out with Eads on planks laid on the superstructure.

By April of 1874, struts, braces and the upper roadway were completed. A 4,480 ft. train tunnel was built on the west end to take traffic past the downtown area to Mill Creek Valley.

The bridge was completed by the end of June. There were many fears that the distance between the piers was too great and that it would not support rail traffic designed for the lower deck below the main roadway. **One of the first to test the bridge was John Robinson, an African-American, who walked across it leading an elephant**. Strange as it may seem, there was a common belief back then that elephants had an uncanny sixth sense that made them balk at going across an unsafe structure. Next, a fully loaded train went across. On July 2, fourteen locomotives with loaded tenders were parked in the middle of the bridge, convincing everyone that the bridge would hold.

A huge 4th of July opening ceremony was officiated by President Grant. Symbolic figures were painted on a canvas, signifying Illinois and Missouri shaking hands. It was a symbolic wedding of East and West. Governor Beveridge was a featured speaker at the dedication.

Ironically, the bridge did not put the Wiggins Ferry Company out of business. It survived until 1913 by reducing rates and by **giving cases of whiskey to those who used their services**. The original St. Louis Bridge Company went bankrupt and the Terminal Railroad Association, created in 1889, eventually gained ownership.

Eads was quickly hailed as one of the greatest engineers of modern times. Roebling, who later built the Brooklyn Bridge, admittedly used many of Eads's ideas for his project.

The Eads Bridge was closed to rail traffic in 1974 and around 1993 the tunnel and lower level started being used by the light rail passenger service system known as MetroLink. The upper deck was closed to cars and trucks during construction but a refurbished top deck was reopened in 2006.

INCREDIBLE FACTS: In 1898, the Eads Bridge, the first people/traffic bridge to span the Mississippi, became the first bridge to be depicted on a U.S. stamp when it was featured as part of a Trans-Mississippi issue.

In its heyday, the Eads Bridge carried more railroad freight than any other bridge in the world.

THE GREAT CYCLONE OF 1896

What is the most destructive event in St. Louis history? The May 27, 1896 cyclone that killed about 140 people

What other significant event happened in St. Louis in 1896? St. Louis was connected to New York and Kansas City by telephone

What event was not as destructive, but caused more deaths than the cyclone? The heat wave of 1936 killed 421 people.

How many people were killed in neighboring East St. Louis by the 1896 tornado? 113

How many people did the tornado kill in **Audrain County** – 100 miles west of St. Louis? Six

What is the difference between a cyclone and a tornado? A cyclone is any cyclonic wind movement while a tornado is a fast-twisting funnel cloud – ergo, not all cyclones are tornadoes.

What neighborhoods were hit by the 1896 storm? Arsenal Street, Shaw's Garden, Compton Heights, Tower Grove Park, Jefferson Avenue, Lafayette Park, City Hospital, South Broadway, Soulard, the river levee

Where did the cyclone cross the river? Near present-day MacArthur Bridge, heading northeast and damaging the east approach to the Eads Bridge in Illinois

What four main newspapers were in St. Louis at the time? *Post-Dispatch*, *Globe-Democrat*, *Star* and *Chronicle*

What were dollar damage estimates? About $40 million

What part of St. Louis did the cyclone leap over and not destroy? Grand Avenue

What kind of damage was done at the river levee? Boats and wharves were blown to the Illinois side.

Lafayette High School in Ellisville/Wildwood (David Lossos collection)

Ritenour High School (David Lossos collection)

Delmar Gardens early roller coaster

How many St. Louis boats were destroyed? Sixteen steamboats, 5 ferryboats, 2 transfer boats and 6 tugs were demolished.

To some, what was the saddest sight of all? 40-year-old uprooted trees that could not be rebuilt or replaced

What was the most unusual death? Francisca Rodriguez, a female patient at a hospital, died of fright.

What were the two chief modes of public transportation at the time of the cyclone? Electric street cars and cable cars

What prominent businesses were damaged? St. Louis Wire Mill, Oriel Glass, National Brewery, Osborn's Harvester Factory, Purina Mills, Shickle, Harrison & Howard Iron, Griesedieck Artificial Ice, Laclede Gas, St. Louis Coffin, Gates Wire Mill, Sawyer Manufacturing, Dodson-Hills Pickle and Sauce, Fairbank Soap, Liggett & Myers Tobacco, St. Louis United Elevator, Iron Mountain freight yards, Enno Sanders Bottling, Merchants' Exchange Building

How did George Simons manage a miraculous survival? He was on the boat *J.J. Odill* which was thrown to the middle of the Mississippi where it overturned. He was dumped into the water and nearly drowned but he managed to grab hold of floating wreckage. He was swept downstream and nearly run over by a steamer. He lost his hold but them grabbed a floating tree and sat astride it, drenched and chilled to the bone. After traveling 4 miles downstream, he was rescued by two men on a skiff near Arsenal Island.

What kept looting to a bare minimum? Self-restraint was more common back then and police announced that **they would shoot looters** and suspicious people milling about.

What oddity existed in **East St. Louis**? A drove of hogs were running free on the Island area near the riverfront. One of them had a piece of tar paper driven into his shoulder and the top of it extended about six inches from the animal's skin. He seemed to suffer no pain from it and all efforts to catch the animal and remove it were futile.

How did two men in a butcher shop on Jefferson Avenue survive the storm? They climbed into a large metal ice box

How did an East St. Louis man profit from the storm? A. Meintz, the owner of a downtown building on Missouri Avenue was planning to add a second story to his building. The storm saved him considerable expense by taking off the roof and leaving everything else undamaged.

How did people describe the storm cloud? Some said it was green and sausage shaped, while others described it as a horizontal black cloud preceded by a yellowish cloud with an interior that looked like a mass of flames. Most said it was not funnel shaped.

How did birds fare in the storm? Poorly! Many were found dead in yards and in the streets. One dead bird was found with all its feathers intact on one side and plucked completely naked on the other side.

Any miraculous bird survival stories? Sara Ruck's bird was in a cage on the back porch. The storm blew her porch away and Sara spotted her bird an hour later, still inside the cage that was entangled in telegraph wires in front of the house. The bird was chirping away as if to say, "never got me!"

Ouija Board (author's collection)

ODD 1909 ST. LOUIS ORDINANCES

1. Every building or room used for gambling is declared to be a public nuisance.
2. It shall be unlawful for any large animal such as a horse, cow, mule, pig or goat to roam free within the corporate limits of the city.
3. No person licensed in the selling of drugs shall sell or deal in vinous, intoxicating or fermented liquors.
4. No person shall boil any pitch, tar, turpentine or resin within the city unless it is 50 feet distant from other buildings.
5. The sale of any lottery, bill or policy to share in any prize is prohibited.
6. Places used for dog or cock fighting are prohibited.
7. It shall be required to bury any person who dies from an infectious disease in an air and watertight casket.
8. It is the duty of every person who discovers a dead body to report such discovery to the Board of Health.
9. It unlawful for any person to take rotting food from any refuse box or barrel and attempt to sell the garbage for profit.
10. No person or corporation shall pile manure within the city limits in an offensive manner.
11. No person shall offer for sale any calf, lamb or pig less than 8 weeks old at the time it was killed for food.
12. Any person who desires to be a night scavenger and remove the contents of privy vaults must secure a license from the city.
13. It is forbidden to spit on sidewalks, elevators, railway platforms, steps or walls of any public building.
14. No person shall use a slaughter house for sleeping or living quarters.
15. All mercantile and manufacturing establishments must provide seats for female employees.

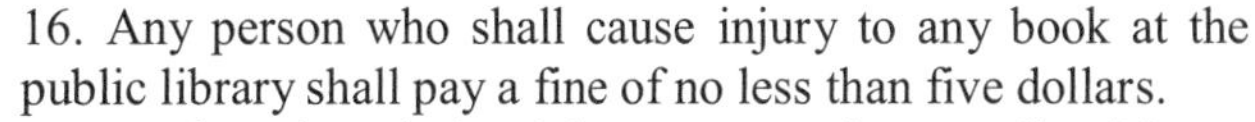

16. Any person who shall cause injury to any book at the public library shall pay a fine of no less than five dollars.
17. No dramshop (saloon) keeper may give or sell spirits to any female unless such female be the licensee or wife of the licensee.
18. No whistle, bell, gong, drum or similar mechanical device may be used to advertise merchandise for sale.
19. No person shall sell or give away literature relating to diseases peculiar to females or about articles or devices or means of preventing conception.
20. No person shall allow a bear or any dangerous animal to run wild.
21. All persons who are idle or dissolute, or who go about begging are declared to be vagabonds and subject to fines.
22. No streetcar shall be allowed to attain speeds of more than 10 miles an hour.
23. Any person who is deformed or mutilated so as to be unsightly or disgusting shall not expose himself to public view.
24. No person shall keep a place or room for the purpose of inhaling or smoking opium.

ST. LOUIS WOMAN POPULARIZES THE OUIJA BOARD

The Ouija game, invented shortly before the turn of the century, was first met by the public with mild interest. The name was derived from the French and German words for *yes*. It became a sensation only after Mrs. John (Pearl) Curran of **Mound City**, Illinois began making fantastic claims in 1913. She told others that the board enabled her to get in touch with the spirit of **a woman killed a hundred years earlier by Indians** in the New England area. This deceased woman, by the name of Patience Worth, now proceeded to dictate to Mrs. Curran thousands of words of poetry and prose that also produced six novels on the eve of World War I. Mrs. Curran eventually left Mound City and moved to **St. Louis**.

DeAndreis High School (David Lossos collection)

In 1919, the American Society for Psychical Research invited Mrs. Curran to come to New York and give a public demonstration. She did, giving an impressive performance before a large audience, receiving words and messages from Confucius and Walt Whitman, along with some esoteric Hindu transcriptions.

Skeptics, of course, called this housewife with the world's busiest Ouija board delusional. They claimed the long-departed Patience Worth was but a figment of Mrs. Curran's imagination. Harvard Psychologist William James explained the phenomenon by comparing her to rare persons with an "alternating personality" who could sit down at a piano and, with no previous training, play a concerto.

Levine's Hats at 14th and Washington (Lorna Nunes photo)

Debunkers claimed that Pearl had this poetry and prose writing ability all along, but hid it so that some day she could make a big splash on the literary scene. Yet Pearl was a woman of limited education, having quit school after completing the eighth grade.

Mrs. Curran went to New York once again in 1928, this time for an audience at St. Marks in the Bouwerie. By now her message of spiritualism was very popular, and she had quite a following. She performed magnificently, producing poems on split-second notice in response to requests from the audience. Mrs. Curran grew quite wealthy from her enigmatic abilities.

As historian Paul Sann explains in his 1967 *Fads and Follies* book, "Miss Patience Worth of New England never called to the bench for a pinch hitter, so the Niagara of words finally dried up when Mrs. Curran died in December of 1937 at age forty-six." The *St. Louis Globe-Democrat* used the following title to introduce her obituary: "Patience Worth is Dead." Was this a case of afterlife communication with the dead or just another hoax? Or is this just another one of those unexplained mysteries?

It is noteworthy that Mrs. Curran's emergence coincided with a rising interest in spirituality. There were those in the 1920s who held séances on each anniversary of the Halloween death of **Harry Houdini** and claimed to have communicated with him.

Arthur Conan Doyle, of Sherlock Holmes fame, was a firm believer in having once lived in a previous life through reincarnation. And then there was **Edgar Cayce**, the man who once a day would lie down on his couch, fold his hands and go into a self induced trance. An observer would then ask him questions about some individual from the past and he would relate answers, called readings, given to him as a result of having communicated with that person.

Black Forest Restaurant (David Lossos collection)

The improbable Ouija board gained even greater notoriety when it became the subject of a murder trial. A lonely Dorothea Turley in the American Southwest found a Ouija board and a handsome cowboy to keep her company. Just one problem - there was still a Mr. Turley. Dorothea asked the board to help her decide between her husband and her young lover. The board replied that her future was with the cowpoke, and that the problem could be solved by having daughter Mattie shoot her father – which she did. Despite the fact that the Ouija board had told them they wouldn't be prosecuted for the act, young Hattie was sent to reform school until she was 21, and mother was given three years behind bars.

In **Chicago,** the Ouija board was involved in another interesting case. In an odd decision the court held that a woman could not be prosecuted for slander against a neighbor because she had been directed to do so by a Ouija board.

The Fuld brothers, of Baltimore, invented the Ouija board in 1892, but they eventually sold out to Parker Brothers. Used by thousands in the hope that it could tell them whether their loved ones would survive the Great War, it remained a popular game throughout the 1920s. The lapboard had ten numbers on it plus all twenty-six letters of the alphabet. The user asked the board a question and relied on the three-legged planchette to "discover" the answer. All you had to do was place your fingers lightly on the planchette and a magical energy guided it to the letters or number that gave you an answer. Women often used the board to determine how many children they would bear or how many times they would be married. For answers to simplistic questions, the board had a *yes* and *no*.

The amazing Ouija board is still around and it has been updated and modernized. You can Google the term "Ouija board" and click on an internet hocus pocus site. There is a reproduced image of a board and you are told to type in a question on your computer. Then you are instructed to place your mouse arrow on the pointer (planchette) and follow it to your answer. Now, I never have believed in nonsensical tom-foolery, but curiosity got the better of me. I asked the talking board if I would ever marry again. Despite the fact that I am over the hill at age 68 and have been, uh, happily married 44 . . . 45, no . . . 48 years, some unseen force took my mouse up to the answer "yes." Hmm!

1932 ST. LOUIS HOUSEHOLD & HEALTH TIPS

1. Always sweep rugs the way the nap runs. 2. Never let milk stand in a tin container. 3. Wash your hands in vinegar after doing the dishes and they will not chap. 4. Coffee grounds should be emptied into the sink as a cleaner for drain pipes. 5. Rub leather furniture occasionally with sweet oil

to prevent cracking. 6. In case of a wound from a rusty nail, place some hot coals in a pan. Put some good wood on the coals, then place the wound over the smoking coals for five minutes to prevent lockjaw. 7. Whooping cough remedy: Take four red onions, peel and cut into fourths, arrange layers in a dish facing upwards like little cups. Sprinkle with sugar and let stand for three hours. Put the juice in a bottle and feed one teaspoon every half hour when awake. 8. A peeled onion hung in a sick room will absorb all the germs. 9. To cure colds, try a spoonful of honey and horseradish, mixed in equal amounts, every hour. 10. Beds, even in the best regulated families, can become infested with occupants that do not belong there. They may be exterminated by the free use of kerosene. 11. Common alum, melted in an iron spoon over fire, forms a good cement for joining glass and iron together. 12. When the firebricks in the stove become covered with clinkers, they may be cleaned by throwing in oyster or clam shells when the fire is very hot and then allowing the fire to go out. 13. Coffee is the easiest thing in the trade to adulterate. When sure of a pure article, buy it in bulk, then roast and grind as needed. 14. The oil of pennyroyal will drive fleas off. Find where the herb grows and then toss the dog or cat whom they infest into a decoction of it once a week. 15. People who are troubled by frost on a window of a cold room may keep them transparent by rubbing them with glycerin. 16. Rub light gloves with fine bread crumbs after each time of wearing to keep them clean. 17. Lard should be kept in a tin and in a cool place. 18. Hair should be brushed with a slow gliding motion, every strand being brushed up and down, right, left, in semicircles from the forehead to the center of the head. 19. The yolk of an egg rubbed on stains on washable goods before laundering will remove spots. 20. Tough meat may be made more tender by laying it a few minutes in vinegar water. 21. Soap should never be used for washing pudding cloths. 22. Tea leaves are most useful for sprinkling over carpets before sweeping for they gather up dust and prevent it from settling on furniture. 23. Rain water is the only water fit to wash the face with. 24. Tumblers that have been used for milk should never be put into hot water until first they have been rinsed in cold water. The heat drives the milk in and gives a cloudy appearance to the glass. 25. It is a good idea to put shot in the bottom of tall vases so they are not so liable to be knocked over. 26. Don't dry your face with a rough towel. Instead, dabble the face with a fine damask one to keep it smooth. 27. Orange juice will polish patent leather. 28. To clean trousers without washing, take a square of dry pipe clay and rub it over the trousers. Allow it to remain for a couple of hours and then brush off. 29. To prevent odor from boiling cabbage, throw a few bits of charcoal into the pot. 30. Kettles may thoroughly be cleaned by boiling potato peelings in them. 31. Clean ivory handles of knives by mixing equal parts of ammonia and olive oil and add to this enough prepared chalk to make a paste. 32. An excellent furniture polish is made of equal parts of vinegar and salad oil. Combine with plenty of "elbow grease."

CARTOONIST CHIC YOUNG

Murat "Chic" Young was born in **Chicago** but grew up in St. Louis. He began working in 1924 for King Features and his first strip was *Dumb Dora*. Then, in 1930, Young created the strip for which he is best known, *Blondie Boopadoop*. Young seemed to have a knack for drawing pretty girls. The strip, which was still running in 2008, took Blondie from a flighty single girl with several beaus to marriage and children with Dagwood Bumstead and, most recently, a new career as a caterer. Bumstead was the son of a wealthy industrialist who disowned him after he married beneath his social class. Bumstead works for J.C. Dithers Construction Company, and his tyrannical boss threatens to fire him when he arrives late, sleeps on the job or pesters him for a promotion or raise. The suburbia couple have a son and a daughter and a dog named Daisey. A running gag in the strip is the outrageously tall **Dagwood sandwich** Bumstead frequently fixes for himself.

The strip was so well marketed that it resulted in 28 movies (1938-1950) starring Arthur Lake and Penny Singleton as well as a radio show (1939-1950) and a television series. Lake and Singleton played the roles on the radio program also. Unfortunately, the TV series only lasted nine months. Young's son Dean eventually took the strip over after his father's death.

Penny Singleton & Arthur Lake

In the film series, Blondie wore the pants in the family and was frequently responsible for convincing Mr. Dithers to give Dagwood his job back. The male character was portrayed as a lovable, bumbling idiot of a husband. A running gag in the series was Dagwood looking at his watch while eating breakfast and realizing he was running late for work. He would go running out the door, crashing into the mailman whose letters scattered everywhere.

Penny Singleton was a natural redhead and dyed her hair blonde to win the role. She became stereotyped and was unable to get other roles once she started playing Blondie. However, she was a shrewd businesswoman and had residual clauses written into her contracts. In fact, **she created the term *residuals.*** This meant that she would receive additional payment every time her radio show was repeated.

In 1995, the strip was honored with the issuance of a classic U.S. postage stamp.

MORE ST. LOUIS AND WW II

INFORMATION

Phyllis Argall was a Caucasian journalist living in Japan when World War II broke out. The **Japanese charged her with espionage** and imprisoned her for six months but then she was released. After the war she resided in St. Louis and wrote about her experiences in *My Life With the Enemy*.

Since the war brought on an acute metal shortage, St. Louisans were encouraged to get involved in scrap metal drives, much to the chagrin of scrap metal dealers. Plastic bicycle frames replaced metal ones. Housewives were encouraged to turn in old pots and pans, kettles, garden tools and worn out appliances. Men were asked to use just one razor blade a week. The metal drives took off when the Fox, Missouri and St. Louis theaters offered free Saturday matinee tickets to kids who brought metal with them.

Grumman Avenger with Emerson Electric gun turrets

The city of St. Louis had a small sales tax back then so shoppers sometimes received a mill with their change at stores. Mills were about the size of a nickel and were stamped with either a 1 or a 5. A 1 was worth a tenth of a penny and a 5 was worth half a penny. This author had St. Louis relatives and I remember them sometimes using mills as poker chips in friendly games. The mills were steel coated with zinc - metals needed for the war effort, so people turned them in and they were exchanged for mills made of vinyl or pressed cardboard.

Female worker in St. Louis

Someone remembered that the giant Ferris wheel from the 1904 Fair was buried somewhere in Forest Park. What a great contribution that would be to the metal drive, especially the six foot diameter, seventy ton axle. Citizens swarmed all over the park with metal detectors and shovels. After much damage, the mayor gave an order to call off the search. Two Civil War cannons were taken from the front of city hall and donated to the scrap drive.

A similar drive was made with rubber as people turned in old garden hoses, overshoes, mats and old dolls.

Year-round daylight savings time was instituted in February of 1942. Downtown stores began staying open late on Monday nights to accommodate the 45,000 St. Louis workers engaging in overtime or night shift work. Betty Burnett, in her *St. Louis at War*, describes a Mardi Gras-like atmosphere in the downtown streets.

Blackout curtains

USOs were instituted to help keep up the spirits of the fighting men. Staffed mainly by volunteers and staying open at late hours, these places provided wholesome alternatives to taverns and houses of prostitution. Prostitution was so bad in **East St. Louis**, particularly in the Valley district near City Hall, officials threatened to declare the city off-limits to servicemen.

St. Louis had about nine different USO locations and occasionally a famous Hollywood personality such as Rudy Vallee would "make the joint jump." The Salvation Army helped staff the USO at 6th and South Broadway.

The Red Cross was noted for serving coffee and donuts to departing servicemen and by holding blood drives. After the St. Louis Cardinals beat the Yankees in the 1942 World Series, every member of the team went downtown and donated blood.

Women who worked in war plants usually earned about half of what the men made – somewhere around fifty cents an hour. They were often required to wear caps or hairnets for safety reasons. Sultry actress **Veronica Lake** was famous for her long peak-a-boo hair style. To encourage women around the country, she cut her hair to set an example for others to follow, making it safer for women who worked around machinery. Sadly, this caused her popularity to wane as an actress since her hair had been part of her mystique.

St. Louis labor unions were a bit unpatriotic during the war. At the beginning of the war, organized labor had given a no-strike pledge. Defense production was stymied time and again by strikes making it hard for factories to meet their production quotas and deadlines. Some businesses also took advantage of the situation to make excessive profits. Missouri Senator **Harry Truman** became famous by heading a committee that investigated fraud, waste and corruption in war plants. In April of 1943, United Mine Workers president John L. Lewis called for a miners strike and, by May 1, 41,000 miners in Illinois were idle. President Roosevelt called out the troops to work the mines until the strike was settled. Initially, Harold Gibbons of the CIO supported the miner's strike, but later reaffirmed the no-strike pledge. After the Teamsters went on strike, the government took over several trucking lines including Brashear Freight, Park Transportation, and Todebusch Transfer.

Cities on both coasts sent some of their priceless art objects to St. Louis museums where they would be safer.

Betty Burnett says the Missouri

Botanical Gardens held a show every October where harvests from Victory Gardens were proudly displayed.

The Veiled Prophet curtailed annual parade and ball activities during the war. A small parade was held during wartime but the floats all had patriotic themes.

When alarm clocks (with those famous luminescent hands and numbers) became almost non-existent at stores, one enterprising woman in University City prospered by starting a wake-up call business. It was mostly women who painted the clocks and watches at the **Elgin**, Illinois plant. Many of them died of radium poisoning, not knowing the risks they were incurring.

Junior WAACS Sewing Kit

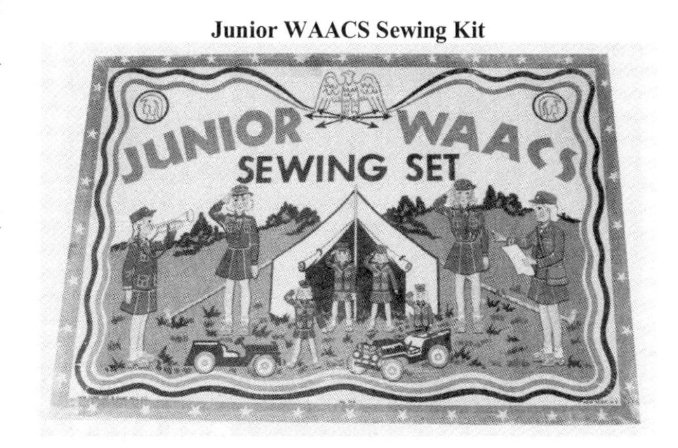

When the government OPA began issuing ration books for things like sugar, butter, coffee and meat, schools sent trained high school students around to individual homes to explain the complicated point system to harried housewives. Amazingly, the schools had 18,000 volunteers for this program.

Stix Baer & Fuller set up a model store on the sixth floor to demonstrate to housewives how to shop wisely and how to prepare nutritious meals with what was on hand. A typical rationed meal might consist of pig heart, collard greens, turnip soup and soybean crackers. Yummy!

During the war, Illinois and Missouri stopped using metal license plates and made them out of soybean-based pressed fiber-board. Back then, you got a new plate every year instead of the sticker that is used today. Logan Hutchcraft (of **East St. Louis/ Collinsville**) said that every time his father got a new plate he took the old one off and nailed it to a stud in his garage. By the time the war rolled around he had a collection of about 15 plates. When the scrap drives came along he took them down and donated them for the war effort.

Typical wartime soybean license plate

Arleigh Jones, of **Tuscola,** Illinois, remembers the time when his uncle once parked his car in a feed lot where hogs could get to it and **they ate both of his soybean license plates**.

Due to meat shortages some places improvised. According to historian Burnett, horse meat was served at the Missouri Athletic Club. Shark was served instead of cod at Miss Hullings. The Mark Twain Hotel served muskrat.

Gasoline rationing was instituted with people receiving A and B stickers, depending on their importance to the war effort. The back of the windshield sticker pointedly asked, "Is this trip really necessary?" The speed limit was reduced to 35 miles per hour. If you were caught taking your car on a long fishing trip, your coupons could be confiscated. St. Louis officials went over to Fairmount Park in **Collinsville** to take down license plate numbers of Missourians who drove to Illinois to bet on the ponies.

St. Louis mothers hung gold stars in their front room window if they lost a son in the war. A silver star meant that a son had been seriously wounded. Families came to dread the teenage delivery boy on a bicycle delivering a Western Union message from the War Department.

Patriotic St. Louis women enlisted in large numbers to become WAACs, (Army) WAVEs (Navy) and SPARs (Coast Guard). They also baked cookies for the USOs, danced with servicemen at USOs and did volunteer work at hospitals.

President Roosevelt stopped by Jefferson Bar-racks in April of 1943 in a surprise visit. He inspected the 15,000 troops and took about 47 minutes touring the place.

That same month there was a **mock battle staged in Forest Park by troops from Jefferson Barracks**. A mock Sicilian village was erected to make the exercise more realistic.

The rivers flooded, in May of 1943, after thirteen straight days of rain. St. Louisans were surprised to see prisoners of war, wearing light blue uniforms, helping with sandbagging efforts. Some German prisoners were kept at Jefferson Barracks while Italian prisoners were kept at **Weingarten**, Missouri.

On Saturday night, over the 4th of July weekend, the St. Louis Browns played the first night game ever held at Sportsman's Park in 1943. The practice of playing double-headers had already been instituted to save fuel from travel costs. The practice of playing the National Anthem before games was started during the war as a patriotic gesture.

Going dancing was a favorite pastime of men and women exhausted by the rigors of defense work and dealing with the frustrations of rationing and shortages. In that respect, St. Louis had plenty to offer. The second floor of the Admiral featured a large ballroom floor. Eddie Howard and Jack Little attracted large crowds at **Tune Town**. The older crowd seemed to prefer the **Showboat Ballroom** on Delmar where they did the "pump handle" more often than the jitterbug. Swing music was featured at the **Casa Loma** and at the Forest Park Highlands. Name bands such as Les Brown, Woodie Herman, Stan Kenton and Lawrence Welk earned big bucks entertaining the crowds in St. Louis. Singers like Nat King Cole and Ella Fitzgerald frequently did gigs in the area.

On August 1, 1943, **East St. Louis**-born Mayor Becker and several other dignitaries (including Thomas Dysart, president of the Chamber of Commerce) decided to show their support for the local aircraft industry. Robertson Aircraft was demonstrating a new glider they had just built.

A crowd of about 5,000 gathered at Lambert Field to watch. The plane was towed into the air and shortly after the cable was released a wing fell off the plane. **Spectators watched in stunned horror as the plane plummeted to earth killing all on board**.

Plane crash that killed Mayor Becker

Inspectors determined that Robertson Aircraft had been negligent by not inspecting a wing fitting that had been milled too much, allowing it to come loose from its slot. The company went out of business shortly before the war ended.

A third war bond drive was launched (September 1943) in St. Louis with a number of Hollywood stars showing up to stimulate patriotic interest. Lucille Ball, Dick Powell, James Cagney and Judy Garland were among the group.

The Cardinals won the pennant again in 1943, but this time it was the Yankees who prevailed in a rematch. The Cardinals lost so many players to the military that at one point they advertised for replacements in the *Sporting News*, published locally.

Emerson's Stuart Symington

Several days after Christmas, railroad employees went on strike so President Roosevelt authorized the railroads to be federalized to keep them running.

St. Louis-made vehicles played an important role in the D-Day invasion of Europe in June of 1944. St. Louis Shipbuilding and Steel cranked out LST boats which St. Louisans could see near the Eads Bridge. Stupp Brothers turned out LCTs. Midwest Pipe made fittings for the LSMs. St. Louis Car converted from making buses and streetcars to Water Buffalos that were tested over at Spanish Lake. American Car Foundry of St. Charles made tanks.

The **Weldon Spring** Ordnance Works produced thousands and thousands of bombs and pounds of TNT. Roughly half of all bombs used by the U.S. in the war were of the 500 pound variety and most of those were produced in St. Louis. After the war, the site was used for uranium processing while chemical weapons were also produced. The plant was shut down in the 1980s and the government spent $1 billion for cleanup. Visitors can walk or bike through a 6 mile trail which is dotted with informational plaques about the site's history.

Battleship Missouri bristling with guns (author's collection)

Stove companies somehow adapted easily to making bombs and this included Empire Stove, American Stove and Wrought Iron Range. The Fischer Body Plant at Union and Natural Bridge made 105 mm howitzers. Carter Carburetor made bomb fuses, Knapp Monarch made grenade launchers, Midwest Pipe made 1,000 pound demolition bombs and Scullin Steel made 12,000 pound earthquake bombs dropped by huge British Lancaster and Halifax bombers. The German battleship *Tirpitz* was sunk by one of their bombs.

Roughly 800 St. Louis servicemen were killed in the war. Unbelievably, over 900 civilians were killed in accidents at work, at home or on the streets of the city.

After the invasion of Europe in 1944, many expected the war to end in a month so workers were laid off and production was halted. By the end of July, it became obvious that this had been a mistake and workers were called back to their jobs. Fourth, fifth and sixth war bond drives were held in 1944. Mayor Kaufmann exhorted St. Louisans to support the efforts and the Boy Scouts went door-to-door handing out leaflets.

St. Louisans were elated when the 1944 election rolled around and Senator Harry Truman replaced odd-duck Henry Wallace as the Vice-presidential nominee. Surprisingly, aldermen passed a bill allowing Negroes to be served at the lunch counters in City Hall, but the regulation did not apply to private eating places.

When the mighty battleship Missouri, a dreadnaught of the Iowa class was launched, Margaret Truman, the President's daughter, did the christening honors with a bottle of champagne.

St. Louis ethnic groups worried about their counterparts in Europe. The Poles were fearful that the advancing Russians might occupy their former homeland and never leave. The French raucously celebrated Bastille Day on July 14, 1944, when it became clear that France would soon be rid of its Nazi oppressors. St. Louis Jews feared the worst for their relatives in Europe, knowing full well Hitler's anti-Semitic diatribes.

There were still about 100 members of the German-American Bund in St. Louis during the war. They secretly sent information about defense plants back to Germany, but did not commit any acts of sabotage.

During the 1944 baseball season, both the Browns and the Cards were in first place in their respective leagues on July 4, and were still there when the season ended. Fittingly, the Browns clinched the pennant by defeating the Yankees at Sportsman's Park on October 2. The Browns actually had a 2-1 lead on the favored Cards but then lost the Series 4-2. Stan Musial went into the Navy after the Series was over.

Roosevelt and Truman won the election in early November and, shortly after that, St. Louisans had another reason to celebrate – the world premier of *Meet Me in St. Louis* at Loew's Theater (10th & St. Charles) on November 22.

When President Roosevelt died in April of 1945 Harry Truman, of **Independence,** became president. As Roosevelt's people were replaced, Charles Ross, contributing editor of the *Post-Dispatch*, became Truman's press secretary, St. Louisan Col. Harry Vaughn became his military aide, St. Louis banker John Snyder became the federal loan administrator, and President of Emerson Electric, **Stuart Symington**, became board chairman of surplus property.

St. Louisans were making plans for a downtown airport, but that was scuttled when a B-25 accidentally hit the side of the Empire State Building. Officials concluded that tall buildings and airplanes didn't mix.

When St. Louisans learned that an atomic bomb had been dropped on Hiroshima on August 6, 1945, few knew about the important role played by Missouri and neighboring Illinois. **Mallinckrodt Chemical** was given the task of refining uranium ore into uranium dioxide. When Enrico Fermi's team set off the world's first controlled nuclear reaction at the University of Chicago in December of 1942, they used fifty tons of St. Louis-processed ore blocks. Dr, Arthur Compton supervised the secret "Manhattan Project" and he later became chancellor of Washington University. On May 4, 1945, Washington University held a gala open house to show off its new atom smashing machine – the cyclotron. So you see, St. Louis helped usher the world into the nuclear age.

St. Louis came close to being the home of the United Nations. When delegates attended the organizational meeting of the U.N. the American representative, Edward R. Stettinius, suggested that the ideal location for the organization would be smack in the middle of America. He selected the old ordnance plant site at **Weldon Spring**. Missouri officials lobbied hard, but in the end lost out to glamorous New York City.

Aside from the jobs and the shot in the arm to revive a post-Depression economy, World War II had a couple of lasting effects on St. Louis. Many mom and pop and small businesses went out of operation due to government regulations and restrictions during the war. And because of post-war affluence and the G.I. Bill, which provided loans to returning servicemen, there was a mad rush to suburbia which resulted in remarkable growth in St. Louis County and a significant decline in the population of the city.

SPOOKY ST. LOUIS

Do you believe in ghosts? Do I believe in ghosts? – nah! Well . . . maybe some. Over the past several hundred years time has woven some incredible supernatural stories into the history of St. Louis. My friend from **Decatur**, Illinois, Troy Taylor has written about many of them. He wasn't the first to do so and he probably won't be the last. Some of these stories will raise goose bumps and make the hair on the nape of your neck stand straight up.

If you're really into this kind of thing, Jason Offutt's ***Haunted Missouri*** (2007) will fit the bill. Reviewer Amy Stapleton says the "book brings Missouri's haunted sites to life and beckons the reader: come visit."

The earliest reasons for hauntings date back to the Mound Builders who gave St. Louis its earliest nickname – Mound City. Explorer Stephen Long made reference to about 27 of these mounds. The biggest of them, La Grange de Terre (earthen barn) was used as a sighting landmark by riverboat pilots. It was located between Second and Broadway. There was another large mound at Kingshighway and Martin Luther King Drive. The French called it Cote Brilliante – Shinning Hill. It was razed in 1877 to make way for Christian Brothers College. Two more mounds, located in Forest Park, were destroyed as preparations were made for the 1904 World's Fair.

Spooky Old Rock House (Mo. Hist. Soc.)

Though long gone from the scene, these Mississippians are best remembered for burying their dead in earthen mounds. As the city of St. Louis grew and expanded, these sacred mounds were razed by insensitive developers. There are those who will tell you that the restless native spirits, whose graves were desecrated, haunt the city.

The **Old Courthouse** on Broadway is said to be haunted, not by Dred Scott but because of historic stone stored there from the Old Rock House that once sat perched at Main and Chestnut. It seems the Spaniard Manuel Lisa was once killed there in a barroom brawl.

The Casino Queen, in East St. Louis, sits on land that was once in the Mississippi River. That famous **Bloody Island** was the scene of several bloody duels that resulted in death for St. Louisans. In 1817 Charles Lucas was killed in a duel with **Thomas Hart Benton**. Thomas Biddle and Spencer Pettis, in August of 1823, killed each other in a duel that was fought from the unbelievable distance of a mere five paces. It seems that Biddle was badly nearsighted. Thousands of St. Louisans watched the duel from the St. Louis levee and riverfront roof tops. Political quarrels were the cause of all

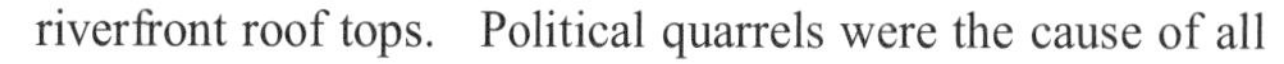

DeMenil Mansion, not far from haunted Lemp Mansion

of the deadly duels fought on Bloody Island. It has been said that boat gamblers, late at night, sometimes hear what sounds like shrieks and moans. They might merely be creaks and groans from moorings, but some think it's the voices of the dead, searching for eternal peace.

The St. Louis side of the river has plenty of cause for hapless spirits to be walking around. Steamboat workers by the scores have been killed in wharf fires, boiler explosions and in the 1896 tornado that raked the area. Some claim to have seen phantom lights from ghost ships during fog-laden nights. Both the *Mississippi Queen* and the *Iron Mountain* were boats that departed from St. Louis and then **mysteriously disappeared without a trace**. Are those strange sounds emanating from the river front at the midnight hour ghostly voices of the passengers who were on board, crying out for help?

Mark Twain, in *Life on the Mississippi*, tells of a psychic experience he once had. He dreamed that he saw his brother lying dead in a metal coffin, dressed in one of Twain's suits, with a bouquet of flowers on his chest. In the middle of the whitish flowers was a single red rose.

McDowell Medical School (Mo. Historical Society)

Not long after, Twain's brother was killed when the boiler on his steamboat, the *Pennsylvania*, exploded. When Twain went to the large room where all the deceased were laid out, he noticed that Henry's coffin was made of metal and all the others were of pine. He was even more startled when he saw his brother was dressed in one of Twain's suits. But the real shocker came when an elderly woman walked up beside him and placed a bouquet of roses on Henry's chest. Lo and behold, there was a red rose smack dab in the middle of the white ones.

Samuel Clemens was born in 1835 at **Florida**, Missouri. It was the same year that Haley's Comet appeared in the heavens. Mark Twain died in 1910, the exact year that Haley's comet, absent for 75 years, was scheduled for another visit.

In 1876, a traveling salesman spent the night in the **Pacific Hotel** in St. Louis. In the middle of the night he was awakened by a noise and was startled to see the ghost of his sister. She had died in a St. Louis cholera epidemic a few years before. The man later said that the quite real and vivid image of his sister was remarkable. He was even able to discern a scratch on the side of her cheek. That morning the salesman went to the house where his parents lived in St. Louis. During breakfast, he told his mother about the realistic apparition. His mother burst into tears. After composing herself, she told her son that when she was preparing her daughter for a one-day viewing in the family parlor, she accidentally scratched her face and then covered it with make-up. Since she never told a soul about the incident, **she was convinced that her son had truly seen his dead sister from beyond the grave.**

Frisco Railroad engine bell competed for in Kirkwood-Webster Groves Turkey Day football game

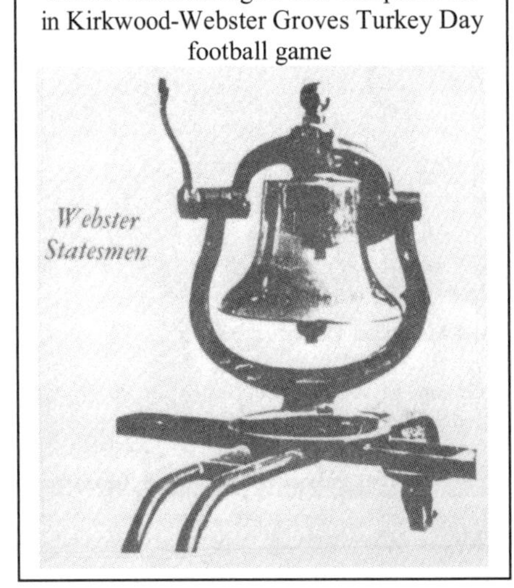

The art of body snatching was first started in St. Louis by an odd duck physician named Joseph McDowell. He built a medical training school at Ninth and Gratiot, near Chouteau's Pond. He had an extreme prejudice against newly arriving immigrants, coloreds and Catholics. McDowell was noted for passing out hateful tracts that espoused his beliefs. Fearing that he had made quite a few enemies, he often wore a metal breastplate under his clothes for protection from attack. His building had a large tower with a deck walk that went around it. The tower was outfitted with six cannon in order to defend it from possible attack by his enemies. One of the cannons was said to have once graced the deck of pirate Jean Lafitte's ship.

The eccentric doctor insisted that his students learn anatomy. Dissection of bodies was against the law, back then, so **McDowell resorted to snatching the dead from potters field where few would object**.

McDowell once stole the body of a German girl who had died from an unusual disease. When local residents learned of the theft they angrily armed themselves and marched off to the medical facility. McDowell hid the body in the attic but then panicked as several from the crowd broke inside to look for the body. Not knowing where to hide, McDowell was astonished to see his dead mother beckoning to him. She pointed to the table where the girl's corpse had been. He quickly lay on the table and pulled a sheet over him, **pretending to be dead**.

As several men searched the room, they pulled down the sheets from various corpses far enough to see their faces. "Here's a fellow with his boots sticking out from the end of the sheet," one of the intruders commented. "He must be a fresh one," another one commented. The men departed without finding the girl or discovering the hoax.

Dr. McDowell had been a strict Calvinist, deriding others who believed in ghosts. But after his dead mother saved his life, he became a spiritualist.

During the Civil War, Dr. McDowell was a secessionist and his facility was commandeered by Union officials and turned into a prison. After the war, McDowell resumed his activities and kept a rattlesnake, a crocodile and a gallows with Abe Lincoln hanged in effigy. Various people in the neighborhood reported seeing ghostly faces of men in tattered prison uniforms staring out the windows of the old Gratiot Street Prison. Cries, wailing and blood curdling screams could also occasionally be heard by those who walked past the building late at night.

The cave in the *Adventures of Tom Sawyer* actually exists just outside of **Hannibal**. It is a dangerous maze cut by nature into the rock beneath the ground. Mark Twain noted in the novel that no man "knew" the cave. It was called McDowell's Cave for the St. Louis physician who owned it.

McDowell had a macabre plan for the cave. He had hung a glass lined copper cylinder **containing the corpse of a teenage girl in an alcohol solution in one of the cave's recesses**. He wanted to see if the cave would reduce the corpse to bones. Hannibal's boys, however, used to go to the cave to sneak a look at the naked dead girl. Sam Clemens was probably one of the girl's regular visitors. With the mix of danger and secrecy, the cave always seemed to Clemens (Mark Twain) a nexus of sex and death.

Movie poster for *The Exorcist*

McDowell died from pneumonia in 1868. His building was razed in 1882 and the St. Louis property is now part of the Ralston Purina complex.

There were two huge **cholera epidemics** in St. Louis that claimed the lives of thousands. The first occurred in 1832 and lasted nearly six weeks. The city was in a state of panic again in 1849. In the belief that foul air was responsible for the disease, heaps of coal, tar and sulfur were burned at nearly every intersection. "Dead wagons" roamed the streets every night collecting bodies that had died that day. Most citizens were too scared to drive the wagons so convicts were used with the promise that their sentences would be reduced. The city lost nearly one-tenth of its population. Disease and epidemics were the main cause of life expectancy being only around 40 years back then. That was part of the reason for large families. Parents considered themselves fortunate if half of their children lived to see adulthood. **The disease did not hit Carondelet** and the city passed an ordnance preventing outsiders, who might be infected, from moving there. Guards were hired to enforce the decree.

Bellefountaine and Calvary Cemeteries were established after the epidemic. Many doctors thought the cause was from eating root vegetables. The cause of the epidemic was most likely a contaminated water supply. Because St. Louis University (9th and Washington) drew its water supply from wells, not the river, the students there escaped the disease.

Chouteau's Pond was also suspected as a source of the disease. The city bought the property for $400, drained it and brought in fill. It then became known as Mill Creek Valley and it later became the locus of railroad yards.

Because of the epidemic, numerous places in St. Louis are said to be haunted due to the restless souls of the dead.

The most haunted park in St. Louis is Lafayette Park. The reason for this dates back to the Civil War era when Union officer James Wilson and his men were captured, in 1863, by Confederate guerrilla leader Tim Reeves. They were summarily executed. When St. Louis commander William Rosencrans learned of the incident he issued a special order for a captured Confederate major and six enlisted men to be executed in retaliation. On October 29, 1864, the prisoners were taken from Gratiot Street prison. They were brought to Lafayette Park and shot by a firing squad. After the deaths of these randomly selected men, residents whose homes overlooked the park reported seeing ghostly images of uniformed men walking around the park late at night, ostensibly seeking justice for their "unjust" deaths.

According to Ron (Johnny Rabbitt) Elz, room 304 at the **Chase Park Plaza Hotel**, on North Kingshighway, is rumored to be haunted. The first sighting took place in 1979. Several people who stayed in the room told stories about being wakened in the night by a beautiful red haired woman. She would smile at them and then disappear through the locked door.

Jefferson Barracks has its very own ghost story. Around 1923, a section of Jefferson Barracks was designated to be a veteran's hospital. A private Halloween party was held there and security officers at the gate commented how one guest was remarkably well dressed in a Civil War uniform. One guest noted that he had even spoken to the man, asking him how he liked the party. The soldier grunted a hoarse reply, "Like it good." When the man talked about the incident with others, hc discovered, to his Aston-ishment, that no one at the party that night wore such a costume.

There is also a long time legend about a ghost that haunts the Jefferson Barracks powder magazine. Those who saw him reported that he had an ugly bullet wound in the head. It seems that, during the Civil War Era, a guard had been killed by a raiding party that attempted to steal munitions.

Building 78, also known as Atkinson Hall, is said to be haunted by a World War I soldier spirit. Like Casper, the friendly ghost, he harms no one and apparently is content to walk the premises making sure that everything is secure.

Remember ***The Exorcist***, the movie that nearly scared you to death? The film was based on William Blatty's best-seller. Historian Troy Taylor refers to the incident upon which the movie was based as **The Year the Devil Came to Town**.

The roots of the story go back to a young boy in Maryland whose bedroom was seemingly under siege by some phantom menace. At night, his bed shook so hard it was difficult for him to sleep. His linens would be torn from the bed. Those who believe the young lad was possessed say its origins go back to when his Aunt Tillie (who was interested in the occult) taught him how to use an Ouija board. Some thought that young Robbie had conjured up a poltergeist who was trying to inhabit his body.

When medical authorities and Lutheran ministers in his home town failed to redress the incredibly frustrating problem, Robbie's parents brought him to St. Louis. The parents had close relatives who lived in **Normandy**. The boy was taken to **Alexian Brothers Hospital** for observation and treatment. If anything, Robbie got worse and was now screaming things in a foreign tongue that linguists later identified as Hebrew Aramaic, the language of Jesus. The weird noises and bed rattling also continued.

William Lemp (National Archives)

Robbie's parents turned to the Catholic Church for help. Two Jesuit priests were brought in and tried to baptize the lad. The ritual, which normally lasts about fifteen minutes, took nearly two hours. When the priests asked, "Do you renounce the devil?" Robby began cursing and thrashing about. When holy water was sprinkled throughout the room, it hissed and vaporized instantly.

Robbie was released from the hospital in March of 1949 and declared to be normal. But he wasn't. Robbie's uncle noticed that strange markings and words began to appear on the boy's body. At night, his bed still shook violently. In exasperation, the priests secured permission from Archbishop Joseph E. Ritter to perform the rarest of ceremonies, an exorcism. Father Bowdern, Father Bishop, Father Kenny and Father O'Hara were all there for the task. Walter Halloran, a seminary student and football player, was asked to hold the boy down. As the prayers commanding the evil spirit to depart began, the boy began to shake violently and utter vile things. It took several exorcism sessions and, as the ordeal continued, Robbie's responses became more violent and obscene. During the process, the young lad was converted to the Catholic faith.

Lemp Brewery (Missouri Historical Society)

The priests were nearly ready to give up, but during one last ritual the boy interrupted with a deep masculine voice and announced that he was Michael the Archangel. In the same masculine voice he ordered the demons to depart his body and suddenly he went into violent spasms. Everything grew quiet and then the boy sat and smiled and in a normal voice said, "He's gone."

Robbie and his family returned to Maryland and he grew into normal adulthood and is married, with three children.

Was this a case of demonic possession or just a hoax? Who knows?

The wing of the hospital where Robbie stayed was razed in 1978. Just before the wrecking ball hit the building, workers reported seeing a rat as big as a cat flee the building.

In January of 2008, the Vatican sent out a directive that more priests need to be trained in the art of exorcism because there was an increase of evil in the world.

One of the most haunted buildings in all of St. Louis is the **Lemp Mansion**. William Lemp, a German immigrant, first came to St. Louis in 1838. He soon built a beer factory at 112 South Second Street, between Walnut and Elm. He introduced St. Louis to its first lager beer, one that was lighter than the dark English ales. He completed the lagering process by storing his beer in a cooling cave at Cherokee and De Menil Place. Lemp opened a saloon that sold only his beer and no hard liquor. Adam Lemp died a rich man in 1862. He left his Western Brewery business to his son, William, and his grandson.

William immediately bought out a five block area around the cave to expand the business. A new brewery was built there and, by 1870, it was the largest in the city. It was still larger than the Busch Brewery when Prohibition closed them in 1920. A bottling plant was added next and, in 1878, artificial refrigeration was added to the plant. By then production had reached 100,000 barrels a year. By the 1890s, Lemp had introduced the popular "**Falstaff**" beer and was a nationally known company. The St. Louis brewery employed about 700 men.

The Lemp Mansion, built in 1868 and extensively remodeled, boasted 38 rooms, marble bathrooms, ornate ceilings and an elevator that had replaced the main staircase, by 1904. At the rear of the house, three massive vaults housed expensive furnishings that were changed along with the seasons. The basement had a silver polishing room where a servant's only chore was to polish silver all day long. Expensive homes typical of this era usually had a ballroom on the third floor. Instead, a tunnel ran from the basement of the house over to the beer cave. Part of the cave was lined with plaster and converted into a large theater and ballroom. There was also a concrete swimming pool with heated water piped in from the brewery's boiler house.

The famous Kennedy family curse pales in comparison to that of the Lemp family. The first to die was the heir apparent, son Frederick Lemp. Around 1901 his health began to fail and he died in December of that year at the age of 28. In 1902, William built a huge mausoleum for Frederick at Bellefontaine Cemetery in north St. Louis. The beautiful ornate building remains the largest structure on the premises.

Arch topping-out ceremony

William Lemp was crushed by the death of his son and his misery increased with the death of his good friend, Frederick Pabst, in January of 1904. He grew despondent and his mental and physical health declined. On February 13, 1904, William Lemp **committed suicide by shooting himself** in the head with a .38 in his bedroom. Adolphus Busch, one of Lemp's chief competitors, served as a pall bearer. William was buried in the mausoleum next to his son.

William Lemp Jr. took over the business and spent the family fortune lavishly. His wife, called the Lavender Lady because she liked to wear that color, was even more of a spender. It was said that she wore a different shade of lavender dress each day of the week. William built a new home in the wilderness near Webster Groves and the old mansion became company business offices.

The advent of Prohibition closed the brewery in 1920. William auctioned off buildings and sold the Falstaff name to brewer Joseph Griesedieck for $25,000. 1920 was also the year that Elsa Lemp committed suicide. She was the youngest of the Lemp siblings. A troubled marriage, headaches, and bouts of depression left her with frayed nerves. **She shot herself** in the bedroom while her husband was taking a bath.

KXOK Dee Jay Nick Charles

William sold the plant property to International Shoe which used it for storage. He now began to suffer from nervousness, headaches, sleepless nights and depression. On December 29, 1922, William Lemp Jr. shot himself in his office. A week before, he had dined with his friend, August A. Busch. St. Louis police began referring to these suicidal episodes as **Dutch Disease**, a play on the German word *deutsch.*

Brother Edwin died of natural causes in 1970, but his will stipulated that a lifetime collection of priceless paintings, family heirlooms, papers and artifacts were to be destroyed by burning. Today, **there are no surviving members of the Lemp family.**

Since then the old mansion has been a boarding house, restaurant, and mystery theater. Dozens of people have reported hearing strange noises, moans and shrieks and seeing doors that lock and unlock on their own.

Life Magazine did an article about America's haunted places and listed the spooky old mansion as **one of the ten most haunted sites in the USA.**

There is one final word of warning that is offered by ghost hunters. **Some dark mist-shrouded night, with eerie diaphanous clouds floating overhead, when you are visiting a haunted site and your inner being senses that deep dismembered voice telling you to get out – do it immediately**!!!

THE GATEWAY ARCH

The Jefferson National Expansion Memorial consists of a 91 acre park near the Mississippi River at St. Louis. It was established to commemorate American westward expansion, the Lewis and Clark journey, the Dred Scott case and the first civil government west of the Mississippi. It is one of the leading national attractions, **drawing roughly four million visitors annually**. It is also the tallest U.S. manmade monument.

The arch was designed by Finnish-American architect Eero Saarinen and structural engineer Hannskark Bandel. It stands 630 ft. tall and is 630 ft wide at the base. The only building in Missouri that is taller is One Kansas City Place in **Kansas City**. The lower half consists of a stainless steel skin covering reinforced concrete and the upper level has carbon steel and rebar under the stainless exterior. The interior is hollow and has a tram that takes visitors to a small observation area at the top.

Underneath the Arch is a visitor's center, accessed from a descending outdoor ramp starting at either base. Within the center is the **Museum of Westward Expansion** with exhibits and a gift shop. It also contains the loading areas for the tram. The Tucker Theater, finished in 1968 and refurbished thirty years later, has 285 seats and shows a documentary, *Monument to the Dream*, on the Arch's construction.

Eero Saarinen died from a brain tumor before the arch was completed. Before his death, **he hired a college dropout, Richard Bowser, to design the tram system**. Elevator companies failed to come up with a workable design, but in two weeks Bowser came up with a system that combined an elevator cable lift system with gimbaled, egg-shaped cars that functioned similar to Ferris wheel gondolas.

The top of the arch can sway up to eighteen inches in high winds. The park grounds are maintained by the National Park Service and the tram is run by Bi-State Development Agency. Leonor K. Sullivan Boulevard is named for the St. Louis congresswoman who helped secure federal funds for the Arch. Sullivan was the **first woman from Missouri to serve in the U.S. House of Representatives**.

On July 21, 2007, **nearly two hundred people were trapped** in the two trams or at the top of the arch due to a power failure. Those who were ambulatory made it down a set of stairs to a service elevator. Others had to wait for the power to be restored. From the top of the arch one can see for 30 miles on a clear day.

Plans for the Arch went back to 1947 when civic leaders held a national competition for the design. Saarinen modified his original design by extending its length 40 feet. In layman's terms, the shape of the arch is similar to that of an inverted hanging chain.

Based on previous construction experience, it was estimated that two or three workers would die from falls during the Arch construction. However, there were no deaths related to the project from beginning to end.

Joe Garagiola, Lou Thesz, Joe Louis, Stan Musial , Yogi Berra, Al Schoendinst (Tettaton picture)

Construction began February 12, 1963, and was completed October 28, 1965. Each leg went sixty feet deep into the ground. The base of each leg at ground level had **an engineering tolerance of one-sixty-fourth of an inch** or the two legs would not mate at the top. Some of the excavated rock and dirt was hauled across the river to East St. Louis to fill in low spots left over from the 1890 street raising project. As each half of the arch moved closer to completion, the weight caused the legs to tilt inward. A brace was inserted near the top to keep them apart until construction was finished. Pittsburgh-DesMoines, the construction company, placed their name on the strut but the government considered it advertising and forced them to remove the name. The letters PDM were allowed on the cranes on each leg of the Arch.

On the day the final piece was to be inserted, it was discovered that there was insufficient room so jackscrews were used to force the two legs apart. It was a bright, sunny day and the south leg heated up from the sun it began to expand. **Firemen used a long hose to spray water on that leg to keep it from expanding too much**. The Boy Scouts organization attached a large U.S. flag to the last triangular keystone piece and the "topping out" process was successfully completed. Vice President Hubert Humphrey and Secretary of the Interior Stewart Udall attended the dedication ceremonies in May of 1968.

The total cost was approximately $15 million. In 1984, monies were set aside by Congress for expansion of the Memorial on the east side, but a moratorium was placed on this when the Casino Queen gambling facility was built in East St. Louis on the riverfront.

Eleven small aircraft have successfully piloted through the Arch, even though it is illegal. In 1980, Kenneth Sawyers tried to parachute onto the top of the Arch, planning to jump back off again with a smaller chute to land on the ground below. Instead, he slid all the way down one leg to his death. In 1984, David Adcock of Houston, Texas, began to scale the Arch using suction cups on his hands and feet, but he was talked out of it after having climbed only 20 feet. The next day he successfully scaled the nearby 21-story Equitable Building in downtown St. Louis.

On 14 September, 1992, John C. Vincent (of New Orleans) was lowered from a helicopter onto the top of the Arch, from which he parachuted to the ground below. A judge gave him three months in jail for the stunt.

The only president or former president to go to the top of the arch was Dwight D. Eisenhower who was responsible for allocating federal funds for the project.

Sometimes those of us who live in the area take the arch for granted. We should all remember the words of Barringer Fifield who said in *Seeing St. Louis*, "**The Arch is where everything comes together. The improbably stainless steel flourish unites not only earth and sky, land and water, east and west, but also St. Louis's past and present, its challenges and responses. Here is where the city begins . . . .**"

FAMOUS PEOPLE BURIED IN BELLEFONTAINE CEMETERY

U.S. Senator Thomas Hart Benton
Suffragist Virginia L. Minor
Fur trader Robert Campbell
Bridge designer James B. Eads
Susan E. Blow – started the nation's first kindergarten
Isaiah Sellers – famed riverboat man who used the same pen name (Mark Twain) that Samuel L. Clemens adopted
Beer baron Adolphus Busch and wife Lilly Anheuser
Laumeier family that established Laumeier Sculpture Park
David R. Francis – St. Louis mayor and Secretary of Interior under President Grover Cleveland
Charlotte Wainwright, wife of millionaire who built first skyscraper in St. Louis. Her tomb was designed by famed architect Louis Sullivan
Shoe manufacturer George W. Brown
Spink family mausoleum, publishers of the *Sporting News*
James S. McDonnell, founder of McDonnell Aircraft
Chris Von der Ahe, owner of St. Louis Browns
Railroad magnate and educational philanthropist John O'Fallon

Falstaff Brewery

U.S. Senator George Vest who helped establish this nation's national park system
William S. Burroughs, inventor of the adding machine
Revolutionary War veteran Stephen Hempstead
General William Clark of the famed Lewis and Clark duo
Beer baron William Lemp and his family (William's wife Lillian hated her husband and said she didn't want to be buried near him. Accordingly, he is in the front of the vaulted tomb and she is in the rear.)
Dr. Joseph (body snatcher) McDowell

(See *Walking St. Louis,* by Galas and West, for a guided tour of the cemetery.)

SUBTERRANEAN ST. LOUIS

It is a well known fact that the entire city of St. Louis is built on top of a complex network of natural caves. According to Ripley's Believe-it-or-Not, **no other city on earth has as many caves beneath its streets, sidewalks and structures**. Many of the local breweries owned caves for lagering and storage purposes. Some of these had stairwells installed and beer gardens built and they became popular night spots for locals. Beer caves stopped being used by breweries when artificial refrigeration was installed in brewing plants.

Making bake goods at Gus' Pretzels (Lorna Nunes photo)

The **Anheuser-Busch** Brewery cave was discovered in 1852 by a German brewer by the name of George Schneider. A soap baron named Eberhard Anheuser gained control of the Bavarian Brewery there around 1857. He formed a partnership with Adolphus Busch and the rest is history.

The Anheuser-Busch Brewery was built on an Indian settlement site called Petite Prairie by the early French. **During the Civil War, arms and munitions from the Arsenal were hidden here to keep them from falling into the hands of the Rebels**.

Trader Vic's Polynesian Restaurant (David Lossos collection)

Cherokee Cave, in South St. Louis, was first discovered by brewer Adam Lemp. In 1945, a pharmaceutical manufacturer bought the property above part of the cave that had an entrance on Cherokee Street at Broad-way. He built a museum building that served as an entrance to the cave. While in the process of digging a passageway, workers unearthed the bones of an extinct peccary (wild boar), dating back hundreds of thousands of years. Also discovered were the bones of an extinct armadillo that was much larger than the common Texas armadillo. These bones were displayed on the premises at the museum which opened in 1950. The cave was connected to the part that contained the old Lemp Mansion underground swimming pool and theater. The cave never became a big attraction and was closed around 1960.

A man named Lee Hess bought the cave property in 1945, renamed it Cherokee Cave (it was on Cherokee St.) and charged admission for tours.

In 1961, the Missouri Highway Department closed the cave and demolished the museum in preparation for construction of Interstate 55. The old Dr. Nicholas DeMenil mansion, located nearby, was also scheduled for the wrecking ball, but preservationists convinced authorities to spare the historic building.

Dr. William Beaumont, a St. Louis surgeon, owned a large tract of land with a cave. It was bounded by Locust Street and Washington Avenue. The land was bought by the Uhrig family which owned a brewery business on Market Street. They enlarged the cave, lined it with brick to prevent seepage dripping, and connected it to others that were nearby. They then installed a narrow gauge train that brought beer to the **Uhrig Cave** from the factory. During the Civil War, the cave became the headquarters for the local militia and Home Guard.

In the 1850s, the Uhrigs built a beer garden and began offering cave tours. After the war, the beer garden was expanded into a small theater entertainment spot.

By 1884, the cave was under the ownership of Thomas McNeary. He and his brother built a stage and installed seating, converting the cave into a vaudeville house. They also installed the **first electric lights used in any St. Louis place of entertainment**.

When the McNeary's lost their liquor license, a syndicate bought the land and built the **Coliseum** on top of it on the corner of Jefferson and Washington. The grand opening was in 1909 and over the years it hosted evangelist Gypsy Smith, horse shows, circuses and, for a while, it hosted the Veiled Prophet Ball. Other performers of note included Enrico Caruso and John McCormack. Evangelist Billy Sunday once held a revival at the Coliseum. In 1916, the Democratic National Convention was held in the building. Bill Tilden played tennis here and Johnny Weissmuller swam in the "**world's largest swimming pool**," built in 1925. The pool could be covered with removable flooring when arena space was needed. Wrestler Ed "Strangler" Lewis even had a championship bout here in 1927. In 1928, nominee Herbert Hoover delivered the keynote speech at the Republican Convention held in the great hall.

The Coliseum began to decline after the Arena was built in 1929 and Kiel Auditorium was constructed in 1934. Lack of parking space was always a problem for the Coliseum after the "tin lizzies" became popular in the 1920s.

The last event staged at the Coliseum was in 1939 – a wrestling match. During World War II it was used as a storage facility for new cars that were "frozen" by government orders for the duration of the war. The building was demolished in July of 1953.

English Cave could be accessed east of present day Benton Park, bounded by Illinois and Jefferson, Wyoming and Arsenal. In 1826, Ezra English built a small brewery next to the cave. He later formed a partnership and they built the first subterranean beer garden in St. Louis, complete with entertainment. Prior to the Civil War, the brewery went out of business.

Gus' Pretzels in South St. Louis (Lorna Nunes photo)

Meanwhile, the city built a cemetery nearby and it began filling up as a result of a cholera epidemic. After the war the bodies were moved to a new cemetery about a mile south of Jefferson Barracks and the old epidemic cemetery was converted into a park. It was named Benton Park to honor Thomas Hart Benton.

In 1877, the cave was once again opened up, this time for the purpose of growing mushrooms. In the 1890s the cave was used by a winery.

Benton Park has a small lake and every once in a while it would lose much of its water, apparently by seepage into the cave labyrinth below. The Park Department eventually solved the problem by lining the lake bottom with concrete.

Winkelmeyer's Cave was used for brewery purposes by four different companies. Julius Winkelmeyer built the first brewery in 1847 at 1714 Market. It was located near the western edge of Chouteau's Pond. As an ever-growing population soon polluted the lake/pond, many thought that the unsanitary conditions there led to the cholera epidemic of the late 1840s. Chouteau Pond was later drained, filled, and it became a railroad yard facility. Winkelmeyer Brewery was eventually superseded by Excelsior Brewery.

By the time Union Station was built, in 1894, the breweries there were out of business and the cave forgotten. The cave was sealed in 1933 when construction was done to widen Market Street.

Park Plaza Hotel and Chase Hotel

Many of these caves would be long forgotten except occasionally there is subsidence that requires buildings to be shored up or sidewalk cave-ins that require fill or support beams. In 1960, there was an incident where a sidewalk in front of the Post Office at Eighteenth and Market partially collapsed because of subsidence. Steel beams capped with large metal plates now support the hollow sidewalk there.

Kerzinger's Ale Cave, located fifty feet beneath the surface, was located at the southwest corner of Broadway and Tyler. After the Civil War, there is no instance in records or newspapers where the cave is mentioned.

The **Falstaff Brewery,** at 1920 Shenandoah, had a cave that was used when the facility was first constructed in 1853. It was owned by a man named Stumpf. The brewery changed ownership on several occasions and by 1911 it was known as the Griesedieck Brothers Brewery. During World War II the cave was designated an air raid shelter.

The **Home Brewing Company** and cave were located on a southeast corner of Salena Street. In the 1890s, the brewery financed the construction of the Highlands Cottage Restaurant. To draw more customers, a horse-drawn merry-go-round was built. After that a picturesque railway was added and **the area was named the Forest Park Highlands**. According to cave historians Hubert and Charlotte Rother, Sophie Tucker, Gypsy Rose Lee and John Phillip Sousa entertained there. The brewery closed in 1909.

Joe Schnaider's Brewery and cave was located on Chouteau Avenue between Armstrong and Mississippi Avenues. In the late 1860s he built a large beer garden and numerous musical groups entertained the customers there, including the St. Louis Grand Orchestra. A number of historians argue that **these musical groups formed the basis of what would evolve into the St. Louis Symphony Orchestra**.

About how many natural caves were under the city of St. Louis originally? 50 – But most were collapsed and filled in as the city progressed.

Whatever happened to Mill Creek? It was converted into an underground storm sewer by the Metropolitan Sewer District. It begins near Kingshighway and Vandeventer and empties into the Mississippi just south of the MacArthur Bridge.

When was this project completed? 1916

What kind of celebration was held to commemorate the event? A huge underground banquet was held, attended by the Mayor and other dignitaries.

How big is the Mill Creek tunnel? About 20 feet in diameter

What was the purpose of the tunnel that went from the Eads Bridge and came out close to where Busch Stadium is located? The trains from the east ran on the lower level of the Eads Bridge and came through the tunnel on their way to Union Station.

Trains stopped using the Eads Bridge a few decades ago. When was it revived? When MetroLink was built around 1993. The Terminal railroad gave the Eads Bridge to St. Louis in return for the MacArthur Bridge, which is closed to trucks and autos, but still carries trains on the lower deck.

Is there a similar train tunnel coming into St. Louis from the north? Yes – it was built by Samuel Insull, the utilities mogul from Chicago, who ran a streetcar line across the McKinley Bridge into St. Louis. Passengers got out underground and walked up stairs to get to street level near Tucker Blvd. It is currently used daily by trains to bring in newsprint for the *Post-Dispatch.*

Modern St. Louis is honeycombed with tunnels, what are some of them used for besides storm sewers? They carry steam pipes, telephone lines, fiber optics and electric lines.

What device is currently being used to connect new tunnels to old ones? There is a circular cutting machine owned by the Sewer District. It cuts a hole through rock ten feet in diameter at a rate of about ten feet a day. When finished, track is laid for a narrow gauge railroad.

Old Ralston Purina building (Missouri H Society)

When were the city's first storm and sewage tunnels built? In the 1850s

River des Peres carries both storm water and sewage. The water is carried on the surface trench and the sewage is carried by a tunnel beneath the river.

Does the River des Peres go through Forest Park? Yes, but it was put underground for the 1904 Fair.

What is the purpose of the cave under the Soldier's Memorial? It is the emergency site for CEMA and police. Messages can be transmitted from there in case of a terrorist attack.

What nuclear war fallout shelter was built under St. Louis in the early 1960s? It was located under a prominent downtown building but officials are mum about which building. The site still has large drums of distilled water, first aid kits and cans of survival crackers.

What company is using caves at an old quarry in South County as a refrigeration facility for its food products? Cuna Food Service

What company built a train tunnel that still exists in St. Louis County? The Frisco Line – 1888

What underground facility exists at the Gateway Arch? The trams that take passengers to the top of the Arch start out underground. That part of the facility is on the same level with the Mississippi and only 700 feet west of the river. Sump pumps are needed to keep everything dry.

(Jerry Mizell photo) Arnold's Ponderosa Restaurant

What was the natural temperature of the Uhrig beer cave? Fifty-seven degrees; ice was hauled in to lower the temperature to thirty-five degrees for beer storage

What oddities were featured in the cave? It had an underground heated swimming pool and an air conditioned theater with a stage and seating area.

Why are the walls of this limestone cave so dark? In its early use people walked around with lighted torches and the soot stained the walls.

Is it true that the cave had electric lights before city streets were electrified? Yes – the electric lights were installed in 1888 and the old gas lights on the streets weren't replaced until 1904.

RALSTON PURINA COMPANY

Ralston Purina was founded in 1894 as the Robinson-Danforth Commission, a horse and mule feed company. Using $12,000 in borrowed capital, William H. Danforth, the company's founder, began selling feed from a storefront on the banks of the Mississippi River in St. Louis. He soon expanded by building a facility at the National Stock Yards in East St. Louis.

In the early 1900s, Danforth began selling a whole wheat breakfast cereal to St. Louis grocers under the Purina label. The word Purina was coined from the company slogan, "Where purity is paramount." The cereal was later renamed Ralston Wheat Cereal after receiving the endorsement of a well known health doctor of the day, Dr. Ralston. In 1902 the names Ralston and Purina were joined, and the company was officially renamed.

The company received a boost from the 1904 World's Fair when its products won first prize at the exposition. The company had a booth at the Fair where it served pancakes made with its wheat flour and Ralston breakfast food.

Ralston Purina's famed "checkerboard" logo was a marketing decision by Danforth, based on his childhood memories of a mother named Mrs. Brown who dressed all of her children in red and white checkered shirts and blouses made from the same bolt of cloth. William's father owned a store in **Charleston**, Missouri.

During the formative years of the business, the emphasis was on agricultural animal feeds and not breakfast cereals. It wasn't until the late 1920s that the first commercial pet food diet was developed by Ralston, giving birth to today's multi-billion dollar pet food industry.

In 1926 the company opened a research facility at **Gray Summit**, Missouri. That same year it purchased the Ry-Krisp health cracker company in Minnesota.

Ralston Purina was listed for the first time on the New York Stock Exchange in January of 1962. Later that day, with the temperature at -7 degrees Fahrenheit, there was a grain elevator explosion and fire that took three days to fully quell.

The Ralston name was mostly associated with soda crackers and cold cereal food such as Shredded Ralston, Wheat Chex and Rice Chex. Most of the human food business was spun off to General Mills. For years Ralston manufactured store brand cereals that were sold in grocery store outlets across the U.S. under the retailer's private labels. In late 2007, Ralcorp acquired Post Cereals brands, thus returning to the major branded cereal business.

In early 2001, the European company Nestlé acquired all the outstanding shares of Ralston Purina and formed a merger. The transaction had an enterprise value of $10.3 billion. Nestlé previously acquired Friskies pet food in 1985. Nestlé acquired Alpo in 1994. The new company name became Nestlé Purina.

Remember those Cold War "duck and cover" drills for school children in the 1950s?

Today, more than a century later, Purina is the world's largest producer of dog food, both moist and dry. The company also makes kitty litter under the Tidy Cats brand name. Tidy Cats was acquired from Edward Lowe Industries in 1990.

Ralston Purina purchased the Eveready Battery Company in 1986 but it was spun off in 2000. It purchased Continental Baking Company "aka" Wonder Bread and Hostess cakes in 1984 but it spun off the bakery business to Interstate Brands Corporation, headquartered in **Kansas City**.

The company has approximately 22,000 employees and dozens of facilities worldwide. The company's headquarters in St. Louis, just southwest of the new Busch Stadium, are known as Checkerboard Square. Its well known brands include Purina dog and cat chow, Alpo, Beggin' Strips, Friskies, Tender Vittles and Fancy Feast.

There is a Purina Farm visitor's center in **Gray Summit** that offers free tours of the facility plus access to animals. Land O' Lakes now owns Purina Mills and makes feed for cows, horses, mules, poultry and swine.

McDONNELL DOUGLAS COMPANY

James S. McDonnell guessed correctly that it was only a matter of time before the U.S. entered World War II so he decided to launch McDonnell Aircraft Corporation in St. Louis in 1939. Meanwhile, Douglas Aircraft was founded in California back in 1921 by Donald Douglas. Douglas aircraft, with a workforce of 160,000, made 30,000 aircraft from 1942 to 1945. Both companies were forced to make drastic layoffs after World War II ended.

1959 Studebaker Hawk

After the war, Douglas began making the DC-6 (1946) and DC-7 (1953). Their first jet plane for the military was the F4D Skyray in 1951. In 1958, they began making the DC-8 to compete with Boeing's 707. McDonnell, a smaller company, supplied the Navy with the F2H **Banshee** and the F-101 **Voodoo**. McDonnell Aircraft became a major player when it produced the F-4 Phantom in 1958. The F-4 Phantom was widely used in the Vietnam War.

Both companies got into the missile business. Douglas became the main contractor of the Skybolt while McDonnell began making the AM-20 Quail. When the lucrative space program came along, the Douglas Co. contracted with NASA to help make the Saturn V rocket while McDonnell Aircraft expanded its work force to make the capsules. Participation in the space race brought enormous prestige for the city of St. Louis.

McDonnell Aircraft played a significant role in the space program making the one-man Mercury capsule, the two-man Gemini and the larger Apollo spacecraft that went to the moon.

The two firms officially merged on April 28, 1967 as the McDonnell Douglas Corporation (MDC). The DC 10 began production in 1968 with first deliveries made in 1971. In 1977, the MD-80 commercial plane was launched. The MD-11 was launched in 1985 and sold 200 units before being discontinued in 2001, after the merger with Boeing, as it competed with the Boeing 777. McDonnell Douglas's final commercial aircraft, the MD-90, was launched in 1988.

The end of the **Cold War** came in 1989 with the collapse of the Soviet Union's empire and the destruction of the Berlin Wall. When Bill Clinton became president in 1993, he severely curtailed the military budget in favor of domestic programs. Naturally, this affected defense contracts and massive layoffs ensued.

Through the years McDonnell Douglas has produced many successful aircraft, including the **F-15 Eagle (1974) which has never been defeated in combat**. The company also made the **F/A-18 Hornet** (with vertical lift takeoff) and the Super Hornet. They also made the **Harpoon** and **Tomahawk (cruise) missiles**. Cruise missiles can be launched from airplanes, submarines or surface ships and are guided by GPS systems. Newer versions can be redirected to other targets in mid-flight. In the motion picture *Under Siege*, a group of mercenaries take over the battleship *U.S.S. Missouri* to gain control of its nuclear-tipped cruise missiles. The Harpoon anti-ship missile can also be launched from an airplane, submarine or surface ship. It is produced at a Boeing plant located in **St. Charles**, Missouri. These missiles have been sold to allies such as Singapore, Spain, Denmark, Pakistan, Great Britain, Nationalist China, Chile and Australia. The Harpoon's chief rival is the French-made Exocet. In 1986, Harpoon missiles sank two Libyan patrol boats in the Gulf of Sidra. They were launched from an A-6 Intruder plane.

In 1984, McDonnell Douglas purchased Hughes Helicopters, paying $500 million. Out of this came the production of the widely-used **AH-64 Apache** attack helicopter.

In January of 1988, McDonnell Douglas and General Dynamics won the Navy Advanced Tactical Aircraft contract. The purpose of the $4.83 billion dollar contract was to develop the A-12 Avenger II, a stealthy, carrier-based flying wing aircraft that would replace the A-6 Intruder. Issues over cost overruns and delays led to a termination of the contract by Defense Secretary Dick Cheney. As of early 2008, the case continued to sit in litigation. The chaos resulting from the collapse of the A-12 program led to layoffs of 5,600 employees. Interestingly enough, the void left by the collapse of the Avenger program would be filled by the Super Hornet. McDonnell Douglas merged with Boeing in 1997 in a $13 billion stock-swap to create the Boeing Company.

After this writer's son (Steve Nunes) graduated from the University of Illinois in 1989, his second job (1991) was with McDonnell Douglas.

Mayor Cervantes & Arch/stadium construction

MAYOR ALFONSO J. CERVANTES

Cervantes was born in St. Louis in 1920. He attended St. Louis University and served in the Merchant Marine during World War II. He married the former Carmen Davis and they had six children. In 1965, he defeated Mayor Raymond Tucker's unprecedented bid for a fourth term in office by winning the primary. He easily defeated Republican Maurice Zumwalt in the general election.

During his term, Cervantes focused on the issue of race relations, crime fighting and city finance. Though many other large cities suffered from black riots during the late 1960s, St. Louis did not. Cervantes kept the peace by conferring with African-American leadership and including them in city government positions and on city commissions.

On his watch voters passed a one per cent sales tax to put policemen on horseback in city parks. Car thefts were reduced by his "lock it and pocket the key" program. He was also successful in getting a $2 million bond issue passed for completion of the Gateway Arch and grounds. A $15 million bond issue for street lighting and a juvenile center was passed in 1972. Cervantes urged the city to buy the **Spanish Pavilion** when the New York World's Fair ended. It was brought to St. Louis and rebuilt downtown as a cultural center. It never caught on and it is now part of the St. Louis Hilton on Broadway, near the ballpark. He also brought an 80 ft. replica of Columbus' flagship ***Santa Maria,*** but it never did well as a tourist attraction. The boat sank at its moorings to add insult to injury.

Cervantes set a precedent for politicians. **He became the first mayor in history to call a disk jockey every morning and give a summary of the previous day's events**. Tom McMahon was the disk jockey he contacted on a regular basis.

Anheuser-Busch Clydesdales in 1933

Cervantes failed in his attempt to get a new airport built in the **Columbia**, Illinois region. He thought it would greatly benefit downtown St. Louis. The proposal met with great controversy, especially from Chief County Executive Gene McNary, who nixed the idea. The brouhaha led to Cervantes' defeat in his bid for a third term in 1973, losing out to John Poelker in the Democratic primary.

Cervantes published his memoirs, *Mr. Mayor*, in 1974 and passed away in 1983 at the age of 62.

Thirty-three years after the flamboyant Cervantes left office, his son, A.J. Cervantes Jr., produced and narrated a documentary called *Mr. Mayor*. According to the documentary, there was no substance to the charges by investigative reporter Denny Walsh, who shared a 1969 Pulitzer Prize for local investigative reporting with Albert Delugach. That coverage for the *Globe-Democrat* was on corruption in Steamfitters Local 562. The documentary also denied that there was anything of substance to a *Life Magazine* article that tied Cervantes to the mob. Cervantes sued *Life* because of the article but it went nowhere in the courts.

Francis Slay is interviewed in the documentary and states a belief that St. Louis would have more air traffic today had the Illinois auxiliary airport been built. He also credits Cervantes for revitalizing a "dying city" with a new convention center, the Arch and a new Busch Stadium

A CAUTIONARY TALE ABOUT DRINKING

There was this father in north St. Louis who took his family, every Sunday, to attend the local Church of God. One day he decided that his son was old enough to teach about the evils of excessive drinking. He took the young lad to the kitchen table where there were two glasses. One was full of water and the other contained 100 proof Kentucky bourbon.

The father took a night crawler and plopped it into the glass of water and it swam around as happy as it could be. Then he retrieved the worm and dropped it into the glass of liquor. The worm shriveled up and died.

"Well, son," the father said, placing a hand on the young boy's shoulder. "What lesson did you learn from that little demonstration?" The boy frowned a bit as he tried hard to come up with the right answer.

"I think I got it, father." "If you drink, you won't get worms!"

MUSEUM OF TRANSPORTATION

The St. Louis Museum of Transportation (314- 965-7998) is located just west of I-270 near the juncture of I-44. Before the interstates the place was accessed by driving on Lindbergh and then taking Big Bend to Barrett Station. According to a former curator for the Smithsonian Institute, it houses one of the largest and best collections of transportation vehicles in the world. It was founded in 1944 by a group of historically interested citizens when they purchased the 1870s mule-drawn streetcar "Bellefountaine." They formed a non-profit educational organization to work toward preserving transportation artifacts. Land was acquired at **Barrett Station**, in St. Louis County, along the right-of-way of the Missouri Pacific Railroad, the pioneer rail line west of the Mississippi River. The line came through **Kirkwood** and was built around 1853. Over the years additional land was acquired and more exhibits were purchased. In September of 1979, the entire operation was given as a gift to the St. Louis County Department of Parks and Recreation to administer.

Museum of Transportation (Lorna Nunes photo)

Located on 150 acres, the Museum is on the site of the first man-made railroad tunnel west of the Mississippi. Visitors can see the entrance to this tunnel that was used by MoPac until 1944. The site also features over four miles of switching and exhibition track, ten buildings and a resource library.

The Museum has over 70 locomotives, old buses, streetcars, an airplane or two, a riverboat and antique autos. One of the most interesting locomotives is a 4-8-8-4 '**Big Boy**" that was used to haul iron ore from the Mesabi Range in Minnesota. It is 132 ft. long and weighs 1.2 million pounds. It had a top speed of 80 mph.

MONSANTO CHEMICAL

Monsanto was founded by John F. Queeny and he named the company for his wife, Olga Monsanto. Queeny was a purchasing agent for Meyer Brothers Drug Company in St. Louis. It was 1900 and Queeny was middle-aged and had only six years of formal schooling.

He discovered that the only U.S. source of saccharin at the time came from Germany. Saccharine was a sugar substitute that was six times less expensive than sugar. One pound of saccharine was the equivalent of 600 pounds of sugar. He built a sulphur refinery in nearby **East St. Louis**, but it burned down the first day of operation, costing him over $6,000. Two years later he decided to try again, bankrolled by Carbonic Acid of Chicago which made ingredients for soft drinks. Queeny sold his manufactured saccharine to Carbonic Acid. They agreed to purchase 6,000 pounds of saccharine every year for five years. He sold it to them for $4.50 a pound. The German saccharine trust tried to kill Queeny's new company by trying to undercut his prices. Queeny sold some property and borrowed against his life insurance policy to keep his company going. By 1905, his company profits exceeded $10,000. At that point, Queeny quit his job with Meyer Brothers and devoted his full energy to his own company. Over the years he expanded his plant and added new products. By the onset of World War I, the company was making a million dollars a year. In 1917, Monsanto began making acetylsalicylic acid, better known as aspirin. Within 60 years his company was the number one maker of that product.

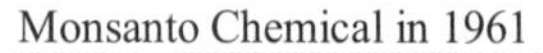

Monsanto Chemical in 1961

Queeny established another plant just outside of **East St. Louis** (on Route 3) and incorporated the town of Monsanto around it. Other manufacturing firms located in his town but in later years, when chemical spills gave the town a bad name, it was rechartered as **Sauget**, Illinois.

There was a post-World War I depression that hit the country and Queeny had to lay off most of his workers to survive. He almost sold out to Dupont back then but changed his mind. In 1925, Monsanto discovered a cheaper way to make sulfuric acid. Queeny, suffering from cancer, turned the company over to his son Edgar in 1928. In the 1940s, Monsanto was a leading producer of plastics and man-made fibers. In 1947, there was a huge explosion of a French ship loaded with ammonium nitrates at Galveston Bay in Texas. Known as the Texas City Disaster, the explosion (which destroyed Monsanto's styrene plant there) is considered the **largest industrial disaster in U.S. history**. Under Edgar's leadership, the company went from $6.5 million in sales to more than a billion in 1962 when he retired.

After 75 years in business, the company had about 150 plants and 60,000 employees. It is the leading producer of the herbicide Roundup, used by farmers worldwide. Monsanto has plants in Belgium, France, Mexico, India and Brazil. In recent years Monsanto has become a biotech giant with genetic engineered products. Monsanto's national headquarters continue be in St. Louis after all these years. This writer's wife's uncle, Jerry Lanius, spent most of his working life with Monsanto.

EMERSON ELECTRIC COMPANY

This writer's sister began working as a secretary for Dick Fox at the Washington Park Emerson plant in 1957. While working there, she met Don Rogier of **Highland** and they were married in 1961. Thanks to her, I began working there in the summer of 1959, after my freshman year in college. I was an inventory control clerk. I went back to college in the fall and returned to Emerson as a summer temp in 1960. My

Emerson Electric Company on Old Florissant Road

fiancée and I decided to get married that September. We had both just finished our sophomore year at **Belleville** Jr. College. I dropped out of college and stayed on at Emerson full time as a tool crib attendant. I was earning $2.22 an hour and our **Collinsville** rent was $75.00 a month. I was laid off six months later, but I barely had enough seniority to bump someone else out of a job in the receiving department at the Emerson plant on Florissant Avenue in St. Louis. In September of 1961, my wife passed a state test and took a full time teaching job in **Summerfield**, Illinois. I quit my job at Emerson to finish my college at SIUE. I graduated in 1963 and taught one year at **Bayless High School** before switching to Collinsville High.

Emerson Electric was founded in 1890 by the brothers Charles and Alexander Meston along with the principal investor, John Emerson. The company manufactured electric motors and fans. Emerson was the first company to sell electric fans in the U.S. (1892). The company soon expanded its product line to include electric sewing machines, electric dental drills and power tools.

During World War II, under the leadership of Stuart Symington, Emerson became the **world's largest manufacturer of airplane armament**. When this writer worked at the Washington Park Emerson plant, it was making fire control systems for the B-52 and the Honest John rocket for the Army.

My cousin, Del Shinn, worked at the St. Louis Emerson plant from 1948-1952, then went off to the Korean War. Emerson had 5,000 factory employees back then. Del's badge number was 54687 – a straight in a poker game. After he came back from the war, he worked for fourteen more years and then was laid off. He and his wife, Doris, who also worked at Emerson, lived on 10024 Pepper Lane, close to the Emerson plant. Their house was near **Dellwood**.

Emerson is a Fortune 500 Company with a worldwide workforce of approximately 138,000 employees.. It has a global presence that spans 150 countries. Emerson is the largest publicly traded NYSE company (by revenue) headquartered in Missouri. Emerson was awarded a record 486 patents worldwide in 2005. Emerson has 100 manufacturing sites in the U.S. and 170 throughout the world. **Emerson is currently ranked # 2 in Fortune America's Most Admired Companies**.

Satchel Page of the Browns

In October of 2006, Emerson filed a lawsuit against NBC regarding a scene that appeared in the pilot episode of the series *Heroes*. The scene depicted Claire Bennett injuring her hand by reaching into an active garbage disposal unit to retrieve a ring. Emerson makes the popular InSinkErator and said that the scene tarnished the product's image. The suit was eventually settled out of court.

ST. LOUIS BROWNS

The Browns first arrived on the St. Louis scene in 1902, moving here from Milwaukee. They assumed the nickname Brown Stockings after it was discarded by the national league club in favor of a new moniker, Cardinals. Browns' uniform colors were brown and orange. Their logo was a statue of Louis IX with a baseball on his shield. They managed to lure away several Cardinal players by signing them to larger contracts. Their first season was successful as they ended with a record of 78-58. In 1905 they lost 99 games. This was a disturbing trend that lasted throughout most of the team's tenure in St. Louis. A saying developed: **St. Louis – first in shoes, first in booze, last in the American League**. In 1911, they set a mark for futility by finishing 56 ½ games out of first place.

The club tried to improve its status by hiring Branch Rickey as a neophyte manager. They still finished in last place. Rickey was fired after a few seasons and was hired by the Cardinals, a club he helped build into a perennial contender. This is the same Branch Rickey who, when he was with the Brooklyn Dodgers, signed Jackie Robinson to a MLB contract.

Roy Sievers of the Browns/Sox

In 1920, **George Sisler** hit .407 for the Browns and had **257 hits**, a record that held up for 84 years. In 1922, they had their best season ever posting a 93-61 record. George Sisler hit .420 and as a team they led the league with a .313 mark. First baseman Sisler was named American

League MVP. Their pitching staff had the lowest ERA in the league but the season ended with the Yankees posting a 94-60 record, edging them by a single game.

In 1933, the Browns set another mark for ineptness. In a game at Sportsman's Park, they drew only 33 paying customers.

With many of the better players in the league off fighting the War, the Browns finally won their only pennant, edging out the Detroit Tigers in the final week of the season in 1944. The Browns started the St. Louis **Trolley Series** with an opening game win, with pitcher Denny Galehouse giving up only one run. The Cards won game two in eleven innings by a score of 3-2, with the Brownies kicking away two balls for errors yielding two unearned runs. In game three, Jack Kramer held the Cards scoreless and the Browns took a 2-1 Series lead. But the Birds came back to win the next three in a row, grabbing baseball's coveted crown.

In 1945, the Brown's team featured **Pete Gray, a one-armed outfielder**. When he was six, Pete fell off a wagon, got his arm tangled in the spokes, and had to have his right arm amputated above the elbow. Determined to play baseball, the kid learned how to bat and throw left-handed. He became an excellent bunter and line drive hitter. As an outfielder, he learned to catch the ball, stick the glove under his right armpit, and throw the ball back to the infield bare handed, all in one quick, deft motion. He lasted just one season and was replaced by regulars who came back in 1946 when World War II was over. He hit .218, had 6 doubles and 2 triples and 5 stolen bases.

Jack Briscoe

In 1949, outfielder Roy Sievers of the Browns was named AL Rookie-of-the-Year.

The Browns made headlines again in 1951 when owner **Bill Veeck** signed aging Negro League star Satchel Paige (Kansas City Monarchs) to a contract. On August 18th the Browns sent a midget (little person) up to the plate as a pinch-hitter. The **three-foot-seven-inch Eddie Gaedel, weighing a mere 65 pounds, walked on four pitches**. The League intervened and prohibited Gaedel from appearing in any future games.

Sam Muchnick

Bill Veeck wanted to move the Browns to Los Angeles, but there was no other west coast team at the time (making travel a problem), so he opted for Baltimore instead. He sold Sportsman's Park to August A. Busch and the rival St. Louis Cardinals. The last Browns' game was played on September 28, 1953, before a sparse crowd of a little over 3,000 fans.

ST. LOUIS WRESTLING

When I wrote ***Coming of Age in 1940s and 1950s East St. Louis***, I sent a copy to Lou Thesz. At the time, he was living in the Chesapeake Bay area. I mailed Thesz a book because in my autobiography I talked about watching pro wrestling on television and admiring him when I was a youth. Three or four months later, the phone rang and my wife answered it. "Bill, pick up the phone – it's Lou Thesz," she shouted down the hall. I couldn't have been happier if it had been the President of the United States calling me.

Dick Murdoch

His voice was clear and strong – pretty much like what I remember it sounding like back in the 1950s. Not at all weak like you'd expect for someone approaching their eighties. He told me one of his earliest professional bouts was at the **East St. Louis** Social Center at 9th and Summit. His pay that night was a meager three dollars because it was 1934 and the country was in the midst of the Depression. The amount would have been two dollars but he earned extra money by helping set up the ring and put out the folding chairs.

I asked him what other reasons he might have had for coming to East St. Louis in the 1950s. He said that he frequented places such as Bush's Steak House (at the foot of Eads Bridge), Buster Wortman's Paddock Lounge and Terry Moore's Playdium on Collinsville Avenue. He said many Missourians frequented these places because St. Louis restaurants could not serve liquor with meals on Sundays due to "blue laws." Lou also sent me a personalized autographed picture. Pretty cool!

The Thesz family moved to St. Louis when he was a boy. His emigrant parents hailed from the former Austro-Hungarian Empire. He attended Cleveland High and, as a teenager, he trained in amateur wrestling with legendary Ad Santel. He made his professional wrestling debut in 1932, at the age of 16. He met Ed "Strangler" Louis, the biggest wrestling star of the 1920s, who taught Lou the art of "hooking," the ability to stretch your opponent with painful holds. The two formed a lasting friendship. By 1937, Thesz had become one of the biggest stars in the St. Louis area, and on December 29 he defeated Everett Marshall for the NWA world heavyweight title. Thus Thesz, at age 21, became the youngest wrestling champion in U.S. history, a record he still holds.

Lou was 6 ft. 2 in. and wrestled at 225 pounds. He is credited with inventing a hold called the German Suplex. Thesz won the title on six different occasions. He retired from full time wrestling in 1979 and became a promoter/announcer/referee. In 1992, he opened the Wrestling Hall of Fame in Newton, Iowa. Thesz underwent a triple bypass heart surgery in 2002 and died about three weeks later from complications.

Saint Louis' **Sam Muchnick** was born in 1905 and died in 1998. He is often called wrestling's equivalent of Pete Rozelle, the NFL Commissioner who turned that sport into a top attraction. He skipped his high school graduation ceremony to go to the Odeon Theater where he saw the great Wladek Zbyszko wrestle in a live event.

In 1926, this Ukranian-born Jewish man joined the sports staff at the St. Louis *Times*, which merged with the *Star* in 1932. While there, he developed acquaintances with Babe Ruth and Al Capone. Muchnick also covered professional wrestling where he formed a friendship with Tom Packs, who was the Midwest's top promoter. Muchnik left the paper in 1932 and became Packs' publicist and booking agent. The duo promoted the Joe Louis vs. Tony Musto fight in 1941 which netted a profit of $14,000. When all Sam got was a $200 bonus, he left his mentor to start his own organization.

Lou Thesz (Nunes collection)

Muchnick's career was interrupted in 1942 when he joined the Air Corps, but after the war he promoted his first event at Kiel Auditorium on December 5, 1945. In 1948, he bolted from the National Wrestling Association to form a rival National Wrestling Alliance. For a while he was rivals with promoter Lou Thesz, but eventually the two joined forces. With Sam as president of the NWA, nearly every other wrestling group in the nation joined his Alliance to gain access to his stars. St. Louis was soon dubbed the **Wrestling Capital of the World**.

Mickey Garagiola

Sam's St. Louis Wrestling Club produced a television program called Wrestling at the Chase on KPLR-TV. It ran from May of 1959 to September of 1983 and it was one of the most popular local productions in St. Louis television history. Colorful Joe Garagiola was the first announcer (from the beautiful Khorassan Room) with male spectators in black ties and women in evening gowns.. Ted Koplar, Harold's son, was the program's director and owner of KPLR TV. Thousands and thousands of Metro St. Louisans became wrestling junkies, transfixed by the thundering spectacle. In 1973, Larry Matysik began calling the play-by-play with Mickey Garagiola as his sidekick. When Mickey wasn't doing wrestling he was one of the main waiters at **Ruggeri's** Restaurant on the Hill. Fans still remember the hilarious charade of bruising, menacing wrestlers losing their cool and going after Mickey at the broadcaster's table.

Playmaker Slater Martin

For 25 years Sam Muchnick was the industry's most influential promoter. His office, at various times, was at the Warwick, Lennox and the Claridge hotels. He was very adept at "matchmaking," which was much more than just pulling names out of a hat. He also shrewdly staged Texas death matches and sent mysterious masked wrestlers into the ring. It was a sellout crowd that saw Johnny Valentine defeat "Hercules" and unmask him as Bobby Graham in 1964.

Sam was seemingly into everything. He showed up regularly in the press box at Cardinal games, was part owner of Cahokia Downs racetrack, and was a longtime member of the Baseball Writers Association, annually casting ballots for the Hall of Fame. Sam and many of his wrestlers were regulars at Jack English's restaurant in west **Belleville**.

January 1, 1982, the day Muchnick promoted his last card, was proclaimed "Sam Muchnick Day" in St. Louis by Mayor Vince Schoemehl.

On reflection, this writer lived through the glorious era when St. Louis was the soccer capital of America, the corkball center of America, the wrestling capital of America. I was in grade school when the Billikens were the national basketball champions, in high school when the Hawks won the NBA title. The St. Louis Cardinals have won seven of their record ten championships in my lifetime, and I hosted a Super Bowl party when the Rams won the NFL title in 2000.

Does it get any better than this?

Other wrestlers this writer remembers include: Chief Don Eagle, Gorgeous George, Johnny Valentine, John Paul Henning, Andre the Giant, Ric Flair, Dusty Rhodes, Vern Gagne, Edouard Carpentier, Dory Funk, Bobo Brazil, Pat O'Connor, Jack Brisco, Terry Funk, Antonino Rocca, Bruno Sammartino, Dick "the Bruiser," Dick Hutton, "Killer" Kowalski, Buddy Rogers, Gene Kininski. And how about those incredible "submission" holds? Fritz von Erich had "the claw, Johnny Valentine had the "brain buster," John Paul Henning had the "bow and arrow," Terry Funk used the "spinning toehold," Buddy Rogers used the figure four grapevine. Others used sleeper holds while a few won matches with the "atomic drop."

ST. LOUIS HAWKS

This basketball franchise was first formed in 1946 and they were called the Tri-City Blackhawks, named for the Tri-cities of Moline, and Rock Island Illinois, and Davenport, Iowa. Coached by Red Auerbach, the Blackhawks made the playoffs the first year. The next year the team drafted Bob Cousy, but made the mistake of trading him to the Chicago Stags. **"Easy Ed" Macauley, who led St. Louis University to a national championship in 1948**, was now playing for the St. Louis Bombers. The last place Bombers folded and Macauley went to the Boston Celtics.

In 1951, the team moved to Milwaukee and changed their name to the Hawks. Big George Mikan and the Minneapolis Lakers were dominating pro basketball at this time. In 1953, the Hawks drafted former 6-foot-10 LSU star, **Bob Pettit**. Despite this, they remained one of the worst teams in the league and moved to St. Louis in 1955. Kerner, with his last place team, discovered that he could not compete with the Milwaukee Braves who had players like Johnny Sain, Warren Spahn, Joe Adcock, Ed Matthews and Hank Aaron.

In 1955, Kerner was offered $100,000 each for Pettit and high scoring guard, Frank Selvy. **Selvy had the distinction of once scoring 100 points in a college game**. Financially strapped Kerner, who had lost over $108,000 of his own money during his ten years of ownership, came within a whisker of accepting the offer from the NY Knicks. Red Holzman was the Hawks' coach at this time.

Kerner desperately searched for an exciting announcer. He knew that the baseball Cardinals had the best in the business with Harry Caray, Joe Garagiola, and newcomer Jack Buck. He finally settled on **"Buddy" Blattner**, a graduate of Beaumont High in St. Louis. The games were carried by KXOK 630 AM. Falstaff beer sponsored most of the games. Charlie Share, Frank Selvy (of Furman), Medford Park, Alex Hannum, and Bob Pettit (Big Blue) played in that first game on November 5, 1955.

Hawks logo

The upstart Hawks, spurred by spirited play from Al Ferrari, defeated the powerful Minneapolis Lakers in the first round of the playoffs, but lost in the next round to the Fort Wayne Pistons, led by George Yardley and Andy Phillip, of **Granite City**, Illinois.

For the 1956-57 season, the Hawks strengthened themselves by acquiring Jack McMahon and Jack Coleman from the Rochester Royals in exchange for Dick Rickets and Chris Harris. However, they lost Ferrari to the Army. The Hawks had the second pick in the draft and they chose All-American Bill Russell. Kerner quickly traded him to Boston for two great players he knew would help the team immediately, **Cliff (Lil' Abner) Hagen and "Easy" Ed Macauley**. That trade ranks as one of the most significant in sports history. Kerner, years later, said if he had it to do all over again he would still make the trade. It took the Hawks to several championship finals and made them a serious contender for a decade. Many analysts think that the Celtic franchise was about ready to fold when they were saved by acquiring Frank Ramsey and Bill Russell in the draft.

Bob Pettit

The Hawks tried to convert Hagen into a guard – a huge mistake. Hagen only got to play forward after Pettit broke his arm in a February game against the Celtics. The Hawks soon realized that if they were going to win a championship they needed a great defensive guard with superior ball handling skills. They acquired **Slater "Dugie" Martin**, who had won several championship rings playing with Mikan and the Lakers. Martin came over from the Knicks in exchange for # 2 pick, Willie Naulls.

Was the Russell trade racially motivated? Kerner says no because they already had a black player in Chuck Cooper.

In 1956-1957, the team started poorly and Red Holzman was fired in mid-season. Player Alex Hannum was made coach. They finished the season with a 34-38 record, but

?, Pettit, Zelmo Beatty, C. Hagen, Len Wilkens, Rich Guerin

barely made the playoffs. The team quickly rebounded and made it to the finals against Red Auerbach's Boston Celtics. With Bob Pettit playing with a cast on one wrist, the Hawks lost a seventh game heartbreaker in double overtime to the Boston Celtics.

The next year they faced the same Celtics, **but this time they won the World Championship in a scintillating game six at St. Louis**. Bob Pettit set a record by scoring 50 points in that contest. I still have fond memories of that game because at the last minute, two of my buddies and I decided to drive over to Kiel and find a last-minute ticket. We must have been the last three people admitted because our seats were in the last row of the balcony, up near the pigeons. The thing I remember most about that exciting one-point nail biter was Pettit scoring 50 and Ed Macauley throwing the ball high up in the air as time ran out so the Celtics couldn't steal the ball. Pettit scored 19 of the team's last 21 points in that storied game.

The next year, Hannum asked for a raise and a two-year contract. Kerner fired him. Ex-Celtic Andy Phillip became the new head coach. Phillip was fired a few weeks into the season and replaced by Macauley. Next, the Hawks made a trade and acquired **Clyde "Boom-Boom Lovellette**, who quickly became a fan favorite. For the 1959-60 season, St. Louis U All-American Bob Ferry was drafted. Sihugo Green was the only African-American on the team. Macauley was 89-48 after two seasons, but was fired and replaced by Paul Seymour – the Hawk's sixth coach in six years.

The Hawks remained one of the premier teams in the league for the next decade. In 1960, under Coach Ed Macauley, the team advanced to the finals again, but lost – once more to the Celtics – in a seven game thriller. The following year, with the acquisition of rookie sensation **Lenny Wilkens**, the Hawks repeated their success, but succumbed to the mighty Celtics again in five games.

The Hawks began to sign more African-American players, including John Barnhill, Cleo Hill, Zelmo Beatty, Chico Vaughn and Bill Bridges. Vaughn's coach at Southern Illinois University at **Carbondale**, **Harry "the Horse" Gallatin** (a **Wood River**, IL native) signed a two year coaching contract in March of 1962. Gallatin, an NBA Hall-of-Famer, was the Hawk's ninth coach in the St. Louis merry-go-round. Gallatin stressed defense and it paid off. Gallatin won "Coach of the Year" honors. The Hawks went 30-7 at home. Pettit was good for 20 points a game, Hagen for 15, Wilkens for ten, Beatty for ten, Vaughn for ten, and Barnhill for another ten. The team was predominantly black but the fans didn't mind because Hagen and Pettit were still the stars.

In October of 1963, 31-year-old Ritchie Guerin became a Hawk. But Guerin never fit in because Gallatin wanted to get the ball to the big men and Guerin was used to being a gunner.

Pettit retired at the end of the 1964-65 season. The Hawks added Paul Silas, a savage rebounder, to the team and he played for four years before being traded away. Ritchie Guerin succeeded Gallatin as coach. The Hawks started poorly in 1965 so Vaughn and Barnhill were traded for "Jumping" Joe Caldwell. For the 1966-67 season, the Hawks obtained Lou Hudson in the draft. He averaged 18.4 points that season. Cliff Hagen, with his patented hook shot, retired that year.

Larry Wilson

During the Hawks' last season in St. Louis, they had **Don Ohl** on their roster, a former graduate of **Edwardsville High**.

As the team became blacker the fan base began to melt away. After Pettit and Hagen retired, the team was essentially all black and attendance fell to about 5,000 per game. Many thought that 6-4 Duke All-America forward **Jeff Mullins** was the next Great White Hope who would bring the fans back. The Hawk's first pick in the 1964 draft, Mullins proved to be a disappointment in his injury-plagued first season. He was traded to Golden State Warriors in 1966 where he blossomed into a three-time NBA All-Star and helped them win a title in 1975.

Owner Ben Kerner became disenchanted with the smallish 10,000 seat Kiel Auditorium. Its seating capacity was the smallest in the NBA. The Hawks played some of their games in the larger Arena, but it was an old building that was not well maintained. City leaders rebuffed his proposal on several occasions and, in 1968, Kerner sold the team and it relocated to Atlanta.

Dan Dierdorf as a rookie

St. Louis Hawks **Hall of Famers** include: Cliff Hagen, Alex Hannum, Red Holzman, Clyde Lovellette, Lenny Wilkens, Ed Macauley, Slater Martin and Bob Pettit. Pettit also won All-Star Game MVP Awards in 1956, 58, 59, 62.

THE FOOTBALL CARDINALS

The Cardinals are the **oldest continuous professional football club in the United States**. The team was first formed in 1898 as the Morgan Athletic Club in Chicago. They began calling themselves Cardinals after they started wearing dark reddish uniforms discarded by the collegiate University of Chicago Maroons.

The Cardinals were charter members of the NFL that was formed in 1920. They were NFL Champions in 1925 and 1947. In 1947, they were led by **former Missouri quarterback Paul Christman** and halfback Charlie Trippi. Their star back of the 1950s was Ollie Matson. Running back Ernie Nevers and defensive back Dick "Night Train" Lane were other standouts of that era.

The team was purchased by Charles Bidwell in 1932.

Bidwell Brothers- "Stormy" & Bill (Globe-Dem.)

They have been under the ownership of the Bidwell family since then. The team moved to St. Louis in 1960. Stormy Bidwell, a co-owner, stayed in Chicago with his family, while Bill Bidwell, a bachelor, moved to St. Louis with the team. Bill ran the team during the week and Stormy flew in from Chicago on weekends to run things.

The last time the grid birds played for a league title was in 1948, losing 7-0 to Philadelphia in a blinding snowstorm. Joseph Griesedieck, of the Falstaff Brewery, and Mayor Raymond Tucker led the efforts to bring the team to St. Louis. Griesedieck became the largest minority shareholder of the team. They played their home games at old Sportsman's Park and did not hold their first game in the new Busch Stadium until August of 1966.

Pop Ivy was the first coach in St. Louis, and one disappointing season after another led to a parade of others including Wally Lemm, Charlie Winner, Bob Holloway and Don Coryell. The Cardinals did manage to win division titles in 1974 and 1975. New stars emerged such as Larry Wilson, quarterback Charlie Johnson, Jim Baaken, Sonny Randle, and Jim Hart.

Perhaps the grid birds' **greatest victory was a 24-17 win in 1965 over the Bart Starr and Paul Hornung-led Green Bay Packers** in a runner-up bowl that was called the Playoff Bowl. When fans began calling the game the "loser's bowl," it was dropped.

In 1973, Don Coryell became the new head coach. In winning back-to-back division titles, the Cardinals were led by QB Jim Hart and a record-setting offensive line that included Dan Dierdorf, Conrad Dobler (said to be the dirtiest player in the league) and Tom Banks. This period was marked by exciting close games, last minute victories, and heartbreaking near misses. The press labeled them the **Cardiac Cardinals**. Team stars from the 1970s included two former Mizzou stars, **Roger Wehrli and Mel Gray**, and running backs Terry Metcalf and Jim Otis. Metcalf was an exciting runner with a penchant for fumbling the ball.

Don Coryell left in 1977 after vehemently disagreeing with management over a first round draft pick, Steve Pisarkiewicz, former quarterback at Mizzou. Pisarkiewicz turned out to be a bust. Another disappointment was **Springfield**, Illinois-born place kicker Steve Little. The former Arkansas star was released after two disappointing years and remains the **highest drafted kicker in NFL history**. Otis Anderson set the Cardinal single season rushing mark with 1,605 yards in 1979.

This writer bought season tickets when the Cardinals drafted Neil Lomax. In 1984, Lomax set the Cardinal record with 4,614 passing yards and with 28 touchdown passes. With RB O.J. Anderson setting rushing records, the Cardinals were a dangerous team. Wide receiver "Three-way" Roy Green also became a star receiver on those early 1980s teams. Amazingly, Green caught passes, fielded punts, and played defense. The grid birds also made the playoffs in 1982, but lost in the first round.

Jim Hart and Terry Metcalf

Two malcontents who were traded away and went on to become All Pros, included Bobby Moore (Ahmad Rashad) and **Bellevillian** Dave Butz. More misfortune! J.V. Cain, an outstanding tight end, collapsed and died from a congenital heart defect. Then there was **hippie misfit, Dave Meggysey**. Meggysey opposed the Vietnam War and would not stand at attention during the National Anthem. He quit football and wrote a tell-all book called *Out of Their League*.

Notable first round loser draft picks included QB King Hill, QB George Izo, RB Larry Stegent and QB Kelly Stouffer.

Receiver Sonny Randle

Owner Bill Bidwell wanted the city of St. Louis to build a new stadium with more seating, but the idea was rejected. They weren't even filling the old Busch Stadium. The team left St. Louis before the 1988 season and went to Phoenix where they became the Arizona Cardinals. They got their first playoff victory since 1947 when Jake Plummer led them to a 20-7 Wild Card win over the Dallas Cowboys in 1998. In 2006, the Cardinals moved into a new state-of-the-art University of Phoenix Stadium with a retractable roof.

Odds and Ends: Chicago Cardinal Ernie Nevers holds the all-time record for points scored in a single game with 46 against the Bears. He was depicted on a U.S. stamp a few years ago.

Cardinal offensive lineman Dan Dierdorf ended up being an announcer on Monday Night football.

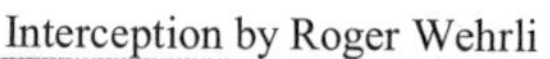

Interception by Roger Wehrli

Running backs O.J. Anderson and Theotis Brown had a radio show in St. Louis called "Otis and Theotis"

The Cardinals were in a very competitive division. It was the best in football with practically everyone else winning a Super Bowl – Cowboys, Redskins, Eagles, Giants.

Neil Lomax had 90 NCAA records by the time he finished his college career. He once threw for seven touchdowns in a single quarter. In 1984, Lomax threw for 28 touchdowns and over 4,600 yards. His passer rating that year was 122. He was selected twice to the Pro Bowl. An arthritic hip prematurely ended Lomax's career (8 years) after the team became the Phoenix Cardinals.

Bellevillian Rusty Lisch, backup to Joe Montana as quarterback at Notre Dame, was drafted by the Cardinals.

Cardinal defensive back Larry Wilson and defensive coach Chuck Drulis **invented the safety blitz**. Wilson once intercepted an opposition pass while playing with casts on both arms.

In the first season of Monday Night Football, the Cardinals defeated the mighty Dallas Cowboys 38-0 (at Dallas) on national television. Johnny Roland, from Mizzou, had a field day and former Cowboy Don Meredith was crying in his beer in the announcer's booth.

The most memorable Cardinals logo was a tough looking redbird with a football tucked under one arm, er wing, and running through the Arch.

Donnie Anderson, a running back from Texas Tech, played for the Birds in 1972.

Jackie Smith made an unfortunate boo boo at the end of his career while playing for the Dallas Cowboys. He dropped a pass in the end zone in the third quarter that would have tied the score against the Steelers in the 1979 Super Bowl. It's considered one of the most famous errors in Super Bowl history because Dallas lost the game. Smith currently holds an executive position with the Casino Queen.

Cardinal football **Hall of Famers include: Larry Wilson, Roger Wehrli, Dan Dierdorf and Jackie Smith**. Other players readers might remember include: RB John David Crow, Mal Hammack, QB John Roach, Joe Robb, Sam (the Rifle) Etcheverry, Prentice Gautt, Pat Fisher, Ernie McMillan, All Pro Bob Demarco, Irv Goode, Jerry Stovall, Sam Silas, Jimmy Hill, RB Bill Triplett, Dale

Meinert, Billy Gambrell, Bill "Thunder" Thornton, QB Charlie Johnson, Willis Crenshaw, Roy Shivers, QB Pete Bethard and Larry Stallings.

THE ST. LOUIS ARENA

The St. Louis Arena opened in 1929 and closed in 1994. Not many years ago it was completely demolished. During its heyday it hosted every conceivable kind of trade show, music concerts, sporting events, circuses, and other forms of entertainment.

Crowds at the St. Louis Arena

My particular fondness for the building goes back to January of 1958. I asked my future wife, Lorna Sanders of Collinsville, for a date. I was working as office boy for Midwest Pipe at the time while she was still a senior in high school. We had known each other since the fifth grade since both of our families attended Washington Park Church of God in East St. Louis.

Lorna was very popular in school and dated numerous boys. For me, a self-conscious awkward kid who wore glasses, it was my first ever date. Originally, we were supposed to attend my church league basketball game at First Church at Riverview and Broadway in north St. Louis. At the last minute, I was able to obtain tickets for the Ice Capades at the Arena.

Blues announcer Dan Kelly

Just getting to her house to pick her up was sort of an embarrassment. Shortly after I left my house in Washington Park, my mom and sister came looking for me. They figured that I would get lost. They were right and they arrived at Lorna's house ten minutes before I did.

I wasn't as embarrassed as most guys would have been, I was too naïve and too happy just to be on a date. We drove to St. Louis in my 1953 Plymouth Savoy sedan. Sitting next to a beautiful girl and watching the Ice Capades was the closest thing to heaven that I had ever experienced.

When it was over, I discovered that I had committed another dating *faux pas*. When we parked I forgot to look and see what row and aisle we were in. We had to wait until most cars emptied from the lot before we spotted my green Plymouth.

When people hear this story they frequently ask my wife, "And you went ahead and married this guy?" We've been married 48 years . . . happily . . . I think.

It was at the Arena that you could also see the Ice Follies, the Police Circus and rodeos. The Auto Show was historically held there until the Cervantes Convention Center was built. There were also horse shows, conventions, tournaments, and the Gypsy Caravan. For a while the Arena was home to an ABA professional basketball team – the Spirits. Marvin "Bad News" Barnes was the star and **Bob Costas** did the radio play by play. It was also home to the Steamers soccer team. (The Steamers lost two championship MISL title games, in 1981 and 1982, to the New York Arrows.) The Arena Bowl was located in an Annex building next door. Because St. Louis was a national bowling hub, numerous championship tournaments were held here.

One of the more memorable events at the Arena occurred when Lou Thesz wrestled and defeated Gorgeous George for the World Championship before a sellout crowd. Other sell-out crowds showed up to see Pavarotti, Neil Diamond and various pop and rock stars.

But the Arena was best known for being home to the Hockey Blue Notes. Ice making equipment was first installed there in 1931. There was one famous incident where the equipment failed and the ice started getting soft. Doors and windows were flung open to the arctic weather outside and fans endured the cold to see the rest of the game.

In the late Forties, St. Louis had the **Flyers** and in the early Sixties the Arena hosted the **Chiefs**, a minor league team. Yet it was the birth of the Blues in 1967 that had the Arena bursting at the seams. Yes! Yes, the Blues. You couldn't beg, borrow or buy a ticket to a Blues game unless you knew someone. Scotty Bowman was the coach and the stars were Glenn Hall, Red Berenson, the Plager brothers, Doug Harvey, Phil Goyette and Dickie Moore. They even went to the Stanley Cup finals three years in a row in 1968, 1969 and 1970. The 19,500 seat arena had the reputation of being the noisiest place in the NHL.

Then the team fell on hard times and Sydney Saloman sold the team in 1977. By the 1990-91 season, the Arena was once again bursting with pride. Brett Hull became a household name. Media coverage grew dramatically. But the glory days were numbered for the Arena. With the completion of the glamorous new Kiel Center, the Blues and the crowds were lured to greener pastures. The International Convention of Lions was the Arena's last hurrah. After 1994, the Arena was a lonely island of concrete.

ST. LOUIS BLUES HOCKEY

The Blues were one of the six teams added to the NHL in 1967, along with the Minnesota North Stars, Los Angeles Kings, Philadelphia Flyers, Pittsburgh Penguins and California Seals. Scotty Bowman was hired as coach. After starting 4-10, the Blues made a trade with the Rangers to get defenseman **Barclay Plager** and center **Red Berenson**. The Blues were the last team to get in the league, chosen over Baltimore at the insistence of the influential Wirtz family of the Chicago Black Hawks. Insurance tycoon Sid Saloman bought the team and spent several million remodeling the 38-year-old Arena. League rules insured that one of the expansion teams would make it to the Stanley Cup finals.

The Blues made it into the playoffs that first season by winning their last game. They advanced to the finals by defeating the Philadelphia Flyers and Minnesota North Stars with numerous thrilling overtime victories. They lost to Montreal in four straight but each game was decided by a single goal. Goalie **Glenn Hall** won the MVP trophy, despite losing four straight, because the opposition had a 151-81 shots on goal advantage. The dominant Blues reached the finals in each of their first three seasons, but were swept by the Montreal Canadiens twice and again by the Boston Bruins in 1970.

Brett Hull

The original stars of the team, Hall, Plante, the Plagers, Goyette, Berenson, Moore, McKenney, Arbor, Harvey and Roberts, were eventually lost to the team through trade or retirement. Red Berenson had an outstanding game in 1968 when he scored **six goals in one night**. The Berenson trade with Detroit, however, brought **Garry Unger**, who ultimately scored 30 goals in eight consecutive seasons and **broke the NHL consecutive games played record**.

Salomon sold out to Ralston-Purina in 1977 and the Arena was renamed the **Checkerdome**. The Blues made the playoffs in 1980 and went on to amass a string of 25 consecutive playoff appearances. Brian Sutter's tenacious play led him to a forty-one goal season in 1979.

Bernie Federko

The Berenson coached team of 1981 was led by **Wayne Babych** who had 54 goals, **Bernie Federko** with 104 points, Brian Sutter with 35 goals, and goal tender Mike Liut, who finished second to Wayne Gretzky for the Hart Trophy. Unfortunately, the Blues were eliminated in the second round of the playoffs by the Rangers.

After the 1983 season, Purina sold out to Bill Hunter who planned to move the team to Saskatoon in Canada. The League vetoed the deal. Harry Ornest bought the team and renamed the Checkerdome back to the Arena. Ornest ran the team on a shoestring budget. They only had 26 players under contract while most other NHL teams had 60 or more (including the farm team). During this time, **Doug Gilmore** emerged as a superstar. Gilmore would go on to become only the second player in the team's history to score more than 100 points in a single season.

In 1986, the Blues reached the semi-finals against the Flames. In the famed **Monday Night Miracle**, the Blues made a furious comeback to tie game six, and won it in overtime on Doug Wickenheiser's goal – one of the greatest moments in team history. But the Blues lost game seven by a 2-1 score. By the early 1990s, the Blues landed **Bret Hull** (from Calgary), **Adam Oates** (from Detroit for Bernie Federko), **Curtis Joseph, Brendon Shanahan and Al MacInnis**. Unfortunately, when the Blues signed Shanahan to a contract an arbitrator unfairly made them give up outstanding defenseman Scott Stevens as compensation. The Blues were always contenders during this period, but never made it past the second playoff round. A consortium of 19 companies then bought the team and built the Kiel Center (now the **Scottrade Center**), which opened in 1994.

Harry Caray

The "Golden Brett" (his father Bobby was the "Golden Jet") had 86 goals in the 1990-91 season.

A dark cloud now arrived on the scene in the name of general manager and coach, abrasive Mike Keenan. Fans thought for sure they had a Stanley Cup when **Wayne Gretzky** was acquired from the Kings, but there was little chemistry between Hull and Gretzky, and the Great One left for the Rangers the next season. Keenan, who traded away several fan favorites, was fired in 1996. Brett Hull scored the 500th goal in his career in the 1996 season. Hull left for the Dallas Stars in 1998, and his team won the Stanley Cup the next year.

In 1999-2000, the Blues won the President's Trophy for having the best regular season record in the league. However, they were stunned in the very first round of the playoffs, losing to the San Jose Sharks. They were competitive for the next three years, but never got past the second round. Chris Pronger, Pavol Demitra, Pierre Turgeon, Al MacInnis and goalie Roman Turek kept the Blues a contender.

In the 2005-06 season, the Blues finished with their worst record in franchise history and missed the playoffs. The crowds dwindled to about 12,000 and fans lost faith in the team.

Columbia native Bill Laurie, who married into the Wal-Mart fortune, sold off most of the name players on the team and quit the franchise. The new owners set about the task of restocking player talent. On June 30, 2007, the Blues signed Keith Tkachuk to a contract. In July, they signed Paul Kariya and Barret Jackman to contracts. They also traded prospect Carl Soderberg to the Bruins for goalie Hannu Toivonen.

Blues players that have made it to the **Hall of Fame** include Bernie Federko, Grant Fuhr, Wayne Gretzky, Glenn Hall, Doug Harvey, Dale Howerchuk, Guy Lapointe, Al MacInnis, Joe Mullen, Jacques Plante and Scott Stevens.

The Blues play their home games at the

Kiel Center. It is a 20,000 seat sports arena located directly behind Kiel Auditorium.

What Blues' record of sorts ended with the 2005-06 season? The St. Louis Blues ended a Guinness Book of Records streak in the 2005-06 campaign when they failed to make the playoffs **for the first time in 25 years**. Sports buffs searched records everywhere and could not find a single instance to match this sports longevity streak.

Young Mike Shannon

What else did the Blues accomplish by having the fewest points of any team during the 2005-06 season? First pick in the draft – something new for them

What St. Louis Blues hockey players have had their numbers retired? Al MacInnis, Bob Gassoff, Barclay Plager, Brian Sutter, Bernie Federko

While the Blues have given St. Louis fans many exciting moments over the decades, they have yet to win the Stanley Cup and have a reputation for amassing a good regular season record and then folding in the playoffs.

CARDINAL MEMORIES

In the days of my youth I had fond memories of listening to hyperbolic Harry Caray describe the heroics of my favorite team. Yes, folks, I bleed Cardinal Red. I was born in September of 1939, and during my three score plus nine on the planet the mighty Redbirds have given me plenty to cheer about, including seven of their ten World Series victories in my lifetime.

The latest improbable story to unfold is the heartwarming saga of **Rick Ankiel**. Back in 2000, he had the best curve in baseball and won eleven games as a rookie. But, in the playoffs against Atlanta, the pressure got to him and he threw something like six wild pitches and was yanked from the game. He spent the next five years in the minors trying to regain his form, but in the history of baseball, no pitcher has ever recovered from such an extreme streak of wildness. His athletic prowess enabled him to try a comeback as an outfielder, but injuries slowed his progress. Ankiel showed signs of promise in 2007 spring training, but was sent to the minors for seasoning where he led the AAA league with 32 homers.

In early August, the Cardinals brought him up to replace Scott Spezio who went to substance abuse rehab. To paraphrase a *Post-Dispatch* writer: "In a script right from a Hollywood movie, Roy Hobbs, er, Rick Ankiel, beat the Dodgers with a late inning home run that resulted in a spine-tingling standing ovation and a tip-of-the-hat curtain call." Ankiel hit two more homers on Saturday, and on Sunday he smacked a double in a 10-2 rout of the Dodgers. When Ankiel hit that first four-bagger, he became **only the second player since Babe Ruth to accomplish the feat of hitting a homer as a pitcher and then hit another one later in his career while playing another position**. His heroics were pure baseball nirvana, and once again Cardinal fans had hopes for a pennant run down the stretch. It's the stuff of which dreams were made.

Rick Ankiel (Topps card)

On August 31, Ankiel pounded a grand slam home run to beat the Reds (8-5) and to enable Tony LaRussa to replace Red Schoendinst as the winningest manager in Cardinal history.

Yes, this writer has witnessed dozens of great Cardinal moments throughout the years. Thank you, God, for the wonderful gift of memory. I have memories, when I was a climber of birch trees, of my dad and uncles excitedly talking about Rogers Hornsby hitting .426 and Grover Cleveland Alexander pitching the Cards to a World Series win. I sat there wide-eyed, eating a Moon pie, as they reminisced about the glory days of the Dean brothers and the Gas House Gang of the 1930s. I hardly believed my ears when they talked about third baseman "Pepper" Martin, the "Wild Horse of the Osage," stopping hot smashes with his chest, and then picking up the ball to throw out hitters.

Jack Buck

The Cardinals have the proudest tradition in the entire National League, leading the Senior Circuit with ten World Series victories. The Redbirds have won two out of three against the Red Sox, two out of three against the Tigers, and three out of five against the mighty Bronx Bombers. What makes it even sweeter is that we beat the pin-stripers in 1926 when they had Ruth, in 1942 when they were led by Joe Dimaggio and in 1964 when they sported the dynamic duo of Mickey Mantle and Roger Maris. Awesome!

What follows is a list of some of my other favorite Cardinal moments. Stan Musial is the only player to hit 475 home runs or more and never once lead the league in round-trippers. I was listening to the game on KMOX radio when Stan hit five homers in a double-header against the Giants at Sportsman's Park. Stan won seven batting percentage titles, but one of my favorite moments occurred when he was a pitcher. Back in the early 1950s, he was locked in a tight batting title race with Frank Baumholtz of the Cubs. It came down to the last day in a game in St. Louis. Musial got a couple of early hits in that game and had the title locked up. The next time Baumholtz came to bat, Musial came in from right field to pitch to him. Baumholtz hit a screaming liner to Red Schoendinst, who couldn't handle it. The official scorer gave the redhead an error. Musial waved from the mound to try to get it changed to a hit, but the arbiter was adamant.

Other great memories: The first two extra-inning All-Star games were won when Stan Musial and Red Schoendinst (from **Germantown**, IL) slugged home runs; Enos Slaughter winning the 1946 Series v. the Red Sox by scoring all the way from first base on a single by Harry Walker; Wally Moon and Bill Virdon winning back-to-back Rookie of the Year honors; Bob Gibson setting a Series strikeout record against Detroit in 1968; Bob Gibson pitching a no-hitter against Pittsburgh; Joe Torre winning the MVP playing first base in the early 1970s; Willie McGee making two spectacular catches and hitting a home run in a Series game at Milwaukee in 1982; Bruce Sutter striking out the last batter to win the 1982 Series; light hitting Tommy Herr leading the league in RBIs at the All-Star game break in 1985; **Jack Clark hitting that dramatic homer** off Tom Niedenfur at Dodger Stadium; Ozzie Smith hitting a game-winning homer off Niedenfur the next game at Busch Stadium; Ozzie Smith doing his patented back flip; Gary Templeton getting 100 hits left-handed and 100 hits right-handed in a single season; Ritchie Allen becoming the first Cardinal since Stan Musial retired (1963) to hit 30 homers in a season; Mark McGuire breaking the home run mark of 61 set by Roger Maris in 1961; slow-footed, third string catcher Glen Brummer stealing home in the 12th inning against the Giants in August of 1982, giving the Cardinals a much-needed win by the score of 5-4; Albert Pujols winning the MVP and Bob Carpenter winning the Cy Young Award in the same year; Jim Edmonds' dramatic homer in the playoffs in 2004 against Houston; Anthony Reyes setting a record last year by becoming the pitcher with the fewest regular season wins (5) to ever start game one of the World Series, and then winning that game; the Cards setting the record two years ago for winning the World Series with the fewest regular season wins (83), and, finally, beating the Cubbies – anytime!

Vic Vac's 1944 World Series cartoon

There was a second baseman named **Bo Hart** a few years back. Like Ankiel, he was brought up from the minors in the second half of the season and injected new life into the team with his spirited play and timely hits. Probably the most dramatic moment came when he struck out instead of getting a hit. Appreciative fans, the best in baseball, gave him a standing ovation. Can you imagine that? A standing ovation for whiffing at the plate! Infielders on the opposing team probably looked at each other in amazement thinking, *I want to play here in front of these fans.*

Albert Pujols

Have there been any heartbreaks? Yep, the agony goes along with the ecstasy for diehard fans. I cried when that bum Frank Lane traded my hero, young and cocky outfielder Jackie Brandt to the Giants. In 1956, he hit .298 and led NL outfielders in fielding with a .990 percentage. Lane broke my heart again when he traded future Hall of Famer Enos "Country" Slaughter to the Yankees. Enos cried when he learned that he had been traded. I get this sick feeling in the pit of my stomach when I think about losing the World Series to the Tigers and Twins, both in game seven. Against the Twins, we won all three games at home, but couldn't get a single win in their nightmarish monstrosity of a domed stadium. Then there was the 1985 loss to Kansas City when umpire **Don Denkinger made the worst call in baseball history**, costing the Birds a Series-winning sixth game. That inept call cost manager Whitey Herzog, of **New Athens**, IL his second title, and probably a trip to Cooperstown, NY.

Yet, over the years, the pluses far outweigh minuses. Stand tall, Cardinal fans, the only team in baseball with a more glorious and historic tradition is the Yanks. In Series play, however, we are the only National League that has dominated them (three or more confrontations). The Cards are 3-2 against the Yanks in World Series play. No brag, just fact!

Odds and Ends: After infielder Ted Sizemore retired from baseball, he became an executive with the Rawlings Company of St. Louis.

Cardinal lefty Wilmer "Vinegar Bend" Mizell, of the 1950s, holds the current National League record by walking 9 batters in a game while managing to pitch a shutout.

Hispanic Cardinal outfielder Jose Cruz was traded to Houston and did so well that they retired his jersey number.

Pitcher Jason Isringhausen holds the Cardinal franchise record for saves with over 200.

Right fielder Preston Wilson (son of Mookie Wilson (NY Mets, 1980s), Houston's second leading RBI man in 2006, was signed by the Cardinals in August of that year.

Cardinal slugger first baseman/ right fielder Chris Duncan was on the **Desmet** High School state championship team.

Travel limitations were placed on the two St. Louis teams during World War II. The St. Louis Browns held spring training in **Cape Girardeau** and the Cardinals were allowed to train in **Cairo**, Illinois.

What issue arose with the new Busch Stadium in March of 2006 concerning the issue of "potty parity?" Originally the new stadium had 352 stalls for men and 313 for women, but complaints forced officials to promise that the Cardinals would play for a tie and the number would be equal.

What infield duo owns the Cardinal mark for most double plays in a season? Mark Grudzielanek and David Eckstein.

What Cardinal relief pitcher, that got the third out in the 1982 World Series win against Milwaukee, was recently elected to the Hall of Fame? Bruce Sutter who is generally **credited with inventing the split-fingered fastball** that dramatically dips as it approaches home plate. Sutter was stolen from the Cubs when the Cards sent Ken Reitz, Leon Durham and Ty Waller up north.

Stan Musial and Red Schoendienst won the first two extra-inning All-Star games with homers.

Stan Musial never homered in downtown Busch Stadium. He retired in 1963 and it was completed in 1965.

When the All-Star Game was held at Busch Stadium in 1966, Casey Stengel commented, "It holds the heat well."

Three St. Louisans lived on "the Hill" and were elected to baseball's Hall of Fame – Jack Buck, Joe Garagiola and Yogi Berra.

Former Cardinal Terry Moore owned a bowling alley complex on Natural Bridge and another one in **East St. Louis.**

Cardinal great Stan Musial was known for playing the harmonica.

In the 2006 World Series Tony LaRussa became only the 2nd manager to win a World Series in both leagues. His first was with the Oakland Athletics.

Cardinal first baseman Jim Bottomley drove in a record 12 runs in a 1924 game against Brooklyn. He went sis for six that day with two homers and a double.

David Eckstein became the first player to start a Series going 0-11 and then becoming the Series MVP (2006).

The Detroit Tigers set a record in the 2006 series. **Their pitchers committed five errors**; the team as a whole committed eight errors and the Cards capitalized on every one of them, scoring eight runs off the errors.

There was something unusual about the Cards win over the New York Mets in the NLCS. They took down the Mets without a win from ace Chris Carpenter and only one RBI from Albert Pujols. The Cardinal with the most post-season hits in 2006 was catcher Yadier Molina with 19 – this after batting only .216 in the regular season.

Scott Rolen had the highest batting average in the 2006 World Series. He went 0-17 in the 2004 World Series against the Red Sox.

The TV ratings for the 2006 World Series were the lowest in history because no east or west coast team was involved. Most dimwitted fans nationwide have no knowledge of the storied history of the Cardinals.

What was the Cardinals post-season ERA compared to the regular season in 2006? Their regular season ERA was 4.54 compared to 2.05 in postseason.

Significantly, what is Tony LaRussa's uniform number? Ten. The 2006 Series win ensures that LaRussa will be elected to the Hall of Fame.

How many National League pennants have the Cardinals won? Seventeen.

Besides Stan Musial, who is the only player to hit five home runs in one day? St. Louisan Nate Colbert – in a double header v. Milwaukee. Musial did it against the Giants.

Dick Schofield was the Cardinal's first Bonus Baby.

The Cardinals played their first home night game in 1935.

Cardinal manager Whitey Herzog, from **New Athens**, Illinois, was known as the "White Rat."

The 1986 Cardinals lacked a true slugger. Slick center fielder **Andy Van Slyke** led the team in home runs that year with 13.

The Van Slyke trade to Pittsburgh was unpopular because he was colorful, a fan favorite, and just about every year with the club his RBI totals and batting average had increased. In his first year with Pittsburgh he hit 21 homers and batted .293. He also won five Gold Glove awards in seven years with Pittsburgh. He still does baseball commentary and lives in St. Louis County.

Marty Marion (Nunes collection)

St. Louis was desperate for a quality catcher and obtained sit-down catcher Tony Pena in exchange for Van Slyke.

Third baseman Terry Pendleton hit .324 in 67 games in 1984, his rookie season.

Will it be easier or harder to hit homers in the new Busch Stadium compared to the old? Harder – The corners and power alleys are about five feet deeper than the old ballpark. The only shorter distance is center field at 400 feet instead of 402.

Who did the Cardinals trade to the Houston Astros to obtain Joaquin Andujar in the middle of the 1981 season? Outfielder Tony Scott – a steal for the Birds

Who was the National League's only 20 game winner in 1984? Joaquin Andujar

How many bases did Vince Coleman steal in 1985, his rookie season? 110

Who were the top Cardinal pitchers in 1986? Bob Forsch led the club with 14 wins and Danny Cox led the team in ERA with 2.90. Todd Worrell had 36 league-leading saves, a NL record for a rookie.

What was Willie McGee's best year as a Cardinal? He hit .296 his rookie year in 1982, but in 1985 he led the league with 216 hits and led the league with a .353 batting average.

What Cardinal had his own brand of chocolate chip cookies? Willie McGee

What Cardinal tied a major league record by hitting **four homers in a single game**? Mark Whitten

What Cardinal won seven batting titles and was never ejected from a game? Musial

What Cardinal pitcher, named "the Cat," was the ace of the Cardinal staff from 1944-1949? Harry Brecheen

What was Brecheen's record in the three different World Series he pitched in? 4-1; his Series ERA is a record 0.83

What St. Louis-born catcher hit .316 in the 1946 World Series and shared catching duties with Del Rice for most of his career? Joe Garagiola

Hammons Field, home of the Springfield Cardinals

What Cardinal third baseman holds the major league record for hitting **two grand slams in one inning**? Fernando Tatis against LA in 1999; his eight RBIs in a single inning is also a record.

What Cardinal was traded to Oakland in the middle of the 1990 season and ended up barely winning the AL batting crown with a .324 average? Willie McGee

Stan "the Man" Musial (author's collection)

Did pitcher Bob Forsch ever have a 20 win season? Yes – in 1977

How incredible was pitcher John Tudor in 1985? Acquired from Pittsburgh, he started off with something like a 1-7 record but ended up 21-8 with a league-leading 10 shutouts and a 1.93 ERA.

What long time Cincinnati slugger/speedster did the Cardinals acquire in 1999? Eric Davis

When the Cardinals won the 1982 World Series, who was the MVP? Catcher Darrell Porter

What was the distance from home plate to the foul poles at old Busch Stadium? 330 Feet

What is ironic about Tony LaRussa's tenure as Cardinal manager? He has over 2,000 wins as a manager, good for 5th place on the all time win list, yet a good number of Metro St. Louis fans think he is mediocre.

What announcer got into trouble because he said Willie McGee looked like the alien in *E.T*? Howard Cosell

What was shortstop Marty Marion's nickname? Slats – He was also called "Mr. Shortstop" because he covered more ground than any other shortstop in his time.

What was third baseman Mike Shannon's nickname? Moonman

What Cardinal hit a key grand slam home run in the 1964 series against the Yankees? Series MVP Ken Boyer

What Catholic high school did Mike Shannon attend in St. Louis? CBC

What Cardinal great was chosen "Player of the Decade" in the 1950s by the *Sporting News*? Stan Musial

Where is the *Sporting News* published? In **Creve Coeur**

What happened to a foul ball hit by Ozzie Smith in a 1979 game? The ball went high and deep into the left field corner and was caught bare handed by Giants outfielder Kevin Mitchell. It is considered one of the great catches in baseball history.

Who is the only player ever to hit a ball out of old Bush Stadium? Reserve 1st baseman Mike Laga – it was a foul ball that he hit in 1986.

Dizzy and Daffy Dean

Why do the Cardinals have very few "seat cushion" promotion nights? In 1987, Tommy Herr hit a grand slam to win a game in extra innings on a cushion night. Thousands of fans went nuts and sailed their complimentary cushions onto the field.

In Cardinals' head-to-head competition with the Cubs, which team holds the edge in total games won? Cubs

Who did computers pick to break Roger Maris' record of 61 homers in a season midway through the 1998 season? Sammy Sosa, of the Cubs, because Sosa played in chummy Wrigley Field and he had a larger "sweet spot" zone for hitting homers than Mark McGuire. The year 1998 is referred to as the "Summer That Saved Baseball" because fans had lost interest because of the 1994 strike. Fan interest was rekindled due to the Sosa-McGuire slugfest.

What Florida State bright prospect's first major league hit for the Cardinals was a homer in September of 1998? J.D. Drew

What Cardinal rookie pitched a no-hitter in 1999 thus becoming only the 7th rookie to hurl a no-hitter? Jose Jimenez, who tossed a 1-0 gem against Arizona

Hailed as the next possible Mickey Mantle, why didn't J.D. Drew pan out for the Cardinals? After several mediocre years where he seemingly was always plagued by injuries, the Cardinals shipped him off to Atlanta where he quickly made the All-Star team the next year.

What Cardinal won the Cy Young award for 2005? Chris Carpenter. Al Pujols won the MVP award the same year but the Cardinals lost to Houston in the playoffs.

What Cardinal set a club record with 14 homers during the month of April in 2006? Albert Pujols; the club also set a record for most wins in the month of April.

Who became the first Japanese player to make the Cardinal roster? So Taguchi – a very solid ballplayer

What player had a dramatic homer in game six against Houston in the 2004 playoffs? Jim Edmonds

What Cardinal 3rd baseman missed two years of playoffs because opposing players keep running into him on the base paths? Scott Rolen

Busch Stadium switched to Astroturf in 1970 – grass returned in 1996. The new stadium of 2006 has Kentucky bluegrass.

Scott Rolen, who batted .314 with 34 homers and 124 RBIs, led the National League All-Star Game balloting in 2004.

What Cardinal pitcher holds the team record for the most wins (14) in his first year as a starter? Adam Wainwright

Mark Mulder won the first game ever played in the new 2006 Busch Stadium in a contest against Milwaukee.

Three Cardinals won Gold Gloves for 2004 - Scott Rolen, Jim Edmunds and Mike Matheny.

The Cardinals lost the 2004 World Series 4-0 to the Boston Red Sox. Had such a whitewash ever happened to them before? Yes – they lost 4-0 to the Yankees in 1928.

Why did the Cardinals not bother signing Mike Matheny to a contract after 2004? They had Yadier Molina, incredibly good at throwing runners out at 2nd base, waiting to take over. He had a one out of thirty start at the plate but ended up having a fairly productive season.

What former Colorado Rockies star outfielder did the Cardinals sign in 2004? Larry Walker – a very good lifetime .314 hitter, he was one of few batters who did well in the 2004 Series against the Red Sox

What Cardinal shortstop, acquired from the Marlins, developed into an all-star hitter and fielder from 2001-2004? Edgar Renteria

What Cardinal star defensive catcher took himself out of the playoffs one year by accidentally cutting his finger with a hunting knife? Mike Matheny

What Missouri town did Albert Pujols call home? **Kansas City**

What nickname was given to the 1987 World Series between the Cardinals and Kansas City? The Interstate 70 Series

What nickname was given to the World Series in 1944 between the Browns and Cardinals? The "Trolley Series" because both teams were from the same city

What former Cincinnati outfielder, thought to be at the end of his career, was very productive for the Cardinals in 2004-2005? Reggie Sanders

How many African-American players were on the Cardinals 2005 roster? Two – Pitcher Ray King and Reggie Sanders – both released in 2006. African-Americans dominate pro football and basketball rosters, but not baseball. Jackie Robinson is turning over in his grave.

Where is the Stan Musial statue at the new Busch Stadium? Gate number 3 (main gate) at Spruce and Eighth streets by the MetroLink station

How far away is the railing on the Poplar Bridge approach from the new stadium? Eighteen feet – which is illegal by MODOT standards, but it was a mistake that was allowed to stand.

What was done to the bridge approach next to the stadium? Construction for the new park undermined the highway so extra pillars, steel cables and support girders were added to the roadbed.

What Cardinal first baseman won the National League MVP in the 1970s and went on to manage both the Cardinals and Yankees? Joe Torre

What was the first band to play in the new Busch Stadium in St. Louis? Bob Kuban and the In Men

What temperamental third base slugger did the Cardinals get in a trade in 1970 with the Phillies? Dick Allen

Did Dick Allen have a good year for the Cards? He hit 30 homers, but was such a disruption that he was traded to the Dodgers in 1971 for Ted Sizemore, a disappointment.

What Cardinal led the National League in ERA in 1979 with a 2.52 average? John Denny

What outfielder was obtained from the San Diego Padres one-fourth of the way into the 1978 season? George Hendrick, who had some very productive years for the Cards. The Cards sent pitcher Eric Rasmussen to the Padres.

What 1980s Cardinal worked as a male model in the off season? Tito Landrum

Who did the Cardinals trade to Oakland to get lefty Mark Mulder? Dan Haren; so far Herrin has been a very productive pitcher while Mulder has struggled with injuries.

By May 29, 2008, outfielder Rick Ankiel had 25 RBIs.

What was 1930s Cardinal Hall of Fame infielder Joe Medwick's nickname? "Ducky"

Al "Red" Schoendinst

What was 1930s Cardinal infielder Leo Durocher's nickname? "Leo the Lip"

How many times did Cardinal pitcher Jeff Suppan pitch against Roger Clemens before he finally beat him? Five

What Cardinal won the 1946 World Series by scoring all the way from first base on a single by Harry Walker? Enos Slaughter

What ex-Cardinal was playing left field for the Yankees when Don Larsen pitched his perfect game against the Dodgers in 1956? Enos "Country" Slaughter, who was also in left field for the Yankees when Bill Mazeroski hit a dramatic game seven homer to win the 1960 Series for the Pirates

What was Ted Simmons' nickname? Simba

Who was the Cardinal manager in 1953? Eddie "the Brat" Stanky

What 1952 Cardinal player was nicknamed "Peanuts?" Harry Lowery – infielder/outfielder

According to scuttlebutt, what took so long for Slaughter to get into the Hall of Fame, despite having a career .306 batting average? In a game against the Brooklyn Dodgers he slid into third base with his spikes flying high. He was accused of being a racist because Jackie Robinson was the third sacker at the time. Those who defend the delay say it's because he was never the dominant player at his outfield position.

What Cardinal right hander joined the team in 1944 and had a 17-4 record his rookie season? Ted Wilks

Slaughter races home to win the 1946 Series

What Cardinal pitcher had a 15-7 record in 1943? Max Lanier

What Cardinal pitcher had a World Series record 7 game winning streak from 1964, '67 and '68? Bob Gibson

What Cardinal set a NL record by playing in 57 straight games at 2nd base in 1950 without making an error? Red Schoendienst

What Cardinal 3rd baseman in the early 1950s was tabbed good hit, no field? Ray Jablonski

What Cardinal hitter has

the highest lifetime average in the NL? Rogers Hornsby at .358. Musial's lifetime average was .331.

How did Wally Moon gain national attention, playing for the Dodgers in 1959 when they were playing at the L.A. Coliseum, while Chavez Ravine was being built? There was a very short distance to left field, protected by a high screen. Moon perfected a hitting style that enabled him to get a lot of "cheap" home runs.

Who did the Cardinals get when they traded Al Hrabosky to the Royals at the end of the 1977 season? Mark Littell

What good hitting, good fielding Cardinal first baseman was foolishly traded to the Mets in the 1983? Keith Hernandez - in exchange for pitcher Neil Allen who was traded away after two mediocre seasons

Curt Flood

What two brothers were pitching sensations for the Cardinals in 1957? Lindy and Von McDaniel; Von developed a sore arm and had only one good year; the duo won 22 games in 1957. (Von won 7)

What Cardinal pitcher was in 987 games, 2nd on the all-time list, when he retired? Lindy McDaniel

What Cardinal won the National League batting title in 1947 with a .363 average? Harry “”the Hat” Walker (he was always fiddling with his hat).

Fans from what city gave Musial the nickname, "the Man?" Brooklyn Dodgers – After Musial clobbered the Dodgers in a double-header, fans moaned when he came to the plate – "Oh, no! Here comes the man again."

What 1950s Cardinal was one of the greatest minor league sluggers in history but was a bust in the majors? Steve Bilko

What diminutive Cardinal lefthander of the 1950s pitched a perfect game for the Pirates in 1959, but lost in 13 innings on a hit by Joe Adcock of the Milwaukee Braves? Harvey Haddix, who won two games against the Yankees in the 1960 World Series

What three professional teams called Sportsman's Park their home? Cardinals, Browns, and football Cardinals

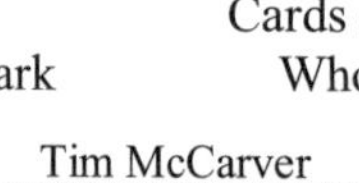

Tim McCarver

What Cardinal clobbered three homers in the 1964 World Series against the mighty Yankees? Ken Boyer

What player hit the most career homers while playing for the Cardinals? Stan Musial – 475

What Cardinal outfielder of the 1990s also played defensive back for the Atlanta Falcons? Brian Jordan

What Cardinal hit the most home runs at the old Busch Stadium? Ray Lankford

What slugging first baseman for the Montreal Expos was a huge disappointment for the Cardinals in the 1992 season, hitting .243? Andres Galarraga – the Cardinals traded him away the next year and he continued to terrorize National League pitchers. In fairness, he did have a wrist injury with the Cardinals.

What Cardinal pitcher broke Bruce Sutter's club record for saves in 1992? Todd Worrell with 128

What Cardinal reliever of the early 1990s had over 200 saves in his career with the Cubs, Red Sox and Cardinals? Lee Smith

What native St. Louisan hit .302 as a Cardinal left fielder in 1992? Bernard Gilkey

Was Lou Brock a lifetime .300 hitter? No – he finished at .295

What former Dodger was picked up by the Cards late in his career and hit .301 as a first base/outfield player in 1975? Ron Fairley

What Cardinal was Rookie of the Year in 1974? Outfielder Bake McBride – the **Calloway Kid** (rural Missouri)

What Cardinal catcher hit .332 and had 18 homers and 100 RBIs in 1975? Ted Simmons

What Cardinal relief pitcher was known as the "Mad Hungarian?" Al Hrabosky

What was Hrabosky's quirky mannerism? Wearing a Fu Manchu mustache, he psyched himself up by turning his back on batters and stomped a ritual-like path around the pitcher's mound.

What Cardinal pitcher threw two no-hitters, one in 1972 and another in 1973? Bob Forsch

What slick fielding, lead-footed Cardinal third basemen led the league in fielding percentage every year he was with the team? Ken Reitz – he was traded to the Giants for Pete Falcone at the end of the 1975 season, but the Cardinals got him back a year later by shipping pitcher Lynn McGlothen to the West Coast.

What nickname did Ken's teammates give him? The Zamboni Machine, because he sucked up ground balls

When the Cubs traded Jerry Morales and Steve Swisher to the Cardinals in 1978, who did they get in return? The Cards sent them Hector Cruz and Dave Rader

Who was the Cardinal manager in 1978? Ken Boyer

What Cardinals manager, for over 11 seasons, overcame tuberculosis as a player in 1959? Red Schoendienst

What Cardinal shortstop/ 2nd baseman of the early 1990s was once brought in as a relief pitcher in a game that got out of hand? Jose Oquendo

What Cardinal outfielder broke Maury Wills' stolen base record with 118 steals in 1974? Lou Brock

What Cardinal catcher of the 1980s stole home against the Giants in a key 1982 pennant race game? Glen Brummer

What Cardinal player won World Series rings with the Phillies, Cardinals (1985), and Royals (1987)? Lonnie Smith

What Cardinal hit over .400 in 1926? Rogers Hornsby - .426

What made Rick Ankiel's first major league homer (2007) significant? It won the game against the Dodgers and the

Cardinals went on to take the series three out of four. In those four games, Ankiel hit three homers and made several outstanding catches. **He received five standing ovations from an appreciative crowd**.

After Rick Ankiel won the game against the Reds on August 31, 2007, with a grand slam, where was his batting average? .328 – tops on the team. The next day, on this author's 68th birthday, he went 3-4 with three RBIs, raising his average to .354.

What was Ankiel's role when the Cardinals swept the Reds (3-2) on Sunday, Sept. 3? He homered again, and then drove in the winning run with a clutch sacrifice fly.

What was the significance of this win for the 2007 team? It put them above .500 for the first time since April.

Julian Javier – Cardinal second baseman for twelve years

In the World Series between the Cards and Twins in 1987, what record was set for a seven game series? The home team won every game.

What first base slugger was the heart and soul of the 1967 and 1968 Cardinals known as **El Birdos**? Orlando Cepeda

What was Cepeda's nickname? Baby Bull

What Cardinal hit a three-run homer off Jim Lonborg to seal the win in game 7 of the 1967 World Series? Julian Javier

What **Granite City** native was the good glove, no hit shortstop for the 1967 Cards? Dal Maxville

What Cardinal 3rd baseman had to retire at age 31 because of a rare kidney ailment? Mike Shannon, who for years has lived in rural **Edwardsville**

When pitcher Bob Gibson broke his leg in mid-1967, who replaced him as a starter? Nelson Briles who won nine straight games

In the 1967 World Series, how many runs did Bob Gibson and Steve Carlton give up in 33 innings? Three

Did Roger Maris have a good World Series in 1967? Yes – he batted .385 and had 7 RBIs.

What three Cardinal catchers went on to become renowned radio-TV commentators? Bob Eucker, Tim McCarver and Joe Garagiola

Who was the first African-American to play for the Cardinals? First baseman Tom Alston

Willie McGee

Trading Steve Carlton to the Phillies probably cost the Cardinals two trips to the World Series. Who did they get in return? Pitcher Rick Wise in 1971 - a bust

What Cardinal outfielder owned a Dodge dealership in **East St. Louis** during the 1970s? Lou Brock

What Cardinal was traded to the Phillies, refused to report, and **set the foundation for "free agency" in baseball**? Curt Flood

What Cardinal infielder set a record by getting 100 hits lefthanded and 100 hits from the right side of the plate in a single season? Gary Templeton

How did Ozzie Smith celebrate important victories? He did a standing back flip.

What Cardinal was traded to the Cubs to get Lou Brock? Ernie Broglio – who turned out to be a bust

What was the first time in the National League Championship Series that the home team won all seven games? Cards v. Houston in 2004

Who defeated the Cardinals in the 1968 World Series? Detroit Tigers, with three game winner Mickey Lollich beating Bob Gibson in game seven

What Cardinal tradition was broken by this Series loss? It was the first time they had ever lost game seven in the World Series.

What two other teams subsequently won Series game seven from the Cards? The Minnesota Twins and Kansas City Royals

What major league record was set by the Cardinals bull pen in the 2006 playoff division series against San Diego? The Cards won the series 3 games to 1 and the bull pen didn't allow a single run in 13½ innings. It had never happened before in either league. This was accomplished by Tyler Johnson, Josh Kinney, and closer Adam Wainwright.

Who was the first Cardinal pitcher to have four straight double digit win seasons since Bob Tewksbury 1990-1994? Matt Morris – he's like that little girl with the curl on her forehead. When he's good, he's very good, but when he's bad he's horrid. Matt retired from baseball in 2008.

What Cardinal pitcher was suspended for several games for allegedly having an illegal substance on his cap? Julian Tavarez

Who quickly became the fan's favorite Cardinal player in the 2005 season? Peppery shortstop David Eckstein

What is Lou Brock's most painful memory as a player? In the 1968 World Series against the Tigers, he failed to slide at home on a key play and was tagged out.

1964 WORLD SERIES

In this segment I thought it would be nice to take readers back to 1964. My wife and I had just moved into a brand new brick house at 203 Bill-Lou Drive, in Lakeview Acres, on the northern edge of **Collinsville**. My cousin, Ray Noones, still lives in that subdivision. My wife was teaching second grade and I was starting my first year as a social studies teacher at Collinsville High. It was some year for me. I was nominated for a Jaycees' award as an outstanding freshman teacher, the Cards won the World Series that fall, and at the end of the school year Collinsville, led by Denny Pace, won the IHSA state basketball tournament.

The exciting 1964 Series pitted the Cardinals against the favored New York Yankees who won 99 games during the regular season. The Cards made it to the Series thanks to a dramatic stretch run and a collapse the last three weeks of the season by the Philadelphia Phillies. It proved to be the last hurrah for the 1950s dynasty of Mantle, Berra, Ford and

Maris. The Cards won the Series in 7 games with Gibson (2-1; 3.0 ERA) being named the MVP. Jim Bouton actually outpitched Gibson in the Series with a 2-0 record and a 1.56 ERA. The series featured the rare brother against brother matchup of Ken and Clete Boyer. Winning manager Johnny Keane quit the Cards when the Series was over and became the Yankee manager, replacing Yogi Berra. It wasn't a smart move because the Yanks fell into last place in 1966.

Roger Maris was traded to the Cardinals for the 1967 season and he hit .385 in the World Series against the Red Sox. Stan Musial barely missed out on the Series, having retired at the end of the 1963 season. Perhaps the most decisive statistic in determining the final outcome was the uncharacteristic nine errors committed by the Bronx Bombers.

The Cardinal strength was in their infield. In the 1963 All-Star game, the starting National League infield consisted of Bill White, Julian Javier, Dick Groat and Ken Boyer – all Redbirds.

Ken Boyer

Mantle, playing in his last World Series, hit three homers, raising his total to a record-setting eighteen, surpassing Babe Ruth's mark of fifteen. Tony Kubek was injured and did not play in the Series. Phil Linz played in his place.

Nearly 31,000 fans at Sportsmans Park saw the Cards' Ray Sadecki win the first game 9-4, sparked by a four run sixth inning that featured a homer by Mike Shannon. New York returned the favor in game two as Mel Stottlemyre bested Bob Gibson and the Pin Stripers won 8-3. Phil Linz hit the game's only homer.

Jim Bouton won game three in front of 67,000 fans at Yankee Stadium as the Yanks pulled out a 2-1 victory when Mickey Mantle homered in the bottom of the ninth off knuckleballer Barney Schultz. It was a knuckleball that didn't flutter.

The Redbirds tied the Series in game four with Roger Craig prevailing over Al Downing by the score of 4-3. The turning point came when Bobby Richardson fumbled a Dick Groat double play grounder and then Ken Boyer hit a grand slam at Yankee Stadium.

Game five is usually seen as pivotal and Bob Gibson won that one 5-2. The game was scoreless until the fifth when Richardson fumbled another double play grounder, this time off the bat of Curt Flood. Lou Brock singled in one run and another came in on first baseman Bill White's grounder. In the controversial 9th, the Yankees rallied when Joe Pepitone hit a smash that caromed off Gibson, who quickly recovered and threw to first. The umpire called the runner out in a close and controversial play. Subsequent film examination showed that the runner was probably safe by a hair-thin margin. Tom Tresh then tied the game with a homer and the Yankees felt that the score should now have been 3-2, game over.

Roger Maris

Catcher Tim McCarver smacked a three run homer in the 10th and the Cards returned to St. Louis with a 3-2 edge.

In game six, Curt Simmons was pounded for homers by Mantle, Maris and Pepitone (grand slam), knotting the Series even with an 8-3 win.

The stage was set for the final decisive game seven. Gibby pitched against Stottlemyre after just two days rest. It was a homerfest as Mantle, Linz and Clete Boyer clouted round trippers. Lou Brock and Ken Boyer homered for the Cards who had a 7-3 lead going into the ninth. Gibson tired and gave up two solo home runs but managed to close out the Yanks with a complete game. Bobby Richardson got his thirteenth hit in this contest, tying a Series record. His two key errors, however, made him the goat of the series. He also made the last out of the Series, popping out to Granite City's Dal Maxville.

The Cardinal announcer for the games was Harry Caray. He was fired in 1969 and the Hall of Fame broadcaster finished his career with the Cubs.

This confrontation is considered a watershed event in the history of baseball since the Yankees had few African-Americans on their roster while the Cards featured Gibson, Brock, Bill White and Flood. David Halberstam wrote in *October 1964* that the 1964 series is seen as an important bellwether point in baseball indicating a permanent paradigm shift demonstrated by the National League's growing enthusiasm for black players. This is somewhat ironic because the current Cardinal roster has few black players. African-Americans have increasingly gravitated to pro football and basketball, and the void has eagerly been filled by Latino players.

This win enabled the fabled Cardinals to be the only team with an edge against the Yankees in World Series competition, minimum of three different contests. The Cards won in 1926 when they had Ruth, 1942 when they had Dimaggio, and in 1964 when they had the M & M boys. The Red Birds lost to them in 1928 and 1943.

1967 WORLD SERIES

The 1967 Series pitted the Cardinals v. the Red Sox. The Sox had Cy Young winner Jim Lonborg and Triple Crown winner Carl Yastrzemski. The Cardinals won 101 games despite Bob Gibson sitting out July and August with a broken leg. **Nelson Briles** filled in admirably for him. Steve Carlton won 14 games in his first full season for the Redbirds. The heavy-hitting Sox were slight favorites going into the Series.

Game one featured Gibson against Jose Santiago at Fenway Park. The Cardinals scored a run in the third on a single by Lou Brock, a double by Curt Flood and a ground out by Roger Maris. Boston tied it in their half of the inning when Santiago homered. The Cardinals scored the winning run in the seventh when Brock singled, stole second and came around to score on ground outs by Flood and Maris. Gibson shut out the Red Sox the rest of the way for a 2-1 victory.

In game two, Lonborg outpitched Dick Hughes and Boston prevailed 5-1. Julian Javier had the game's only hit for the Cardinals. Yastrzemski drove in four runs with two homers.

Ted Simmons

In game three at Busch Stadium, Nelson Briles bested Gary Bell as the Cardinals won 5-2. Briles won 14 games for the Cards that year with a 2.43 ERA. The Redbirds scored a run in the first on a Brock triple and a Flood single. Shannon hit a homer in the second with McCarver on board. The Cardinals added an insurance run in the sixth when Brock singled and went to third on a wild throw. Maris, who had ten hits in the Series, singled him home. The Cards got another run in the eighth when Maris singled and Orlando Cepeda doubled him home. Boston scored their final run on a Reggie Smith round tripper.

Gibson pitched a shutout gem in game four and the Cardinals went up 3-1 in the Series. Jose Santiago suffered his second defeat. The Cards scored four in the first off hits by Brock, Flood, Maris, McCarver, Javier and Dal Maxville. McCarver and Javier drove in the final two runs of the game for a 6-0 triumph.

Jim Lonborg outpitched **Steve Carlton** in game five as Boston prevailed 3-1. Boston scored one in the third and Carlton departed after the sixth, with the score tied 1-1. The Sox scored two in the ninth when manager Red Schoendinst erred by replacing reliever Ray Washburn with Ron Willis. George Scott, Rico Petrocelli and Reggie Smith did most of the damage. Maris spoiled the shutout bid with a ninth inning homer.

In game six, at Fenway Park, rookie Gary Waslewski bested one-year Cardinal wonder Dick Hughes (16-6). Boston had their hitting shoes on as they clobbered the Cardinals 8-4. Petrocelli, Smith and Yastrzemski homered for the "Beantown Bombers" with only Lou Brock answering for the Cards. The game was tied 4-4 in the seventh, but in the bottom half the Sox put the game out of reach with four more runs. Cardinal reliever Jack Lamabe took the loss.

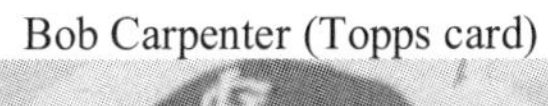

Bob Carpenter (Topps card)

In game 7 it was ace against ace – Gibby v. Lonborg. Boston newspapers angered Gibson with the boastful headline, "Lonborg and Champagne." But Lonborg struggled on only two days rest. The Cardinals scored two runs in the third. Then **Gibson hit a homer** in the fifth and the Cards got another when Brock singled, stole two bases (**a Series record 7th**), and came home on a Maris' sac fly. Javier also hit a three run homer in the fifth. The final score was 7-2. Gibson, with three complete game wins, was the Series MVP. Only two other pitchers in Series history had three wins in one series. Both teams committed four errors.

Cepeda, Maxville, Flood, McCarver and Shannon barely hit .200 in the series. **Javier, Brock** and **Maris** were the hitting stars. Yastrzemski hit .400 and had three homers.

1982 WORLD SERIES

The 1982 World Series matched the Cardinals against the slugging Milwaukee Brewers, with the Cardinals winning in seven games. The Cardinals won the East division by three games over the Phillies, then defeated the Atlanta Braves in three games to move on. My son and I were at Busch Stadium for the first game of that series. The Series was referred to as the **Suds Series** because of Anheuser Busch and Miller Brewing calling the two towns home to their facilities.

Paul Molitor set a Series record by becoming the first player to have two four hit games. Catcher Darrell Porter won the MVP award in the Series. The two teams seemed unevenly matched. The 1982 Brewers hit 216 home runs for the season, earning them the nickname Harvey's Wallbangers, after Coach Harvey Kuehn. The light hitting Cards had mustered a mere 67 homers. Gorman Thomas and Ben Ogilvie combined had 74. The Brewers were without the services of 1981 MVP Rollie Fingers due to a torn arm muscle. A loss in the Series would have been galling because the Cardinals had traded Rollie Fingers, Ted Simmons and Pete Vuckovich to the Brewers, getting very little in return.

Game one at Busch Stadium was all Brewers as Mike Caldwell shut out the Red Birds on three hits with a 10-0 score. Paul Molitor and Robin Yount had 9 hits between them. Former Cardinal Ted Simmons homered in the game.

The Cards, playing Whitey Ball (speed, pitching, defense), eked out a 6-4 victory in game two. When Simmons hit his second homer in as many games, the Brew Crew, behind Bob McClure, had a 3-0 lead after three innings. The Cardinals bounced back with two in the bottom half of the third with a hit and stolen base by Willie McGee, followed by a Tom Herr double and a Ken Oberkfell single. The Brewers stretched their lead to 4-2 in the fifth on hits by Yount and Cecil Cooper.

Darrell Porter tied it in the sixth by doubling in two runs. In the bottom of the eighth, the Cards loaded the bases and reliever Pete Ladd walked Steve Braun for the go ahead run. Bruce Sutter got the save with a scoreless ninth.

Both team's aces faced each other in game three at County Stadium. Willie McGee had one of the most memorable games in Series history by making two sensational catches and belting a three run homer plus a solo shot. The game was scoreless until McGee hit a three run blast in the fifth. The Cards scored two more in the seventh when Lonnie Smith hit a triple and came in to score when the throw at third was wild. McGee then hit his second homer resulting in the final score of 6-2. Sutter gave up a two run homer to Cecil Cooper in the ninth.

The Brewers tied the Series by winning game four 7-5 behind Jim Slaton and Bob McClure. Dave LaPoint held the Brewers to three hits in six innings before the roof fell in. The Brewers scored six runs in the seventh inning after sure-fielding Keith Hernandez made an error at first base. Jeff Lahti and Doug Blair were totally ineffective in relief. The most unusual play in the Series occurred in the second inning when Tom Herr hit a sacrifice fly that plated two runners – a series record. McGee and Smith scored, with Ozzie taking advantage of left fielder Ben Ogilvie taking too much time to get the ball back to the infield.

Ozzie Smith

In game five, the Brewers took a 3-2 Series lead as the Brewers won 6-4 behind the pitching of Mike Caldwell. The Cardinals staged a ninth inning rally as Keith Hernandez doubled in a run and George Hendrick singled him in. Bob McClure closed out the game by retiring pinch-hitter Gene Tenace. The Cardinals now had their backs to the wall but were going home to the friendly confines of Busch Stadium.

Game six was unusual in that two rain delays totaled over two and a half hours, and the game did not end until well after midnight. Fans shivered through rain, sleet and snow on a cold October 19 night.

The Cards staved off elimination by winning a blowout. Darrell Porter and Keith Hernandez had two run homers and Hernandez added a two run single. Dane Iorg had two doubles and a triple as rookie John Stupor went the distance, scattering four hits.

Joaquin Andujar and Pete Vuckovich squared off against each other in the finale. The Cards scored first with a run in the fourth on a Lonnie Smith RBI single. Ben Ogilvie tied it the next inning with a solo homer. The Brewers took the lead in the sixth by scoring two runs. In the bottom of the sixth, the Cardinals loaded the bases and Kuehn brought in reliever McClure. Hernandez tied the game with a two run single and then George Hendrick gave the Red Birds the lead with an RBI single. They added two more in the eighth on singles by Porter and Steve Braun. Sutter pitched a scoreless eighth and ninth to clinch the victory. The Brewers hurt themselves by committing ten errors in the Series. Andujar won two games in the Series.

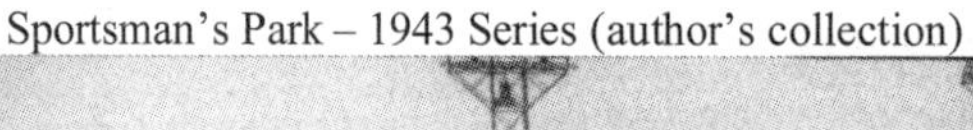

Sportsman's Park – 1943 Series (author's collection)

Sixto Lezcano was the big name in the 1980 trade with Milwaukee in 1980. Lezcano came over from Milwaukee in a multi-player deal. He had decent stats in seven years with the Brew Crew but was terrible with the

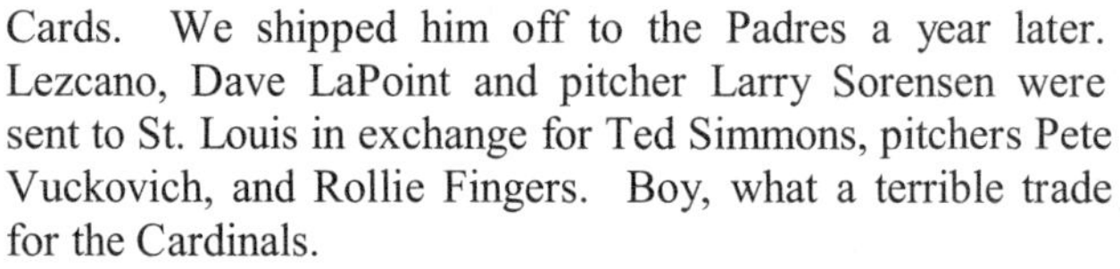

Cards. We shipped him off to the Padres a year later. Lezcano, Dave LaPoint and pitcher Larry Sorensen were sent to St. Louis in exchange for Ted Simmons, pitchers Pete Vuckovich, and Rollie Fingers. Boy, what a terrible trade for the Cardinals.

Dave LaPoint turned out to be the best player in the deal for the Cardinals. LaPoint gave up only 3 runs in 8 -1/3 innings his 1982 World Series start against the Brewers

Dane Iorg set a World Series record for the Cardinals. He had three hits in one game as a designated hitter.

How fearsome were the Brewers as a group of sluggers? They averaged 5½ runs a game during the regular season.

1985 WORLD SERIES

In one of the most dramatic moments in Cardinal baseball history, Jack Clark hit a key 9th inning homer against Dodger pitcher Tom Niedenfur in the NL championship playoffs. Ozzie Smith hit an incredible homer two days later at Busch Stadium to win another dramatic game against the same Dodger pitcher, sending the Cards to the Series.

This was the first Series in history to feature all night games and it was the first time an American League expansion team won the World Series. It was also the last time a designated hitter was not used at an American League park during a World Series game.

The Cards went into the Series with a huge handicap. Vince Coleman, their offensive spark plug, did not play due to a **freak accident**. The Cardinals were practicing at Busch Stadium when it started to rain. The ground crew activated the machine that rolled out the infield tarp and Coleman was standing too close to it and his leg was injured.

The Series was dubbed the **Interstate 70 Showdown**. Ken Daley and John Tudor won the first two games at Royals' Stadium in low-scoring affairs. Bret Saberhagen bested 20 game winner Joaquin Andujar 6-1 in game three at Busch Stadium. John Tudor pitched a 3-0 shutout and Tito Landrum, filling in for Vince Coleman, hit a home run, putting the Cards up three games to one. KC won the next game by defeating Bob Forsch 6-1.

Game six was back at Royals' stadium. Danny Cox had a 1-0 lead going into the bottom on the ninth. Todd Worrell and the relief staff had not given up a single ninth inning lead the entire season. Disaster struck when Jorge Orta grounded to Jack Clark who tossed the ball to Worrell covering first base. Umpire Don Denkinger made the **worst call in World Series history** by saying Orta was safe when he was obviously out. The Cardinals lost their composure and the Royals won the game 2-1 on a hit by former Cardinal, Dane Iorg.

John Tudor didn't have anything on the mound the next night and MVP Bret Saberhagen won game seven by a score of 11-0. Andujar and Herzog were ejected from the game for disputing calls by infamous Don Denkinger, who was now behind the plate.

The light hitting Cardinals set a Series mark for futility with a collective .185 batting average – the lowest ever for a seven game series.

Russ Carter – St. Louis Hop

SPORTSMAN'S PARK

What was the last band to play at the old Sportsman's Park in St. Louis? Bob Kuban and the In Men

What record does Sportsman's Park hold? More games were played there than in any park in history; the Cardinals and Browns called it home.

What was probably the best feature of Sportsman's Park? Fans were closer to the action and could hear the players talking.

What was the biggest drawback of the old stadium? Fans could end up with a seat behind a support pillar.

Which team came first, the Browns or the Cardinals? The Browns went back to 1866 but they evolved into the Cardinals. The new Browns were affiliated with the American Association.

Babe Ruth normally played right field but when he came to Sportsman's Park he switched to left – why? Because the afternoon sun was so bad in right field

Which team started the concept of the Knothole Gang at Sportsman's Park, the Browns or Cards? Cardinals

How did the term "knothole gang" originate? In the days of early baseball the outfield fence merely consisted of plank boards. These boards often had knots in them that fell out. Youngsters could then watch the game free by peeping through the hole.

How much did it cost to join the Knothole Gang? It was free, all one had to do was fill out a request and they sent you a membership card.

Where did the Knotholers sit at the games? The worst seats in the ballpark – in the left field stands near the foul pole

Where were photographers stationed to take pictures? They were allowed on the field, often near what today is called the on deck circle.

Why did lefty Stan Musial enjoy playing at Sportsman's Park? Because of the chummy right field screen

Delicia Devon – Prom Magazine rep at Rockin' 'n' Rollin' teen beauty salon on 9th floor of Famous Barr - circa 1961

How was music piped over the loudspeakers in the early days of Sportsman's Park? It wasn't – high school bands provided music.

How were the starting lineups announced back in the late 1920s? By a man with a large megaphone

When did Gussie Busch buy Sportsman's Park? 1953

What major change did he make? He got rid of the billboards on the outfield walls advertising things like City Ice, Gem razor blades and Sealy mattresses.

What kind of advertising did Gussie put up for Anheuser-Busch? A lighted eagle on the scoreboard that flapped its wings every time the Cardinals hit a homer

What was the last World Series played at Sportsman's Park? 1964 – the Cards beat the Yanks in 7 games.

In the 1930s and early 1940s, what did the outfielders do with their gloves at the end of an inning? They left them in the outfield. This dates back to the days when players shared gloves because of limited incomes.

What were the four streets that surround the old Sportsman Park? Spring and Sullivan, Grand and Dodier

SAINT LOUIS UNIVERSITY

This Jesuit university, established in 1818 by Bishop Du Bourg of Louisiana, is the **oldest university west of the Mississippi River**. With an enrollment of nearly 12,000 students, it is the fourth largest Jesuit school in the U.S. Archbishop John Glennon approved a desegregation policy in 1943. In the early 1970s, a group known as the St. Louis Jesuits released Bible-based liturgical music that enjoyed wide acceptance. Its Griesedieck Complex has some of the largest dormitory rooms in the country with full baths in each 12 x 27 room.

St. Louis University for years was synonymous with college soccer. The men's team has won 10 national titles (between 1960 and 1973), **the most in NCAA history**. They also hold the record for most NCAA Tourney appearances with 43. Billikens who have gone on to play professionally include Shane Battelle, Brad Davis, Vedad Ibisevic, Brian McBride, Matt McKeon, Dipsy Selolwane, Mike Sorber, Joe Clarke, Bob Madison, Martin Hutton, Jack Jewsbury, Tim Ward and Will John. Pat McBride was another SLU standout. He played three times for the U.S. Olympic team in the 1960s. The team plays their home games at Hermann Stadium on campus.

In 1948 the basketball Billikens were ranked number one in the first AP basketball poll ever taken. Led by NBA Hall of Famer Easy Ed Macauley, SLU won the NIT tourney that season and became national champions. (The NCAA title game did not yet exist.)

The last time the roundball Billikens made it to the NCAA Tourney was in 2000 and they have made only a total of six NCAA appearances. St. Louisan **Larry Hughes**, who was drafted by the Cleveland Cavaliers, led CBC to the prep state title in 1997. He is one of the top defensive players in the NBA. In 1998, he led the Bills to the NCAA Tourney where they defeated U- Mass before losing in the second round. Hughes left for the NBA after his freshman year and once scored 44 points against Denver. Hughes missed much of the 2005-2006 NBA season with a broken finger. He was traded to the Chicago Bulls in 2008.

Budweiser All-Star Bowling: Front: Tom Hennessey, Dick Weber, Ray Bluth Middle – Don Carter, Whitey Harris, Back – Pat Patterson

The Billikens managed to set an odd record in their 2005-2006 season. It became a national phenomenon when they started off winning one game and then losing the next one, with the streak reaching 20. Statisticians came up with the odds of win one and lose one for 20 straight games at 24,000 to one. In the 2006-07 season, the Billikens finished with twenty wins.

In 2007, the team had a new coach with an expensive six year contract, **Rick Majerus**. The rotund coach led Utah to the Final Four in 1998 and once was an assistant coach for the Milwaukee Bucks. Two of his players, Tommie Liddell of **East St. Louis** and Kevin Lisch of **Belleville**, were picked to the pre-season All-Conference Team. Unfortunately, the team got off to a horrible start and had a sub-par season.

Midfielder (2003-2007) Brian Grazier of **Edwardsville** was a prep soccer All-American. He had an outstanding freshman year but sat out his junior year due to an ankle injury. Early in his senior year, the Billikens upset #2 ranked Indiana. As a senior, Grazier was the team leader and had a career high five points and helped the Billikens to their third conference title in a row. At the end of the season the Billikens were ranked 12th in the nation. They lost in the NCAA Tournament to Illinois-Chicago via penalty kicks and ended with a record of 12-2-5.

Lonnie Tettaton once worked as a pin setter

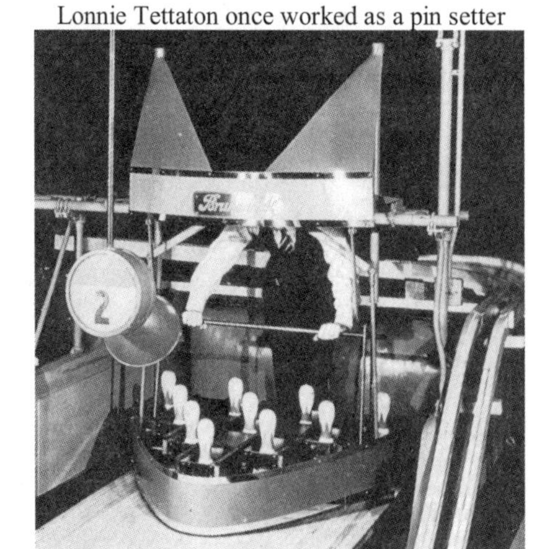

The St. Louis soccer Billikens had an amazing year in 2005-06. They were picked to finish 13th out of 14 teams in the Atlantic Ten. With two games to go they were in 2nd place and lost to 1st place George Washington, out of D.C., by one goal.

Chaifetz Arena, in March of 2008, replaced the Scottrade Center as the university's primary location for large events such as basketball games. The basketball Billikens moved their home games from the Arena to the Scottrade/ Savvis/Kiel Center (at 14th and Clark) in 1994.

BOWLING HALL OF FAME

The Bowling Hall of Fame is located in St. Louis at 111 Stadium Plaza, just northwest of the new Busch Stadium. Bowling was probably invented in Germany around 300 A.D. King Edward III of England once banned the game to force his troops to concentrate on their archery prowess.

In the Washington Irving story, Rip Van Winkle is awakened from his sleep by the crashing of ninepins. Many St. Louis kids earned extra money as pinsetters until the invention of the automatic pin-setting machine by the Gottlieb Company of Chicago. As with wrestling, the national center of this sport seemed to be in St. Louis with the emergence of stars such as **Ray Bluth, Don Carter**, and **Dick Weber**. In 1970, Don Carter was voted the **greatest bowler of all time**. Carter was a member of the "Budweisers" who broke all kinds of bowling records. Ray Bluth, Dick Weber, Tom Hennessey and Pat Patterson were on that team. Dick Weber's son (Pete) is also in the Hall of Fame. He grew up in **Florissant** and started bowling at age two. Pete was temperamental and had a stormy personal life. Despite the troubles and controversy, Pete has 34 PBA tour event wins, tying him for third on the all-time list. Pete's trademark is wearing sunglasses during competitive matches. Other St. Louisans on the elite list include Norm Meyers, Nelson Burton Sr., Nelson Burton Jr., Tom Hennessey, Charles O'Donnell, Pat Patterson and Birdie Humphreys.

In the Fifties, there were televised programs such as *Make That Spare, Bowling for Dollars*, and *Celebrity Bowling*.

Bowling is a worldwide sport participated in by more than 95 million people in 90 countries. Admission to the Hall of Fame is around $7.00. Visitors can even bowl on an old fashioned alley. Since opening in 1984, the museum has dedicated itself to collecting bowling artifacts and memorabilia. There is also a small theater there which shows footage of Hall of Fame members. (314) 231-6340

GOLFER HALE IRWIN

Irwin was born in 1945 at **Joplin**, Missouri, and started golfing at age four. He graduated from the University of Colorado where he was a two-time All-Big Eight defensive back, as well as an academic All-American in football. He also won the individual NCAA Division I golf championship in 1967 and turned professional the following year. Irwin has been a long time St. Louis resident.

Overall, Irwin had 20 victories on the PGA Tour winning prize money of just under $6 million. His great iron play enabled him to defeat opponents on the toughest of courses. His three major titles were the 1974, 1979 and 1990 U.S. Opens. Irwin also played on five Ryder Cup teams with wins on four occasions. During 1975-78 Irwin made 86 consecutive cuts which **ranks fourth in golf history** behind Tiger Woods, Byron Nelson and Jack Nicklaus.

Irwin began playing on the Senior Tour in 1995 and leads the pack of 50 and older golfers with 45 Champions Tour titles and earnings of about $23 million. He was inducted into the World Golf Hall of Fame in 1992.

ST. LOUIS RAMS

When the football Cardinals left for Arizona, St. Louis was left without a team. Despite the Rams being one of the storied NFL franchises, they had fallen on hard times in Los Angeles and attendance was down. This set the stage for a move to St. Louis.

Kurt Warner (author's collection)

The Rams first began playing in Cleveland in 1937. The team moved to Los Angeles in 1946 and played their games at the Coliseum, built for the 1924 Olympics. The 1950 L.A. Rams held the single season team scoring mark until it was broken by the 2007 New England Patriots. From 1980 to 1994 they played their home games at Anaheim Stadium in Orange County, but they kept the name L.A. Rams.

The NFL owners wanted the team to go to Baltimore but owner Georgia Frontiere preferred St. Louis. They relented only after Frontiere agreed to share PSL (Permanent Seat License) money with them. Rich Brooks coached the Rams in the 1995 and 1996 seasons and then former Philadelphia Eagles coach Dick Vermeil was hired. He coached them to a Super Bowl win in 2000 and then announced his retirement. Offensive coordinator "Mad" Mike Martz was hired to take over the reins. The **Greatest Show on Turf** lasted about three years and then Curt Warner, due to lack of protection from a woeful offensive line, was injured. His performance deteriorated dramatically and Martz made the controversial decision to bench him in favor of Marc Bulger. Warner left for the New York Giants after the 2003 season.

Dick Vermeil (author's collection)

Mike Martz was fired in 2005 and Scott Linehan took over for the 2006 season; the Rams started slowly but won their last three in a row to finish at a respectable 8-8.

In 2007, the Rams, beset with numerous injuries, fell to a woeful 3-13 record.

2 SUPER BOWL SEASONS

Going into the 1999-2000 season, the Rams had the worst record of any NFL team for the decade. They sent fumbling QB Tony Banks to Baltimore and signed former **Desmet High** star Trent Green as a free agent. In pre-season Green was electric with 28 completions in 32 attempts. Rams hopes were crushed when Green's leg was broken in a preseason game and they were left with a little-known backup quarterback from Arena Football, Kurt Warner. After playing in college for Northern Iowa, he was drafted and cut by Green Bay. Then he went to work in a supermarket for $5.50 an hour. The next year he signed with the Iowa Barnstarmers. Then he played a year for the Amsterdam Admirals in NFL Europe, while connected to the Rams by a contract. Not much of a resumé. But this was to be a season of miracles and Warner would have a stellar season in the most fantastic Cinderella story in the history of the NFL. The Rams ran roughshod over practically everybody and ended at 13-3. The last loss was a meaningless game at Philadelphia where all the regulars were pulled after the first quarter.

In Warner's first playoff game, against the Minnesota Vikings, he threw for 395 yards and 5 touchdowns. The Rams won the game 49-37 with former Illinois QB Jeff George throwing for 423 yards and 4 touchdowns.

The Rams made it to the Super Bowl by coming from behind to defeat Tampa Bay in the NFC Championship Game. The high-powered Rams, stymied by a stout Buccaneer defense, led by a scant 5-3 at the end of the first half. Tampa Bay took the lead 6-5 with a third quarter field goal, but Warner put the Rams ahead 11-6 near the end of the game with a long throw down the sideline that **Ricky Proehl** hauled in for "the catch."

In the 2000 Super Bowl in Atlanta, the Rams played the Tennessee Titans, one of only three teams that defeated them in the regular season. The Titans barely made it to the Super Bowl, thanks to the last-minute trick lateral play on the kickoff known as the "Music City Miracle" in NFL lore.

The Rams, **led by the lowest paid starting quarterback in the NFL**, started fast and had four first half drives that made it to the Red Zone, but then the Titans stiffened and the Rams could only muster three field goals for a 9-0 halftime lead. St. Louisan **Tina Turner** provided the halftime entertainment.

In the third quarter Kurt Warner threw a 9 yard touchdown pass to **Torry Holt** and the Rams went up 16-0. The Titans, led by quarterback Steve McNair and running back Eddie George, made a furious comeback and tied the score late in the fourth quarter. This was the largest deficit ever erased in a Super Bowl game. On the first play of the ensuing drive, Warner threw a deep pass to **Isaac Bruce,** but Jevon Kearse hit his arm just as he let go of the ball. Bruce came back for the ball and then dodged his way 73 yards past defenders into the end zone. With 1:54 left in the game, McNair drove the Titans from their own ten yard line to the Rams ten yard line with six seconds left, enough time for one more play. McNair completed a pass to Kevin Dyson who turned to dive into the end zone but was miraculously stopped inches short by Mike Jones who made what is known as "**the tackle**." The ending is considered the **most exciting in Super Bowl history**.

Other Rams' stars on this team were tight end Ernie Conwell, RB **Marshal Faulk**, receiver Az Akim, offensive end Orlando Pace and defensive Pro Bowlers Grant Wistrom and Kevin Carter (17 sacks). Punt returner Tony Horne had a league-leading 29.7 return average. Warner was Super Bowl MVP, passing for 414 yards and **breaking Joe Montana's previous record**.

In 2001, the Rams offense once again dominated the league. Their defense was highly ranked, led by defensive end, Leonard Little. They rolled to an impressive 14-2 regular season record and were 14 point favorites to win the 2002 Super Bowl. However, the Rams had defeated New England during the regular season by a mere 7 points. They had practically all of their offensive weapons back from their Super Bowl winning season. Marshal Faulk won the Offensive Player of the Year Award for the third year in a row. Kurt Warner was spectacular as he threw for nearly 5,000 yards to Holt, Bruce, Akim, Proehl, Faulk and Conwell. Kurt also won the league MVP award. London Fletcher, Aeneas Williams, Dre Bly and Dexter McCleon led a tenacious defense.

However, what won the Super Bowl for New England was rarely discussed until 2006. New England defenders were told by their coach to block, hit, grab, push, hold – do whatever it took to knock Ram receivers off their pass routes. Their coach guessed correctly that in a premier event such as the Super Bowl, referees, not wanting penalties to determine the outcome of the game, would be cautious about throwing flags in that situation. Not long after the Super Bowl it was noticed that referees were lax about enforcing the five yard rule and had to be given special instructions to get them to follow procedure and throw the flag. In 2007, the same New England coach was caught cheating by videotaping coaching signals by the opposition. They were only mildly penalized by forfeiting their late first round draft pick.

Cleveland High (Donna Mizell Bullock photo)

The first quarter of Super Bowl 36 ended with the Rams leading 3-0 with Jeff Wilkens making one field goal and missing another. In the second quarter, Ty Law intercepted a Warner pass and returned it for a touchdown, giving New England a 7-3 lead. New England scored again after a Ricky Proehl fumble and led at halftime 14-3. No Super Bowl team had ever come back from more than a 10 point deficit at halftime.

In the third quarter, Warner threw another interception leading to a New England field goal and a 17-3 lead. The Rams responded with a furious rally and tied the game with 1:30 to go in the fourth quarter. The Rams went into a "prevent defense" which allowed New England to march down the field and kick the winning field goal as time expired.

Warner finished the game with 365 yards passing, a Super Bowl mark eclipsed only by his 414 yards in Super Bowl 34. He threw two interceptions, but one was caused when Torry Holt slipped and fell coming off the line of scrimmage. Az Hakim led all receivers with five catches for 90 yards. Marshal Faulk led the Rams with 76 rushing yards and four passes good for 54 yards. This was the first Super Bowl won by a score on the last play of the game.

Ram fans are irate as new revelations about New England cheating have been swept under the rug by the league office. Just before the 2008 Super Bowl, it was also learned that they had illegally taped the Rams' final practice session before the 2002 Super Bowl.

Who scored the first touchdown on the ground for the Rams after they moved to St. Louis from LA? Jerome Bettis

Who caught the first touchdown pass in the dome after they moved to St. Louis? Isaac Bruce

Who was the starting quarterback for the Rams when they first came to St. Louis? Chris Miller

What was Miller's record after six games? He was 5-1 but then suffered a career ending concussion.

What was Miller's most impressive win? A victory over Brett Favre at Green Bay

What was the original name of the Edward Jones Dome? The TWA dome but TWA was bought out by American Airlines and they dropped St. Louis as a hub.

How many fumbles and interceptions did Warner commit in the 2000 Super Bowl? None

What was Kurt Warner doing just five years prior to winning the Super Bowl? Stocking groceries

What did defensive lineman Kevin Carter do with less than 30 seconds to go in the 2000 game that stunned coach Vermeil? He took himself out of the game because he was exhausted chasing after Steve McNair.

What three great accolades were achieved by Warner for the 1999 season? NFL – MVP, Super Bowl MVP, and starting quarterback at the Pro Bowl

Why did Kurt Warner choose number 13 for his jersey? He chose that number to underscore his aversion to luck or superstition and demonstrated his faith in God.

What low water mark was set by the inept Rams in the 2005 season? On December 24 they lost 24-20 to the lowly San Francisco 49ers, their fourth loss in a row at home for the first time ever under the dome.

In what 1978 film did actor Warren Beatty play a Rams quarterback who wins the Super Bowl? *Heaven Can Wait*

What was ironic about the Rams' 1999 season? Until then, the Rams had the worst NFL won—lost record in the 1990's.

What was the Rams' record in 1998 under QB Tony Banks? 4-12

What Rams quarterback was MVP of the 2002 Pro Bowl? Marc Bulger

What Pro Bowl record did Bulger set? He threw for four touchdowns. Remember, quarterbacks in the Pro Bowl only play for a little more than a quarter.

Remember DA Haircuts

By defeating the Dallas Cowboys in the last game of the 2005 season, what was the Ram's overall record? 6-10

What winning streak did the Rams manage to keep alive with this victory? It was their fourth win in a row on nationally televised Sunday Night Football on ESPN.

What streak of ineptitude did the Rams break in this game? It was the first time in 28 games that the Rams didn't have a turnover.

In all fairness, what news did the Cowboys receive earlier in the day that deflated their motivation? They were knocked out of the playoffs by a Washington Redskins victory over the Eagles. However, the Rams had Jamie Martin at quarterback instead of starter Marc Bulger, and aged Marshal Faulk was the running back instead of the injured Steven Jackson.

What amazing feat was accomplished by quarterback Marc Bulger after the first five games in 2006? He set a Rams mark with 214 consecutive passes without an interception, against Green Bay on October 8, breaking the old record of 207 held by Roman Gabriel since 1968.

John Claiborne wearing those unique socks

What Rams receiver won the Good Hands competition at the 2006 Pro Bowl? Torry Holt – defeating Chad Johnson and Steve Smith

What 2003-2005 Kansas City kick return/punt return specialist is one of the most feared in the league? Dante Hall – signed by the Rams for the 2007 season

What Rams offensive lineman has two Super Bowl rings? Adam Timmerman – one with the Packers

What St. Louis Rams radio announcer **died in 2005 from a staph infection** following hip replacement surgery? Jack Snow

What St. Louisan and Rams quarterback attended **Vianney** High and stuck out like a sore thumb because he was only one of eleven Protestants at the school? Trent Green

At the beginning of the 2006 season, what NFL quarterback had the best home record? Marc Bulger 20-4

Cleveland High Dutchmen

In 2006, how close did Marc Bulger come to besting Curt Warner's 1999 records? When he gave way to third stringer Ryan Fitzpatrick in the season ending 41-21 win over Minnesota, Bulger needed only 5 more completions and 52 yards. Amazingly, Bulger had 24 touchdown passes and only 8 interceptions for the season.

What three Rams went to the Pro Bowl in 2006? Torry Holt, Marc Bulger and Steven Jackson. Unbelievably, Leonard Little was left off the team despite having 13 sacks, the second highest total in his career.

What receiving mark did Steven Jackson set in 2006? He led all NFL backs with 90 receptions.

In what sense was Steven Jackson a better football player than MVP LaDanian Tomlinson? Tomlinson finished the 2006 season with 2,323 total yards while Jackson bested him with 2,334 – unbelievable for an 8-8 team.

What was mainly responsible for the Rams' woeful 2007 campaign? Orlando Pace was out for the season after an injury in the first game. Leonard Little missed half the season due to an injury. Bulger missed numerous games due to broken ribs and a concussion; Steven Jackson missed four games, Dante Hall missed most of the season due to injury and Jeff Wilkens started missing easy field goals and was released at the end of the year. Game thirteen, against Cincinnati, saw the Rams use their 9th different offensive line due to numerous injuries. Torry Holt did manage to reach the 1,000 yard receiving mark for the eighth straight season.

Grover Cleveland High was part of the Public School League that consisted of Soldan (Maroons), Southwest, McKinley (Goldbugs) Beaumont (Blue Jackets), Roosevelt (Rough Riders), Sumner (Bulldogs), Central, Hadley Tech (Hornets) and Vashon (Wolverines). Its colors were orange and blue and the teams were nicknamed the Dutchmen. The building itself, marked by two memorable Norman Towers, was referred to as the "Old Castle." The football stadium and track and field complex was directly across the street from the main entrance. Their yearbook was called the *Beacon*. Arthur Svoboda was principal in 1957. Cleveland had a January graduating class as well as a June class.

John Claiborne lettered in football, baseball and basketball at Cleveland. He would go on to become Vice-president of the St. Louis baseball Cardinals. He was an end in football, a catcher in baseball and a forward in basketball. Wes Bokal, who works at St. Louis City Hall, remember him as a teammate on the Wash U. Bears football team. Wes said John also did kickoffs and field goals when they played together in the early 1960s.

Cleveland's 1956-57 basketball team consisted of Charles Hasser, Don Jansen, John Dyn, Bruce Mills, Bill Blasberg, Ray Wichmann, Barry Herr, Bill Rayburn, Norm Harrison, John Claiborne, Baylor Kohut, Stewart Cloud, Carl Weber, Frank Zavadil, Ron Yanker and Coach Earl Jansen.

Most Intelligent: Madeline Lange & Roger Bernhardt; Likely to Succeed: Renee Ryter & Alan Brennecke; Best All Around: Janine Renaud & Jerry Catron; Prettiest/Handsome: Jane Haag & Don Webb; Cutest Smile: Jean Davis & Rich Brandon; Best Dressed: Mary Towns & John Payton; Prettiest Eyes: Diane Gerlitz

& Dan Ekman; Prettiest Hair: Carolyn Robinson & Mike Russo; Best Athlete: Sue Bockrath & Don Jansen; Most Spirited: Mickey Moore & Charlie Wicker; Most Bashful: Mary Battoli & Ron Dencker; Best Musician: Mary Pieske & Norm Nottmeier; Best Laugh: Connie DeArriba & Dave Vogler; Personality: Kay Kaspar & Mel Jackson; Best Dancer: Sue Caldwell & Earl Kestler; Best Singer: Marilyn Moss & John Petri; Chatterbox: Gail Hawkins & Norm Harrison; Artistic: Ginny Funke & Ron Poppen; Most Popular: Pat Hurley & John Claiborne; Cutest Couple: Betty Reed and Don Pasek.

CASA LOMA BALLROOM by David Lossos

The building on the northeast corner of Cherokee and Iowa streets was constructed in 1927. During the first eight years there were no less than five different attempts to make a go at the ballroom business. All ended in financial failure. It wasn't until 1935, when partners Art Kawell and H.J (Nap) Burian took over the reins, that the Casa Loma Ballroom came to be. Art and Nap had teamed up years before, and successfully managed dances at the Triangle Hall, Concordia Turners Hall, and, finally, the Alhambra Grotto prior to taking on the Casa Loma Ballroom. During those early years nearly every big name, and quite a few soon-to-be big names, graced the stage at the Casa Loma.

Original Casa Loma Ballroom interior (David Lossos)

Today you will find that much is the same as it was in the beginning. Stepping onto the smooth oak dance floor is like stepping back in time. On most Friday evenings the "big bands" still play the same tunes that resonated off the walls in 1935, and the "Rock 'n' Roll" sounds of the 50s and 60s return on Saturdays.

One of the rare photos is the Casa Loma Ballroom as it appeared when first built in 1927. Note the ornate ceiling and balcony railings, along with the various "advertising booths" around the perimeter of both floors. They were all local businesses in the immediate area, including Kriwanek Brothers, the Hat Mart, Dilg Schuesser Co., Wessel's Texaco, Cherokee National Bank, A.G. Maass Printing, Wilshire I-on-A Co., the new Cherokee Tom-Boy Market and Schonberg's Markets.

Pianist Russ David

Harry James is best remembered today for his colorful trumpet playing and as the husband of pin-up girl Betty Grable. In 1935, he joined Ben Pollack's Orchestra, leaving in December 1936 for the Benny Goodman band. During his time with Goodman, James became very popular with the jazz crowd for his flamboyant, eardrum-shattering trumpet playing. He became so popular that when he decided to leave Goodman (in December 1938) to form his own band, Goodman himself financed the outfit. The Harry James Orchestra debuted in February 1939. In June of that year, James lured an inexperienced Frank Sinatra as his male vocalist. It was on November 5, 1939 that the relative unknown Sinatra made his debut at the Casa Loma Ballroom, barely being mentioned at the bottom of the nightly bill.

Not even a disastrous fire on the evening of January 19, 1940 could keep the Casa Loma from flourishing. Within the same year it was completely rebuilt on the same site.

The Casa Loma thrived during the Depression, and continued to draw huge crowds into the war years. Servicemen home on leave, or getting ready to ship out, packed the ballroom. Many individuals met their spouses at the Casa Loma during this period of turmoil in the world.

A mainstay of Saturday TV in St. Louis during the 50s and 60s was a program called the "**St. Louis Hop**." The hometown version of the highly popular Dick Clark's "American Bandstand" was hosted by **Russ Carter**. He was the emcee of this dance show in St. Louis from 1958 to 1973. The show had several homes, including the Arena Roller Rink, the Casa Loma Ballroom and the Sheraton-Jefferson Hotel before finally ending its run in 1973 at KSD studios. During the 1950s and 1960s the Casa Loma was THE place to be for high school students on a Saturday afternoon.

In 1967, the remaining owner, Art Kawell, sold the ballroom to Ellen and Norman Reichert. Once again, in 1960, after a brief hiatus, the ballroom reopened under new ownership in the person of Pat Brannon and his wife. Under the management of the Brannons, the Casa Loma continues to evolve. Two constants are the big-band sound and Rock 'n' Roll, both still very popular. Currently, the Casa Loma Ballroom features many great touring acts in addition to the area's top name bands. Ballroom, Rock 'n' Roll, Imperial Swing Dancing and many other activities ensure a schedule of excitement at the St. Louis Casa Loma Ballroom.

For nearly three-quarters of a century the Casa Loma Ballroom, a landmark of entertainment in St. Louis, has provided a wide range of popular music and dancing.

Here's a few of the artists that have appeared on its stage:

Al Alberts (4 Aces), Steve Allen, Ray Anthony, Gus Arnheim, Mitchell Ayres, Pearl Bailey, Count Basie, Tony Bennett, Jack Benny, Ben Bernie, Bill Haley and the Comets, Jules Blattner, Blue Barron, Blue Notes, Teresa Brewer, Butch Wax & The Hollywoods, Bill Carlsen, Steve Carlton, Russ Carlyle, Russ Carter, Chubby Checker, Ernie Collins, Perry Como, Ellen Conner, Bing Crosby, Bob Crosby, Xavier Cugat, Bobby Darin, Russ David, Johnny "Scat"

Davis, DeCastro Sisters, DeJohn Sisters, Johnny Desmond, Tony DiPardo, Jimmy Dorsey, Tommy Dorsey, Shep Fields, Ted FioRito, Ella Fitzgerald, Chuck Foster, The Four Freshmen, The Four Lads, Jan Garber, Judy Garland, The Gaylords, Benny Goodman, Gray Hayworth, Skitch Henderson, Woody Herman, The Hilltoppers, Marion Holmes, Bob Hope, Eddy Howard, Russ Hughes, Joni James, Henry Jerome, Jimmy Joy, Catherine Joyce, Dick Jurgens, Max Kaiser, Art Kassel, Herbie Kay, Sammy Kaye, Hal Kemp, Stan Kenton, King Sisters, Bob Kuban, Kay Kyser, Dorothy Lamour, Abbie Lane, Lloyd LaParie, Jerry Lee Lewis, Guy Lombardo, Johnny Mathis, Billy May, Ray McKinley, Fred MacMurray, Glenn Miller, Mitch Miller, Mills Brothers, Modernaires, Vaughn Monroe, Buddy Moreno, Russ Morgan, Nick Mucci Orchestra, Donald O'Connor, the Poni Tails, Dick Renna, Alvino Rey, King Richard, Gale Robbins, Buddy Rogers, Mickey Rooney, Royal Canadians, Joe Sanders, Artie Shaw, Stan Shaw, Julie Sherwin, Tom and Dick Smothers, Teen Tones, Al Trace, Orrin Tucker, Billy Vaughn, Bobby Vinton, Fred Waring, Chick Webb, Ted Weems, Lawrence Welk, Andy Williams, Dallas Wilson, Jonathan Winters and Frank Yankovic.

1947 Mercury "woody"

The Spanish translation of Casa Loma is "happy house," but the owners said the name was chosen, not because of any meaning. They simply liked the sound of it.

MISSOURI COAL MINES

Back in the old days when we threw a shovel of coal into the furnace, few of us realized that we were handling a product that had its origins billions of years ago. This was when the surface of the planet was mainly covered with water and swamp land. The climate and conditions were perfect for the growth of carboniferous plants – giant ferns, trees and shrubs. The air buzzed with mammoth insects of infinite variety, while gargantuan beasts (dinosaurs) and reptiles inhabited the waters and land.

Jefferson Barracks Powder Magazine Museum (L. Nunes)

Coal is a blackish rock that is made from plants that lived and died about 200 million years ago. Because coal is made of once living plants, it is called a fossil fuel. Coal was first discovered in Missouri 200 years ago in 1806. Its presence was noted along the Osage River south of the present site of Prairie City in Bates County. Nearly half of the electricity used in Missouri is generated from coal. Neighboring Illinois has the nation's largest reserves of bituminous coal. It has more BTUs than the oil reserves of Saudi Arabia and Kuwait.

Missouri never had as much coal as neighboring Illinois. Perhaps that was fortunate. Here is the way writer James Deakin put it. "Coal mining regions are hard, harsh, unforgiving and burdensome. Coal was the master; man was slave. The people ground away in the mines, and the mines ground away at the people, turning their skins gray and seamy, giving them black lung, maiming them, and then in the Depression years casting them away. They never had hope; now they had no work either. They sat on the sagging porches of old frame houses, in faded dungarees, staring into an indefinite distance. They coughed and coughed, and then they died."

A typical Missouri coal miner currently earns about $45,500 a year. Missouri has two surface mines and no underground mines. Each day the average Missourian uses about 100 gallons of water and 20 pounds of coal (coal-based electricity). Roughly 83 percent of Missouri's electricity comes from coal, mostly imported from western states.

About one-third of the state had underground coal reserves when the white man first arrived here. Currently, coal mining in Missouri is a relatively small industry, although coal bearing beds still underlie 35,000 square miles, mostly in the northern and western part of the state. Surface mining in Randolph County accounted for 90 percent of the state's output in 1992. Unfortunately, like southern Illinois coal, most of it is high sulphur content. Virtually none of the coal mined in Missouri is shipped out of the state.

It has been estimated that the original amount of coal deposits in the United States exceeded three trillion tons. In Missouri, the coal beds were formed when our inland sea receded and Missouri became a great marsh or swamp with luxuriant plant growth. Peat beds were formed year after year as these plants formed layer after layer. (Peat is an early stage of coal formation.) There was relatively little earth disturbance, so most of our coal is found in beds that are relatively level.

In April of 1885, remnants of an ancient city were discovered near **Moberly** at the bottom of a coal shaft 360 feet deep.

Scott K. Williams has researched St. Louis coal mines, gaining info from a map published by the Missouri Department of Natural Resources at **Rolla,** 573-341-4616. Most of these listed existed between 1850 and 1915. The Chouteau Mine was along Berthold near Kingshighway. The Highlands Mine was near Oakland. The David Jones Mine lay underneath portions of the St. Louis Zoo. There was a slope mine in the 1920s near Deaconess Hospital. The Diggins Mine was in the Dogtown area. The Sublette Mine was at Shaw and Hereford. The Evans and Howard Mine was located south of the River Des Peres. The Laclede Mine was near the south bank of the River Des Peres. The Russell Coal Mine was at Morganford and Bent. The McDonald

Mine was near Arsenal, Grand, Gravois. Peter Delore's Mine was south of Morrow and McGreggor and east of Gravois. The Bingham Mine was at Osceola and Gravois. The Kemper College Mine was along Arsenal between Hampton and Kingshighway.

From about 1850 to 1950, about a third of all coal produced in the state was used by the railroads. And for years, about half the coal produced has been consumed by St. Louis and Kansas City.

What many people don't realize is that most seams of coal are only about two and a half to fourteen feet thick. In the early days of mining, for every ton of coal mined, there was about one and a half tons of coal wasted or left in the mines as supporting pillars. Modern methods of mining and improved equipment have greatly reduced this percentage.

There were three methods of mining coal in early Missouri: the drift, the strip, and the shaft. Where the coal bed outcrops on a hillside or a ravine, the drift or slope method is used. A drift mine differs slightly from a slope mine in that the former follows the seam in on a level, while the slope mine is driven downward at an angle from the surface to reach a vein of coal that does not outcrop.

Another problem faced by miners was the danger of the roof of a mine collapsing. Timbers were used to shore things up, but many mines chose to spray the underside of a roof with a cement mortar called "gunite." It was sprayed on one to three inches thick with a "gun." Mines that were about 300 or 400 ft. deep had temperatures that hovered around 60 degrees. It was necessary to create numerous air passages in mines to provide adequate ventilation to insure the dilution of poisonous and explosive gases generated by the coal, mine water and explosives. It was common in area mines to use the room and pillar method of mining. The greater the depth of the mine the closer the natural pillars were spaced. It was not uncommon for the tremendous weight on the pillars to push down on the clay floor causing the floor to heave, a condition known as a "squeeze." If the floor was hard, the pressure on the pillars sometimes caused them to collapse, closing the mine.

Strip mining, also called open-pit mining, is possible when the seam of coal is an exposed outcrop or close to the surface. The loosened cover or "spoil" can be thrown aside, and large power shovels can be used to load the coal onto trucks or railroad cars. When there is no outcrop, the digging must be started by cutting a 70 ft. wide ditch next to the seam. This ditch is called a box cut. Surface coal usually has lower sulfur content because of oxidation. In the early years, strip mining left ugly scars on the land with a series of furrows, with topsoil mixed with subsoil. The state legislature enacted laws requiring mine companies to restore and reforest the land after the coal has been extracted.

Consumption of coal in America reached a peak around 1918 with over 700,000 men employed.

Back in 1915, a large ocean liner, in making a record trip across the Atlantic, used 4,725 tons of coal, enough to keep 945 families in fuel for an entire year. In a single year, one great steamship company paid seven million dollars for the coal necessary to operate its fleet of steamships, or fifty percent more than it paid for provisions for crews and passengers.

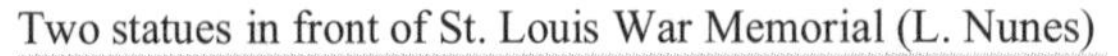
Two statues in front of St. Louis War Memorial (L. Nunes)

Coal was first brought to the St. Louis area from an Illinois mine (about eight miles from the Mississippi) in the bluffs near a small village named Pittsburg (near present-day Routes 157 and 15. The coal was first hauled by mules and horses along tracks with wooden rails. Pilings had to be driven in Pittsburg Lake (Grand Marais) so that a bridge could be constructed across the body of water. **East St. Louis** was in a rudimentary stage of development at that time (around 1834) and the coal was delivered to the riverfront. From there it was loaded on Samuel Wiggins' ferryboats and transported across the Mississippi to the city of St. Louis. The Illinois & St. Louis Railroad fared poorly in its early years because the company overestimated the demand for coal by St. Louis. Wood was still the preferred fuel, even in steam locomotives that came along. But demand for coal slowly increased, and by 1855 the eight-mile long railroad, now with iron rails and a steam engine, was the **richest dollar-per-mile railroad in the nation**. By 1875 coal could be delivered to any part of St. Louis on a railroad track for six cents a bushel. Manufacturers could buy in bulk at $1.50 a ton.

In 1950, there was a general formula used in estimating the amount of coal a family would need to get through a typical St. Louis winter. Experts generally figured one ton per room per season, plus an extra half-ton. So, on this basis, a typical five-room house would ordinarily require almost six tons of coal. Coal was delivered by truck and emptied into the coal bin of the house, located in the basement. Access was gained by a metal door, usually located in the block foundation. By the early-to-mid 1950s, many homes converted to a stoker. This was a machine with a hopper that was attached to the furnace. Instead of using lump coal, stoker coal was pellet sized and was automatically fed to the furnace by a motor-operated worm screw at the bottom of its hopper. Instead of an ash residue, stoker coal produced "clinkers" which were very abrasive on the hands. By the late 1950s, many homes converted again, this time to natural gas. Old coal furnaces were often retrofitted with gas burners.

Historian C.H. Quackenbush says that the most common gas used in St. Louis was coal gas – artificial gas made from coal. This was manufactured by placing coal in a superheated clay retort, which was then closed to exclude air. The heated retort freed the volatile or gaseous matter from the coal. These gases were then carried through a series of pipes and appliances which condensed, washed and scrubbed the crude gas, and by mechanical and chemical means removed the impurities from the product and made it ready for the 400 uses for which gas is applicable.

A second method of making gas from coal was known as the carbureted method. The gas is manufactured by passing steam through a bed of coal or coke in an incandescent state. The action of the hot fire on the steam passing through it decomposed the steam into hydrogen and oxygen. These gases were united with carbon gases from the fuel bed to create water gas. The mixture in that state had little illuminating value, so it was then passed to another machine where it was mixed with an oil vapor. This whole mixture was then fixed into a permanent gas by contact with superheated fire brick. It was then scrubbed and cleaned in a similar manner as the coal gas. Water gas was often used to enrich coal gas, thereby giving it greater illuminating value. The distribution of gas from the storage holder was carried on through a system of about sixty miles of cast iron pipe of diameter varying from four to sixteen inches. The flow of gas through mains is similar to water flowing through pipes, but the pressure is much less, being about 1/9 of a pound per square inch. Wrought iron pipes were laid from the main to the consumer's basement at no charge. Contrary to public opinion, gas meters, which measure the amount of use, are very accurate. They cannot register unless gas at that time is passing through it.

Missouri currently has 20 coal-powered energy producing plants that have a total of 49 coal boilers. It is also the national headquarters for Peabody Energy Company (314-342-3400) and Arch Coal Inc. Peabody is the largest coal producer in the world. Of all the energy sources in use, coal puts more carbon dioxide into the air than any other source.

One of the coal powered plants is in **Springfield**. Springfield's Murray Germany says that trains from Wyoming, pulling 110 coal cars, can be seen coming into the town on a regular basis. In order to make it up some of the steep grades, five diesel engines are required – three in front and two in the rear. Once the terrain levels out, the two at the rear are removed.

Missouri currently has nearly 50 billion tons of coal lying beneath the surface.

WELL WITCHING IN PRAIRIE COUNTRY

By Don Rogier

I grew up on a farm during the Depression. When I was a young teen, I helped my brother Dale dig a well on the family farm. Unlike digging for oil, you don't have to worry much about looking for a specific terrain. You mostly decide upon the approximate location where you want it, usually close to a house or barn.

Next we used the services of a reputable man good at "witching." He used an apple tree branch, stripped of extraneous growth, with a fork in it – much like a Thanksgiving turkey wishbone. The witcher held each branch of the fork in a hand and pointed the remaining piece up in the air in front of him at a 45 degree angle. Then he started slowly walking toward the area where we wanted the well. When he came to the spot where he was perpendicular to an underground stream, the pointer section moved downward, as if propelled by some magnetic force. Now there are those who claim witchers are secretly responsible for the downward turn of the stick. Yet I was once witness to a well hunt where the witcher held tightly to the stick and this strange force was so strong it twisted the bark off the branches.

He then marked the spot with a stake and then walked away from it at a 90 degree angle. Then he slowly walked toward it again, now looking for a place where two separate underground streams crossed. Again, the witching stick bent downward to indicate the presence of water.

Now this process tells you where the water is, but it doesn't tell you how deep it is. For that the man took a six foot long fruit tree branch and held it horizontal to the earth at the spot where the two streams crossed. My brother and I stood in amazement as the branch moved up and down in his hand thirty times. We asked him what that meant, and he said that we would hit water around 30 feet down. "Had it gone up and down forty times," he explained, "that would have indicated a depth of 40 feet."

After the man left, we set about digging the well. It was about three feet in diameter. My brother Dale dug with a shovel and when he got down about four feet we built a frame over the hole to support a winch with a bucket at the end of the rope. Dale would fill the bucket, and I would haul it to the top and empty it. Because digging was the hardest, we regularly switched positions.

We were digging the well in late summer, and we ran into some blue clay that was as hard as concrete. As the going got tougher we went to a nearby rock quarry and bought a case of dynamite with appropriate fuses and blasting caps. We put a stick of dynamite in the hole and set it off. All it did was blow the winch off the top and create a very wide crater. We later learned that what we should have done was cut the stick of dynamite into three pieces and placed them around the perimeter equidistant. Done in that fashion, and set off electronically in simultaneous fashion, the blast would have gone inward instead of outward. We finished digging the well by hand. The dynamite came in handy later when we needed to remove some tree stumps. We also used it a few times for 4th of July celebrations and occasionally to go fishing.

St. Louis Science Center on Route 40 (Lorna Nunes photo)

We struck water about 29 feet deep, and then we pumped the trickling water out and dug down another eight feet to make sure there would be a reservoir of water in the well during dry spells. We knew of other farmers who dug wells on their property and had to go down only nine feet because they encountered a spring.

When we got to the bottom, my brother and I switched places. Dale sent bricks down the bucket and I started laying them in circular fashion. No mortar was used because this method allowed for water to seep in through the cracks. About four feet from the top, we used mortar on the joints to keep out groundwater, which is more easily contaminated. Nowadays the EPA requires mortar to be used ten feet from ground level.

After reaching ground level we went up another foot and capped the well with a solid piece of cast concrete that had a ready-made hole. A pipe was inserted down in the hole and connected to the metal hand pump. The pump had a rubber or leather gasket inside to insure proper suction. But you first had to "prime" the pump by pouring some water into the pump shaft to create the proper suction.

Some farmers would continue the mortared brick another three feet above the ground. Then they built a wooden A-frame roof with shake wood shingles and support beams to hold the winch, rope, and drinking bucket.

When I was married and teaching in **Rolla**, Missouri, during the early 1960s, we needed to drill a well where we were living. We hired a company and they brought in a truck with a drilling rig. The man said there was no need for witching in the area. "There's water anywhere you drill in Missouri, as long as you go deep enough."

The first 20 feet down was all gravel, which required casing. But after that it was all rock which required no casing. They used a rotating hammer drill with a diamond bit, and in the middle of the drill was a pipe that sent down air and water. The compressed air and water forced the ground up rock to the top. It took eight hours to drill 350 feet deep.

For modern three foot diameter wells, installers use concrete tiles instead of bricks. If they drill an eight inch hole they use perforated plastic PVC pipe.

Nowadays witchers often use two bronze brazing rods or metal coat hangers as "divining rods." The two metal rods are bent 90 degrees into an L shape and they grab hold of one end of the rod in each hand while the other piece sticks out horizontally. If they come across a stream the rods will line up parallel to the stream. In recent years witchers were not needed to locate pipes in the ground because metal detectors could be used. But metal pipes rust and corrode and for several decades PVC pipe has usually been used instead of metal. Today, witchers are sometimes used to find where these plastic pipes are buried.

I recently discovered a new and unique use for a witcher. I was doing genealogy research on my family, and I found my great, great, grandmother's grave. I figured my great, great, grandfather was probably buried next to her, but there was no marker for him. I heard about a man who was known for witching graves. At first, I didn't believe it, but reliable sources told me the man could actually witch graves. He uses two metal wires bent at a 90 degree angle with wooden handles. When he searched a vacant spot next to my grandmother's grave, the two rods began to bend inward. "There's a man in that grave; probably your great, great grandfather." He explained that if a woman had been in the grave the rods would have moved off to the side. If a grave site is empty, the rods don't move.

I was very skeptical about this "grave witching" until I blind tested him with graves where I already knew who was in them.

Do I believe in witching or divining rods? Yep. Seeing is believing!

MISSOURI OZARKS FOLKLORE

(sent to me as an E-mail by a friend: source unknown)

A good ol' boy in the Ozarks had two really good coon dogs and this other old boy had a pet monkey. The first man was always wantin' to go coon huntin' with the other guy. So this other boy told him one night, "Yeh, you can go with me." So he told him what time to be there. He got there and this other guy had his pet monkey with 'im.

The guy looked at him and said, "Man, you can't take that monkey out there, the coons'll kill 'im."

"Well," this other guy said, "The dogs trail and that coon'll go right up in a tree. You give this monkey a pistol and he'll go right up there and shoot 'im between the eyes. You see, I've got this monkey trained to kill game. He'll shoot a pistol right at 'em."

The first guy says, "Ah . . .ah . . h, I don't think I can quite believe that."

But they went hunting and this other guy brought his monkey along. The first time the dogs treed a coon the men were able to see him and they shot him dead with their rifles. But the next time the dogs treed a coon the branches were so thick they couldn't see him. Finally, the one man said, "Let me send my monkey up that tree to git that coon." The monkey scrambled up the tree with a small pistol in one hand. Not long after they heard a shot and the dead coon landed at their feet.

The man who owned the dogs shook his head. "I don't believe it, there must be a catch to this somehow."

"No, there ain't either. You saw the monkey come back with a shell missing, didn't yah?"

So time went on and this guy with the monkey, he got sick with the grippe. So the first old boy with the dogs was itchin' to go coon hunting again. He asked his friend if he could borrow the monkey and the pistol, and the man readily agreed.

"Just be sure and bring 'im back when you're through huntin'."

So the first old boy, he took the monkey and he had great success shooting a couple of coons. Finally, the dogs treed a coon and he couldn't see it. He sent the monkey up the tree with the gun and he was gone and gone and gone. Finally, the monkey came back and as soon as he hit the ground he shot both dogs. Killed 'em. Made that guy so mad he would have killed the monkey, but it didn't belong to him. When he got back to the other man's house he was cussin' a blue streak. He told this other guy, "You know what that crazy monkey done? It killed both o' my dogs. They treed a coon and I put that monkey up there. He was gone a long while and then he finally came back and shot both my dogs."

The other guy says, "Oh-h-h yeah-h-h-h, I forgot to tell you something. One thing that monkey hates is dogs that lie!"

Vintage Vinyl in the Delmar Loop (Lorna Nunes photo)

SALT LICKS

Salt, composed of NaCl (each poisonous in its isolated form), has long been recognized as a necessary compound for sustaining life in mammals. In the Bible, Jesus is quoted as saying, "Ye are the salt of the earth." In Roman times soldiers received part of their regular pay in the form of salt. Indeed, the word soldier comes from the Latin *sal dare*, meaning to give salt. Elephants in Africa are known for making long and dangerous treks up to mountain caves that have salt deposits in them. Farmers everywhere buy blocks of salt and place them next to animal watering troughs. Around the globe wild animals make regular visits to salt licks. The animals lick the surrounding earth near the spring which is saturated with salt.

There are places in Missouri that were once 3,500 feet under ground and were brought to the surface by a geological upheaval/anticline. This area is part of the Ozarks, a range older than the Rocky Mountains. This fault system was responsible for the salt springs. These springs attracted deer and bison in early pioneer days. Before that, it was a gathering area for Ice Age mammals such as the Mastodon, Saber toothed tiger, Pleistocene Horse, Giant Bison and Giant Sloth.

Example of an old salt kettle

Southeastern Illinois had an impressive salt lick near the town of **Equality**. In 1803, seven Indian tribes entered into a treaty with the United States whereby our government promised to deliver 150 bushels of "white gold" a year (from the Saline Salt Springs) to the council chiefs. In return, the Native-Americans relinquished claim to some 14,800,000 acres in southern Illinois, virtually abandoning the area. Territorial Governor William Henry Harrison was so eager to secure land for settlement, he frequently didn't bother to check whether the signatories had the authority to sign such treaties.

When Illinois was admitted to the Union, Congress gave the salt licks to the State. In 1819, the Gallatin County salines at **Equality**, commonly known as the "Nigger Works," using over 1,000 slaves, produced nearly 300,000 bushels of salt. **It was the only place in Illinois where slavery was legal**. The Great Half Moon salt lick was one of the largest in the U.S. and covered about 13 acres. This was a crescent-shaped depression in the earth that was caused by numerous animals over the years coming to the spot and licking away at the earth to gain access to the salt it contained. It was the only place in Illinois where slavery was legal.

It is estimated that by 1823, income from the salt works in Gallatin County provided 1/7th of the state revenues. In addition to seasoning, salt was a necessity for preserving food and for tanning hides. Probably its greatest use was for preserving meat.

The brine was collected in large metal kettles that were brought in from Pittsburgh. The kettles held about 60 gallons of water. A fire was kept constantly burning under the kettles. The fuel was wood from nearby trees. The water was brought from the salt wells to the kettles by wooden pipes made from twelve-inch diameter trees that had the centers bored out. Iron bands were fitted over the jointed sections of the logs. The final salt product was then hauled by oxen to **Shawneetown** and then loaded into keelboats. Much of this salt was shipped to **Cape Girardeau** and **St. Louis**. Around 1840, coal came to be used as fuel instead of wood and new furnaces were built. The making of salt at Equality ceased about 1870 because it could be produced cheaper elsewhere.

Many similar salt operations existed at various places in Missouri, but on a smaller scale. Daniel Boone and his sons went up the Missouri River to the central part of the state to obtain salt at a salt lick. It came to be known as **Boone's Lick**. The area where they lived was about 20 miles west of **St. Charles**. Daniel Boone tried to enlist to fight in the War of 1812 but was rejected because he was 78-years-old. He died at age 86.

Saline County is named for its salt springs and licks. Daniel Boone, and a friend named Stephenson, used to carry on horseback a large iron kettle to the salt springs in Saline County. In it they would boil the water used in making salt. The kettle remained in the Stephenson family until 1918 when it was placed in the museum of Central Missouri State at **Warrensburg**.

THE GREAT 1925 TORNADO

Mother Nature flexed her muscles around 1 PM on March 18, 1925, and created a record-breaking tornado that started in southeast Missouri, crossed into Illinois and, three hours later, was wreaking havoc in Indiana. It remains the **deadliest storm in U.S. history**.

The storm originated just north of **Ellington** and it began snapping trees along its destructive path. Fortunately, most of the Missouri landscape that it ravaged was sparsely settled. However, as the storm continued along at a speed of about 55 mph, it hit the Missouri town of **Annapolis**, destroying about 90 percent of the structures. Annapolis is 111 miles south of St. Louis and is located on the Missouri Pacific Railroad. The entire lead industry of that town was devastated as two citizens were killed and 50 were injured. Brick buildings crumbled as easily as if they had been log cabins. In the area just north of **Cape Girardeau**, there were reports of 12 dead and fifty injured. The storm then continued to **Biehle** where it killed ten residents. After hitting Biehle, the storm crossed the Mississippi and devastated the Illinois town of Desoto. It roared all the way across southern Illinois and proceeded to wreck towns in Indiana.

Path of 1925 tornado

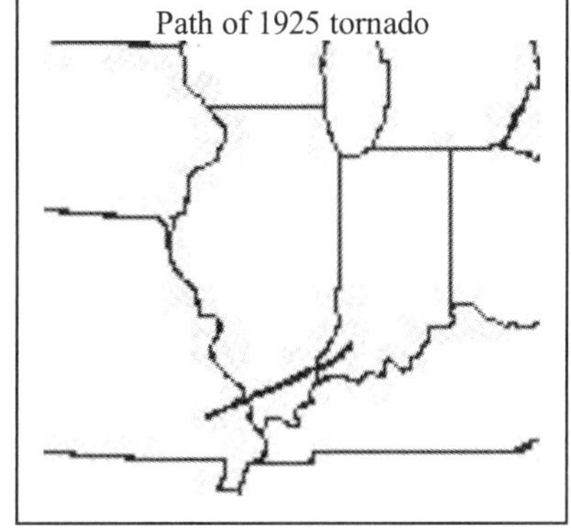

Doctors from **Poplar Bluff** and surrounding areas made haste for **Annapolis** to treat the injured, many of whom were taken by train to **St. Louis** hospitals. The Missouri Pacific Railroad brought in Pullman cars to house the homeless. Damage to the Annapolis Lead Company was estimated to be $200,000 and total damage to the town was $800,000. Of the 300 structures there, only three were left standing. A brick schoolhouse, on the edge of town, survived because it was not in the tornado's path.

Strangest of all, a residence in the middle of town, housing a bed-ridden woman and her family, was surrounded by other destroyed buildings, but was left untouched. However, it was eventually devoured by flames from fires that started because of the storm.

It is estimated that the storm stayed on the ground for 219 miles, a new record. This deadly tri-state tornado killed over 1,000 people and injured over 2,000.

The 1925 storm, in today's terms, would probably be described as an F-5 as measured on a scale developed by University of Chicago scientist Theodore Fujita. The cyclonic winds within the storm might have varied between 200 and 250 miles per hour.

Historian Wallace Akin says that one reason the devastation was so widespread was that the U.S. Weather Bureau had no tornado warning system in place. **In 1925, government meteorologists were forbidden to use the word "tornado," fearing the term might scare people** and ruin commerce for that day.

The terrain of Midwest geography played a significant part in the story since the vast expanse of flat land between the Rockies and the Appalachians allows storms to ravage the area, unimpeded by mountains. The Great Tornado was spawned when moist air coming up from the Gulf of Mexico clashed with a cold front, brought down from the north by the Jet Stream. In 1925, scientists were not yet aware of the Jet Stream. **The Jet Stream was first discovered by Japanese scientists during World War II when they sent incendiary balloons aloft in an attempt to set fire to the woods of the Pacific Northwest.** The southernmost tip of the Jet Stream path pretty well coincided with the path of the 1925 storm through Missouri and Illinois.

Remember the milkman making deliveries?

The parent storm actually started out in Montana and Wyoming two days earlier. As the two air masses collided and moved east, the warm air began to override the cold air and it then shifted counterclockwise, producing a cyclonic wind and a super cell thunderstorm.

The swirling death wind, which swept over the southern part of three states, caused property damage in excess of ten million dollars. The death and injured figures were based on bodies recovered from the stricken area, and upon the number of persons still unaccounted for in the storm-ridden territory. The original figures were revised upward daily.

Dave was once a newsboy

Nine were killed in an 1871 St. Louis tornado. Four more were dead after an 1890 storm. Three were killed and 100 injured in a 1904 cataclysm. Yet another tornado hit St. Louis and **Granite City**, Illinois, in 1927, leaving 79 dead and 550 injured. Finally, in 1959, 21 more St. Louisans were killed and another 345 injured. The 1927 tornado was the **second deadliest storm in U.S. history**. This storm touched down in **Maplewood** and

A wrecked building in Missouri

traveled in a northeasterly direction, barely missing most of downtown St. Louis.

A 1959 tornado hit St. Louis once more, killing 21 and injuring 345. Since big cities are not usually hit by tornadoes (because of their relatively small area geographically), **this makes St. Louis the deadliest large city in America – weather wise**.

ST. LOUIS MEMORIES BY DAVID LOSSOS

I was welcomed to St. Louis on September 4th of 1943 at DePaul Hospital, the fourth child of Ed and Helen Lossos. My family was of modest means, neither rich nor poor. Dad owned a Texaco Service Station at the intersection of Hebert, Elliot and Glasgow, in north St. Louis (dominated by Democrats), but we were always a Southside family (an area dominated by Republicans). My first home was located at 3654 A Folsom, a four family flat. I have vague memories of this home (long since paved over for a parking lot near St. Louis University's Hospital). It must have been crowded though, considering that six of us lived in such a small abode. Dad's sister and her family lived in one of the ground floor flats. I assume that we lived in this neighborhood because my grandfather, John Lossos, was still residing nearby at 2901 LaSalle, the Lossos family home in which he and my late grandmother raised eleven children. We were in **St. Margaret of Scotland parish**, and that is the school that I began my seventeen years of Catholic education. My most vivid memory of kindergarten year involved the annual Halloween practice of school children painting pictures on the outside of various retail stores' plate glass windows. To this day I have no idea how I managed to get this "honor" as a five-year-old. I certainly had no artistic talent, a trait I've managed to maintain my entire life. Anyway, I remember slopping paint on the window of a grocery store on 39th Street. As I recall there was no way to discern what the finished product was supposed to be, unlike the jobs done by my schoolmates in the other eight grades. In spite of that, I remember waiting with baited breath for my dad to see my "work of art" on the way to church the next day. I was devastated when we passed the window and someone had washed just the window that I had painted.

Childhood marble memories

I recall three significant things that took place in 1950. The first was that my mother was pregnant with her fifth child. This was a especially significant since I was giving up possession of the title "the baby" that I had held for eight long and glorious years. Almost as important was the arrival of the first TV. For some reason I still remember my dad and brothers lugging it up all those stairs, plugging it in, and all of us mesmerized watching the **test pattern**. And lastly, my parents finally recognized the need to move to bigger quarters. Mom and Dad choose to move a little further south, to the other side of Tower Grove Park, at 3825 Connecticut, the address that was home until right after graduation from Saint Louis University.

Dave's old TV test pattern

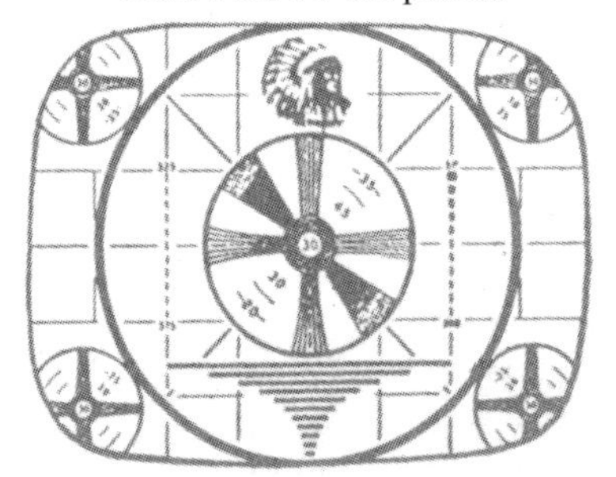

I have nothing but happy memories of growing up. I started 2nd grade at St. Pius V, and later went on to SLUH (1961 grad) before SLU. Along the way I grew up. Tower Grove Park was my true home, where my friends and I spent endless hours riding bikes, climbing the stone ruins of the Southern Hotel near the pond, and taking square dancing lessons behind the tennis courts. I wore the required uniform of white tee-shirt and heavy denim Levis regardless of the 100 degree temperatures of summer. I actually remember the first time I ventured out of the house dressed in bermuda shorts on my way to a "teen-town" at St. Pius - I felt like I was stark naked. I also remember spending so much time at Carpenter Branch Library, where I learned to love books.

For a while I tried delivering **newspapers**, and then a job cleaning up the behind-the-scenes area of a butcher shop. I also managed to pick up easy money by parking cars at my dad's service station that was near Sportsmans Park. Sunday was the only day he didn't work, which worked out well for me during the St. Louis Football Cardinals season. Each summer during high school **I worked at the Muny Opera** as a drink vendor. I not only made good money, but I was able to see every show. During college I was very fortunate to obtain three months work each and every summer in the warehouse of Western Electric Company.

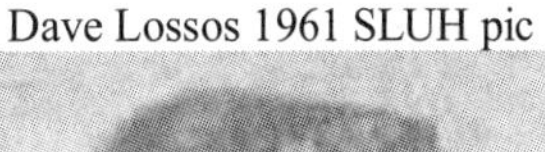

Dave Lossos 1961 SLUH pic

I treasure so many things of my youth that are uniquely St. Louis. I have a website entitled "Genealogy in St. Louis" that has a large following. Back in 2001 I posted some memories I had of growing up in St. Louis including:

I remember when my phone number was MOhawk 2343.

I remember going to see a double feature at the Ritz Theater for 25 cents.

I remember coming into the movie in the middle and eventually saying to the person I was with, "This is where we came in".

I remember the way to get your friend to come out to play was to stand in front of their house and yell their name.

I remember (as a ten year old) being sent to the corner tavern to get my grandma a pail of draft beer.

I remember riding the Grand Avenue electric street cars.

I remember riding my bike in Tower Grove Park (even after dark!).

Much to my surprise folks started sending me their fond memories, so I started appending them to mine. Over the years I've received more than 5600 individual memories, and have posted them all at **http://genealogyinstlouis.accessgenealogy.com/memories2008.htm**

The Hidden Youth of Helen Tappeiner Lossos

by Dave Lossos

Helen Tappeiner Lossos (aka "Mom") was masterful in **hiding the truth about her childhood**. We never heard of her childhood friends, of neighborhood streets where she whiled away the hot days of her St. Louis summers. We never knew about her grade school activities, about teenage crushes. There were never any class pictures, or baby pictures, or, any pictures at all. Of course, she didn't really have to lie about all this because I can't once remember having directly asked her. She simply never told us about the parts of her life that she didn't want to remember.

Mom was born August 31, 1908, the daughter of Conrad Peer Tappeiner and his young bride, the former Philomena (Minnie) Marseiler. In order to understand the conditions under which mom came into this world, it's necessary to give a little background on her parents.

Minnie was born on May 28, 1881, in the small village of Schluderns, in the Tyrol area of the Austrian Alps, the daughter of Louis Marseiler and Filomena Rupp. On another hill above the village lies a castle. Minnie was a twin, her sister being Louisa. We know little of Minnie's youth, but we do know that her two sisters immigrated to the United States before she did. We can only assume how difficult it was for her parents to say goodbye forever to the last of their three daughters.

Minnie arrived at Ellis Island on April 22, 1902, only twenty years old, and had twenty dollars in her pocketbook. At that time in American history, the large influx of immigrants dictated that only those in good health and capable of earning a living were allowed to settle here. When Minnie arrived on these shores, her two sisters were already ensconced in the United States.

Dave wonders if his mom got to enjoy roller skating time while living in an orphanage?

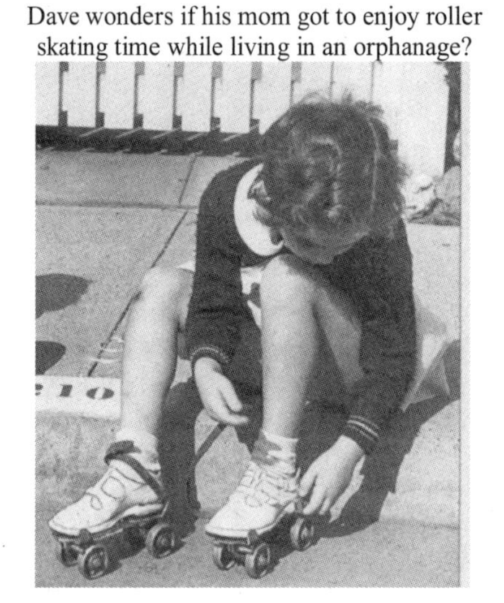

According to the naturalization papers filled out by Minnie, "Coonie", as he was called, was born in Matsch, Austria (which is now part of Italy) on December 12, 1880. He was the fifth of five illegitimate children of Philomena Peer. Why she never married the father, Edward Tappeiner, we will probably never know. Conrad arrived in this country in 1902. Matsch and Schluderns are only about a mile or so apart, which automatically leads one to believe that Conrad and Minnie knew each other before arriving in the U.S.

They married in St. Louis on November 15, 1907, by a Justice of the Peace. A mere nine months later Mom was born, on August 31, 1908. At the time, they were living at 4501 Gravois (near the **Bevo Mill**). Mom was baptized in Holy Family Church (ironically close to where we all lived for so many years). The following year Conrad and Minnie separated on October 11, 1909. We don't know for sure what transpired during Mom's first year, but can certainly gain some information from the divorce papers. In the documents she tells the courts that Conrad was "in the habit of drinking intoxicating liquors, and was in the habit of coming home intoxicated, and when in this condition was extremely violent in his abuse" of her. Minnie goes on to say that Conrad struck her "with his fist" "four or five weeks after their marriage". Also, according to Minnie, Conrad showed no fatherly feelings and affection toward mom, and "on one occasion choked (Helen) in an attempt to suppress (her) crying". Even during the tumultuous first year of the marriage **Minnie had to work as a servant** to help make ends meet. Apparently Conrad, because of his drinking, was unable to hold down a job in spite of the fact that he was a trained carpenter.

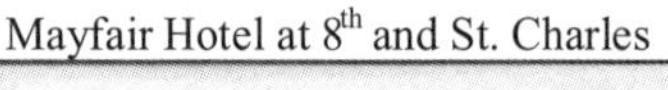

Mayfair Hotel at 8th and St. Charles

The courts granted the divorce in December of 1909. Mom was only 14 months old, and undoubtedly would not have remembered any of that time in her life. The court decreed that Conrad pay Minnie $25 per month in alimony. From what we understand Minnie seldom received it, and therefore was forced to look for work to support herself and mom. As far as I can tell, Minnie's older sister, Josephine, was quite settled, and already had two girls, aged ten and thirteen. In addition, Minnie's twin sister, Louisa, was also living in St. Louis, and had three daughters of her own. It's hard to understand how Mom was confined to an orphanage here in St. Louis for nearly eighteen years with two aunts, both in stable marriages, in the same vicinity.

Minnie never remarried after her divorce from Conrad. I can find no trace of Minnie until 1913 when she was a live-in servant for the wealthy Buss family in **Jennings**. The address was 2601 Hord Avenue, at the corner of Orchard Avenue.

Conrad remarried Anna B. Mueller (nee Klein). He first shows up in the St. Louis County Directories in 1917 as a farmer living on Zeiss Avenue in **Affton**.

We do have the record of Mom's induction into St. Ann's Foundling Asylum and Widows' Home. The register shows that Mom entered the asylum on November 6, 1909, less than a month after Conrad and Minnie separated (and before the divorce was even granted). She remained in the care of St. Ann's Home until September 5, 1913. As St. Ann's Home cared for boys and girls from birth to age five, she had reached the age limit for that facility. St. Ann's, at Page and Union was the building that mom first knew of as "home". The building no longer exists.

On September 14, 1913, at age five, never having known life outside of an orphanage, Minnie committed Mom to another "home" that she was to be in for the next eleven years of her life. These eleven years are a complete blank relative to what events took place in Mom's life. I've requested all information that pertained to mom during her confinement in both St. Ann's and St. Mary's. All the "Catholic Services for Children & Youth" organization could provide was a date in and a date out of each institution.

Minnie took Mom out of St. Mary's Asylum on August 2, 1924, and placed her, as a boarding student, at St. Elizabeth's Academy, on Arsenal Street. Mom's "Sweet Sixteen" birthday began the final portion of her youth, still within the confines of an institution. It should be noted here that the fate that befell most of Mom's friends (namely Mary, Eleanor, Corine, Adele, and Rose) at St. Mary's were to be sent to St. Philomena's Industrial School on August 30, 1924.

St. Philomena's was the proscribed institution for young orphan girls in the last phase of their youth to learn a trade. I'm sure Mom looked at St. Elizabeth's as a marvelous alternative.

By the way, St. Mary's Girl's Orphan Asylum is no longer in existence. The building that mom knew as home for so many years is now the San Francisco Christian Assembly Multiplex Center. It is located at 5341 Emerson (a block away from Calvary Cemetery).

It's unclear when Minnie moved out of St. Louis, and found employment as the live-in housekeeper of Our Lady of Mt. Carmel Parish in Chicago, Illinois. We do know that she remained in this position for a long time.

Meanwhile, Conrad and his wife Anna, and Anna's daughter Susan, were living close to Grant's Farm in the early 1920s. Conrad never adopted Susan. Susan and Conrad didn't get along, and she left home when only 15. However, in 1923 Conrad and Anna adopted the four year old orphan son of Anna's sister. His name was Oscar. He took the Tappeiner name. I found Oscar in early 1982, and was able to have a "reunion" between him and mom. It was from Oscar that I first saw a photo of Conrad. Mom was like a giddy school girl when she met her "brother." This happened just months before Mom's death in June of 1982.

Oscar was able to share some interesting stories of Conrad. Apparently Conrad, being a carpenter, worked at the construction of portions of the Busch estate on Grant's Farm. Oscar recalled that Conrad would sometimes play cards with Gussie Busch in the horse stables of the farm.

While all of this was happening, Mom was settling into the new routine at **St. Elizabeth's Academy**. Mom spent all four years here as one of the "residents." About 17 of the 45 students in mom's 1928 graduating class were fellow boarding students. Sisters Innocentia and Laetitia were the prime "Mother" figures in Mom's life at this time. St. Elizabeth Academy provided a firm foundation for their students in many aspects of life. Mom learned to play the piano here. She was also a frequent contributor to the yearbook in her final year. That yearbook reflects the following "prophecy" for Helen Tappeiner: "(that) her captivating style of story-telling" is now useful in urging the youngsters to bed." One can only imagine what the story was behind that comment.

It was also during her four years at St. Elizabeth that Mom began a regular familial relationship with her cousin, Mrs. Anna Glinz Kendrick, the second daughter of Minnie's oldest sister, Josephine Marseiler Glinz. Anna's daughter Frances was only six years younger than Mom. John Kendrick, Anna's husband, would drive down to St. Elizabeth's nearly every weekend to pick up mom for a visit. The 1928 St. Elizabeth Academy Senior Yearbook also gives us a nice time-line of events that mom experienced in 1927 and 1928. For example, the infamous September 29, 1927 tornado, that killed 86, injured 500, and lay waste to six square miles of buildings, inflicted limited damage to the school Mom called home. October 12th was a field day to nearby Tower Grove Park to celebrate Columbus Day. October 19th the girls got off to attend the **Veiled Prophet** Parade. December 16th mom and the rest of the seniors got a tour of the brand new gymnasium. February 21, 1928 was a double-header for Mom. In the morning she attended a lecture entitled "What Catholic Women can Accomplish in the World". That afternoon she helped the boarding seniors defeat the boarding juniors in a basketball game in the new gym. The seniors attended a play at **Fontbonne** on April 21st. In late May, Mom participated in the school play called "The Making of Miss 1928". Mom played the part of a mannequin. On May 16th Mom attended a tea at **Webster College**. June 2nd was a Farewell Party at the **Mayfair Hotel**, followed on June 6th by a luncheon on the roof of the Hotel Chase. Finally, on June 11, 1928, **Mom ended nearly 19 years of imposed "incarceration" when she graduated from high school and started her life as an adult**.

We know that Mom lived with her cousins the Kendricks at 2914 Hebert, and assume that she probably did so directly after leaving St. Elizabeth Academy in June of 1928. She was nearly twenty years old, and a stunning beauty.

Mom went to work at J. C. Penney's. One day, while

Helen and Ed Lossos

waiting for the bus in front of the Texaco Service Station just a few houses down from her home on Hebert, Mom struck up a conversation with the owner. They began dating, and made quite a striking couple. **Ed Lossos** was nine years older than her, and still lived at home with his father and sister. His mother had passed away that year (1930). He felt an obligation to care for his father, who was 68 at the time. They continued to date, and finally in 1933 decided to marry. They went to **Al Smith's Restaurant** at the corner of Meramec and Grand for a "wedding dinner".

ST. LOUIS MUNY OPERA

By David Lossos

The concept of a permanent outdoor theater in Forest Park probably began with the success of the 1904 World's Fair. However, it wasn't until an outdoor production, between two large oak trees, of Shakespeare's "As You Like It" in 1916 that the concept started to become a reality. Following this success, the "Muny" was built in just 49 days - from scratch. The massive stage was constructed, an orchestra pit built, dressing rooms built behind the stage. Crowds in 1917 saw six performances of Verdi's "Aida".

In November of 1918, Mayor Kiel, and other prominent St. Louisans, met and decided to incorporate the theater. The "Muny" was born. Six operas were performed in 1919. Tickets were just 25 cents up to a dollar, and 1,620 of the 9,000 seats were set aside as free.

This tradition continues to this day. On June 10, 1919, the Municipal Theatre Association gained official status, and six days later the curtain rose on "Robin Hood," with a packed house. Mayor Kiel himself proudly appeared in the production as King Richard!

During all but two years Mayor Kiel served as president of the St. Louis Municipal Opera, until his death in 1942. A commentary contained in the Silver Anniversary Souvenir brochure, published in 1943, seems to be as true today as it was when written 65 years ago:

"Certain cities have traditions which have spread their fame throughout the world. And as their fame has gone forth it has attracted visitors from great distances - eager to see and enjoy the unusual and spectacular wonders which nature has created or which man has built. St. Louis has brought forth another wonder, and given it to the world, and seen it grow to world fame within the short span of twenty-five years. St. Louis' Municipal Opera is one of the renowned institutions of our day, and it has grown to greatness during our own generation."

On a personal level, I feel I had a small part in the unqualified success of the Muny. In the late 1950s, during my high school years, I was a vendor each summer at the Muny. I personally kept many patrons from parched throats and heat stroke with my hawking of "ice cold" drinks before the show and during intermissions. For four seasons I was able to see every performance (no vendors were allowed during the performances). Many times I remember sitting backstage and watching the performers scrambling to get ready for their next scene. It was a magical time for a young teenager, and I treasure my memories of that period of my life.

In 1930, the stage was equipped with a turntable to enhance performances. It was refurbished in 1997 due to dilapidation. In 1994, the Muny Kids was founded featuring a select group of performers from the ages of 7-13 who travel around St. Louis performing. In 1998, a similar group called Muny Teens, ages 13 to 18, was formed for the same purpose.

The Muny seats about 11,000 people with 1,450 free seats in the back of the theater (bring your binoculars). In August of 2007, the Muny completed its 89th annual season with over 440,000 attending the productions. The Muny is a not-for-profit organization.

Here are a few of the folks that appeared on-stage at the Muny over the years: Anna Maria Alberghetti, Eddie Albert, Don Ameche, Ed Ames, Andrew Sisters, Lauren Bacall, Burt Bacharach, Pearl Bailey, Gene Barry, Mikhail Baryshnikov, Beach Boys, Leonard Bernstein, Theodore Bikel, Michael Bolton, Jack Buck, Jimmy Buffett, Carol Burnett, Sid Caesar, Cab Calloway, Glen Campbell, Carpenters, Jack Carson, Cyd Charisse, Imogene Coca, Hans Conried, Walter Cronkite, Crosby, Stills & Nash, Tyne Daly, Bette Davis, Pam Dawber, Dennis Day, Gloria De Haven, The Debonairs, Yvonne DeCarlo, Doobie Brothers, Bob Dylan, Barbara Eden, Douglas Fairbanks, Jr., Morgan Fairchild, Alice Faye, W.C. Fields, Gale Gordon, Leslie Gore, Betty Grable, Peter Graves, Joel Grey, Dorothy Hamill, Richard Harris, Al Hirt, Bob Hope, Linda Hope, Engelbert Humperdinck, Davy Jones, Shirley Jones, Stubby Kaye, Stacy Keach, Gene Kelly, Julius La Rosa, Patti LaBelle, Dorothy Lamour, Angela Lansbury, Archie Leach (prior to changing his name to Cary Grant), Julian Lennon, George Maharis, Marsha Mason, Ethel Merman, Steve Miller, Liza Minnelli, Agnes Moorehead, Jim Nabors, Joe Namath, Harriet Nelson, Ozzie Nelson, Stevie Nicks, Rudolph Nureyev, Carroll O'Connor, Donald O'Connor, Sarah Jessica Parker, Pat Paulsen, Minnie Pearl, George Peppard, Bernadette Peters, Tom Poston, Juliet Prowse, Tony Randall, Martha Raye, Debbie Reynolds, Cathy Rigby, Linda Ronstadt, Dan Rowan, Rod Stewart, Mel Tillis, Leslie Uggams, Ben Vereen, Betty White

The Magic House on South Kirkwood Road (Lorna Nunes photo)

RIP-ROARING PRAIRIE FIRES IN MISSOURI COUNTRY

The great English writer Charles Dickens visited his brother in **St. Louis** in 1842. He decided to kill two birds with one stone by also visiting the prairie in nearby Illinois.

Muny Opera in Forest Park (David Lossos collection)

His group traveled by coach going through Illinoistown and on to **Belleville**. Then they reached **Lebanon**, situated on a stately hill, and pushed beyond its outskirts to reach the Looking-glass Prairie. Here his memory failed him as he wrote about facing the *setting sun*. Since he was looking east, the diminishing orange orb would have been to his back – towards St. Louis. Despite his anticipation from having read much about the Illinois prairie, Dickens was disappointed. "There it lay, a tranquil sea without water: a few birds wheeling here and there, and solitude and silence reigning paramount around. The grass was not yet high; there were bare black patches on the ground; and the few wild flowers that the eye could see, were poor and scanty. I felt little of that sense of freedom and exhilaration that a Scottish heath or an English down awaken. It was lonely and wild, but oppressive in its barren monotony."

How unfortunate that Dickens, with all his brilliance, was unable to see that which deTocqueville clearly perceived. Illinois and Missouri prairie had become the locus of freedom and democracy – a beacon to oppressed peoples of the world and home to a great experiment in government that made despots and tyrants tremble in their boots.

The Missouri prairie fooled many people. Explorer Stephen Long erred when he labeled the prairie and plains area as the **Great American Desert**. Future president James

Monroe visited what then was called "the west" and remained unimpressed. Easterners who visited the Midwest tended to classify all grasslands as "swamps." Because the terrain was treeless, most thought it to be infertile and its land was among the last in the state to be settled upon. Its tall bluestem prairie grass grew high enough to nearly engulf a rider on horseback. Its towering growth and tangled roots made it nigh impossible for the seed of a tree, dropped from the wing of a bird, to take hold and grow. Trees did not find the denser glacial soil so friendly as did the grass roots of the bluestem.

Colorful legend gives us yet another explanation. The prairie was once covered with thick trees, but then along came **Paul Bunyan** and his fabled axe, and the land was once again pancaked as in days of yore when the great glaciers from Canada came down and flattened everything. Then Babe, his famous blue ox, hauled the trees back east where the lumber was used for home construction and railroad ties.

This same heavy, unbroken sea of grass made plowing in the early years quite difficult. The cast iron plow, consisting mostly of wood with a few strips of metal, hadn't changed much since medieval times. Thomas Jefferson spent considerable effort toward drawing up mathematical specifications of a proper plow. Not until John Deere was there a modern steel plow of sufficient design to handle the tough, fibrous prairie soil. Yet the wondrous new plow created a new problem, for the traditional team of oxen was not strong enough to pull the implement through the resisting grass and soil. Four and six oxen, yoked together, were now required for the task.

The great annual growth of tall, thick prairie grass, covering vast areas of surface, when killed by autumn frosts and dried to tawny by Indian summer suns, was vulnerable to accidental and malicious fires. A conflagration of this abundant kindling often formed a contiguous line of many miles in length. Driven by high winds, early pioneers described prairie fires that made the earth tremble and quiver beneath one's feet as if the embattled columns of flame had the weight of a Roman legion. One Missourian said the prairie fire had a low sullen roar, like a distant Niagara. "The insistent noise accompanied its march as if Pluto, from his fiery regions, lent it subterranean music. Flame, light, motion and sound combined to make a terrifying spectacle unequalled in grandeur – a panorama that would have made Nero proud. Alarm for safety of property, home and human life often added to the intensity of the stark drama of power and splendor. Billowy swaying clouds of black smoke, lifting skyward, would suddenly explode into brilliant flame, lighting the entire landscape and heaven above. Everything of combustible substance melted and vanished before this crucible of heat and flame. Its progress was swift as the wind. The fleetest buffalo could hardly escape it by utmost strain of speed. Birds of the air and wild beasts of the prairie and grove fled before its scathing march with cries, screams and yowls of fright and terror. Frequently, they were overtaken and burned to a cinder despite the fleetness of Mercury, that swift Roman messenger. When it was over, there was an eerie silence, wisps of smoke and a barren tableau that was as lonely and desolate as a Salvador Dali landscape."

Early Missouri settlers, from experience, learned how to guard against danger and loss from prairie fires by plowing wide and numerous furrow strips around fields, cabins, stables, stacks of hay, grain, fodder and all exposed property. But, sometimes great shears of flame, driven by strong winds, would be torn from the line of fire and leap across the barriers, threatening life and property. If instant sufficient help were not present, all might be swept away in one fell swoop of fire and devastation. Sometimes such fiery visitations came in the darkness of night and neighboring homes were added to the smoking ruins of the same fire. To skillfully fight and rescue life, homes, sheds and barns from loss by prairie fire often required the same daunting courage as facing the tomahawk and scalping knife. The diaries and letters of the day are replete with stories of men and women who became heroes and heroines in desperate time of need on the Missouri prairie.

A tip of the hat to our courageous forefathers who bridged the streams, fought the floods, plowed the land, battled the Indians (who were understandably angered) and tamed a wilderness that today ranks as one of the great states in America.

COLORFUL MISSOURI AND ILLINOIS INDIAN LEGENDS

My state of Illinois came to be inhabited by various Algonquin tribes who migrated to Illinois country from back east. The Illinois Indians consisted of the Kaskaskias, Cahokias, Tamaroas, Peorias, Michigameas, Moingwenas and several minor groups. They were haughty of step and referred to themselves as Illiniwek, which meant "**superior men**" (as if other Indians were mere beasts). It was the early French explorers who shortened the name to Illinois.

These Indians planted corn, tomatoes, squash, tobacco, beans and pumpkins. Tobacco was used mainly for ceremonial purposes and was smoked in a special long pipe called the calumet. After planting season, they hunted rabbits, buffalo, deer, bear and wild fowl. They supplemented this diet by catching fish in rivers and streams. The Illini, consisting of about 12 tribes, worshiped Manitou, the Great Spirit.

Henry Schoolcraft

Warfare was common and the calumet war dance has been vividly described by early French explorers. Sundry migrations of other tribes into the area brought conflict. Some of the outsiders were the Fox, Kickapoo, Winnebago, Pottawatomie, Sauk, Ottawa, Miami and Shawnee. The Pottawatomie settled around the shores of Lake Michigan. The Sauk and the Fox roamed the wooded lands of the northwest part of the state. The most feared and hostile of the Illini enemies were the Sioux, from the West, and the Iroquois from back East. The Iroquois were the first Indians to acquire firearms. As English settlers pushed the Iroquois out of the Mohawk Valley in New York, they moved east, invading Illinois country around 1655. Around 1667, several of the Illinois tribes, subject to fierce warfare, were forced to leave the area and move westward across the Mississippi River into Missouri. Such was the state of affairs when the white men first arrived on the scene.

Until recently, Native-Americans in the Missouri area were not treated kindly by most historians. Here is a depiction of them in a 1925 textbook. "The savages were wild men indeed, for they knew nothing of the mineral wealth and almost nothing of the farm value of the lands. One could hardly call the inhabitants men; yet these savages loved to call themselves superior men. Their influence on history amounts to little, for they gave up their lands to the white men with hardly a protest and left practically nothing behind except a few barbarous relics and some Indian place names."

Yet, the first Americans had a distinct culture and part of that heritage included fascinating stories and tales that were passed down from generation to generation. Here is a sampling of some of that lore.

Evangeline Falls, the highest waterfalls in the state of Missouri, are also known as Mina Sauk Falls. What is the legend behind this? Mina Sauk was the daughter of Chief Sauk. She was made love to by the chief of an enemy tribe. When he was captured he was killed by being impaled on spears. His grief-stricken bride uttered a curse on her tribe and leaped to her death from the top of the cliff. The Great Storm God caused a cyclone to come along and destroy the people of her tribe. Then he hurled a lightning bolt at the top of the mountain and caused water to gush from the top, cascading to the bottom to wipe away the blood of the young lovers. This water-blood mixture caused flowers to spring up on the banks of the stream below which are known as "Indian Pinks."

Devil's Toll Gate is a tall cliff less than a mile away from Mina Sauk Falls. It was so named because wagons on the trail were forced to unload before they could make it through the narrow pass – almost as if the Devil were exacting a toll on travelers.

There is a rugged cliff called **Virgin's Bluff** located on the banks of beautiful Table Rock Lake in southern Missouri. It was given that name from a legend that has existed in that area for generations.

During the time of Spanish occupation one of the soldiers met Moon Song, the beautiful daughter of an Indian tribal chief. The two fell in love and she agreed to marry her lover and return with him to Mexico. The chief refused to give his permission for she was his only daughter. He already had selected a handsome young brave for her and he wanted a grandson to carry on tribal leadership in years to come.

The chief sent a band of warriors to kill the Spaniard who learned of the plot and left the area, never to return. The Indian maiden, overcome with grief, went to the bluff and **leaped 325 feet to her death into the James River below**. The chief had the medicine man cast a spell on the bluff, forbidding any member of the tribe to go near it.

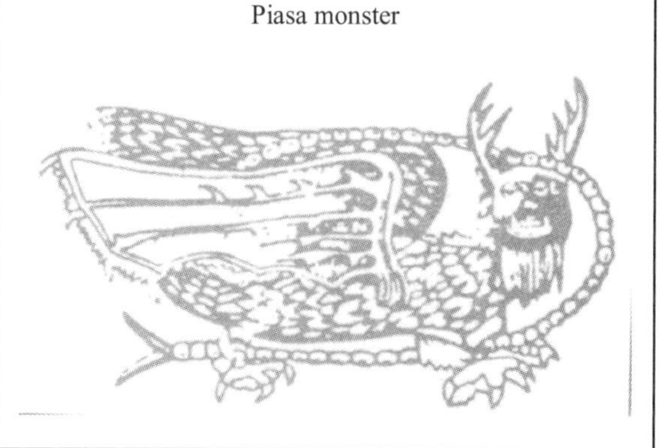
Piasa monster

Early whites heard about the spell but shrugged it off as just another tall tale. However, the water below the bluffs soon became known as "Virgin's Swirl" and they were the most dangerous waters on either the James or White River. Over the years many boats capsized at that spot resulting in numerous deaths. On several occasions, hunters have been found shot near the top of the bluff.

Most believed that the curse would be ended by the waters of Table Rock Lake, built in the later 1950s. That proved not to be the case. There have been numerous tales of freak accidents and cabin fires, keeping the legend alive.

Night fishermen claim to occasionally hear sounds that are similar to a woman's moan. Many believe it is Moon Song pining away for her lost love.

The state of Missouri has more natural caves than any other state in America. There is an old cave in south St. Louis that was used for storing beer by a local brewer named English. English Cave could be accessed east of present day Benton Park, bounded by Illinois and Jefferson, Wyoming and Arsenal. The cave was associated with an early Indian legend. A young brave and a maiden fell in love. The young lovers fled to the site to escape the ire of an angry chief who wanted the beautiful girl for himself. The chief discovered their whereabouts and guarded the entrance. The two inside eventually starved to death.

Ginger Blue Resort, dating back to 1915, took its name from an Indian chieftain buried on the property. The chief's daughter fell in love with a brave. One day as they strolled by **Mystery Cave** they were attacked by a large bear. The brave wounded the bear with his knife, and the animal ran into the cave. The brave followed him in to finish him off and neither the bear nor the brave ever came out.

Each day after that the maiden would go to the cave and sit on a nearby rock to mourn the only man she ever loved. During a lifetime of weeping, her tears falling on the rock carved out an image of her lover which can still be seen by present day visitors.

Located in the extreme Southwest corner of the state, the resort burned several years ago and is no longer operative.

In 1818-1819, **Henry Schoolcraft** and a companion, Levi Pettibone, led an expedition from **Potosi** to what is now **Springfield**. Schoolcraft was an American geographer, ethnologist and geologist who also published books about early Illinois. In 1819, Schoolcraft published the book, *A View of the Lead Mines of Missouri*, which led to Missouri becoming the leading lead producing state.

Schoolcraft's wife was also an ethnologist and her writings were part of Longfellow's material that became the *Song of Hiawatha*. What follows is a story about Missouri Indian lore from Schoolcraft.

The early Indians believed in two spirits, Kitchemonedo, the good spirit, and Matchemonedo, the evil spirit. Kitchemonedo made the world and everything in it. He peopled the earth with men and women who, as years passed, became ungrateful and full of hate. The Great Spirit plunged the world into a huge lake and drowned everyone. Feeling remorse, and lonely, he made a man. But then the man grew lonely so he sent him a sister. One night the man had a dream and when he awoke he talked about it with his sister. "Five men will come to your lodge tonight, but you must not talk to any of them except for the last." As she repulsed each suitor, they fell down and died. But when Tamin presented himself, she received him kindly. Tamin buried the bodies of the other four suitors and from each of their graves sprang crops of tobacco, beans, melons and pumpkins. Tamin and the girl were married and from this union sprang all subsequent Indians. When Tamin died and was buried, the never before seen crop of corn sprouted from his grave.

Along the bluffs of the Mississippi, north of **West Alton**, is the painting (a reproduction of an Indian pictograph) of the legendary Piasa Bird, known by the Indians as the Bird of Evil Spirit. The fiendish looking creature, first seen by Marquette and Jolliet in 1673, and first sketched in 1826, had the body of an alligator and feet with talons, pointed teeth, enormous wings, and the face of a man with antlers on its head. It is generally regarded as the **greatest Indian painting in North America**.

Named for a local creek, the bird was presumably the thunderbird or storm spirit of the Iliniwek. The monster pictograph was seen by Marquette and Jolliet in their early voyage down the Illinois and Mississippi rivers.

Liberty Bell of the West at Kaskaskia

The creature was said to have lived in a cave and feasted on local Indians, swooping down and carrying them away to be devoured in its lair. Finally, the brave young chief of the Illini, Ouatoga, took twenty armed warriors with him and stood brazenly on a rock to defy the monster. The evil one swooped down to kill its intended victim, and at the last second, the hidden warriors emerged and killed the beast with their poisoned arrows.

The original painting, in red, green and black, was quarried away for railroad ballast in 1847. Local Boy Scout groups erected a metal picture on the bluff face in the 1980s.

Marquette and Jolliet also floated past **Tower Rock** in their canoes during their 1673 exploration of the Mississippi River. They talked to local natives who warned them about the rock (near present-day Grand Tower). They told the duo not to go past the place for near it lurked demons and monsters that would devour them. The native custom, they were told, was to offer gifts or sacrifices to the Manitou to appease the treacherous spirits.

Marquette and Jolliet ignored the warnings because they believed in the one true Christian god. Marquette gave us the first written description of the most prominent protuberance between the source and the mouth of the Great River. He wrote, "At the great rock, there was a violent struggle between the waters which force one another with a great din and inspires fear in the savages."

British Union Jack

This 62 ft. high rock also occupied a place in colorful Indian lore with a tale about a thwarted romance. According to legend, there was a Wyandotte brave who was loved by a Fox Indian maiden. But she told him that she had already been promised by her father to a warrior of the Fox. Despondent, she climbed Tower Rock and leaped to her death in the dreaded waters below. Saddened by the loss of the love of his life, he followed her in death, making this place known as "**Lovers Leap**."

Another popular Native-American tale was about an Indian maiden named Esmeralda. She fell in love with a dashing young riverboat pilot and wished to marry him. For years she pined away until one day she heard that her true love had been killed in a boiler explosion. The very next day, Esmerelda's lifeless form was found at the jagged base of the rock.

If you read any of the haunted Illinois and Missouri books by Troy Taylor, he'll tell you about strange moans around the Grand Tower area. On those spooky nights, where much of the moon is blurred by diaphanous clouds pushed along by chilling winds, if you listen hard enough, you can hear the soulful wail of Esmerelda's mournful voice. He'll also tell you that if you cup your hand behind your ear, you just might hear the muted roar of the evil Manitou that dwells at the base of **the nation's smallest national monument**.

INDIAN CURSE PUTS KASKASKIA IN MISSOURI!

Do you believe in curses? Best-selling **Decatur** author (*Haunted Illinois*) Troy Taylor does. Did you know that **14,000 acres of Illinois land are physically in the state of Missouri**? How is that possible you ask? It's enough to make you scratch your head and say, "gee whiz!" Here's what happened.

In 1703, the French village of Kaskaskia was established by Jesuit priests who came down from the Starved Rock area (on the Illinois River) where they had founded the Immaculate Conception Church in 1675. A new Immaculate Conception Church in Kaskaskia was constructed (of logs with a thatched roof) that same year. Kaskaskia thus became one of the oldest, and possibly the oldest town in Illinois. The settlement was named for the Kaskaskias, one of the five tribes of the Illinois Native-American confederacy.

The town that grew around the church was located on a peninsula between the Mississippi and Kaskaskia rivers. A new church, made of stone, was built in 1714 at the expense of the French government. The stone church was enlarged in 1737. Yet a third church of vertical palisade posts was built around 1775. It was torn down in 1838 and a new brick church was constructed. It lasted until the 1881 flood, and the materials were used to build a new church farther west and south at the site of New Kaskaskia, Illinois.

Kaskaskia, with a population that quickly swelled to about 7,000 inhabitants, was the largest town in Illinois at its zenith. It ruled as the social and commercial center of "Upper Louisiana" for more than a century. French inhabitants in Canada were attracted to Kaskaskia due to its warm climate and rich soil. The site was so prosperous that the gay social life earned it the title, "The Versailles of the West."

The French government decided to protect the settlement of Kaskaskia and strengthen its hold on Illinois by building a fort near the town. In 1718, Pierre du Boisbriant, the French military commander of Illinois, built Fort de Chartres, located 18 miles north of Kaskaskia. Wood was taken from the virgin forest and stone was secured from the nearby bluffs. The star-shaped fort was similar in outline to the more famous Fort Ticonderoga, captured by Ethan Allen and Benedict Arnold in the Revolutionary War. The fort was named in honor of the Duc de Chartres, the French regent's son. In 1753, it was refurbished by Jean B. Saucier and Richard McCarty. McCarty was an Irishman who later became the fort's commander. The wooden walls were replaced with stone, over a three year period, at an astounding cost of one million dollars. The sum nearly bankrupted the French government. This largest and best-built French fort in North America, covering four acres, protected settlers from the nearby Chicasaws, Piankashaws, Kickapoo and the fierce Fox who made periodic raids from the north. By 1771, Fort de Chartres was officially abandoned because it was in a state of neglect.

Kaskaskia before the 1881 flood

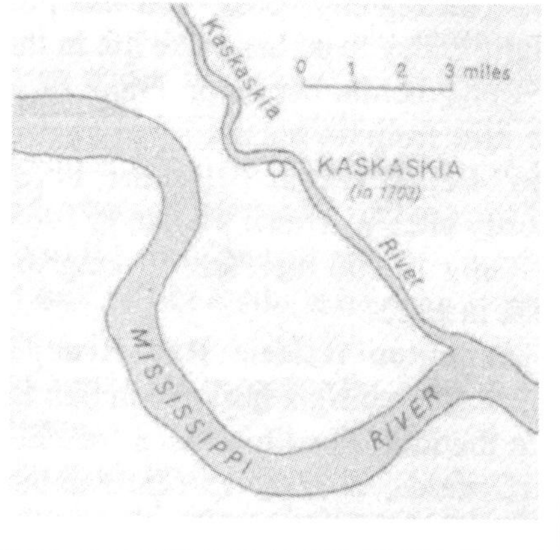

If you visit the site today there is a partially reconstructed fort, a museum, and a research library.

Britain took control of Illinois after winning the French and Indian War (1756-63). In 1766, just before the British took possession, the French burned Fort Kaskaskia, which was near the town and much smaller than Fort Chartres, but up on the bluffs. It was the only bluff overlooking Kaskaskia where a fort might be built to protect the town. When Fort Kaskaskia was completed, the garrison at Fort Chartres abandoned the place and occupied the new fort. After the British took over, they built Fort Gage near the town and on the flood plain.

It was from Kaskaskia that George Rogers Clark launched his intrepid campaign to evict the British from Illinois during the Revolutionary War (1776-1783).

Kaskaskia after the 1881 flood – now located in Missouri near St. Marys

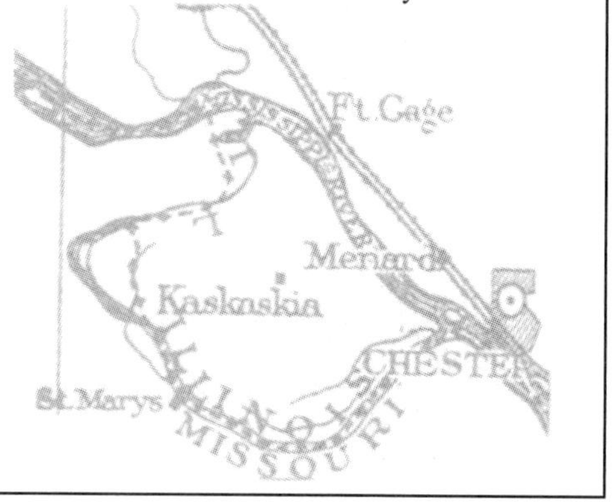

In 1741, King Louis XV presented the parish at Kaskaskia with a 650-pound cast bronze bell. The bell, which is still preserved and on display, bears the inscription (in French): "For the church of the Illinois, with the compliments of the King from beyond the sea." It took many months to bring the bell up the river from New Orleans on a raft. In time, new bells (1878) were procured from St. Louis and the old one was placed in storage. When George Rogers Clark took control of the territory, French citizens retrieved the bell and rang it loudly to proclaim their new freedom from the hated British. This historic Illinois "Liberty Bell of the West" is actually **11 years older than the more famous Liberty Bell** in Philadelphia. It took about four months for men to tow the bell up the Mississippi with the bell sitting on a raft.

Yet Kaskaskia, so proud and so prosperous, was doomed. According to legend, a curse was placed on the town by an Algonquin Indian who was not allowed to marry a French maiden that he loved. The Indians around Kaskaskia were friendly, with many of them having been converted to Christianity. A good number of natives lived on the fringe of town. This particular Indian brave, educated by French missionaries, worked at a house and plantation owned by an affluent man named Bernard. No one knows for sure how it happened, but the handsome native met and fell in love with Marie, the man's daughter.

Now Marie was the beautiful "Belle of Kaskaskia," with numerous hot blooded suitors, but she loved only the Indian. It was quite common, back then, for French men to marry Indian maidens, but quite unusual for a white woman to marry a native. When the Indian asked the father for his daughter's hand in marriage, he was refused. The Red Man simply wasn't suitable. Not long after that, the couple ran away to begin a new life together. Outraged, the father and some of his close friends chased after them. The lovers were tracked down and finally apprehended near **Cahokia**. The Indian was beaten and tied to a pirogue, and then banished from the community. As the log moved down the river, the Indian turned and cursed the father. He said that Bernard would be dead within a year and that Kaskaskia was damned with even the dead of the town being disturbed from their graves. Then he looked up to the sky and prayed to the Great Spirit that the girl's father would one day be killed by his own people. Next, he implored that the town of Kaskaskia would be destroyed by the Mighty River. The river then swallowed the Indian beneath the muddy water.

The damning words were quickly forgotten. But as time went on the curse seemed prophetic because the economic fortunes of the town declined as French inhabitants, unhappy with Americanization of the settlement, moved away and went to **Ste. Genevieve**, Old Mines (near **Potosi**), St. Louis and New Orleans. The population would eventually shrink to less than a thousand. In 1881, the dark curse dramatically worked its magic. In April, after weeks of rain, the raging Mississippi overflowed its banks. The big river was about to change its course and unearth dead bodies in the local cemetery. The swollen flow of the river current fed into the Kaskaskia River that was not capable of carrying such a volume. Since the eastern bank of the Kaskaskia River was composed of limestone rock, the additional riverbed needed to handle the huge volume of water was gouged out when the Mississippi savagely cut through the earthen neck of the peninsula and **placed most of the town on the Missouri side of the river**.

Thanks to the Indian's curse, much of Kaskaskia was now on the other side of the river, within the boundaries of Missouri. The Church of Immaculate Conception survived, but was also on the west side of the river. The Kaskaskia cemetery was washed away and the bodies of those buried there were disgorged into the raging waters. The old and impressive Menard House (the "Mount Vernon of the West") remained with what was left of old Kaskaskia, eventually becoming a popular tourist attraction. The forgotten "Liberty Bell of the West" was recovered from an old building and transferred to Kaskaskia Island. In 1948, the state of Illinois erected a new brick structure to house the historic bell.

Chief Pontiac

With old Kaskaskia now on the west side of the Mississippi River, those sly rogues in the state of Missouri tried to claim it. There was a huge legal battle that the U.S. Supreme Court finally settled in favor of Illinois. It ruled that Kaskaskia had historically been part of Illinois and that a whimsical act of nature should not change its attachment to that state.

And what, you ask, ever happened to old man Bernard? He got into a quarrel with a local man and was killed in the ensuing fight. **Now do you believe in curses?**

EARLY HISTORIANS WERE POLITICALLY INCORRECT

Pick up a book on Missouri history written near the turn of the century and you will find descriptions of Native Americans to be unkind, to say the least. Here is an example. I am not going to cite the source because in light of modern interpretation, it would be totally unacceptable. We should remember that this was standard fare back then.

The savages who greeted . . . Marquette and Jolliet . . . were wild men indeed. Their camps were laid out in no order whatsoever and were composed of rude huts made of bark and skins. One could hardly call these settlements towns; one could hardly call the inhabitants men.

Murder of Chief Pontiac (ISHL)

How else were early historians unkind to the Indians? In a 1953 history and geography book, the author wrote: "The Indians of Missouri ignored most opportunities. They contented themselves with hunting, fishing and crude agriculture. We are fortunate that Missouri was finally occupied by an advanced and energetic people (whites)."

Current political correctness no longer allows such judgments in textbooks.

What famous Indian is buried in an unmarked grave somewhere near Broadway in St. Louis? The famed chieftan Pontiac, who led a rebellion in 1764, was murdered by another Indian near **Cahokia** in 1769 and he was buried in St. Louis near Fourth and Walnut. Over the years the whereabouts of his grave became lost. His rebellion was the most significant one in late colonial history.

What is the buried treasure legend of the Chickasaw Indians of **Bread Tray Mountain**? Bread Tray, 1,425 ft. high, is in Stone County (southwest Mo) near **Lampe**. The Indians of the mountain learned how to make crude jewelry of silver and even used it as currency. They were finally overcome by an enemy tribe but before leaving the area they sealed everything in a cave, hoping someday to return. Happy hunting you treasure seekers!

Why will nothing grow on top of Bread Tray Mountain? A young maiden from another tribe arrived one day and informed the people that the Great Spirit told her that if she married the chief's son there would be peace and prosperity. The wedding took place and the prophecy came true. Everyone was pleased except the Medicine Man who had previously prospered on the misfortunes of others. He conspired against her and drove her away. Before leaving she placed a curse on the mountain.

What is the legend behind the naming of the town of **Arrow Rock**? According to tradition, two braves were competing for a maiden and her hand in marriage was promised to the warrior who could shoot an arrow the farthest. The winner's arrow lodged in a stone bluff.

How was the town of **Femme Osage** named? Around 1800, some French fur traders named an area in St. Charles County Femme Osage for an Indian woman who, according to folklore, drowned in a local stream.

LOST YOKUM SILVER MINE

In 1541, the Spanish discovered rich deposits of silver near the confluence of the James and White rivers in Southwest Missouri. A fort was built atop Breadtray Mountain and the Spanish began the smelting process converting the silver into bars that would be taken back to Spain. The Spaniards were suddenly forced to flee the area as they were threatened by a large band of Indians.

Their mine was not rediscovered until 1810 when a Chickasaw Indian raiding party entered the cave as they sought shelter from a violent storm. The Indians began making silver jewelry which they traded for supplies as far away as St. Louis.

Around this time, several members of the Yokum family settled in the area and became close friends with the natives. Then, the Indian Removal Act forced the natives to leave the area for lands farther west. They revealed to the Yokums the site of the mine in return for wagons and supplies.

The Yokum brothers acquired some blacksmithing tools and made molds for the minting of U.S. silver dollars. Now the Yokum dollar was counterfeit, but no one objected since its silver content was slightly greater than the ones that came from the U.S. Mint.

When the U.S. government finally became aware of the Yokum dollar, it sent agents to the area to find the mine. They threatened the Yokum family with jail unless they revealed the source of the mine, which they refused to do. A bargain was finally struck whereby the case against them would be dropped if they stopped minting the coins. James Yokum died soon afterward and the other brothers left for the California gold hills. The mine's entrance was sealed before they left. The secret location of the mine was never revealed and undiscovered riches are there for the taking.

Tower Rock in the Mississippi River near Altenburg

THE NATION'S SMALLEST NATIONAL MONUMENT

Tower Rock is a large chunk of limestone jutting up from the Mississippi River in southern Missouri near **Altenburg**. Its location in the river presented a hazard to steamboats, and in earlier days legends of romance, mystery and evil were associated with the swirling waters surrounding its base. Just below the island of Tower Rock there is a dangerous eddy of water that early boatmen labeled the "**Devil's Whirlpool**."

How did Mother Nature create this unique and interesting piece of geology? During the great Ice Age, popularly known as the Liman Advance, a great glacier came down from Canada and pushed the bed of the Mississippi westward. This radical change forced the river to flow over a bed of limestone. Eventually, the relentless eroding waters created its present bed and left the rock in its present location. It has existed for eons, undisturbed by the scouring waters of the Mississippi which have swept its base. Prior to the glacier that changed its course, the river was between a massive rocky ridge and a large hill now known as Fountain Bluff.

In 1679, Henri de Tonti (LaSalle's faithful lieutenant) and several missionaries placed a large wooden cross at the top of Tower Rock in the Mississippi River. They called it Le Cap de Croix, **Rock of the Cross**. The Indians called Tonti "Iron Hand" and marveled at his metal claw in place of a hand. Tonti, an Italian, had previously lost his hand in a European battle.

In 1699, a French explorer by the name St. Cosme traveled down the Mississippi and confirmed the Marquette/Jolliet sighting of the one acre landmark known as Tower Rock. St. Cosme was another one of those ubiquitous Jesuit missionaries who came down from Canada to convert the "heathens." Tonti's cross had been stolen so St. Cosme was determined to erect another one to prove to the natives that the Christian god was more powerful than the Indian Manitou.

Over the years the place took on a number of names including Tower Rock, La Roche de la Croix (rock of the cross), Castle Rock, Devil's Tower, Rock of St. Cosme, and Passage of the Cross.

During the Ulysses Grant Administration (1870), the Army Corps of Engineers cleared the area around it of other rocks that might have proved dangerous to navigation. This created a nice clear channel between Tower Rock and the Missouri shore. There were plans to dynamite the rock and eliminate the shipping hazard completely, but it was left standing because Grant thought it to be a suitable support for a future bridge.

Just north of the rock there was a ferry business that took passengers to the Missouri town of **Wittenberg**, a place originally founded by German Lutherans. It was this group that later became the nucleus of the current Lutheran Church-Missouri Synod.

The difficult passage past the rock made it a natural site for river pirates. Around 1800 there was a notorious band of renegades who thrived by attacking and pillaging boats that went past. After committing their heinous acts of murder and robbery, they retreated to a hideout that came to be known as "Sinner's Harbor." It took a detachment of U.S. cavalry to clean up the problem.

Mark Twain, in his riverboat pilot days, knew Tower Rock quite well and noted that it was the site of many a steamboat wreckage. James B. Eads, of future bridge fame, spent many hours on the bottom of the river near the rock salvaging cargoes in his specially made diving bell. The waters around Tower were a veritable treasure trove for salvage operations.

MISSOURI GEOLOGY AND GEOGRAPHY

It was British writer Rudyard Kipling who said that "**geography is destiny,**" and Missouri is one of the finest examples of that dictum. Missouri has an advantageous location because it is practically in the geographic center of the United States. For several decades it has been the population center of America. Its fine prairie soils up north place it in the "Breadbasket of America." The beautiful, rugged Ozarks in the southern half give it unmatched scenic beauty and make that region a tourist magnet that brings an influx of millions of dollars annually to local and state coffers.

Missouri is that rarest of states that boasts flat farmland, rolling hills, rich river bottom land, glaciated plain, dense forests, breathtaking valleys, flowering meadows, rock-lined river bluffs, volcanic rock formations, clear blue springs, wide meandering rivers, spectacular caves, **the oldest mountain range in the USA**, karst sinks and granite cliffs. Quite a rich diversity of landscape, eh? There's nothing boring here about God's handiwork.

What makes Missouri significant is its moderate climate, Missouri Valley location and its water resources. Missouri belongs to neither East, West, North or South, but is the focal point of all four regions. It is almost a near perfect microcosm state where roads, rail, waterways and airlines intersect.

During a national political campaign Thomas Reed of Maine, riding through Pike County, exclaimed, "Such a country, such lands! Why, **if we had such soil back in New England, we would sell it by the peck for seed**."

What is the basic geography of Missouri? Millions of years ago much of the state was covered by an inland sea. Marine animals lived and died here and their fossils can be found in most of the state. Ages later the great sea receded leaving great swamps with giant ferns and other vegetation. These growths died and were replaced by succeeding layers of vegetation that over time formed into coal deposits. Eons later (about one-half million years ago), the great glaciers, hundreds of feet thick, came down from the north reaching slightly south of the Missouri River. Before the glacier completely melted (about 15,000 years ago) it carved out ditches and formed rivers, depositing boulders and leaving gravel, rock and pulverized stone, much of which can still be seen today.

By comparison, the earliest Native Americans arrived on the scene about 10,000 years ago.

Missouri geology is a fascinating story spawned in fire and explosion, submerged in shallow seas, eroded into hills and hollows and bulldozed pancake flat by mile-thick sheets sent down from the ice gods in Canada. Missouri is sometimes breathtaking in its natural beauty, displaying an interesting ruggedness that is absent in most Midwestern states. Missouri is home to some of the oldest rocks in the Midwest: gray-purple rhyolite and red granite. Rhyolite can be seen in the bed of the Black River at Johnson's Shut-Ins State Park (**Lesterville**) and the granite may be observed at Elephant Rocks Park at **Graniteville**.

Mound City has granite and diorite boulders that were carried down from Minnesota. The golf course there has made a large sundial from red granite stones and an oversized golf club.

Missouri's state fossil is the sea lily, formed during the Pennsylvanian period. Its official state rock is mozarkite, named for the state and one of its regions. The term mozarkite is derived from "Missouri" and "Ozarks." Mozarkite is a form of one of the most common rocks found in the state, chert, which is composed of quartz. Chert may not be a very familiar term but when it is grayish in color it is usually called flint. Missouri natives, of course, made their arrowheads from this mineral. When it is found in a pinkish color the rock is referred to as mozarkite. According to rock collector Doug McCain, the best mozarkite is in Lincoln County where it weathers out of 450 million year old dolomite.

Don't confuse the state rock with the state mineral, which is galena – lead ore.

At Hawn State Park, near **Farmington**, one can see exposures of Lamotte sandstone that has eroded to form canyon-rimmed valleys with near-vertical cliffs.

The oddest rocks in the state are to be found at Elephant Rocks State Park on Highway 32 near **Graniteville**. Proof of the earth's antiquity can be found in these billion-year-old monolithic boulders that dwarf human visitors to the area. The rocks are believed to have been formed during the Cambrian period when molten rock broke through the earth's crust and came to the surface. As the magma cooled, it hardened into rock. Years and years of weathering produced the rounded look of the boulders. The biggest rock, named Dumbo, is 27 feet tall and 35 feet long. It weighs about 680 tons.

At Washington State Park, between **Potosi** and **Desoto**, there are petroglyphs – Indian carvings on dolomite rock. It is thought that these markings were made by inhabitants of the Middle Mississippian Era, a group related to the mound builders in St. Louis.

Another interesting geological site is Johnson Shut-ins, located north of **Lesterville** on Highway N. These convoluted rock formations were formed eons ago by prehistoric volcanic eruptions that spewed forth magma that eventually hardened into rock. Then, an inland sea encroached the region, covering up the existing rock and then planting layer after layer of sedimentary rock. (We're talking about the passage of 250 million years or more, folks!) After the sea retreated and violent uplifts created the Ozarks, water action began to cut a deep river valley, sculpting chutes and spectacular gorges.

Bayless High on Weber Road, where this author taught from 1963-64 (my room was on the top floor, extreme right)

If you don't believe that something as soft as water can cut through stone, visit a place that carves names and dates on cemetery headstones. In older times, the words were gouged out by sandblasting. Nowadays, they use a high powered stream of water. Truly amazing!

The "shut-ins" are tucked away in the St. Francois Mountains; the box canyon gives one a claustrophobic sense of being isolated, hence the term shut-in.

Southwest Missouri is fascinating to rock and mineral collectors at such places as Truitt's Cave at **Lanagan**, Ozark Wonder Cave at **Noel**, the Tiff Mines near **Seneca**, and the Marble Quarry at **Carthage**.

Southeast Missouri even has terrain that resembles a Louisiana bayou. The Alfred Lake Natural Area, in Butler County, consists of about 53 acres of swamps, bottomland forest, swamp oak, swamp tupelo, and bald cypress trees that are more than 500 years old.

It is believed that Missouri coal was laid down in the northern part of the state millions of years ago during the Pennsylvanian Period. Missouri has extensive coal deposits but most seams are only two or three feet thick and, as in neighboring Illinois, there is high sulfur content. Nevertheless, the coal provided heat, power and jobs for many small towns until clean air mandates in 1950 started shutting the mines down.

If you subtract organic material in soil, what else is left? Soil comes from decayed and eroded rock.

What kind of rocks are found in Missouri? 1. Sedimentary (limestone) formed from mud, sand and animal shells and bone 2. Igneous (granite) formed from melted material inside the earth and hardened as it was pushed upward and cooled 3. Metamorphic (marble) sedimentary rock transformed and hardened by pressure

What is a knob? A small dome-shaped hill

In what state park is Onondaga Cave found? Daniel Boone State Park near **Leasburg**

What record is held by Onondaga Cave? Its Big Room is **the largest living cave room in the world.**

What famous Missouri cave is near **Stanton**? Meramec Caverns

What made this cave so famous? The cave's owner, Lester Dill (to boost tourism) began advertising that this was a famous hideout for the Jesse James gang and that there might be some of his robbery gold still undiscovered in the cave. Further, Stantonites perpetuate the myth that **Jesse James was not murdered in May of 1882**. Jesse ostensibly arranged for the death of a remarkable look-alike so that Governor Crittenden would quit hounding him and he could start living a peaceful life.

What is noteworthy about the St. Francois Mountain region? For over 70 years it was the **greatest lead-producing region in America**.

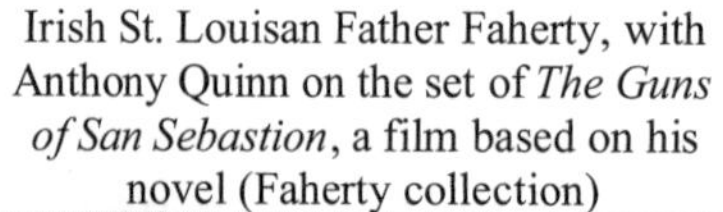

Irish St. Louisan Father Faherty, with Anthony Quinn on the set of *The Guns of San Sebastion*, a film based on his novel (Faherty collection)

What are two notable exceptions to the flat land of the Southeast Lowlands? Crowley's Ridge and Commerce Hills, which rise 150 feet above the surrounding plain

After the Pennsylvanian Era, nature settled down and began the slow weathering process that gave the state its famous caves and sinkholes. Known as **karst topography**, the process was created by rain falling on the ground and eating away at the limestone and dolomite. It is able to do this because the rain is slightly acidic because of carbon dioxide in the air. This mild form of **carbolic acid** slowly eats away carbonates from the rock creating paths for the rivulets to follow. These slowly widen and when they find an exit from the ground, *voila* – you have a spring. Caves are formed when the water drains away from an enlarged passage and air enters into the equation. When just a portion of a cave roof collapses, it leaves behind a natural stone bridge.

Some parts of the state have a landscape that is marked with depressions called sinkholes. This is referred to as karst terrain. The soil cover in these areas is usually thin which allows rainwater to seep into limestone bedrock below. Instead of the water running above the ground in streams, in these areas it flows through cracks and fissures in the bedrock forming tunnels and caves. Rainwater combines with carbon dioxide in the air and forms carbolic acid which slowly eats away at limestone and dolomite. When a cave collapses a sinkhole or sunken landscape is formed. Overlying rock and soil collapse into the cavity forming a bowl-shaped depression on the surface.

What are Missouri's physiographic regions? Southeast Lowland Region, Salem Plateau, West Osage Plains, Springfield Plateau, St. Francois Mountains, North Glacial, and Loessial Till Plains Region

What is the dividing line between the Ozark region and the rest of the state? The Missouri River

Why is the Ozark Plateau unique? It is the only considerable elevated area between the Rockies and Alleghenies.

What important metal was being mined near **Joplin** by 1872? Zinc

What notable hill area in southeast Missouri was formed by soil deposited by the wind? Cayley's Ridge

There is a large granite boulder in Sullivan County (near **Bairdstown**) that is 12 ft. high and 25 ft. long. How did it get there? It was brought down from Canada and deposited by a glacier

What are the main rivers in Missouri's prairie region? The Lamine, Osage, South Grand and Blackwater

What is Missouri's annual rainfall? It varies from 34 inches in the north to 46 inches in the south. A similar pattern exists in Illinois.

How long is the growing season? It averages 170 days.

In what Missouri counties is most karst landscape found? St. Louis, Perry, Genevieve, Cooper, Greene, Boone, Christian, Phelps, Pulaski and Howell

How many commercial caves are in Missouri? There are 28

Where is **Little Dixie**? Centered in Boone and Calloway counties, it received its name because its southern slaveholding settlers rejected Yankee St. Charles and St. Louis in 1810 and settled in the middle of the state. Surrounding counties often like to think they are part of this unique region.

What four rivers help form Missouri's boundaries? Mississippi, St. Francis, Missouri, Des Moines (extreme northeast corner)

What explains the current path of the Missouri River?
As the North American glacier melted, its waters followed the southern rim of the glacier.

What name is given to that part of the state north of the Missouri River? North Glacial and Loessial Region

What is the translation for the French Bourbeuse River? "Muddy"

What historic roads are in Missouri? Route 40, going from St. Louis to Kansas City, Route 66 the "Mainstreet of America" which cuts across the state diagonally from St. Louis, and U.S. 65 running perpendicular to Route 40 and called the Lakes to Gulf Highway

What are Missouri's principal rivers? The Mississippi, Missouri, Platte, Grand, Chariton, Osage, Gasconade, Meramec, Current, Black, St. Francis and White

How many states east of the Mississippi River are bigger than Missouri? None

Where is the largest single outlet spring in America? Big Spring near **Van Buren;** the flow is 276 million gallons a day.

Where is the highest point in the state? Taum Sauk Mountain, 1,772 feet above sea level in southeast Missouri; Taum Sauk was a local Indian chief.

What is the lowest point in Missouri? St. Francis River – 230 feet – southeast Missouri

How tall is nearby Lead Hill, 2 miles east of **Cedar Gap**? 1,744 feet; nearby Seymour Hill is 1,740

Where is the highest waterfall in the state? Evangeline Falls, so named because the site is allegedly referred to in Longfellow's poem

The Pinnacles natural area is a 27-acre area eleven miles north of **Columbia** off Highway 63. Kelly Branch, Rocky Fork and Silver creeks have formed narrows, pinnacles, cliffs and arches in the Burlington limestone.

Cowards Hollow is a 56-acre portion of the Mark Twain Natural Forest southwest of **Van Buren**. The area contains an unusual chert shut-in, shelter cave, a 20 foot waterfall and a chert cliff.

Castor River Shut-ins is a 209 acre area of the Amidon Conservation Area in Madison County off Highway 72. These are Missouri's only known granite shut-ins. The pink granite is from the Bread Tray formation. The eastern collared lizard can be found in these glades.

Where is **Devil's Toll Gate**? This tall cliff is less than a mile away from Mina Sauk Falls. It was so named because wagons on the trail were forced to unload before they could make it through the narrow pass – almost as if the Devil were exacting a toll on travelers.

St. Louis Soccer star / NY Jets kicker Pat Leahy (from *The St. Louis Irish* by David Lossos)

Where are the Elephant Rocks? In Iron County at the northwest edge of **Graniteville; t**he biggest rock, called Dumbo, is 27 feet high.

What Piankisha Indian legend is associated with the Devil's Toll Gate? A maiden of the tribe living in the area became lost and was accosted by a monster. When her escape was cut off by a big wall of granite, her death seemed imminent. She was saved when **the Great Spirit hurled a bolt of lightning that split the wall** with a narrow passageway, allowing her to escape.

In what part of Missouri did the French mine lead? The St. Francis and Meramec river valleys

Why did early settlers avoid the treeless prairie region of Missouri? Since there were no trees, they thought it was infertile.

What is the best explanation of why there were no trees in the prairie regions? Paul Bunyan cut them down to build his cabin and barn.

What area of Missouri is suitable for growing cotton? The Mississippi valley area south of **Cape Girardeau**

What river goes under the St. Louis Muny Opera? River des Peres

Where is Missouri's most famous igneous Precambrian knob? Pilot Knob, north of **Ironton**

Where is the Devil's Honeycomb? A few miles southwest of **Irondale**; on top of Hughes Mountain, it is an example of igneous rock that cooled to form large columns.

Where is the rugged Lincoln Hills area of Missouri? Northeast Missouri along the Mississippi up by **Hannibal;** it includes The Pinnacle – the highest point on the river at 840 ft.

What is one of the best examples of twin windblown peaks in Missouri? In St. Charles County; the French named them Les Mammelles (twin mammary glands) and were easily seen from the floodplain of the Missouri.

Where is the Balds region of Missouri? Southern Missouri in the Shepherd of the Hills country; a bald is a mountain with a grassy area surrounded by trees.

Who were the Baldknobbers? A vigilante group formed to combat lawlessness of the post Civil War Era that sometimes violated the law themselves. Anti-baldknobber groups were often formed.

Where is Blue Mound? It is a 200 ft. tall, mile long hill that was used as a burial mound by Chief White Hair of the Osage Indians; it is located northeast of **Nevada**, Missouri.

Carthage was the marble capital of Missouri. The White House, the Missouri Capitol building and the U.S. Capitol are all faced with marble from Carthage.

How many states border Missouri? Eight – the same number as Tennessee and the most in the USA

How did an area on the Big Piney River come to be called **Devil's Elbow**? Logs for railroad ties were floated down the river to the town of **Jerome**. There was a near 90 degree bend in the river that caused log jams and lumber jacks said it was a devil of an elbow.

In 1900, how much extra money could Missouri farmers earn by hand hewing railroad ties with a double bladed axe? Ten cents per tie

Where was the largest Indian shelter cave in Missouri? At Onyx Mountain Cavern near **Powellville**

How was the Gasconade River named? The French named it for the area of Gascony back in their native land.

What metal was mined at the town of **Webb City**? Lead

What were some common uses of Missouri lead? Lead was used to make lead pipes (replaced by PVC), pewter tableware (lead and tin), red paint, batteries and ammo for guns.

Where does Missouri rank among states in lead production? First

What were Missouri's early lead centers? **Potosi**, **Herculaneum** and **Joplin**

What other metals are found in lead as by-products? Cobalt, silver, nickel, copper and zinc

Where was Missouri's center in 1950 for mining copper, cobalt and nickel? **Fredericktown**

Where is the mining belt in Missouri that produces the most zinc? It begins at **Springfield** and extends to the western border.

The rock residue from lead smelting is called "chat" and it was piled in great heaps beside the mines. Did it have any value? Yes, it was used extensively in road pavings and more than a million tons were sold each year.

Metal ores have to be smelted to separate the metal from the rock. What geographic advantage did Missouri have over most other smelting states? Missouri was next to the rich Illinois coal fields for fuel.

What were some common uses of Missouri zinc? It was used to coat nails, wire, gutters and sheet metal in a process called galvanization.

What state, plagued by drought, does Missouri object to drawing water off from the Missouri River? North Dakota – long a thorn in Missouri's side concerning this issue

How good are Missouri's water resources? With one acre of running water to every hundred acres of land, **it is the best watered state in the Union.**

What metals are smelted from Missouri rocks? Lead, tungsten, zinc, iron, copper, silver, barite, cobalt and nickel

Where is Missouri's Royal Gorge? It's eight miles south of **Arcadia** (Iron County) on Highway 21.

Missouri and Kentucky are the only two adjoining states separated by a river, that aren't connected by a bridge. How did that happen? Missouri, Illinois, and Kentucky all come together near **Cairo**, Illinois. To go from Kentucky to Missouri, travelers cross the Ohio River Bridge near Cairo and then go into Missouri by crossing an Illinois bridge that spans the Mississippi River.

Where is Missouri's Little Grand Canyon? Also known as Marthasville Grand Canyon and Devil's Den Hollow, it is in Warren County.

Where is the biggest spring in Missouri? Big Spring is about four miles south of **Van Buren** in Carter County.

What is Missouri's rank in size among states? Nineteenth

A TRAIL OF TEARS IN SOUTHERN MISSOURI

During the winter of 1838-39, thousands of Cherokee Native-Americans were uprooted from their homelands in the Great Smoky Mountains and forcibly removed by the U.S. government to Oklahoma Territory. The Cherokee nation included about nineteen thousand natives and their ancestral lands covered several southeastern states, but were concentrated mainly in eastern Tennessee and northwest Georgia. The Cherokee were among the proudest, most civilized and most advanced Indians in America. Sequoia, one of their leaders, had developed a Cherokee alphabet. They learned the ways of the white man and owned businesses, ran plantations and printed a newspaper. Some of them even owned slaves. They are also credited with an independent development of the log cabin.

The white man had long been known for forcibly removing Indians from their lands, but when Indian-hater Andrew Jackson was elected president in 1828, the Cherokee knew this spelled trouble. As the white population in Georgia grew, the demands to solve the "Indian problem" increased. In 1830, Congress passed the Indian Removal Act and Jackson quickly signed the bill into law. Many Americans thought this was an injustice, including Tennessee congressman, Davy Crockett. The matter went to court and in the case of Worcester v. Georgia, the Supreme Court held the law to be unconstitutional. But Jackson proceeded with the removal saying, "Mr. (Chief Justice) Marshall has made his decision, let him enforce it."

It was Jackson's hand-picked successor, President Martin Van Buren, who finally enforced the Removal Act. The law affected Five Civilized Tribes: the Seminole, Cherokee, the Creek, Choctaw and Chickasaw. In April of 1838, General Winfield Scott began rounding up the "savages" and herding them into stockades. Hundreds of natives died from disease in the makeshift forts during months of waiting for the trek to begin. Instead of one big procession, the Cherokee were divided into several groups and took three different routes, making it easier for them to forage for food along the way. The group that went across southern Illinois and Missouri had the northernmost route and suffered the most. Horses and wagons were loaded with possessions that those on the forced march held dear. Salt pork and corn meal were their only daily rations. The march did not begin in earnest until October, with over 15,000 Cherokee, including women and children, participating. The U.S. military actually played only a supervisory role in the march, as native leaders were allowed to make many of the decisions along the way.

Trail of Tears map

A distance of about 1100 miles had to be covered by people who were on horseback, in wagons, or on foot. It didn't take long for the emigration to run into bad weather, starting when they arrived in western Kentucky and Tennessee. Blankets and rations provided by the U.S. government proved to be inadequate. Medical care was nearly non-existent. On reaching southern Illinois, many of the braves deserted the march, disappeared into the forests and sneaked back to their homelands.

Entry into Illinois was made at **Golconda**, on the Ohio River. The Buel House and Davidson Cabin at Golconda are the state's only remaining structures along the Trail of Tears. Mr. Buel was one of those who gave aid and comfort to the refugees. It took several days to transport everyone across the river by John Berry, who operated the ferry at the site. Berry made a nice sum of money for his efforts. He charged $1 a head when his normal fee was 13 cents for a Conestoga wagon. A marker a few miles southwest of Golconda notes that 9,500 Cherokee passed the site on the way to their new home in Indian Territory (Oklahoma). Thus Berry made $9,500 dollars off the starving natives. While staying near Golconda, several Cherokee were murdered by local whites.

Southern Illinoisans who witnessed the event were surprised to hear some of the natives singing "Amazing Grace" to bolster their spirits. The song had been translated into Cherokee by an American missionary. It has since become sort of a Cherokee anthem. As the sick and weak died along the way, they were quickly buried where they fell. Cholera, whooping cough and smallpox spread among the tribe during the journey. There is no way to accurately know how many Cherokee died during this sad saga. Most estimates place the number who died in camps (mostly from disease) at 2,000 and the number of those who died along the journey at another 2,000.

After entering Illinois at Golconda, the trail dipped slightly south and went through a town called Wartrace. Then it moved on to Alley Springs which was slightly below **Dixon Springs**. From that point on, the trail pretty much followed an old deer and buffalo trail that would eventually become Illinois Highway 146. The town of **Wetaug**, in Pulaski County, was named for one of the tribes of the Cherokee.

The trail exited Illinois at Bainbridge's Mississippi River ferry site, located just north of **Cape Girardeau**. There were significant amounts of ice in the river which caused further delay and even more deaths. From there the difficult trek continued across southern Missouri, past **Waynesville**, and into Indian Territory.

Jean Baptiste duSable – Founder of Chicago (Chicago Hist. Society)

The winter of 1838-39 was unusually harsh, causing more suffering and deaths than would have otherwise occurred. Reactions of the local white inhabitants were mixed. Some had lost loved ones to Indian attacks and resented them. Others were indifferent. And there were those who felt sorry for their plight and donated food and clothing. The town of **Vienna,** Missouri, has a Trail of Tears Memorial Park to help memorialize the event. Another tribute to the Cherokee exists near **Jonesboro,** IL at the Trail of Tears State Forest.

Cape Girardeau County is home to Missouri's Trail of Tears State Park (573-334-1711). The Bushyhead Memorial in the park is a tribute to Nancy Bushyhead Hildebrand, a native woman who was a sister to Reverend Bushyhead and a wife to Lewis Hildebrand, who led one of the detachments. She died and is buried somewhere within the park's boundaries. This Northern group went through **Springfield** and exited the state near Fayette, Arkansas. A more southerly group came into Missouri near **Cairo**, Illinois, and went into Arkansas near the southeast part of the bootheel area and went towards Batesville, Arkansas. The different groups then crossed into Oklahoma Territory from Arkansas. **Jerome**, Missouri, also has a memorial to the Trail of Tears.

In 1986, the National Park Service designated a Trail of Tears Route through Missouri that travels through **Cape Girardeau, Fredericktown, Farmington, Flat River, Potosi, Steelville, Rolla, Lebanon and Springfield**.

Descendants of the displaced Cherokee refer to the event in their language as Nynna-daul-tsuni – "The Place Where They Cried." For more information read Joan Gilbert's book, *The Trail of Tears Across Missouri.*

AFRICAN-AMERICAN HERITAGE

Where is the Black Madonna Shrine? Operated by Franciscans, it's just off Interstate 44 between **Pacific** and **Eureka.**

What founder of the city of Chicago gave up his trading post there and moved to **St. Charles**? Jean Baptiste DuSable

Moses Gunn was born in St. Louis in 1929, the oldest of seven children. He served a stint in the Army and then attended Tennessee State University where he received a Bachelor's degree. He portrayed a gangster in two of the ***Shaft*** films and was Booker T. Washington in the movie, ***Ragtime***. He was nominated for an Emmy in 1977 for his role in the mini-series, ***Roots***. Gunn died from the complications of asthma in 1993.

Robert Guillaume was born Robert Williams in St. Louis in 1927. Guillaume is French for the name William. He pursued an acting career after a stint in the Army. His first big role was Benson the butler on the series, *Soap*. Then he did the spinoff *Benson* which ended in 1986. He became the TV pitchman for Ocean Spray cranberry juice and Phillips Milk of Magnesia. He is an accomplished singer and replaced Michael Crawford in the role of the *Phantom of the Opera*.

Redd Foxx was born in St. Louis but his family soon moved to Chicago. His electrician father abandoned the family when he was four. He once worked as a dishwasher in a speakeasy where Malcom X was a waiter. Fox was ¼ Seminole and was dubbed "Chicago Red" due to his red hair. He took the stage name Foxx from baseball star, Jimmy Foxx. Foxx became known as a stand-up comedian known for raunchy humor. He was the star of *Sanford and Son* until it was cancelled in 1977. After *Sanford and Son*, Foxx had numerous legal battles with the IRS. On one occasion they seized his house and snatched some expensive jewelry right off his body. Foxx died in 1991 after suffering a heart attack.

Maya Angelou was born in St. Louis in 1928 and became an important figure in the Civil Rights movement. In 2001, the *Ladies Home Journal* named her one of the 30 most powerful women in America. Her 1969 biography, *I Know Why the Caged Bird Sings*, was nominated for the National Book Award and she has won wide acclaim for her poetry.

Maya was her childhood nickname. After being raped by her mother's boyfriend, she became mute for nearly five years. Her last name was Johnson but she changed it to Angelou after divorcing her first husband, a Greek sailor named Angelous. Since the 1990s she has gone on the lecture circuit, charging a standard fee of around $15,000 per appearance.

Leon Spinks was born in St. Louis in 1953. He enlisted in the Marines while still an amateur boxer. He won the gold medal in the light heavyweight division at the 1976 Olympics in Montreal. Brother Michael Spinks also won a gold medal at those games. He rose to the top of the heavyweight rankings after only seven fights. He made history in 1978 by besting an aged and out of shape champion, Muhammad Ali in 15 rounds. Spinks liked to party and failed to train. He lost the title to Ali in a rematch. Spinks continued his outlandish living, even hiring Mr. T as his bodyguard. In ten years Spinks went from champion to homeless and was found working at a McDonalds in

Nebraska. Brother Michael Spinks beat champion Larry Holmes in 1985, making them the only brothers to ever hold the heavyweight title. His son **Cory Spinks** later won the welterweight title.

Josephine Baker was born in St. Louis in 1906 and for a while lived in Chestnut Valley at the corner of Targee and Gratiot. Her mother worked for a German family and it is thought that her father was white. She was living with her family in Boxcar City, on the **East St. Louis** riverfront, at the time of the 1917 race riot there. She talks about the terror she experienced in her biography.

Josephine started her career as a street performer, dancing in the streets as a child. She entered vaudeville joining the St. Louis Chorus at 15. She headed to New York City during the Harlem Renaissance but became an expatriate when she left for Paris in the middle of the decade to escape segregation. She was an instant success thanks to her erotic dancing where she appeared practically nude on stage at the *Folies Bergeres*. She often appeared on stage with Chiquita, her pet leopard who wore a diamond studded collar. She often performed the *Danse sauvage*, wearing a skirt of artificial bananas.

She became the first woman of African descent to star in a major motion picture, *La Sirene des Tropiques*. She returned to the U.S. on several occasions but she never obtained the same reputation as in France. She refused to perform before segregated audiences.

Baker was so well known that when the Nazis occupied Paris they were hesitant to cause her harm. She was awarded the *Croix de Guerre* for her underground intelligence work during the war. Josephine Baker was often criticized in the American press for her loose morals and numerous marriages. The "Black Pearl" died in April of 1975.

J.B. "Jet" Banks

J.B. "Jet" Banks was elected state representative in 1968. In 1976, he was elected to the Missouri Senate where he became the first African-American in that body to become the Majority Leader. He received a degree from Lincoln University and has done graduate work at Washington University and St. Louis University. He is in banking and real estate and is director of several Missouri corporations. Banks has also received over 100 awards and citations for St. Louis community service.

St. Louisan **Henry Armstrong** won the featherweight boxing title in October of 1937. He is the only man to hold three titles simultaneously as he was also the welterweight and lightweight champion.

CHURCHES AND RELIGION

When was the first Baptist Church organized in St. Louis? With the help of John Mason Peck, a log church was built on Fee Fee Creek in 1815.

When was the first Presbyterian Church organized in St. Louis? 1817, with the help of Calvinists Clement Penrose and Charles Gratiot

What started the recent problem between the Catholic hierarchy and St. Stanislaus Church in North St. Louis? Quite some time ago St. Stanislaus parishioners asked the bishop for permission to form a corporation and a Board of Directors with the priest still having the final say. About twenty years ago, the Catholic hierarchy took the power away from priests and gave it to the board. Parish members defied hierarchy officials by refusing to accept the authority of the local pastor. As punishment, the archbishop dissolved the parish and took away the sacraments from the defiant church. St. Stanislaus members say its all about the hierarchy wanting their money – they are worth about $15 million. They will also probably make more money when they sell land to the state for the new bridge coming in across the Mississippi in the near future. It's a Polish church and they play accordion music there.

This Protestant author was Best Man at a north St. Louis Catholic wedding at St. Pius X Church in 1963. When did it close? Police officer Ken Hoelker was married in St. Pius X, but it was closed a little over two years ago due to declining attendance. The two of us became acquainted when we worked at Emerson Electric.

Where is the St. Stanislaus Jesuit Museum? On Howdershel Road in north St. Louis.

Do both bell towers of St. Stanislaus have bells? No – only one

What brewery was located near St. Frances de Sales Church (Ohio near Gravois) in St. Louis? The German Griesedieck Brothers who donated large sums to the church

What church on South Broadway (near Soulard) has the oldest bell **made in the U.S.**? Sts. Peter and Paul Catholic Church – the 1850 bell was in the original church but when a new and larger church was built, it was replaced. It sits on the lawn with a special marker.

What St. Louis church was built on top of an old cemetery? St. Bridget of Erin; the basement has dirt floors and old stone grave markers.

What is the new function of the old United Hebrew Temple? It now houses the library of the Missouri Historical Society. The new Temple/Congregation is in Creve Coeur at 13788 Conway Rd.

Where is the **only mechanically operated carillon in the state of Missouri**? At Concordia Seminary; a carillon has numerous bells that can play a tune.

What church has the largest steel bell in the state of Missouri? Christ Church Cathedral in St. Louis

Why does this church have a statue of Daniel Tuttle? He is considered the **Father of the Episcopalian/ Anglican Church in the West**, and he greatly expanded the work of the church in Missouri as well.

Of what material are most of the clappers of steel bells made? Iron

What is the most common material for church bells? Bronze

WITCHES, GHOSTS AND GOBLINS

Halloween was always a fun, but scary, proposition back in the 1940s. This author's head is still filled with spooktacular memories of ghouls and ghosts, witches and goblins. Carving the Jack-O'-Lantern was unfailingly a

highlight of the season. I would help my mother select a medium sized pumpkin. Mother wanted one that was symmetrical and blemish free, but I usually talked her into buying one that was misshapen and had character. Once we got home, mother cut the obligatory round hole in the top and scooped out the innards for making scrumptious homemade pies. Then she gave me a butcher knife to carve the face on front. "Don't cut your finger off and get blood all over my clean floor," she always warned. "Okay, Mom," I nonchalantly answered in my best Henry Aldrich voice. I had the choice of making it a "happy face" or a "spooky face." I usually opted for the sinister design with a menacing look.

Spooky Halloween memories

It wasn't easy for kids in my neighborhood to go trick or treating in that area. My older cousins warned me that witches were on the prowl and they liked to swoop down on their broomsticks and snatch kids off the streets. They would then whisk them off to some horrible cave, plop them in a cauldron of boiling water (bubbling with lizard tails, newt eyes, and salamander toes), and make stew of their flesh.

"**If you ever encounter an evil witch that begins chasing you on her broom, be sure to take off your left shoe and spit in it**. That will break the evil one's magic powers and she will be forced to search for a different victim," they explained.

1942 Chevy Highway Patrol Car with siren on fender

Being caught in the clutches of evil monsters wasn't the worst thing that could happen to a kid back then. We also had to contend with the ghost of Henry Lee. According to the legend, Henry was a religious man who attended the Assembly of God Church. He worked the night shift in Washington Park at the St. Louis Bridge Company, next to the B & O tracks.

It was Halloween Eve in 1930. Henry Lee lived in a desolate area called Jackass Flats. He loved going to the shallow Spring Lake next to the tracks to go **frog gigging**. A long pole with a two-pronged mechanism on the end proved useful for plucking the green amphibians from their murky habitats.

1942 Highway Patrol weigh station

One fog-laden night, he was walking home from work, carrying a kerosene lantern to light his way through a heavy mist that was as thick as pea soup. He accidentally stumbled upon a group of moonshiners who thought he was a "revenuer." One of them quickly picked up a shotgun and fired. **The powerful blast knocked Henry clean out of his shoes**. The unlucky fellow never made it home.

After the incident, on every subsequent Halloween, people reported seeing a ghostly apparition, wandering around the area, carrying a lamp. The headless spirit of Henry Lee was just trying to find his way home.

Kids in my neighborhood were afraid to trick or treat. We usually made our rounds in the opposite direction where we were less likely to run into Henry Lee. But one year, when I was eleven years old, I foolishly mustered up the courage to go looking for Henry Lee. I took along a Brownie box camera so that I would have proof of the encounter. It was a dark Halloween night barely lit by a gothic crescent moon. The cold night mist settled on my hands and face and sent a chill down my quivering spine. Undaunted, I made my way along an old gravel road hoping for success – yet praying that the grisly story had been a mere figment of someone's imagination. Suddenly, out of the ink-black darkness of Hades, there it was. My hands trembling, I hurriedly snapped a picture and ran as fast as I could back to the safety of my home. When the roll was developed, I quickly shuffled through the snap shots looking for my prize. I gasped in shocked disbelief when I came upon the picture. **All that you could see in the photograph was a lantern about three feet off the ground, slightly to the left of an empty pair of brogans**!

MISSOURI HIGHWAY PATROL

Courtesy of St. Charles Patrolman Ken Hoelker Ret. Badge 351

The Missouri Highway Patrol was created in 1931; 55 men were chosen from 5,000 applicants. The original cars did not have a red light on top. Instead, they had two Klaxon horns. The first trooper salaries were $125 a month.

Thirty-caliber rifles were issued to troopers in 1934. Highway Patrol headquarters were moved to **Jefferson City** in 1938, from **Springfield.**

Recruits were being trained in 1939 at Camp Hawthorne, near **Kaiser.** There were two big events patrolmen were being assigned to by 1939, the State Fair at **Sedalia**, and Mizzou football games in **Columbia.**

Patrolmen did not get two-way FM radios until 1941.

Women were first employed by the Patrol as radio operators in 1943 due to wartime manpower shortages. The

Highway Patrol purchased its first aircraft in 1946, a war surplus Stinson L-5.

The Patrol was placed in charge of the Missouri Training School for Boys at **Boonville** to restore order and improve conditions in 1948. Tom Pasley, in 1948, was the patrolman who designed the first large door decals.

The monthly income for troopers in 1949 was $250.

Some truck weigh stations by 1950 included: **Cameron, Dexter, Harrisonville, Matthews, Parkville, Poplar Bluff, Republic, Moberly, Savannah, Kansas City, Macon, Hannibal, Imperial, St. Charles, Gray Summit, Carthage, Springfield, Cape Girardeau and Kingdom City.**

1943 first women radio operators

The Patrol helped quell a riot in September of 1954 at the State penitentiary at Jeff City; three inmates were killed.

Patrol members received their first retirement system in 1955; before that, they were only on Social Security.

Patrol cars first received seat belts in 1955.

Troopers first started using blackjacks in 1958.

The Highway Patrol obtained its first helicopter in 1959.

By 1962, 505 men were in the highway patrol.

Driving while intoxicated was reduced from a felony to a misdemeanor in 1963; thereafter, it only was a felony on the third offense.

Missouri's first African-American trooper was David McPherson, 1965.

Men going into the Highway Patrol in 1966 were issued guns from state funds, but the uniform, hat and shoes were out of pocket expenses.

Post-Dispatch Building in 1904

In the mid-Sixties, the pay of a rookie patrolman was about $5,100.

Troopers were first issued chemical mace in1967.

Troopers were sent in May of 1969 to Lincoln University in Jeff City to quell student anti-Vietnam War riots.

Trooper William Brandt was killed by a tornado in June of 1970 when the winds blew his car into a bridge abutment near **Macon.**

The first bomb and arson unit was organized in 1971.

The first two female Patrol members were Patricia Wright and Bridget Cronin, 1975.

The last full-size car to be used in large quantities by the Highway Patrol was the 1978 Mercury.

Missouri got its first seat belt law in 1987, signed by Governor Ashcroft; Ashcroft would go on to become Attorney General under George W. Bush.

What famous people have been escorted by the Missouri Highway Patrol? Winston Churchill, Harry Truman, Ronald Reagan, George H.W. Bush, George W. Bush, Pope John Paul II and Mikhail Gorbachev

The Patrol's first K-9 Unit completed its training in November, 1989.

Semi-automatic pistol (Glock .40 caliber Model 22) replaced the old Smith & Wesson revolvers in 1991; every officer had his badge number as a serial number on the gun.

What was the main provision of the 1994 law that allowed Highway Patrol officers to retire early? Eighty and Out – an employee's age and years of service had to total 80.

Troopers started riding bicycles to patrol the State Fair in 1995.

What became the new speed limit on Missouri interstates in 1996? 70 on rural and 60 on urban interstates

In what year did the state law dictate that Missouri highway patrolmen would be called "troopers?" 2007

When did Missouri's "proof of insurance" law go into effect? 1998

Did Missouri troopers ever wear badges? No - their distinctive uniform is enough.

Why were wallet badges issued at one time and then taken away? Officials discovered that patrolmen were using them to get into movies free. They currently are issued wallet badges and are told it is against regulations to accept such favors.

Where did the first group of recruits to Highway Patrol train? St. Louis Police Academy; they are currently trained at the Highway Patrol Academy in Jeff City.

Did early Missouri troopers use motorcycles or cars? They had open Ford roadster cars and the Colonel would not let them put the tops up – even in winter – because he wanted the public to recognize them as troopers.

Were troopers ever allowed to shoot at speeding cars if the driver failed to pull over? Troopers were told to first pull alongside and wave them over. If that didn't work they were allowed to shoot out the tires.

When did Highway Patrol cars switch from the single rotating red light to a bar of lights on top of the car? Around 1967

In the 1960s, approximately how many miles did the highway patrol put on their cars before trading them? 25,000 miles – currently, it is 50,000; Illinois waits until 150,000.

In the mid-Sixties, what did it cost the highway patrol to trade for a new car? One dollar – car companies subsidized the police because they wanted the public to see patrolmen driving big cars to encourage the buying public to purchase bigger cars.

What happened to the practice? It ended around 1970 because the federal government said it was "unfair" trade practice.

Are retired Missouri patrolmen allowed to carry their guns into restaurants? Yes, but they have to qualify on the firing range once a year. They are allowed to carry their weapons anywhere a working police officer can carry his weapon.

Illinois, a more liberal (anti-gun) state, does not allow retired policemen to carry weapons.

What happens to fine money collected by the Highway Patrol? Unlike St. Louis city or county, it's donated to Missouri schools.

What Missouri troopers have been killed in the performance of their duties? B.O. Booth, V.O. Dosing, F.L. Walker, J.N. Greim, C.P. Korbin, R.S. Creach, W.W. Allman, J.R. Jenkins, W.R. Brandt, H.C. Bruns, R.W. Harper, G.W. Snodgrass, D.H. Marion, J.M. Froemsdorf, J.E. Linegar, D.C. May, R.A. Guilliams, M.E. Webster, R.G. Kimberling, R.J. Kolilis, Kelly Poynter, Kevin Floyd, Jay Sampietro, Ralph Tatoian, Dewayne Graham Jr., Michael Newton

AMAZING MISSOURI TRIVIA

(at least in our opinion)

How should a knowledgeable person pronounce the state of Missouri? TV broadcasters usually say Muh-zur-e but traditionally its been pronounced Muh-zur-uh. It's an absolute no no to say Muh-zur-ree.

What couple founded Lindenwood College in **St. Charles**? Missourian Rufus Easton, the founder of **Alton**, Illinois, later moved across the river. His daughter Mary was wed to George Sibley and they later founded Lindenwood.

Early picture of St. Louis City Hall

What is the proportion of males to females in Missouri? Males constitute 48.85 percent of the population and females 51.15 percent; it's a genetic thing.

What is the ethnic makeup of the state? 85.35 percent white; 11.56 percent African-American; 1.33 Asian; .45 Native American; .17 Hawaiian; 2.3 Hispanic

How many electoral votes does Missouri have in a presidential election? Missouri has 11 electoral votes based on its population.

J.C. Penney, the large retail store, had its beginnings in **Hamilton**, Missouri.

What is the origin of the word "Missouri?" Missouri is most likely a French rendition derived from an Algonquian word meaning "place of large canoes."

J.C. Penney

What other states besides Missouri claim to be the "Crossroads of the Nation?" Indiana and Illinois, although Indiana has long been eclipsed by the other two states

How long is Missouri? About 460 miles long – measured from the northwest to southeast corners as the crow flies

What is the highest point in the state of Missouri? Proffit/Taum Sauk Mountain off Highway 21 at 1,744 feet. In order to qualify as a mountain, a peak must be at least 1000 feet high.

Where is the lowest point in the state? Cottonwood Point in southeast Missouri on the St. Francis River which is only 230 feet above sea level

What are the longitude and latitude boundaries of Missouri? The state is roughly between 36 to 40 degrees north latitude, and 90 to 95 degrees west longitude, making it about ¼ of the way around the globe from the prime meridian in England.

How large in area is the state? 69,674 square miles – 18th overall in size

How many states border Missouri? Eight – a number that only Tennessee can match They include Illinois, Kentucky, Tennessee, Arkansas, Oklahoma, Kansas, Nebraska and Iowa.

How many counties are in the state? 114. Illinois has 102.

For whom is the state capital named? Thomas Jefferson

What is Missouri's official nickname? The Show Me State

How much larger is Missouri than Rhode Island? With 69,674 square miles, it is 57 times larger

What is unique about St. Louis? It is the only independent city in the state and it is a city that has the functions and offices of a county.

What is Missouri's largest county in size? Texas (south of Rolla) is the largest county – 1,180 sq miles - making it larger than Rhode Island. Its county seat is **Houston**.

What is the state's smallest county? Worth County – 266 sq miles

What are the ten largest cities in Missouri? Kansas City – 444,387; St. Louis - 343,279; Springfield - 150,704; Independence – 111,023; Columbia – 89,593; Lee's Summit (south of Independence with part of it resting in Jackson County) - 78,659; St. Joe - 72,628; O'Fallon – 67,009; St. Charles 61,411; St. Peters 53,907 Jackson County has two of the largest cities in the state (Kansas City and Independence, and part of another, Lee's Summit).

What are the three distinct regions of Missouri? The state is located in the central plains region of the US and it has the Prairie region in the north and west, the Ozark region in the Southwest, and the Southeast lowlands near the bootheel.

What school won the state basketball title in 2005? **Poplar Bluff**, led by Tyler Hansbrough who now plays for North Carolina

What Kansas City newspaper has been listed as one of the six best newspapers in the country? *Kansas City Star*

When Missouri State U. tried to cut $350,000 from its budget by getting rid of 5 sports, including women's tennis, what happened? The 2006 action was followed by a class-action lawsuit claiming discrimination and violation of Title IX.

Back in the 1930's what did the letters RFD stand for on Missouri farms? Rural Free Delivery; prior to RFD, people living on farms had to go to the nearest town to pick up their mail. RFD led to the building of roads and bridges in rural America.

How many traffic related deaths were there in Missouri in 2005? 1,213 – slightly higher than 2004

Who was Rocky Sickman? From **Washington**, Missouri, he was the only American hostage held by Iranians (Carter administration) for 444 days who returned home with a diary.

Cinderella Theater at 2735 Cherokee

As of 2006, how well has Missouri done in recovering from the 2001 recession caused by the attacks on 9-11? Missouri is one of thirteen states not to have recovered completely with employment growth and manufacturing slightly lagging.

What change in handicapped parking signs did the Missouri House pass in 2006? "Handicapped Parking" was deemed politically incorrect and the new signs will read "accessible parking."

Old St. Louis Shriners Hospital – Kingshighway at Clayton

What else is on the state flag beside the three horizontal stripes? The state seal

The state tree is the white dogwood.

The hottest temperature ever recorded in Missouri is 118 degrees on July 10, 1954, at **Warsaw.**

What controversial gun legislation became Missouri law in 2004? Permission for qualified Missourians to carry concealed weapons

What has been the net result? Crime rates did not drop but accidental or unjustified shootings have not risen. All the brouhaha was for nothing – it has become a non-issue.

When the Missouri Highway Patrol writes a ticket for speeding, where does the fine money go? To a special fund for schools; the legislature passed a law some years ago hoping it would lessen motorist complaints. It didn't!

What World War II general was the son of a Missouri country school teacher and a seamstress? Omar Bradley

What was the name of Omar Bradley's Piper Cub plane that he used in World War II? *Missouri Mule*

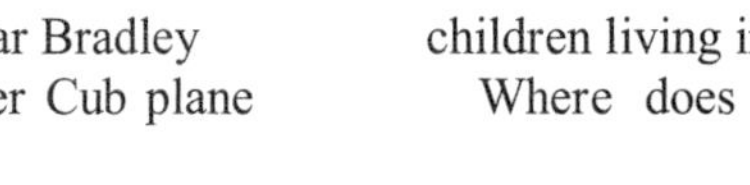

Ronnie's Drive-in at Crestwood on Route 66

Why did Missouri officials order 2,000 Missouri truckers to retake their tests in April of 2006? Facilities in **Sikeston** and **West Plains** (mostly school districts) were lax, and perhaps fraudulent in administering the tests. A license clerk in **Independence** blew the whistle on the scheme.

What is the specific southern border of Missouri, excepting the bootheel? It should be easy to remember because it's the 1820 Missouri Compromise line of 36 degrees, 30 minutes north latitude

Glen Miller bought his first trombone in **Grant City**; the family lived there when he was 12.

Sheldon "Red" Chaney opened a restaurant in **Springfield** (1947) where you drove up to an open window and yelled your order inside. He painted everything inside blue and green; you'd think you were outside at a picnic. It was called Red's Giant Hamburgs and it was on Route 66. It is **considered the nation's first food drive-thru window**.

Red called them hamburgs because he misjudged the size of the sign and ran out of room for the letters.

The Missouri town of **Marionville**, southwest of **Springfield on Highway 60, is home to white (albino) squirrels.** There is a $1,000 fine for harming any of the critters. **Olney**, Illinois, is also famous for its white squirrels (rats with bushy tails.

Missouri's nicknames include: The Show Me State, The Cave State, The Lead State; some say Missouri is second to Tennessee in total number of caves, but is first in caves open to tourism.

The State Flower of Missouri is the White hawthorn "wild haw" flower.

The state song of Missouri is "The Missouri Waltz," written in 1914 and adopted in 1949.

The state mineral of Missouri is Galena, or lead sulfide – lead.

The three main colors on the state flag are Red (valor), white (purity), blue (vigilance, justice).

The state motto of Missouri is "The Welfare of the People Shall be the Supreme Law."

Where does Missouri rank compared to other states regarding the number of people with college degrees? 37th

Where does Missouri rank regarding the fewest number of children living in poverty? 37th

Where does Missouri rank among the states for life expectancy? 26th

Where does Missouri rank compared to other states when it comes to being "friendly" to small businesses? 22nd

Where does Missouri rank with other states in per capita income? 29th

How many states were in the Union when Missouri was admitted? Missouri was the 24th state; it has 24 stars on the state seal.

When is Missouri Day? The third Wednesday of October; schools are supposed to spend time that day devoted to Missouri history.

According to the 2000 census, what is the state's population? 5,754,618

What disturbing news did Missourians receive in 2007?

According to national statistics, Missouri had more illegal meth labs than any other state.

What infamous incident occurred in August of 2007 at **Potosi**? A crazed gunman killed three and wounded several others at the First Congregational Church of **Neosho.**

Where did the infamous "Ma" Barker and her sons live for a while in Missouri? **Webb City**

Stetson's only hat manufacturing site in the U.S. is located at **St. Joseph**.

The U.S. center of population (2008) is about seven miles east of **Edgar Springs**

How did the town of **Arlington,** on Route 66, get its name? The name came from Arlington, Virginia, home of P.C. Harrison, the town's founder.

How did the town of **Avilla,** on Route 66, get its name? It was named for the Indiana hometown of David Holman, the town's founder.

How was **Ballwin** named? It was named for John Ball who laid out the town in 1837.

Kansas City is the only large town within 200 miles of both the geographic center and population center of the U.S.

How did the town of **Ozark** gain national prominence in 1887? A group of law enforcement officers raided a Baldknobbers' stronghold and administered justice to the night riding vigilantes.

This author's wife had a cousin, Wayne Armistead, who lived in **Richland**. What was he noted for? He was the town's only dentist. This author once fired an Uzi he accepted in lieu of money.

In what town did Cole Younger and his gang commit their first bank robbery? **Liberty**, Missouri – 1866; they made off with $60,000 in gold and currency.

Did the outlaw Frank James enlist to fight for the Confederacy? Yes, in 1861

Where did Jesse James usually hide out after he robbed a bank or stagecoach? At his mother's house; he was a mama's boy.

Did the Younger brothers and James brothers ever join forces? Yes – they robbed banks at **Richmond** and **Gallatin**, Missouri.

Did Jesse James ever kill anyone? He killed the engineer in an 1873 train robbery in Iowa.

Where did Jesse and Frank hide out after robbing the Iron Mountain mail train in 1874? **Roscoe**, Missouri

What happened at the attempted bank robbery at Northfield, Minnesota in 1876? The citizens, sensing something was wrong when the James gang rode into town, alerted the sheriff and they fought back, killing several members of the gang. No loot was obtained in this failed attempt.

When did the James gang commit their last bank robbery? At **Glendale**, Missouri in 1881

Vess Soda Sign

World's tallest man – Alton's Robert Wadlow as a young teen - International Shoe made his footwear free in exchange for promotional appearances at St. Louis area shoe stores

Why is Jesse sometimes known as Mr. Howard? Howard was a pseudonym he used for three years while laying low after the Northfield raid.

Who portrayed Jesse in *The Great Northfield Minnesota Raid*? Robert Duvall; Cliff Robertson played Cole Younger in the 1972 film.

ST. LOUIS/MISSOURI TASTE BUDS

As a native Illinoisan I was amazed to discover my state's significant connection to certain foods and drink. Cracker Jack originated at **Chicago's** 1893 Columbian Exposition. The confection known as caramel was invented by a **Peru**, Illinois candy maker. The first Dairy Queen opened in **Kankakee** in 1938. Miracle Whip salad dressing was invented by Max Crosett of **Salem**. Ray Kroc opened his first McDonald's franchise in **Des Plaines**. Twinkies was a snack food first concocted by James Dewar of **Schiller Park**. The ice cream sundae was invented in **Evanston**. The first Steak "n" Shake appeared in **Normal** in 1934. Chuckles were first made in **Danville**.

Yet Missouri has a pretty good list of its own. **Crab Rangoon** is thought to have been invented in St. Louis at Trader Vic's Polynesian Restaurant – though some dispute this. Trader Vic's was near the Eads Bridge on 4th and Washington Avenue. It had one of the finest New Guinea primitive art collections in the world and was on the lower level of the Bel-Air Motel Complex. It closed in 1985 and is now part of a Ramada Inn complex.

Toasted ravioli was invented at Oldani's on The Hill and served to Mickey Garagiola – Joe's brother. Some sources claim it was invented at Angelo's. Angelo's has been replaced by Charlie Gitto's. Read Joe Pollack's *Toasted Ravioli* for an interesting culinary tour of St. Louis restaurants.

A **Prosperity Sandwich** is one of those foods typically found only in the St. Louis area. It consists of an open face sandwich with turkey, ham, bacon, and melted cheese with a special cream sauce. The sandwich was invented by the Brit known as the Earl of Sandwich. He loved to spend so much time at the gaming tables that he hated to take time out to leave, so he put sliced meat between two pieces of bread. When Captain Cook discovered the Hawaiian Islands, he gave them the name Sandwich Islands.

Another food peculiar to St. Louis is **bar-b-qued pork steak** – pork butt sliced thin into steaks.

The **car window food tray** (1920s), making drive-in restaurants feasible, was invented by Louie McGinley, the man who built the famous **Parkmoor**

Restaurant at Clayton and Big Bend. It was torn down a few years ago and replaced by a ubiquitous Walgreen's.

The **Hacienda** in Rock Hill has great Mexican food.

The **Concrete** was an ice cream treat invented at **Ted Drewes**. It consists of ice cream mixed with candy, fruit, and/or nuts. When Dairy Queen failed to secure rights to it, they came up with the name Blizzard – a poor imitation. Ted Drewes started in 1929 and has two locations, one (1931) on Grand (south of Gravois) and the other on Watson Road/Route 66 (1941).

That reddish brown condiment known as bar-b-que sauce is consumed by St. Louisans in a volume per capita that is **more than any other American city**.

Carol Charlwood Block of St. Louis/Collinsville at McDonnell Aircraft computer room – circa 1964

Around 1890 there was a St. Louis physician who convinced a food company owner (George Bayle) to make a paste from ground peanuts so that his patients with dental problems could obtain protein – **voila, peanut butter**. Remember the children's song? "Little peanut, sitting on a track/ heart was all a'flutter/ along came a choo choo down the track/ woo, woo peanut butter."

Provel cheese was developed especially to be a topping for thin St. Louis-style pizza that is traditionally cut into squares. It is a processed cheese made from provolone, Swiss and cheddar. Food historian George W. Baltzell believes the name comes from the words **pro**volone and **Vel**veeta.

Whistle orange soda ("Thirsty? Just Whistle") was developed around 1919 by a man working for Vess Jones Soda. **7-Up** was developed around 1929 by Charles Grigg of the St. Louis Howdy Company and originally carried the name Bib-Label Lithiated Lemon-lime Soda. It was originally made with 7 ingredients and placed in a 7 ounce bottle. By the end of World War II, 7-Up was the third best selling soda in the country.

In the 1970s, 7-Up made one of the fifty greatest commercials of all time. It depicted a large black man (Geoffrey Holder) on a tropic isle explaining that the drink's secret came from the "uncola nut." The commercial ended with his husky "Ha, ha, ha!" – similar to what he did in the James Bond film, *Live and Let Die*. It has been said that the red spot on the bottle came from the fact that the owner was an albino, although I have found nothing to substantiate this. In case you're wondering, the drink no longer contains lithium.

Missouri walnut tree

TUMS antacid tablets (calcium carbonate) were first developed in 1928 in a St. Louis basement laboratory by pharmacist Jim Howe. He gave the tablets to his wife to calm her upset stomach. He kept the tablets in a Mason jar and took them along when they went on an ocean voyage. He gave the tablets to other passengers on the voyage and they were an immediate hit. He started producing TUMS commercially in 1930. It is still the nation's #1 selling tablet for indigestion.

Hot dogs, on a specially sized bun, were served for the first time at the 1904 World's Fair. So was **iced tea** and ice cream served in a cone. They ran out of paper cups so the ice cream was served in a cone-shaped waffle. The brand name soft drink **Dr. Pepper** was introduced to the world at the St. Louis Fair, but it was created in Waco, Texas.

The apple is thought to be one of the single healthiest foods in existence. J. T. Stinson gave an address at the 1904 Fair and in it he proclaimed the famous homily, "**An apple a day keeps the doctor away**."

For decades Mavrakos was the ONLY chocolate in St. Louis worth eating, followed closely by Bissinger's. Many St. Louisans remember buying rocky road Easter eggs from their store on Grand near Arsenal. There was another Mavrakos store downtown near Miss Hullings.

O. T. Hodge's Chili Parlor in downtown St. Louis set the standard. A relative of his started Edmond's Chili Company so consumers could buy the product in cans.

As previously mentioned, Twinkies were first made in Schiller Park. Jimmy Dewar came up with a sponge cake with banana filling. Jimmy was traveling to St. Louis when he spotted a sign for Twinkie Toe Shoes and this gave him the name. Due to a banana shortage during World War II, vanilla filling was used.

This author's favorite Italian restaurant is **Pisano's**.

Red Robin currently serves a French Onion soup that comes close to what was made at Famous-Barr, but not quite. When my wife and I came over from Illinois to shop downtown, we almost always ate onion soup at Famous or fish at Miss Hullings.

Missouri supplies about 70 percent of the world supply of black walnuts. When on the trees they are about the size of a yellow-green tennis ball and have a similar coloration. The state produces about 25 million pounds of walnuts a year. Hammons Products at **Stockton** is the only processor of black walnuts in the world. Nearly 45 percent of walnuts are used in the making of black walnut ice cream. Walnut shells are so hard that they can be pulverized and used to clean jet engines. In 1989, the black walnut was designated the state tree.

SPRINGFIELD, MISSOURI

Springfield is the third largest city in Missouri and is called the "Queen City of the Ozarks." Its population is about 151,000. It was either named for a field and a spring near the town or it was named after Springfield, Tennessee. Another version says it was named for Springfield, Massachusetts.

Springfield was served by the Missouri Pacific and the Frisco railroads. It was once home to the headquarters and main shops of the Frisco. Springfield still has about 65 trains going through it daily. However, passenger service to the city stopped in 1967 and it is not served by Amtrack. Its location was on old Route 66 (now I-44) and U.S. 166 and U.S. 60 once terminated at Springfield. Springfield is known as the Birthplace of Route 66 due to its early connection with the road.

The City Council has recently passed several controversial ordinances. In 2003 smoking was prohibited in most restaurants. In 2006 a bar ban was instituted for anyone under 21 in any bar or restaurant after 9 pm that made most of its profit selling liquor. This caused an uproar from college students from Missouri State, Drury and other schools. They maintain that most bars are already strict on checking IDs and that many underage students went to the bars to support local music groups or remain sober to drive for older friends.

Springfield's Central High was attended by **Bob Barker** of *The Price is Right*. Hillcrest High was attended by **John Ashcroft**. **Brad Pitt** attended Kickapoo High. Greenwood School was attended by golfer **Payne Stewart**. Missouri State University (SMS) was attended by actors **John Goodman** and **Kathleen Turner**.

John Ashcroft

Rockabilly singer **Robin Luke** is from Springfield. His "Susie Darlin'" was a Top Forty hit and was featured in the Molly Ringwald/Robert Downey Jr. film, *The Pick-up Artist.*

Mafia don John Gotti, Timothy McVeigh, Robert Stroud (the Birdman of Alcatraz), and Ramzi Yousef (1993 World Trade Center bomber) were all incarcerated, at one time or another, at the Springfield U.S. Medical Center for Federal Prisoners.

Jimmie Angel, famed **Springfield** aviator, was **the man who discovered Angel Falls in Venezuela**, the highest waterfall in the world.

JOPLIN, MISSOURI

Joplin, with a population of about 48,000, is located in the southwest corner of the state. The town was named for an early Methodist minister, Reverend Harris Joplin.

The town's main growth came after the Civil War because of lead and zinc mines. For a while, **Joplin was the lead and zinc capital of the world**. As a result, 75 percent of Joplin is undermined. Eagle-Picher Lead is still a noted employer. As one might expect, frontier Joplin was wild and woolly with the three-story House of Lords being the dominant restaurant, gambling den and place of loose women.

In the 1930s, **Bonnie and Clyde** spent time in the city and robbed several prominent businesses and banks there. They killed two policemen making their escape, but left most of their possessions behind, including a camera. The Joplin *Globe* developed the film and it contained the most famous existing photos of Bonnie and Clyde, including the one with her holding a gun and smoking a cigar.

Joplin has a park system that features the **world's largest Chert Glades** (silica/sedimentary rock often containing fossils).

Springfield poet Langston Hughes

Joplin is surrounded by the bedroom communities of Webb City, Neosho, Pittsburg and Carthage. Joplin is also home to the 30,000 square foot John Q. Hammons Convention and Trade Center.

Joplin was located on old Route 44 and the town's name is mentioned in the lyrics to the song, "Route 66." The city was once a beehive of railroad activity, but passenger trains have not served the city since about 1966.

Famous people born in Joplin include actor **Robert Cummings**, poet and writer **Langston Hughes**, golfer **Hale Irwin**, actor **Dennis Weaver** (Gunsmoke), and Rams football player, **Grant Wistrom**.

Famous people who at one time lived in Joplin include **Mickey Mantle** (Joplin Miners), artist **Thomas Hart Benton**, Cardinal manager and announcer **Gabby Street** and **James Thrash**, wide receiver for the Washington Redskins.

KANSAS CITY

Kansas City is still thought of as a western cow town by many, but it is quite cosmopolitan. **It has more miles of tree-lined boulevards than Paris** and more fountains than any other city in the world except Rome. It has more miles of freeway per capita than any other metro area with a population of one million or more.

Zoot Suit

Kansas City is not flat like Chicago or Dallas. It sits atop 150 ft. high bluffs overlooking the rivers. Kansas City proper is bowl-shaped and is surrounded by cliffs that were carved by glaciers.

Kansas City is the largest city in the state, but St. Louis (thanks, in part, to the Metro-East) has a larger metropolitan area. Kansas City, at the confluence of the Missouri and Kansas (Cansez) rivers, was founded in 1838. Lewis and Clark visited the site in 1804 and noted it was a good place to build a fort. Francois Chouteau reached West Port/ Kansas City in 1821 and established Chouteau's Landing. In 1833, John McCoy established West Port along the Santa Fe Trail. Westport Landing was established a year later. A group of investors known as the Kansas Town Company brought in many of the early settlers. It incorporated in 1850. The city was the scene of several battles during the Civil War (almost all Union victories), including the battle of Westport.

Three major trails all originated in Jackson County – the Santa Fe, California, and Oregon. The monument at Pioneer Square in Westport honors Pony Express founder Alexander Majors, Westport founder John McCoy, and Mountainman **Jim Bridger**, who owned Chouteau's Store.

After the Civil War, the selection of West Port/Kansas City over Leavenworth, Kansas by the Hannibal & St. Joseph Railroad brought significant growth. The population exploded after 1869 when the Hannibal Bridge, designed by Illinoisan Octave Chanute, opened for business. West Port became Kansas City in 1889.

Pioneer Square KC Monument: Alexander Majors/ John McCoy/Jim Bridger/

By 1925, the city was under the thumb of the dominant Democratic political machine, headed by boss Tom Pendergast.

After World War II the city experienced urban sprawl as an affluent population headed for the suburbs. Like St. Louis, the inner city began to decline. There were several riots in Kansas City during the Civil Rights upheavals of the 1960s. By 1970, the city had 316 square miles, more than five times its size in 1940.

There is an old saying about the character of Kansas City and St. Louis. It is said that Kansas City is the easternmost western city in America, while St. Louis is the westernmost eastern city in America.

Kansas City corn flag

The city's water was recently rated the cleanest among the fifty largest cities in the U.S., containing no detectable impurities.

Kansas City is sometimes called Paris on the Plains, the Barbeque Capital of the World and the City of Fountains.

Hallmark Cards, the world's largest maker of greeting cards, is headquartered in Kansas City. The company was founded in 1910 by Joyce Hall. More than **11 million cards with the Gold Crown are produced daily**. Hall was named for an Episcopal bishop, Reverend Joyce.

Eads Bridge in 1887 (MHS)

The *Kansas City Star* won a Pulitzer in 1952 for covering natural disasters.

The Nelson-Atkins Museum is the best known art museum in Kansas City.

Kansas City has an annual Groundhog Run every Sunday closest to Groundhog Day. The fundraiser is entirely underground, carved out of 270 million year-old limestone. SubTropolis, as it's called, was built by Lamar Hunt, owner of the Kansas City Chiefs and Wizards soccer team. Over 50 companies are located there for low utilities and high securities reasons. The underground wonder consists of more than 400 acres.

The Airline History Museum in Kansas City has a restored Lockheed Constellation. This prop-driven craft is considered by many to be the most beautiful airplane ever built.

The Kansas-City based firm of H& R Block was sued by the state of New York in March of 2006. The suit alleged fraud and claimed customers were steered into a faulty IRA plan with high fees.

Kansas City has a final assembly Harley-Davidson plant that gives tours. It is located at 11401 North Congress, just south of the airport. 816-270-8488

The nation's only intact 1860s woolen mill in just northwest of Kansas City at **Lawson**. The Watkins Mill is open year-round and is powered by a sixty horsepower steam engine from a salvaged boat. Men and women in period costumes demonstrate the workings of the mill complex. 816-580-3387

The town of **Peculiar** is in Cass County, just south of Kansas City. Just how it received its unusual name is an interesting story. When the postmaster sent in an application to the federal government he chose the name Excelsior. The government informed him there was already a Missouri town with that name. Several more potential names were rejected for the same reason. Exasperated, the man asked the Post Office Department to assign the town some peculiar name. The next letter said he had received his commission as postmaster of Peculiar, Missouri.

One hundred eleven people were killed in the 1981 accident at the Hyatt Regency Hotel in Kansas City. A large crowd of people were dancing to big band music on the skywalks, and the skywalk suspension rods collapsed.

The Crown Center, a $500 million redevelopment project with hotels, restaurants, shops and offices, was funded by Hallmark Cards.

FAMOUS FIRSTS

What was the first city in the USA to have a professional fire department? Cincinnati – St Louis was second (1850)

What was the first school district in the state to adopt a salary schedule for teachers, based on performance instead of length of service? Ladue, in St. Louis – 1953

What state was the first to bid out contracts for the new interstate highways system created under Eisenhower? Missouri, 1956

What city boasts the nation's oldest tradition of a Chamber of Commerce organization? St. Louis – over 164 years old. The St. Louis Chamber dates back to 1915.

The St. Louis Symphony is the nation's second oldest.

Where was the largest Standard Oil Service Station sign in the USA? At Skinker and Clayton in St. Louis

The world's first turnstiles were introduced at the 1904 Worlds Fair at St. Louis.

The world's first all steel bridge was built in 1878 at **Glasgow**, Missouri. Many feared that a steel bridge would not be as strong as an iron one so in 1899 a new bridge was built and the old one was demolished.

The Eads Bridge (1874) was the first arched steel truss bridge in the world.

Where was the **first "cloverleaf" west of the Mississippi River**? The Watson Rd./ Kirkwood Rd. (bypass Route 66) cloverleaf

Paris, Missouri, has a three-section tombstone that was for the three wives of Daniel Dulaney. The tombstone has been featured in Ripley's Believe it or Not.

For years the Pea Ridge Iron Ore Company (near **Sullivan**) has been the only underground iron ore plant in the U.S.

Jesse James committed the world's first daylight bank robbery at **Liberty**, Missouri, in 1866.

The world's first school of journalism was founded at the University of Missouri in 1908.

Grand Avenue Viaduct (Dave Lossos postcard collection)

Country Club Plaza in Kansas City was the nation's first major shopping center planned especially for automobile traffic (1922).

The nation's first pedestrian push button **traffic control light** was at Delmar near Union in St. Louis.

What well known St. Louis lawyer/farmer became the nation's first secretary of agriculture in 1889? Norman Colman

The first air mail delivery of letters in the U.S. took place when a couple of balloonists took off from Kinloch Field on a flight to the east coast. The Wright Brothers and their exhibition team later visited Kinloch Field with one of their aircraft. **Teddy Roosevelt was on hand and went up in the plane and became the first president to fly**. In 1920, Mayor Albert Lambert bought the field and the city built a hangar and landing strip, thus the origin of Lambert Airport.

Nation's first pushbutton traffic control light

In the late 1920s, Lambert Field became the first in the nation to have an air traffic control system. A man named Archie League stood out on the runway and communicated with pilots with the use of flags.

Glen Echo (off Lucas and Hunt) was **the first 18 hole golf course west of the Mississippi (1901)**, followed by the Normandie Club on the Rock Road.

The St. Louis World's Fair of 1904 was the first to take up as much as 1,272 acres. That record has never been surpassed by any subsequent fair.

Second Baptist Church at Kingshighway and Washington Boulevard (Dave Lossos postcard collection)

Kirkwood was the first planned residential suburb west of the Mississippi (1854).

Carrie C. Catt, at a 1920 women's convention in St. Louis, suggested the creation of the League of Women Voters to inform females on political issues. The idea was adopted at once.

The first political primary in America occurred in St. Louis in 1854 when Democratic voters went to the polls and chose Thomas Hart Benton as their nominee for the Senate.

When it came time to transport Abe Lincoln's body for burial in Springfield, the only undertaker in the area with a four horse hearse was Jesse Arnet of St. Louis. He knotted his reins so that he could drive the four horses with one hand and he tied a similar knot in his tie. **Thus was born the four-in-hand tie knot.**

The world's first successful dirigible flight took place in 1904 at the World's Fair. In 1907, the first international balloon race was held in St. Louis.

MISSOURI CRITTERS

What unusual animal was one of the first to cross the Eads Bridge after its completion in 1874?

A Negro named John Robinson led an elephant across the bridge. It was done to refute claims that the bridge was unsafe. According to long-held belief, elephants were said to have a sixth sense that would prevent them from crossing an unsafe bridge.

What was the name of Meriwether Lewis' dog that went on the Lewis and Clark Expedition? Seaman; he saved a couple of lives on the journey during a fierce storm.

Does southern Missouri have armadillos? Yes – they are common road kill. They tear up yards looking for worms, grubs, and other insects. They also eat scorpions and spiders. Their name is Spanish for "little armored ones." Careful, armadillos are one of the few creatures that can transmit the plague.

Is it unlawful in Missouri to shoot dogs if they trespass on one's property? No, unless the dog is posing a threat to humans or is attacking farm animals.

What critter did the St. Louis City Museum try to sell on E-bay for $150,000? A rare albino two-headed rat snake; the highest bid was only about $50,000.

When did Missouri begin issuing hunting licenses? 1905, for the price of one dollar

Does southern Missouri have tarantulas? Yes – at Branson, Missouri, they warn guests about them in their brochures. Tarantulas are the only spiders that make good pets.

Where can one find scorpions in Missouri? In southeast Missouri; be sure to shake out your shoes before putting them on if you stay in a bed and breakfast down there.

What is mobbing? It's when crows, jays, chickadees, titmice and blackbirds swoop down en masse to drive away predators or people from nesting places.

What about collared lizards, those funny creatures that run in an upright position on their hind legs? Yep, they're also in dry parts of southeastern Missouri.

How does going into a Missouri cave during the winter and disturbing thousands of bats contribute to their demise?

Gray and Indiana bats are hibernating. Each time they are disturbed they use up vital fat reserves that cannot be replaced. Excessive disturbance can cause bats to die.

What is unique about Tumbling Creek Cave in Taney County? It has the highest biodiversity of any cave west of the Mississippi. The cave harbors 115 species, including three endangered species: gray bats, Indiana bats and a nearly extinct cave snail. It has been featured on National Geographic.

Due to a declining area suitable for habitat, about how many prairie chickens are left in Missouri? 500

Which animal lives the longest, the horse or the mule? The mule, which can also withstand heat better

Why was **Lathrop** once known as the **Mule Capital of the World**? Dealers there named Guyton & Harrington sold $37 million dollars worth of mules to the British government during World War I.

Who was "Freckles?" He was a firehouse dog in **Richmond Heights**. When an alarm came in he barked to attract attention and jumped into the front seat of the fire truck. He put on demonstrations by jumping out of second story windows into a safety net. After being killed by a car in 1937, his body was stuffed and displayed in the public library.

What is the Missouri record for an alligator snapping turtle? 316 pounds

How do alligator turtles catch their prey? There is an appendage on the tip of its tongue that looks like a worm. When a fish swims by to have a closer look, it becomes a meal. Alligator turtles do not have teeth.

How long do alligator turtles live? About 70 years

Who was Rex McDonald? He was a Missouri-bred show horse that won so many titles he had to retire because no owner would show a horse against him. At the 1904 World's Fair, **Rex was named the Champion Saddle Horse of America**. Rex died in 1913.

What prehistoric-looking, bottom feeding game fish was almost extinct in Missouri by 1910? Due to habitat destruction and over harvesting, Missouri's largest and longest-living fish, the lake sturgeon was nearly decimated. It has been a protected species since 1974.

What is unusual about the lake sturgeon's reproductive pattern? They don't start reproducing until they're 20 years old and after that, they only spawn about every three years.

Why was Jim the Missouri "Wonder Dog" famous? For seven straight years **he predicted the winner of the Kentucky Derby**. He was a Llewellin setter owned by Sam Van Arsdale. The dog started out by predicting the sex of several newborn babies born to neighbors. One day his owner wrote the names of the horses entered in the Kentucky Derby on a slip of paper and handed one slip to seven different men. Old Jim went over to one man and the name on his slip won the race. In 1933, the dog entertained a session of the state legislature. The state telegrapher was asked to send the dog a message in Morse code that told him to pick out a specific member of the legislature. The dog roamed the aisles and finally put his paw on the correct knee.

What is the oldest fish in North America that can still be caught at the Lake of the Ozarks? The spoonbill paddlefish, which produces delicious black roe caviar; to keep them they must be at least 24 inches long.

How was the case of **Old Drum** (a dog), one of the most unusual cases in the history of Missouri's Supreme Court? In the 1870 case of *Burden v. Hornsby*, Charles Burden sued Leonidas Hornsby for shooting his favorite dog. Dog lovers all over the world were touched by the prosecuting attorney's "man's best friend" closing arguments. Burden was awarded $50 in damages. A statue of Old Drum stands on the courthouse lawn at **Warrensburg**.

In professional bull riding (at rodeos), how long is the rider required to stay on before he can dismount? Eight seconds; prominent Missourians who do this include Dustin Hall of **Springfield**, Matt Bohon of **Cole Camp**, Willy Ropp of **Trenton**, and Luke Snyder of **Raymore**.

What Missouri town was named for the local postmaster's favorite pooch? **Rover**, in Oregon County

What kind of critters (with lit eyes that blink) guard the main stairway at the Fox Theater in St. Louis? Lions

Who wrote a ballad about a dog named Jim that made him the most famous dog around after the turn of the century? Missouri politician Champ Clark; the song expressed outrage at the way rural folk were treated by city folk. "Every time I come to town/ The boys keep kickin' my dawg aroun'/ Makes no dif'erence if he is a hound/ They gotta stop kickin' my dawg aroun'."

What animal is a state symbol for Missouri? Mule

What is the official name of the feline exhibit at the St. Louis Zoo? Big Cat Country

Huge Alligator Turtle

What important conservation role is played by the red fox, found throughout the state of Missouri? The red fox feasts on crop-damaging species such as rodents, rabbits and grasshoppers.

What was voted the official state bird by the legislature in 1927? The eastern bluebird

What is the name of the huge stuffed gorilla at the St. Louis Zoo? Phil

What mythical creatures, facing in opposite directions, grace the top of the Civil Courts Building in St. Louis? Half sphinx and half griffin hybrids

What two critters are on the state flag of Missouri? bears

In what downtown hotel is there a metal statue of a man walking a dog? Adams Mark Hotel

What type of fish is most common to Lake Wappapello? Crappie

What legend is associated with Missouri's purple martin swallows? They always return to the state in the spring on Good Friday.

What myth concerning mosquitoes is associated with purple martins? They are voracious consumers of mosquitoes; skeeters only comprise about three per cent of their diet.

What is the standard house for purple martin birdwatchers? An aluminum house with 12 six-inch by six-inch rooms

Why are Missouri goats destructive to trees? They eat all of the bark and this kills them. They are useful because they also eat underbrush.

How does the Missouri Department of Conservation dispose of its old cars? It sells them to the public when they have 120,000 miles.

What state ranks second to Texas in cattle production? Missouri – which also ranks second in the total number of farms.

Why did branding return to Missouri in 2006 as a popular form of marking cattle? It seems that rustling was making a great comeback.

Do Missouri blue jays stay in the state year round? Yes – their favorite pastime is chasing other birds away from backyard feeders filled with sunflower seeds.

Can Missouri owls turn their necks completely around? Almost – Extra vertebrae allow them to rotate their heads 270 degrees in both directions.

Why do Missouri owls always look as if they're staring? Their eyes are fixed in their heads and cannot move sideways in the manner of human eyes.

Does Missouri still have any black bears? Yes – they migrate north from Arkansas and they are becoming more common.

Does Missouri have any mountain lions? Though rare, they still exist and are a protected species.

Is it legal to use duck or turkey decoys for hunting purposes in Missouri? Yes – as long as they are not live

Why are Missouri wetlands important for migrating ducks? Waterfowl from Canada or North Dakota fly nonstop to Missouri wetlands and spend about two weeks here to recover the fat reserves expended in flight. After a fortnight of refueling, the fowl continue to their southern wintering grounds to produce ducklings the next spring.

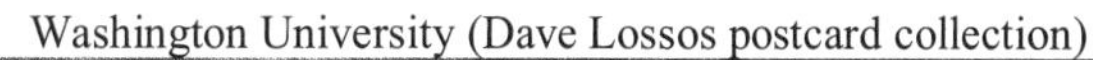
Washington University (Dave Lossos postcard collection)

What is the result of farmers planting crops right up to the edge of a tree line? The crops near the trees are stunted and the yields are low. Missouri Conservation Dept. has a program to encourage planting crops about 15 feet away from a tree line and allowing natural cover to grow there. The cover often quickly becomes a refuge for quail. Farmers who cooperate in this program get federal reimbursement.

Why is fishing often good in mid-winter at the Thomas Hill Reservoir in Macon and Randolph Counties? The 4,950 acre lake was built to provide cooling water for the Associated Electric power plant. The warm water discharged from the plant into the lake attracts schools of shad, and hybrid striped bass often follow them. Catfish can also be caught there.

How expensive is it to order tree seedlings from the Missouri Conservation Department? A bundle of 25 seedlings sells for anywhere from $3 to $12, depending on the tree variety.

About how many deer do hunters take each season in Missouri? A little over 200,000

How do deer hunters perform a valuable service? If the deer weren't killed, the population would rise dramatically and large numbers would starve to death.

What is the latest alien invader to threaten Missouri wildlife? Called "rock snot" due to its yellow-brown slimy appearance, this single celled diatom can form an impenetrable mat that can choke out native plants and animals.

How much training is required for newly hired conservation agents? Six months

What frontier-type of lawlessness has become commonplace in the Ozark region of Missouri? Cattle rustling, due to rising beef prices. Bob Herndon of **Marionville** lost $18,000 worth of calves when thieves cut his fences in October of 2005.

ROUTE 66 AND OTHER ROADS

EARLY ROADS IN MISSOURI: As soon as the Louisiana Purchase agreement was signed in 1803, settlers from the East began streaming into Missouri Country. Most came down the Ohio River on flatboats that carried three or four families.

Daniel Boone was our country's first "trailblazer" and he brought settlers into Kentucky by what became known as the Wilderness Road. Early wilderness roads in Missouri were often mere paths used by deer or buffalo to reach salt licks, water sites, or feeding grounds. As the settlers followed the old trails, the hooves of their horses and oxen and the wheels of their heavy wagons widened the trails into roads.

Indians and early settlers often marked the way with these trails by bending saplings, sometimes called **thong trees**. For many years such elbow-shaped trees could be seen on the state's landscape. These trees were bent in a certain direction to indicate the direction of a trail, a path to water or the way to a salt lick. The bending process was done by using a forked stick called a "thong." The tree would then grow in the desired direction until its natural quest for sunlight caused it to once again grow straight up.

In 1818, our nation's first "highway" was

completed. The National or Cumberland Road went from Cumberland, Maryland, to Wheeling, Ohio. It reached **Vandalia**, Illinois, in 1852. It was originally planned to reach the Mississippi at the bustling river port of **Alton** but Alton's fortunes went downhill after the murder of newspaper editor Elijah Lovejoy. The road instead went further south and ended at **East St. Louis**. It eventually became known as Route 40 and it extended into Missouri and went from St. Louis to Kansas City.

The National Road was a far cry from modern highways as we know them today. It was merely a clearing through the woods. When Congress appropriated funds for the road the requirement was that it should be 33 feet wide "with stumps to be very low."

An 1822 Missouri law required that limbs and branches were to be cleared from roads and no stump higher than ten inches could be left. These stumps became major hazards for wagons and buggies. One traveler wrote in his diary that in wet Missouri weather "It is a fairly decent road if the mud does not quite go over your boot tops when you are sitting in the saddle." There is a story about another traveler who encountered a man's hat in the middle of the road after a heavy thunderstorm. When he stopped and picked it up he was shocked to see a man's head protruding from the mud. "Here, let me help you," the Good Samaritan offered. "Are you all right?"

"I suppose so," the man replied, "but there's a horse and buggy below me that are in a bad fix."

Three Notch Road, which went from **Ste. Genevieve** to **Mine La Motte**, is considered **the oldest road in Missouri**. The name comes from the custom of notching trees back then to identify the path of a road. The process was also referred to as "tracing," hence the origin of early roads being called traces, such as Natchez Trace.

Red Cedar Inn Restaurant at Pacific, MO, dating back to1932 – artwork by Joseph Squires: squires.j@sbcglobal.net

Early roads were often named for the place of their final destination. Outside of St. Louis, North Broadway was called Bellefountaine Road because it led to the big or beautiful spring near the Missouri River. Conversely, South Broadway was called Carondelet Road. Manchester Road led to Manchester. James Morgan owned the land at the shallow point where the River Des Peres could be forded by wagons. This became known as the road to Morgan's Ford which evolved into Morganford Road. Similarly, Halls Ferry, Tesson Ferry, Dougherty Ferry and Lemay Ferry were all roads that led to ferries operated by the men with the aforementioned names.

The first significant improvement in Missouri transportation was the **corduroy road**, so named because it resembled ribbed corduroy cloth – *cor du roi*, cloth fit for a king. These roads consisted of trees that were felled, stripped of their branches and placed side by side. This took care of the quagmire problem when it rained, but the roads were hard on wheels and axels, and the ride was bone jarring.

These corduroy roads were especially important in swampy areas, such as those in southeast Missouri. One such road, called the pole road by locals, ran from the Mississippi and went west for about ten miles, just south of **New Madrid**. Ash, oak, catalpa, and cypress withstood the weather better than softwoods such as silver maple, box elder or cottonwood. According to Missourian Otto Kochtitzky, the Missouri legislature did not authorize funds to construct a log road until 1855. It was for a road that went from **New Madrid** to West Prairie (**Malden**). A ten cent toll for a horse and wagon was accepted by farmers because it enabled them to carry heavier loads and make fewer trips.

Next came the introduction of the plank road. Poles and planks were an integral part of the Spanish Camino Real (Royal Road/king's highway) that connected the towns of **New Madrid** and **Cape Girardeau.** The old plank road from St. Louis to **St. Charles** became Easton Avenue. The original Kingshighway that went between the two towns is considered the second oldest road in Missouri. Telegraph Road is in south St. Louis. The name for this route was derived from the telegraph line erected along it in the 1850s.

The longest plank road, approximately fifty miles, went from **Ste. Genevieve** to Iron Mountain via **Farmington**, a route now approximated by Highway 32. Missouri built seventeen plank roads during this craze and almost all of them went bankrupt.

Plank roads did not last long because the state was taken with "railroad fever." Within about six years the plank roads became unusable and the lumber was sold for firewood or used for fuel by steam engines. The road that went to the city of St. Charles was originally a plank road. When the boards finally rotted they were taken up and small rocks were spread on the road – hence the name St. Charles Rock Road. Olive Street Road was also once a plank road.

With the coming of the railroads, roads used by stagecoach lines and wagons reverted to dirt paths. These roads became quagmires when it rained and were nearly impassable during the January thaw.

These swampy areas of Missouri were not overcome until after the Panama Canal was built. Drainage in the bootheel area began around 1910 and was finished by 1920. After the Canal was built (in 1914) many of the engineers came to southeast Missouri to dig drainage ditches. In fact, **the digging of these ditches involved more dirt removal than the building of the Panama Canal.**

After the horseless carriage was invented, automobiles in significant numbers appeared in the state around the turn of the century. As late as 1910, about 95 percent of Missouri's roads were still dirt. Ironically, when horseless carriages became stuck in the mud, they were pulled out by teams of horses. Drivers soon began pushing for paved roads. However, the state legislature was still largely dominated by rural interests and farmers did not care to pay the costs for a city man's pleasure. The problem was solved when a state law was passed transferring money collected for license fees into road improvements. When that later proved to be insufficient, a tax on gasoline sales was imposed in 1917.

The Hawes Road Bill of 1917 was significant because it shifted responsibility for constructing roads from counties to the state.

The **first paved road in the state** did not occur until St. Louis began paving Gravois in 1915. By 1918, it was completed all the way to River Des Peres. Mr. A. Busch requested that the paving be continued all the way to Grant's Farm, which he owned. He paid for half of the paving costs.

Hardscrabble – Grant's home in St. Louis (author's collect.)

The number of automobiles increased dramatically and by 1918, there were 130,000 cars in the state. Wartime prosperity and Henry Ford's innovative assembly line made cars affordable to more citizens. Soon the auto became much more than just a rich man's toy.

In 1921, the state legislature passed the Centennial Road Bill that authorized the sale of bonds for the purpose of building hard roads to connect Missouri's major urban centers.

The need for hard roads was not deemed a necessity until large numbers of Americans began buying the "horseless carriage" after World War I. When alternate paths of Route 66 were built during the Depression, they were often bricked instead of concreted. The brick process was used because it was labor intensive and WPA projects like this put more men to work during the Depression.

Wagon Wheel Motel at Cuba, MO (dating back to 1934) – artwork by Joseph Squires – squires.j@sbcglobal.net

The Missouri highway known as Route 60, between **Charleston** and **Neosho**, was once part of a main transcontinental route from Virginia to California.

Springfield is often considered the birthplace of Route 66. It was at a Springfield meeting in 1926 where highway officials suggested the label, Route 66, for the U.S. highway that was to go from Chicago to California.

Jensen's Point, on 66 near Pacific, was named for the 1st director of Shaw's Arboretum in Gray Summit, Lars Jensen

Missouri has four of the most famous motels on Route 66. What are they? Coral Courts in **Marlborough**, Munger Moss in **Lebanon**, Wagon Wheel in **Cuba**, and Boots Motel in **Carthage**; the first motor hotel in Missouri (1929) was the Big Chief in **Pond**. The original restaurant building on Route 66 is still there.

What north-south highway intersects Route 40 at right angles? U.S. 65, known as the "Lakes to Gulf Highway"

What was the most important Missouri highway in 1955? Route 40, which went from St. Louis to Kansas City

What 1940s restaurant, recommended by Duncan Hines, was billed as the "Home of Unusual Sea Foods?" Edmonds – on Old Route 66

What Club Beautiful, owned by Mittino, offered a steak dinner for $2.75 in 1947? The Shangri La – on old Route 66

Nelson's Café, on old Route 66 in the 1940s, later became what modern restaurant? The Viking

Steiny's Inn, near Times Beach on old Route 66, later became a building used by what government agency? EPA

What motel on old 66 featured 35 rooms in brick cottages and offered "a phone in every room" in 1940? The Wayside Court

How did the town of **Albatross,** on Route 66, get its name? The village was chartered in 1926 and received its name for the Albatross Bus Lines that stopped there.

Where was **Suicide Alley** on Route 66 in St. Louis County? As Route 66 headed west from the Coral Courts area it was three lanes wide. The middle lane was a passing lane. Unfortunately, cars headed in either direction could use the middle land and this resulted in some horrible crashes.

Where is Missouri Wine Country? Missouri's Rhineland area starts along Route 66/I-44 just past **Fenton** and follows the highway all the way to the edge of the state at **Joplin**. To prevent strokes, this author drinks small amounts of Red Velvet from the **St. James** Winery, owned by Mary K. Malone. It was built in 1970 by Jim and Patricia Hofherr. Forget the vidal blanc. They say red wine three times a week reduces the chance of a stroke by 40 percent. I'm not much of an oenophilist (I hope I spelled that right), but I'm getting long in the tooth.

What St. Louis Art Deco Motel units featured closed door garages and became famous as a No-Tell Motel? Coral Courts on old Route 66

A MOST PROLIFIC KILLER

Tom Horn was born (1860) near **Memphis** in Scotland County, Missouri. He left home as a teen with a desire for adventure. In his lifetime, he was an Old West lawman, scout, soldier, hired gun, detective, outlaw and assassin.

At age 16 he became a scout for the U.S. Cavalry and was involved in the Apache Wars. Next he became a hired gun and participated in an Arizona war between sheepmen and cattlemen. Tom worked in Colorado for a spell as a deputy sheriff, where he drew the attention of the **Pinkerton Detective Agency** due to his skills as a tracker. During his four years with the agency, Horn killed 17 men. When Horn committed a robbery, while in their employ, he was forced to resign.

In 1895, he was working for the Wyoming Cattle Association in a range war. During this time he killed cattle thief William Lewis and his rustler partner, Fred Powell. After killing rustlers Matt Rash and Isom Dart, he made the statement that "killing was his specialty." He was being paid $600 for every rustler that he killed. His trademark was to rest the head of each victim on a rock. During this time he clashed with the likes of Kid Curry and the Wild Bunch, led by **Butch Cassidy** and the **Sundance Kid**.

Tom joined the Army for a stint in the Spanish-American War in 1898, but he spent most of his time recovering from a bout of malaria.

In 1903, Horn was accused of murdering a 14-year-old boy in the Iron Mountain country of Wyoming. There is disagreement among historians as to whether Horn committed this murder. Although Horn might have been innocent of the specific murder for which he was hanged, he certainly committed enough others. Horn's reputation, proximity to the murder scene and past history made him an easy target by the local sheriff. It was said that while Horn sat in a cell awaiting his execution, he made the thirteen knots in the noose with which he was hanged.

Tom Horn (National Archives)

In all, it is **estimated that Horn killed between 40 and 45 men**. Horn was hanged in Cheyenne, Wyoming a day before his 43rd birthday.

BANDIT QUEEN BELLE STARR

She was born Myra Maybelle Shirley on February 5, 1848 on a farm near **Carthage**, Missouri. Her family called her May. Her father was a Carthage innkeeper and a slave holder. She received a classical education and took instruction on the piano. After a Union attack on the town of Carthage (1864), her family moved to Texas. While at Scyene, Texas, according to legend, she became acquainted in the ways of the lawless by associating with the James boys and the Younger brothers. She knew them, of course, because she grew up with them in Missouri. The outlaws used the Shirley home in Texas as a hideout. Her brother, John A. Shirley had ridden with Quantrill's Raiders. John was killed at **Sarcoxie** while he and another Quantrill scout were eating at the home of a Confederate sympathizer.

Belle Starr

In 1866, she married a Quantrill Raider by the name of Jim Reed. She gave birth to a daughter in 1868. Her husband was wanted for murder, so the family moved to California where a son was born in 1871. After things cooled down a bit, the family moved back to Texas. Jim became a wanted man again, this time for a stagecoach holdup. Jim Reed was killed in Paris, Texas in 1874. The worst thing Belle did back then was running a livery stable and selling horses that her husband stole.

By 1880, May was now using the name Belle. That same year she **married a Cherokee Indian named Sam Starr**. They lived with his family in Oklahoma Territory. In 1884, Belle and Sam were charged with horse thievery. She was found guilty and served six months in the Detroit House of Corrections. Sam Starr was killed in a gunfight in 1886.

To keep her residence on Indian land, Belle married another Red Man. In 1889, Belle was killed by ambush while out riding. One researcher believes she was killed by her own son whom she had allegedly beaten for mistreating her horse. Her murder was never solved. There is no hard evidence that Belle ever participated in a murder, robbery, or stage holdup.

Another version holds that Starr died when she was shot and killed while feuding with a neighbor. Starr is thought by some to have had an illegitimate daughter with Cole Younger.

Although most of her life Belle Starr lived a quiet and obscure life, her story was picked up by a writer for *Police Gazette* who wrote an autobiographical novel (sold for 25 cents), ***Belle Starr: the Female Jesse James***. It was published in 1889. She was sensationalized as an amoral, amorous adventuress known as the "Bandit Queen."

Gene Tierney played the title role in the 1941 Hollywood production, *Belle Starr*. Sex pot Jane Russell took on the role in the 1952 film, *Montana Belle*.

WILLIAM QUANTRILL: SOLDIER OR MURDERER?

Quantrill, the oldest of eight children, was born in Ohio in 1837. He was raised in a pro-Unionist family and initially espoused Free-Soil beliefs. For a while, he worked as a school teacher in **Mendota**, Illinois. In 1859, he was living in Lawrence, Kansas, and again was teaching school. When charges were brought against him for murder and horse thievery, Quantrill fled to Missouri.

With the outbreak of the Civil War, he joined the Missouri State Guard. He quit after discovering a huge dislike for military discipline, forming his own bushwacking guerrilla unit. At times they skirmished with the Jayhawkers, undisciplined Union militia from Kansas who made border raids into Missouri.

The Confederacy officially made Quantrill a captain. Instead of wearing a uniform, he sported a slouch hat, woolen shirt, and high heeled boots. When the Union Army issued an order for all captured guerrillas to be shot, Quantrill ceased taking prisoners and started doing likewise.

Quantrill's **infamous raid on Lawrence**, Kansas, took place on August 21, 1863. Lawrence was known as the stronghold of anti-slavery forces in Kansas. It was also the home of Senator James Lane, infamous in Missouri for his rabid anti-slavery views and a leader of the **Jayhawkers**. These people had plundered Missouri for years prior to the war.

Immediately preceding the "massacre," Union General Thomas Ewing had ordered the detention of females giving aid to Quantrill's raiders. Several female relatives of the raiders were imprisoned in a makeshift jail in **Kansas City**. On August 14, the building collapsed killing four women and seriously injuring several others. One of those killed was Josephine Anderson, sister of Quantrill Raider, "Bloody" Bill Anderson. The Unionist burning of the Missouri town of **Osceola** was another contributing factor for the raid.

Quantrill attacked Lawrence, early in the morning, with an estimated force of 450 men. Senator Lane, a prime target, escaped through a cornfield wearing only a nightshirt. However, the raiders killed nearly 200 men and young boys, dragging many from their homes to execute them before their families. When Quantrill's men left around 9 a.m., most of Lawrence's buildings were in flames. The local saloons were also drained of whiskey and the banks relieved of their money. The raid is considered **one of the most gruesome events of the entire war**.

William Quantrill

On August 24, in retaliation for the raid, General Ewing issued General Order #11. **The edict ordered the depopulation of three and a half guerilla-infested Missouri counties** along the Kansas border. Thousands of civilians were forced to abandon their homes. Union troops marched along behind them, burning houses, destroying crops, and slaughtering animals during the process. The area was so thoroughly devastated that it became known as the **Burnt District**. **There was an 11-year-old girl in one of the families that was forced to vacate. She would eventually become the mother of Harry S Truman**. (The S in his name was merely a letter.)

Quantrill and his men fled to Texas, but later participated in fighting north of the Missouri River. In the spring of 1865, Quantrill and a few dozen men staged a series of raids in western Kentucky. He rode into a Union ambush on May 10 near Taylorsville, Kentucky, and was fatally wounded in the chest, **dying at the age of 27**.

During the war, Quantrill met fourteen-year-old Sarah King at her parent's farm near **Blue Springs**, Missouri. Her father disapproved of the relationship so they eloped when she was fifteen. They married and she lived in camp with Quantrill and his men. She was seventeen at the time of his death.

Historians are divided on Quantrill's legacy. Some regard him as a daring horse soldier and a folk hero. Others describe him as a bloodthirsty outlaw. Rumors persist to this day that gold from Quantrill's bank robberies is still hidden beneath Missouri soil or squirreled away in some small undiscovered cave.

In the John Wayne movie, *Dark Command*, he opposes William "Cantrell" in the early days of the Civil War. In the movie *True Grit*, it is strongly implied that Wayne's character (Rooster Cogburn) once rode with Quantrill.

"BLOODY" BILL ANDERSON

Born in Kentucky, Anderson grew up near **Huntsville** in Randolph County, Missouri. Anderson's father was shot dead in March of 1862. Anderson and his brother later confronted the neighbor who allegedly killed their father and murdered him.

By the spring of 1863, Anderson and his brother had become bushwackers and joined Quantrill's Raiders. Three of Anderson's sisters were imprisoned for assisting Confederate partisans. Union soldiers removed partitions and supports in the building to make more room. On August 14 the building collapsed killing one of Anderson's sisters. Anderson's sister Mary survived, but she was a permanent cripple. It is thought that this incident sparked Anderson's hatred for Unionists.

During the winter of 1863/64, Bill Anderson married Bush Smith of Sherman, Texas. Anderson participated in the raid on Lawrence, Kansas. After the raiders fled to Texas, he and William Quantrill quarreled. Anderson returned to Missouri in March of 1864 as the leader of his own unit.

Anderson gained notoriety for his particular savagery against his enemies. He and his men usually shot their prisoners and often scalped them. He wrote letters to the newspaper in **Lexington**, Missouri, claiming that his actions were revenge against wrongs that would otherwise not be righted.

He and his raiders were joined by Frank James and sixteen-year-old Jesse James, former Quantrill raiders. Anderson and his men soon adopted the practice of **dangling the bloody scalps of their victims from their horses' bridles**.

On September 27, 1864, Anderson and his bushwackers stopped a train near **Centralia**, Missouri. They killed and mutilated 21 Union soldiers who were returning home on furlough. When Union soldiers pursued the guerillas, they were lured into a trap. Aided by other guerrilla groups, Anderson and his men killed and mutilated about 120 Union soldiers.

Colonel Samuel Cox was assigned the Union task of eliminating Anderson's guerrillas as an effective force. They set a trap for the bushwackers near the hamlet of Albany (now **Orrick**) on October 26, 1864. Anderson was shot in the head and killed, his surviving men retreating. A silken cord with 53 knots was found on Anderson, believed to be the number of men he had killed.

An injured Cole Younger

Anderson's remains were taken to **Richmond**, Missouri, and put on public display. His body was then dragged through the streets before being posited in a grave. In 1967, a veteran's tombstone was placed over his grave.

In the movie ***The Outlaw Josie Wales***, Clint Eastwood's title character (a Missouri farmer) is visited by Bloody Bill Anderson and his men after the slaughter of Wales' family by Kansas Jayhawkers. Wales then agrees to ride with Anderson to "set things right."

While most partisans think him to be a hero, Unionists generally call him the devil; his grave marker in Richmond merely reads, "Captain, Confederate States Army."

There were many who thought that the killing of "Bloody Bill" did more for Union morale than the defeat of Missouri Confederate General Sterling Price.

THE JAMES BROTHERS

Jesse W. James was born in Clay County, September 5, 1847, near the town of **Kearney**. He was of medium height and build but had striking blue eyes.

Frank James

His father Robert was a farmer and Baptist minister from Kentucky who had a hand in founding William Jewell College in **Liberty**. His father died while prospecting for gold in California when Jesse was three. His mother Zerelda remarried twice after that. Prior to the Civil War, the family owned seven slaves and grew tobacco on their farm.

Jesse had an older brother named Frank and a younger sister, Susan. The threesome also had four half-siblings.

When the war broke out, Frank enlisted in the pro-Confederate State Guard and participated in the battles of Wilson's Creek and Lexington, both Southern victories. After falling ill, Frank surrendered and was allowed to go back home after signing a loyalty oath.

Jesse in death: dots represent Civil War wounds

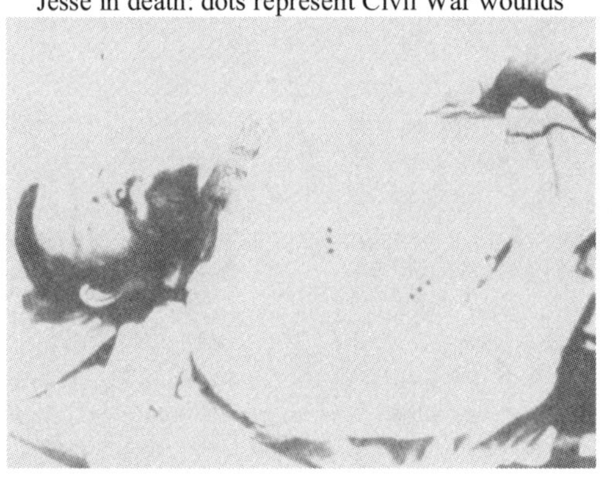

Federal troops came to the farm in 1863, seeking information about Confederate guerrilla groups. Sixteen-year-old Jesse was beaten and his stepfather was hanged, but miraculously survived. Shortly after, Jesse joined the Confederate Army, headed by guerrilla leader, Bloody Bill Anderson. For a while, Jesse was also part of Quantrill's Raiders. At one point in the war Jesse killed eight people in one day. At war's end he was shot and wounded by Union militia while trying to surrender. His first cousin, Zee Mimms, nursed him back to health, and that was the beginning of a nine year courtship that ended in marriage.

Zee Mims – Jesse's wife

In postwar Missouri many communities were bitter about what had happened during the war and were more interested in revenge than forgiveness. Ex-Confederates weren't welcome no matter how sorry they were for their prior actions. In some instances, grand juries indicted individuals even though they had been pardoned by President Johnson. It is thought by some historians that this bitter atmosphere is what led Jesse James down a road of crime and lawlessness.

In 1866, Jesse and some of his old bushwhacker friends held up the Clay County bank in **Liberty**. This was the first armed robbery of a U.S. bank in post-Civil War times. During the holdup, Jesse deliberately shot and killed a bystander, a student at William Jewell College. The main reason for the robbery was to get back the deed to the family farm, but the holdup also netted $60,000.

In 1868, Frank and Jesse joined Cole Younger in robbing a bank at Russellville, Kentucky. In December of 1869, Frank and Jesse robbed another bank in **Gallatin**, Missouri. The take was small but Jesse shot and killed the cashier, mistaking him for the Union officer who killed Bloody Bill Anderson during the war.

Gallatin would become famous for its "squirrel cage" rotary jail. The idea of a circular jail enabled a centrally located guard to keep an eye on all prisoners.

The James brothers teamed with Bob and Cole Younger to rob banks, stagecoaches, trains and even a fair in **Kansas City**. Missouri became known infamously as the **Robber State**. By occasionally hamming it up for bystanders and treating ladies in a chivalrous manner, Jesse acquired the label "Robin Hood." In all, the James brothers robbed 14 banks.

The James gang pulled off its first train robbery in 1874 at Gads Hill, 100 miles south of St. Louis on the Iron Mountain Railroad. Victim's hands were examined for calluses. The hold up men didn't rob the working people, only the rich.

Jesse sent letters to the ***Kansas City Star*** and the editor fed his ego by publishing them. In the letters Jesse rationalized his actions and blamed his lawless activity on vindictive Unionists and harsh Reconstruction policies. Editor John Edwards had an axe to grind. An unreconstructed rebel, he was trying to return treasonous old Confederates to political power.

Frustrated authorities brought in the Pinkerton Detective Agency from Chicago. The Pinkertons were foiled by Confederate sympathizers with two of their men being killed. One agent turned up dead **with all but his hands eaten by hogs that freely roamed around the hills**.

Founder Allan Pinkerton took personal charge of the case and staged a raid on the James homestead on the night of January 25, 1875. One of the half-brothers was killed and Jesse's mother lost an arm when an incendiary bomb was set off. The net result was that Jesse became an even more sympathetic figure in the eyes of the public.

Jesse married Zee Mimms in April of 1874 and they had four children. Two twin sons died in infancy, but another son, Montgomery, grew to manhood and became a **Kansas City** lawyer.

On September 7, 1876, the James-Younger gang planned the heist of a Northfield, Minnesota bank. The robbery was thwarted by an assistant cashier who lied and told the gang that the vault was on a time lock. Meanwhile, angry citizens took note of what was happening and formed a militia to fire upon gang members as they fled. Two of the gang were killed and the group split up, with the James brothers returning to Missouri. The two Youngers were eventually captured and the gang was essentially destroyed.

Jesse and Frank left for Nashville, Tennessee, and grew beards and changed their names. Jesse was now Thomas Howard. They soon became restless and started up the robbery business again. In October of 1879, they robbed a bank in **Glendale**, Missouri. Then they later staged two different train robberies. Internal squabbling led to the breakup of the new gang and the two brothers returned to Missouri. Jesse bought a house in **Saint Joseph**, but Frank decided to head east to Virginia.

Jesse next formed an alliance with two brothers, Bob and Charlie Ford. Jesse didn't suspect that Bob Ford was conspiring with Governor Crittenden to capture or kill Jesse and collect a $10,000 reward. On April 3, 1882, James took off his gun belt to climb on a chair to dust and straighten a framed embroidery that his mother had made. Both brothers drew their guns but Bob was faster on the draw and his bullet struck Jesse in the back of the head, killing him.

Jesse's killer, Bob Ford

News of the killing spread like wildfire and large crowds came to the house to see the dead gunman. The Ford brothers were charged with murder and sentenced to hang, but were paroled by the governor. The Fords were given part of the reward money and then they fled Missouri, fearing reprisals. Charlie Ford committed suicide in 1884 and Bob Ford was killed during an argument in 1892.

Jesse's epitaph reads: *In loving memory of my Beloved Son, Murdered by a Traitor and Coward Whose Name is not Worthy to Appear Here.*

It didn't take long for rumors to appear that said Ford didn't kill Jesse, but a look-alike someone else in a convoluted plot to escape justice. A man named J. Frank Dalton, who died in Texas in 1951, **claimed to be Jesse James** shortly before he passed at age 103. In general, no serious historian gives much credence to the survival claims. DNA tests performed in 1995 proved once again that the body in the grave was indeed that of Jesse James.

Wyatt Earp – Wickipedia

Jesse James soon became the subject of dime novels, short stories, biographies, poems, songs and newspaper articles. As a youth, I remember seeing the black and white 1949 film, *I Shot Jesse James*, which was largely sympathetic to the legendary outlaw. Reed Hadley portrayed Jesse James and John Ireland, one of my favorite actors, played Bob Ford.

Five months after Jesse's murder, Frank James surrendered to Governor Crittenden, telling him that he wanted to give up his life of crime. He was put on trial for two of the robberies, but no jury would convict him. For the last thirty years of his life Frank worked at a variety of jobs, including a St. Louis theater guard and ticket puncher. He even went on the lecture circuit for a while with his old friend, Cole Younger. His final years were spent giving tours of the James home (in **St. Joseph**) for twenty-five cents. He died in February of 1915 at the age of 72. In accordance with his wishes, Frank James' body was taken to St. Louis by train where it was cremated and the ashes placed in an engraved metal urn. The ashes were then placed in a metal safety deposit box behind vaulted doors in a Kansas City bank.

After the Northfield raid, **Cole and Bob Younger** surrendered to authorities and pled guilty to avoid hanging. Both were given life sentences at Stillwater, Oklahoma. Bob died in prison of tuberculosis, and Cole was finally paroled in July of 1901. In 1903, Cole and Frank James began touring the lecture circuit as part of a Wild West Show. Cole became a Christian in 1912 and died in 1918 at the family farm in **Lee's Summit**, Missouri.

THE RENO BROTHERS

The Reno brothers (Frank, Sim, William, John) grew up in Indiana and came to hate school and the religious instruction that they received during their formative years. **They are notorious for being the first peacetime gang in history to become train robbers, heisting an Ohio & Mississippi (B & O) train in 1866**.

After terrorizing southern Indiana they decided to move on to another state. On November 17, 1864, several gang members raided the treasurer's office at the Daviess County Courthouse in **Gallatin**, Missouri and made off with over $23,000 in cash and bonds. John Reno, one of the robbers, was arrested by some Pinkerton Detective men at Seymour, Indiana, in December. Reno pleaded guilty and was sentenced to twenty-five years in the state penitentiary at **Jefferson City**.

Reno was released after serving fourteen years. By the time he got out all the rest of his brothers were dead. William, Frank and Sim were **lynched by a vigilante mob** that broke into a jail where they were being held.

Randolph Scott, in *Rage at Dawn*, portrayed an underground Pinkerton Detective agent who was mostly responsible for the breakup of the gang.

WYATT EARP

When it comes to that part of U.S. history about the Old West – cowboys, cattle drives, gunslingers and shootouts – one normally doesn't associate this era much with the

Missouri past. Yet, once again, Missouri surprises us because the connections are spectacularly varied and frequent. Take Wyatt Earp, for instance – the man who tamed Dodge City and prevailed over the Clantons in the famous **gunfight at the OK Corral** at Tombstone, Arizona. He was born in **Monmouth**, Illinois. His full name was Wyatt Berry Stapp and he was named for a member of the Illinois regiment who was his father's commanding officer in the Mexican War. His father was a constable for three years in Monmouth, but the family left and headed west when their property was sold at auction. It seems father Nicholas had a secondary source of income – bootlegging. He was caught and when he was unable to pay the fines his property was sold.

Wyatt's first job as a constable (1870-71), at the tender age of twenty-two, was at the town of **Lamar** in Barton County, Missouri. Wyatt posted a $1,000 bond to accept this position. (Future president Harry Truman was also born in Lamar on May 8, 1884.) Wyatt married Urilla Sutherland in January of 1870. They were married by Wyatt's father who was a justice of the peace. Wyatt's respectable in-laws owned the Lamar Hotel. Urilla died of typhus within the first year of marriage and is buried in the Howell Cemetery, six miles northeast of Lamar. (One version claims she died in childbirth.)

Several lawsuits were filed against Wyatt while he was a lawman and he chose to leave the state rather than face them.

When Wyatt was sheriff at Dodge City, Kansas, he became acquainted with a certain **Ned Buntline**. Buntline was an erstwhile newspaper editor who lived in **St. Louis** in the 1850s and helped organize the anti-immigrant Know-Nothing Party there. Buntline was once lynched by a mob in Nashville, left for dead, cut down, and revived by his friends. He was involved in a nativist riot at St. Louis and jumped bail, fleeing to **Carlyle**, Illinois, where he became a newspaper editor. Buntline, born Edward Judson, quit the newspaper business and headed west where he became an adventurer extraordinaire. He made friends with Earp, **Bat Masterson** and William F. Cody. He purchased a pair of specially made long-barreled revolvers from the Colt factory in Connecticut. He gave one Buntline Special to Masterson and another to Earp, reportedly in exchange for colorful stories that he could write and sell for publication. If you remember the old television series where Hugh O'Brien portrayed lawman Earp, the Buntline Special was used to pistol whip drunken cowboys who were shooting up saloons.

Ned Buntline

Remember the old television series where Guy Madison portrayed **Wild Bill Hickok**? Yes, folks – Hickok is another Missourian who became famous in the Wild West. Wild Bill Hickok, a famed frontier sheriff from **Troy Grove,** Illinois, was shot and killed by Jack McCall. Hickok was playing cards in Deadwood, South Dakota, at the time and was holding aces and eights, now known as the "**dead man's hand**" in poker. Hickok customarily sat next to a wall with his back protected while playing cards. On that fateful day in 1876, he could not find such a seat at the poker table and was sitting with his back to the door when McCall, whom Hickok had earlier slighted, shot him in the back of the head.

Wild Bill Hickok (Wikipedia)

McCall was acquitted at his trial, but when he began to brag about the cowardly deed he was tried again and hanged. When **Hickok's gun was examined there were seventy-two notches on it**. Hickok, who was in declining health, had gone to South Dakota as a gold seeker.

Hickok left his father's farm in 1857 to become a stage coach driver on the Santa Fe and Oregon trails. His gunfighting skills led to his nickname, "Wild Bill."

While a constable in Kansas he invented the concept of "posting" men out of town. He posted a list on "**dead man's tree**" and proclaimed he would shoot them on sight if seen in town the following day. As his legend grew, few stayed around to challenge his threat. When the Civil War broke out Hickok became a scout for the Union Army.

After the war, Hickok went to **Springfield**, Missouri, where he participated in what is believed to be the first "western-style" quick draw gunfight (July 21, 1865) in history, exemplified by the opening shootout scene in the Matt Dillon *Gunsmoke* series on television.

In a Ned Buntline novel titled *Wild Bill Hickok: King of the Border Men*, Hickok leads a group of Army scouts in a shootout with Missouri Border Ruffians, led by Dave Tutt, the man Hickok fought in Springfield in 1865. Tutt, a former Confederate soldier, became friends with Hickok. However, they quarreled after a drinking bout and had a street shootout in Springfield's town square.

Later, he became marshal of Abilene and in a famous incident ran outlaw John Wesley Hardin out of town after disarming him. Hickok, who was once married to Calamity Jane, was the first "dime novel" hero of the western era.

Historians are skeptical of the 72 notches on his gun, but there is little doubt that Hickok was a fearless and deadly fighting man, equally at home with a revolver, rifle or knife.

William F. Cody was born in Iowa and at the tender age of fourteen became a rider for the Pony Express – **St. Joe** to Sacramento. His father had been a freesoiler and Cody became involved in the "bleeding Kansas" controversy. He was one of the Jayhawkers who once fought against a bunch of Jesse James-led Missouri Ruffians.

After his mother's death in 1863, Cody joined the Union Army and **saw action in Missouri**. After the war he earned the name "Buffalo Bill" by shooting 4,000 buffalo to feed the men who were building the Kansas Pacific Railroad.

In 1869, he was immortalized by Ned Buntline's novel, *Buffalo Bill: King of the Border Men*, extolling his exploits against Missourians. While a scout for the Army he killed a Sioux warrior named Yellow Hair (1876) and exclaimed, "This scalp is revenge for Custer's massacre."

It was Ned Buntline who convinced Cody to do a traveling Wild West Show which became a spectacular success. When the Columbian Exposition opened in Chicago in 1893, Cody sought permission for his show to be part of the celebration. He was turned down. Undaunted, he rented space near the Exposition and wowed thousands with his spectacular battle scenes. Cody hired Annie Oakley and Sitting Bull to be part of his show.

Charles Bolles, (**Black Bart**), was living in Missouri when gold was discovered in California in 1848. In 1850, he and his brother left for the gold fields, spending the winter of 1849-50 in **Independence**, Missouri. He later returned to **Decatur**, Illinois, where he met and married a woman named Mary. They had two daughters. They were living in Decatur when the Civil War broke out. Bolles was a private in Company B of the 116th Illinois Regiment that fought at Vicksburg and participated in Sherman's "march to the sea." He was a brave soldier who rose to the rank of 1st lieutenant. He returned to his life on the Decatur farm after the war but eventually left his wife and headed west in search of adventure. He began the career of a highwayman, robbing numerous Wells Fargo stages. Inspired by colorful dime novel stories, he began wearing black, took the name "Black Bart," and left poems with his victims. A notorious outlaw, he nevertheless was known for his politeness during robberies, eschewing foul language. He was finally apprehended and served four years in San Quentin Prison. While he was in prison, his wife Mary was living in **Hannibal**, Missouri. After his release from prison he lived in San Francisco a bit before he disappeared and was never heard from again.

Gratiot School at 1615 Hampton (Dave Lossos collection)

WHOLE LOTTA SHAKIN' GOING ON

The San Francisco earthquake was mere child's play. The Alaska quake of the 1960s hardly moved the state. The absolute worst earthquake in U.S. history, according to some experts, occurred in Southern Illinois and Missouri due to the nearby New Madrid fault in Missouri. The San Francisco earthquake affected some 60,000 square miles, but the New Madrid jolt affected an area sixteen times greater – over a million square miles.

DuBourg High School on Eichelberger (David Lossos collection)

The Big One struck on December 16, 1811, and a series of lesser aftershocks continued through February 7, 1812. The largest quake, estimated by scientists to have been an 8.2 on Richter's deadly scale, was strong enough to ring church bells in belfries as far away as Philadelphia. The air was filled with the smell of sulfur, with the screeching of birds, thunderous roaring sounds and dust that turned day into night. Most deaths occurred on the Mississippi where boats were swamped or struck by uprooted trees or collapsing banks. Some areas sank and formed new lakes. Mother Earth shrugged and earthen cliffs fell into the Mississippi; boats disintegrated and sank at their moorings. The tremors radiated all the way to Canada and as far south as Mexico. Part of Missouri broke away from its moorings and ended up in Kaintuck (Kentucky). Much of **New Madrid**, in the bootheel of Missouri, was destroyed. William Clark, the territorial governor, requested federal aid for the area, a precursor to FEMA. Five towns in three states were swallowed up. Nicholas Jarrot's two story mansion in **Cahokia**, the oldest brick structure in Illinois, sustained a large crack in a wall. Islands in the Mississippi disappeared, and new lakes were formed on previously solid ground. Ripley's Believe-It-Or-Not reported that the cataclysmic quake had caused the Mississippi River to ***flow backwards*** for a spell.

The steamboat *New Orleans* was traveling on the Mississippi at the time. That night the ship was moored to an island in the river. The next morning, the crew reported that the **quake caused the island to disappear**.

The massive earthquake destroyed Fort Massac, near present-day **Metropolis**, Illinois. It had fallen into disrepair but had been rebuilt after the Revolutionary War, so ordered by George Washington. It was quickly restored after the earthquake as a fortification for the War of 1812. A replica of the 1794 fort, with French *post en terre* vertical timbers, has been reconstructed and features tours and a historic museum.

The earthquake, caused by slippage of tectonic plates, collapsed some bluffs along the Mississippi River and formed Reelfoot Lake on the Missouri-Kentucky-Tennessee borders. Because the area of southern Missouri was so sparsely settled, there were few deaths. The entire state of Missouri had a population of only about 4,000 at this time. This "prime event," the "great shakes" as old timers called it, was said to have shaken the ground in long waves that would rock and roll. Due to the basket-like construction of pioneer homes back then, where no iron or nails were used, there was minimal damage. Reports talked about horrible smells and dark sulfur vapors filling the air. One eyewitness said that the stock was very much disturbed and frightened; horses nickering, cattle lowing, hogs squealing, chickens squawking. The domestic animals all came running to the house for protection. One neighbor woman collapsed and died from fright.

The New Madrid quake turned solid ground into a swampy morass overnight. A region in Missouri near the area is named Pemiscot County and the name literally translates into "**liquid mud**." Sand boils – geysers of sand and water dredged up from the bowels of the earth – shot up more than 100 feet into the air. There are some places where evidence of these nearly 200 year-old boils still exist as infertile spots on Southern Missouri farms. They can readily be observed from the air.

Seismologists are on a continuing lookout for another big quake from the New Madrid fault. In 1990, a respected St. Louis climatologist named **Iben Browning** said there was a 50/50 chance that another quake would occur on or near December 3. He based the prediction on a series of circumstances including the gravitational pull of the moon. Everyone knows that earthquakes can't be predicted, but a media frenzy ensued and ***millions of tax dollars were wasted*** in useless drills and preparations for the impending disaster. School officials, terrified of criticism or lawsuits, caved in and ordered school buses with drivers to park beside the schools on standby in case evacuations were necessary.

The designated day came and went with nothing happening. T-shirt sellers were quick to capitalize on the non-event with clothing that shouted "**I Survived the 1990 Earthquake**."

W. Atkinson wrote a book in 1989 titled *The Next New Madrid Earthquake*. He predicts that a big new quake will kill about 5,000 people and result in billions of dollars in property damage. The probability of a 6.5 magnitude quake hitting again by the year 2040 is rated at 90 percent. Such an event would destroy about 60 percent of Memphis, Tennessee. Southern Missouri is particularly vulnerable since few of its large buildings possess earthquake resistant construction.

Concordia Seminary (David Lossos postcard collection

In 1900, geologists concluded that the 1811 quake was due to slippage from great artesian pressure, which for centuries had undermined beds of clay by the steady removal of sand. Its axis extended from **New Madrid** to **Caruthersville**. Sinkholes were formed as far north as St. Louis.

Abraham Bird was a farmer near New Madrid who lost his land when it was swallowed up by the earthquake. The federal government issued him an "earthquake certificate" which entitled him to other unsettled land in Missouri. The town of **Hannibal** was established on land first deeded to Abraham Bird.

In 1998, Peter Hernon, an editor for the ***St. Louis Post-Dispatch***, penned the novel *8.4*. It is a terrifying story about a contemporary New Madrid earthquake of massive proportions. America's luck finally runs out. Cincinnati, Louisville, Memphis and St. Louis are devastated. Kentucky Dam collapses. The center span of several Mississippi River bridges fall into the drink. In Chicago, people on Michigan Avenue are injured by falling glass from high rise buildings. Several buildings in the Loop area collapse. The death toll for the affected area climbs to 130,000. A continuing cycle of earthquakes causes great concern for President Nathan Ross (former governor of Illinois), because the New Madrid fault zone triggers quakes in other nearby fault areas.

Finally, a plan to end the cataclysm is developed. It calls for the detonation of a small nuclear bomb, placed in a Kentucky coal mine shaft eighteen hundred feet below the earth's surface. A group of scientists and engineers successfully detonate the bomb, reducing the stress that has built up along the fault line over the last 200 years. The risk was huge because there was a chance that if the blast were too strong or improperly located, it would restart a geological process that ground to a halt millions of years ago. Worst case scenario: the Gulf of Mexico would extend as far north as southern Missouri. There was also the danger that the bomb blast might vent, causing a cloud of radioactive dust to settle over a large area.

Hernon's scary best-seller was selected for inclusion in a *Reader's Digest* condensed book volume.

New Madrid residents face the uncertain future with black humor. Stores sell T-shirts that read, "**It's Our Fault**." The historic and scientific aspects of the 1811 earthquake can best be studied by visiting the New Madrid Museum on 101 Main Street, New Madrid, Mo. (573-748-2378)

What is author Peter Hernon's background? He was a city editor for the *Post-Dispatch* and wrote *Under the Influence*, an unauthorized biography of the Anheuser-Busch beer dynasty.

Why would a new quake probably be worse than the San Francisco quake of 1906? The bedrock here is harder so the quake will travel farther.

What started the 1990 quake scare? On September 26, 1990, there was a quake with a magnitude of about 4.1 in the **Cape Girardeau** area with an epicenter at **New Hamburg.**

How long is the New Madrid fault line? 140 miles long, directly affecting eight states. It crosses the Mississippi River near **Caruthersville.**

Is it possible to outdistance a Missouri tornado in a car? Yes – they only travel at speeds of 20-40 miles per hour.

Abraham Bird, before moving to **New Madrid**, owned the land in Illinois at the confluence of the Ohio and Mississippi rivers. Near **Cairo**, it is still known as Bird's Point. The waters of twenty-five states flow past the site.

MEDICINE IN EARLY MISSOURI

The pioneer doctor was a far cry from today's modern practitioners. A foot gashed by the slip of an axe . . . a man stricken with ague, an outbreak of smallpox, a soldier dying of a gangrenous wound – these and other hazards in pioneer life created a desperate need for doctors in early Missouri.

The prevailing medical wisdom back then was based on Galen's ancient humoral theory – that all human diseases had their origins in bodily fluids. This is a theory that lasted for over a thousand years. Around 1800, doctors were still using leeches on patients to suck out the "bad blood."

Unlike doctors of today, their reward was meager for there was little hard currency available on the frontier. The simple equipment of a country doctor included a mortar and pestle for mixing herbs and medicines, a set of balances for weighing amounts of powders, homemade splints, bandages, a few simple drugs, syringes, hot water bottles and an assortment of crude instruments. Among these were a saw for amputations (hence the nickname "sawbones"), pliers (tooth extraction) and a "**puls-ometer**." This dumbbell-shaped device was about six inches long and contained a red liquid. It was used to impress dubious patients that they were getting a thorough and accurate diagnosis. The patient grasped one end of the contraption and bubbles rose up in the other. This, of course, had nothing to do with the patient's condition, but it was usually quite impressive. The early doctor had to make his own pills and tinctures; in fact, he mixed up all his medicines.

Elaine Viets (Dave Lossos collection/John Forbes photo

Most often the doctor rode a circuit over his territory as he made house calls. Ague consisted of alternate intervals of chills, fever and sweating. The most common treatment for ague (malaria) was quinine water. Quinine, which was derived from the bark of the South American chinchona tree, was also used to treat leg cramps. One woman in **Springfield** was noted for making a home remedy served at her husband's hotel called Mrs. Slough's Vegetable Anti-Bilious Dispeptic Pills. Her pills not only cured ague but purportedly healed a wide variety of ailments including closed pores and impurities of the blood.

Doctor fees were usually small and, even then, they were often paid in promises, seldom money. Farm vegetables were the general medium of payment.

There were no anesthetics and for amputations patients were held down and given a bullet to clamp down on to suppress screams. This is the origin of the phrase, "bite the bullet." Cautery was another method of treating wounds. To stop the flow of blood and kill infection, a hot poker was pressed to an injury for several seconds.

Most doctors went along with home remedies, superstitions and the use of charms. The right front paw of a mole was tied around a child's neck to ward off attacks of "croup." A ball of asafetida, tied in a white cloth and worn around the neck, ostensibly prevented milk sickness. Gum camphor worn around the neck supposedly warded off malaria. For colds, a child wore a spider in a pouch around his neck until it died. For a case of poison ivy, patients were told to take a slice of watermelon and rub it over the affected area. This would give immediate relief from the itchiness and within a day or two the affected area was supposed to dry up and flake off with dead skin. Many pioneer women swore that a solution made from boiled peach tree leaves worked even better. A slice of dill pickle was often applied to bee stings. For cold sores you were supposed to take a finger and rub the back of your ear. Then you were to take that finger and rub it on the affected area. Drinking sassafras tea was used to shorten the duration of a cold. The Indian method was to make a necklace out of sliced onion and wear it for three days. To stop nosebleeds, a small coin was placed inside the mouth with one edge resting on one's lower teeth while the top pushed the upper lip toward the nose. Tea, made of white ants and a lick of a lump of alum, plus eating some Indian turnip, ground in molasses, were other folk cold remedies. Another common treatment for colds was to rub the throat and chest with goose grease.

In case of fever, pioneers consumed a mixture of the juice of garlic and onions, crawled toward the east under a double-rooted raspberry briar, and then ate a mixture of ground flax seed and licorice, vinegar, raisins, and sugar-candy. If children, sick with fever, didn't respond to these treatments, the child would be put to bed, covered well, and given tea made from snakeroot, dogwood, willow or sassafras.

Conventional wisdom said that the elderberry had ingredients that contributed to longevity so pioneers consumed this fruit as much as possible, often converting it into wine.

The first use for Missouri oil was medicinal. The Indians skimmed it off pools of water and used it on insect bites and stings. The white men bottled it and sold the balm as **Seneca Oil**. Oil for lubrication came from castor beans. Missouri pioneers made a cough syrup for croup from sorghum, ginger, pepper and vinegar.

Another deadly health issue for early pioneer settlers was **milk sick**. Abe Lincoln's mother died (in 1818 when he was only ten) from the poisoning when the family briefly lived in Indiana. Dr. Anna Bigsby (Bixby) studied medicine in Philadelphia, but came to practice in Southern Illinois. Her fame spread quickly when she solved the riddle of milksick that caused mysterious deaths. Superstition usually attributed the sickness to witches, but Bigsby proved it was caused by the white snake root plant, also known as nightshade. Farmers in Illinois and Missouri eliminated the problem by destroying the deadly plant wherever it was found.

SHOW BIZ: ACTORS & ACTRESSES

What St. Louis actress starred in the hit TV series, *McMillan and Wife* with Rock Hudson? Susan St. James

Where is the world's largest outdoor stage? St. Louis Municipal Opera in Forest Park

What St. Louis/Granite City man stared in B westerns and was similar to Lash LaRue? Whip Wilson, who is buried in **Edwardsville**

St. Louis actor John Goodman invested in what radio station? KTRS

What St. Louisan played the part of Michael Anthony (the man who delivered the money) on the TV series, *The Millionaire*? Marvin Miller

What St. Louisan played the role of "Egghead" on the old *Batman* TV series? **Vincent Price**

Vincent Price

What was the name of the liberal-minded sitcom where Susan St. James shared top billing with Jane Curtin? *Kate and Allie*

What was the name of the 1966 TV series where Susan St. James played Anthony Franciosa's "girl Friday?" *Fame is the Name of the Game*

What quirky eating habit does Susan St. James have? She is a vegan or vegetarian who also has five children.

What tragedy befell Susan St. James and her husband? Her husband and two sons were in a private plane crash. One son was able to pull his father from the wreckage and save his life, but the plane burst into flames before the other son could be saved. The sad story was retold on a 2006 episode of Oprah Winfrey.

Susan St. James starred in one of this author's favorite movies – a 1982 love story set in Vietnam co-starring Dennis Christopher (*Breaking Away*). Can you name the movie? *Don't Cry, It's Only Thunder*

What **Pattonville** High School grad married hockey star Wayne Gretzky? Janet Jones, who starred in *A Chorus Line*

What part did Janet play in *A League of their Own*? The 1961 **Bridgeton**-born actress was a pitcher for the Racine, Wisconsin, ball team.

John Goodman

How did she get into trouble in February of 2006? She was indicted for placing illegal bets via a New Jersey gambling ring. The assistant coach of the Phoenix Coyotes was connected with the ring. The whole legal thing fizzled out.

What kind of bets did she make? She claimed that she never bet on her husband's hockey team, but she allegedly placed a $10,000 bet on the coin toss at the Super Bowl and a $75,000 bet on the outcome of the game.

What St. Louisan starred in the classic horror movie, *House of Wax*? Vincent Price

What St. Louis actress starred in *The Poseidon Adventure*? Shelly Winters

What **Springfield** native gradated from the University of Missouri and starred in the film, *Meet Joe Black*? Brad Pitt

What creator of Mickey Mouse was born in Missouri? Walt Disney

What Missouri actor had a more famous brother known for his lumpy face? Noah Beery was a brother to character actor Wallace Beery.

What **Springfield** high school did Brad Pitt attend? Kickapoo High School

Did Brad Pitt graduate from Mizzou? He majored in journalism and left for California two credits shy of graduation.

How did Pitt support himself before hitting it big as an actor? He drove strippers around in limousines.

What actor in the film *Stripes* formerly attended Washington University in St. Louis? Harold Ramis

What actress, who starred in *Black Rain*, (with Michael Douglas) grew up in St. Louis? Kate Capshaw

Kate Capshaw is the second wife of what famous movie director? Steven Spielberg, who divorced Amy Irving

Was St Louisan Betty Grable ever in love with Dwight Eisenhower? No! Why on earth would you think that?

During what World War II battle were soldiers asked to identify themselves by identifying Betty Grable's husband? Battle of the Bulge – Her husband was bandleader Harry James.

With what type of film was St. Louisan Vincent Price most associated? Horror films such as *House of Wax* and *The Fly* – He was dubbed the "Master of the Macabre."

To what famous playwright was St. Louis actress Marsha Mason married? Neil Simon

St. Louisan Redd Foxx was the star of what hit television series? *Sanford and Son*

What munchkin for the *Wizard of Oz* lived in St. Louis and once engraved tombstones for a living? Mickey Carroll

What movie, filmed in St. Louis, was about the work of Father Dismas? *The Hoodlum Priest* – Starring Don Murray

What St. Louis-born actress is the great, great, great granddaughter of the founder of the city of **East St. Louis**, Captain James Piggott? Virginia Mayo

Affton-born **John Goodman** was the star of what television series? *Roseanne*

Who is St. Louisan Kevin Kline's actress wife? Phoebe Cates; Kline's family owned Kline's Department Store and The Record Bar. Kline graduated from Priory School in 1965.

What St. Louisan starred in two successful television series, *Quantum Leap* and *Star Trek Enterprise*? Scott Bakula

What spooky St. Louis native was featured on Michael Jackson's top-selling album, *Thriller*? Vincent Price

What movie – that starred James Spader – featured the White Knight hamburger joint in St. Louis? *White Palace*

What were the four movie theaters on Grand Avenue near Shenandoah in St. Louis? Shenandoah, Arsenal, Ritz and Melba

When was the Tivoli Theater (on Olive St.) in University City constructed? It was completed in 1924.

What was the name of the movie theater on DeBaliviere near the north side of Forest Park? The Apollo

What leading-man actor died of a cerebral hemorrhage one day before he was scheduled to appear at the Sheldon Concert Hall, near Grand Ave? Cary Grant – November 1986

What 1934 **Clayton-born**, Missouri, man died at age 57 from emphysema? Handsome **James Franciscus**

What were some of Franciscus' main TV shows? *Naked City, Mr. Novak*, and the blind sleuth, *Longstreet*

What were some of his noteworthy film credits? *Marooned, Youngblood Hawke* (my personal favorite) and *Beneath the Planet of the Apes*

What part of St. Louis was home to actress Marsha Mason' coming-of-age years? **Crestwood**

What are some of Marsha's more memorable film roles? *The Goodbye Girl, Chapter Two* and *The Cheap Detective*

When was the first 3-D movie shown in St. Louis? 1952 – ***Bwana Devil*** at the Ambassador Theater; it starred Robert Stack and the plot revolved about the African man-eating lions of Tsavo. The Ambassador also showed the first Cinerama movie, *This is Cinerama,* narrated by Lowell Thomas (seen by my sister Jackie while on a date). This author saw *Bwana Devil* at the Majestic in **East St. Louis**.

What movie theater evolved into Powell Hall? St. Louis Theater on Grand, north of the Fox

What was the name of the original theater at Grand and Washington Ave? Midway

What three St. Louis theaters were owned by the famous Loews chain? Loew's State. Loew's Orpheum, Loew's Mid-City

What downtown nickelodeon (near the bus station) started out as a 24 hour newsreel theater? The World art theater on St. Charles

What were the three movie theaters located on The Hill? Columbia, Macklind and Family

What movie theater in St. Louis had exclusive rights to *Ben Hur*? This author saw the film at the Pageant on Olive St.

OTHER FAMOUS MISSOURIANS

St. Louisan Chuck Berry signed his first record contract with what company? Chess Records of **Chicago**

What St. Louisan gave Annie Mae Bullock the name Tina Turner? Ike Turner

Who was Albert King? He was a tall, famous blues guitarist who competed with Ike Turner at the St. Louis scene. During his stay in St. Louis, he began using the Gibson Flying V guitar named Lucy that became his trademark.

What famous smooth jazz saxophonist grew up in **Kirkwood**, Missouri? David Sanborn, who suffered from a bout with polio at an early age

What white "blue-eyed soul singer" was born in St. Louis in 1952? Michael McDonald

What singer, recently linked with cyclist Lance Armstrong, was once a school teacher in St. Louis? Cheryl Crowe, who originally was from the boot heel area

What NBA basketball star was from **Crystal City**? Bill Bradley, who graduated from Princeton, won NBA championships with the Knicks, and became a U.S. Senator

MISSOURI TOWN & PLACE NAMES

What town was founded by the Frenchman Pierre Laclede? St. Louis in 1764; traveling north from the Illinois settlement at Fort Chartres, he named it for the French king Louis IX who was killed on his way to one of the Crusades. There is a statue of Laclede in front of St. Louis City Hall.

Who was with Laclede at this time? His 14 year old step-son, Auguste Chouteau

How did **Canton** get its name? Originally named Cottonwood Prairie and dating back to 1827, there was a steam ferry that operated nearby named the *Cantonia.*

How did **Clarksville**, on the Mississippi, get its name? The name honored General William Clark of the Lewis and Clark expedition.

How did **Kiddville,** in Sullivan County, get its name? Matthew Kidd platted the town in 1858. The town died out with the coming of the Quincy, Missouri & Pacific Railroad which missed it. Most folks moved to nearby Green City.

St. Louis has a street called Gravois Avenue. What is the translation for the French word Gravois? Gravel

How did the town of **Fenton** get its name? It was named for founder William Long's Welsh grandmother, Elizabeth Fenton Bennett.

What South St. Louis town had a large park with bear pits? Carondelet Park; Ken Hoelker says he remembers seeing empty bear pits at Fairgrounds Park when he was a teen. St. Louis has a total of 105 parks.

How did **Shrewsbury** get its name? It's named for a hamlet in England.

In what community was the old 66 Park In (drive-in theater) located? **Crestwood**

James Franciscus

What was Kirkwood's original name? Dry Ridge – it was named for James Kirkwood, chief engineer of the Pacific Railroad who laid out the route to the town.

What is the name of the science museum for children located in **Kirkwood**? The Magic House

Where is the new Missouri home for Clifford, the big red dog? In 2006 a new display for Clifford was opened at the Magic House.

Where is the IMAX Theater located in St. Louis? At the Science Center across from Forest Park on the south side of Route 40

What is the meaning of the name Meramec River? It's an Indian word meaning "catfish."

Why is the River des Peres quite often dry? It's basically a drainage canal to channel excess storm water in west and south St. Louis to the Mississippi River.

The town of **Festus** was founded in 1886 and was named for a prominent banker, Festus J. Wade.

Sikeston was established in 1860 by John Sikes,

Warrenton was named for General Joseph Warren who was killed at the battle of Bunker Hill during the Revolution.

Herculaneum was named for that old town in Italy that was buried when Mt. Vesuvius erupted in 79 A.D.

Wentzville, established in 1855, was named for the chief engineer of the St. Louis, Kansas City & Northern Railroad.

Webster Groves was named for statesman Daniel Webster.

Times Beach was a promotional idea of the St. Louis *Star Times* that in 1925 gave six month subscriptions to people who bought lots there for a summer resort on the Meramec River. Times Beach made national headlines in 1982. During the summer the town's streets were sprayed with waste oil to keep the dust down. The EPA discovered that the oil had contained dioxin and everything was contaminated.

Eureka is a Greek word that means "I've found it." A surveyor for the Pacific Railroad discovered that a line through this gap in the hills would eliminate steep grades.

O'Fallon was named for a railroad developer, John O'Fallon, with Illinois having a town of the same name for the same reason.

Pine Lawn is named for the pine trees planted by Charles Clark, son of explorer William, on the front of his property. When a train depot was built there it was called Pine Lawn.

How did **Allenton** get its name? The town was named for Thomas Allen, president of the Pacific Railroad Company who laid out the town.

What town (next to Allenton) was also laid out by the Pacific Railroad Company? **Pacific**

The town of **Mehlville** was named for Charles Mehl, an early settler.

Brentwood was named for its first settler, J.T. Brent.

Overland was named to honor the Overland Trail, which headed westward from the Mississippi River.

Ferguson was named for William B. Ferguson who was a real estate developer.

Riverview was named for the fact that it overlooked the Mississippi River.

Black Jack was a name that came from a trio of blackjack oak trees at the intersection of Old Halls Ferry and Parker Roads.

Hanley Hills was named for a local farmer named Martin Hanley who was a Confederate sympathizer.

Hazelwood was named for the estate of Richard Graham. Tradition says that when the great Henry Clay of Kentucky visited there in 1828; he called it Hazelwood.

Bellerive was named for Louis de Bellerive, a French commandant who left Illinois and came to St. Louis shortly after it was established.

How did **Manchester** get its name? Most think it's named for Manchester, England. It was originally called Hoardstown.

What town is a fusion of the towns Ballwin and Manchester? **Winchester** – incorporated in 1935

How did **Ballwin** get its name? For resident John Ball who platted the town in 1837

How was the town of **Grover** named? Originally called St. Friedling, the town was awarded a post office during Grover Cleveland's presidency.

How was **Fox Creek** named? It was given that title by a local resident who shot a large fox there while hunting. The town was located at the headwaters of Wild Horse Creek.

Where was the first U.S. fort west of the Mississippi? Bellefontaine Neighbors – 1805 (St. Louis)

What is the translation of the French word Bellefontaine? Beautiful spring or fountain

What is the meaning of the town name of **Florissant**? From the French word *fleur* for flower, it translates to flowering valley.

State Fair at Sedalia (Missouri State Manual)

How did **Bridgeton** obtain its name? In its early history one had to cross a stone bridge to get into town. The place was originally called Cottonwood Swamp.

How did **Maryland Heights** get its name? A prominent doctor in its early history gave his estate (on a hill) that name because he originally came from Maryland.

How was **Frontenac** named? Located on bypass Route 66, it honored Louis Comte de Frontenac, an early governor of New France.

How was **Gray Summit** named? Daniel Gray owned a prominent hotel in the area and it was the highest point on the rail line between St. Louis and Jeff City.

When was San Carlos changed to **St. Charles**? Charles was the king of Spain who inherited Missouri territory by the Treaty of Paris that ended the Revolution in 1783. When it became part of America via the 1803 Louisiana Purchase, the name was Americanized to **St. Charles.**

What was the early capital of Missouri after it became a state in 1821? St. Charles

How did the town of **St. Joseph** receive its name? It was named for the patron saint of Joseph Ribidoux, the town's founder who was an employee of the American Fur Company.

How did **St. Joe** become nationally famous in 1859? It was the eastern starting point of the famed Pony Express that delivered mail out West.

How long did the Pony Express last? Eighteen months

Kirkwood High School in St. Louis (David Lossos collection)

What did William Waddell, the man who organized the pony express, think was its greatest achievement? Keeping California in the Union during the Civil War

How was **Sedalia** named? The town's founder named it Sedville for his daughter, whom he called Sed. When he filed a second plat in 1860 he changed the name to Sedalia, which he thought sounded better. The Sedalia stockyards were at the end of the Rawhide Trail.

Why is **Sedalia** currently such a prominent Missouri town? The State Fair is held there every August.

Is **Sleeper** one of those quant, sleepy Missouri towns? Yes, but it was named for J. Sleeper, construction gang foreman on the Frisco Railroad.

What town was named because it was out there by itself, far away from other towns? **Solo**, in Cooper County

What town was originally called New Palestine but was changed in 1898 to honor a friendly conductor on the Missouri Pacific Railroad? **Speed**, for the man Austin Speed

What town was named for an entrepreneurial Wyandotte Indian? **Splitlog** – named for Mathias Splitlog who unwittingly helped finance a fraudulent real estate scheme based on fraudulent mining assay reports.

How did James Wilson convince citizens to change the name of Campbell to **Springfield**, for the town in his native state of Massachusetts? He bribed them with a "pull" of whiskey.

Why is this James Wilson feller famous? He's the James Wilson of the Civil War battle of Wilson's Creek fame.

How was the town of **Tightwad** named? According to locals, it had something to do with a local store owner who squeezed a nickel until the Indian rode the buffalo.

How was Polk County's **Tintown** named? It was named for a local siding salesman who convinced large numbers of store owners to place siding on their wooden buildings.

How was the town of **Vulcan** named? Ore mined here was sent to the Vulcan Iron Works in St. Louis and it was important to the town's economy.

How was **Windyville** named? During a town meeting, held to discuss a name for incorporation, someone commented, "You people sure are long winded."

How did **Villa Ridge** get its name? Villa is Spanish for town and ridge was tacked on by railroad officials because it was a high point between the Missouri and Meramec rivers.

How was **Hall's Place** named? Hall was a local bootlegger who owned a gas station, store, numerous illegal stills, a bar and a dance hall.

How was **St. Clair** named? Originally called Traveler's Repose, officials thought it sounded too much like a cemetery and it was named for a railroad official on the Frisco line.

How did **Stanton** get its name? It was named for local copper mine owner, John Stanton. Stanton also owned a powder mill and supplied Confederate forces with gunpowder. He was hanged by Union forces.

How was the town of **Sullivan** named? Originally labeled Mount Helicon, it was changed to honor James Sullivan who built the railroad depot for the Frisco Railroad. Sullivan operated a gunpowder factory at Saltpeter Cave (Meramec Caverns). The Confederate sympathizer was hanged by Union troops.

Bonnie Parker in a tough gun moll pose

Is the town of **Carthage** named for a place in Africa? Yes. It was Hannibal's home town noted for its democracy. The town square of Carthage was duplicated in a movie studio for a scene in the movie, *Back to the Future.* The infamous duo of **Bonnie and Clyde** once obtained a car from Carthage and used it to rob a bank in nearby **Oronogo.**

What explains the origin of **Bourbon's** name? A local resident named Richard Turner ran a place labeled the Bourbon Store because he sold liquor to railroad construction crews.

How did a landlocked state like Missouri get a town on Route 66 named **Cuba** – an island? In 1857, two gold seekers returned to the area from California via ship, around Cape Horn. The ship put into port at Cuba and they were duly impressed.

How did **Rosati** get its name? It was named by local Italian vineyard owners to honor Joseph Rosati, the first Italian bishop of St. Louis.

Was **St. James** named to honor a Catholic Saint? Yes. It was the name-saint of Thomas James who owned the Maramec/Meramec Iron Works. The place was platted in anticipation of the westward extension of the St.L-SF Railroad.

Why does the town have a significant German population? During the Civil War a detachment of German volunteers encamped near town. They were so impressed that they brought their families there to live after the war.

How did **Rolla** get its name? This Pacific Railroad construction town had numerous people from North Carolina so the place was named for Raleigh in that state. The Missouri town was spelled the way easterners pronounced it, Raw-la – hence Rolla.

How was **Caffeyville** named? It was named for businessman Floyd Caffey. Much of the town was razed when Route 66 was built.

What circumstances led to the naming of **Carterville** on Route 66? Named for an early settler, the town was a booming lead mine place until the mines played out after World War I.

What was the town of **Clementine** noted for along Route 66? Stands along the highway sold baskets and souvenirs and it became a popular stopping point for travelers.

How did the Route 66 town of **Gascosark** receive its name? The name is a combination of the nearby Gasconade River and the local Ozark Mountains.

How was the Route 66 town of **Fanning** named? The town was named for early settlers, the four Fanning brothers.

How was **Halltown**, on Route 66, named? Early settler George Hall located here in 1870.

For what person was **Conway**, on Route 66, named? J. Conway was the person responsible for bringing the railroad to town in 1869.

How was **Crestwood**, on Route 66 named? The name came from the crest of a hill that had a grove of trees. One of the trees, over 200 years old, is still standing.

How did the town of **Dadtown**, on Route 66, receive its name? Betty Lewis and her father built a general store in the area and the place was named to honor her dad.

Is **Doolittle** named for the World War II hero? Yes. Originally called Centerville, the name was changed in 1946 and General Doolittle flew in his own bomber to attend the ceremonies.

How did **St. Robert** get its name? Robert Arnold was pastor of a Catholic church in the area and the town was named for his patron saint, St. Robert Bellarmine.

Was **Waynesville** named for a Revolutionary War hero?

Yes. It honored "Mad" Anthony Wayne who fought like a madman at Stony Point. The courthouse there flew the Confederate flag until Union troops arrived and took it down.

How was **Buckhorn** named? It was named for the Buckhorn Tavern that was established along a stage coach line.

How did the town of **Marshfield** come to be named? It was derived from the name of Daniel Webster's home in Massachusetts.

What was the worst disaster suffered by the town? About 80 people were killed by tornadoes that struck there in 1880.

Why was the town of **Strafford** listed in Ripley's Believe it or Not? It was hailed as the only American town with two main streets and no alleys. The town is named for Strafford, Connecticut.

How did **Nogo** obtain its unusual name? A meeting was held to determine the town's name but agreement couldn't be reached. Someone used a popular phrase of the day and called the effort a no-go.

Is **Jefferson City** named for President Thomas Jefferson? Yes

How was **Bois d'Arc** named? It's French for "wood of the bow," referring to the Osage Orange bush from which the Indians made their hunting bows.

How did **Paris Springs** obtain its name? E.G. Paris was the proprietor of a local hotel and some mineral springs were nearby.

How did **Mexico** come to receive that name? It was named by veterans who fought in the Mexican War.

How did the burg of **Rescue** get its unusual name? A family traveling west got stranded and some locals gave them food and shelter while their wagon was fixed. They said they were lucky to have been rescued.

What is the origin of the name Missouri? It is a corruption of an Algonquin or French word (referring to the Osage Indians - Oumessouri) that means "people in big canoes," although there are several variations of how it might have originated.

How did the town of **Advance** get its name? The Houck Railroad kept retreating due to frequent flooding and the town "advanced" with it.

How did the town of **Agency** get its name? It was the site of an Osage and Fox Indian agency set up near the Platt River.

How was the settlement of **Aid** named? It was named for the son of an early settler.

How did **Anutt** in Dent County get its name? It was named for local teacher Annet Lenox by one of her formal pupils who never mastered spelling.

How was the town of **Augusta** named? It was named for the wife of the town's founder, Leonard Harrold.

How did **Ava** get its name? It is a biblical town in the book of Judges.

How did **Bachelor**, in Callaway County, get named? The area was noted for a number of males who refused to "git hitched."

Early postcard of St. Louis University (Dave Lossos collection)

How was **Baring** named? It honored the Baring brothers of London who helped the Atchinson, Topeka & Santa Fe Railroad that skirted the edge of town.

How did the name **Bellflower** come to be applied to a town in Montgomery County? No one knows for sure, but the man who first settled there probably named it for bell-shaped flowers in the area.

How was **Bendavis** named? A prominent orchard owner wanted to promote his Ben Davis type apples.

What is the origin of **Bland's** name? Bland was chosen to honor Dick Bland, the Missouri politician who favored bi-metalism as a government coinage system.

How in the world does a town get a name like Blue Eye? The postmaster had blue eyes (I'm not making these up!)

How did **Branson** get its name? R. S. Branson was the first postmaster.

How was **Buffalo** named? A prominent early settler was from Buffalo, NY.

What did whiskey have to do with the naming of **California**? A man named "California" Wilson gave the town fathers a jug of whiskey in exchange for naming the town after him.

Cape Girardeau sounds French. Is it? The southeast Missouri town was named for a French fur trapper and trader named Girardat.

Isn't **Chamois** a deer? Yes, but the hilly area reminded early settler Morgan Harper of the alpine deer landscape in his native Switzerland.

Isn't **Charity** a woman's name? Yes – it was the Christian name of the town's postmaster.

How did **Cherry Box** get its name? The town's mailboxes were fastened to local cherry trees.

What town was named for Henry Clapper, the man instrumental in persuading the MKT Railroad to come through the area? **Clapper**, of course

How did **Clayton**, on Route 40, west of St. Louis, get its name? Local land baron John Clayton donated 100 acres of his farm.

Why did Newburg change its name to **Competition**? When it was given a post office there was already another town with that name. Town fathers held a competition for a new name and apparently town folk lacked imagination and Competition won by default.

Were residents of **Defiant** really defiant? Apparently so; there was angry and defiant competition with the town of **Matson** as to which would be the recipient of a rail spur line.

Does Des Peres translated mean "good place to settle?" No, it's French for "of the Fathers."

How did **Devil's Elbow** on Route 66 come to be named?

It was named for a 90 degree bend in the nearby Big Piney River that caused frequent log jams. They said it was a "devil of an elbow."

How did the small burg of

Flat (in Phelps County) get its label? An early settler looked around and noticed it was the only flat terrain in the area.

How is **Foil** an appropriate town name? Residents moved the town to higher ground due to possible flooding and this saved them much grief, having foiled the flood waters.

Was the town of **Folk** named for someone famous? Kinda! It was named for local boy Joe Folk who became Missouri governor in 1904.

How did **Frankenstein** secure its unusual name? Gottfried Franken donated land and stone (stein) to build a local church.

How did the town of **Greasy** get such a name? It comes from nearby Greasy Creek, so dubbed when a wagonload of pork and bacon overturned in the stream.

The town of **Half Way** must be in the middle of something, right? Uh, huh! It's the mid point between Bolivar and Buffalo.

Lambert Airport (Dave Lossos postcard collection)

Hanging Hollow! Is it the result of vigilante justice? Almost! A man thought to be a robber and murderer was standing under a tree limb with a rope around his neck when someone rode up with a note from the sheriff saying that someone else confessed to the crime.

How was **Hannibal**, Missouri named? It was named for the man who nearly conquered Rome a few thousand years ago.

How did the town of **Harvester** in St. Charles County get its name? It was due to the bountiful wheat harvests.

Is there any connection between the town of **Herculaneum** and the Roman village buried in lava in 79 A.D? Yes! Moses Austin, who ran a lead smelter, gave the town its name because the smoke from the smelter reminded him of the Vesuvius volcano.

Who was Steven Austin? He was the son of Moses Austin and was the founder of Texas. Their state capital is named for him.

How was **Hollywood** named? The label came from the many holly trees in the wooded area.

Does **Holstein** have a German connection? Yes! It was named for the German province famous for the breed of cattle the settlers brought with them.

Actor Robert Cummings of Joplin

Was the town of **Hooker** named for the famous Civil War general? No - it was named for an early settler in the area. A 1929 *St. Louis Post-Dispatch* article said Hooker had "Missouri's Smallest High School."

How did the town of **Ink** obtain its odd name? During a meeting to decide the town's name a bottle of ink was spilled. The post office had just requested that new town names be shorter to better fit on the postal stamp so the name was adopted.

How was the distinctive name of **Japan** adopted? The name was adopted to remind the community of Spanish and Portuguese priests who went to Japan and were killed by authorities in 1597.

What did the name **Joplin** honor? Reverend Harris Joplin, who established the first Methodist church in Jasper County. In 1872, the towns of Union City and Blytheville merged to form the new town. The two early towns were such bitter rivals that children would stand on opposite sides of nearby Turkey Creek and throw rocks at each other.

What is Clyde Barrow's connection to **Joplin**? On April 13, 1933, the notorious bank robber killed Detective Barry McGinnis and Constable J.W. Harryman in Joplin.

What Indian tribe is honored by the name **Kansas City**? The Kansa Native-Americans

Is **King City** another one of those places named for a local postmaster? Yes! Horatio King

What Missouri town had the **nation's first college of Osteopathic medicine**? **Kirksville**

How was **Kirksville** named? Jesse Kirk's wife promised a group of surveyors a turkey dinner, washed down with whiskey, in return for naming the new town after her husband.

Is **Kirkwood** another of those Missouri towns named for a railroad engineer? Yes! James P. Kirkwood, chief engineer of the Pacific Railroad that platted the town

How was **Knob Noster** named? It translates to "our hill." A knob is a hill and noster is French for "our."

Is **Ladue** French? Ladue was named for Peter Ladue, an early French settler.

How was **Lebanon** named? It was named for Lebanon, Tennessee, original home of many of the town's settlers. Lebanon has a barrel factory (Independent Stave Co.) that gives tours. It is located on the north side of Interstate 44. You can contact Barrels of Fun at 417-532-7700. Next door is Walnut Bowls factory outlet.

Also in Lebanon, along the outer road that parallels I-44, is **Nancy Ballhagen's Puzzles** with 2,400 different puzzles in their inventory. 417-286-3837

Why was Lebanon important during the Civil War? It was located on the Military Road between St. Louis and Springfield.

What was Lebanon's quarrel with the railroad? When the town refused to build a depot for the railroad, they laid the tracks a mile away from the city. The town of Lebanon then packed up and moved to the new location on the mud flats.

How was the town of **Laquey** named? It was named for Joseph Laquey (Lackway) who became postmaster in 1898.

How was **Leasburg** named? It was named for Samuel Lea, a native of Yorkshire, England. The town's early name was Harrison Station, for the five members of the early Harrison family.

How did **Lee's Summit** get its name? It was named to honor a certain Dr. Lea who was kidnapped and shot. It also happened to be the highest geographical point in the area. As so often happens, the misspelling of Dr. Lea's name was never corrected.

Does the town of **Liberal** (in Barton County) reflect its true nature? Its founder, George Walser, hoped it would attract free thinkers of the liberal persuasion. Since then, Missouri has become a bit conservative.

How was **Licking** named? For the nearby salt lick that attracted deer and buffalo

Was **Log City**, on Route 66, actually made of logs? Yes – isn't that obvious?

Are there any other Missouri towns named for local creeks? That's how **Longrn** got its name.

How does **Loose Creek** make any sense as a town name? It doesn't, until you discover that the name comes from the French word for Bear Creek. The French word for bear is L'Outs with the "t" being silent.

What Missouri town was named for the sweetheart of a prominent judge? **Lulu**

Is **Lynchburg** another one of those old vigilante towns? No! It was named for prominent land owners with the name Lynch.

What Missouri town was named for the month when a post office was established? **March**

Is the town of **Marshfield** swampy? NO! Remember, it was named for the Massachusetts home of Daniel Webster.

The town of **Midway** is equidistant between what two points on Route 40? St. Louis and Kansas City

Are there any other towns named for the postmaster's wife? **Minimum** was named for Minnie Farr.

Is **Neosho** an Indian word? It's Osage for "clear water."

What happened to the Spanish town name of Nuevo Madrid, honoring the capital of Spain? After the Louisiana Purchase it was Americanized to **New Madrid.**

What place in McDonald County receives thousands of Christmas cards every year so they will be postmarked with the town's name? **Noel**

Is the town of **Niangua** derived from an Indian word? Probably – it ostensibly means "I won't go any farther."

How was **Northwye** named? It was due to a "Y" created by the juncture of U.S. 63 and Route 66, north of Rolla.

How did **Notch** receive its unusual name? In pioneer times roads were identified by trees on the side that had distinctive notches. One notch meant it was a major road, two notches indicated it was big enough for a wagon, and three notches meant it was merely an Indian trail.

How was the town of **Vienna** in Maries County named? It was either for a woman named Vie Anna or the capital of Austria.

Does the town name **Ozark** come from an Indian word? No! It's a corruption of the French word Aux Arcs, a term for Arkansas.

How was the town of **Phelps** named? The village was named for Colonel Bill Phelps, an attorney for the Missouri Pacific Railroad.

Was **Plano** named after the town in Texas? Yes – it was a Texas town with which Missourians conducted extensive trade.

Was the town of **Plato** named for a Greek philosopher? Yes, since it was hoped that wise thinkers would migrate to the town.

Wainwright Building in St. Louis

What do the nearby medicinal springs have to do with the town of **Ponce de Leon**? The mineral springs allegedly restored youth to those who used them, reminiscent of Ponce de Leon, the Spanish explorer who discovered Florida while searching for the fountain of youth.

How did P**oor Man's Chance** receive its unusual name? Located on Turkey Ridge, in Pulaski County, a local man sold ten acre plots at a bargain price to poor farmers.

How did **Portage des Sioux** obtain its name? It was situated at the spot where local Indians began carrying (portage) their canoes to reach the Missouri River, thus escaping their enemies in 1796.

How did **Racket** (in Benton County) obtain its name? It was thought to be due to the honking noise made by migrating geese in the area.

How was **Raytown**, in Jackson County, named? For a local settler

Near what small towns is Union Electric's Calloway County nuclear power plant located? **Reform/Fulton**

What Missouri town honors the only Italian bishop of St. Louis? **Rosati** – so named by local winegrowers in 1930

How did **Springvale** receive its name? The town was named for its topographical features.

How was **Stafford** named? The town was named for a prominent resident. It was on land that originally belonged to the Kickapoo. In 1819, in the Treaty of **Edwardsville**, Indians ceded lands in Illinois in return for this land. Then, in 1932, the Treaty of Castor Hill (St. Louis County) exchanged this land for a new home in Oklahoma.

Lambert Field, 1945 (Dave Lossos postcard collection)

How was **Stone City** named? The town, a popular resort frequented by nearby **Carthage** residents, was name for its construction materials.

Who platted the town of **Webb City** in 1875? John Webb. The town experienced a zinc mining boom during World War I due to Europe's need for foreign zinc.

BRANSON NASHVILLE WEST

When this author's children were young, in the early 1970s, my wife and I took them on vacation to Silver Dollar City. There we rode the train, visited the saloon entertainment at Miss Kitty's, toured Marvel Cave, watched craftsmen blow glass and make such items as leather goods, old brooms and carvings. Then we rode the mine train roller coaster and merry-go-round. They also had a play about the Baldknobbers and a music group called the Presleys. That was it!

East St. Louisan Bob Tyler and Branson performer "Boxcar" Willy who was in Belleville Ill.

About twenty years went by and we didn't pay much attention to the place. One night we were watching the *Tonight Show* on TV and they were talking about how Branson had taken the country music title away from Nashville. My wife and I looked at each other and shrugged, wondering what on earth they were talking about.

We telephoned Bob and Judy Hrasky of **O'Fallon**, some St. Louis friends who had a cabin on the Lake of the Ozarks, and asked them about it. They said we wouldn't believe how the place had grown and stars such as Wayne Newton, the Rockettes, Bobby Vinton, the Platters, Andy Williams and Charley Pride were all down there. They invited us to come down and stay with them at a timeshare they had at Stonebridge, right across from Silver Dollar City.

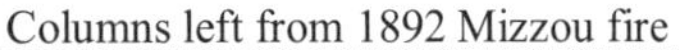

Columns left from 1892 Mizzou fire

When we arrived we couldn't believe our eyes. The quiet little town was now throbbing with excitement and the main road along Route 76 was so jammed with traffic, pedestrians were making better time than the cars.

We had never heard of a time share so they sat down and explained it to us. They said they did all kinds of research and that Stonebridge was a good investment. The intriguing part of a timeshare was that you could "bank" it and trade it for other time shares all over the world.

"Where do you buy one of these?" I asked. "Their sales office is in the main club house next to the golf course," they said. We went over there and found a salesman. I told him I wanted to buy a timeshare. "We'll have to sit down while I explain everything to you and then we'll take a tour," he said. He nearly fell off his chair when I curtly replied, "Let's skip that part. Just get out a contract and I'll sign on the dotted line." He later told us that it was the easiest sale he ever made. My wife got all flustered because she knew we didn't have the $10,000 in the bank. She went over to a couch, lay down, and took a Valium. I told her that I would sell my red 1965 Mustang convertible to cover the expenses.

A few years later we went down to Disneyworld. It was one of those three-day trips where a company paid all your expenses and in return you had to listen to an hour and-a-half time share presentation. We took a tour of their facilities and then went back to the sales office. The salesman was gushing with pride, telling us how his timeshares were among the most desirable in the world because of their proximity to Disneyworld. "Are you kidding?" my wife asked rhetorically. "This place can't hold a candle to our time share in Branson, Missouri," she said emphatically with hands on hips. I thought the man was going to have a stroke of apoplexy.

We only go to Branson once a year, but my wife loves it so much that not once has she banked it and traded it in for another somewhere else in the USA.

If you go to Branson, be sure you see the hilarious ventriloquist on the *Branson Belle*. Don't miss the Rockettes, if they ever come back. Shoji Tabuchi's pool table in his massive and ornate men's room is a must. The urinals actually have crushed ice in them. The gun and doll museum, at the nearby **College of the Ozarks**, is a feast. The War Museum at the east end of 76 Boulevard is another must, as is the Roy Rogers Museum. My favorite eating place is the **Hard Luck Café.** While you are there, the waiters and waitresses take turns singing songs, backed by recorded music. We eat at that establishment once a day when we are in Branson.

Back in 1939, Branson was a sleepy little tourist town with a population of about 1,000. Harold Bell Wright's 1907 book, *The Shepherd of the Hills*, made the town a tourist attraction. Its location on Lake Taneycomo helped make it a cheap tourist attraction during the Depression. To get there from St. Louis, you drove Route 66 to **Springfield** and then went south on Route 65. Back then, Branson was on State 80, an asphalt road that followed high winding ridges vividly described in Harold Bell Wright's novel, the *Shepherd of the Hills*. **Dewey Bald**, mentioned in the story, sits majestically at 1,341 feet, qualifying as a mountain. From its summit can be seen the beautiful White River. One of the attractions back then was old **Matt's Cabin**, a log cabin with shingled roof and a fieldstone fireplace, overlooking Mutton Hollow, one of the settings in the book.

The highway continued on to **Inspirational Point**, a high hill overlooking an appealing scenic Ozark panorama. There was no Silver Dollar City back then. In case you're wondering, Silver Dollar City took its name from the fact that visitors were given change back from cash spent in the form of silver dollars. Silver Dollar City came about when

Mary Herschend decided that people waiting to get into Marvel Cave needed a diversion.

Marvel Cave: For $1.25 you could tour one of the most majestic and largest caves in Missouri. Inside the chamber is Pike's Peak, a massive rock formation 175 feet high. It took nine hours to tour the ten miles of passageways, but most visitors shortened their stay to about an hour and a half, looking at bats, stalactites and stalagmites and visiting the **Cathedral Room, "Devil's Head," the Grand Canyon, Lost River and the Egyptian Room**.

The final attraction was Uncle Ike's Post Office (mentioned in the novel), a small crib like structure that did a small business netting a mere $100.00 a year. The original Ike was dead and buried in the small town of **Notch**.

The town's first music attraction was the Baldknobbers Hillbilly Jamboree. Forty-one years ago, the **Presleys** moved out of a cave and opened a theater on what became known as The Strip. Four generations of Presleys have entertained the folks with their musical talent. According to the story, the tradition started in 1934 when Don Presley traded his favorite hound dog for a guitar. From the late 1950s until 1967 the Presleys performed at Springfield's Fantastic Caverns and the Underground Theater near **Kimberling City**. Fantastic Caverns is the only cave tour in North America where tourists ride on a tram. In 1967, the Presleys took a big risk by buying ten acres and building a small theater on the near-desolate 76 Strip. Gary Presley said in an interview that for the first three years they didn't make a penny. The only money they made was the change that fell out of people's pockets as they sat and watched the show.

Boxcar Willie, now deceased, became the first celebrity to move his show to Branson. The largest theater in town is the Grand Palace with 4,000 seats.

Faurot Field during football game

UNIVERSITY OF MISSOURI

Mizzou, located south of downtown **Columbia**, is a land grant university that was founded back in 1839. It was the first public university west of the Mississippi River. Thomas Jefferson's original tombstone was given to the university by his heirs in 1883. **The world's first school of journalism was founded on the campus in 1908**. Current enrollment exceeds 28,000 with students from every state in the nation and 100 foreign countries represented.

Operations were suspended in 1862 due to the Civil War. During the war the citizens of Columbia formed a "home guard" unit that became notoriously known as the "Fighting Tigers of Columbia." In 1890, an alumnus of the school suggested the university's newly-formed football team be called the "Tigers."

Memorial Union Hall at University of Missouri

On January 9, 1892, Academic Hall, the institution's main building, fell victim to **a fire rumored to have been caused by the first electric light bulb west of the Mississippi**. The columns from that building, which still stand today, form the center of Francis Quadrangle.

In 1935, a black graduate of nearby Lincoln University was denied admission to MU's graduate school. The case went to the U.S. Supreme Court which voted 6-2 to compel the school to admit Lloyd L. Gaines.

In athletics, former football coach Dan Devine holds the school record for the most victories at Faurot Field and the gridiron. Former coach and alum Norm Stewart maintains the record for the most wins on the hard court. Memorial Stadium was built in 1926 and has an official capacity of 68,349. It features a nearly 100 ft. wide "M" behind the north end zone. Truman the tiger, born in 1986, is the school mascot. In a 2004 competition, Truman was acclaimed the "**Best Mascot in the Nation**."

Mizzou is credited with establishing the tradition of the name "Homecoming" in the United States, which was subsequently adopted by most colleges across the country. The tradition began in 1911 when athletic director Chester Brewer invited alumni to "come home" for the big football game against traditional rival Kansas University.

Sam Walton, Brad Pitt and Cheryl Crowe all attended the University of Missouri.

MIZZOU FOOTBALL

Don Faurot was born in Mountain Grove, Missouri, on June 23, 1902. Faurot's association with the University of Missouri started when he was a young boy who would sneak into old Rollins Field to watch the football Tigers play and practice. He was the eldest of four brothers to win a football letter at MU. Faurot was a three-sport letterman from 1922-1924. A lightweight fullback in football, he captained the basketball team, and was an infielder in baseball.

After college, Faurot was appointed head coach at Kirksville State Teachers College (now Truman State University, where he spent nine years. In 1935, he was named head coach at Missouri, where he would remain until 1956 - with three years out for service in the U.S. Navy during World War II. His prime contribution to football was his innovation of the Split-T formation at Mizzou in 1941. In the post-World War II era, countless universities adopted the Faurot formation — and more than 60 years later, it is still in vogue today at all levels of football. Several of football's most notable formations — the Wishbone, Wingbone, Veer or I-attack and others — utilize Faurot's option play as their basic concept.

In 19 years as the Tiger football coach, Faurot's record was 101 wins, 79 losses and 10 ties. His 1939 team, featuring All-American Paul Christman, won Faurot's first Big Six title and a bid to the Orange Bowl. His 1941 team also won the Big 6 and played in the Sugar Bowl. In 1956, he stepped down as head coach but he remained as athletic director until 1967.

Dan Devine's success at Arizona State University resulted in the University of Missouri hiring him as head coach on December 18, 1957. At first, Devine was reluctant to accept the position, having traveled to Missouri in a plane that developed engine trouble. In addition, Devine had hot chocolate spilled on him by a stewardess during the flight, which arrived six hours late.

However, over the next 13 years, Devine would turn the once-dormant program into a consistently competitive school that finished with a Top 20 ranking nine times. His record of 92-38-7 during this span included four bowl game victories, with his winning percentage passing that of Don Faurot, the legendary coach who had preceded him.

After finishing 5-4-1 in his first year, Devine (with two years left on his contract) gained even more job security when a Missouri alumni group funded a $150,000 life insurance policy that covered him as long as he remained as head coach of the Tigers. The investment paid off as Missouri never lost more than three games a season over the next decade.

In 1960, the Tigers began the year unranked, but after shutting out Southern Methodist University, 20-0, in the season opener, moved up to 16th and continued to head upward in the weekly rankings. Following that win with eight straight victories, Missouri became the top-ranked team in the country following a 41-19 victory over the University of Oklahoma.

Needing only a victory over the University of Kansas to clinch a national championship, the Tigers (favored by a touchdown) instead, were stunned in a 23-7 upset loss. After an Orange Bowl victory over legendary Heisman RB Joe Bellino and Navy on January 1, 1961, Missouri finished the year ranked fifth. The team earned a small consolation when they were awarded the win against Kansas after the Jayhawks were penalized for using an ineligible player. Mizzou officially finished 11-0.

While never again reaching that level, Missouri maintained its strength throughout the 1960s, with Devine taking on the added duties of athletic director in 1967. During his three years in the latter role, he made a key hiring when he selected Norm Stewart to head the fortunes of the school's men's basketball squad.

After finishing 9-1 in 1969, Missouri faced Penn State University in the 1970 Orange Bowl. The Nittany Lions entered the game with a 28-game winning streak, and extended the string by intercepting seven Tiger passes in a 10-3 defensive battle.

Devine had four lackluster years as head of the Green Bay Packers and then ended his career by winning a national title at Notre Dame.

The 1983 Tigers lost the Holiday Bowl to BYU when All-American Steve Young pitched the ball to his running back who went to his right, stopped, and threw a pass to his left that found Steve Young in the end zone.

In a game at Columbia in 1990, the Tigers made an incredible goal line stand to defeat Colorado, the team that would be declared the national champions. Unfortunately, the refs didn't keep track of the downs and the Buffalos won the game illegally on the **FIFTH** down.

At the end of the 2005 season, what Mizzou player had the NCAA Division I record for yards rushing as a quarterback? Brad Smith with over 4,000 yards

Who is the only NCAA quarterback to pass for 8,000 yards and rush for 4,000 yards? Brad Smith

Who did Missouri defeat in the 2005 Independence Bowl? Steve Spurrier's South Carolina - 38-31, finishing the season with a 7-5 record

How bad was Missouri in the first half? At one point they were down 21-0 and Brad Smith had only 26 yards rushing– it was the greatest Independence Bowl comeback in history.

What was the low point in the game for Mizzou? Missouri executed a beautiful drive that included a fake field goal play that got the ball to the one yard line. They couldn't punch it in and to make matters worse Adam Crossett missed a 22 yard field goal.

What was the turning point in the game? As South Carolina was going in for another score, a Missouri cornerback intercepted a pass on the one yard line and ran it back 99 yards for a score.

At what point did the Tigers first take the lead? When Adam Crossett hit a fifty-yarder that put them ahead 31-28; late in the fourth quarter South Carolina made a field goal to tie the game. Crossett, incidentally, has yet to miss an extra point at Mizzou, and has never missed a field goal against a Big 12 opponent. Brad Smith scored the winning touchdown with just 2:13 left in the game.

What play sealed Mizzou's victory? Cornerback Darnell Terrell of **Eureka** intercepted a pass with only 1:29 remaining as the Gamecocks were moving down the field to tie the score.

St. Louis music icon Bob Kuban grew up in Bellefountaine (Lossos/ Pat Brannon)

How important was the play of Missouri's tight ends? Tight ends Chase Coffman and Martin Rucker combined for 13 catches for 182 yards and a touchdown. Their blocking also enabled Brad Smith to run wild in the second half.

What was Brad Smith's record as a starter at Mizzou? A mediocre 25-23

How many games did Brad Smith miss due to injuries as a starter in his four years at Mizzou? None

How many records did Smith rack up during his illustrious career? 60 Missouri, Big 12, and NCAA records

How was Missouri's pass defense in the S.C. game? Terrible! South Carolina receiver Sidney Rice set an Independence Bowl record by making

12 catches for 191 yards. However, he was limited to just three catches for 21 yards in the second half.

What were Smith's mind boggling totals for the game? He passed for 282 yards and ran for 150, giving him 432 of the Tiger's 504 yards of total offense.

Who was Mizzou's backup quarterback in this game? Chase Daniel – he got in the game twice – once when coach Pinkel put him in to try and jump start the offense, and again briefly when Smith suffered a minor ankle injury.

Who did Mizzou dedicate the game to? Aaron O'Neal who collapsed and died during a pre-season scrimmage

What impressive statistic did Chase Daniel have as a senior for his Texas high school team? He passed for over 4,000 yards as a senior and was Texas' "Player of the Year."

With Chase Daniel as quarterback in 2006, where did Missouri rank in the NCAA with total offense? They were 8th in the nation. After ten games into the 2007 season they were averaging over 40 points a game and were ranked 7th in total offense.

Where was Mizzou ranked in preseason polls at the beginning of the 2007 season? 26th; Ron Zook's Illini were unranked and finished at #13, upsetting #1 ranked Ohio State in the process and led the nation as the most improved team, going from two wins last year to nine this year plus a BCS bowl bid.

After the 5-0 Tigers administered a 41-6 thrashing (Oct. 6, 2007) to Nebraska, what was their ranking in the polls? Eleventh in the nation; after whipping Colorado 55-10 in early November, Mizzou moved up to the 6th spot, just behind undefeated Kansas and once defeated Oklahoma. They lost to 6th ranked Oklahoma on October 13th. When they defeated Texas A & M in their tenth game, they matched Dan Devine's 1969 club with a 9-1 record. When they defeated Kansas State on November 17, this was the first time a Missouri team had ten wins since 1960.

Typical delirious "Braggin' Rights" crowd

After the November Kansas State win, the Tigers moved up to the number four spot in the rankings. Tight end Martin Rucker was leading the nation's tight ends with over 60 receptions. Jeremy Macklin set a freshman NCAA mark for the most total all-purpose yards in a single season.

The Missouri-Kansas "Border Showdown" at Arrowhead Stadium in Kansas City took on even more significance when number one ranked LSU lost to Arkansas the day before. The **Mizzou-Kansas rivalry ranks second in the nation in number of games played**. Coach Pinkle's team had the lead all the way, but Kansas mounted a furious comeback that fell just short. The final score was 36-28 and the new ratings **put Mizzou at #1 in the nation**. The next week they would play Oklahoma in San Antonio for the Big Twelve title. Against the Sooners, the Tigers looked inept and were held to less than 30 points for the first time in the season. The loss was devastating as they dropped to 6th in the rankings. Kansas and Illinois, two teams which they had beaten, received BCS bowl bids while Missouri had to settle for playing Arkansas in the Cotton Bowl. Mizzou made the best of it by defeating the Razorbacks 38-7 and finishing at 12-2, the most wins ever for the Tigers. Running back Tony Temple set two Cotton Bowl records by running hog wild with four touchdowns and 281 yards.

Illinois finished the season ranked 13th in the nation and played powerhouse Southern Cal in the Rose Bowl. Four turnovers were turned into 28 points by the Trojans and Illinois was crushed 49-17.

Chase Daniel was named one of four finalists for the Heisman Trophy.

MISSOURI BASKETBALL

The Stipanovich/Sunvold years are the ones remembered best by Mizzou fans. Both players were recruited by Coach Norm Stewart, Steve from Desmet and Jon from **Blue Springs**. Stipanovich, at 6-11, was one of the most heavily recruited players in the nation. In the 1979-80 season the duo teamed with Ricky Frazier, a **Charleston** native who transferred from St. Louis University after his freshman season. Curtis Berry, Steve Wallace and Larry Drew were the rest of that team's core.

The team started quickly out of the gate, and with an 11-2 record were ranked thirteenth in the nation. Then came a bombshell. Steve Wallace lost his academic eligibility. It was at this point that Sunvold moved into a starting position but it left the team with a weak bench. The team stumbled, with conference losses to Oklahoma and Kansas State, but jelled quickly. They made up for an early season loss to Kansas by trouncing them by an 88-65 score. By beating Kansas State, the team finished with an 11-3 conference record and Norm Stewart won his second Big Eight title.

The end of the season went badly as Missouri lost to Kansas in the semi-finals of the Big Eight Tournament. Worse, Curtis Berry re-injured a knee and was lost for the rest of the year, crippling Tiger hopes in the NCAA Tournament. Mizzou vanquished San Jose State and Notre Dame in the Midwest Regional, but lost to LSU 68-63 when Stipanovich got into foul trouble.

Still, it was a spectacular season as the Tigers set an NCAA record by shooting 57.3 percent from the field.

During Stipo's three years at Desmet, his Catholic school won two high school state championships. In college, Stipo had several off-court incidents. He missed part of his sophomore year when he **accidentally shot himself** while playing with a gun at a party on campus. There was another incident at a White Castle where he got into a fight with a fan who made disparaging remarks about his play. His biggest triumph came as a senior when Mizzou played top-ranked Virginia, led by another tall center, All-American Ralph Sampson. The shorter Stipo outplayed Sampson and Mizzou won the game. In the 1983 NBA draft, Stipo was selected second overall by the Indiana Pacers. Knee problems limited his career to five seasons.

After his NBA career, Stipo moved to Oregon for a while but later returned to St. Louis where he is an executive with

the only company operating a coal mine in Missouri.

Sunvold was drafted by Seattle but wasn't an impact player because Coach Lenny Wilkens couldn't decide whether he was a point or off guard. The 6-2 Sunvold was traded to the Spurs for a second round draft pick. John was a good shooter but was an average ball handler and lacked quickness. Jon then went to the Miami Heat in the 1989 expansion draft and led the NBA in 3-point shooting percentage (.522). That was good for second place in the NBA record book. He quickly became a fan favorite.

After his NBA career, Sunvold became a television announcer for ESPN basketball games.

One of the best non-conference basketball rivalries in the nation is the **Braggin' Rights game** at the Savvis Center between the Missouri Tigers and the Fighting Illini. The series dates back to 1980 when Lou Henson and Norm Stewart were the coaches. After 1999, Illinois led the series by a slim 11-8 margin, but since then have reeled off a gob of wins in a row. James Augustine and Dee Brown had the heady experience of never having lost to Mizzou in their careers. One of the most dramatic wins for Mizzou came in 1995 when the final buzzer sounded with the game tied. Unfortunately, one of the Missouri players had just fouled Kewane Garris, the Illinois guard. Garris had already scored over 30 points in the game. With no other players on the court, a shaky Garris missed both free throws. Missouri ran wild in overtime and won by a score of 96-85. Later that week, Garris received a package in the mail. He opened it and **was astonished to find two bricks, courtesy of a Mizzou fan**.

St. Louis musician Jules Blattner (courtesy Dave Lossos/Carol Kawell Ellis)

Former Duke University star Quin Snyder was hired to replace legendary coach Norm Stewart in 1999. He was hailed as a sensation upon his arrival. His first team, although seriously undermanned, knocked off a ranked Illinois team in the Border War game and then defeated the archrival Kansas Jayhawks.

Snyder, who three times led his Blue Devils to the final four as a player, is married to NBA coach Larry Brown's daughter.

In Snyder's second season, his Tigers once again toppled a ranked Kansas team and then won their first NCAA tournament victory since 1995. The next year Snyder did something that had been accomplished only two other times in 100 years of Missouri basketball. The Tigers made it to the Elite Eight. In the process, the Tigers defeated 5th seeded Miami, then pummeled the Big Ten Champion Ohio State Buckeyes. Next to fall were the UCLA Bruins. They then lost a close game to the Oklahoma Sooners.

In 2002-03, Missouri again reached the NCAA Tournament. Their five NCAA wins in three seasons was unmatched in Mizzou roundball history. In January of 2003, point guard Ricky Clemons was arrested on charges of assault and battery against his former girlfriend. While in jail, Clemons accused other players of receiving payments from Snyder's assistant coaches. As the scandal began to unravel, so did Missouri's season. Picked to finish first in the Big Twelve, and once ranked #3 nationally, they finished the year with a dismal 16-14 record. In the fall of 2004, the NCAA put Mizzou on probation after a lengthy investigation. It was discovered that Clemons had received academic credit for work he hadn't completed.

Snyder's 2005-06 team had an up and down season. Snyder resigned after losing to the Baylor Bears, leaving Mizzou with three more conference games to play. Despite the controversy, Snyder, with trips to the NIT his last two years, is the only Missouri coach to take his teams to post-season tournament play every year in his tenure. Snyder is currently the coach of the Austin Toros. He was succeeded by interim coach Melvin Watkins.

University of Alabama Birmingham coach Mike Anderson was hired to coach the Tigers in March of 2006.

In November of 2007, former coach Norm Stewart was inducted into the Basketball Hall of fame. Stewart had 731 career wins, including 634 in 32 seasons at Mizzou.

In the 2007 Border War game at the Scotttrade Center, Mizzou lost its eighth straight game to Illinois, this time by a single point, 59-58. It was a heartbreaking loss for Mizzou had a 58-56 lead but turned the ball over on its last three possessions. For further info, read Michael Atchison's *True Sons*.

In January of 2008, five players, including the team's leading scorer, were suspended for violating team rules. It was discovered that they had gone to a Columbia nightclub. Senior guard Stefhon Hannah was banished back to Chicago after suffering a broken jaw in an altercation.

KANSAS CITY CHIEFS

Lamar Hunt was the founder of the Dallas Texans football team in 1960. The team moved to Kansas City in 1963 because it could not compete with the Dallas Cowboys. Hunt wanted to call the new team the Kansas City Texans. Some suggested the Kansas City Mules. They finally settled on the Chiefs. Kansas City's mayor Roe Bartle's nickname was "the Chief."

The Chiefs played their home games at Municipal Stadium with a 49,002 seating capacity. They moved into Arrowhead Stadium in 1972. The Chiefs, with **Hank Stram** as coach and **Len Dawson** of Purdue as quarterback, lost to Vince Lombardi's Green Bay Packers in the first Super Bowl, 35-10. They got their revenge three years later in 1969 by upsetting Bud Grant's Minnesota Vikings, who are best remembered for losing four Super Bowls, 23-7. Five members of the Hank Stram era made it into the Hall of Fame – Len Dawson, Bobby Bell, Willie Lanier, Buck Buchanan and kicker Jan Stenerud. Coach Stram was also enshrined. Other notable players were Otis Taylor, Jim Lynch and Mike Garrett.

Marty **Schottenheimer** became the new coach in 1989 and compiled an impressive 101-58-1 record. The Chiefs were the NFL's winningest team of the 1990s. Arrowhead

Stadium began to sell out every game with stars such as Derrick Thomas, Christian Okoye and Deron Cherry. The Chiefs traded for **Joe Montana** prior to the 1993 season and also signed running back **Marcus Allen**. They lost the AFC Championship game to Marv Levy's Buffalo Bills who are best remembered for losing four Super Bowls. Montana retired after the 1994 season. The Chiefs lost in the 1996 playoffs to the Indianapolis Colts when kicker Lin Elliot missed multiple field goals. In 1997, there was a quarterback controversy between **Elvis Grbac** and Rich Gannon. Gannon went 5-1, but Grbac started for the playoff game against Denver, which they lost. That odd choice still remains a controversy. Conservative "Martyball" was gone after the 1998 season; when Schottenheimer resigned. Gunther Cunningham became the new coach but lasted only two seasons. In 1999, the Chiefs missed a playoff berth when kicker Pete Stoyonavich flubbed a chip shot field goal against the Raiders.

Dick Vermeil came out of retirement in 2001 to coach the Chiefs. Kurt Warner made **Trent Green** expendable for the Rams, so the St. Louisan was traded to Kansas City. He led the Chiefs to a 13-3 record, but they lost 38-31 to the Colts in a game that set a playoff mark because neither team punted.

Tony Gonzalez, Priest Holmes, Dante Hall and Larry Johnson emerged as stars. Vermeil retired at the end of the 2005 season and Herm Edwards became the new coach. The 2006 Chiefs lost the Wild Card playoff game 23-8 against their nemesis, Peyton Manning's Colts.

For the 2007 season, **Damon Huard** became the starter and the Chiefs traded injured Trent Green to the Miami Dolphins, but Green suffered a near career ending concussion in the middle of the season. The Chiefs struggled through a losing season that year.

What KC running back set an NFL record with 27 touchdowns in a single season? Priest Holmes

What Kansas City linebacker was left paralyzed from the waist down after a car crash in January of 2000? Derrick Thomas

What coach won a Super Bowl, retired, and then came back to coach the Kansas City Chiefs? Dick Vermeil

What KC receiver led the Chiefs in total yards for the 2005 season? Former Ram, Eddie Kennison

What KC receiver led the Chiefs in receptions for the 2005 season? All Pro Tony Gonzalez

What is the name of the trophy that is the prize for the winner in the annual preseason game between the St. Louis Rams and the Kansas City Chiefs? Governor's Cup

Who led KC in rushing for the 2005 season? Larry Johnson, who was drafted out of Penn State

What KC player led the AFL in receiving four of his first five years in pro football? Lionel Taylor

What miracle enabled KC to make the playoffs in the 2006 season? They needed a season-ending win against the Jaguars, plus losses from Denver, Cincinnati and Tennessee.

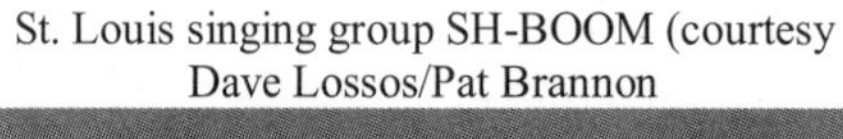
St. Louis singing group SH-BOOM (courtesy Dave Lossos/Pat Brannon

Actress Agnes Morehead

KANSAS CITY ROYALS

Kansas City entered the Central Division of the American League in 1969 as an expansion team. They took the name "Royals" from the American Royal Livestock Show, held in Kansas City since 1899. The club was founded by Ewing Kauffman, a local businessman. The city began looking for a team after the Athletics moved away to become the Oakland Athletics.

Kansas City had good early success, winning their inaugural game against the Minnesota Twins 4-3 on April 8. They traded for Lou Pinella who won the Rookie of the Year award. They also invested in a strong farm system which developed such future stars as pitchers Paul Splittorff and Steve Busby, infielders George Brett and Frank White, and outfielder Al Cowens.

In 1971, the Royals had their first winning year, with manager Bob Lemon guiding them to a second-place finish. In 1973, under Jack McKeon, the Royals adopted their powder blue road uniforms and moved from Municipal Stadium to the brand-new Kauffman Stadium.

Manager **Whitey Herzog** replaced McKeon in 1975 and the Royals quickly became a dominant team, winning three straight division championships. This record was marred when the Royals lost three straight League Championship Series encounters to the Yankees.

Herzog was fired after a second place finish in 1979. He was replaced by Jim Frey. The Royals vanquished the Yankees in three straight, but lost the World Series to the Philadelphia Phillies in six games.

In 1980, third baseman George Brett was hitting .400 or better until the middle of September. The pressure of trying to break Ted Williams' 1941 .406 mark finally got to him, and he ended the season with an impressive .390 mark

The 1983 season was marked by future Hall of Famer **George Brett's** legendary pine tar incident. Brett hit a home run against the Yankees. The umpires examined his bat and decided that the pine tar was too high up the handle and disallowed the homer. George Brett "went nuts" and was ejected from the game. The league later reversed the umpire's ruling and allowed the homer to count.

In 1985, **Bret Saberhagan** won the Cy Young Award and led the Royals to the World Series against the St. Louis Cardinals. In the playoffs, they fell behind three games to one against Toronto, but rallied to win the series. Against the Cards, the Royals once again fell behind 3-1, but rallied to win in seven games.

In the late 1980s and early 1990s, the Royals developed young stars such as **Bo Jackson**, Tom Gordon, and Kevin Seitzer.

Starting in 1995, the team went into a long decline. Team owner Ewing Kauffman died in 1993. The Royals decided to cut their payroll by trading star pitcher **David Cone** and outfielder Brian McRae. MLB salaries continued to rise and the Royals kept cutting, trading outfielder **Johnny Damon**, **Kevin Appier** and **Jermaine Dye**. In 2002, the Royals set a new low in franchise history by losing 100 games.

Superstar **Albert Pujols** played high school ball at Fort Osage High in **Independence**, Missouri, but the Royals didn't even make an effort to draft him, letting him slip away to the St. Louis Cardinals where he led them to a World Series win in 2006.

In 2003, manager Tony Pena led them back to a winning record, but they fell apart again in 2004 and compounded the problem by trading superstar **Carlos Beltran** for prospects. In four out of the next five seasons the Royals lost 100 games and have become the doormat of the American League.

Other noteworthy Royals players include Dan Quisenberry, Amos Otis, Willie Wilson, Cookie Rojas, Frank White, Hal McRae and Fred Patek.

How many battling titles did George Brett win? Two – 1980 and 1990

What unusual physical ailment bothered George Brett? Hemorrhoids

What Royals player won the batting title in 1982 with a .332 average? Willie Wilson

What Royals player led the league in hits in 1975 and 1976? George Brett

What Royals player led the league in hits in 1987? Kevin Seitzer

Has any member of the Royals ever led the American league in homers? No

What Royals player led the league in RBIs for 1982? Hal McRae – 133

What Royals player led the league in stolen bases four years in a row from 1965-1968? Bert Campaneris

What Kansas City player led the league in winning percentage in 1977? Paul Splitorff, who went 16-6

What Kansas City player led the league in winning percentage in 1989? Bret Saberhagen who was 23-6

What Royal led the league in ERA in 1993? Kevin Appier – 2.56

Has any Royal pitcher ever led the league in strikeouts? No

What Kansas City pitcher led the league in saves in 1993 with 45? Jeff Montgomery

What Kansas City pitcher led the league in saves four different years? Dan Quisenberry in the 1980s

Author/poet Calvin Trillin

Actress Kathleen Turner

FAMOUS MISSOURIANS

Missouri has provided more than its share of people who have gained fame as actors, writers, inventors, poets, merchants, artists, dancers, sports stars and the like. What follows is a list of some of the more notable.

Robert Altman, film director born in Kansas City; Burt Bacharach, songwriter who married Angie Dickinson, born in Kansas City; Josephine Baker, singer and dancer, born in St. Louis; E.L. Cord of Warrensburg – built the Auburn, Cord and Duesenberg; Wallace Beery, actor, born in Kansas City; Howard Hughes of Lancaster, inventor of an oil drilling bit that made him a fortune; William Bent of St. Louis, noted pioneer and fur trader; Robert R. Bennett, composer, born in Kansas City; Yogi Berra, Yankee baseball player from St. Louis - won more World Series rings than anyone in history; Thomas Hart Benton, painter from Neosho; artist George Caleb Bingham of Franklin; Bill Bradley, basketball player and U.S. Senator from Crystal City; WW 2 General Omar Bradley of Clark; Emmett Kelly, famous clown (born in Cabool); Grace Brumbry, opera soprano from St. Louis; writer William Burroughs of St. Louis; opera director and conductor Sarah Caldwell of Maryville; frontierswoman Calamity Jane of Princeton; public speaking author Dale Carnegie of Maryville; agronomist George Washington Carver of Diamond Grove; actor Don Cheadle (*Hotel Rwanda*) of Kansas City; writer/humorist Mark Twain of Florida; newscaster Walter Cronkite of St. Joseph; singer Cheryl Crowe from the bootheel area; actor Robert Cummings of Joplin; actress Jane Darwell of Palmyra; comedienne Phyllis Diller of St. Louis; cartoonist Walt Disney of Marceline; inventor (father of inertial navigation - gyroscopes) Charles Draper of Windsor; Jeanne Eagles, actress from Kansas City; poet T.S. Eliot; inventor of the LCD (liquid crystal display) James Fergason of Wakenda; Eugene Field, the "children's poet" from St. Louis; Cliff Edwards of Hannibal, the voice of Jiminy Cricket; St. Louisan Dave Garroway, the first host of television's Today Show; Senator James Fulbright of Sumner (fought against McCarthyism and the John Birch Society, helped establish a scholarship program for exchange students, and opposed the Vietnam War); actor John Goodman of Affton; actress Betty Grable of St. Louis; comedian/activist Dick Gregory of St. Louis; actress Jean Harlow of Kansas City; astronomer Edwin Hubble of Marshfield; inventor (the integrated circuit) Jack Kilby of Jefferson City; poet Langston Hughes of Joplin; inventor William Lear (Lear jet) of Hannibal; conservative radio talk show host Rush Limbaugh of Cape Girardeau; film director John Huston of

Nevada; outlaw Jesse James of Centerville; physical culturist Bernarr MacFadden of Mill Springs; Mary McBride of Paris/ St. Louis, historical and contemporary romance author; inventor (optical fiber for communications) Robert Maurer of St. Louis; boxer Archie Moore grew up in St. Louis - he learned how to box in reform school where he was sent for nearly two years for stealing; after 16 years as a pro he became light heavyweight champion at age 39; Moore amassed more knockouts (145) than any known boxer in history; Moore is the only boxer in history to have fought Rocky Marciano, Floyd Patterson, and Cassius Clay; actress Agnes Moorehead (Endora the witch on *Bewitched*), who grew up in St. Louis; Pulitzer Prize poet Marianne Moore of Kirkwood; actress Geraldine Page (*Sweet Bird of Youth*, with Paul Newman) of Kirksville; merchant J.C. Penney of Hamilton; zoo director Marlin Perkins; W W I General John J. Pershing of Linn County; actor and master of the macabre, Vincent Price of St. Louis; George McManus, creator of the comic strip, Maggie and Jiggs; dancer/actress Ginger Rogers of Independence; artist Charles M. Russell of St. Louis; Wyoming Governor Nellie Tayloe Ross of Saint Joseph; choreographer Ted Shawn of Kansas City; baseball manager Casey Stengel of Kansas City; soprano Gladys Swarthout of Deepwater; poet Sara Teasdale of St. Louis; music composer (*The Plow That Broke the Plains*) Virgil Thomson, of Kansas City; President Harry S Truman, of Lamar; author/humorist Mark Twain of Florida; actor Dick Van Dyke of West Plains; actor Dennis Weaver (Chester on *Gunsmoke*) of Joplin; actress Pearl (*Perils of Pauline*) White of Greenridge; novelist Laura Ingalls Wilder (*Little House on the Prairie*) of Mansfield; civil rights leader Roy Wilkins (NAACP) of St. Louis. Conservative author Phyllis Schlafly is a Washington U. graduate.

What Missouri mountain man served as a guide for explorer John Fremont, The Pathfinder? Kit Carson

Who is **Calvin Trillin**? He is an author, poet and columnist who was born in Kansas City in 1935. Many of his columns were humorous articles about food and restaurants. He contributed many articles to *The Nation* magazine.

What famous star of the 1981 movie *Body Heat* was born in Springfield, Missouri? Kathleen Turner

St. Louis-born pin-up girl, Betty Grable

What college did Turner attend for two years? Missouri State University at **Springfield**

What were some of Turner's other notable films? The "new Lauren Bacall," with the deep sexy voice, stared in *Romancing the Stone, The War of the Roses, Jewel of the Nile*, and *Peggy Sue Got Married.*

Where was writer/author Richard Rhodes born? **Kansas City**, Missouri in 1937 Two of his most noteworthy books are *The Making of the Atomic Bomb* (Pulitzer Prize winner) and *James Audubon.* When Rhodes was a youngster, the police discovered that his step-mother was starving and abusing him. He was sent to the Andrew Drumm Institute, founded in 1928 at **Independence**. It is still in operation today.

Rapper Eminem was also born in **Kansas City**. **Chuck Berry** was once arrested for armed robbery and was sentenced to ten years in the Reformatory at **Jefferson City**.

Dolly Parton wrote the song "I Will Always Love You" for **Porter Wagoner** who was from **West Plains**.

Yogi Berra

Saxophonist Charlie "Yardbird" Parker was born in Kansas City.

Where was actor Robert Cummings born? **Joplin**, Missouri in 1908

Who taught Cummings how to fly an airplane? His godfather, Orville Wright

What were some of his more notable films? *Saboteur, Dial M For Murder*, and *King's Row* with Ronald Reagan

What was Cummings' big television hit show? The *Bob Cummings Show*, named *Love That Bob* in reruns

What Missourian wrote the novel, *The Shepherd of the Hills*? Harold Bell Wright of **Lebanon**, Missouri

Missourian Walt Disney making cartoons, drawings and films for the military - WW 2

Who was the WNBA 2001 Rookie of the Year? Shooting sensation **Jackie Stiles**, a graduate of Southeast Missouri State

What happened to Jackie's pro basketball career? Thirteen surgeries put her on the sidelines

Who was Dick Bland? "Silver" Dick Bland of **Lebanon** was a Missouri congressman who favored a U.S. dollar based on gold and silver and was favored to win the Demo-cratic nomination for president in the 1896 race until William J. Bryan gave his Cross of Gold speech. He was co-sponsor of the Bland-Allison Act of

1878 which required the U.S. Treasury to purchase between two and four million dollars worth of silver every month.

What Missourian is the **founder of osteopathic medicine**? Dr. Andrew Taylor Spill

In what Missouri city was actress Joan Crawford (Lucille LeSueur) reared? Her family moved to **Kansas City** in 1916.

What school did she attend? St Agnes Academy

What college did Joan attend in 1922? Stevens College in **Columbia**

How was Joan's movie name determined? A producer decided that her last name sounded too much like the word "sewer" so a contest was held by *Movie Weekly* magazine and a fan won $500 for suggesting the name Joan Crawford.

For what 1945 role did Joan win the "Best Actress" Academy Award? *Mildred Pierce*

How many times did Joan Crawford marry? Five – including once to Douglas Fairbanks Jr. from 1929-1933

What movie was Joan's last big hit? *What Ever Happened to Baby Jane*; Joan campaigned against her co-star, Betty Davis, who lost the "Best Actress" Academy Award to Ann Bancroft.

What 1969 biography, by one of her five adopted children, showed Joan to be a cruel mother? *Mommy Dearest*

Who was Frederick Niedermeyer? He was an early Missouri aviation pioneer who was born in 1896 at **Columbia**, Missouri. After he was killed in a 1922 plane crash, the U.S. military began requiring all pilots to wear parachutes.

Who was Ben Hogan? Hogan won the 1946 PGA Western Open, held at the Sunset Hills St. Louis course.

What receiver from **Chesterfield**, Missouri, made the key catch against Tampa Bay (from Curt Warner) in the playoffs, sending the Rams to the Super Bowl against the Tennessee Titans? Rickey Proehl

What St. Louisan starred in **The Babe**, a 1992 film about Babe Ruth? John Goodman

What high school did Goodman attend? **Affton** High

What was Goodman's major at Southwest Missouri State?
Drama – his first job was eating a Whopper in a TV commercial.

What St. Louisan (**Clayton**) starred in the 2002 film, *The Emperor's Club*? Kevin Kline

Name the film that made a big splash and won Kline an Oscar for Best Supporting Actor. *A Fish Called Wanda*

How many seasons did St. Louisan Yogi Berra play? He played 19 seasons from 1946 to 1965 and participated in 14 World Series competitions.

Kevin Kline and wife Phoebe Cates

Actress Joan Crawford

Musician/composer Scott Joplin

What team did Berra play for after he was released by the Yankees? New York Mets

St. Louisan Yogi Berra is famous for one-liners and malapropisms. What is Yogi Berra's best line in his famous commercial for Afflak Insurance? Sitting in a barber shop, he extols the virtue of having this insurance. To paraphrase: "If you get hurt in an accident and can't work, they pay you cash, which is just as good as real money."

What is Berra's best quote? "Baseball is 90 percent mental. The other half is physical."

What did Yogi say he would do if he found a million dollars? "I'd find the fella who lost it and, if he was poor, I'd give it back."

Berra has become a cultural icon because of these goofy misstatements. What are they called? Yogi-isms. "It ain't over till it's over."

What was Berra's most controversial play as a Yankee? In a 1950's World Series game v. the Brooklyn Dodgers, Jackie Robinson tried to steal home and was called safe. Berra protested vehemently, but to no avail. Close examination of the play shows that Berra was right.

What girl has won the state cross country championship the last three years in a row, setting a record for time in the process? Meredith Snow of **Eureka** High

If **Scott Joplin** was born in Texas in 1868, how does Missouri get to claim him? He moved to St. Louis around 1890. The house he lived in is at 2658 Delmar.

What is Joplin's music legacy? He is called the "King of Ragtime" His best piece was "Maple Leaf Rag" (my opinion, of course).

What is Ragtime? It is a blend of European classical music combined with African harmony and rhythm

What 1970s movie made his music, especially "The Entertainer," well-known to most Americans? That Paul Newman/Robert Redford buddy flick, *The Sting*

What was **Scott Joplin** doing at the Chicago Columbian Exposition in 1993? He played the local taverns and dance halls trying to earn a buck.

What is the subject of his composition, *The Great Crush Collision*? A Staged crash of two railroad locomotives near Waco, Texas in 1896

How did Scott come to write the *Maple Leaf Rag*, one of his best known compositions? He wrote it while working at the Maple Leaf Club when he was living in **Sedalia**, Missouri, in 1899.

What kind of work did Scott Joplin do after he moved to New York City in 1911? He became the first African-American to compose an opera when he wrote *Treemonisha*

What caused Scott Joplin's premature death in the year 1917? A severe case of third stage syphilis

What is composer W.C. Handy's connection to St. Louis? While living with his wife in Memphis, and playing in the night clubs on Beale Street, the "**Father of the Blues**" wrote his most famous composition – *St. Louis Blues* (1914). As a result, St. Louis claims to be the "Home of the Blues."

What is **Tina Turner's** connection to St. Louis? Tina was born Anna Mae Bullock in Nutbush, Tennessee, but came to live as a teenager with relatives in St. Louis.

How did Tina meet Ike Turner? She dropped out of school and started hanging around night clubs where Ike and his band were playing. When Ike bought a house in the Alta Sita section of **East St. Louis** in 1958, she moved in with the boys.

Who was **Daniel Bissell**? He commanded the fort at Bellefontaine Neighbors, the first fort west of the Mississippi River after the 1803 Louisiana Purchase. The Bissell Mansion is now a tourist attraction. The place also features a whodunit mystery dinner theater. 800-690-9838

What famous Missouri slave was born in 1864 on the **Diamond Grove** farm of his master, Moses Carver? George Washington Carver; Carver received a college education at Iowa State University and later accepted a position at the Tuskegee Institute, run by Booker T. Washington. Carver did research on devising alternative crops for southern farmers when it was discovered that years of cotton production had worn out the soil. Carver came up with 105 food recipes using the peanut. He also came up with many innovative commercial uses of the peanut but none were successfully marketed. Carver, who never married, may have made the biggest contribution to his race by merely showing that black men had intelligence.

Carver became nationally famous after he gave lengthy testimony before a Senate committee about the many uses of the peanut. His testimony resulted in peanuts being included in the Fordney-Mc-Cumber Tariff of 1922. He gained more fame by claiming that massaging the legs of polio victims with peanut oil could produce dramatic effects. It was soon proven that any beneficial effects came from the massage, not the peanut oil.

It is a widely held fiction that Carver invented peanut butter while on a visit to St. Louis. That food was invented by a St. Louis physician.

What is significant about Diamond Grove National Monument? It was the first National Monument Park dedicated to an African American.

If Carver developed so many innovations, why does he only have three patents? He felt it wouldn't be fair to profit that much from his research. "God gave them to me" he frequently said. Carver was honored in 1998 by being depicted on a 32 cent U.S. stamp.

JOHN J. PERSHING

Where was John Pershing born? On a farm near **Laclede**, Missouri in 1860

What colleges did Pershing attend? The Normal School at **Kirksville**, then West Point

What was Pershing's main motivation for wanting to attend West Point? It wasn't out of a burning desire to serve the military. He merely wanted to get the best education available. He graduated first in his class in 1886.

What tragedy befell Pershing in April of 1886? His father died, followed by his mother a week and a half later.

What honor did Pershing achieve in 1886? He was in charge of the honor guard at President Grant's funeral.

What was Pershing's assignment in 1895? He led a cavalry group of Buffalo Soldiers and became an ardent supporter of allowing Negroes to serve in the military. This was an unpopular stance that earned him the nickname "Nigger Jack." World War I reporters softened it to "Black Jack."

What did Pershing do in the Spanish-American War of 1898? He participated in the battle of San Juan Hill and was awarded a Silver Star for bravery.

What tragedy befell Pershing in August of 1915? His wife and three daughters were killed in a fire at the Presidio in San Francisco. His six-year-old son Warren was the only survivor.

Who was one of Pershing's aides during the ill-fated 1915 expedition that sought to capture the bandit, Pancho Villa? George Patton

Did Pershing receive the lion's share of credit for the Allied victory in World War I? Yes

What did Douglas MacArthur dislike about Pershing? He thought he commanded too far from the front to be an effective general. MacArthur would later refer to Pershing as a "desk general."

Father Marquette

What significant promotion was given to Pershing after the war? He was given the title, General of the Armies, the only person to hold that rank.

Was Pershing a candidate for the Republican nomination in 1920? Yes, although he did not actively campaign for it. Many Republicans thought Pershing was associated too closely with President Wilson's policies and the nomination went to Warren Harding of Ohio.

How did Pershing win the Pulitzer Prize for history in 1932? He wrote, *My Experiences in the World War.*

When did Pershing die? July 15, 1948 at Walter Reed Hospital; he was buried at Arlington Cemetery.

MISSOURI HISTORY – 1600 - 1821

The two main Native-American tribes, when the white men arrived, were the Missouri and the Osage. They buried their dead in mounds which were so numerous that St. Louis at one time was called **Mound City**. The main hunting ground of the Osages, first mentioned in 1763 by Marquette, were located in what is now Bates and Vernon counties. This flat plain became known as the Osage Prairie.

The Osages lived in villages and individually were housed in tepees. Osages were tall, many of them well over six feet. In some early accounts they were described as giants. They shaved their heads, leaving only a clump on top that was decorated with feathers and wampum. The Osages had the unusual habit of plucking their eyebrows. They painted their ears vermillion; if they were grieving over a death they painted them black. They frequently painted their faces with black, white, and green stripes. During warfare, they **scalped their enemies**. They smoked a pipe as part of their religious ceremonies, revering the Great Spirit, the sun and the moon. Missionaries found that they were very reluctant to adopt Christianity. The women of the tribe did most of the work, except for hunting and warfare.

The Missouri, first described by an explorer in 1687, lived near the place where the Missouri and Mississippi rivers joined, 17 miles north of St. Louis. In 1789, the Missouris were conquered and dispersed by the warlike Sac and Fox tribes. The Missouris were noted for their bravery and friendliness to the whites.

Madam Chouteau – owner of slaves (MHS)

Most likely, who were the first white men to set foot in the state? Desoto's Spanish conquistadors who came as far north as **Cape Girardeau in 1541**

What French explorers visited Missouri in 1659? Radisson and Groseilliers

What other early whites visited Missouri? Marquette and Joliet during their 1673 trip down the Mississippi

What explorer claimed Missouri for France? LaSalle – 1682; it was LaSalle and his assistant Henri "Iron hand" Tonti who devised a scheme to strengthen French control of the Mississippi valley by building a series of strategically located forts.

Seal of the French Jesuits

Early Missouri was part of what French territory? Upper Louisiana

Who was the first Frenchman to explore the Missouri River -1714? Etienne (Steven) Veniard de Bourgmond who probably made it up to either the Kaw or possibly the Platte River; Bourgmond was looking for the "south sea" and the Northwest Passage.

Who discovered Missouri's lead deposits in 1715? LaMotte Cadillac, who was looking for silver; ten years later Phillip Renault was mining it commercially.

Who made the first recorded overland trip across Missouri? Charles Claude de Tisne in 1719

What Frenchman, in 1720, founded the town of **Cape Girardeau**? Jean Girardot abandoned his post on the Illinois side of the river and set up a canoe landing at what formerly was called Cape Rock. The town was further established by Pierre Lorimier, who hated Americans and paid Indians in gold for their scalps.

Pierre Chouteau (MHS)

What Frenchman brought the **first slaves to Missouri**? Philippe Renault, who put them to work in lead mines in the Meramec valley – circa 1722; Renault was head of mining operations for Company of the Indies. The company was bankrupt by 1744.

Who built Fort Orleans near the mouth of the Grand River (Carroll County) in 1723? Etienne Bourgmond; it was the first European fort in Missouri. The town of **St. Genevieve** was founded by the French around 1733 and claims to be **Missouri's oldest town**

Where did the early French make salt in Missouri? Saline Creek.

What immigrant group was responsible for introducing this country to the drink known as the **mint julep**? It was first concocted by the French at Kaskaskia and St. Louis. It consists of bourbon and molasses, garnished with a green mint leaf.

What were the principal crops of early French settlers at St. Louis? Tobacco, rye, buckwheat, flax, cotton, barley and beans

What were the favorite pastimes of the early French? Drinking, dancing, card playing, horse racing and billiards; most Americans thought the French to be lazy and more interested in these pastimes than hard work.

What kind of presents did Pierre Laclede give to the various Indian tribes engaged in the fur trade at St. Louis? Blankets, knives, awls, liquor, uniform jackets, guns, cloth and medals

Why did the early Spanish explorers give up on Missouri? They found no gold/silver

When did the French establish St. Louis? 1764, by Pierre Laclede, **Madam Chouteau** and their fourteen year old son, Auguste Chouteau, whom Laclede had adopted. They first obtained a land grant from King Louis XV of France. In the early years it was called "Laclede's Village."

What was the long lot system used by the French? Instead of square farming lots, the French ones were long and narrow, giving more farmers access to the river.

What did the French use for land measurement instead of acres? Arpents

What was the most profitable "crop" for the French at St. Louis? The fur trade

What method of river transportation was used by the early Indians? Hollowed out logs known as pirogues

What is odd about the date St. Louis was founded? France had just lost the French and Indian war and ceded the territory to her ally, Spain. News traveled at a snail's pace in those days.

When did the first Spanish official arrive in St. Louis? 1767, although lieutenant governor Don Pedro Piernas did not arrive until 1770. St. Louis was the capital of what the Spanish called Upper Louisiana.

Who was Antoine Soulard? He was a naval officer who was the French king's surveyor for Upper Louisiana and a prominent St. Louis land owner. **Julia Soulard**, wife of Antoine Soulard, gave land to the city for use as a market. Soulard Market has existed since 1779.

The village of Carondelet was founded in 1770. St. Louisans often went there to gamble for it had a racetrack for horses.

Were there any battles at St. Louis during the American Revolution? Yes – at Cahokia and St. Louis in 1780. The British wanted control of the fur trade centered at St. Louis and they were upset that St. Louis was a supply base for George Rogers Clark. Sauk, Fox and Winnebago Indians crossed the river at present-day **Bremen Street** (McKinley Bridge) and came back with about 43 scalps. St. Louis population at this time was barely over 500.

Both France and Spain sided with the Americans in the war. A British force supplanted by 200 Sioux warriors came down from Wisconsin but were beaten back.

When George Rogers Clark made his expedition in 1779 to capture Vincennes, what help did he receive from Missourians? St. Louisans donated money to him for his cause when he was in **Cahokia**.

Auguste Chouteau (MHS)

What happened in the British and Indian attack on **St. Louis** in May of 1780, during the Revolutionary War? The residents were forewarned by scouts and, with help from **St. Genevieve**, were able to fend off the Indians. The invaders were beaten off and did not return. The Indians were also discouraged when they learned that George Rogers Clark had arrived unexpectedly in Cahokia. After the war, many French inhabitants moved from New Orleans to Missouri because they disliked the new American government and its inflated currency. The Spanish permitted slavery and gave each settler 160 acres of free land plus 42 acres more per child.

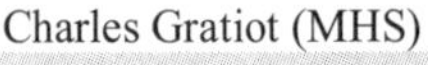

Charles Gratiot (MHS)

Why did many French in Cahokia and Kaskaskia move to St. Genevieve and St. Louis after the French and Indian War? They did not want to be ruled by Protestant England.

What three Missouri areas grew under Spanish rule? St. Charles, Cape Girardeau and New Madrid; there were five governing districts including the above plus St. Genevieve and St. Louis.

When Spanish officials actually arrived in St. Louis to take possession of Louisiana, what unprecedented action did they take? They granted 800 acres of free land to Americans who wanted to come there and settle, thinking this would discourage the British from coming down and invading from Canada. There was a fee of $40 for clerical and survey costs.

How did Julien Dubuque trick the Sac natives in 1788 into letting him mine lead? Back then, no whites were allowed in Indian Territory north of the Missouri River. He had a pow wow with them and said if they didn't give in to his demands **he would set the river on fire**. Two of his partners, unknown to the Indians, poured turpentine in a nearby creek and marked it with a floating piece of wood. When it came by he set the water on fire. The terrified Indians quickly made the concessions.

The early French gaily dancing (ISHL)

What legacy did Spain leave on Missouri during her ownership from 1770-1804? Very little – only about 20 Spanish families ever moved to St. Louis.

How did native slaves, owned by Missouri Indians, earn their freedom? By killing one of the enemy in battle

Who discovered Onondaga Cave in 1798? Daniel Boone

How did France get Missouri back in 1800? It was transferred from Spain when Napoleon signed the secret treaty of San Ildefonso.

What St. Louisan provided Lewis and Clark with wooden matches tipped with phosphorous 20 years before the friction match came into general use? Dr. Antoine Saugrain of St. Louis; he also made them thermometers by scraping the mercury off the back of a mirror and enclosing it in glass.

Who was Missouri's first postmaster? Rufus Easton was appointed by President Thomas Jefferson in 1804.

Who was Edward Hempstead? He was an American lawyer (1805) for numerous prominent French families in St. Louis. Hempstead Ave. in St. Louis is about three blocks long and in the 1950s it was a telephone exchange.

Who was Missouri's first territorial governor? James Wilkinson, 1805; he most likely plotted a treasonous scheme with Aaron Burr to separate the western part of America from the rest of the country. Meriwether Lewis became the new territorial governor in 1807.

In 1812, a small market opened along a St. Louis road the French called Rue de la Place (place of the market). The Americans changed it to Market Street making it the oldest street in the city with an American designation.

Who was the territorial governor of Missouri from 1813-1820? William Clark, younger brother of George Rogers Clark

How was Calloway County named? It was named for Captain James Calloway, a grandson of Daniel Boone who was killed in 1815 by Indians.

Where was Missouri's first bank located? St. Louis - 1816

What states sent the most immigrants to Missouri in its early pioneer years? North Carolina, Virginia, Tennessee and Kentucky

After Missouri statehood, what were its two largest immigrant groups? Germans and Irish

What was Jefferson's plan for Indians east of the Mississippi? He planned to send them to Missouri

What political purpose would the Indians in Missouri serve? They would be a buffer between the Spanish further west and the whites east of the Mississippi

Who was the Baron de Carondelet? He was a prominent Frenchman in St. Louis involved in the fur trade and land acquisition. He was a friend of August Chouteau. The Spanish later appointed him governor general of Louisiana

Territory and the town of **Carondelet** is named for him.

What founder of Texas once operated a lead mine near **Potosi**? Moses Austin, the father of Stephen Austin. Austin's shot tower was at **Herculaneum.**

What is the purpose of a shot tower? Molten globs of lead are dropped into water from the tower. When the lead hardens it forms a perfectly round pellet.

What pioneer metallic tableware was often made from Missouri lead and tin? Pewter in the form of dishes, bowls and goblets

What road did Austin contract to have built? A road about 8 ft. wide that went from **Potosi** to St. Louis. He stipulated that no tree stump should project more than eight inches high.

What caused Austin to plan to leave Missouri for Texas? He was ruined financially by the panic of 1819. He died in 1820, but son Stephen finished the Texas settlement project.

Who was Charles Gratiot? He was a Swiss immigrant who came to Cahokia and helped George Rogers Clark during the Revolution. He moved to St. Louis in 1781 and married Victoire Chouteau, becoming a prominent merchant. Gratiot Avenue is a couple of blocks north of Chouteau.

Who was the first settler in **St. Charles**? Louis Blanchette – 1780; the St. Charles Interstate 70 Bridge over the Missouri River is named for him.

L. Purchase flag raising ceremony at St. Louis

When Americans arrived in St. Louis after 1804, what notable changes took place? The French were a peaceable lot but the new arrivals from the East were adept at cursing, fighting, brawling, eye gouging and dueling. Before the Americans arrived there had been no murders in St. Louis for 40 years.

What was Missouri's first newspaper? The *Gazette*, printed in St. Louis in 1808

After the American Revolution was over in 1783, what was the strategy of the Spanish in St. Louis? To try and get settlers west of the Alleghenies to form a confederation with them instead of joining the Union

What road did the Spanish build from **New Madrid**, through **Ste. Genevieve** and on to St. Louis? The old Spanish Kings Highway

What action, by the Spanish in 1802, caused westerners to demand U.S. government action? Spanish officials ended the right of free deposit at New Orleans. This meant that American imports and exports could no longer be stored there. American commissioners went to France to buy only the port city of New Orleans and were astounded when Napoleon, strapped for cash, offered all of Louisiana.

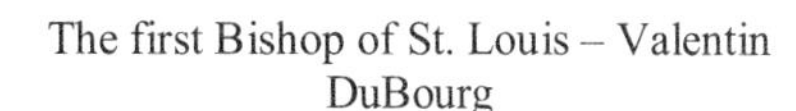

The first Bishop of St. Louis – Valentin DuBourg

Where was Missouri's head of government in 1805? The Territory of Louisiana, located at St. Louis, had a governor and three judges.

In 1806, **Zebulon Pike** led an expedition from Fort Belle Fountain to explore the source of the Arkansas River. During this trip the group discovered what came to be called Pike's Peak in Colorado. The year before, Pike tried (unsuccessfully) to find the source of the Mississippi.

Who was Jean Cabanne? He was a prominent French citizen of St. Louis who was elected to the Board of Trustees when St. Louis incorporated in 1809.

Who was Clement Penrose? He was elected to the Board of Trustees in 1811 and proposed all sorts of nuisance taxes on gambling, card playing, Sunday sales, billiards, acrobats and animal acts.

Why did Daniel Boone leave Kentucky and come to Missouri? He was disgusted because he had been swindled out of his property. Also, he had sons already living in Missouri.

In what Missouri town is the home of Nathan Boone, Daniel's son? The two story brick house is in **Defiance.**

How did Boone's sons make a living in Howard County? They processed salt from what came to be known as Boone's Lick. Boone's Lick Trail went from St. Charles to Old Granklin and the salt lick in Howard County.

What soon-to-be-famous child was brought by his family to Boone's Lick in 1811? Kit Carson

What other Missouri town has a stone house built by Nathan Boone? **La Charette**

Who organized the Missouri Fur Company in 1808? Manuel Lisa who married a woman from the Omaha tribe; he introduced the turnip, the bean and the potato to Indian tribes that previously knew nothing of these vegetables.

In the last battle of the War of 1812, Andrew Jackson inflicted defeat on the British at New Orleans. It was St. Louisan John Mullanphy's (Irish) cotton bales that Jackson used to shield his men from the fire of General Packenham's troops. The buckshot and bullets that Andrew Jackson used to win the Battle of New Orleans (1815) were made at **Herculaneum**

What St. Louisan killed his political rival in a duel on Bloody Island in 1817? Thomas Hart Benton shot Charles Lucas from a murderous distance of only 10 feet; the "affair of honor" made national news and cemented the view of St. Louis in the wild Kentuckyan image. Benton was the **greatest duelist that Missouri ever had**. He fought several duels on Bloody Island and killed two men there.

What was the first steamboat to pass the mouth of the Ohio River and reach St. Louis? ***Zebulon Pike*** – 1817; The Indians called it the "Thunder Canoe" Early St. Louis settlers Hempstead and Gratiot also died in the year1817.

What feat of discovery was accomplished by Missourian "Broken Hand" Smith? He discovered the famed elusive "south pass" through the Rockies for pioneers.

What was the population of St. Louis in 1818? About 2,500; Chicago at the time was a mere trading post.

Who was Peter Lindell? An important grocer retailer in early St. Louis

Why did many well-to-do immigrants skip through southern Illinois and settle in Missouri instead? They owned slaves and slavery was forbidden in Illinois by the Northwest Ordinance of 1787.

What was the only serious Indian problem encountered by Missourians? The Sac and Fox made trouble for northeast settlers during the War of 1812.

What British outpost was captured by 200 St. Louisans, led by William Clark, in 1813? Prairie du Chien in Wisconsin

When did the War of 1812 end officially for Missourians? A peace treaty was signed in St. Louis in 1816.

How was Boone's Lick country defended against the Indians during the War of 1812? Seven forts were built in the area.

Who negotiated a treaty with the Indians in 1816? At Portage des Sioux, near St. Charles, Ninian Edwards of Illinois, William Clark, and Auguste Chouteau

Illinois was admitted to the Union in 1818 as the 21st state, even though Missouri's population at the time was larger. In fact, census takers in Illinois were bribed to pad their figures, making Illinois the smallest state (population wise) to enter the Union after the original thirteen. Because of Missouri's large geographic size and mineral wealth, northerners feared the admission of Missouri as a slave state. Missouri is larger than any state east of the Mississippi River. Missouri statehood was rejected again in 1819 and Alabama was admitted instead.

What famed "King of the Keelboats" claimed to be half horse and half alligator? The outrageous **Mike Fink**

What was the significance of the **Edwardsville**, Illinois, Treaty of 1819? Thousands of Indians in Indiana and Illinois agreed to a treaty that required them to move to Missouri and take up residence there. Missourians eventually sent them packing to Indian Territory in Oklahoma.

What currency was used in St. Louis at this time? The barter system was giving way to Spanish silver coins that were scored with 8 "bits," and paper currency issued by banks in Ohio, Kentucky and Pennsylvania. John Mason Peck labeled this rag currency "shinplasters."

When was the Bank of Missouri chartered? 1817; it was insolvent by 1821

In 1819, the *Western Engineer* went up the Missouri River as far as the mouth of the Platte River. Running along the keel and extending from the **front of the boat was the image of a huge black serpent** with its mouth painted red and its tongue the color of red-hot coals. The steam exhausted from the mouth of the serpent. The Indians looked with wonder at the strange boat for in it they saw in it the Great Spirit.

What explains this lack of Indian trouble for most Missourians? For unknown reasons, Native Americans never settled in Missouri in large numbers.

Mike Fink (University of Nebraska Press)

How many Native-Americans were living in Missouri at the time of statehood in 1821? About 6,000

What were Missouri's dominant tribes? Sac, Fox, Shawnee, Kansas, Sioux, Iowa and Delaware, although the Missouri and Osage were dominant

What kind of shelter was used by the Osage? Traditional wigwams with long poles covered with grass mats

When did the Osage Indians surrender their last Missouri land holdings? 1825 - Treaty of Fort Osage near **Independence**; they left the state and went west to Kansas

In 1832, St. Louis University received a charter from the Missouri legislature, making it the oldest university west of the Mississippi.

What was the last Indian war in which Missourians participated? The 1837 Seminole War in Florida; President Martin van Buren asked Thomas Hart Benton if he thought Missourians would travel that far to help their country. "Missourians will go wherever their services are needed," Benton replied. Missouri sent a regiment that helped subdue the natives in the swamp lands.

What person was largely responsible for the peaceful relations between the Indians and the early white settlers? William Clark who treated them fairly and kept his word; when he signed treaties with the natives he always managed to find land further west that was acceptable.

What happened to the explorer by the name of Du Tisne? While exploring Missouri he was captured by Indians. He guessed by their pointing and conversation that they were going to scalp him. He was bald but wore a wig. Thinking quickly, he took his knife and pretended to cut away his hair, throwing it on the ground. The **natives were impressed that a man could scalp himself so they let him go**.

What happened to the tribe known as the Missouri Indians? They were defeated and scattered by the Sac and Fox tribes in 1789.

Where did the Missouri tribe of natives live? According to a French explorer in 1687, around the juncture of the Missouri and Mississippi rivers

When was the town of **LaGrange** (French for barn) established? In 1795, making it the oldest Missouri town north of St. Louis

Why were the Shawnee and Delaware brought into the St. Genevieve area by the Spanish government around 1798? To act as a buffer against the warlike tribes in the West

What area, thought to be ideal as a reservation land by the federal government, was set aside for the Indians in the 1830 Treaty of Prairie du Chein. The rich bottom land of the Missouri, Platte and Nodaway rivers in the northwest. The Indians were pushed out of the state further west.

When greedy whites demanded this fertile area, what happened to the Indians? The treaty was abrogated and the northern boundary of the state was pushed west to the Missouri River.

How did **chamber pots** save one family during this period of Indian attacks? At the village of Cote Sans Dessein, the savages tried to storm the blockhouse that was being defended by only 3 men and 2 women. After hours of attack and siege the natives grew frustrated and launched fire arrows. But the women were able to put the fire out with a small amount of water they had inside. When another arrow was launched they thought they were doomed until someone remembered a pitcher of milk. When yet another arrow came flying in, the occupants were seized with despair. There was nothing left. Then one of the women went into a bedroom and came out with her eyes lit. She held high a chamber pot that contained liquid more valuable than gold. At last, the Indians finding their efforts stymied at every turn, stomped away in disgust.

What problem arose when Missouri sought admission to the Union in 1819? Missouri was a slave state and this was now becoming a sectional issue.

What was the Talmadge Amendment? It was a measure in the U.S. House of Representatives that would have prohibited the introduction of more slaves into Missouri and gradual emancipation for those already there. It was voted down in the Senate. This event is important since it was the opening round in a series of events that would lead to the Civil War. It was the first time since the adoption of the Constitution that the issue of slavery was debated nationally.

Kit Carson (Library of Congress)

What was Jefferson's quote about the issue? The bitter debate that now arose over the issue of slavery was like "a firebell in the night."

What compromise was suggested by Senator Thomas of Illinois and pushed through Congress by Henry Clay and Senator Jesse Thomas of Illinois? That the line between slave states and free states west of the Mississippi be the southern boundary of Missouri – 36 degrees and 30 minutes. Much of Missouri's first constitution drew heavily on the constitution of Illinois. According to the Missouri Compromise, Maine was admitted to the Union as a free state and Missouri joined as a slave state. Missouri was admitted in 1821, the same year Mexico received its independence from Spain.

According to **Scott K. Williams**, St. Ferdinand's (in Old **Florissant, Number 1 Rue St. Francois**), completed in 1820, is the oldest Catholic Church building between the Mississippi and the Rocky Mountains.

How did Missouri come to be known as the number one mule raising state? It happened as a result of trade on the Santa Fe Trail in the 1820s where Missouri traders took cotton hose, eyeglasses, cutlery, handkerchiefs and woolen goods and brought back mules and other items.

Current Missouri Capitol under construction

Who were Missouri's first two U.S. Senators after it achieved statehood in 1821? Thomas Hart "Old Bullion" Benton and David Barton

How is it that Thomas Hart Benton once nearly killed Andrew Jackson in a fight circa 1815? Jackson acted as a second for a man who fought a duel with Benton's brother Jesse. When Thomas Benton heard about the incident, he became angry and said if he met Jackson on the street he'd horse whip him. Jackson and a friend went to Benton's home and attacked the two brothers. Jackson was severely wounded in the melee.

How did Thomas Hart Benton become a U.S. Senator in 1821? David Barton was the first one chosen by the legislature, but there was a bitter contest to decide who would be the second senator. Barton wanted Benton as his colleague but was one vote short of confirmation. After much arm twisting and political dealing, the Benton forces had enough votes for confirmation. Just as the vote was being taken a key voter fell ill. Desperate, Benton's men had four Negroes carry Daniel Ralls on his sickbed to the House chamber where he cast the deciding vote.

What was "squatter sovereignty" championed by Benton? Many pioneer farmers did not have enough money to buy land when they first started. They settled (squatted) on public land, built a cabin and a barn and worked the land before it was surveyed and offered for sale at public auction. When the land was sold, they were thrown off their property. Benton secured the right for them to buy the land before it went up for sale. The passage of the **Homestead Act in 1862**, after his death, was a vindication of his policies.

In 1820, the Irish held their first St. Patrick's Day parade in St. Louis

MISSOURI HISTORY 1821-1850

Who was the first Mayor of St. Louis – 1823? Pennsylvanian William Carr Lane, a physician

Why are so many St. Louis streets named for trees like poplar and elm and olive? Mayor Lane persuaded the Board to discard the 62 year-old system of French names and adopt this practice which he was familiar with in Philadelphia; curiously, there were no olive trees in St. Louis.

What famous men went on a fur expedition from St. Louis in 1823? **Jim Bridger**, **Jedediah Smith** and **Mike Fink**; the purpose was to build forts out West and rely more on white trappers rather than Indians. Mike Fink murdered a man and was killed by another man on this expedition. During Smith's travels he discovered two new overland routes to California. In the next fifteen years 148 "mountain men" were killed by Indians, grizzlies, drowning and other hazards. Smith was killed by Comanches. Men like Bridger, Smith and **Kit Carson** probably did more to open up the trans-Mississippi than any other persons or groups.

When was Jefferson Barracks established south of St. Louis? 1826 with 500 troops being stationed there by 1829

When was the first veto of a bill by a Missouri governor? It happened in 1824 when Governor Bates vetoed a bill that **outlawed dueling and made violations punishable by public whipping**.

When was the first state capitol building constructed? 1826 – It burned in 1837 and a new structure was completed by 1840.

When did voters approve construction of the current state Capitol? 1911, with a final cost of $4,215,000, styled in Roman Renaissance with the exterior done in Carthage limestone.

How many columns are in the capitol building? 134

How wide is the grand stairway at the capitol? 65 ft.

What is unusual about the site where the capitol building is located? It sits atop an old Indian burial mound.

What **Creve Coeur** man built the first wagon to traverse the Continental Divide and take settlers into Oregon? Irishman Joseph Murphy; when the Mexican War broke out he won a government contract to supply the army with wagons. The Murphy wagon, as it came to be known, was one of the most durable in the country. Most of the wagons that traveled on the Oregon Trail were Murphy wagons. His company built 200,000 wagons before it went out of business in 1894.

When were the city limits of St. Louis extended to 18th Street? 1831

Current Missouri Capitol Building

When did the first cholera epidemic hit St. Louis? 1832

Who or what did the locals blame for the epidemic? Not understanding the nature of germs and disease, they blamed it on cabbage and sauerkraut eaten by German immigrants.

Where were victims of the disease quarantined? On Arsenal (Quarantine) Island at south St. Louis

What famous Missourian died as a result of the disease? U.S. Senator Alexander Buckner

Who was the most famous doctor in Missouri at this time? Lewis Lynn of **St. Genevieve**

What caused him to become endeared to so many people in the state? His self-sacrificing work during the cholera epidemic

Why is Dr. Lynn called "**The Father of Oregon**? As a U.S. Senator he sponsored the bill that organized Oregon as a territory and encouraged settlers to go there.

The first daily newspaper in the country was the St. Louis *Herald*, begun in 1834.

What statue is on top of the Capitol in Jeff City? Ceres, the Roman goddess of grain

What nickname did the city of St. Louis have at this time? The "Memphis of the American Nile" (Memphis, Egypt)

Bloody Island at St. Louis where Benton fought his duels

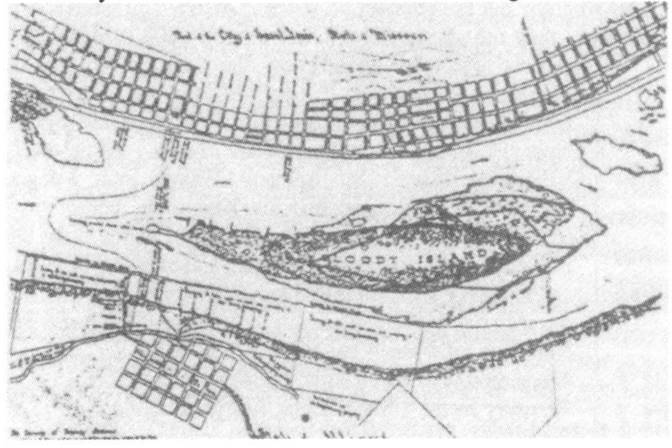

What Missourian of this era is considered **America's First Geographer** Jedediah Morse

What Missourian is the **Father of the Santa Fe Trail**? William Becknell, who led a wagon train along the trail in 1822. It was on the Santa Fe Trail that pioneers learned the techniques of traveling long distances, later used on the Oregon Trail. The Santa Fe Trail's jumping off point was Independence, on the Missouri River. Independence was also the rendezvous point for settlers traveling the Oregon Trail. **The Mexican burro, by way of the Santa Fe Trail, entered Missouri and mated with Belgian draft horses in German settlements, producing the famous Missouri mule**. Oregon Fever hit the country in the 1840s, promoted by Senator Lewis Linn of Missouri. It was said that "out in Oregon the pigs are running about under the great acorn trees, round and fat, and already cooked, with knives and forks sticking out of them so that you can cut off a slice whenever you get hungry."

What famed mountain man joined William Ashely's American Fur Trade Company in 1822 at St. Louis? Famed mountain man Jedediah Smith who saw more of the American west than any white man up to that point of time

A shave and a haircut back then cost two bits in Missouri. Where did that expression originate? Spanish and Mexican milled silver dollars were scored and could be broken into halves or quarters and half quarters. A half quarter was called a "bit" and it was worth 12 and ½ cents.

Is this the reason the New York Stock Exchange gave quotes figured in fractions of 1/8 of a dollar for over 200 years? Yes, although the market dates to 1790, and back then it was the Spanish "pieces of eight" that was a dominant coin

What did Smith accom-plish in 1827? He was the first white man to cross the Sierra Nevada Mts. Men like Bridger, Smith and Carson were significant forces for opening up the West.

What Missourian is thought to be the first white to see the Great Salt Lake and was one of the first to see Yellowstone? Jim Bridger, but he thought the Salt Lake was an arm of the Pacific.

What did Bridger discover in 1850? The South Pass through the Rockies which shortened the Oregon Trail by 61 miles; Bridger died at **Washington**, Missouri, in 1881.

What was Bridger's favorite story? He told a yarn about the time he was chased by 100 murderous Cheyenne warriors for several miles until they finally cornered him in a box canyon. At this point Bridger would go silent, prompting eager listeners to ask, "What happened next, Mr. Bridger?" His eyes twinkled as they darted around as he replied, **"Why . . they kilt me!"**

What did Daniel Webster call Missouri in 1837? An infant Hercules

What were Missouri's major products at this time? Hemp, tobacco, cereals, poultry, min-ing, dairy products and beef

How did the Missouri Com-promise, as it came to be called, appeal to both the North and South? Missouri came into the Union in 1821 as a slave state and Maine came in as a free state, maintaining the sectional balance in the U.S. Senate. The North and South each had twelve states.

Was the "bootheel" area in southeast Missouri part of the original state? Yes – the people living in that region lobbied to be included since Arkansas had only recently been made a territory in 1819

Where was the state's early capital, intended to be temporary? San Carlos/**St. Charles**

Why was **Jefferson City** chosen as the new site for a capital? Its central location in the state was on the Missouri River. The choice was unpopular since no settlement existed there at the time.

Who was John Rice Jones? Oxford-educated **John Rice Jones** migrated to America and began practicing law in Philadelphia. He heard about the western frontier and decided to explore the excitement. In 1786, he reached the falls of the Ohio River at Louisville where he joined **George Rogers Clark** and his army of 1,000 to suppress the hostile Wabash Indians. For his service, he received a grant of 100 acres near Vincennes. He located at **Kaskaskia** in 1790 and became the first man to practice law in Illinois. He acquired more land and became an extensive owner of property in Indiana and Illinois. His law practice prospered and, in 1808, he paid taxes on 16,400 acres in Monroe County alone. In 1801, General Harrison commissioned him as Attorney General for the Indiana Territory. His son, Rice Jones, began practicing law in Kaskaskia in 1806. John Rice Jones later made his home in Kaskaskia, the capital of Illinois Territory. Jones supported the move to set aside for 10 years the 6th article of the Northwest Ordinance of 1787 forbidding slavery in the Northwest Territory. Although not a slave owner himself, many prominent leaders in Illinois at the time were slaveholders.

Jones later became involved in Missouri politics and helped draft that state's first constitution at St. Louis in 1820. His son, Rice Jones, once met to fight a duel with Shadrach Bond, who went on to become the first Governor of Illinois. The site of the duel was an island in the Mississippi not far from **St. Genevieve**. Bond remembered that the quarrel was political and not personal and called the affair off at the last second. The elder John Rice Jones was murdered on the streets of **Kaskaskia** by a man named James Dunlap in 1808.

What companies had the dominant beaver fur trade business in the 1820's? St Louisan William Ashley competed with John Jacob Astor with his Rocky Mountain Fur Company.

What two ethnic groups dominated St. Louis by 1850? 43 percent were either German or Irish

In 1827, Congress authorized the building of an arsenal in St. Louis. Construction began on what is now 2nd and Arsenal streets. The site was considered remote since it was about a mile south of the city limits.

What was tragic about the duel between Spencer Pettis and Joshua Biddle that took place on Bloody Island near St. Louis in 1831? Biddle's eyesight was defective so the men walked off a mere five paces before they turned and fired. **Both men were killed**.

What was the subject of the quarrel? Pettis had been assaulted by Biddle for criticizing the Bank of the United States. Biddle's brother (Nicholas) was president of the bank.

Most assumed that Thomas Hart Benton of Missouri would be the next Democratic nominee after Martin Van Buren. What happened to his presidential aspirations? Benton, a political maverick, allied himself with the northern faction of the Democratic Party and control passed to the southern wing, led by John Calhoun. Benton also opposed the annexation of Texas, believing it would cause a war with Mexico. Southern Democrats supported the annexation of Texas. Benton was one of the moving forces behind what would come to be known as The Jacksonian Democracy Movement, championing the cause of the common man.

When did the Methodists organize state-wide groups in Missouri? 1816; the first permanent Methodist church in Catholic dominated St. Louis was established in 1821 by Jesse Walker.

When did the Masons organize at St. Louis? 1821

What Missouri preacher, turned mountain man, helped open up the Santa Fe Trail and worked as a guide with Kit Carson? Bill Williams, whose brother John had a daughter who is thought to be the **first American white child born in St. Louis**.

When was the Catholic Diocese of St. Louis organized? 1826; the Presbyterian Synod organized in 1832

When did Missouri get a branch Bank of the U.S? 1829 at St. Louis with John O'Fallon, William Clark and Pierre Chouteau among its directors; Andrew Jackson vetoed its rechartering and the bank closed in 1835.

Leonids meteor shower

St. Louis grew so rapidly after 1835 that it acquired a new nickname. What was it? Lion of the Valley

The paving of the riverfront wharf area with cobblestones began in 1835.

What newspaper went out of business in 1832? Missouri's second newspaper, the *Western Journal*, (now called the *Beacon*) dating back to 1815

In 1831, Major Nathan Heald and his wife, who were living in a cabin in **St. Charles** County, were surprised by a guest – an Indian. Back in the War of 1812 Major Heald was in charge of the garrison at Fort Dearborn (Chicago). The fort was attacked by Indians allied with the British. Heald and his wife were captured by different tribes. This event is known as the **Fort Dearborn massacre**. About 26 people, including soldiers, women and children were killed. Heald managed to escape and immediately began looking for his wife. He paid a friendly Indian a mule and a jug of whisky to find his wife and bring her back, which he did. Their surprise visitor was the Indian who had rescued Mrs. Heald.

Who established the first Catholic parish in Kansas City, 1833? Father Benedict Roux

Startled Missourians witnessed a Leonids meteor shower on November 12, 1833, and refer to it as the "night the stars fell." A firestorm of shooting stars, silent but spectacular, filled the night sky. One eyewitness account said, "The sky was scored in every direction with shining streaks illuminated with fireballs." Their numbers, during the nine hours that they fell . . . were estimated to be 240,000.

What penal bill was passed by the legislature in 1833? The new law established funding for Missouri's first state prison. For decades the stone prison was called one of the worst in the nation until reforms were made in the 1870s.

When did Missouri get its first "beer cave?" 1835 – Ezra English owned the St. Louis Brewery at Benton Park

When was the Baptist Conference organized in St. Louis? 1836

What German immigrant set up **Missouri's first weather station at St. Louis** in 1836? Dr. George Englemann had a thermometer, a barometer (pressure) and hydrometer (humidity). He also started the state's first German newspaper, the *Anzeiger*

What was a shinplaster? It was an oversized paper currency issued by state banks that printed money in the 1830s without the proper backing by silver and gold. If these banks failed, and many of them did, the money was worthless.

Chouteau's Pond at St. Louis (MHS)

Who were the "hards" and the "softs?" Missouri split into two factions at this time. The "hards" favored gold and silver only for currency while the "softs" favored paper money to supplement gold and silver, which were in short supply. Thomas Hart Benton was a noted hard.

When was the Platt Purchase added to Missouri's boundaries? 1837; it includes Atchison, Nodaway, Holt, Andrew, Buchanan and Platte counties.

Where was this "add-on" territory located? Along the Missouri River in the northwest corner of the state

How was this land obtained for Missouri, since it had been given to the Indians a few years earlier by treaty? Captain William Clark purchased the land from the natives.

When was the Bank of Missouri created? 1837 - it was given a 20 year charter by the legislature.

What was lost when the state capitol burned in 1837? The original 1820 state seal; a new one was designed with the two bears facing each other instead of looking at the viewer.

How much did a dinner at a typical roadside tavern cost in 1837? A meal with cornbread and chicken fixings cost 37½ cents or three bits.

How much was lodging with two people in a bed at this time? 12 ½ cents. Lodging in a separate bed was 25 cents.

Alexander Von Humboldt predicted that St. Louis would become the Memphis of the American Nile (Mississippi).

Who opened the first stage line from St. Louis to **Jefferson City** in 1838? Thomas L. Price

Who found the first bones of a Missouri mastodon (glacial age Pleistocene animal) in 1838? Albert Koch - on the Bourbeuse and Pomme de Terre rivers; In 1839, Dr. Albert Koch, working near **Kimmswick**, uncovered the bones of what he called the Missouri Leviathian. It was later reclassified as a mastodon. Mastodon State Park is currently near Kimmswick.

Missouri and Iowa fought over bee trees in the **Honey War of 1839**. Honey was an important source of natural sugar to early settlers. Bees, first imported to America in 1638, created hives in tree hollows. When the pioneers found these trees, they cut them down and stole the honey. Beeswax was also used in the making of candles.

The ill-defined border between the two states became a source of conflict. Surveyors, over the years, had laid out four different boundary lines, leaving some 2,600 square miles in dispute.

The budding controversy became known as the Honey War when an Iowa sheriff tried to arrest a Missouri man after he cut down several bee trees in the disputed no-man's land. "**Death to the Pukes**" became the rallying cry of irate Iowans. Each governor mobilized the State Militia, but in the end the dispute was settled peacefully by the U.S. Supreme Court in 1849. Missouri, which currently produces 4 percent of the nation's honey, eventually declared the honey bee to be the State Insect.

What are the roots of the St. Louis *Globe-Democrat*? It started out as the *Workingman's Advocate* in 1831 and became a Republican newspaper sometime between 1856 and 1860.

How many newspapers were operating in Missouri by 1839? 25 - by 1860 there were 162

What were typical Missourians like in 1840? Frontier life in Missouri attracted criminals and adventurers as well as decent citizens. Liquor was sold without restriction, while gambling at cards and horses were popular amusements. Shooting matches, wrestling and bare-knuckle fighting were popular pastimes. Though many were illiterate and rough in manner, they were hospitable and upright. Chewing tobacco was common. The country people enjoyed house raisings, quiltings, square-dances, corn-husking, camp meetings, militia-mustering days and political stump speeches. Townsmen gathered in taverns for drinking and sociability. The women were kept busy butchering hogs, working at the spinning wheel, making candles and soap, cleaning house, making clothes, cooking, washing, raising the kids and trying to keep their husbands civil.

When did the German William Lemp begin his brewery business on 2nd Street in St. Louis? 1842 - He introduced St. Louis to bottom-brewed, light, clear lager beer.

What German enclave on North Broadway incorporated in 1844? Bremen, located at Broadway and Bremen Avenue near the future McKinley Bridge

Where is the oldest continually operated Missouri ferry on

the Mississippi River? The Canton Ferry that connects with Meyer, Illinois, dating back to 1844

Where were the two main sources of iron ore for St. Louis at this time? Iron Mountain and Pilot Knob; the ore had to be hauled in wagons. Iron Mountain, with 200 million tons of ore, was the **largest known deposit of ore in the world**.

How did Page Avenue in St. Louis receive its name? It's named for Daniel Page, a prominent owner of Star Flour Mill, banker and mayor in the 1840-1850s time period. Lindell Blvd. is named for Peter Lindell, a prominent banker citizen of St. Louis in the 1840s era.

What new frame of government did Missourians adopt in 1845? Another constitution

St. Louis grew so fast that by 1845 it overtook what eastern city in population (35,390)? Pittsburgh

The Economic Rivalry Between St. Louis and Chicago was written in 1847 and what conclusions did the author draw? Chicago was overtaking St. Louis as an economic giant because of its progressive wide-awake leadership. James Primm, in *Lion of the Valley,* asserts that it was much more due to Chicago's superior geographic position and closer ties with New York and Boston.

What group founded one of the first co-educational colleges in Missouri? German Lutherans established Concordia Seminary in St. Louis in 1849.

What disease hit St. Louis in 1849? A dreaded cholera

Albert Koch and his Missouri Leviathan near **Imperial**

epidemic caused city fathers to drain and eliminate Chouteau Pond.

What caused the Nativist riot of 1849 in St. Louis? Nativists, also called Know-Nothings, were against foreign immigrants and Catholics. The riot happened when poll watchers began to carefully scrutinize Irish naturalization papers at the polls on election day. Angry Irish voters committed some stabbings and an angry mob soon formed. Irish homes and businesses were attacked. A mere 63 policeman were insufficient to contain a city that had grown to 95,000.

There was a similar election riot in August of 1854 that resulted in 10 deaths, 33 wounded, and over 90 buildings damaged. It took 700 armed citizens to bring order to the city.

THE MORMON WAR IN MISSOURI

In the early 1820s, a devout man named **Joseph Smith** prayed to God and asked him what church he should attend. Smith claims he was visited by an angel named Moroni who led him to a cave near the family farm at Palmyra, New York. Smith was given a record of God's dealing with former inhabitants of the North American continent. He put on a pair of "magical" spectacles that enabled him to translate the strange writings on golden plates into English. This became the basis for the *Book of Mormon* and the beginning of a new Christian religion. The Mormons believed that Native Americans were one of the lost tribes of Israel. They also believed that Jesus Christ had come to America after his crucifixion and Resurrection, and ministered to the natives.

Smith founded the Mormon Church in 1830 at Fayette, New York. Believers were urged to avoid the use of tobacco, alcohol and coffee. Their most controversial belief, adopted later, was the practice of polygamy – having more than one wife. The movement spread westward, first to Kirtland, Ohio, and then to **Independence**, Missouri (Jackson County). In each instance they were met with pressure and opposition from their neighbors, causing them to move on. They were strong in Jackson County, numbering a third of the total population. In July of 1833, a mob broke into a Mormon printing office, destroyed it, and threw the press into the Missouri River. The Mormons moved across the river to an unsettled area in Clay County, which they reorganized into Mormon County. For political, economic and religious reasons, they once again came into conflict with their "Gentile" neighbors. The Mormons were also against slavery.

In 1838, the Missouri governor signed an "**Extermination Order**," saying that the hated Mormons needed to be driven from the state. The heavily armed Mormons were prepared to fight it out, but threw down their arms when surrounded by militia units under General Samuel Lucas. About 10,000 Mormons (led by Brigham Young) fled the settlement in 1839 and left for **Quincy**, Illinois, where they found sympathy from local citizens in a free state.

Joseph Smith (The Prophet), who had been imprisoned in **Liberty**, Missouri, escaped and joined his flock at Quincy. The Mormon leaders then purchased land in nearby Commerce and renamed it **Nauvoo** – Hebrew for "beautiful place of rest." Previously the land was occupied by Fox and Sac Indians.

It is thought that the practice of polygamy did not begin until around 1841. Non-Mormons were referred to as gentiles. The Mormons were adept at missionary work, and converts migrated to the new city from Canada and Europe. By 1846, Nauvoo, with about 15,000 people, was the **largest city in the state of Illinois**.

The Mormons established a militia and its "legion" was the largest military force in the state and **second in size only to the U.S. Army**. Mormons were also feared for their political activism. They voted as a large bloc and had significant influence in the state legislature. This gave them control over the balance of power between Whigs and Democrats.

One prominent writer accused the Mormons of plotting to take over about five Midwestern states, including Missouri, so they could establish a religious oligarchy. This was seen by opponents as a threat to democracy. Other rumors spread like wildfire. One said that women from local communities were being kidnapped, and forced to live and serve in

polygamous Mormon harems. Nearby local communities feared Mormon manifest destiny and took to mob violence and lynchings against the "saints."

Smith was seen as a fugitive from justice back in Missouri. Perhaps the straw that broke the camel's back was when Smith and his army destroyed an opposition printing press, *The Expositor*, which opposed polygamy. Joseph Smith and his brother Hyrum were arrested for treason and taken to the jail in **Carthage**, Illinois.

In 1844, an angry Illinois mob, led by members of a disbanded militia, stormed the Carthage jail and **both men were killed**.

Persecution and mob violence by "gentiles" dropped off after the murders but soon became resurgent. A two-year period of violence following the murders is referred to as the **Mormon War**. Governor Thomas Ford finally sent a commission, headed by Stephen Douglas, to persuade the Mormons to leave Illinois. In 1846, **Brigham Young**, the new leader, led 5,000 of the Mormons from Nauvoo in a westward trek that would end with the establishment of Salt Lake City, Utah. Joseph Smith's first wife (Emma Hale Smith) stayed behind because she did not care for polygamy. She later married a non-Mormon.

Brigham Young

When Brigham Young died, one enterprising political cartoonist drew a picture of "Bigamy" Young's wives in mourning. Six of them were depicted crowded together in a large bed, wiping their tears with handkerchiefs.

Nauvoo had been unique. It was a carefully planned city, with farms located on the perimeter. Many of the houses were constructed of brick. Their Nauvoo House was the largest hotel in the entire area. The Temple, built of bluff limestone, was situated on the highest point in the city. A huge restoration effort was started in 1962, led by James Kimball, resulting in the town becoming a huge tourist attraction.

What mistakes, made by several other states, including Illinois, did Missourians avoid in the 1830's and 1840's? The state did not waste money on too many hugely expensive plank road and canal projects.

What does historian Stanley Vestal believe was the real cause of the white man's triumph over the Red Man in Missouri? The buffalo hunters exterminated their main source of food and, having nothing to eat, the natives were willing to submit.

How did the state university at Columbia come to be built in 1841? At the time of statehood, the U.S. government donated two townships, with the money from land sales there going to support the school. It was determined that whatever centrally located area raised the most money by subscription would win the site. Boone County won with nearly $118,000 and the school was built at **Columbia**.

What **7th governor of Missouri committed suicide** in 1844? Thomas Reynolds, the man who in 1842 proclaimed the **state's first official observance of Thanksgiving**. That same year he signed a state law doing away with imprisonment for debt. Thomas was depressed because he was hounded by political enemies. Reynolds County would be named for him.

How was the Missouri Compromise of 1820 part of the Compromise of 1850? By its terms, California was admitted as a free state and the Missouri Compromise line of 1820 was extended to California.

How did Missouri manage to escape the worst of the 1837 national depression? Missouri, led by reverence for Jeffersonian values and the wisdom of Benton's conservatism, did not teeter on the verge of bankruptcy with grand schemes to build plank roads, canals and railroads. As banks of other states were failing, the Bank of Missouri thrived.

When did public education in Missouri begin? 1838 when two elementary schools opened supported by income from the old French commons area in St. Louis

What were two popular Thomas Hart Benton nicknames of the era? "Old Bullion" (hard currency) and the "Gibraltar of the West"

Who were the Millerites? William Miller of New York predicted that the world was going to end in 1843. He had a large following in **Hannibal.**

What plans for a Missouri town were destroyed by the great Mississippi and Missouri rivers flood of 1844? Julius Malinckrodt laid out and sold plots for a St. Charles County town called Dortmund, the place of his birth in Germany. Many of the lots overlooked the river. The flood changed the river's course, moving the river away from the town, and Mallinckrodt had to refund the money.

What was Missouri's famous **"monster hunt" of 1844**? The steamboat *Flora Jones* was the first boat to ascend the Osage River at **Harmony Mission** in Bates County. The captain gave a blast on its shrill whistle and the locals thought it was the cry of some horrible monster. The neighbors were aroused and a posse was formed to hunt down and kill the monster. As the group neared the river they could actually hear the monster huffing and puffing and blowing smoke. The men hid behind trees and took cover behind rock as the sea monster came down the river. Just as they were preparing to shoot they saw passengers on the deck and realized it was some kind of newfangled boat.

Where was Berry Meachum's school for "coloreds" located in St. Louis during the 1840s and 50s? On a steamboat in the Mississippi; children rafted their way to learn the three Rs

What law did Missouri pass against coloreds in 1847? It became illegal to teach Negroes or mulattoes to read or write.

Boatman's Bank of St. Louis, the oldest such institution west of the Mississippi, was established in 1847.

What three trails west started from Independence, Missouri? The Oregon Trail, the Santa Fe Trail, the California Trail

In what year was the California Trail established? 1849 – Winding its way to the gold fields of California

What town in New Mexico was subdued by **Alexander Doniphan** and 500 mounted Missourians in the Mexican War? Santa Fe

Doniphan and his men were under the command of what other notable Missourian? **Stephen Kearny** – the expedition began at Fort Leavenworth, Kansas, and followed the Santa Fe Trail.

At what Texas border town did Doniphan's men defeat a larger Mexican force? El Paso

When Doniphan and his men won the Battle of El Brazito, how many of his men were killed? None

What Mexican town did Doniphan and his men capture? Chihuahua

When Doniphan and his men returned to Missouri, what was their notable achievement? They made what is considered the **longest military march in history – 1846-47 (about 3,000 miles)**

What leader of a Missouri regiment in the Mexican War went on to become governor of the state? Sterling Price – 1853-1857

What other Missourian participated in the conquest of California and the defeat of Mexico? Kit Carson; during the Civil War, as Indian Agent he was responsible for holding the southwest natives loyal to the Union cause.

Why is Missouri called the "**Mother of the West**?" After the Mexican War many of its noble sons and daughters settled in Texas, Oklahoma, Kansas, Nebraska, Oregon and California

How did Missouri Senator **David Atchison claim to be President *de jure* of the USA for one day**? On Sunday, March 4, 1849, President Polk and his Vice-president left office. The new President, Zachary Taylor, refused to be sworn in on a Sunday. Atchison was sworn in as President *Pro Tem* of the Senate (next in line for the presidency) before Taylor, and this is the basis for his claim.

Where is David R. Atchison buried? At his home in **Plattsburg**, Missouri

What two things are named for him? Atchison, Kansas and Atchison County, Missouri

As a proslavery Democrat, what famous law did he play a large part in getting passed in 1854? The Kansas-Nebraska Act, which nullified the Missouri Compromise line of 1820 and allowed the people in these two territories to vote slavery up or down.

In the 1855 elections in Kansas, what made it obvious that both sides were stuffing the ballot boxes? There were 3,000 residents but 6,000 ballots were cast.

After he refused to stand for re-election in 1856, what illegal action did David Atchison take? He became involved in border ruffian attacks on a few settlements in Kansas, including the town of Lawrence. The town was pillaged and three citizens died. Atchison was close friends with Jefferson Davis.

Did John Brown and his five sons retaliate? Yes, they murdered a Missouri slaveholder and liberated 11 of his slaves; in May of 1856, after pro-slavers raided Lawrence Kansas, John Brown and his sons killed five proslavery settlers in what was called the Pottawatomie Massacre.

What did naturalist **James Audubon** do in 1843? He made his last big trip as he went up the Missouri River in search of mammals to include in his new book about quadrupeds of North America. When Audubon went into the wilderness, he brought along his horse, gun, knapsack and his dog.

James Audubon (Library of Congress)

Of the 121 St. Louis-based steam-boats in 1848, one fifth did not survive more than three navigating seasons.

AUDUBON DISLIKES STE. GENEVIEVE

In February of 1814, James Audubon traveled on a keelboat (from Henderson, KY) up the Mississippi to Ste. Genevieve, Missouri. He was partners with a man named Ferdinand Rozier, and they planned to sell the merchandise they were hauling to make a profit.

The pair found the river up north to be filled with ice so they stopped and made camp in Alexander County, Illinois, near the last big bend in the Mississippi before it joins the Ohio River. This lowland area was called the Tawapatee Bottoms.

Audubon was not discouraged by the delay as he set about searching for new birds to observe and paint. When the ice melted, they made their way to Ste. Genevieve. He immediately disliked the place, **referring to the French inhabitants as lazy, uncouth and uneducated**. He and his partner soon parted ways as Audubon longed to return to his wife and family. He crossed the Mississippi and arrived at thriving **Kaskaskia**, Illinois, which was almost directly across from Ste. Genevieve.

MISSOURI HISTORY 1850-1860

How did the street known as Lucas & Hunt receive its name? It was named for prominent land owner of this period, James Lucas and his sister, Ann Lucas Hunt. In 1850, they laid out a large residential site called Lucas Place on land inherited from their father.

What West Point grad (6th in his class), named for a famous Indian chief, was assigned to Jefferson Barracks in St. Louis in 1850? William Tecumseh Sherman

By 1850, what was the only slave state to have a smaller black population (percentage wise) than Missouri? Delaware

When California entered the Union as a free state in 1850, what St. Louisan represented her in Congress? John C. Fremont, who had earlier led an expedition – backed by prominent St. Louisans – to find a railroad pass through the Sierra Nevadas

What was the population of Missouri in 1850? 682,000

What famous singer entertained enraptured St. Louis audiences in 1851? Jenny Lind – the Swedish Nightingale

According to its masthead, when was the St. Louis *Globe-Democrat* founded? 1852

What forerunner of the important town of Kansas City was incorporated in 1850? Kansas/ Westport Landing/City of Kansas, originally established by the French as a fur trading post

What Missourian became famous for serving as a guide on the exploring expeditions of John C. Fremont? Christopher "Kit" Carson of **Franklin**, Missouri; Fremont was called "the

Pathfinder."

What happened to Carson's town of **Franklin**? It was swallowed up by a Missouri River flood. Carson was born in Kentucky but spent most of his childhood in **Boone's Lick**.

What state capital honors Kit Carson? Carson City, Nevada

What is the Missouri connection to the old song, "Sweet Betsy of Pike?" The Pike in the song refers to where Betsy was from, Pike County, Missouri.

What famous expression came out of pioneer experiences on Missouri's Salt River? "We're up Salt River without a paddle." By the time of this author's youth it had changed to "Up Salt Creek without a paddle." The uncouth had yet another variation on those words.

Where did St. Louis rank as a port city in 1854 as demonstrated by the number of steamboats stopping at her harbor? Third, behind New York and New Orleans

From 1835-1860, **Independence** experienced a boom as a jumping off point for settlers headed west. Why did it experience a decline after the Civil War?

It was due to the railroads and the fact that it wasn't on the Missouri River.

When was Missouri's first railroad built? 1852 – The Pacific Railroad went from St. Louis to Kirkwood and Sulphur (correct spelling) Springs; it reached **Jefferson City** in 1855.

What was the first co-educational institution of higher learning west of the Mississippi? Culver-Stockton College, organized in 1853 at **Canton**.

What **communal village** was established six miles west of St. Louis in 1858? It was a group of Icarians founded by Etienne Cabet. The utopians had previously lived in Nauvoo, but the colony split and one of the factions moved to Missouri. The short lived colony was called Cheltenham.

Were most Missourians slaveholders during this period? No

What were Beecher's Bibles? Henry Ward Beecher, a Brooklyn minister, urged his congregation and others to send arms to the anti-slavery settlers who were moving into Kansas. Crates marked "bibles" were shipped to Kansas and, when opened at their destination, Sharps rifles were found inside. The rifles became known as Beecher's Bibles. It was his daughter, Harriet Beecher Stowe, who wrote *Uncle Tom's Cabin*.

Who is known as the "Father of the State University?" James S. Rollins because of his lifelong support

A railroad bridge built by Chicagoan Lucius Boomer fell into the Gasconade River on November 1, 1855, killing 44 and injuring 100. Bridges back then were so poorly constructed that nearly one out of four eventually collapsed. Due to high winds, tornado or poor engineering (take your pick), a 640-foot section of the Mississippi River Bridge connecting **Chester**, Illinois, and Missouri fell into the water in 1944.

Where was the focus of Missouri support for the newly formed Republican Party in 1856? In Gasconade and St. Charles counties, led by Frank P. Blair; Blair was largely responsible for keeping Missouri in the Union during the Civil War. There is a statue of him in Forest Park at Kingshighway and Lindell.

The first public high school in St. Louis opened in 1856 on the northeast corner of 15th and Olive.

What was the first railroad from the east to reach St. Louis? The Ohio & Mississippi (1857), although it ended in Illinoistown (**East St. Louis**) because the Eads Bridge was not yet built.

Did John Brown and his sons ever make a raid into Missouri? Yes – December 1858; border raids by both sides became so common that Governor Stewart called out the militia to patrol the area and the Kansas governor did the same thing.

Why did the Dred Scott case inflame sectional rivalries? It upset abolitionists because the court ruled the Missouri Compromise unconstitutional and slave owners could now take their human property anywhere they wanted. The decision also ruined Illinoisan Stephen Douglas' bid for the presidency since his "popular sovereignty" doctrine was now passé.

The **world's first airmail delivery** took place in 1859 when four St. Louisans took off in a balloon from Washington Square in St. Louis to test the theory that the Earth's rotation caused prevailing west to east air currents. The men landed near Henderson, New York. The mail had been thrown overboard to remove ballast and regain altitude, but it was recovered and delivered.

MISSOURI RAILROADS

When did Missouri first pass a law to subsidize railroad building in the state? 1851, supported by Thomas Hart Benton, an ardent advocate of Manifest Destiny

What railroads were the first to receive grant money? The Pacific (Missouri Pacific) and the Hannibal & St. Joseph (Burlington); these railroads were needed because the Missouri River was often closed to navigation two or three months of the year due to ice.

What city is currently the third largest rail center in America? St. Louis

What was significant about the Pacific Railroad? It was the first railroad in the state and the first one west of the Mississippi.

What disaster befell the Pacific on its maiden run from St. Louis to **Jefferson City** in 1855? The bridge over the Gasconade was not completed, but the contractors agreed to install enough supports for the initial run. When the train, and ten cars loaded with passengers, crossed the bridge, the supports gave way and the engine and cars fell into the river thirty feet below, killing many prominent St. Louisans, including Henri Chouteau.

What strange proposal was made by Thomas Hart Benton and John C. Fremont in 1854 at the Farmer's Hotel in **Kansas City**? They devised a plan to import camels as beasts of burden for crossing the western plains during the hot months. Camels were imported for this purpose but the project failed.

Early trains had a cowcatcher. It was a V-shaped bumper fitted on engines to clear the track of animals and debris.

On early trains a diamond stack was an oddly shaped stack (engine chimney) designed to diminish the amount of hot embers emitted that might start disastrous prairie fires.

Who invented the pneumatic air brake for railroad cars? Chicagoan George Westinghouse – before that, brakes were mechanical.

By 1858 the Butterfield Overland Mail Route took postings from St. Louis to San Francisco by stagecoach.

Who invented the railroad "mail car" in 1861? According to historian Walter Williams, it was William Davis who submitted plans to Postmaster General Blair. A special car was made for the purpose of sorting and delivering mail.

The only railroad completed in Missouri during the 1850s was the 207 mile long Hannibal & St. Joseph, which connected those two cities in 1859. By 1860 only 810 miles of railroad track had been laid in the state. The Pacific Railroad was intended to link St. Louis with Kansas City by following the Missouri River. It stopped at **Sedalia**, ninety-five miles short of its destination. There was a southwest branch of the Pacific line that went from St. Louis through the town of **Pacific**, then through **Rolla, and from there to Springfield**. The North Missouri line was an effort to connect St. Louis with Iowa. It built a bridge over the Missouri River at St. Charles in 1871. It intersected with the Hannibal & St. Joseph when it reached **Macon**. The St. Joseph & DesMoines was organized in 1877.

The Pacific, Hannibal & St. Joseph, and the Southern Branch all received land grants, totaling 127,000 acres, from the federal government to encourage the development of railroads and encourage western settlement. The land was actually given to the state of Missouri which passed it on to the railroad companies. In return, the railroads paid about six or seven percent of their annual gross revenues into the state treasury. Land grants usually consisted of about six miles of land on either side of the railroad tracks. This land was then sold by railroads to settlers or speculators.

Railroad mogul John O'Fallon (MHS)

By 1860, all Missouri railroads, except for the Hannibal & St. Joseph, had gone bankrupt and were sold to other investors at public auction. Inexperienced management, poor construction, faulty equipment and high costs led to a multitude of problems.

What Missouri railroad, completed in 1858, was principally built to haul ore? The **Iron Mountain** line ran from St. Louis to **Pilot Knob** and Iron Mountain. John C. Fremont headed a consortium of financial backers, although most Missouri railroads were subsidized by the state. Tracks were later extended (1869) to **Belmont** near the Kentucky border. Three years later the line reached the Arkansas border and, in 1874, the line was connected to Texas railroads at Texarkana. In 1881, the line was taken over by the Missouri Pacific Railroad. The Iron Mountain line was robbed twice, once by the James gang and once by the Dalton gang. In 1881, it became part of the Missouri Pacific which, in turn, became part of the Union Pacific.

What was the route of the **North Missouri Railroad**? It ran 167 miles from St. Louis to **Macon** where it linked up with the Hannibal & St. Joseph. From there it went to Bloomfield, Iowa. **John O'Fallon** was president of the line, and the Board of Directors included Lewis Bissell, Charles Drake and James Rollins. Another line that connected to Iowa was the Kansas City, St. Joseph & Council Bluffs. It afterward became a branch of the Wabash. In 1871, the Hannibal & Central Missouri line was completed to **Moberly**. This line was conveyed to the Missouri, Kansas & Texas in 1873. The MKT line, over 2,000 miles long, went from Denison, Texas, across Kansas, and then to **Hannibal**. In 1879, the Wabash, St. Louis & Pacific line was incorporated and it eventually evolved into the Wabash Railroad.

The **Missouri Valley Railroad** was organized to link Kansas City with St. Joseph and the Iowa border. It was eventually absorbed by the Chicago, Burlington & Quincy.

By 1918, only the Missouri counties of Dallas, Douglas and Ozark were without railroads as Missouri had 8,529 miles of track. The railroads quickly replaced the steamboat as the major carrier of passengers and freight.

Despite numerous problems with financing, speculation and corruption, railroads transformed life in Missouri. They connected Missouri with the rest of the nation, increased property values, gave farmers a market for surplus crops, ended isolation in numerous small towns, provided employment, made it easier to travel and created new towns that sprang up along their routes.

What Missouri town was second only to St. Louis in population in 1860? **St. Joseph** (8,932) – thanks to a railroad and the Pony Express

What was the population of St. Louis by 1860? 190,500; of that number, about 1,750 free Blacks were living in St. Louis; Blacks in Missouri were forbidden, by law, to attend school after 1847.

When did Missouri see its first streetcar? 1859 - The St. Louis line ran on Olive Street from Fourth to Tenth Street and was pulled by horses.

What railroad line had its completion spike driven at **Chillicothe** in 1859? The Hannibal & St. Joe; the Hannibal & St. Joseph eventually became part of the Burlington Railroad.

What was the only early Missouri Railroad not to default on its bonds and revert to the state? Hannibal & St. Joe

How much land was given to the railroad company by the federal government as an inducement to build the railroad? 600,000 acres

---

What were Missouri's leading church denominations in 1860? Methodists numbered first, followed by Baptist, Presbyterian, Christian, Catholic, Lutheran, Episcopal and Jewish

How many slaves were in Missouri by 1860? Only 115,000 comprising 9.8 percent of the population; in St. Louis only one percent of the population consisted of slaves.

What were Missouri's largest cities in 1860? St. Louis (160,773), St. Joseph, Hannibal, Kansas City, St. Charles, Independence, Jefferson City, Cape Girardeau, Springfield

Where was Hiram Revels' school for "coloreds" located in 1860? Near the levee on the St. Louis riverfront; Revels would become famous after the war as the nation's first black U.S. Senator (from Mississippi).

What two Missourians have statues in the federal Capitol's Hall of Fame? Francis P. Blair Jr. and his mentor, Thomas Hart Benton; Blair was a Republican who became so disgusted with the vengeful politics of the Radical Republicans that he switched over to the Democratic Party.

THE PONY EXPRESS

The Pony Express flourished eighteen months (1860-61) at **St. Joseph**, Missouri. It began there because railroad construction had not progressed beyond that point. The invention of the telegraph eventually killed off the service. The 1,996 mile route from St. Joe to Sacramento had 190 relay stations spaced about ten miles apart. An average trip took ten days. The young riders received $100 a month as pay, if they lived long enough to collect it. The job was so hazardous handbills stated that **orphans were preferred as riders**. Riders could weigh no more than 125 pounds. A rider usually traveled about 75 miles before passing his leather pouch to another rider. The riders were generally lightly armed because they discovered that a fast horse was their best defense against Indians. The route followed the Oregon Trail, then headed south along the Mormon trail, then went the rest of the way along the California Trail. The Pony Express grossed $90,000 and had expenses of about $200,000. After the Civil War, the assets were sold to Wells Fargo for well over a million dollars.

Donuts were invented when the girl friend of rider Johnny Fry passed them to him as he rode by.

Of the four national candidates running in the 1860 presidential election, which candidate received the fewest votes in Missouri? Abe Lincoln

Which 1860 candidate got the most? Stephen Douglas – the moderate candidate; Lincoln garnered the most votes in St. Louis.

If there was so much pro-slave sentiment in Missouri, why did it remain in the Union when the Civil War arrived? According to James Primm, Missouri's course was set by men of influence, whose Unionist ideas were shaped by Thomas Hart Benton, who died in 1858.

What was the value of Missouri slaves in 1860, according to estimates by the governor? A hundred million dollars

Could Missouri slaves sue for their freedom if they were being held illegally? Yes

What law did Missouri adopt in 1847 concerning free Negroes? They were forbidden to enter the state.

Did Missouri get a new constitution in 1865? Yes. It was narrowly defeated by voters but then absentee ballots from soldiers in the war passed it by a margin of about 2,000 votes.

Abe Lincoln tries to intimidate James Shields as he prepares for the saber duel

Francis Preston Blair Jr.

What was the most interesting feature of the new constitution? It granted immediate freedom to all slaves, **making Missouri the first state to free all its slaves.**

Why was it called Drake's Consti-tution? Charles Drake, a Missouri senator, was the guiding force behind the creation of a new frame of government.

What were some of the most prominent German communities in pioneer Missouri? Hermann, Dutzow, Augusta, Altenburg, New Melle, Westphalia, Wittenburg and Frohna

In what years did failed revolutions in Germany cause many intellectuals to migrate to Missouri? These occurred in 1832, 1833 and 1848.

What influential Missourian helped Abe Lincoln defeat William Seward for the 1860 Republican presidential nomination? **Francis Preston Blair** Jr. (Francis P. Blair's son) had met and formed a friendship with Lincoln back in 1857 when visiting William Herndon, Lincoln's law partner. Seward led for two ballots but couldn't get the necessary majority. Blair led the move for Missouri delegates to switch from favorite son Edward Bates to Lincoln and this paved the way for Lincoln's nomination.

In 1860, the average St. Louisan drank 658 glasses of beer a year.

MISSOURI AND THE CIVIL WAR

Where did Abe Lincoln almost fight a duel with a saber in Missouri? Near **West Alton**; Lincoln was challenged by a political opponent named James Shields. The person challenged gets to pick the weapons and Lincoln chose sabers. The two men traveled by stage from **Spring-field** to Alton. From there they rowed across the Mississippi to fight their duel on an island near West Alton. The duel was called off at the last minute.

When the South seceded from the Union, Abe Lincoln issued a call for 75,000 volunteers. Missouri, being one of those Border States with slaveholders to the south and abolitionists in the north, discovered that its citizens had fiercely divided loyalties. About two thirds of its people were of white southern stock. However, most of Missouri's prominent men in leadership positions favored the Union cause. Governor Claiborne Jackson thought Missouri should stand by her sister slaveholding states. James Primm tells us that voters sent mostly slave owning delegates to a March 1861 convention that opposed Missouri secession by a 98-1 vote. The slave owners were mostly professed Unionists.

After the fall of Fort Sumter, Lincoln issued a call for 75,000 volunteers. The governor refused to send troops but Congressman Frank Blair volunteered 4,000 Home Guard paramilitary units, which Lincoln accepted. The Home Guard was augmented by the German Turnverein Society which had a small arsenal of their own at the Turner Hall. Secessionist sympathizers countered with their own Minute Men group, led by Lieutenant Governor Thomas C. Reynolds.

In a sense, the war started in Missouri long before the first shots at Fort Sumter in the spring of 1861. Missouri Bushwackers had been clashing with Kansas Jayhawkers ever since the passage of the Kansas-Nebraska Act. Missouri, with its breathtaking scenic beauty, would be host to over 1,160 recorded engagements during four long years of Civil War within its borders.

Historian Carolyn Bartels says that the greatest terror for Missouri citizenry was not so much the pitched battles or enlisted soldiers of either army, but the renegade lawless bands that roamed the countryside. These ruffians did not seem to wage war by the same rules as bona fide soldiers.

Missouri sent more men to war, in proportion to her population, than any other state. Missouri was the scene of 11 percent of the total engagements in the war. At the battle of Vicksburg, for example, Missouri furnished 39 regiments – 17 Confederate and 22 Union.

Map of Missouri Civil War Battles

Had St. Louis fallen under Confederate control the state likely would have gone into the Confederate column. Thirty-one thousand slavery-hating Missouri Germans wore proud blue uniforms, thus saving the Western frontier for the Union.

Missouri, ranking eighth in population in 1860, was a keystone state for the Union forces because the important Missouri, Mississippi, and Ohio rivers touched its borders or bisected its land. The nation's major lines of communication were anchored in the state. Missouri Iron and lead furnished bullets and cannonballs. Missouri crops and animals fed the soldiers and the population.

It was a war of divided loyalties as brother fought against brother, business partner fought against business partner. The war was a catalyst of terror in many Missouri counties as barns were destroyed, houses were burned, men were killed in their front yards, women were hung, and hundreds left the area where they lived for safety of life and limb.

The Civil War battle of **Hog Hollow** took place in the Missouri Ozarks. How the site came to be named is of interest. There was this man who lived in the community and he was known as being a hard bargainer, usually coming out on top whenever any deals were made. One day he went into town to buy supplies and while there a man came up to him and offered to sell him three pigs.

The piglets were in a burlap sack, known in the Ozarks as a poke. "How much do you want for them?" The man asked. The stranger said he wanted a dollar for all three. The man thought that was too much and chiseled the price down to 75 cents.

"Let me see the pigs first," the man said to the stranger.

"I can't. If I open the bag the pigs will get out," the stranger replied.

"Oh, well. I guess pigs is pigs," the man said with a shrug. The wily old man laughed all the way home and couldn't wait to tell his wife what a bargain he had made.

When he got back to the farm and opened the poke he was surprised to discover that the piglets were unlike any he had ever seen. As the months passed the pigs grew into very large wild boars with long dangerous tusks. One day he sent his son to the pen to feed the boars and **they ate the boy and then escaped into the woods**, thus the name Hog Hollow.

This occurrence is what started the old saying, **"don't buy a pig in a poke**."

The prominent Dorthea Dix was in charge of the Union Army Nurse Corps during the war. On a visit to St. Louis, she made it clear that **all young and pretty applicants were not welcome**.

A good number of captured Missouri Confederates were taken to **Alton**, Illinois, and imprisoned there in what used to be the state penitentiary. At its peak, the facility held more than 2,000 men. The conditions there, like most POW camps at the time, were filthy and overcrowded. About 1,300 men would later die from smallpox. The epidemic lasted from the winter of 1863 to the spring of 1864. The city eventually erected a tall obelisk to honor the Confederate war dead.

Missouri was in a rather unique situation when the war began because it was a slave state surrounded by free states. Missouri had just elected a pro-slave governor named Claiborne Jackson, yet anti-slave forces were given voice by General Nathaniel Lyon and Congressman Francis Preston Blair. In Missouri, "brother against brother and neighbor against neighbor" wasn't a cliché. No where were loyalties more heated and divided than they were in Missouri. With more than 1,100 battles and skirmishes within the state, **only Virginia and Tennessee saw more bloodshed**.

LINCOLN PROPOSED TO COMPENSATE SLAVE OWNERS. Abe Lincoln did not favor immediate emancipation of the slaves because he thought it would be too disruptive socially. Instead he proposed gradual emancipation that would end slavery by 1900. Southern firebrands and aristocrats rejected this plan and thought any war between the North and South would be brief, disparaging the fighting ability of northern "mudsills." (To southerners, mudsills were people of the lowest social order.) Southerners derisively referred to free Negroes as "smoked Yankees."

Nathaniel Lyon

St. Louisan **Edward Bates** has a statue dedicated to him just west of the Art Museum in Forest Park. Bates was the attorney general in Lincoln's administration. Bates' family was the perfect microcosm – one son served in the Union Army and another fought for the Confederacy. He favored the idea of colonization for newly freed slaves, as did Lincoln. African-American leaders, such as Frederick Douglass, rejected the idea.

Camp Jackson at St. Louis

It was Bates who told Lincoln that St. Louis had the wherewithal to design and build alligator **ironclad ships**. The government placed orders for the boats and James B. Eads supervised their construction at **Carondelet**. The four ships were named the *St. Louis, Benton, Carondelet*, and *Mound City*. The ships were built at the Union Iron Works at a point where the River Des Peres flows into the Mississippi. The Marine Railway Company was already at that site and boats could be lifted out of and into the water by a crane and placed on a railway car whose tracks went partially into the river. Eads also used an existing facility at **Mound City**, Illinois, not far from **Cairo**. These ships were responsible for the North gaining control of the Mississippi River, a vital element to winning the war. The *St. Louis* was the **first ironclad in the world**, and it was used by U.S. Grant to capture forts Henry and Donnelson on the Tennessee and Cumberland rivers. The *St. Louis* was sunk later in the war when it was hit by a Confederate torpedo (mine). The aforementioned ships played an important part in the capture of Island #10 in the Mississippi. Island # 10 was the **first victory on either side where the winners suffered no loss of life in battle**.

Jesse Benton Fremont

The war was a disaster for St. Louis because the Confederacy closed the lower Mississippi early in 1861 and it was not reopened until Farragut captured New Orleans and Grant took Vicksburg. William T. Sherman was among the first to recognize that the Mississippi River was the "backbone of the nation."

When was the last slave auction in St. Louis? January 1, 1861; the auction crowd stuck together and bid a pathetic eight dollars. The discouraged auctioneer called off the proceedings.

What decision was made at a special convention in March of 1861? The group saw no reason to vote for secession at that time and held out for some sort of national compromise.

Where was the Missouri governor C. F. Jackson on this issue? He ultimately planned for Missouri's secession.

What happened to Missouri after the South fired on Fort Sumter (South Carolina in April of 1861? Governor Jackson refused to heed Lincoln's call for troops to put down the rebellion.

When did Missouri go 46 days without being represented by a senator in the nation's capitol? On January 10, 1862 Missouri's two senators were expelled because they were too loyal to the Confederacy.

What provocative action was taken by Claiborne Jackson on May 6, 1861? He sent a group of militia to organize Camp Jackson, located on the outskirts of St. Louis. Their objective was to capture the arsenal at St. Louis. **The arsenal was significant because it was the largest among all the slave holding states.** Claiborne Jackson's actions were opposed by St Louisan Frank Blair, who organized his own militia, the Wide Awakes

What happened on the day Jefferson Davis was inaugurated as president of the Confederacy? Missourians went to the polls and elected men to a convention to decide whether Missouri would join the Confederacy. The pro-Unionists won and Missouri stayed loyal.

What happened at **Liberty**, Missouri on April 20, 1861?
Missouri rebels captured the arsenal located there.

What special connection did Congressman Blair have to the Lincoln Administration? His brother Montgomery Blair was in the President's cabinet.

Who was placed in charge of the military command in St. Louis? Nathaniel Lyon – a hothead rather than a conciliator

What happened to the state militia at Camp Jackson? Lyon surrounded and captured it (without bloodshed) with his forces on May 10, 1861. The day before Lyon had **reconnoitered the camp in a carriage, wearing a veil and wearing a dress that concealed two pistols**. He noticed the street names in the camp were "Beauregard" and "Jeff Davis."

What happened as the troops returned to Jefferson Barracks? They were fired upon by civilians. They returned the fire and killed 28 people, sending the state into an uproar. Businessman William Tecumseh Sherman was among the spectators at this event. The state assembly met in night session and gave the governor dictatorial powers.

What St. Louis institution exists on the old Civil War site of Camp Jackson? St. Louis University

What was Lyon's next military objective? On June 15, 1861, Lyon's forces came up the Missouri River on steamboats and occupied **Jefferson City**. This quick action probably kept Missouri from going over to the Confederacy.

Who became the new pro-Union provisional governor of the state? Hamilton Gamble, who pursued a conciliatory policy toward the secessionists. Members of the old rump government fled to Arkansas.

Where was Missouri's first big battle of the Civil War? Claiborne Jackson and his forces retreated to Springfield and Lyon chased after them. Meanwhile, ex-governor Sterling Price helped train Jackson's forces. The opposing groups met August 10 at Wilson's Creek in **Springfield**. Lyon's forces were outnumbered nearly two to one. It was a bloody battle, won by the secessionists. Two Union groups wore gray, two Confederate groups wore dark blue, and the Missouri State Guard wore civilian clothing, causing confusion during the battle. Lyon was killed and his forces retreated to the railhead at **Rolla**. Lyon was the **first Union general killed in the war, thus making him a hero in the North**.

Confederate Sterling Price

What was the significance of the Battle of Wilson's Creek? It allowed the Confederacy to retain control over Southern Missouri.

Who succeeded Lyon as commander of Missouri's Union forces? John C. Fremont, Thomas Hart Benton's son-in-law

Fremont declared martial law in St. Louis to counteract the Secesh actions of the Police Board. Lincoln relieved Fremont of command in November of 1861 due to his rash actions and inept military leadership.

When Fremont became famous for his exciting and positive writing about the West, who actually did his writing for him? His wife, the beautiful and articulate **Jesse Fremont**, daughter of Thomas Hart Benton

Heroic Nathaniel Lyon at Wilson's Creek

Did Jesse become involved in her husband's presidential campaign of 1856? Yes – "Fremont and Jesse too" was the slogan.

Did Jesse become involved in her husband's Civil War activities? Yes – she was quite astute politically and she was often referred to as "General Jesse."

What was odd about the Benton-Fremont relationship? Thomas H. Benton was a Democrat and opposed his son-in-law when he ran for president on the Republican ticket in 1856.

What action, early in the war, did Fremont undertake in Missouri that was rescinded by Lincoln? He emancipated the slaves, a move wildly applauded by the Germans and abolitionists.

Henry Halleck replaced Fremont and was just as inept, but he had able commanders in Grant and Samuel Curtis. Women who too zealously promoted the Confederate cause were banished from the state as were wives of Confederate officers who were suspected spies.

What St. Louis Underground Railroad site is listed as one of sixty-four sites by the National Park Service's Network to Freedom list? The Mary Meachum Freedom Crossing, an 11 mile paved greenway

When did the battle of Lone Jack take place? August 16, 1862 – it was a bloody five hour battle at **Lone Jack**, Missouri (660-566-2272).

How did the Union keep in touch with its California supporters during the Civil War? They used the Pony Express at **St. Joseph.**

What Missourian during the war was known as the "**Swamp Fox**?" Meriwether Thompson earned his reputation leading his men in the swampy areas near the Kansas border. He raided the bank in **Charleston** in 1861, taking $56,000. He briefly captured **Sedalia** and **New Madrid** and participated in the Battle of Westport (Kansas City).

What military road went into **Weston** during the Civil War? The Leavenworth Road, which today is East Bluff Road

How did Fremont cause more chaos in Missouri? He considered Missouri a conquered province and freed the slaves in places of rebellion. Lincoln forced this premature emancipation to be rescinded. Fremont, egged on by his wife Jessie Benton, abused his authority and mimicked Julius Caesar. He blundered by jailing Frank Blair for insubordination. On August 14, 1861 he placed St. Louis under martial law.

Who was the **first slave in the nation freed** by federal authority (Fremont's executive order)? Hiram Reed of St. Louis

Why was the Civil War disastrous for St. Louis trade? The Confederates closed the lower Mississippi/New Orleans and cut off trade with the East and foreign countries. Sales to Union armies partially made up for the loss.

Where is Grant's Trail? It is a six mile trail that runs through south St. Louis and goes by Grant's Cabin and his wife's childhood home at White Haven.

Where is secessionist governor Claiborne Jackson buried? Sappington Cemetery at **Arrow Rock**; he died of pneumonia in December of 1862 at his Missouri capital in Arkansas.

Where was the northernmost skirmish of the Civil War west of the Mississippi? The **Battle of Athens**, Aug. 5, 1861. At this battle, Unionist Colonel **David Moore led a bayonet charge against the enemy that included two of his own sons.**

What happened to Grant after his failed effort to make his farm in St. Louis a success? He moved to **Galena**, Illinois, and worked in his father's leather tanning business, which he hated.

Where was U.S. Grant's first battle? Grant led a move, in November of 1861, to drive Confederates out of their camp at Belmont. Grant, stationed at Cairo, led forces to keep the Confederates from attacking nearby Columbus, Kentucky. The Confederates regrouped and drove the Union forces away but their designs on Columbus were thwarted.

According to historian James Priddy, there were **four times in one day that U.S. Grant escaped by seconds or inches, death or capture during the battle of Belmont.**

What organization in St. Louis pushed for the victory of Democrats (in the 1864 election) and the overthrow of the Unionists in St. Louis? The OAK – Order of American Knights, led nationally by Clement Vallandigham – a Copperhead

Bloody Bill Anderson in death

Where did the October 1864 clash between Gen. Sanborn and Joe Shelby's Confederates take place? At Wilkins Bridge near **Billingsville; at war's end, Shelby was the only general who refused to surrender, fleeing to Mexico instead.** It was Shelby who led the longest cavalry raid of the war, covering 1,500 miles in 41 days in 1863. His men raised the Confederate flag over the Missouri statehouse.

Where was *Stars & Stripes*, the newspaper that kept fighting men and families informed, first published? **Bloomfield,** which currently features annual chuck wagon races on Memorial Day weekend (573-568-3157)

Who was Sam Hildebrand? He was a Civil War bushwacker and notorious outlaw who used a cave in **Bonne Terre** as his hideout. Hildebrand, in his autobiography, claimed to have killed 100 men. Officials credited him with at least thirty. Hildebrand was tracked down and killed in **Pinckneyville**, Illinois, in 1872. Incidentally, Bonne Terre currently boasts the **largest underground lake in the world**. Divers love to explore the five-level mine that was abandoned in the 1960s and filled with water. The 80 square miles has been listed by National Geographic as **one of America's Top Ten Adventures**. 314-209-7200.

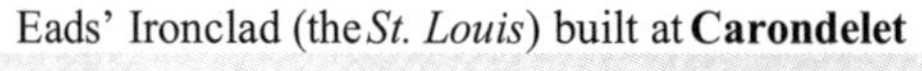

Eads' Ironclad (the *St. Louis*) built at **Carondelet**

Where is the oldest of Missouri's four remaining covered bridges located? Next to a mill in **Burfordville** that was destroyed by Union troops to keep it out of Confederate hands

What moderate program of emancipation did Missouri adopt in 1863? All slaves were to be freed on July 4, 1870, except for slaves that were over 40 years of age who would remain permanently indentured to their owners.

Were there any battles at **Cape Girardeau**? The most notable one took place on April 26, 1863.

What Missouri battle took place 17 days before the First Battle of Bull Run? The Battle of **Carthage**, July 5, 1861 – hence **the first battle of the entire Civil War took place in Missouri**. The town was destroyed by guerilla warfare in 1864.

Who was "Bloody" Bill Anderson? A Confederate who was responsible for a massacre at **Centralia,** killing 24 Federal soldiers from a passing train

The Battle of **Lexington** began on September 12, 1861. Lexington, on the Missouri River, was about 40 miles east of Kansas City. About 8,000 men of the Missouri State Guard were led by Sterling Price. They laid siege to a Federal military post housed in a Masonic college building commanded by James Mulligan. This is sometimes referred to as the **Battle of the Hemp Bales** because Price's men wet down hemp bales and used them as moving breastworks as they advanced against the Union forces, trapping them with the river at their backs. Mulligan's troops surrendered on September 20th. There were about 73 men killed on both sides combined with 270 wounded. **It was during this battle that the first land mines were used in the Civil War**. Lexington was known as a center for Quantrill's Raiders during the war.

Lexington is one of the few Civil War battlefields never cultivated. The trenches and earthworks are still visible.

What Missouri town, in 1895, was reputed to have **more millionaires per capita than any other U.S. city**? Carthage, which became a magnet after the Civil War for developers and entrepreneurs

How is the Missouri Battle of Carthage depicted at the museum in that town? With a detailed mural and diorama 417-368-6643

What famous building material does **Carthage** produce?
Gray marble and limestone

An infamous Massacre occurred in **Palmyra** on October 18, 1862. Union commander John McNeil (the "Butcher of Palmyra") ordered the execution of ten prisoners of war in retaliation for the abduction and murder of a well-known Union supporter in that town by Colonel Porter and his men. Both Lincoln and Jefferson Davis called the Palmyra Massacre the **Darkest Crime of the Civil War**.

Was **Hannibal** a stop on the Underground Railroad? Yes, and many of the slaves hid out in the Mark Twain Cave.

Did Mark Twain fight for either side in the war? Twain fought briefly (two weeks) for the Confederate side as a lieutenant. Then he quit the war and joined his brother Orion in **St. Joseph**. From there they headed west and escaped the war.

How did Lincoln plan to reward the border state of Missouri for remaining loyal to the Union? He wanted to compensate slave owners for their losses. $15 million was appropriated for the Border States, but Radical Republicans kept it from passing in Congress.

What was General Thomas Ewing's infamous **General Order Number 11**, 1863? Ewing issued a decree ordering that people living in the area of Westport/Kansas City, (thought to be a desperadoes' nest) had to evacuate their homes. George Caleb Bingham devoted one of his paintings to this topic.

U.S Grant, Julia Dent, and four children

What former schoolteacher, from **Mendota**, Illinois, made a raid on the town of Lawrence, Kansas, and massacred over 100 men and boys, burning the town in the process? William Quantrill – whose men were mostly from Jackson County. He was killed by his enemies in Kentucky – 1865.

What eventually happened to John Brown? He was captured after making a raid on the federal arsenal at Harper's Ferry, Virginia, and hanged for murder and treason.

Who were the Jayhawkers? Anti-slave groups in Kansas that crossed the border and made raids on pro-slave forces in Missouri

What is the oldest collegiate sports rivalry west of the Mississippi? Kansas/Missouri

What is the significance of this Civil War conflict on the current collegiate sports scene in Missouri? There is a bitter sports rivalry between Missouri and Kansas. Missouri coaches might not win the conference title, but they had better win the game against Kansas.

What August, 1862 battles helped the Union gain control of northeast Missouri? Two battles at **Kirksville**

What town was known as the **Bushwhacker Capital** during the war? **Nevada,** Missouri; it now houses a Bushwhacker Museum

What group did Grant command early in the war at **Mexico**, Missouri? The 21st Illinois Volunteer Infantry – July, 1861

Confederate forces were effectively driven out of Missouri at what battle in northern Arkansas? Pea Ridge where nearly 6,000 Confederates died

Jenny Hodgers/Albert Cashier

Who invaded Missouri with a force of 12,000 men on September 19, 1864? Sterling Price – his objective was St. Louis. He hoped the attack would force Sherman to send a significant number of troops from back East, thus relieving pressure on besieged Atlanta. General W.S. Rosecrans was the military commander in charge of St. Louis at this time.

How well did the invaders succeed? They tore up railroad tracks and destroyed much property, but they were punished at **Pilot Knob** by General Tom Ewing of the Union forces. The victory ended the threat of Confederate attacks on Carondelet and Jefferson Barracks. Ewing was Sherman's brother-in-law.

When Price feared that St. Louis was too heavily defended, what became his next objective? **Springfield**, but he bypassed that also because it was heavily defended as well. His new strategic objective became the federal installation at Leavenworth.

Where was Price finally defeated? In late October, 1864 he was defeated by General Curtis at the **Battle of West-port**, near Kansas City. Remnants from the encounter fled to Texas. Westport was called the **"Gettysburg of the West" as it was the largest battle west of the Mississippi** After the war, at the bidding of Emperor Maximilian, Price tried to establish a colony of ex-Confederates in Mexico.

What flamboyant Missourian unsuccessfully challenged Lincoln for the 1864 Republican presidential nomination? John C. Fremont

Where was the "Cracker Castle?" St. Louis at Chouteau and Fourteenth St.; so called because its owner, James Pearce, made his fortune selling hardtack (a hard, saltless biscuit) to the Union Army.

What made Missouri's situation after the war unique? There had been so much division and hatred and chaos within the state during the war, there was probably no other state that had as much guerilla warfare and internal dissention. These hatreds, born of the killings and revenges of the war, lasted long after the war was over. It was the war that spawned the likes of the James gang and the Younger brothers.

What was Missouri's debt after the war? Thirty-eight and a half million dollars

Why is **Springfield** National Cemetery unique? It's one of the few cemeteries where both Confederates and Yanks are buried.

Missouri is the only Union state to have a star on the Confederate Battle Flag, although it was honorary since Missouri technically stayed in the Union.

About 8,344 Blacks from Missouri served in the Union Army during the war – all under white commanders.

H.C. Thruston, a Texan, served in the 4th Missouri Cavalry, CSA, Marmaduke's Division. **He was the tallest man in the world at the time**, standing at seven feet, seven and a half inches tall. Robert Wadlow, the **Alton Giant** who died in 1940, was about eight feet, eleven inches tall.

During the Civil War there were many teenage boys with high-pitched voices who served in the CSA or Union army. There were also a number of **women who dressed like a man** and enlisted to fight in the conflict. The most interesting story is that of an Illinois woman named Jenny Hodgers. She **holds the record for remaining undetected the longest**. She joined the army in 1862, at age nineteen, under the name Albert Cashier. She passed the physical which consisted of a cursory look at the eyes, ears, mouth and limbs. No undressing was required. Cashier was with Grant's forces at Vicksburg and acquitted herself/himself well.

Cashier avoided detection by going behind trees or bushes when nature called. He/she didn't mix socially with other men and was known as a loner. Cashier did occasionally darn other soldier's socks. When asked about this skill, he shrugged and said he grew up with three sisters who taught it to him.

When the war ended Cashier went back to Illinois and continued the ruse, living the life of a bachelor and earning his keep by doing odd jobs. Cashier voted regularly in presidential elections, **making her the first woman to vote**.

Her gender was not discovered until she was in a 1911 car accident and was sent to a veteran's hospital for treatment. Her story ends sadly because authorities thought that only an insane woman would want to dress as a man. She was forced to wear dresses and spent the rest of her life in a mental institution. Jenny Hodgers passed away in October of 1915 and was given a soldier's burial in Illinois, dressed in full uniform.

MISSOURI HISTORY 1860-1904

By 1860, Kaycee – Kansas City - was now the **biggest cattle market in the world.**

Missouri's population rank in 1860 was eighth (with a little over a million) – moving up from 23rd in 1820.

By 1860, only 25,000 out of a population of 1,200,000 citizens in Missouri owned slaves.

During Abraham Lincoln's campaign for the presidency, a dyed-in-the-wool Democrat named Valentine Tapley, from **Pike County**, Missouri, swore that he would never shave again if Abe were elected. **Tapley kept his word and his chin whiskers went unshorn from November 1860 until he died in 1910, attaining a length of twelve feet six inches**.

The only completed rail line in Missouri, when the Civil War broke out, was the 206 mile long Hannibal & St. Joseph.

Once the slaves were freed by the 13th Amendment, Missouri cotton production became practically nonexistent, as did hemp production which had relied heavily on slave labor. Tobacco production remained strong after the war but went into a long slow decline.

The Pacific Railroad reached Kansas City in 1865.

Another cholera epidemic hit St. Louis in 1866. It led to the construction of a new waterworks. This, too, proved to be insufficient and not until a new plant was built in 1904 in north St. Louis, near the Chain of Rocks, was the problem finally solved.

In 1867, the city of St. Louis purchased 36 acres on the highest point in the city called **Compton Hill**. The purpose was for building a reservoir to solve the city's water problem. The distinctive water tower still stands in Reservoir Park.

William and Marcella Magnan note in their *Streets of St. Louis* that the town's air, weather and drinking water had a poor reputation. When Jenny Lind, the "Swedish Nightingale" came to sing, her manager caustically remarked, "It is muddier in wet weather and dustier in dry weather than any other part of the United States. It is a huge reservoir devoted to manufacturing mud on a grand scale. The air is so rich (with dust and smoke) along the Mississippi River that one is satisfied by an afternoon walk in St. Louis, as if one had eaten a heavy dinner."

In 1867, the U.S. Supreme Court handed down a landmark decision in the case of *Cummings v. State of Missouri.* Immediately after the Civil War, many states (including Missouri) passed laws that required an "iron-clad oath" before one could teach, preach, practice law or enter politics. Having just fought a war due to actions of hothead southern firebrands, northerners had no desire to see these people returned to positions of leadership. The Missouri oath required one to swear that he/she had never fought for the Confederacy or supported it in any meaningful way. Six months in jail and a fine of $500 was the penalty for violating the law.

Mark Twain (Wikipedia)

Father John Cummings refused to take the oath and on Sunday, September 3, 1865, he delivered a sermon to a small congregation in the town of **Louisiana** in Pike County. Many opposed the oath and thought it to be a violation of constitutional rights. They lost in the Missouri Supreme Court but the U.S. Court ruled that the Missouri law *was* ex post facto, a bill of attainder and violated Cummings' personal rights. The ruling abolished the hated loyalty oaths.

In 1868, Henry Shaw gave Tower Grove Park to the city of St. Louis. The 190 acre park was almost treeless at the time. The perimeter was reserved for fine homes, following the English tradition. It was later extended to 277 acres.

In 1870, two Burlington Railroad men bought five acres of ground in **Kansas City** and set up a stock yards exchange. The next year they nearly tripled its size. They incorporated as the Kansas Stockyards Company. Several packing companies built plants there. Within ten years the Armour

Company was employing more than 600 men. By the turn of the century only Chicago and East St.
Louis surpassed the massive yards.

In 1871, the water tower at 20th and East Grand was built. **According to Ripley's "Believe-it-or-Not," it is the tallest free-standing Corinthian column in the world**, soaring 154 feet tall. The tallest water tower in St. Louis is at Blair and Bissell streets and stands 190 feet high.

Mark Twain humorously remarked that St. Louis water was so thick you could chew it. He said there was so much mud in the water that **a man could grow corn in his stomach**.

Twain probably wasn't exaggerating too greatly for it was customary for letting a glass of St. Louis water stand for an hour before drinking it so the dirt could settle to the bottom.

Joseph McClurg was elected governor of Missouri in 1868. He was the first governor to recommend a prohibition law in the state.

Ella Ewing was born in **Memphis**, Missouri, in 1872. Due to a tumor on her pituitary gland, she grew to a height of 8 feet 4 inches. She became known as the **Missouri Giantess** and toured with P.T. Barnum's circus and Buffalo Bill's Wild West Show. Curious onlookers paid ten cents to see her and 25 cents to shake her hand. She died in 1913 as a result of her disorder.

In 1874, the city of St. Louis bought the 1,375 acre tract of land that became known as Forest Park. Carondelet Park and O'Fallon Park were created at the same time. A citizen named Hiram Leffingwell (founder of Kirkwood) used his influence to get city officials to buy the land. He undoubtedly was influenced by a trip to NYC where he toured Central Park. He pushed for 2,754 acres but the city only bought 1,375 acres at a cost of $800,000. Much of the land at the time was owned by William Forsythe, John Cabanne, Thomas Skinker and the Chouteau family. All, including Leffing-well, would have streets named for them.

Governor Gratz Brown

Most residents did not like the idea of establishing a park that was considered too far west from the downtown area. In the next election, all the officials who voted to buy the land were thrown out of office. The land was pretty much undeveloped until the 1904 Fair came along.

In 1869, Kansas City was forced by prudence to build a railroad bridge across the Missouri River to connect with a rail line that came out of Chicago and stayed north going through Hannibal and St. Joseph. Kansas City was now a fiefdom of the Windy City. This made it clear that Chicago was the dominant Midwest city – not St. Louis or Kansas City.

Joseph Pulitzer

Twenty-four year old Missouri con-gressman Richard Bland became famous after the Civil War by advocating bi-metalism – minting U.S. currency on gold and silver, not just gold. Bland quickly earned the title, "Silver Dick."

Oliver H. Kelly, founder of the Grange farmer's movement in 1867, organized the Missouri Grange in 1870.

By 1875, the city of St. Louis was over 100 years old but the only develop-ments past Grand Boulevard were Shaw's Garden, Tower Grove Park, and William Russell's property.

When **Gratz Brown** became governor in 1870, what important service did he render to the state? He was elected as a Liberal Republican and led Missourians back toward unity and away from bitterness and hatred of Democrats who had supported secession. The "**Ironclad Oath**" was repealed in 1870, thereby restoring the vote to 75,000 Missourians.

In 1868, Franz Schwartzer began selling a stringed instrument in **Springfield** called a zither.

The KKK made its first appearance in the state in 1868 when it put up placards in **Boonville** advertising for membership.

When did the Atlantic & Pacific line reach Springfield? 1870

When did St. Louis annex the **Carondelet** area? 1870; St. Louis was so jealous of Chicago that when the 1870 census was taken, the city inflated its figures by more than 50,000 to make sure it would rank ahead of Chicago. By the 1880 census, Chicago had moved ahead of its rival.

What president of the St. Louis Board of Health in 1870 was responsible for inventing a wire splint to ease the pain of people with fractured thighs? John Hodgen, who also served as President of the American Medical Association, invented the stomach pump as well.

A railroad bridge across the Missouri River at **St. Charles** collapsed in 1870, killing 129 people.

Who blocked Gratz Brown's path to national fame at the 1872 Democratic Convention in Cincinnati? Brown was expected to get the presidential nomination of the Democratic Party, but at the last minute Missourian Carl Schurz abandoned his support of Brown and threw his support to Charles Francis Adams. Horace Greeley eventually got the nomination and Brown became his running mate. They were easily defeated by Grant and his supporters.

Who was the first governor to live in the current Governor's Mansion - 1872? Gratz Brown, who had stones for the columns taken from a quarry in Iron County that he owned. Prison labor was used to help construct the building.

In what year was the "Drake Constitution" of 1865 replaced by yet another Missouri Constitution? 1875, and this time it lasted for 70 years. The old constitution was a product of Radical Republicanism. Radicals believed the state had not acted strongly enough in punishing disloyal citizens and freeing slaves. It also said that anyone who killed another in a duel could not hold political office – thus ending the practice engaged in mostly by lawyers and politicians.

Was the Grange (farmer's alliance) movement successful in Missouri in 1875? Yes, it had more than 2,000 separate groups in the state at that time, having first been formed in 1874 at **Boonville**.

What was the chief complaint of the Grange concerning the railroads? The farmers felt victimized by big business, the banks and the railroads – especially the railroads that charged exorbitant rates for hauling their products to market.

When did the Iron Mountain Line first stretch from St. Louis into the bootheel? 1872

After the Chicago fire of 1871, St. Louis passed an ordinance requiring that all downtown buildings were to be made of brick. This led to the operation of numerous clay mines in and around the city.

When did Joseph Pulitzer (pull-it-sir) found the St. Louis *Post-Dispatch*? He acquired the *Post* in 1872 and bought the *Dispatch* in 1878, merging the two papers.

Was Pulitzer a Republican or Democrat? Republican. Currently the newspaper leans heavily to the side of the Democrats.

Who was the founder of "yellow journalism?" Joseph Pulitzer – sensational and lurid stories designed to sell newspapers

What innovation did Pulitzer introduce in his *New York World* newspaper? The first color comics

What Biblical plague hit Missouri in 1874? Locusts

When did the St. Louis *Globe* buy and merge with the *Democrat*? 1875

When was Sumner High School established for "coloreds?" 1875 - on 11TH Street between Poplar and Spruce; it was named for Charles Sumner, the famous Radical Republican of the Civil War era.

What happened to Missouri's growth rate after 1875? It declined as many prominent citizens left for greener pastures and more progressive states.

When were the corporate limits of St. Louis fixed? 1876 – It was a decision by St. Louis and St. Louis County voters that proved to be a crippling deterrent to the future development of St. Louis. Some historians believe the split occurred because of the tax dispute over Forest Park. The county people were still bitter about the Civil War. They owned slaves and had supported the Confederacy. They were angered that St. Louis city had housed the Union Army. The city had caused them to lose their slaves so why should they pay higher taxes to help the city finance the park. The **Municipal Divorce Bill** also allowed the city of St. Louis to extend its boundaries past the three county parks.

Other historians claim that the separation had little to do with old war grudges and that the split was merely due to short sightedness by politicians and voters of that era.

Who pushed Grant to seek an unprecedented third term in 1876? His wife Julia, who fell in love with D.C. social life; Carl Schurz helped nip the movement in the bud.

Vandeventer Place (Missouri Historical Society)

When did long distance telephone lines reach Missouri? 1877

Who was the largest plug tobacco maker in the world in 1878? Liggett & Myers of St. Louis

In 1878, technicians completed the telephone exchange in **Hannibal,** making it the first in the state and **the second in the world**.

What invention revived the Missouri mining industry since her surface deposits had been exhausted? The diamond drill (1879) to cut through rock

William R. Nelson arrived in Kansas City and became the owner/editor of the *Kansas City Star* in 1880. Through his editorial urgings, Kansas City grew from a roughshod cow town to a beautiful city with many beautiful parks and scenic boulevards. He left much of his fortune to build an art museum in Kansas City.

What St. Louis school superintendent was nationally famous as a leading educator in the 1870s and 1880s? William Torrey Harris; he trained teachers through his own normal school, discipline was very strict and emphasis was on a classical education. St. Louis schools were thought to be **among the best in the nation**.

What prominent woman helped establish the kindergarten movement in St. Louis? **Susan Blow**, daughter of Henry Blow, a civic leader of the 1850s who helped establish the St. Louis Philharmonic Society in 1859.

What was the purpose of the kindergarten? It was assumed that children reared in the homes were undisciplined scalawags. Children were taught silence, obedience, punctuality and self-control, which would help correct the problem.

What two groups fought range wars during this period of Missouri History? The cattlemen and the nesters (sod-busters) who wanted to fence the open range

What was the population of St. Louis in 1880? 350,518 – with 54,901 German and 28,588 Irish immigrants

What exclusive residence area in St. Louis was laid out in 1770? **Vandeventer Place**, with a ¾ mile long private street, became home for the *nouveaux riches.* It was a few blocks north of Olive and it extended from Grand to Vandeventer.

Who lived there? The Lionbergers, the Carrs, Henry Clay Pierce, Thomas Niedringhaus (founder of Granite City) Daniel Catlin (tobacco millionaire), Edward Mallinckrodt (ammonia manufacturer)

What were the five leading industrial products in the state in 1880? Flour and grist mill products, meat packing, foundry and machine shop products, tobacco, lumber

What were Missouri's three top agricultural products in 1880? Corn, wheat, tobacco

Faultless Starch Company was founded in 1887 at **Kansas City** and is still in operation.

Where did William T. Sherman live after his Civil War career? St. Louis, until 1886 when he moved to New York; he was brought back for burial in 1891.

The first cable cars in St. Louis were installed in 1886 on Locust, Olive, Easton, Broadway and Fourth streets.

What native Missourian became governor of Illinois during this era? John Peter Altgeld

The Democratic National Convention was held in St. Louis in 1888. To attract visitors, streets in the Shaw neighborhood were named for Grover Cleveland, his young wife Frances Folsom, and his opponent, James G. Blaine. Another street was named for Henry Flad, the man who helped Eads build his bridge.

In 1889, **Aunt Jemima** pancake flour was introduced in **St. Joe**, Missouri. **It was America's first self-rising flour for pancakes and the first ready-mix food to be distributed commercially**.

The Grand Boulevard viaduct over railroad tracks was completed in 1889. It took four years to build.

The St. Louis Terminal Railroad Association was formed in 1889.

What was the population of St. Louis in 1890? 451,770

Where did St. Louis rank in beer production in 1890? Second only to NYC nationally

How did Missouri get the name "the Show Me State?" A Missouri congressman, speaking in Philadelphia said, "I come from a country that raises corn, cotton, cockleburs and Democrats. **I'm from Missouri and you've got to show me**."

Absorene Mfg. Co. (wallpaper cleaner) was established at 209 Pine St. in 1891. The company later relocated to the old Mullanphy Emigrant Home and extensively remodeled it in 1938.

The People's Party, better known as the Populists, was organized in Missouri at **Sedalia** in 1892. The party argued for the abolition of child labor, the eight hour working day, equal pay for men and women for equal work, a graduated income tax and the direct election of U.S. senators. All of these items eventually became U.S. law.

The nation was hit by the depression of 1893, but a magazine writer noted that "St. Louis suffered no ill effects from the financial panic."

In what year did the Forest Park Highlands open? 1896, just in time for the 1904 Fair

In the 1890s, Swift Packing Company built a plant in **St. Joseph** giving a big boost to its fledgling stockyards.

By 1899, St. Louis had 26 shoe factories employing more than 5,500 workers.

What was the population of St. Louis in 1900? 575,238 – ranking 4TH in the USA behind New York, Chicago and Philadelphia. St. Louis was at its zenith in this decade.

Popular brands of chewing tobacco at this time were My Wife's Hat, Scalping Knife, Lock and Chain and Wiggletail Twist.

What was the largest brewery in the world in 1900? Anheuser-Busch took up 50 square blocks in south St. Louis

After the 1900 streetcar strike, where 15 people were killed in riots, what label was applied to St. Louis? **America's Worst Governed City**

What governor from **Gallatin**, elected in 1900, had 8 children, with 6 dying in infancy and none living past the age of 7? Alexander Dockery, whose wife also died while he was in office

When did Missouri reach its apex in terms of rural population? 1900, with 2 million people living on farms

How many steamboats were left on the Mississippi by 1900? Only about 300

Why is **Carl Schurz** a prominent Missouri figure? He started out as a newsman in St. Louis and ended up becoming a U.S. Senator (1869-75) – the first German-born man to achieve that distinction.

Schurz came to America shortly after the famous failed Revolutions of 1848. He became co-owner of the *Westliche Post*, the largest German language newspaper in the country. Schurz (a liberal Republican) was appointed Secretary of the Interior by President Hayes in 1877.

What was his most famous quote? "Our country right or wrong. When right, to be kept right; when wrong to be put right." This was a twist on Stephen Decatur's, "My country, may she always be right, but right or wrong, my country." His name and face are on a four cent stamp. Also, at the University of Missouri, a residence hall bears his name.

According to tradition, what is one supposed to do When passing under the archway of the Memorial Union at the University of Missouri? Tip one's hat

How did Lackland Avenue receive its name? The street is named for Rufus Lackland, a wealthy St. Louisan and major stockholder in the St. Louis Gaslight Co.

What happened to Grand Avenue when streetcars were electrified in the 1890s? It went from residential to commercial.

What did elegant homes or this era have instead of garages? Carriage houses

What was the shocking Meeks murder at **Milan,** in Sullivan County, on May 18, 1894? Gus Meeks, his wife, and three children were brutally murdered and thrown into a shallow grave. One daughter, Nellie Meeks, miraculously survived, threw off the dirt and straw and ran to tell her neighbors. William and George Taylor were convicted of the crime. The Meeks were going to testify against the Taylors in a court matter. William was a prominent banker. Both brothers disappeared soon after the tragedy, but were captured a month later in Arkansas. William Taylor was hanged at **Carrollton** on April 30, 1896, but George escaped due to the carelessness of the sheriff, who was nearly lynched by an angry mob. He was never captured. Nellie grew to womanhood and married Albert Spray of **North Salem**. She died in 1910 shortly after giving birth to a daughter.

What famous great-grandson of President John Quincy Adams lived in **Kansas City** around 1900? John Q. Adams, the son of Charles Francis Adams

What black piano player and composer was entertaining people in **Sedalia** brothels in 1900? Scott Joplin – who remained largely undiscovered until 1973 when his music was featured in the movie, *The Sting*.

The first battleship *Missouri* was completed in 1901. It had a top speed of 18 knots and carried a contingent of 561 crew and officers. It was part of the Great White Fleet that Roosevelt sent around the world. The ship was never in battle and was scrapped in 1922 due to an arms reduction treaty.

What was the "**Missouri Idea**" that gained national attention around 1904? In essence it stated that the only thing required for the well being of a state was that honest leaders enforce plain and basic laws. The progressive concept was cobbled together by Governor Joseph Folk. Folk, a Democrat, saw his name mentioned often by the national press as a possible presidential candidate.

How did Anheuser-Busch become connected to the famous painting of "**Custer's Last Fight**?" Cassily Adams did the painting, but the brewery company paid him $35,000 for the right to reproduce and distribute it. Placed behind the bar in hundreds of thousands of saloons, the painting, with the Anheuser-Busch name at the bottom, became one of America's most recognized works.

What infamous article about corruption in St. Louis was written in 1902 by Lincoln R. Steffans? "Tweed Days in St. Louis" in *McClure's Magazine.* St. Louis was a corrupt city back then and Irish politician Ed Butler was among the most notorious.

Who was James Campbell? He was a turn-of-the-century millionaire who owned large amounts of land and invested in railroads, streetcars and public utilities. He lived at Westmoreland Place.

Who was Joseph McCullagh? He was the owner and publisher of the *Globe-Democrat.*

What town, near Sikeston, was declared the **Watermelon Capital of the World** at the 1904 fair? **Blodgett**, where the current Beggs Family Farm is located; visitors love going through the 12 acre corn maze. 573-471-3879

By 1904, St. Louis, the nation's **fourth largest city**, was the world's largest producer of beer, shoes, stoves, wagons and several other products.

W.H. Ray was a midget from **Hornersville** who was dressed up to personify Buster Brown, the little boy comic strip character, for the Brown Shoe Company at the St. Louis World's Fair of 1904. The 42-inch tall Ray and his 37- inch wife were billed at Sells Brothers Circus as the **World's Smallest Couple**.

MISSOURI HISTORY: 1904-1940

CARING FOR THE POOR IN YE OLDEN TIMES

In this day and age of the "welfare state," it is hard to imagine the financial difficulties faced by our antecedents. Most Missouri counties, by the turn of the century, had a "poor farm." And every town had a "potters field" where those with no means of support were buried. I grew up in 1940s and 50s in **East St. Louis** and vaguely remember a potters field over by Bunkum Road.

Dwight Davis

A check of old county record books reveals a bit of insight into the manner in which these problems were handled. It must be remembered that these were the days of "rugged individualism," before New Dealism came up with the concept of social security, make-work projects and welfare payments.

Children who had no parents or relatives to look after them were sent to orphanages. Most counties had a panel of three judges who appointed someone to be an "overseer of the poor" for a particular township. It was the duty of auditors to see to it that the accounts were in good order and that the money was spent frugally. The county was required to look after and give aid to the poor, usually referred to back then as paupers. The amount of help the counties could provide was always meager.

Records indicate that all of the money expended in one year for a single county would not equal that given to a single family today. At one such meeting, the minutes show that Conrad Murphy was allocated $3.00 for the care of a Mrs. Willoughby. Another man was given enough specie (hard money) to buy a shirt, a pair of pantaloons and socks for a certain James Sanders. Another man, named O'Brien, was allocated $8 for making a coffin for "old Mrs. Adams."

Indenturism was still alive in 1826, for records tell about a John Osgood, age 12, being "bound out" or "sold out" to a certain Abraham Tilghman until the age of 21. Most certainly, this meant that Tilghman was to provide food, clothing and shelter, in return for work on the farm.

In *The American Commonwealth*, James Bryce said that governance in the cities was the one great failure of the American Experiment. St. Louis, full of municipal corruption, was a prime example of his thesis. Yet, St. Louis was growing substantially in population and was still producing wealth. A leading commercial and agricultural center, the city was second only to Chicago as a leading rail center. With a population of 575,238 in 1900, it was fourth behind New York, Chicago, and Philadelphia. St. Louis, **St. Joseph**, **Kansas City**, and **East St. Louis** were all major packing house complexes. St. Louis ranked fourth in overall industrial production. However, the city lost its national milling title to Minneapolis. It ranked fifth in beer production, behind New York, Chicago, Philadelphia and Milwaukee. There were about nineteen breweries operating in the city in 1900. Anheuser-Busch, with its huge complex, boasted the largest beer plant in the world. Adolphus Busch, a German immigrant, married Lilly Anheuser in 1861 and after the Civil War captured a large share of the southern market by pioneering in the use of refrigerated railroad cars. He introduced pasteurized beer in 1871. His sales jumped when he introduced a beautiful label that made his product resemble a wine bottle. He increased sales by giving away pocket knives with the company logo.

St. Louis was also known for dress making, furniture making, shoe manufacturing, book publishing, lumber products and periodical publishing. By 1904, Liggett and Myers had moved to North Carolina, but its Mill Creek Valley plant still led the world in production. The American Wine Company, at Cass and Garrison, was producing nearly 19,000 bottles of spirits a day.

The wholesale grocery trade and dry goods trade gave St. Louis a number of philanthropic millionaires, including Wayman Crow, who helped found Washington University. Washington University was so named because its charter date happened to be on February 22 (Washington's birthday) in 1853. S.C. Davis was another big dry goods wholesaler who also sold boots and shoes. One of his grandsons, **Dwight Davis**, became Secretary of War in 1925. He also established the **Davis Cup competition and the tennis center in Forest Park is named for him**.

St. Louis's first and largest department store was operated by William Barr. Located in the old Railway Exchange Building, it occupied an entire block, bounded by Sixth, Seventh, Olive and Locust streets. The company's principal rivals were Grand Leader (Stix, Baer and Fuller) and the Famous Company. Hargadine and McKittrick, owners of the Barr Company, built the city's tallest building in 1908, the 24-story Railway Exchange. Sol Loewenstein and Jaccard were the city's largest wholesalers in the watch, silverware, jewelry and clock business.

Life was hard for the working class in 1900. Only about 23 percent of St. Louisans owned their homes. Slums were prevalent. A smoke pall hung over the city due to the prevalence of soft, sulfur-ridden, Illinois coal that was burned in homes and factories. The famous Irish "Kerry Patch" area, on the north side, was notorious for its poverty and violence. Lucas Place, Carr Square and Lafayette Square, once prominent islands where the *hoi poloi* lived, were beginning to decline. Vandeventer Place, Clayton, Westmoreland Place and Compton Heights were on the rise. **The deed restrictions in Compton Heights were the first in Missouri** and were soon emulated by other neighborhoods. In 1903, *National Magazine* said that St. Louis outranked all other cities when it came to ostentatious homes.

Tony Faust's Restaurant (David Lossos collection)

In April of 1966, Mayor A.J. Cervantes rode in a motorcade around the perimeter to celebrate historic preservation at Compton Heights, which became an even more isolated neighborhood with the construction of 1–44.

Cable cars were introduced on the city's streets in 1896 and street cars were common by the 1890s. Grand Avenue was rapidly changing from residential to com-mercial. Castle-like homes were owned by tin maker Thomas Niedringhaus (founder of **Granite City**), Wiggins Ferry heiress, Mary Scanlan, ammonia maker Ed-ward Mallinckrodt and tobacco millionaire, Daniel Catlin.

James Neal Primm notes that it was Erastus Wells who built a narrow gauge railroad that allowed the country squires to live in the west and have easy access into the city. The train went by Wells' home, hence **Wellston**.

William Reedy, an escapee from the Kerry Patch, became the publisher of the highly respected literary magazine, *The Mirror*. The *Post-Dispatch* was becoming famous for its muckraking articles against big business barons and corrupt officials. Joseph McCullagh, of the *Globe-Democrat*, was a Republican mouthpiece, but still managed to fire broadsides at both parties.

Homer Phillips Hospital

A bitter transit strike gave the city a big black eye in 1900. Strikers and their families threw dead frogs at scab workers, cut trolley lines and piled timbers and garbage on the tracks to block passage. **A vicious battle on June 10 left three dead and fourteen wounded**.

In 1905, Governor Folk signed the state's first compulsory school attendance law for youngsters between the ages of eight and fourteen. That same year, racing horses for the purpose of betting was also banned.

In 1908, Henry Perry, who would become known as the **Father of Kansas City Barbecue**, began operating a barbecue stand in an alley by the Garment District of that city. As his business grew, he moved to 18th and Vine and ran his business out of an old railroad car.

What two reform political measures were adopted by Missourians in 1904? The initiative and referendum

What did Missourians do in 1904 that they hadn't done since 1868? They voted for a Republican (Teddy Roosevelt) in the presidential election.

What St. Louisan successfully prosecuted "Boss" Edward Butler and then became Missouri's youngest elected governor in 1904? Joseph Folk

What Missouri town set the state record for a low temperature in 1905? **Warsaw**, at -40 degrees; -40- degrees is the temperature at which the Fahrenheit and Celsius scales are the same (-40F equals 40 C)

How was the Terminal Railroad Association hurting St. Louis at this time? The Terminal Railroad, in St. Louis and East St. Louis, was owned by the 22 railroads that converged on the area. This association levied an additional charge on all freight that moved through the area. The Merchant's Bridge, built in 1888, and the Municipal Bridge, were efforts to circumvent this burden-some monopoly. Two years after its completion, the Merchant's Bridge, located north of the McKinley Bridge, fell under control of the Terminal Railroad Association.

The tradition of horse racing started at the Missouri State Fair in 1909 when Dan Patch raced Minor Heir.

In 1911, the Missouri AAA secures passage of the Hull law which established rules of the road. The Municipal Bridge (later the MacArthur Bridge)

opened in 1917 as voters approved a bond issue for $2.75 million, but another $1.5 million was required for cost overruns and approaches.

What group put up some of the extra money that was needed in return for free use of the bridge until it recouped that amount? Terminal Railroad Association

What happened to the Missouri Capitol Building in February of 1911? It was struck by lightning and burned. Voters authorized a bond issue of $3,500,000 to construct a new one.

By 1910, what other state had more of its native born people living in Missouri than any other? There were 186,691 Illinois-born residents living in Missouri.

When did Kutis Funeral Home begin operating in St. Louis? 1910 at 1006 Geyer Avenue; the company relocated to Gravois Avenue in the 1920s.

The city purchased Fairgrounds Park from the now defunct Agricultural and Mechanical Fair Association in 1910.

What Missourian became Speaker of the U.S. House of Representatives in 1911? James Beauchamp "Champ" Clark; **he is the only Missourian to hold that position**.

How did Champ Clark, the favorite, lose the presidential nomination to Woodrow Wilson in 1912? Clark, from **Bowling Green**, actually won a majority vote after the 9th ballot at the convention. But the rules said that a 2/3 majority was needed to win. William Jennings Bryan abandoned his friend Clark in favor of Wilson.

What man **made the nation's first successful parachute jump from a moving airplane** at St. Louis in 1912? A man named Captain Berry

Who was Mary Scanlan? She was the wealthy heiress of the Wiggins Ferry fortune. She lived on Grand Avenue and entertained notable guests to the city, including Mrs. Grover Cleveland.

How did the St. Louis Zoo originate? The St. Louis Zoological Society was organized in 1910. During Republican Henry Kiel's successful mayoral campaign, he advocated the establishment of a zoo. Dwight Davis opposed the zoo but Kiel didn't listen to him. By 1914, there were bison, elk, zebras, monkeys, bears, mountain lions and a kangaroo. St. Louis school children contributed pennies to buy an elephant. The bear pits were completed in 1919.

Who was **Homer Phillips**? He was a leader of the St. Louis NAACP at this time. The hospital for coloreds was named for him.

What was the main provision of the St. Louis segregation law of 1916? No person of color could move into a neighborhood that was more than 75 percent white.

The Orpheum Theater, at 9th and St. Charles, was built shortly after the war.

How did St. Louis get an immediate influx of hundreds and hundreds of Blacks on July 2, 1917? They fled across the Eads and Municipal bridges to escape the **East St. Louis** race riot that killed 39 Blacks and 9 whites.

Where was "Little Italy" at this time? 10th and Carr at Columbus Square

Why did Italians flee this area and move to "the Hill?" Coloreds began to crowd "Little Italy."

The company town of **Ilasco**, about a mile south of **Hannibal**, was built by Atlas Portland Cement. The name was an acronym for the materials used to make the product – iron, lime, alumina, silica, calcium and oxygen. Eastern European immigrants who lived here made the cement that was used to build the Panama Canal and the Empire State Building.

What Missourian was sent to the southwest to capture the Mexican bandit Pancho Villa? John J. Pershing was sent on a mission that was unsuccessful.

Who did a majority of Missourians support in the 1912 and 1916 elections? They preferred the Democrat, Woodrow Wilson, over Taft and Roosevelt in 1912 and Wilson again in 1916 over Charles Evans Hughes.

How did Republican governors Herbert Hadley and Elliott Major try to lead Missouri into progressivism during the years 1909-1917? They convinced voters and legislators that the role of government should be expanded to address problems in health, environment, highway improvement and child welfare legislation.

Where did these two men fail in their efforts? The legislation was passed, but then voters rebelled when they realized that enlarging the responsibilities of government meant a significant rise in taxes.

What Missouri senator voted against Wilson's request for war in 1917? William Stone was one of only six senators to vote against the war. Four of Missouri's members in the House of Representatives voted against the war.

What was Missouri's rank in the value of its food crops in 1916? Fourteenth, but by 1917 it had jumped to fifth.

In 1916, August Busch Sr. built **Bevo Mill** on Gravois, which quickly became a landmark. The sixty foot windmill building cost $250,000 to build.

1920: the Missouri AAA began sponsoring the school boy safety patrol program with orange belts and silver badges.

During World War I, Berlin Avenue had what name change? It became Pershing Avenue.

When did the top three St. Louis car makers go out of business? The Moon and Dorris called it quits in 1926 and the Gardener went out of business in 1932.

Why was the Soldiers Memorial at 13th and Pine built? To honor the veterans of the Great War (World War I)

When was the memorial built? During the Depression by the WPA

How many St. Louisans were killed in the Great War? 1,075

How many Missourians participated in the war effort and how many of them were killed? 140,257 men were mustered into the service (one-third were volunteers) with 3,466 of them being killed.

What Missouri man was in charge of the draft during the war? General E. H. Crowder

Northside Catholic High in St. Louis (David Lossos collection)

How well did Missourians respond to the sale of war bonds during World War I? The state oversubscribed its quota for all five loans.

During the war, Missouri farmers increased their grain production by 87 percent. Monsanto and Mallinckrodt Chemical experienced prosperous growth because the war cut off access to German chemicals.

When World War I ended, how many St. Louisans came back from the war in 1918? About 30,000, including members of the Missouri 138th Infantry; in all, about 156,232 Missourians served in the war including Harry Truman who was with the "Brave 35th " Division.

When the victory parade for World War I was held, how many women fainted, according to estimates? As the parade progressed, they swooned at the rate of one a minute. Was fainting really that big of a problem back then? Apparently so. Many Missouri households had what were commonly known as "fainting couches."

By 1917, thanks to efforts by the WCTU and the Anti-Saloon League, 96 of Missouri's 114 counties had voted to become "dry."

Prohibition was difficult for local brewers to swallow. What helped Falstaff and Anheuser-Busch survive? Falstaff made root beer soda pop and the Anheuser Company made pancake and waffle syrup.

It was estimated that there were 100,000 members of the Ku Klux Klan in Missouri after the war. As a group they saw America changing for the worse. They were anti-immigrant because most of the radicals and anarchists in America seemed to come from dissatisfied immigrants. There was evidence that they were behind much of the labor unrest and violence. The KKK strongly supported immigration restriction laws that were passed by Republicans during this decade. They were strong supporters of Prohibition and disliked the Irish and Catholics who opposed it. They abhorred Jews because they were non-Christians. The Bolshevik revolution in Russia led to Communist organizations dedicated to over-throwing capitalist governments by force. The KKK opposed godless Communists and spoke out against them. Nor did the KKK like black people, and they were vehemently against Blacks marrying whites.

When did St. Louis get its first setback (stair-step) skyscraper? 1924 – The Southwestern Bell Company

With what other phone company did Bell merge? Kinloch Phone Company

The dog race track at Hanley Road and Olive was a magnet for gamblers, pickpockets and bootleggers during the 1920s.

When was the MoPac Building built? March of 1927, a few blocks up the street from the current phone building

What big building on Lindell went up shortly thereafter? The Park Plaza Hotel

What new St. Louis suburbs were built in the Twenties? Richmond Heights, Clayton and St. Louis Hills

The Chain of Rocks Amusement Park, at 10783 Riverview, opened in 1926. It was high on a bluff, offering a spectacular view of the Mississippi River, the water treatment plant and the Chain of Rocks Bridge. It had a fun house, an arcade, a carousel, a Ferris wheel, The Octopus Ride, bumper cars, a picnic area, a wooden roller coaster, a swimming pool and various other attractions. A steel roller coaster called the Mad Mouse, featuring sharp turns, was built in 1959. The park closed in 1977.

What street marked the limits of St. Louis in the Twenties? Big Bend – anything west of that and people thought you had moved to Springfield.

How much did a five room bungalow cost in 1927? $3,200

How much did a decent pair of shoes cost in 1927? $3

Who was the recognized "Toastmaster of St. Louis" in the Twenties? Ed Lowry of the Ambassador Theater

When did St. Louis get its first Drive-in restaurant? It was the Parkmoor on 6737 Clayton Road, 1930

When did St. Louis get its first two radio stations? KSD arrived in 1922 and KMOX in 1925. WEW, at St. Louis University, began broadcasting in 1923.

When did St. Louis get its first air service from New York? 1927 – Trans-continental Air

What was unusual about the service? Passengers rode a train at night to Columbus, Ohio, and flew from there the next morning to St. Louis. Radar was yet to be invented.

How were departing and arriving flights at Lambert Field announced? By megaphone

Who were the two stars of the 1926 Series-winning baseball Cardinals? Grover Cleveland Alexander and Rogers Hornsby

Who hit three homers for the Yankees in a single game against the Cards in the 1926 World Series? Babe Ruth

When was the last time a professional St. Louis sports team had won a title? Back in 1886, the St. Louis Browns led the American Association in wins.

Who wrote in reference to St. Louis and the Browns, "First in booze, first in shoes, and last in the American League?" Ernest Kirschten

Why was **John Pershing** in Kansas City on November 1, 1921? He was there to help dedicate the Liberty Memorial that was being constructed there. Vice-president Calvin Coolidge also attended.

In what year were Missourians first required by law to elect a county superintendent of schools? 1921 – for the purpose of improving educational standards

John J. Pershing

Where was the squalid and violent Irish "Kerry Patch" neighborhood in 1922 St. Louis? On the near north side

What European countries had the most immigrants living in Missouri by 1920? Germany with 55,776, Russia with 18,769, Ireland with 15,022, Italy with 14, 609, Great Britain with 14,272, Austria with 8,676 and Poland with 7,636

What type of controversial platform did Senator James Reed of Missouri use to win a highly improbable victory in 1922? He opposed Prohibition, denounced the League of Nations and scorned woman's suffrage.

During the 1920s what musician personified **Kansas City Jazz**? Count Basie

Lindell emerged in this era as St. Louis's showcase street with its wide boulevard, hotels such as the Coronado, Melbourne, Chase and Park Plaza, and magnificent structures like the Masonic Temple and Scottish Rite Cathedral.

What famous bank robber was arrested in 1925 at St. Louis? Pretty Boy Floyd, after he committed his first robbery

What St. Louis landmark opened in 1926 at 1103 Locust Street? Miss Hulling's Cafeteria; Florence Hulling invested her life savings of $600 to begin the business. When she grew too old, her son Steve continued the tradition. It went out of business a few years ago.

The Loews State Theater was built in 1923 and the Ambassador Theater was built in 1926. The Fox, Missouri and St. Louis theaters were all built in the Twenties. During this period the Imperial Burlesque Theater was located at the northeast corner of 6th and Pine. The St. Louis police headquarters were built in 1927.

What Missourian, from **Clay County**, promoted the Dempsey-Tunney fight at Chicago in 1927? Tex Rickard

What St. Louis high school at 1020 N. Grand was destroyed by a tornado? Central High School in 1927; Roosevelt High opened in 1925, Beaumont High was started in 1926 and Vashon opened in 1927.

What St. Louis suburb was hit by a tornado in 1927? The tornado touched down at **Maplewood**, headed northeast, crossed the Mississippi, and finally dissipated after wrecking a few things in **Granite City**, Illinois.

Why did St. Louis Union Electric build the huge power plant across the river in Cahokia in 1927? The facility produced a million horsepower with its huge turbines and six smoke stacks that were twenty-eight feet in diameter. Since the prevailing winds blow from west to east, the downtown area would be spared from the emissions. Locating across the river also eliminated the exorbitant rates charged by the Eads Bridge/Terminal Railroad monopoly. The company bought forty acres of land cheaply and saved $350,000 a year in bridge tolls. With its transmission cables under the river, it was only two miles from the center of its power load.

McKinley High School in St. Louis (David Lossos collection)

The Missouri Pacific Building in St. Louis (23 stories tall), near the current elevated part of routes 40/64, just east of the Sheraton Center, was completed in 1928. The 18-story Army Support Center, built in 1931, became a JC Penney warehouse, an Edison Brothers warehouse and, finally, was remodeled as the current Sheraton complex.

The 1929 film, ***St. Louis Blues***, starring Bessie Smith as a nightclub singer, has the only footage of this legendary singer in existence.

By 1930, what percent of Missourians lived in either St. Louis or Kansas City? One-third

St. Louis drops to 7th place as it is passed by Los Angeles in the 1930 census. The city now has a population of 821,960. This will be the city's peak figure as it slips to 8th place in the 1940 census with a slight decrease in population.

What was Missouri's population in 1930? 3,629,367 with 821,960 people living in St. Louis, 399,746 living in Kansas City, and 80,935 in St. Joseph, the third largest city.

St. Louisan Dr. Isaac Kelly was kidnapped in 1931 by gangsters and held captive for eight days at an unknown location on the east side. A grand jury indicted Mrs. Nellie Tipton Muench and four hoodlums for the kidnapping. The hooligans were killed, gangland style, on the east side, before they could be brought to trial.

Nellie lived at fashionable Portland Place and ran a midtown dress store (Mitzi Shop) that catered to the society trade. Her father was a Baptist minister and her brother was a judge on the Missouri Supreme Court. She was acquitted by a jury in 1935. Not long thereafter, she was arrested again and this time was sentenced to ten years in jail for claiming (at age 42) that she had given birth to a baby. It was revealed she had taken the baby from a young Pennsylvania girl.

For months and months no story dominated the newspaper columns like those devoted to her unsavory past as reporters relished digging up as much dirt as they could on this society dame to sell more newspapers. (See Kirschten's *Catfish and Crystal* for in-depth coverage of this topic.)

How and when was Lake of the Ozarks created? It was created when Union Electric built Bagnell Dam in 1931 at a cost of $33 million. **It was the largest artificial lake in the USA at the time.** Before the dam, the town of Bagnell was called the "Tie Capital of the World."

What river was dammed to create Lake of the Ozarks? Osage River; Bull Shoals Dam and Table Rock Dam were built in the 1950s by the Corps of Engineers.

What river was dammed at Branson to create a lake? The White River

How did Tom Pendergast of Kansas City acquire a fortune? In the concrete business

Why did Tom Pendergast go to prison in 1939? Failure to report substantial amounts of income to the IRS – the same rap that put Capone away

A 1936 heat wave in St. Louis killed 375 people.

Coal-smoke polluted skies over St. Louis were so bad in December of 1939 that one particular foul day is remembered as **Black Tuesday**.

KANSAS CITY WORLD WAR I MUSEUM

The only national World War I museum in the USA is located at Liberty Memorial in Kansas City. It opened back in 2006 to rave reviews. This magnificent building houses more than 50,000 artifacts, ranging from documents to post cards, from uniforms to weapons.

The exhibits are viewed from a specially-built transparent walkway that goes over a no-man's land replica filled with 9,000 blooming poppies, symbolic of the fallen heroes.

The original museum was much smaller and was cobbled together from funds and artifacts donated by veterans. The

Great War Memorial was dedicated by President Calvin Coolidge in 1921. Future President Harry Truman, a war veteran, served on the decorating committee for the event. General John Pershing was present, along with top military leaders of Belgium, France, Italy and Great Britain. This is the only time in history where all of these great men were together at the same place.

The museum pays tribute to the role of women in the war who worked as nurses to attend to sickness, disease and injuries suffered by the valiant troops. There is a special exhibit that highlights the role of the Army Nurse Corps that became part of the American Expeditionary Force.

There is also a small theater which documents the war by showing actual footage and documentaries about the cataclysmic event.

One can also glean a spectacular view of the greater metropolitan Kansas City area by taking the elevator to the top of the building.

Pretty Boy Floyd

THE KANSAS CITY MASSACRE

The Kansas City Massacre involved the shootout and deaths of four law enforcement officers and a criminal fugitive at the Union Station railroad depot at Kansas City, Missouri, on the morning of June 7, 1933. According to the official FBI report, the incident occurred as the result of an attempt by Charles **"Pretty Boy" Floyd**, Vernon Miller, and **Adam Richetti** to free their friend, Frank Nash, a federal prisoner. At the time, Nash was in the custody of several law enforcement officers who were returning him to the U.S. Penitentiary at Leavenworth, Kansas, from which he had escaped three years earlier.

Vernon Miller (FBI)

The incident occurred in the parking lot in front of the east entrance of Union Station. As the agents and the prisoner began to climb into their car, they were fired upon. Officers Groom and Hermanson were killed immediately. Agent Caffrey was the next victim with a fatal shot to the head.

Inside the car, Frank Nash and Chief Reed were killed. Agents Lackey and Smith were able to survive by falling forward in the back seat of their Chevrolet. Lackey was severely injured by three bullets while Smith escaped unscathed.

Adam Richetti (FBI)

As a result of the infamous incident, President Franklin Roose-velt sought and received permission to arm all FBI agents.

The FBI later theorized that Nash, Caffrey, and Hermanson were accidentally killed by friendly fire from Lackey's shotgun, a weapon with which he was unfamiliar. The entire episode lasted only about 30 seconds.

When the attacking gunmen looked inside the lawmen's car, they concluded that everyone was dead. They began running for their getaway car. Just then, a Kansas City policeman emerged from Union Station and began firing in the direction of the killers, wounding Floyd. The outlaws jumped into their getaway car, sped away and disappeared.

A huge FBI manhunt ensued. Vernon Miller's mutilated body was found in a ditch outside Detroit on November 29, 1933. Police theorized he had been killed by a rival gang from New Jersey.

Richetti was arrested following a shootout near Wellsville, Ohio, on October 20, 1934. Floyd was found hiding on a farm in Clarkson, Ohio, on October 22, 1934. He was killed in the ensuing shootout. A watch with ten notches was found on Floyd's body, ostensibly carved by Floyd as an indication of the number of people he had killed.

Four other individuals who had helped plan the conspiracy were later apprehended. They were fined $10,000 each and received two years in the penitentiary.

Hollywood made a film about the Kansas City Massacre in 1975. The movie starred Dale Robertson, Bo Hopkins and Scot Brady.

Things were bad in Kansas City, but **Springfield was the site of the largest single massacre of law enforcement officers in U.S. history**. Six officers were slain on Jan. 3, 1932, by Harry and Jennings Young. The officers went to a farm at **Brookline** (near Springfield) to arrest the brothers, who were wanted for murder. Six men were killed in the ensuing gun battle and the brothers fled the state. A group of Texas Rangers trapped them in a Houston house and killed them with a murderous barrage of gunfire.

THE DOOLITTLE RAID: APRIL 1942

Former St. Louisan Colonel James Doolittle was a great hero. After Pearl Harbor, Americans were desperate to get a few licks in against Japan. On April 1, 1942, following two months of extensive training, 16 highly modified B25 medium bombers, with five man crews, were loaded onto the *USS Hornet* at Alameda, Calif. Each plane carried four 500 pound bombs and extra fuel tanks. Dummy guns were mounted in the tail section to discourage attacks from the rear. The *Hornet* joined up with a protective task force led by the *Enterprise*. The two carriers proceeded under radio silence towards their intended launch points in enemy waters near Japan. The group was sighted by a small Japanese ship so Captain Mark Mitscher launched the planes immediately, 200 miles farther from Japan than intended. The pilots were led by **Jimmy Doolittle**. None of them had ever taken off from a carrier but all 16 planes were launched successfully. They flew single file at wavetop level to avoid detection. They arrived at their targets around noon on the 18th of April. Their targets were Tokyo, Yokohama, Kobe, Osaka and Nagoya. No bomber was shot down or severely damaged.

After releasing their bombs the planes headed for landing fields in unoccupied China. Low on fuel and in rapidly deteriorating weather, most crash landed in China. Doolittle and his crew received assistance from an American missionary in China, John Birch, who later became the namesake of the conservative **John Birch Society**. The Japanese captured eight airmen and shot three of them. One died in captivity and the other four were freed by American troops in August of 1945.

Since Doolittle lost all 16 planes with only light damage done to Japan (50 dead, 400 injured), he told his men he expected to be court martialed. Instead, the raid bolstered American morale so greatly he was given the Medal of Honor and promoted two grades to Brigadier General. As of April of 2006, only 16 of the original raiders remained alive. The raid was the subject of two films, ***Thirty Seconds Over Tokyo*** and ***Purple Heart***. Doolittle Raid memorabilia is on display at the Air Force Museum in Dayton, Ohio.

Jimmy Doolittle

The 2001 film, ***Pearl Harbor***, with Josh Hartnett, Kate Beckinsale and Ben Affleck, ends with scenes of B-25 Mitchells taking off from the *Hornet* and heading for Japan. Say what you will about the love story, the special effects during the attack on Pearl Harbor are spectacular in this film.

As it became evident that the war in Europe was going to be won by the Allies, Hollywood shifted its focus to the Pacific Theater. Spencer Tracy portrayed Lieutenant Colonel James Doolittle in ***Thirty Seconds Over Tokyo***, a film that showed Americans paying Japan back for the treacherous raid at Pearl Harbor. Van Johnson, Robert Walker and Robert Mitchum were additional cast members.

GENERAL MAXWELL TAYLOR

Maxwell D. Taylor was born in **Keytesville,** Missouri, and graduated from the U.S. Military Academy in 1922. During World War II he commanded the 101st Airborne. On D-Day he jumped into France with his men and **became the first Allied general to land on the continent**.

During the Korean War he was Army Chief of Staff.

During the Little Rock desegregation crisis in 1957, Eisenhower ordered Taylor to deploy 1,000 troops from the 101st Airborne to enforce Federal court orders.

Taylor was critical of Eisenhower's over reliance on nuclear arms and sided with Kennedy's "flexible response" stance. Taylor became close friends with Kennedy brothers John and Bobby. After the Bay of Pigs, Taylor was made Chairman of the Joint Chiefs.

When problems in Vietnam came to the nation's attention, the Joint Chiefs favored going in with massive force with a plan to win. Unfortunately, Taylor succeeded in keeping these opinions away from the president which allowed Secretary of Defense Robert McNamara's dismal policy of "gradual response" to dominate.

Taylor succeeded Henry Cabot Lodge Jr. as Ambassador to South Vietnam in 1964.

Taylor died of Lou Gehrig's Disease in 1987 and was interred at Arlington Cemetery.

OMAR BRADLEY

Omar wanted to attend college but he couldn't afford it. After high school he started working for the Wabash Railroad in **Moberly**. One of his mentors suggested that one way to get into college was to go where they paid the students – West Point. He wrote a letter to his congressman, but was told that the principal appointment had already been given to someone else. The best he could do was an alternate. Applicants had to pass an exam and Bradley was afraid his study habits were weak because he had been out of school a year. He almost didn't take the test. Then he was afraid he had flunked. Weeks later he received a letter telling him that the other man failed the test and the appointment was his if he wanted it. He reported to West Point, on the Hudson River, August 1, 1911. Bradley graduated from West Point in 1915, the same year as Dwight Eisenhower.

During World War I, most of his colleagues were off to Europe while he was stationed in Butte, Montana, guarding the copper mines. By 1929, he had graduated from Command and General Staff School where he learned the basics of command from General George Marshall, then a lieutenant colonel. In 1936, he became Assistant Secretary to the General Staff. In 1942, Marshall sent Bradley off to participate in the fighting by giving him command of a unit in North Africa. For the first time in his 32 year career he was going off to war.

Omar Bradley first arrived in North Africa in February, 1943, but he was basically serving as Eisenhower's eyes and ears to correct what had gone wrong at Kasserine. It turned out that inexperience was the main problem.

Patton didn't want anyone looking over his shoulder so he convinced Ike to appoint Bradley as deputy corps commander. The great triumvirate was now in place – Ike the coordinator, Bradley the thinker and Patton the fighting machine. Bradley was given his third star just before the Sicily campaign. Thanks to a recommendation from Patton, he was commander of the II Corps. Bradley made a shrewd decision during the Sicily campaign. Instead of placing captured enemy Sicilians in POW camps, he allowed them to go back to their farms if they promised to quit the military.

Bradley established good relationships with journalist Ernie Pyle and cartoonist Bill Mauldin, creator of "Willie & Joe." Conversely, "spit and polish" Patton hated cartoonist Bill Mauldin and his unkempt, wisecracking, scruffy cartoon soldiers.

Bradley got to meet President Roosevelt in September of 1943 to brief the President on how our green troops had seasoned in battle. Roosevelt surprised Omar by telling him about the atom bomb project.

After the Tunisia and Sicily campaigns, Ike called him back to Europe to gear up for the Normandy invasion. Ike placed him in command of the Channel assault on D-Day. He was the American equivalent of Britain's Montgomery. Bradley described what it was like to observe the big battleships firing their salvos on D-Day. He said it was as if Zeus were hurling thunderbolts across the sky. Bradley thought the bravest man and most devoted soldier he ever saw was Brigadier General Theodore Roosevelt who resolutely braved death with indifference at Utah Beach and destroyed its terror for thousands of younger men with him.

An odd situation existed between Bradley and Patton after the breakout from the Normandy beaches. In North Africa and Sicily, Patton had been Bradley's boss. Due to Patton's demotion because of the famous soldier- slapping incident, the roles were now reversed.

His job in France was made more difficult when Ike, on several different occasions, told him to pull units away from Patton and give them to "Mr. Cautious," General Montgomery. What was Bradley's overall assessment of General Montgomery? Although Montgomery had a big ego and was often a pain in the neck, Bradley admitted he was beloved by his troops and was the master of the "set" battle.

Rare photo of Harry Truman and Jimmy Connors' grandfather, John Connors (Mayor of East St. Louis), giving Truman key to the city

What was Bradley's role in Operation Market Garden – the battle for Arnhem? Very little. Monty sold the idea to Ike before Bradley even found out about it. When he learned of the plan he opposed the ill-fated operation.

In retrospect, Bradley had one big regret concerning Patton. Patton was always begging for more gasoline. If it had been given to him, instead of Montgomery, there is a good chance his 3rd Army would have reached the Rhine by September of 1944 and ruined German plans for Von Rundstedt's final offensive known as the Battle of the Bulge.

Why did Bradley threaten to resign shortly after the Bulge? The press made it seem as if Montgomery had saved the day at the Bulge and clamored for the Brit to be given equal status with Ike. Omar told Ike he would quit if that happened. Fortunately, the truth came out that it was Patton who had saved the day – not Montgomery.

In 1950, Bradley was given his fifth star and made General of the Army. He reorganized the Veteran's Administration and then became Chairman of the Joint Chiefs from 1949-53. The man who was known as the "GI's General" died in 1981 at age 88. After Bradley's death, the U.S. Post Office issued a stamp in his honor.

Karl Malden played the part of Omar Bradley in the Academy Award-winning movie, *Patton*.

World War II General Enoch Crowder was from **Grundy County** and Rear Admiral Coontz was from **Hannibal.**

SOLDIER IN GREASE PAINT

Historian Bob Priddy gave the above title to Jane Froman. She was born in St. Louis and attended Christian College in **Columbia**, where her mother taught music. After graduating, she enrolled at the University of Missouri to study journalism. In 1927, she saw her name in lights for the first time when she grabbed the lead in a musical production. That landed her a contract with a week-long show in St. Louis where she shared a dressing room with a very young Betty Grable. Jane obtained a contract to sing on WLW in Cincinnati, and that led to a contract in **Chicago** with Paul Whiteman and NBC. Within six months she had her own show. She sang on five different occasions for President Roosevelt.

After the Japanese attacked Pearl Harbor, **she was the first entertainer to go overseas with USO troupes** Early in 1943, she was on a plane with other entertainers headed to Europe to entertain the troops. The plane crashed in the Tagus River in Lisbon, Portugal and she suffered severe injuries. Her left leg was fractured, her right leg was nearly severed, she had several cracked ribs, and there were multiple fractures of her right arm. It took 25 operations to keep her leg intact. Her hospital bills amounted to $350,000.

Later, in 1943, still in great pain, with her leg in a 35 pound cast, the 85 pound Froman sang for 3,500 soldiers in Boston. They gave her a standing ovation. In 1944, she was named to the Philco Radio Hall of Fame. After the war, she had recovered enough to go back to Europe and entertain the occupation troops. Congress appropriated $200,000 to help pay her bills. In 1952, she was given her own television show, "Jane Froman's USA Canteen." Actress Susan Hay-ward portrayed her in a 1952 film biography, *With A Song in my Heart.* Hayward did the acting and Froman did the song voice-overs.

Jane Froman

November 10, 2007, the 100th anniversary of Fro-man's birth, was declared **Jane Froman Day** at Columbia. For further read-ing see Barbara Seuling's recent biography of Jane Froman.

Missouri contributions to World War II were significant

in areas of leadership (Harry Truman, Omar Bradley), entertainers (Betty Grable, Jane Froman), and vehicle, airplane and ordnance production. What follows are a few other interesting tidbits about Missouri's ties to the war.

George Wightman, of **Sedalia**, was the **first American airman killed in World War II**. He was at Wheeler Field, trying to get his plane in the air, during the attack on Pearl Harbor. At the end of the runway he was hit by Japanese bullets, causing his plane to crash and burn. Wightman Air Base at **Knob Noster**, near Warrensburg, was named in his honor. It first was a base for B-47 bombers and years later ICBM missiles were installed in silos. Today it is home to **B-2 Stealth bombers** that look like a flying wing.

Major League baseball thought about canceling their season after Pearl Harbor, but Roosevelt urged teams to continue playing since it would be good for home front morale.

Sunday doubleheaders became the standard fare at Sportsman's Park in St. Louis because it cut down on the amount of travel. Due to gasoline rationing, teams were not allowed to travel to faraway places in Florida for spring training. Thus the Cardinals held their camp at **Cairo**, Illinois, and the St. Louis Browns practiced at **Cape Girardeau**, Missouri. Because of their proximity, they played against each other for practice games.

Baseball announcers were not allowed to talk about the weather for fear it might help the enemy. One time, when Dizzy Dean was doing a Cardinal game, it started to rain and he had to improvise. He said, "I cain't say what the weather condition is, but it sure ain't sweat the players are wiping off their foreheads."

Southwest High School in St. Louis (David Lossos collection

The origin of the famed Tuskegee Airmen, in part, has a Missouri connection. An African-American man named Cornelius Coffey trained Blacks how to fly at Harlem Field in Chicago. With strong support from the *Chicago Defender*, two of his pilots flew from Chicago to Washington, D.C, to lobby Congress for a Black fighter squadron. They met with Senator Harry Truman of Missouri and he promised them support. Under pressure from Truman, Eleanor Roosevelt and the NAACP, the Army Air Corps created the 99th Pursuit Squadron. The program came to be called "the experiment," and there were many in the military who wanted to see it fail rather than succeed.

Post-Dispatch weather bird

Quite a few navy people grumbled about the battleship *Missouri* being chosen, in deference to President Truman's native state, as the site of the Japanese war surrender in September of 1945. The ship saw limited action in the war. The *Missouri* was 13 stories tall, cost $100 million, had 16 inch guns, 16 inch armor, and had 15,000 valves, 844 doors, 5,000 light sockets and 800 telephone headsets.

Senator Harry Truman of Missouri made a name for himself during the war by exposing waste and corruption connected to wartime government contracts. He and his committee became the arch enemy of those who collected government money and produced a shoddy product.

During the war, St. Louis-born Betty Grable was voted America's favorite pin-up girl by American GIs. During the Battle of the Bulge, soldiers were asked to identify her husband (musician Harry James) to make sure they were Americans and not infiltrating Germans dressed up in fake U.S. Army uniforms.

What four star Missouri general commanded more troops than any other general in history? Omar Bradley, who became Chief of Staff of the U.S. Army in 1948

What St. Louisan was head of the War Department's personnel board? Malin Craig

What St. Louis private rose through the ranks to become a general? Walter Krueger

When was Fort Leonard Wood built? 1940 at **Waynesville**

When was camp Crowder built? 1941 at **Neosho**

For whom was the camp named? Missourian Enoch Crowder, who administered selective service in World War I

MISSOURI HISTORY 1941-1960

In 1944, the Jefferson Barracks Bridge was completed, connecting **Columbia, Dupo and East Carondelet** (Route 3) with south St. Louis County.

Dan Stewart discovered the bones of a duck billed, herbivore Hadrosaur near **Glen Allen**. In 2004, it was adopted as the State Dinosaur.

Why was the Municipal Auditorium in St. Louis changed to Kiel Auditorium in 1943? To honor St. Louis Mayor Henry Kiel

What was on the spot before the auditorium was built in 1934? It was the tavern where Frankie Baker shot her lover in 1899, inspiring the song, "**Frankie and Johnny**." It seems that Miss Frankie Baker, age 22, was a regular of the "tenderloin" or red light district on Lucas Place. Frankie died in a mental institution in 1950.

When did Life Magazine do a story on the KKK in the Missouri Ozarks? May 27, 1946

When did Missourians adopt their 4th constitution? 1945 – It was a bridge to the future, meant to enable the people to better manage problems in a modern world. Though amended many times since, this document still remains in force.

Harold Koplar was the managing owner of four St. Louis hotels – the Chase, Forest Park, Park Plaza and the Congress.

Archbishop Ritter desegregated St. Louis parochial schools in 1947. By law, public schools were still segregated.

St. Louis population in 1950 stood at 856,000 residents.

What 1950s television show told tales of a cattle drive between Texas and **Sedalia**? *Rawhide*

When did the Veteran's Bridge open? 1951 – tennis star Jimmy Connors' father was in charge of toll collections.

The Milkman, a 1951 film starring Donald O'Connor and Joyce Holden, had its world premier at the Fox Theater in St. Louis. Pevely Dairy had a major role in this production and worked closely with the producer and stars.

On Friday, July 13th, 1951, the Kaw and Missouri rivers overflowed their banks and flooded about five million acres in Kansas City. After the waters receded, about 6,000 dead hogs, cattle, cats, dogs and horses were hauled away.

Arch and Old Cathedral (courtesy William Weiss)

In 1952, Harriet Fordyce donated the 25-room mansion, Hazelwood, to St. Louis University for use as a retreat house. Harriet was the daughter of Daniel Frost. General Frost was in charge of the Confederate state troops located at Camp Jackson in Lindell's Grove. Frost ultimately surrendered to Lyon. She also donated a large sum of money to the school with a quid pro quo that Union General Nathaniel Lyon's statue be removed. General Lyon can now be seen at Lyon Park on South Broadway, near the Busch Brewery.

Ronald and Nancy Reagan were in **Springfield** in 1952 for the world premier of the film, *The Winning Team* - Grover Cleveland Alexander

Bobo Holloman pitched a no-hitter in his first major league start for the Browns in 1953, a feat that has remained unmatched. It was the only complete game in his brief career.

When was the current main terminal at Lambert Airport built? 1954

There was an inmate riot at the 120 year old state penitentiary in 1954. Four inmates were killed at the 47 acre Jeff City facility and thirty injured. Damages amounted to nearly $4 million in the stone purgatory that was built in 1835.

In 1955, voters in St. Louis passed a $110 million bond issue for civic improvement and slum clearance.

In 1956, Missourians voted for Adlai Stevenson in greater numbers than for Dwight Eisenhower. **Since 1904 to the present, this is the only time Missourians voted for the loser in a presidential election**, thus making Missouri the nation's foremost bellwether state.

The film ***Spirit of St. Louis*** was released in 1957 with actor Jimmy Stewart playing the role of Charles Lindbergh. Actor John Kerr turned down the role because he disagreed with Lindbergh's isolationist politics.

Interstate 70 opened in 1957 and it was dubbed the Mark Twain Expressway. When Interstate 55 opened it was referred to as the Ozark Expressway. When the Poplar Street Bridge opened, it was officially named the Bernard F. Dickmann Bridge for a St. Louis mayor in the 1930s. **There is a historical marker at St. Charles that indicates it was where the Interstate Highway System began**. From St. Charles, it headed in two directions, east and west.

CBC, led by Garry Garrison and Bill Eigel, won the Class L high school basketball championship in 1959

East St. Louis, Alton and **Desoto**, Missouri, are named All-America Cities by Look Magazine in 1959. Only 12 such cities in the U.S. received this award.

There was a 1959 strike at the *Globe-Democrat* that lasted for 99 days. The main issue was pension benefits.

Soccer was instituted at St. Louis University in 1959 and the St. Louis team **went on to win the national champion-ship** that year.

St. Louis ranked tenth in size (according to the 1960 census) and its population was down to 750,026.

When were the Plaza Apartments completed – St. Louis' first Urban renewal project? 1960 – Most of the Mill Creek Valley slums were torn down to make room.

MISSOURI HISTORY 1961 – 2008

Missouri Attorney General Thomas Eagleton condensed a 10,000 word proposal to unify St. Louis with the County down to 25 words. It was put on the ballot in 1962 and rejected by voters. If such a proposal were adopted in 2008, St. Louis would become the 5th largest city in the U.S.

Noted attorney William L. Weiss wrote a book titled, *St. Louis: Past, Present and Future*, citing many reasons why St. Louis and the County should be reunited.

St. Louisan **Ron Hunt** had his rookie year in baseball with the NY Mets in 1963. He finished second to Pete Rose as Rookie of the Year. Hunt was also the first Met ever selected to an All-Star team. He played for the Dodgers, Giants, and Expos, finishing his 12 year career with the Cardinals. He set a major league record for being hit by a pitched ball 243 times.

When did the St. Louis Plane-tarium open? 1963

In 1964, the tallest building in St. Louis was the 31-story South-western Bell Building.

In 1964, Myles Standish was the newspaper drama critic for plays at the downtown American Theater.

Clarence Gideon of **Hannibal** won a historic U.S. Supreme Court case in 1963 that said indigents had the right to free legal counsel.

When did St. Louis celebrate its Bicentennial? 1964

Who became Missouri's first two-time governor? Warren Hearnes, who took office in January of 1965

The last remaining streetcar lines in St. Louis were abandoned in 1966.

What St. Louis County supervisor stopped the East-West Gateway Council plan to build a new regional airport in the **Columbia-Waterloo** area of Illinois in 1967? Gene McNary

What Democrat was elected Missouri's U.S. Senator in 1968? Thomas Eagleton; he did not seek a fourth term in 1986; Eagleton died in March of 2007, having previously been given a star on the St. Louis Walk of Fame.

Spirit of St. Louis Airport in Chesterfield

Kutis Funeral Home at this time was at 2906 Gravois. The phone number was PRospect 2-3000

What Democratic nominee for president put Thomas Eagleton on the ticket with him in 1972? George McGovern; both men were opponents of the war in Vietnam

Why was Eagleton removed from the ticket? It was learned that during the 1960s he had twice received electric shock therapy treatment for exhaustion.

What CBS documentary upset Webster Groves in 1966?

"Sixteen in Webster Groves" was an award-winning documentary focusing on the experiences of growing up and living in Webster Groves. Narrated by Charles Kuralt, the one hour program concluded that the typical middle America, middle-class town was superficially friendly, prosperous, progressive, religious, charitable and arts and education oriented, whose adolescent culture – with the complicity of the adult population – was clique-ridden, status oriented, hyper-competitive, hypo-critical, prejudiced and materialistic.

St. Louis Cathedral on Lindell (MHS)

When the documentary aired, many town citizens felt that their community had been unfairly portrayed. It was a dishonest portrayal. When the students were categorized as depressed, the program did not mention that the depression was temporary due to the death of a popular student.

In 1968, after the murder of Martin Luther King Jr., African-Americans demanded that the Kansas City schools be closed the day of his funeral to honor him. Officials refused and Blacks rioted causing looting (360 jailed) and millions of dollars in damages. Six African-Americans were killed during this time. There was no similar race riot in St. Louis or East St. Louis.

When was the speed limit on Missouri highways reduced to 55 MPH? 1974, under President Carter due to the Arab oil boycott

What Osage Beach resort, back in the 1970s, offered a ski trail with artificial snow? Tan-Tar-A – Lodge of the Four Seasons; Marriot's Tan Tar A is one of the most popular convention sites in the state.

Who designed Tan Tar A's golf course? 573-348-3131 Bruce Devlin

What is the Native-American meaning of Tan Tar A? It's Blackfoot for "one who moves swiftly."

Worlds of Fun opened in **Kansas City** in 1973 with 60 rides, shows and attractions.

Lambert's Restaurant in **Sikeston** started throwing rolls on May 26, 1976, and they have continued ever since. They also have a location in **Springfield**.

Who was elected governor in 1972? Christopher "Kit" Bond, who lost to Joe Teasdale in 1976, then defeated Teasdale in 1980. Bond defeated Lieutenant Governor Harriet Woods in 1986 and won again in 1992.

What was unusual about Bond's election in 1972? At age 33, he became Missouri's youngest governor

Prince Charles of the UK visited the Gateway Arch October 21, 1977.

Joe Shatto, the Grand Titan of the Northeast Missouri KKK Chapter, made a presentation about the KKK to a sociology class at NEMS/Truman State University in **Kirksville**. Downstairs in the Adair County Historical Society Building, which was formerly the town library, a bathroom door still read "Coloreds" until it was painted over in the late 1990s.

What is unusual about Kit Bond's son, Sam, completing a tour of duty in Iraq as a Marine in 2006? Bond is one of very few federal lawmakers with a child serving our country in the military.

In 1980, the U.S. population center was near **Desoto**, Missouri (Jefferson County), and in 2000 it was located in Phelps County near **Rolla**, Missouri.

By 1980, **Branson** had only six entertainment theaters.

Who was Missouri's Attorney General in 1980? John Ashcroft, who later was elected governor in 1984 and in 2001 was appointed U.S. Attorney General by President George W. Bush

What St. Louis church has the **largest amount of religious mosaics** of any in the world? The St. Louis Cathedral

Why did a vigilante group in **Skidmore** (1981) murder Ken McElroy in broad daylight? McElroy was a known bully who, for years, spent his time drinking, fighting, shooting people, burning down houses and abusing women – always somehow managing to escape punishment. He was shot to death as he sat in his Silverado truck, next to his wife. His wife was not injured.

Skidmore made the national news again in 2004 when Lisa Montgomery cut open the abdomen of pregnant Bobbie Jo Stinnett and stole her baby. M. William Phelps wrote about the incident in *Murder in the Heartland.*

What well-known conservative radio commentator's grandfather was a well-respected lawyer in **Cape Girardeau**? Rush Limbaugh, who was a shoe-shine boy at age 13 and later worked at KGMO radio

Ava Lanius gives 1980 commencement address at Lindbergh High

Who were Missouri's two U.S. Senators in 1980? Thomas Eagleton (D) and John Danforth (R)

What St. Louis company did Danforth's grandfather establish? Ralston Purina

Who was on Danforth's staff when he became Missouri's Attorney General in 1968? Clarence Thomas

How did this bode well for Thomas in the future? Danforth's considerable influence was critical for the controversial Thomas in winning U.S. Senate approval for his appointment to the U.S. Supreme Court (remember Anita Hill?).

What St. Louisan **started the Tree of Lights national campaign for the Salvation Army** in 1968? Ralph W. Coldewe of the Absorene Mfg. Co.

What happened back in 1970 when Danforth ran against Stuart Symington for a U.S. Senate seat? He was defeated.

What strange circumstances led to the election of Danforth as U.S. Senator in 1976? Symington retired. There was a three-way race for the Democratic nomination and Jerry Litton won the nod. Sadly, Litton and his entire family were killed in a plane crash (at **Chillicothe**) on their way to a victory rally in **Kansas City**. Hearnes replaced Litton on the ticket, but he was easily defeated by John Danforth.

Dick Gephardt (Library of Congress)

Whom did Danforth narrowly defeat for re-election in 1982? Harriet Woods of **University City**; had she not been so anti-Reagan in that election, "Give 'em Hell, Harriet" might have won.

What Missouri Democrat did Danforth crush in the 1988 U.S. Senate race? Jay Nixon; Danforth then retired in 1994 and Ashcroft won his vacant seat.

What position did Danforth almost achieve in 2000? Danforth, a political moderate, met with George W. Bush and expected to be named as his running mate on the Republican ticket, but Bush chose Dick Cheney instead.

Missourian **Nancy Cruzan** was in an automobile accident that left her in a persistent vegetative state. In a case that went to the U.S. Supreme Court, the justices ruled in favor of "the right to die" and her feeding tube was removed. She died 11 days later on December 26, 1990. Her father later committed suicide.

When was St. Louisan Richard Gephardt first elected to the U.S. House of Representatives? 1976; he retired in January of 2005.

What important positions did Gephardt serve in as a member of Congress? He was Majority Leader (1989-1995) and Minority Leader (1995-2003).

When did Gephardt run for the Democratic presidential nomination? Twice, in 1988 and again in 2004

Was Gephardt ever considered for the Vice-presidency? He was on the short list twice, but lost out in 1988 to Lloyd Bentsen and in 2000 to Joe Lieberman.

What Bill Clinton policy did Gephardt strongly oppose? NAFTA – North American Free Trade Agreement; Gebhart received strong support from organized labor.

The St. Louis Children's Magic House was started in 1979 by two young mothers. It was located in a 1901 Victorian house built for George Edwards, first president of A.G. Edwards brokerage firm. It has been consistently rated as one of the top children's museums in the country. A favorite attraction is the electrostatic ball. By touching it, one is given a "hair-raising" experience. The museum is undergoing expansion and should be ready in late 2008.

In 1985, the state legislature declared that the honey bee was the State Insect. The fiddle was declared the State Musical Instrument and the State "wiggle" was the Square Dance.

Where was the **largest enclosed shopping mall in the nation** when it opened in 1985? The four-tiered St. Louis Center that housed Famous & Barr and Dillards; St. Louis Center is currently closed but the Famous section (Macy's) put up a Christmas train window display in 2007. The big stores in downtown St. Louis failed because patrons prefer to shop at the numerous suburban malls where parking is easier. Northwest Plaza was once the largest outdoor mall in the nation.

Wendy Wiese of **Ballwin** became a news anchor on KMOX radio in 1986. Her first radio position was at **Montgomery**, Missouri.

Who visited **Columbia** in March of 1987? President Ronald Reagan

In March of 1988 Missouri held its first presidential primary.

In 1989, the crinoid was voted by the state legislature to be the "State Fossil." This particular creature was chosen thanks to lobbying efforts by a group of school students from **Lee's Summit.**

Where was the first Arnold Palmer-designed golf course in Missouri? Osage National Golf Club - Lake of the Ozarks

Where is the St. Louis City Museum located? Near 15th and Washington; it features lots of scrap metal items that kids can bang on and slide on. There are many slides (made of roller bars) to play on. It also has dinosaur remains, caves, an aquarium and more. 314-231-2489

In 1988, St. Louis was the nation's second largest inland port, with barge connections to 29 metropolitan centers around the world.

By 1990 **Branson** had 22 music entertainment theaters.

The 1990 population center of the U.S. was at **Steelville**.

How many people attended the 2007 annual St. Louis balloon races, held on September 15? Forest Park opened at noon, the balloons weren't supposed to start the race till 5 P.M., but by 3 P.M. all entrances were closed because the park was filled with 11,000 people.

Senator Jim Talent (State of MO Manual)

How did St. Louis lose millions of dollars and numerous jobs to New Jersey due to recent base closings?

The Air National Guard, which had long been located by the main airport at Lambert Field, was relocated by the Defense Department. Lambert was supposed to have built new facilities when they built a new runway, but failed to do so when money became tight. Had the new facilities been built, the Closure Commission would have kept the facility in St. Louis.

In a 2006 survey, where did Missouri roads rank, nationally, with truckers? Second only to Pennsylvania as the worst in the nation

What Creve Coeur native bought the *Sequoia*, the presidential yacht? Gary Silversmith, a graduate of **Ladue** High School. The first president to use the yacht was Herbert Hoover.

What mathematical formula determines the shape of the St. Louis Arch? Y = 68.8(COSH0.01X-1)

What is the technical term for the shape of the Arch? Imagine loosely holding a drooping chain at each end. The parabolic Gateway Arch is an upside-down version of the catenary.

What **Krakow**, Missouri, native started his acting career as a singing cop on General Hospital? Jack Wagner

Why did the Bosnian newspaper *SabaH* (Sunshine) move to St. Louis in 2005? Because St. Louis has one of the largest Bosnian communities in the United States

Jean Carnahan

Where is the center of the Bosnian community in St. Louis? In South St. Louis (Gravois and Morganford) near the area around Bevo Mill

What calamity befell Johnson's Shut-Ins State Park (in Reynolds County) on December 14 of 2005? The Taum Sauk Ameren/Union Electric reservoir earthen dam (on Proffit Mountain) collapsed, flooding the park with a massive tidal wave of an estimated billion gallons of water.

What criticisms were made of the reservoir's construction in a post-mortem report? The dam was doomed to fail - the foundation was not scraped clean of soil; rock fill was not compacted during construction; too much fine-grained material was used.

According to internet gossip, what caused the dam to collapse? A 1.8 earthquake at the New Madrid (MAD-rid) fault a few days earlier

What is the origin of the phrase Johnson Shut-Ins? Shut-in is another word for the gorge cut by the swift Black River current, whose valley was constricted, causing it to be narrow. The rhyolite/granite rocks located there are over a billion years old.

What was the purpose of Ameren/UE's hydro electric plant at the site? The plant generated electricity for peak usage by allowing water to flow through turbines and fall into a collection pool below. The water was then pumped back up to the top during non-peak hours to keep the cycle going.

How many truckloads of dirt and silt had to be hauled off to clean up the park, located in Reynolds County? 3,052 truck loads

Where is Route 66 State Park? Off Interstate 44 near **Eureka/Times Beach**

What other attraction is featured at the park beside Route 66 info? There is a section devoted to the Times Beach dioxin disaster.

What caused the disaster in Times Beach? A contractor, to control dust on the roads, sprayed them with oil that contained deadly dioxin. The federal government made history by buying out the entire town and forcing evacuation.

Who became Missouri's first Miss America in 1990? Debbye Turner, an African-American

What was the population of St. Louis in 1990? 396,685; the population of St. Louis County was 993,529.

The Timber Wolf at **Kansas City's** Worlds of Fun was ranked second best roller coaster in the world in 1990.

What president celebrated the 4th of July in Missouri in 1991? George H.W. Bush; he officially opened the Show-Me-State Games and visited **Springfield** and **Marshfield.**

What Russian delivered a speech at Westminster College (**Fulton**) in May of 1992? Mikhail Gorbachev

Missouri voters adopted an amendment to the state constitution in 1992. **Term limits** were imposed on the total length of service in the legislature to 16 years. A person could serve a maximum of eight years in the house and eight years in the senate.

What Democrat was elected Missouri Governor in 1992 and re-elected in 1996? Mel Carnahan; his opponents derisively called him "Tax Man." Carnahan. Mel was born at **Birch Tree** in central south Missouri.

Was anything flooded at Jeff City during the 1993 flood?
Yes, the state capital is on the Missouri River, which flooded.

What happened to the Greater St. Louis Air and Space Museum, established in 1982, at the Spirit of St. Louis Airport? It was devastated by the 1993 flood. This museum has been re-established at **Cahokia**, Illinois, in a hangar built in 1929 for Ozark Airlines.

In 1994, the Emperor and Empress of Japan visited St. Louis, costing the city more than $90,000.

In 1994, KSDK-TV weatherman **Bob Richards crashed his red plane** into the ground near Chesterfield Airport. Bob reportedly was upset that a woman he was seeing broke it off and then talked about him flying over and "buzzing" her house on the 'Steve and DC Morning Radio" talk show. The shock jocks were fired for once telling a woman on the air that she was "acting like a nigger."

In 1997, Michael Cuffey, state coordinator for the KKK, sought to help sponsor a program on station KWMU at the University of Missouri in Columbia. Cuffey submitted this message to be read on air: "The Knights of the Ku Klux Klan, a White Christian organization, standing up for the rights and values of White Christian America since 1865. For more information please contact the Knights of the Ku Klux Klan at Box 525, **Imperial**, Missouri, 63052. Let your voice be heard."

Officials at the university declined the offer, and the Klan filed a lawsuit which it lost when the U.S. Supreme Court refused to hear their appeal. University officials testified that they feared losing as much as $5 million from underwriters and donors by acknowledging KKK support on the air.

Where was a 98 car pile up in Missouri in April of 1998? Interstate 70 - near **O'Fallon** and **St. Peters**; 40 injuries but no deaths; obviously too many drivers on the interstate were tail gating.

Mel Carnahan

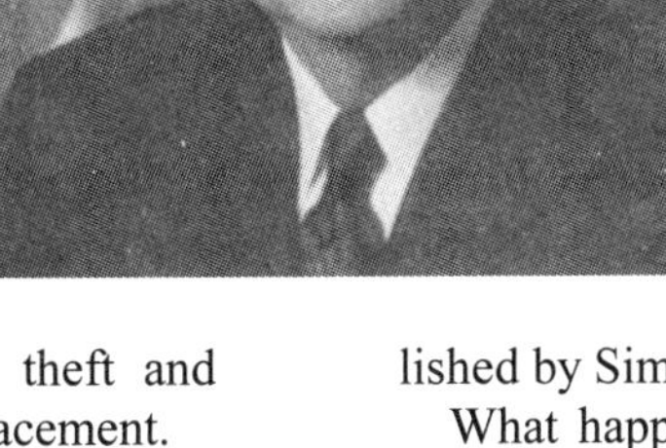

What St. Louis university has hosted several presidential campaign debates in recent years? Washington University (2000 – Bush-Gore)

In March of 2001, the U.S. Supreme Court ruled that the KKK would be allowed to participate in Missouri's Adopt A Highway program. Civil Rights groups said they would put up a billboard next to the KKK sponsored sign in an effort to promote diversity.

The KKK sign was erected on I-55 near **Arnold**, but after several replacements due to theft and vandalism, highway officials declined further replacement.

How many St. Louis schools were closed in 2003 as a cost-saving measure? Sixteen

When U.S. Congressman Tom Delay of Texas ran into ethical problems, what Missourian took his place in 2005? Roy Blunt became House majority leader; he had been the House majority whip.

What relationship is Matt Blunt, the current Missouri Governor, to Roy Blunt? Matt Blunt is his son.

Governor Matt Blunt

What happened to Missourian Roy Blunt's effort to remain the House majority leader in 2006? Considered the favorite to win, Blunt was upset by Ohioan John Boehner who promised a "fresh start."

What is Missouri Governor Matt Blunt's annual salary? $120,087

Why was State Auditor Claire McCaskill critical in 2006 of bonuses paid to those who manage Missouri pension funds? The Chief Investment Officer earns $190,000 and can increase that amount by another 50 percent, depending on how well he/she manages the money by investing it.

Is this salary more than the State Auditor earns? Yes – McCaskill's salary is only about $96,455.

What St. Louisan held the position of County Executive when he suddenly died of a staff infection a few years ago? Buzz Westfall

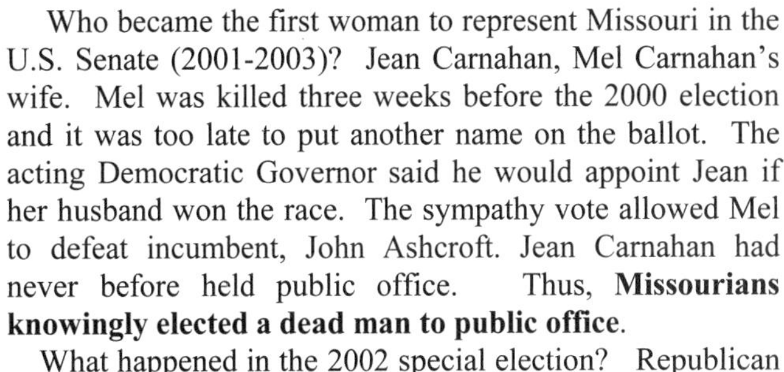

Who became the first woman to represent Missouri in the U.S. Senate (2001-2003)? Jean Carnahan, Mel Carnahan's wife. Mel was killed three weeks before the 2000 election and it was too late to put another name on the ballot. The acting Democratic Governor said he would appoint Jean if her husband won the race. The sympathy vote allowed Mel to defeat incumbent, John Ashcroft. Jean Carnahan had never before held public office. Thus, **Missourians knowingly elected a dead man to public office**.

What happened in the 2002 special election? Republican Jim Talent narrowly defeated Jean Carnahan.

What happened to Talent in the 2006 election? He lost to the Democrat, Claire McCaskill.

In 2004, Sarah Steelman (of **Rolla**) became the first Republican woman in state history to be elected to the office of State Treasurer.

The St. Louis Science Center, on Oakland Avenue, was recently named by Forbes Magazine as one of America's top 25 most visited museums.

What high school had a drama teacher resign (2006) because her students were not allowed to perform "The Crucible" (Salem Witch Trials) or "Grease" (students drinking and smoking)? Fulton High School

Where is William Jewell College? In **Liberty**

What Missouri Senator co-authored a book on terrorism in Southeast Asia with AP reporter Lewis Simons in 2006? Republican Senator Kit Bond – published by Simon and Schuster

What happened to worker Jimmy Belfield while he was painting the Jefferson Barracks Bridge across the Mississippi in 2006? Sadly, while trying to help three other painters dangling from safety tethers, he fell 90 feet and was swallowed up by the river.

Where is Missouri's only castle? At Ha Ha Tonka (laughing water) State Park in Lake of the Ozarks; it was built by a Kansas City businessman Robert Snyder in 1905 and he employed Scottish stone masons to insure authenticity. Snyder was killed in an automobile accident a year later and his sons completed the project. A fire, caused by a spark from a fireplace, gutted the castle and what remains today are the ruins.

Where is the largest factory outlet mall in Missouri? The 61 acre facility is at Osage Beach with about 110 stores. 573-348-2065

What recent graduate of Missouri State holds the NCAA record for best career free throw percentage in basketball? **Blake Ahearn** at 94 percent

Missouri native sons involved with NASCAR racing include Rusty Wallace (St. Louis), Carl Edwards (**Columbia**), Jamie McMurray (**Joplin**), Mike Wallace (St. Louis), Ken Schrader (**Fenton**), Kenny Wallace (St. Louis).

According to the 2007 movie, Jason Bourne's (Matt Damon) true identity was David Webb, who was born in 1971 in **Nixa**, Missouri.

About how many policemen are employed by the city of St. Louis? 1,200 – by contrast, New York City has about 30,000.

For what two companies has former Cardinal manager Whitey Herzog become the spokesman? Group Health Plan and Southwestern Hearing Centers

What is the average dollar amount of free meals and gifts given to Missouri lawmakers? In 2005, the average was $839.00.

Missouri U.S. Senator, Kit Bond

What unusual city ordinance concerning decibels was passed in 2006 by St. Louis aldermen? Persons with boom boxes of more than 140 decibels or cars with sound systems having over 300 amps could be subject to fines.

What was the 2006 name of the St. Louis entry in the National Indoor Football League? River City Rage which moved its home games from the Family Arena in St. Charles to the Savvis Center

What large St. Louis downtown department store was bought out and became Macy's in March of 2006? Famous and Barr

In 2006, my former 1957 classmate at East St. Louis High, **Benita Weissman Boxerman,** co-authored a book with her St. Louis County husband, ***Jews in Baseball***. Her parents ran a pharmacy on Caseyville Avenue, about seven blocks from where I lived.

What traditional African-American parade has St. Louis had for nearly 100 years? The Annie Malone Parade which usually draws 75,000-95,000 people

How many Missourians were killed in the March 13, 2006, tornado? Nine – the last March death in the state was in 1982. The deadliest of 113 reported tornadoes was at **Renick** where four people were killed.

In 2007, Connie Stevens was at work in **Boonville**, Missouri directing ***Saving Grace***, starring Tatum O'Neal and Piper Laurie. It tells about events that happened when she was visiting relatives in Boonville during the 1951 flood. Back in the 1990s, Missouri became the first state to offer tax credits to production companies in order to encourage films being shot within the state.

A young Jesse James

The now closed Kemper Military Academy was home to Chucky in ***Child's Play 3***. It was featured again in George Clooney's 1986 TV movie, ***Combat High***.

In January of 2008, Bill Nunes' daughter-in-law (Stephanie Strohman) performed in the Metro Theater Company's production of *Go, Dog. Go*! (book written by P.D. Eastman). She was also the props designer for the play. It was performed at the West County Family WMCA (**Chesterfield**) and at the Center of Creative Arts near the Delmar Loop in **University City**. She was also in the production of *Hanna's Suitcase*, performed at the Edison Theater on the Washington University campus.

The Wash U's men's basketball team won the NCAA Division 3 basketball crown in March of 2008 – the school's first such national title. The win for the 11th ranked Bears was especially satisfying because no Missouri or Illinois team made it to the NCAA Division 1 tournament, a rarity. Mark Edwards is the coach and the Bears were led by Troy Ruths and Tom Blount. The school also won 2007-08 championships in tennis and women's volleyball. Tuition, plus room and board at Wash U. in 2008 was $49,000 a year. When author Bill Nunes attended Southern Illinois University (1962), tuition was $180 a year.

According to meteorologist Cindy Preszler, rainfall in March of 2008 set a record and made it the **wettest March in St. Louis history with over fourteen inches**.

In February of 2008, Charles Lee Thornton shot and killed five people at a **Kirkwood** City Hall meeting. Two other people were injured, one critically. The berserk gunman was shot and killed when the police stormed the building. It is believed that Thornton's frequent clashes with council members at meetings, and his loss in a lawsuit is what set him off. His commercial vehicles had been repeatedly ticketed by officials for illegal parking.

YOU KNOW YOU'RE A MISSOURIAN IF . . .

What follows is one of those Jeff Foxworthy-type lists that someone sent me by E-mail - author unknown.

You think everyone from the big city has an accent
You failed high school geography because you thought Cuba, Florida, Nevada, Houston, California and Mexico were cities in Missouri
The phrase "I'm going to the lake this weekend" can only mean one thing
You go to Branson four times a year
You know in your heart that Mizzou can beat Oklahoma in football
You know in your heart Mizzou can beat Illinois in basketball
You rooted for the South to win the Civil War
You think **Jesse James** is a hero
The best thing on earth is sitting on your front porch during a thunderstorm
You'll pay for your kids to go to college, unless it's KU
You know what cow tipping and outhouse tipping are
You think frog gigging should be an Olympic sport
There's a tornado warning and the whole town's outside watching for it
The local gas station sells live bait
You measure distance in minutes
You've ridden the school bus an hour each way
You pronounce Missouri with an "ah" on the end
You know what's knee-high by the Fourth of July
You go fishing with quarter sticks of dynamite
You see people wearing bib overalls at funerals

Your four major food groups are beef, pork, beer and grits
You think a flannel nightie is sexy lingerie
You think deer season is a national holiday
You know which leaves make good toilet paper
You put a red bow on your car grill at X-mas
You have a squirrel tail trailing from you car antenna
Motorists only tap their brakes and roll through stop signs

MISSOURI TOURISM

For years, tourism was Missouri's third most important source of income behind manufacturing and agriculture. In recent years, it has significantly narrowed the gap.

Interior of the beautiful Fox Theater in St. Louis

What new attraction was added to Six Flags for the spring of 2006? Superman, the Tower of Power 636-938-4800

What new theme park was added? Bugs Bunny National Park

St. Louis has a Dental Health Theater that features a set of sixteen three-foot tall teeth that serves as an educational facility for youth. It is located on Laclede's Landing and **it is the only display of its kind in the world**. It is free, but reservations are required and presentations are 45 minutes long. 314-241-7391

Marthasville has an Annual Spring Mud Bog the second Saturday in June. Off roaders and spectators have loads of fun with this slop and sludge fest.

Crown Ridge Lodge in **Ste. Genevieve** is on a 5,000 acre winery which is also a tiger sanctuary. There is an optional tour where visitors can feed the tigers. 573-833-9909

The town of **Weston** bills itself as the "Town That Time Forgot." Located on the Missouri River, about 25 miles from Kansas City, the bustling town once was second only to St. Louis in population. Located on a wide spot in the river, it had an excellent harbor for steamboats. In 1841, Ben Holladay became the first postmaster and began operating a stage coach line. His holdings became so extensive that he became known as the "**Stagecoach King**," supplying numerous Mormon treks that went to Salt Lake City. William F. Cody even lived in the town for a while. The town was torn apart by the Civil War and further reduced by two disastrous fires and two traumatic floods. The 1881 flood changed the course of the river putting its main channel two miles away and ending all river traffic.

Yet the town refused to die and its many historic buildings have enabled Weston to become a popular tourist attraction.

Weston is home to the largest tobacco warehouse west of the Mississippi and it is the only place in Missouri where tobacco is still grown. Most of Missouri's cotton and rice is produced in the delta lands in the southeast part of the state. Unlike most neighboring states, Missouri produces almost no crude oil.

Glore's Psychiatric Museum in **St. Joseph has been declared one of the fifty most unusual museums in America**. It has a macabre collection of instruments and devices used to treat insane people over the past few hundred years. It all began in 1872 when the state was convinced by locals to build a Lunatic Asylum on the city's outskirts. The mentally ill were locked in cages, forced to take ice baths and given rides inside giant wooden spinning wheels. The brochures say that after you view these exhibits you'll come away glad that you're not insane (assumeing that you're not already crazy). 816-387-2310

Licking is noted for its water tower that is painted to look like a baseball. Some claim it's the World's Biggest Baseball. This is where all the baseballs in America were once manufactured before everything was moved to the Rawlings plant in St. Louis. The town was called Licking because it was near a buffalo and deer salt lick.

Where is the dog museum in St. Louis? It's at the Jarville House in Queeny Park. (314) 821-3647

The tiny hamlet of **Hornet**, Missouri, has a supernatural phenomenon known as the **Ozark Spook Light**. To those who claim to have seen it along a gravel road, called the Devil's Promenade, it looks like a flaming bouncing sphere about the size of a basketball. According to tradition, it was first seen by the Indians along the Trail of Tears. Some researchers attribute the sightings to will o' the wisps, a luminescence caused from decaying organic matter.

St. Clair, Missouri has two water towers. One is labeled hot and the other cold.

What is the big attraction at Mastodon State Park near **Imperial**? When woolly mammoths and mastodons roamed the state, some of them were trapped in the mud of the nearby mineral springs. When the ooze hardened to stone it preserved their remains. The Kimmswick Stone Bed is one of the biggest Pleistocene fossil deposits in America. (314-464-2976)

Brunswick is the self-proclaimed pecan capital of Mis-Missouri. George James, owner of the Nut Hut, began marketing a thin shelled pecan in 1955 which he named the Starking Hardy Giant. He put a giant 12,000 pound reproduction on display next to his store on Highway 24. Ripley's calls it the **World's Largest Pecan**.

What three Metro-east attractions are in Illinois, but are so close they are almost considered part of Missouri? Louis and Clark Interpretive Center in **Hartford** on Route 3 (618-251-5811); Cahokia Mounds State Museum on Route 40 near **Collinsville** – 618-346-5160; Raging Rivers water park north of **Alton** 618-786-2345

Beverly Hillbillies: their truck is at College of the Ozarks

The University of Missouri at **Rolla** has a **half scale replica of Stonehenge**, England. The megalith was created by engineering students in 1984 and was carved by high water pressure. It took one month to carve 160 tons of granite.

Richland has an unusual Bar B-Q and Steak House. It's called The Caveman and it used to be a Roaring Twenties speakeasy where liquor flowed and flappers danced the Charleston and Black Bottom.

What historic site has a petting zoo and is free, but charges $8.00 for parking? Grant's Farm - closed on Mondays 314-843-1700

Farris Truck Stop in **Faucett** features a complete tractor/ trailer on steel 50 ft. high pillars for advertising. It is located on Interstate 29, south of St. Joseph. The oddity was erected in 1976.

The University of Missouri at **Columbia** has a life-sized replica of cartoon character Beetle Bailey. Like Willie & Joe, Bailey was controversial because it was thought he fostered disrespect toward officers among enlisted men. In 1970, cartoonist Mort Walker introduced the character Jack Flap into the cartoon, making it the **nation's first integrated cartoon strip.** Walker is a University of Missouri graduate.

The World's Largest Gas Pump, two stories tall, is a roadside attraction in **King City** at 508 North Grand.

There is a rock farm at **Alexandria**, located in northeast Missouri near the Iowa border. Visitors can pay $15.00 to find their very own geode, a rock that contains dazzling quartz crystals. Betty and son Tim Sheffler run the place. When Ferdinand Marcos was in power, he used to buy Sheffler geodes to decorate his palace in the Philippines.

6th and Washington – Stix, Baer & Fuller on Right (MHS)

What town features a Wolf Sanctuary that features a slide and film presentation about wolves? **Eureka,** at the Wild Canid Center 636-938-5900

Walt Disney grew up in **Marceline** and the town has a museum dedicated to his memory. It is said that Disney's idea for the Matterhorn ride came from the slag heap of the town's coal mine.

In what town can one find Whiskey Jack's Museum of Prohibition-era Memorabilia? **Washington**

In what quaint German town can one find the Seven Sisters Bed and Breakfast? **Hermann,** which bills itself as **the Sausage Capital of Missouri;** Hermann also features a Grape Stomp at the Stone Hill Winery the second Saturday in August. 800-932-8687

What town has an Oktoberfest and the **world's largest wine hall**? **Hermann**, at the Hermannhoff Winery Festhalle; Hermann, on the Missouri River, was founded in 1837 on land owned by the German Settlement Society of Pennsylvania.

At what town, near Route 63, can one find one of Missouri's nine swinging bridges? **Vienna**, near Ball Park Road

What place in **Rolla** has over 60 antique cars? Memoryville, USA in Rolla (314-364-1810)

What brought famed oceanographer Jacques Cousteau to **Bonne Terre**? Old flooded lead mines with crystal clear illuminated water in the **world's largest manmade caverns**

Where is the Missouri Mine State Historic Site? Near Flat River, just east of Highway 67

Where is Our Lady of the Miraculous Medal shrine? At **Perryville** on Highway 61

Schindler's Tavern, in **New Hamburg**, is famous for its baloney burgers and a preserved 6-foot-10-inch gar caught in 1912. The town also has an annual Kowpasture Klassic charity golf event. Tennis balls are used rather than golf balls. 573- 545-3709

Where in southeast Missouri can one see an annual Civil War battle re-enactment? At **Jackson** near the Iron Mountain Railroad tourist excursion site

Where can tourists see a mill that has been in operation 190 years? Bollinger Mill at **Burfordville** on Highway 34 East; you'll also find one of four remaining covered bridges in the state.

Maxie is a 5,500 pound goose replica in **Sumner**, which calls itself the **Wild Goose Capital of the World**. Its Swan Lake National Wildlife Refuge is a huge stopover for large numbers of migratory waterfowl.

What museum at **Independence** has hands on exhibits for kids? Frontier Trails Museum

Queeny Park, in west St. Louis, is home to the American Kennel Klub Museum of the Dog, featuring such notables as Rin Tin Tin and Lassie. 314-821-3647

Jasper Giardina has an Antique Radio Museum at 2022 Cherokee in St. Louis featuring 10,000 radios. 314-421-8313

What happened to the old Museum of Medical Quackery on Lindell in St. Louis? It closed and the exhibit was moved to the Science Center at Forest Park.

Where is the most photographed water mill in the state? Hodgson Mill on Route 181 in Ozark County

Where is Powder Valley Nature Center? In **Kirkwood,** on Cragwold Road north of the juncture of I – 270 and I – 44 (314) 301-1500. It features a large exhibit center, an auditorium, a fish aquarium, gift shop and nature trails. Its name comes from the Civil War Era when a nearby cave was used to hide explosives in case of a possible invasion of St. Louis by Confederate troops.

Where is **Bennett Springs**? About 10 miles from **Lebanon**, off Interstate 44; there is a fish hatchery there and a nice spot for fishermen.

Where is the World's Greatest Sporting Goods Store (according to ads)? The Bass Pro Shop in **Springfield is second only to the St. Louis Arch, attracting over three million visitors annually.**

Churchill Museum at Fulton

Where is the best railroad museum in the state? The Museum of Transportation near I 270 and I 44 at St. Louis 314-965-7998

Where is the Missouri College of the Ozarks where students all work to pay their tuition? Point Lookout on Highway 65, not far from **Branson**

Where is the largest permanent Titanic museum in the world? The Titanic Museum in **Branson**

Does Branson have a World War II museum? Yes – but the Veterans Memorial Museum also covers other wars since World War I. It's the museum with the North American P-51 Mustang out in front. 417-336-2300

The Presleys at Branson

When this author first visited Branson in 1961, what were the only shows? The Baldknobbers and the Shepherd of the Hills play – plus Silver Dollar City

What are the main features of the Ralph Foster Museum located on the College of the Ozarks campus? A huge antique gun collection and the truck used by the Clampetts in the *Beverly Hillbillies* TV show, plus a Thomas Hart Benton painting, "The Departure of the Joads" (Dust Bowl) – 417-334-6411

What is the big attraction in old Downtown **Branson**? Dick's Five and Dime store on West Main featuring 50,000 items

Where can one get meals cooked on an antique wood-burning stove? At the Briar Patch near **Anderson** on Route 76 – 417-845-3925

Forest Park Tour Bus (Missouri Historical Society)

What three presidents have attended the State Fair at **Sedalia**? Taft, Truman and Reagan

Where is Missouri Bison World where you get to feed members of a herd of 1,000 animals? Missouri Ozarks, near **Potosi** – 573-438-4449

Webb City, north of Joplin, has a sculpted pair of 32 feet tall "Hands in Prayer." Jack Dawson is the man responsible for completing this religious work of art on Business Route 71.

How long is the KATY Trail? 200 miles long from **Sedalia** to **St. Charles** paralleling the Missouri River and it is part of the Rails to (bicycle) Trails national program (Missouri-Kansas-Topeka MKT Railroad)

What Missouri town has a 243 ft. long railroad tunnel that filled with 4 ft. of water in the 1993 flood? **Rocheport** – on the KATY Trail

What town is home to Stevens College? **Columbia;** founded in 1833, it is the second oldest women's college in the nation.

What was the first public university west of the Mississippi? University of Missouri at **Columbia**, 1839

What did it cost in 2006 for a student to attend one year at Mizzou? $14,308

Where is Lincoln University located? In **Jefferson City** on 52 rolling acres 573-681-5599

What is significant about the six Ionic columns that adorn the center of the Francis Quadrangle? They once supported the portico of Academic Hall, the first building constructed on the campus at Mizzou.

What relatively new theater in **Columbia** offers live music every Saturday? Lighthouse Theater – 573-474-4040

Where are the world headquarters of the Church of the Latter Day Saints? **Independence** – 816-833-1000

What are the six flags that fly over Six Flags theme park off Interstate 44 in southwest St. Louis County? U.S., British, French, Spanish, Confederate, Missouri

Where can you see a Civil War cannonball embedded in a courthouse column, a relic of an 1861 Confederate victory? **Lexington** 660-259-4711

What town has a Christopher Wren Church of St. Mary the Virgin that was brought from England and reassembled stone by stone? **Fulton**; the church houses the **Winston Churchill Museum**. 573-642-6648

Did Mikhail Gorbachev of the Soviet Union ever visit Missouri? Yes, he visited the Winston Churchill Memorial and library at Fulton.

What town hosts a Scott Joplin Festival every June? **Sedalia**

Where is Central Missouri State University located? **Warrensburg**, founded in 1871 660-543-4677

What town boasts Powell Botanical Gardens? **Kingsville** with 835 acres 660-697-2600

What **Carthage** bed and breakfast is in the Marble Home, built in 1900? The White Rose – also a winery and a restaurant – 417-359-9253

What Lake of the Ozarks town has the Morgan County Historical Museum? **Versailles** (pronounced ver-sayles)

Where is the 3,600 sq. foot aviary known as the House of Butterflies? **Osage Beach** 573-348-0088

What is the largest state park in Missouri? Lake of the Ozarks State Park 800-386-5253

What Lake of the Ozarks town features Fantasy Caverns? **Eldon** 573-392-2115

Where are Ozark Caverns? **Kaiser** 573-346-2500

Where is Bridal Cave, site of a legendary Indian wedding ceremomy in the early 1800s? At Thunder Mountain Park at the Lake of the Ozarks; more than 1,200 couples have been married at the cave's chapel. 573-346-2676

Painter Thomas Hart Benton

Where is Jacob's Cave? **Versailles**; it is the only walk through cave in Missouri that is handicapped accessible. 573-378-4374

What town features a yearly Cyclone Day in April with interesting informational displays about a severe and destructive storm that hit the area in the 1800s? **Kirksville** – 660-665-6502

What town features a Frontier Shootout in April where visitors can test their skill with a cap and ball revolver? **Kearney** – 816-628-6065

Where is Summit Lake Winery? **Holts Summit**, Missouri – 573-896-9966

What town has a reconstructed 1850s village with more than 30 structures? **Blue Springs** 816-795-8200

Where is the oldest Thespian Hall west of the Alleghenies? **Boonville** – 888-588-1477

What German-American town holds a Maifest and an Octoberfest? **Hermann** 800-932-8687

What town bills itself as the "place that time forgot?" Quaint little **Kimmswick**. Kimmswick was founded in 1859 by a German immigrant named Theodore Kimm who was also the town's postmaster.

Princess Theater on Grand near Olive (Missouri Historical Society)

What winery is located near Tower Rock in the Mississippi? Tower Rock Winery at **Altenburg** – 573-824-5479

What Missouri town features Persimmon Hill Berry Farm? **Lampe** – with a tempting and delicious array of jams and jellies and more (800-333-4159)

What town has Liberty Farms featuring 11 acres of blueberries, blackberries and nearby wineries? **Farmington** (537-756-2860)

What town boasts Huckleberry Hollow's U-PICK-IT Farm with neat rows of succulent berries amid wandering chickens and peafowl? **St. Clair** (636-629-0668)

What town features a berry picking farm with a beehive under glass to watch honey making? **Cleveland's** The Berry Patch (816-618-3771)

What town, an hour west of St. Louis, features berries and friendly farm animals for petting? Thierbach Orchards at **Marthasville** (636-433-2299)

Where is **St. James Winery**? It's at St. James on the north side of Interstate 44. 800-280-9483

Where is the Dalton Gang Homestead in Missouri? **Red Oak II** a restored rural town northeast of Carthage on Route 1 (417-358-9018)

What town features Lakeview Farms, with you-pick berries and kid activities that include hunting for gem stones and a Bonnie and Clyde-themed treasure hunt? **St. Peters** (636-978-8830)

Where is the Jesse James Bank Museum? **Liberty** (816-781-4458)

Where is the last 19th century woolen mill with original equipment in America? **Lawson** 816-296-3357

What is unique about **Jamesport**? It has the state's biggest Amish community. 660-684-6146

What former Jesse James home town holds an annual festival every September? **Kearny** (816-635-4506)

Where is the only iron/ manganese mineral water springs in the USA? **Excelsior Springs** 816-637-0753

Where are Missouri's old-time carousels located? Silver Dollar City, Perryville, Eureka, St. Louis Zoo and Independence

What bed and breakfast in **Fulton** is situated in one of the most beautiful Victorian houses in the Midwest? Romancing the Past – (573-592-1996) William Woods University, Westminster College, and the Winston Churchill Library are only blocks away.

In what year was Onondaga Cave discovered? Originally discovered by Daniel Boone, it was rediscovered in 1886 by Charles Christopher, John Eaton and Mitis Horine; it is one hour southwest of St. Louis off I-44 near **Leasburg**. The park is open year round but cave tours are not held during the winter. 573-245-6600

Was the cave a tourist attraction for 1904 Fair visitors? Yes! Showman Lester Dill acquired the cave in the 1950s and the state of Missouri bought it in 1982.

What is the name of the river that meandered through the openings in the dolomite rock, forming the Onondaga cave over a period of several million years? Lost River because its origin was unknown

How did the name Onondaga come to be applied to the cave? Myrtle Land submitted the winning entry in a naming contest. It is an Iroquois word that means "spirit of the mountain."

What proposed dam in 1967 would have flooded most of the cave? A dam on the Meramec River; Missourians protested so loudly that the project was abandoned.

What owner of Meramec Caverns bought the cave in 1953 and promoted it as a Jesse James hideout? That great showman and exaggerator, Lester Dill

The Big Room at Onandoga Cave is second only to Marvel Cave as the largest cave room in Missouri.

Where is Marvel Cave? Silver Dollar City on the outskirts of West **Branson**

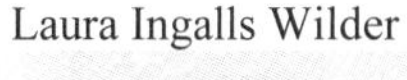
Laura Ingalls Wilder

MISSOURI ARTISTS AND WRITERS

Were Missouri's two Thomas Hart Bentons related? Benton, the painter, was a great nephew of Benton, the politician.

For what type of painting is Benton most noted? Murals

Where can one find the best exhibit of Benton's murals? On the walls of the house lounge in Jefferson City; Benton was paid $5,000 in 1936 to execute it.

Why was the mural controversial? Along with traditional scenes it depicts racism and vigilante hangings and other messy and corrupt things Missourians did in building the state.

What is Thomas Hart Benton's most erotic painting? *Persephone* – showing a voluptuous naked girl about to be dragged off to Hades on an old farm wagon.

Artist George Caleb Bingham

In what year did the WPA's *Missouri: A Guide to the Show Me State* get published? 1941; It can be purchased new on Amazon.com or used on E-bay.

What **Olivette** native is the head writer for the 50 year old TV soap, "As The World Turns?" Jean Passanante, a graduate of **Ladue's** Horton Watkins High

What other famous Missouri artists were there besides George Caleb Bingham and Thomas Hart Benton? Charles M. Russell. Russell was born in 1864 in **Oak Hill**. Russell attended Oak Hill School on Morganford. Growing up, he had an intense fascination of the West and read about it and made clay figures of wild animals.

Painter Charles M. Russell

He had an intense dislike for school and, at age 16, left home and went to Montana. He came back home three years later and his parents persuaded him to enroll in art school. He quit after half a day, complaining that they spent most of his time teaching him how to hold a drawing pencil.

Russell went back to the West and began to seriously draw, paint and sculpt things related to the west. In his lifetime he executed more than 2,000 works, making him one of the most important artists of his time. Russell died in 1926.

What Missourian became a famous Harlem Renaissance poet of the 1920's? Langston Hughes

What writer was born the year Haley's comet streaked across the heavens and died 76 years later when it streaked across the heavens again? Mark Twain

Where in St. Louis is there a statue of poet Friedrich Schiller? In the park directly across the street from Kiel Opera House

When was *Tom Sawyer* published? 1876

When was *Huck Finn* published? 1884

What novel was written by Ed Howe? *The Story of a Country Town* (**Bethany**)

What town was home to Laura Ingalls Wilder, author of *Little House on the Prairie*? **Mansfield**

What was the title of Sarah Teasdale's book of poems, published in 1907? *Sonnets to Duse and Other Poems*

How many copies did Harold Bell Wright sell of *The Shepherd of the Hills*? Eight million – an astounding sum for 1907; John Wayne starred in the movie.

Who wrote *Tess of the Storm Country*? Rupert Hughes of **Lancaster**

Aurand Harris is the most produced children's playwright in the U.S. His works include "Punch and Judy" and "Androcles and the Lion."

What was the subject of author Winston Churchill's 1901 book, *The Crisis*? Life in St. Louis during the Civil War

As a youth, Benton attended the Western Military Academy in **Alton** and drew cartoons for a **Joplin** newspaper.

During World War II, Benton did a series of eight paintings showing the threat of the Axis Powers to western democracies.

Who is the father of the St. Louis *Globe-Democrat*? J.B. McCullagh, who was a war correspondent during the War Between the States and **invented the practice of interviewing**. He lost everything in the 1871 Chicago fire and came to St. Louis to serve as editor of the *Democrat*. In 1873, he resigned and took a position with the *Globe*. He was managing editor when the two papers merged a few years later and led it out of $200,000 debt to become one of the great newspapers in the country.

Who was Missouri's (**Wright City**) most distinguished writer and theologian? Reinhold Niebuhr; his magnum opus was *The Nature and Destiny of Man.* In the 1920s he was a pacifist, socialist and critic of Henry Ford's dehumanizing assembly line. In the 1930s, he became a new Deal supporter and an advocate of welfare capitalism.

What Missourian painted Missouri scenes such as *The County Election*? George Caleb Bingham

What is Bingham's most famous painting? "Daniel Boone Escorting Settlers Through the Cumberland Gap" – in the Kemper Art Museum at Washington University.

In what Missouri town was Mark Twain born? **Florida** – his parents moved to Hannibal in 1839.

What actor is famous for portraying Mark Twain on stage in a one man show? Hal Holbrook

Writer Harold Bell Wright was quite prolific, churning out one novel every two years between 1900 and 1935, with many of them making the national best-seller list. *The Calling of Don Matthews* was a 1909 novel about a man called to pastor a small church. It was based on his experiences when he lived in **Lebanon** and the book angered its citizens. After this, his third book, Wright left Missouri and spent the rest of his days in California. Wright's Shepherd of the Hills did more to publicize the Missouri Ozarks than any other single piece of literature.

What internationally famous St. Louis-born writer, apparently weaned on a pickle, penned the acerbic poem, "The Wasteland?" **T.S. Eliot**

Where did Eliot obtain his character from in "The Love Song of Alfred J. Prufrock?" Prufrock was a furniture dealer in St. Louis.

What St. Louis playwright wrote *The Witching Hour*? Augustus Thomas

Who was Marianne Moore? Born in **Kirkwood**, she edited *The Dial* in the 1920s and also won the National Book Award.

Who is the most famous playwright to hail from St. Louis? Tennessee Williams

What Tennessee Williams work is based on the time that he lived in **St. Louis**? *The Glass Menagerie*

What notable St. Louis poet died in 1904 after walking six blocks to and from the St. Louis Fair on a hot summer day? Kate Chopin

What ethnic group published the *Journal of Speculative Philosophy*? St. Louis Germans – 1867-1893

What Missourian won the first Pulitzer Prize for poetry? Sara Teasdale

What St. Louis woman read a poem at President Clinton's inauguration? Maya Angelou

What St. Louis-born writer is known as "the Children's Poet?" **Eugene Field** – a title that he despised

Nellie Tayloe Ross

Rachel Stix Michael – 1935

Poet Eugene Field

What are Field's most famous poems? "Little Boy Blue" and "Wynken, Blynken and Nod"

What Missourian wrote the novel *Back Street*? Fanny Hurst

Who wrote *Deliver us From Evil*? St. Louisan Dr. Thomas A. Dooley (St. Louis University) who treated the sick in Vietnam and Laos in the 1950s during the Communist insurgency against the French. He died of cancer in 1961 before he could finish his work.

Iowa-born MacKinlay Kantor (*Andersonville*) drew upon the time he lived in Missouri to write *The Voice of Bugle Ann.*

Missourian Henry Bellaman wrote *King's Row*, which was made into a movie starring Ronald Reagan.

MISSOURI WOMEN

Sarah M. Peale, the niece of artist Charles Wilson Peale, moved to St. Louis in 1847 where she resided for the next forty years. She painted dozens of portraits and still lifes and counted the Marquis de Lafayette among her clients.

Princeton's Calamity Jane was a Pony Express rider and a scout for General George Custer's 7th Cavalry.

Hannah Cole is generally credited with establishing **Boonville**, even though it wasn't named for her. She (left a widow by Indians) and her nine children built homes near Franklin.

This was the first white settlement south of the Missouri River. During the War of 1812, she armed her cabin, which was situated on a high bluff, with cannon. By 1815, the place was being referred to as Hannah's Fort. When Cooper County was organized in 1818, her fort was chosen as the county seat.

St. Joseph's Jill Eikenberry appeared as Anne Kelsey on the popular television series "L.A. Law."

Fan dancer Sally Rand was born near **Cross Timbers** in Hickory County and was famous as a star attraction at the Chicago fair of 1933.

Linda Bloodworth-Thomason of **Poplar Bluff** was the creator and writer for the television series *Evening Shade* and *Designing Women.*

Kathryn Grayson attended St. Louis schools. This singing actress starred in *Showboat* and *Kiss me Kate.*

Missourian Marcie Burks claims to have invented the frenetic 1920's dance called the Charleston. In 1925, Marcie gave a Demonstration of the dance for guests at a hotel in **Excelsior Springs**.

Kate O'Flaherty Chopin was born in 1851. Her father died in the famous Gasconade bridge collapse. She married Oscar Chopin, a St. Louis banker. They moved to New Orleans, but she returned to St. Louis after her husband died of swamp fever. She began writing children's stories and novels. *The Awakening*, a novel published in 1899, was criticized for having a heroine who was not content to be a wife and a mother. Outwardly she conformed to society's expectations, but inwardly she wondered if there was more to life besides being a convenient fixture in her husband's life. In recent years, her character has become a hero in the women's movement.

What St. Louisan donated a huge sum to help rebuild Christian College in **Canton** after a disastrous 1903 fire? Along with Robert Stockton, Mary Culver made a sizeable bequest and the college was renamed Culver-Stockton.

What St. Louis woman established **the nation's first kindergarten**? Susan Blow

Statuesque **Elaine Viets**, who grew up in South St. Louis, wrote a column for the *St. Louis Post-Dispatch* for 25 years. Her specialty was writing about the quirky habits of south St. Louisans who put pink flamingoes in their front yards. She also did a brief stint with KMOX radio before moving to Washington, D.C. where she became a mystery writer. Four of her novels are set in St. Louis and the heroine is a fictional newspaper columnist. Viets suffered a stroke in April of 2007 and is on the long road to recovery. Another Viets book is *Urban Affairs: Tales From the Heart of the City* (1988). In 1997, she wrote *How to Commit Monogamy*.

Ginger Rogers

Kathleen Nolan was born Jocelyn Schrum at St. Louis in 1933. In 1975, she achieved fame by becoming **the first female president of the Screen Actor's Guild**. She was nominated for an Emmy for playing Kate McCoy on *The Real McCoys*. During her career she appeared in dozens of television programs as a guest star.

Why was **Nellie Tayloe Ross** significant? Born near **St Joseph**, she went on to become the first woman governor in the U.S. (Wyoming, 1924), and she later was appointed by FDR (1933) to be director of the U.S. Mint. She was an ardent supporter of Prohibition.

Phoebe Hearst

Rachel Stix came to St. Louis in 1884 and married Elias Michael who became president of Rice-Stix Dry Goods. After the death of her only child in 1894, Rachel devoted her life to volunteer causes. During World War I, she headed up a committee that trained women to take positions of men who left for the military. Later, she helped found the St. Louis School of Occupational Therapy. In 1922, Mayor Kiel appointed her to the Board of Education, the first woman to serve in that capacity.

Who was "Unsinkable" Molly Brown? Margaret Brown of **Hannibal** was on board the ***Titanic*** and, as it was going down, it seemed as if she would meet a cruel fate because there were too few lifeboats. At the last minute she was put into a boat because the woman ahead of her backed out and chose to go down with her husband.

On the rescue ship *Carpathia,* she worked to help the sick and injured. She raised money to assist the widows. She later moved to Denver where the woman with crude and unlearned manners often clashed with the city's cultural elite. Debbie Reynolds starred as the legendary woman in the movie that was based on a musical of Molly's life.

What Missouri woman **founded the PTA**? Phoebe Apperson **Hearst** of **St. James** and **Steelville** was the **mother of William Randolph Hearst**, born in 1863. Her husband George was a rich U.S. Senator and she spent his money on philanthropic enterprises. She established a training class for kindergarten teachers. In 1897, she and another woman founded the National Congress of Mothers which changed its name in 1924 to National Congress of Parents and Teachers.

Who was the nation's first female lawyer? Phoebe Couzins, who graduated from Washington University's school of law in 1871. Phoebe was referred to as a "female bachelor." She also became the **first woman U.S. Marshall** when she was appointed to replace her father when he died in 1887.

What **Columbia** woman was one of the most famous sculptresses of her era? Vinnie Ream, who had a degree from Columbia College; her two best-known works were of Abraham Lincoln and Thaddeus Stevens.

Who was known as the **Fulton Flash**? Helen Stephens was working out one day with the boy's track team at Fulton High. The coach timed her in the 50 yard dash and she ran it in 5.8 seconds, which unofficially tied the national record. In a 1935 AAU meet in St. Louis, Helen beat favored Stella Walsh and set a new world record in the 200 meters. The two were competitors again in the 1936 Berlin Olympics. She set a new world record in the 100 meters, a mark that stood until Wilma Rudolph bettered it 20 years later.

Who was only the second woman in the nation to become a U.S. Postmaster? Ann Gentry, whose husband was killed fighting the Seminoles in Florida. Thomas Hart Benton secured the post for her because she was left to raise a large family.

Who was Missouri's first woman lieutenant governor? Harriet Woods of St. Louis, who died in February of 2007

What woman grew up in St. Louis, attended the University of Missouri, taught special ed at Southern Boone County High, became an actress and starred in *Indiana Jones and the Temple of Doom*? Kate Capshaw, who is currently married to director Stephen Spielberg

There are a number of St. Louis streets named for women. According to research by William and Marcella Magnan, this includes: Alcott Street, named for the writer Louisa May Alcott; Alice Avenue, named for a relative of John O'Fallon; Annie Malone Drive, named for the Black businesswoman; Clara Street, named for Clara Bircher, the wife of Dr. Rudolph Bircher. She also named Thrush, Wren, Robin and Oriole streets; Folsom Avenue is named for Frances Folsom, the young wife of President Cleveland who visited St. Louis; French Avenue is named for Mary Field French, a cousin to poet Eugene Field; Julia Dent Drive is named for the St. Louis wife of Ulysses S. Grant; Lillian Street was named by Clara Bircher for her mother; Lucille Street is named for a daughter from the Jennings family; Mary Avenue is named for a relative of John O'Fallon; Rosalie Street is named for the wife of Henry Von Puhl; Sarah Street is named for Sarah Coleman, niece of Peter Lindell; Vivian Street is named for Vivian Switzer.

What Missourian once said that she did everything Fred Astaire did, only backwards while wearing high heels? Ginger Rogers.

Ginger's ancestors came from **Arrow Rock** and she grew up in **Kansas City**. As a young teen she worked the vaudeville circuit with her mother acting as manager and chaperone. In 1929, she left for Broadway and worked in musicals. She became the highest paid nineteen-year-old working girl in America. By the age of 31 she had earned over a million dollars appearing in numerous Hollywood films. In 1933, she made it big as Fred Astaire's dancing partner in *Flying Down to Rio.* Together they made nine musicals for RKO. Sometimes she rehearsed for eighteen hours straight and on several occasions left the studio with bloody feet. After the musicals, she was quite successful doing dramatic and comedic roles, earning a Best Actress Oscar for *Kitty Foyle*. She married actor Lew Ayres (*Dr. Kildare*) who lost his popularity when he became a pacifist during World War II. They divorced in 1941. Rogers eventually married three more times.

Rogers was a Republican and a staunch anti-Communist and named names before the House Committee on Un-American Activities which led to numerous actors and actresses being blacklisted for their dabbling in radical left-wing causes. She died in 1995.

Missourian Candy Tockstein

FLORENCE "CANDY" TOCKSTEIN
(Interviewed by the author in 2002)

Candy Tockstein was born in 1925 at **Vienna**, Missouri. Her family moved to **East St. Louis** where her father worked for Hunter Packing Company. After she graduated from high school in 1943, she went to work for Emerson Electric in St. Louis. While there, she won the "Miss Emerson Electric" contest and that led to a modeling career at Stix Baer & Fuller and at the Chase Park Plaza. While working as a St. Louis model, she once dated drummer **Buddy Rich**. Agencies said that her German-Irish name was too long so they shortened it to Toxton.

She moved to Chicago to further her career. While there, she dated bandleader **Tommy Dorsey** for three years. She thought he was going to ask her to marry him but somehow it never happened. She left Chicago and began modeling in New York City. While there, she dated **Frank Sinatra** who was doing the "Your Hit Parade" radio show.

I asked Candy if Sinatra was a good date. She said he was a very good date and that he really knew how to treat a lady. One night she was with Sinatra at the El Morocco Club and a man from the Charles Feldman Agency gave her his card and told her that she should be a movie star. Candy said she had no acting experience. He told her to do some summer stock and then come to Hollywood and he would get her a contract.

Candy did summer stock at Yardley, Pennsylvania and then left for Hollywood. Feldman secured a contract for her with MGM where she had bit parts in six movies. After a year her contract was picked up by Harry Cohn of Columbia Pictures. Harry changed her stage name to Susan Perry and she was cast as **Humphrey Bogart's** wife in *Knock on Any Door* (1949). This was the picture that introduced handsome actor John Derek to movie audiences. Candy had minor roles in three other films, *Julia Misbehaves* (1948), *Moonrise* (1948), and *Act of Violence* (1949).

While in Hollywood, Candy dated **Peter Lawford**, Mel Tormé and Frank Sinatra, who was now on the west coast acting in films. She began going steady with Mel Tormé and wanted to celebrate Christmas with his family in Chicago. Columbia Studios told Candy they wanted her to date stars like Frank Sinatra and Peter Lawford, and that Tormé was "small potatoes." She was told, in no uncertain terms, that if she went to Chicago her career would be finished. When she went anyway, Columbia dropped her contract.

At Candy and Mel's engagement party, Frank Sinatra showed up with his pal, songsmith Jimmy Van Heusen. Sinatra had a little too much to drink. He knocked on the door and said, "Where's Candy, I want to see Candy." Mel's friends convinced Frank to leave without further incident.

Candy and Mel (the Velvet Fog) were married in Chicago in February of 1949 at the Ambassador Hotel. **Nat King Cole, Peggy Lee** and **Dorothy Kilgallen**, among others, were at the gala affair.

Candy gave birth to their son Steven, on January 29, 1953. They bought a house on Fontenelle Way in Bel-Air. On July 9, 1955, Candy gave birth to a daughter, Melissa. Mel's singing career took him on the road a lot and their marriage began to deteriorate as Candy grew lonely staying at home with the children.

One day, Candy told Mel that she had fallen in love with one of his best friends, television personality **Hal March**.

Mel was a fast-draw gun enthusiast. He owned a very extensive gun collection and was afraid he would have to sell it in the divorce settlement. Candy told Mel that she didn't want anything except his signature. She explained that Hal was making good money as host for *The $64,000 Question,* and that Mel was still struggling as a young singer. It wasn't a bitter divorce because Mel knew that he had neglected his marriage.

Candy was married to Hal March for 14 years. They had three children – Jeffrey, Peter and Victoria. After Hal died she raised her children and then married industrial designer, Jerome Gould. They lived in Encino, California until his death 14 years later. Candy was living at Rancho Mirage, California, when she passed away about two years ago.

This author was responsible for placing her biography on the International Movie Data Base several years ago at www.imdb.com.

MISSOURI WOMAN INVENTS KEWPIE DOLL

Rose O'Neil invented the Kewpie Doll in the late 1800s. They were made of various materials including pulped wood, bisque (tinted porcelain), vinyl, plaster and metal. The sexless figures were that of a naked baby, posed in a variety of charming positions, sometimes clothed only with a hat or a narrow belt. The Kewpie had a distinctive wave of blondish hair that ran in a narrow swatch from the front to the back of the head.

The Kewpie craze first began when Kewpie stories appeared in the *Ladies Home Journal* in December of 1909. Children began asking for a Kewpie doll of their own, so Rose created twelve varieties and had them manufactured by a German company. When World War I came along, she was forced to switch to an American firm. The cherub doll was quite popular with poor children because the Kewpie was affordable. The dolls became popular items to win at games of skill at carnivals. The fad began to fade after the mid-1930s.

Rose made a fortune off the porcelain cherubs and she and her husband spent a lot of time at the family retirement estate (Bonnie Brook) in the Missouri Ozarks. After she upgraded her Ozarks estate she referred to it as "a good place to unbutton."

Although Rose traveled the world and rubbed elbows with the literary giants of her day, she retired to Bonnie Brook and completed her memoirs before she died in 1944.

There is a Kewpie doll collection at the museum located at the School of the Ozarks near **Branson**.

JAMES EARL RAY'S MISSOURI CONNECTION

By Lonnie Tettaton

Although James Earl Ray was born in **Alton**, Illinois, he had several interesting Missouri ties.

Ray's father (George) was arrested for forgery in 1935 and sent to prison. George's mother-in-law helped the family buy 60 acres of land in Missouri near **Ewing**. George skipped bail and hid out from authorities. James Earl Ray flunked the first grade while at Ewing. Small for his age, he was picked on by other boys at the school. He started wetting the bed and began to stutter. Tragedy struck in 1937. Ray's sister Marjorie was playing with matches and she accidentally set her hair and clothes on fire. She died the next day. The Ray family was so poor that, in the winter of 1940, they were forced to start tearing rooms apart for kindling so that they could keep warm. The house was reduced to a one room shack and Ray had to sleep on the floor.

Ray in Ewing, Missouri (white sweater)

After numerous scrapes with the law, Ray was given a 20-year sentence in Missouri after a failed 1959 robbery attempt of a Kroger store in **St. Louis**. It was his fourth major offense. Life behind bars was tough. The 100-year-old prison had twice the number of inmates (2,000) for which it had been built. **The place was once described as "square foot for square foot, the bloodiest 47 acres in America."**

Ray had two botched escape attempts, in 1961 and 1966. In prison, he had repeatedly made disparaging remarks about **Martin Luther King Jr.**, and **H. Rap Brown**. He escaped from Missouri State Penitentiary at Jefferson City in April of 1967. In July he bought a 1962 Plymouth from Bundy Olds in **East St. Louis**. He drifted around, spending time in **Edwardsville**, **St. Louis**, Chicago, Indianapolis, Detroit, Toronto, Atlanta, Los Angeles, Mexico and Birmingham, Alabama, where he began stalking King.

James Earl Ray

King was murdered around 6:01 PM on April 4, 1968. He had gone to Memphis, Tennessee with Ralph Abernathy, **Andrew Young** and **Jesse Jackson** to lead a civil rights march in support of about 1,300 striking sanitation workers, nearly all of whom were black. Strangely, about a month before shooting King, Ray graduated from bartending school in Los Angeles. He used a Remington 30.06 rifle he had purchased in Birmingham about a week earlier. Ray had stalked King previously when he was in Atlanta but could never find the opportunity to kill him. He fired just one shot from the rear bathroom window of a dingy complex where he had rented a room. The walls were paper-thin, and the tenants next door said they remembered that the man in 5B spent a lot of time in the bathroom but seldom flushed the toilet. The bathroom window gave Ray a good view of the balcony of King's room in the Lorraine Motel in Memphis, 200 feet away.

Ray pulled the trigger while standing in the cast iron tub. The powerful shot tore a hole in King's jaw about the size of one's fist. The bullet severed his spine and caused severe brain damage. King was rushed to a hospital where doctors worked to save his life, but he died about an hour later. Ray probably killed King because he was a racist and sought recognition by slaying "The Dreamer." About 3,500 FBI agents were immediately assigned to the case. They eventually found Ray's abandoned white Mustang, parked at a housing project in Atlanta.

There was much talk about the shooting being a conspiracy and that Ray was probably dead, killed by the other conspirators. Author **Truman Capote** voiced that very opinion on the *Tonight* show. Ray was arrested about two months later on June 8, 1968, at Heathrow Airport near London. He was carrying a loaded .38 revolver at the time. Ray also had an airline ticket for Africa and two Canadian passports with the name Ramon Sneyd, another alias. He had disguised himself by letting his hair grow longer, wearing dark-rimmed glasses, and by having plastic surgery performed on the tip of his nose.

Many assumed it was a conspiracy from the start. It was thought that only a hired killer would have enough money to go to Canada (in Montreal he used the alias Eric Gault), then to London, to Portugal, and back again to London. After Ray was captured, he claimed innocence. Ray said he had been in Memphis with a swarthy man named Raoul and was involved in a deal that went sour, smuggling drugs and guns to South America. Ray said it was this Raoul who probably killed King and set him up as the fall guy. Ray claimed that when the alleged deal went south, and he later heard about King's murder, he got scared and decided to leave the country.

"Oh, God, I feel so trapped," was about all Ray had to say when he was apprehended. Ray was extradited from London and flown to Memphis. The 65-day manhunt was over. Ray's two brothers, John and Jerry, set up a defense fund in Memphis on his behalf. Judge W. Preston Battle presided over the trial, and Arthur Hanes was to be his counsel. Shortly before his trial was to begin, Ray changed his mind and asked for famed Houston lawyer Percy Foreman to represent him, thus delaying the trial. Ray wanted to plead *not guilty*, believing that "no southern jury would convict a white man for killing a nigger." In the end, Foreman convinced Ray to plead guilty in exchange for a life sentence because the jury would make an example of him and give him the chair.

MAKING BROOMS FROM BROOM CORN

When making a broom pioneers used a maple, birch, or ash sapling for the broom handle. The bark was peeled off and the stick was allowed to cure for a year. Waxed linen thread was used to bind the broom stalks to the handle. Sometimes strips of rawhide were used for binding. As the rawhide dried out and shrunk the fastening became more secure. It was soon discovered that the bristles were less likely to fall out by drilling two holes and inserting wooden pegs in the lower handle to help secure the binding. It was too difficult to make round pegs to exact specifications, so square ones were used instead. **This is the origin of the expression, "a square peg in a round hole."**

HOG KILLING TIME ON MISSOURI FARMS

I grew up in urbanized East St. Louis, but my wife's parents were from small towns in Missouri and grew up on farms. My wife's meat-hungry parents spent all summer eating fried chicken, stewed chicken with noodles, baked hen with sage dressing, boiled rooster with dumplings, and chicken salad. By fall they said they were so tired of chicken they could hardly look one in the face.

Sometime in late November or early December, after the first hard frost, came pig-killing time. Folks had to wait for cold weather so the meat wouldn't spoil. Catsup was invented by ancient Europeans who mixed spices with tomatoes to disguise the taste and smell of slightly tainted meat.

My wife's parents looked forward to relishing big platters of hot sausage, snoots, pork tenderloin, scrapple, liver, head souse, head cheese, pickled pigs feet, bacon, shoulder, ham and fat-back.

They had a smokehouse on the rear of their property. It was a nearly airtight room in which a fire was built in an open stove and it gave off thick smoke from burning hickory. Just enough oxygen was allowed in the smokehouse to keep the fire smoldering. The smoke enveloped the meat, hanging from ceiling hooks and it dried, cured and became tasty.

One year, when my wife (Lorna) was eight, her family visited their Missouri relatives at **Wesco** (near **Steelville**). The first week in December saw the arrival of weather deemed cold enough for hog butchering. They got up at 5:00 AM one morning and her dad and uncle began to make preparations. They had a breakfast of biscuits, gravy and eggs. Then Lorna followed her dad and uncle out to the barn where they fed the horses and mules. Before they finished, she went over to the chicken coop and collected eggs from the laying hens.

My future wife, Lorna Sanders, feeding a baby pig

The men dug a shallow trench about one and ½ feet deep and about eight feet long. They filled the trench with kindling and moved a metal scalding trough over it. Then they lit a crackling fire and poured in tubs of water that had been placed by it. Soon, the water was steaming in the cold air.

Then Lorna's uncle took a rifle and he and her dad walked down to the hog pens. They told her to get back to the house because they didn't think children should view the killing. She dutifully started to trudge back to the house, but her curiosity got the better of her and she turned back and crept along the board fence and peered through one of the cracks.

She blinked at the sharp crack of the rifle and closed her eyes as the hog staggered off and fell, dying. The two men dragged the hog onto a wooden sled and the horse pulled the sled to the trough. The hog was then placed in the trough of boiling water, turned over, and then taken out. Her dad and uncle then began scraping the skin with huge corn knives. The hair came off like magic.

Next, the hog was hoisted by the hind legs and hung from the fork of a large tree branch with the help of a block and tackle. Then his throat was cut. Her aunt quickly shoved a clean milk bucket under the hog to catch the bright red blood that came gushing out. Then the hog was gutted.

Lorna viewed the whole affair wide-eyed with some misgivings for she had enjoyed slopping the hogs, scratching behind their ear with a corncob, and listening to their friendly grunts. She felt a lump in her chest wondering why it had to be like this. She had that same feeling when her aunt would wring the necks of chickens so they could have meat with their dumplings.

Her aunt and mother carried the buckets of blood away, chattering over the kind of German recipe and seasonings that would be used to make blood sausage.

Then, on tables made with boards placed on sawhorses, her dad and uncle began the task of gutting and butchering the hog. Her uncle was an expert and showed her dad how to carve off the hams, shoulders, head and other parts, placing them in large tubs and pans. The women brought dish-pans and filled them with meat for making sausage. Lorna went back to the kitchen with the women and turned the handle of the meat grinder. It was fun seeing the pieces of lean and fat go through the grinder and come out in long streams.

Corn growers Liberty League Poster

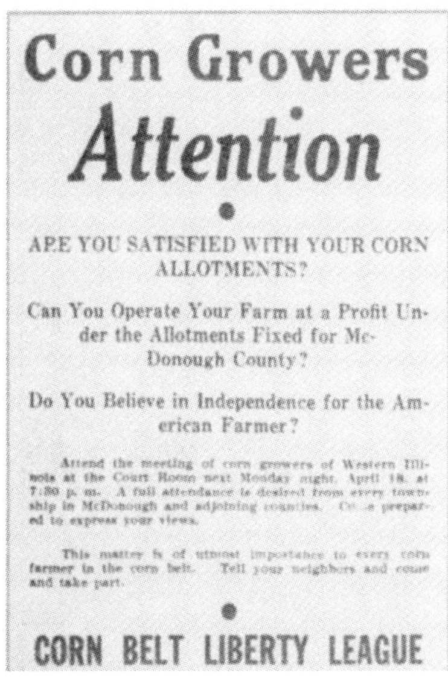

The gruesome task of scraping and washing entrails, for the casings to hold the sausage, fell to the women.

The huge hams, shoulders and sides of bacon were taken to the smokehouse, salted and put on hooks. The smoking process over a hickory fire preserved the meat and added a taste quality.

Then her mother and aunt used a big iron skillet and cooked some sausage. They opened jars of pickles and jars of canned green beans. Then they sliced some cucumbers, tomatoes and onions and poured sweetened vinegar over them.

After the work was done they all gathered around the table, gave thanks, and stuffed themselves with delicious food. Lorna usually went light on the meal and made up the difference with yeasty slices of home baked bread, smothered with freshly churned butter and thick, dark sorghum molasses.

After butchering the hog, all the fat was carefully trimmed and saved. The next day, this was placed in a big black-iron kettle under which a hot fire was kept burning. Cans of lye were added and the mixture was cooked and stirred until the proper consistency was obtained.

The residue rose to the top and was ladled off and the remaining thick, white mixture was poured or ladled into wooden forms. When it hardened it provided bars of soap that took care of laundry needs. When using the soap, the housewife scraped off some shavings from the bar of soap into the hot wash water. As it dissolved, it left a sudsy water in which the family clothing was washed. It was a harsh detergent that was hard on the body (chapped skin) and clothing, but it cleaned fairly well.

The rinds or pork "cracklings" remained after the fat was cooked from them and youngsters considered them a delicacy.

MOO, MOO – OINK: MISSOURI FARMS

It has been said that all of mankind's inventions, all of our accomplishments and dreams, would be for nothing were it not for six inches of topsoil and the fact that the sun shines and it occasionally rains.

Missouri agricultural rankings among the 50 states are as follows: hay – 3, rice – 6, soybeans – 7, corn – 9, cotton - 10, beef cows - 2, turkeys – 3, chickens – 16, milk cows - 17

In pioneer times it was quite common for our ancestors to plant certain shrubs close enough together that they formed what was known as a hedgerow fence. Osage orange, used by Indians to fashion their bows, was the most common. The stout limbs and thick foliage was strong enough to turn cattle and settlers often referred to it as "pig tight." Another shrub that was sometimes used was the black thorn. If you scan old issues of *The Prairie Farmer* it is easy to find articles encouraging the use of hedges.

When Joe Glidden, of neighboring **Dekalb**, Illinois, invented barbed wire fencing, hedgerows began to decline. Historians believe that the practice of planting hedgerows was brought over from England where it was quite common.

What is the definition of the phrase "growing season?" It is determined by the last killing frost of spring and the first killing frost of fall.

What is Missouri's average length of the growing season? 178 Days – somewhat less in the north and over 200 in the bootheel

The only fruit native to early Missouri was the pawpaw. The tree grows to a height of 25-30 feet. Its fruit ripens in September and was once referred to as "Missouri bananas."

Most Missouri farms have wells to provide drinking and bath water. What is the advantage of a well that is deep enough to reach bedrock? Deep wells are less likely to run dry, but bedrock water has high mineral content producing "hard water."

What is the average annual rainfall in Missouri? Nearly 40 inches – less in the north and more in the south. St. Louis gets about 36 inches a year.

In frontier Missouri, what was "broadcasting?" Seed was placed in a cloth bag with straps that slung over the shoulders. As the farmer walked along the field, he sowed the seed by scattering handfuls to his left and right.

In pioneer times what animal was probably used for plowing more than the horse? An ox – often yoked in pairs

Home-made skate scooters (Lonnie Tettaton)

What soil problems hamper farming in much of southwestern Missouri? Where rock formations are near the surface the soil is too thin to hold enough moisture to sustain agriculture. In these parts of Missouri corn is the leading crop and hog raising prevails.

What happens to most Missouri corn? It goes to market "on the hoof;" that is, it is fed to cattle and hogs.

What is the name for a female donkey? Jenny – the male is a Jack

In 1931, Missouri led the nation in the production of what fruit? Strawberries

Back in the 1950s, why were geese useful on cotton farms in Southeastern Missouri? They were loosed on cotton fields to eat grass and weeds growing between the rows.

What was the minimum amount of land early settlers could buy from the government at a dollar or $1.25 an acre? Forty acres or a quarter-quarter section; increased amounts had to be bought in multiples of 40.

When the Pacific Railroad was completed and the company sold land to prospective farmers, what were the terms? Prices were low and terms were liberal. A down payment of only fifty cents an acre was required with seven years to pay the remainder.

Why was cholera so prevalent in pioneer days? The concept of germs was unknown. Cholera occurred under conditions of filth, often caused when several families lived under one roof with no running water or indoor plumbing.

Young girls played hopscotch (Lonnie Tettaton sketch)

What fruit, that could be made into wine, was thought by early pioneers to help them live to a ripe old age if they grew and consumed it? Elderberry

When was it estimated that Missouri had lost 90 percent of its wetlands? 1968

What wild-growing Missouri plant was used by natives for arrow shafts? The Wahoo

What percentage of Missouri land is devoted to crops? 43 percent; 11 per cent is wooded and 11 percent is pasture

What do you call kernels of corn that have been soaked in a caustic solution and have had their husk removed? Hominy; you get grits when hominy is ground up into a coarse matter

How big is a township? Six miles square consisting of 36 sections; each section has 640 acres

Section 16 was reserved for what purpose? The money obtained from the sale of section 16 went to support public education, mostly to build one-room schoolhouses where students of several grades were combined.

How were wagons designated in pioneer times? By the number of bushels they could hold. A typical wagon was designated as an 80-bushel wagon.

What caused the lack of trees on the Missouri prairie? Frequent prairie fires and thick grass that prevented tree seeds from taking root.

What were squatters? Some people moved on a piece of land and started herding or farming before it was put up for sale by the government.

What were squatter's rights and pre-emption laws? When the land was offered for sale, squatters were given the first chance to buy the property if they had a certificate of entry.

What is the cheapest price that land was ever sold for in Missouri? Twenty-five cents an acre; Uncle Sam was so hard up for currency after the Civil War that land was sold at bargain prices.

Why has red long been the predominant color for Missouri barns? When paints were first produced for barn use, it was discovered that the cheapest and most durable were from a red pigment that came from an iron oxide base.

Tripe and chitlins were common food items eaten by the poor during the Depression. What are they? Tripe is cow stomach and chitlins are hog intestines.

What was a "Poor Farm?" The Missouri legislature, before the Civil War, passed legislation that established the almshouse system. This allowed county governments to build a place to house the indigent. Two story structures were often built in rural areas. The overseer and his family lived on the first floor and the poor lived in small rooms upstairs. The poor worked (farmed) small plots of land near the house and grew fruits and vegetables to assist in their keep.

Is a tomato a fruit or a vegetable? Fruit

What unique method of rat control was invented by farmers? Rats can't burp so they set out quantities of Coca-Cola for them to drink. The carbonated beverage caused them to explode. (Yes, I know – unbelievable.)

How many soybeans are in a pod and what determines the number? Anywhere from 2-4, the number depending on how good the growing season has been.

Is a soybean round like a pea or kidney shaped like a lima

bean? They are round and yellow, marked with a black dot

Has Missouri ever been a significant tobacco producer? Yes – The soil and climate of southern Missouri was suitable for tobacco production in the state's early years.

What is the origin of the term "quarter horse?" In the old days race tracks were straight and a quarter of a mile long. Race horses were called quarter horses.

What is Missouri loam and where is it found? It contains a mixture of clay, sand and lime, mixed with humus. It is not stiff like clay soils and is more fertile than sandy soils. It exists in the northern prairie region and is a dark, rich color. The central part of the prairie region has gray shale loam and the southern section has sandy loam.

What type of soils are found in the glacial area of Missouri up north? There is alluvial soil in the bottom lands, loess (windblown) soil and glacial soil. There are numerous small streams and this part of the state has good drainage.

Where are Missouri's richest soils? The southeast lowlands are dominated by rich Mississippi alluvial soil. An early visitor from Maine exclaimed, "Why if we had soil this rich back in New England we'd sell it by the peck."

What is the most famous quote about this soil? It's so rich you can plant nails and harvest crowbars. Alternate: It's so rich you can plant straw and harvest wheat.

What about the Ozark region? The limestone and flint soils of this region are uniformly poorer than in other parts of the state. Fruits, berries and grapes prosper and cattle, poultry and goats are raised.

What crop dominates Missouri agriculture? Because of the varying terrain and differing soil types, Missouri is not a one crop state like Iowa. **Missouri leads the nation in the variety of her agriculture**.

What is actually Missouri's number one crop? Corn, but it goes to market "on the hoof" in the form of cattle and hogs

How long does it take for a hog to mature to full market size? 10 months

Currently, **Missouri is the only state that produces corncob pipes.** What famous general smoked a Missouri Meerschaum corncob pipe made in **Washington**, Missouri? General Douglas MacArthur; the company supplied all the pipes for the Robin Williams *Popeye* movie. Washington is known as the **Corn Cob Pipe Capital of the World**. Production averages about 5,000 pipes a day. 636-239-2109

Host Russ Carter: Steve Carlton and his wife are guests at the St. Louis Hop (courtesy Mrs. Carter/David Lossos)

Where was Missouri's "tobacco belt?" Central Missouri

What is Missouri's leading orchard crop? Apples – most of them are grown in orchards north of the Missouri River.

Who owned the **first and largest commercial fruit tree nursery** in the U.S? The Stark Brothers of **Louisiana**, MO, with their world-famous Stark Delicious apple – dating back to Judge Stark in 1816. Luther Burbank worked with the Stark brothers to market new varieties that he developed.

What is Missouri's most famous peach type? Elbertas

In 1950, what were the three main milk condensing companies in Missouri? Carnation, Pet and Pevely

Why do farmers generally avoid killing non-poisonous snakes? Farmers like it when snakes take up residence in barns because they eat mice.

How much water is required to process and produce a pound of grain? An astounding 1,000 pounds of water

How much Missouri water is required to process and produce one pound of meat for consumer's tables? 1,300 pounds of water

Why are Missouri soybeans good for people with diabetes? Soybeans have very little sugar and very little starch which the human body converts to sugar.

What type of cow generally is the best milk producer - Jersey, Gurnsey, Holstein or Hereford? Holstein; the Hereford is raised mostly for beef; a Jersey is the best butterfat producer

What weed commonly found on farms is used to make deadly ricin? Jimson weed

What weed's seeds did the French immigrants bring with them because they were afraid it didn't exist here? Dandelion – for greens and dandelion wine; According to Mildred Rongey of **O'Fallon**, Illinois, lambsquarter is an edible weed that her mother sometimes mixed with dock and dandelion greens for salads during the Depression.

Soil in the spring must be 58 degrees before planting.

What price were farmers getting for a bushel of soybeans in 2002? About $5.50 a bushel – not a whole lot more than what farmers were getting 25 years ago.

What was a general price for farmland in 1942? About a hundred dollars an acre; this meant that one could buy a farm, raise a large crop of soybeans, and pay off the farm in about a year. This is impossible today due to low grain prices and the high cost of land.

How many rows of kernels are there on a typical ear of corn? Sixteen or eighteen – it's never an odd number.

What caused the farm crisis of the 1980s? In the mid-1970's, in the early years of the Carter administration, the price of farmland started to rise. Farmers decided to buy up as much cheap land as they could at a six percent variable loan from banks. Interest rates were deregulated in 1977. Farmers figured that in a few years their farm would be worth twice the amount they had paid for it. Then along came the energy crisis and interest rates shot up to nearly eighteen percent. With high interest rates, farmers stopped buying acreage and prices fell from less demand. Instead of a three hundred dollar a month payment, the bank was now demanding almost $900 due to increased mortgage rates. When farmers couldn't make the payments, the banks foreclosed and farms that had been in the family for over a hundred years were lost.

Most people remember that pre cut homes could be bought from a Sears catalog. Was it also possible to order a pre-cut barn from Sears? Yes

Can you hear corn grow? Farmers claim they can sit on their porch on a hot summer night, after a drenching rain, and hear the nearby corn in the field growing.

Is grain dust in storage silos explosive? Very – that's why they all have spark arrestors in their electrical systems.

In the old days were hogs driven to market the same as cattle? Yes – drovers brought hogs long distances to the Chicago market.

Why do you have white meat and dark meat on a chicken? Parts of the chicken where muscles get used a lot such as the neck and legs are dark. The muscles that get used the least, such as the breast and wings, are white meat.

Long hair at Lindbergh in 1980

Can chickens be trained to beat humans at tic tack toe? Yes – by rewarding them with grain. Chickens who can do this are popular attractions at state fairs and carnival side-shows. They are usually nick-named "Birdbrain."

Butter is made on a farm by churning cream long enough that all the fat particles clump together. What do you call the liquid substance that is left over? Buttermilk

How did Missouri farmers make cottage cheese in the old days? An animal enzyme called rennin was added to milk to make it curdle. Then the mixture was strained through a muslin cloth and the left over liquid was fed to hogs.

In the course of time, what name came to be applied to this cloth that was used to strain cottage cheese? Cheesecloth

What principle of physics is used in a farmer's cream separator? Centrifugal force

Lindbergh High logo

What term does a chicken farmer use to describe a nest of several eggs? Clutch

In the fall, farmers went out into the woods and cut up dead trees, stacking the wood near the house in cords. This wood was used to heat the house in wintertime. What was done with the left over sawdust? When the pond or river froze, blocks of ice would be cut and stored in an icehouse. The sawdust was placed between the blocks to keep them from sticking together and freezing back into one big lump.

From what part of a cow is brisket obtained? The lower chest – it is low in fat and is cured in a solution of brine.

Where did the expression "rough as a cob" originate? Corncobs and the pages from Sears or Montgomery Ward catalogs were used instead of toilet paper in outhouses.

Why were three corncobs used per visit to the outhouse – two red and one white? You'll have to talk to a farmer or call this author if you can't figure this one out.

Farm fertilizer (often bought in 100-pound sacks) is associated with three numbers. What do these numbers represent? The first number is the nitrogen content; the second is the percentage of phosphate; the third is the percentage of potash or potassium – NPK designation; currently it is often bought in bulk by farmers.

Why are hogs able to kill poisonous snakes? Their skin and fat layers are so tough and thick, the venom doesn't get into their bloodstream.

Why do "druggies" steal anhydrous ammonia from farmers? They use it to make "meth," known by the common name of "speed." The mixture is highly volatile and inexperienced people sometimes blow themselves to smithereens because they store it in propane tanks that are not made for high pressure.

What high school club is popular with teenagers in rural areas? FFA – Future Farmers of America

In 1960, if you saw a Fordson tractor, what color was it? Blue; a 1950 Allis Chalmers tractor was orange

What color were Caterpillar tractors? Yellow, of course

Rhode Island Red, Leghorn, Bardrock and Plymouth Rock are all types of what farm animal? Chickens

What slang term do farm kids use to describe cockleburs? Porcupine eggs

What were primogeniture laws? Before the Revolution, it was common practice that when the head of the household died, and he had several sons, only the oldest inherited the land. It was done to prevent the large estate from being divided. This practice dates back to medieval times. The landless sons were expected to become monks or soldiers.

What was long a favorite Halloween prank pulled by Missouri farm kids? Pushing over outhouses

Why are authorities suspicious of non-farm people buying large amounts of farm fertilizer? It can be used by terrorists for making bombs.

Did Timothy McVeigh use farm fertilizer to make the Oklahoma City bomb? Yes. It was mainly ammonia nitrate and fuel oil (anfo), stored in a rented van and ignited with a stick of dynamite.

How did Missouri farmers in 1950 remove tree stumps? They bought sticks of dynamite at a quarry and blasted them out.

What did farm kids often use for excitement on the Fourth of July instead of firecrackers? One-quarter sticks of dynamite

Missouri farm kids also used calcium carbide for entertainment. How did this work? A can was placed over a small amount of calcium carbide with a small amount of water added. Then a fuse was added and then lit. The water and calcium carbide produced acetylene gas that exploded, sending the can high into the air.

How did yeoman farmers make their own gunpowder? It was a mixture of saltpeter, charcoal and sulfur.

Why were early Missouri settlers referred to as yeoman

farmers? The term referred to small, independent freeholders who owned their own land.

What was the old farm prank related to saltpeter? If a small amount was mixed in with food, it led to temporary impotence.

Why did tractor makers switch from gasoline engines to diesel? Gasoline engines run hotter, wearing out the valves and other engine parts quicker.

Bowling Hall of Fame in St. Louis

Were baby chicks ever delivered to farmers through the regular mail by the postman? Yes – in reinforced cardboard crates that were perforated

What was the purpose of making hybrid plants? To produce healthier plants with higher yields

What determines the length of time it takes for corn to mature? The amount of sunlight it is exposed to. There is also a genetic factor. If a farmer gets his crop in late due to excessive spring rain, he buys seed that matures faster.

What determines the amount of time it takes for soybeans to mature? Soybeans mature based on the length of the nights. Soybeans planted near a streetlight or nightlight take forever to mature.

Why are potatoes planted in mounds instead of on flat ground? Too much water causes the potato plant to rot.

Are potatoes grown from seeds? No – they are grown from "shoots" or the "eyes" of the potato.

Is horseradish grown from seeds? No – it is grown from the tip of the root on the plant that is cut off.

Lorna Nunes says Blueberry Hill in U City has the best hamburgers in St. Louis

What causes popcorn to pop? The heat causes moisture inside the kernel to expand and literally explode.

What was a "husking bee" in pioneer times? Again, neighbors got together and "shucked" corn, often followed by a large meal cooked by the women with music and dancing afterward.

Are phases of the moon related to Farmers Almanac recommendations? Yes – Charlie Oliver of **Belleville** was once getting ready to plant some fence posts. He was told by a neighboring farmer that the moon was in the *wrong phase*. "If you want the posts to be true and straight and firm, they should be inserted when the moon is dark (crescent moon)." He explained that a bright moon would pull the posts an inch or two out of the soil and they would lean and be weak.

What animal did farmers use in their front yards to trim grass instead of a lawn mower? Sheep; goats can be used but they also eat the bark off trees.

Do cows fall asleep while in the standing position? Most do after they are about a year old, giving rise to the teen sport of "cow tipping" since cows can't move laterally.

Why was water from a rain barrel preferred to well water for washing clothes? It was "soft water" because it had fallen from the sky. Groundwater in wells is often "hard water" because it contains dissolved minerals.

What happened to odd parts of the pigs such as the ears at butchering time? They became part of "head cheese." Some think the ears are used for making silk purses but there is an old saying about that.

Were bees indigenous to Missouri? No – they were brought in by settlers from the East. Indians called bees "white man's flies."

A human intestine is about twenty feet long. How long is the intestine of a horse? One hundred feet

Does Missouri raise ostriches in significant numbers? Yes

Is it true or is it an urban legend that the eye of an ostrich is larger than its brain? True

Everyone knows ostriches cannot fly. How fast can they run? Up to forty miles per hour

How often do farmers milk their cows? Usually twice a day, but improved feed and breeding has bumped it up to three. Cows are given feed mix with hormones to improve productivity; some environmental groups consider this controversial.

What Missouri crop has 60 percent more vitamin C than a lemon? Horseradish

Is it true or an urban myth that rabbits and horses can't vomit? True – it has something to do with the structure of their esophagus.

Since 1972, does Missouri have more trees or fewer trees? Incredibly, despite shrinking forests due to urban sprawl, there are more trees. That's because homeowners are planting more trees and farmers are planting more trees on their acreage.

How much of Missouri's forested land is privately owned? 85 percent; two-thirds of Missouri was originally forested.

How much wood does a typical Missourian consume each year? A little more than a ton; typical Missourians in urban areas consume 100 gallons of water a day through toilet use, cooking food, washing clothes, taking showers, etc.

How many acres of forest land does it take to build a typical new, two-story Missouri home? Three acres

Name two common Missouri farm animals that have four parts to their stomachs. Cows and sheep are ruminants. When they eat grass it goes to the first of four stomachs. Later, when they are resting, they regurgitate and chew their cud. A cow typically chews on its cud approximately 45-50 times before swallowing it again.

What are the only livestock native to Missouri? Turkeys (although they were wild and not domesticated) – old timers called them "Carolina parrots."

Is the following true or an urban myth? Some turkeys are so dumb they look up to see what is hitting them on the head when it starts raining and they drown. Urban myth – although they *are* dumb; all birds are fairly dumb - hence the epithet, "birdbrain."

What are the only two animals on a Missouri farm that must worry about sunburn? Pigs and humans are the only animals that can sunburn, unless it's an albino animal.

Do pigs have teeth? Yes

What Missouri animal and its worldwide cousins out-number humans? Chickens

How did soybeans originally come to this country? They were originally brought over from Asia as ballast in a ship.

Why are soybeans an excellent thing for crop rotation? They are a legume – their under-ground nodules add nitrogen to the soil.

Originally on Chippewa, now in St. Charles off I-70

When farmers took their hogs to the large slaughter-houses in Kansas City, what was the only part of the hog wasted? The slaughterhouses bragged that they used every part of the hog except the squeal, and they were trying to sell that to Henry Ford for horns in his Model T Fords.

What do you call a castrated male pig? Barrow – a castrated bull is called a steer.

What is the purpose of castration? It makes the animal less aggressive, and, in the case of a pig, they put on more weight. Less testosterone also makes the meat more tender.

Diesel fuel sold to farmers for agricultural purposes is taxed at a lower rate than urban fuel for highways. How are the two fuels differentiated? A red dye is placed in farm fuel.

What crop did Missourians raise as a source of lubricant before oil wells came into existence? Castor beans were once a big crop in the state. (Castor oil – ugh! I took it as a kid.) Castor beans on your property perimeter are also rumored to keep moles out of your yard.

In 1950, if you saw a gray tractor with red trim, what make was it? Ford; if you saw a red tractor with white lettering it was an International Harvester. A Farmall was very similar to International Harvester.

In 1950, if you saw a green and white tractor, what brand was it? Oliver; if you saw a yellow/beige and brown tractor it was a Case

In 1950, if you saw a green and yellow tractor, what brand was it? John Deere; a Minneapolis-Moline was red and yellow, sometimes red and black

What color was a 1950 Ferguson tractor? Gray – it looked like a Ford, had a similar wide stance, but did not have any red paint.

Why did farm residents sometimes have health problems with early lids used on canning jars? The old one-piece lids had a zinc coating, and this sometimes leeched into the preserved food.

When making jars of jelly preserves, what kind of wax was poured on top of the jar to preserve freshness? Paraffin

What do you call a female cow that has never borne a calf? Heifer – If, like my wife, your answer was "unmarried virgin," that is a very poor alternate answer.

What do you call a female pig that has never given birth? Gilt – which becomes a sow after she has given birth to piglets; a male pig is a boar.

How are Missouri farmers helping our nation to cope with gasoline shortages? Missouri corn is used to produce ethanol to the tune of about 400 million gallons a year.

Is ethanol about the same type of alcohol that was produced illegally during Prohibition? Yes – the formula is CH_3 CH_2 OH in case you're interested

How much are the construction costs to produce a gallon of ethanol? Since 1982 it has dropped from $2.25 to $1.00.

Is a gallon of ethanol more or less energy efficient than a gallon of gasoline? Less – but 10 percent ethanol in gasoline increases its octane and the gasoline with it burns cleaner. Cars with flex fuel capability can burn either E – 85 ethanol (up to 85 percent) or gasoline.

What is done with the grain substance left over in the ethanol producing process? It's used for animal feed.

Are yeast and fermentation part of the ethanol making process? Yes

Can companies such as Pioneer and Monsanto develop hybrid corn that is more suitable for producing ethanol? Yes – also more suitable byproducts /co-products

How many ethanol plants are there in the U.S.? About 78

About how many million gallons of ethanol does a typical Missouri ethanol plant produce in a year? 40

Is America the leading ethanol producer in the world? No – it's Brazil. They decided to become free of dependence on OPEC oil back around 1970.

How long does it take before a female chick begins laying eggs? It takes a hen about seven months to mature, depending on the breed.

What unit of measurement is used to describe the height of a horse? Horses are measured by "hands" with one hand being the equivalent of four inches. A "hand" is also used to describe a bunch of bananas or a group of tobacco leaves tied together.

Why did some farmers prefer mules to horses? Mules are thought to better withstand heat and humidity and they eat less because they are smaller. Mules are usually sterile.

How many pecks make a bushel? Four; remember when

potatoes were sold in grocery stores by the peck?

What is the origin of the expression, "sucking the hind teat?" The weakest piglet always got shoved down to the last teat by the others. The first pair of teats produced more than the last, so that little piggy became the runt of the litter.

How many teats does a sow generally have? Anywhere from ten to fourteen; cows have four spigots

Where were eggs and butter stored on a farm before refrigerators? In the well

What is no till farming? The seed, fertilizer and insect control are all planted together in a narrow strip of ground. The field is not plowed first.

For what purpose was GPS (global positioning system) originally sold to farmers? For yield monitoring so they could determine what parts of their fields needed more fertilizer.

William Clark (National Archives)

Why did GPS systems not catch on with most farmers? After cost-benefit analysis, the farmers decided they weren't worth the price.

What determines the straightness of row after row of corn or soybeans? The skill level of the farmer driving the tractor

How did farmers who weren't very good at plowing a straight row rationalize? They claimed the yields from crooked rows were higher. (Think about it!)

What is the secret to making a straight furrow? Most farmers say you have to fix your gaze on an object at the end of the field and keep your eye on that object.

What do the four H's represent in Four H Clubs? Head, Heart, Hands, Health

What is a typical farmer's response to a dumb question where the obvious answer is "NO?" It's something like – "Do pigs fly?" or "Do chickens have lips?"

Is it true or is it an urban myth that a mule won't sink in quicksand but a donkey will? Urban myth

What logo is the symbol of Four - H Clubs? Four leaf clover

People who raise sheep often include a llama in the flock. Why? The llama protects the sheep from predators. The llama has the uncanny ability to direct its caustic spit into the eyes of an attacker, causing severe pain, driving them off. (I know, I don't believe this one either.)

Meriwether Lewis (National Archives)

What happens to laying hens that fall off in production? They are sold to somebody such as Campbell's and become chicken soup.

What did farm wives in the 1930's and 1940's do with empty 50 lb. feed sacks? They used the cotton material, imprinted with colorful designs, to make house dresses, pillowcases, aprons, and underwear. Sugar and flour were also packaged in imprinted cloth bags.

Who was thought to make better cow milkers, men or women? Women, because they were gentler and had more patience.

What did farmers in 1945 do with empty burlap feed sacks? They were placed over the seat of a tractor. The open weave of burlap was good for this purpose.

What is a long ton of wheat? 2200 pounds – A regular ton is 2,000 pounds.

If a farmer in a wagon yells the command "haw" to a horse, what does it mean? Go left; "gee" means turn right

In central Missouri, when is winter wheat normally harvested? At the end of June

During what month is winter wheat normally planted? Late October, early November

What part of corn is male and what is female? The tassels are male and the silks are female.

In Missouri, what was supposed to be "knee high by the Fourth of July?" Field corn – with modern techniques it's "head high by the Fourth of July.

What is the state's definition of a farm? Mostly for tax purposes, it's a piece of land that produces crops or raises animals at a minimum value of $1,000.

What popular Missouri crop came from Manchuria and was not grown here until the 1920's? Soybeans

What determines the prices farmers receive for their crops and animals? Market demand and speculators/investors at the Board of Trade in Chicago

What are the two main farmers' unions? The NFO and the Farmers' Union

What part of the horseradish is used in making the condiment? The upper part of the root

Back in the 1920s, how did egg producers determine which eggs had chick embryos in them? They held them up to a candle or a strong light.

About how often does a good laying hen produce an egg? It used to be about one every five days but improved feed and breeding has improved on that.

What is a big complaint among animal rights activists about the way chickens are being raised? They no longer run around the barnyard. They remain caged from birth until slaughter.

Where did the phrase "pecking order" originate? The barnyard; the dominant chickens exercise control and the subservient ones demure or wait their turn at the feed or watering mechanism. To assert dominance, the aggressive ones peck at the weak ones.

What bumper sticker do farmers use to counter criticisms? "Don't complain about the cost of food with your mouth full."

What is a pullet? A young female chicken less than seven months old

Where does forestry, fishing and agriculture rank in the Missouri economy? Seventh – behind services, finance, manufacturing, government, transportation, retail trade, wholesale trade and construction; mining is ranked eighth.

What slang term do some Missouri farmers use to describe chicken eggs? Cackleberries

LEWIS AND CLARK EXPEDITION

There is a historical marker on Route 67 in Madison County, Illinois. It is the site where Lewis and Clark set out in May of 1804 with 43 unmarried men from Camp Dubois at **Wood River**, across from the mouth of the Missouri River, to begin their twenty-eight month exploration of Thomas Jefferson's Louisiana Purchase. This was the most significant exploring expedition ever sent out by the U.S. government. One of the men on the expedition, on the return trip, stayed out west and **discovered Old Faithful** at present Yellowstone Park.

Daniel Boone (Wikipedia)

Both Illinois and Missouri would play a significant role in the trans-Mississippi expedition. In preparation for the journey, the group of about 22 men floated down the Ohio River from Louisville in a keelboat and landed in Illinois Territory at present-day Gallatin County. Also on board was Lewis' 140 pound Newfoundland dog named Seaman. He was adept at killing squirrels in the river and bringing them back to the boat for food. He also warned the group when grizzly bears would approach the camp. They continued south to Fort Massac on November 11, 1803 where they conferred with Commander Daniel Bissell. Here, several more men were recruited for the expedition. They left Massac and arrived at present-day **Cairo** on November 14. Clark then sketched a map of the confluence of the Ohio and Mississippi. Forty miles up the Mississippi they landed at Cape Rock, the site of **Cape Girardeau,** where they conferred with a man named Lorimier who owned a trading post. They passed Tower Rock (which Lewis climbed) on November 25 and Lewis and Clark's boats landed at Fort **Kaskaskia** on November 26 where they recruited 12 more men. Lewis rode on horseback to **Cahokia** while Clark brought the party in boats. They stopped briefly for provisions at **Bellefontaine**. Clark's group landed at the mouth of Cahokia Creek on December 7. The party then traveled further up the river to establish a camp for the winter at River Dubois (Wood River). For five months the group trained and prepared for the quest that lay ahead. Actually, Clark did most of the training while Lewis stayed most of the winter in St. Louis with Auguste and half-brother Pierre Chouteau.

Lewis and Clark Wood River fort replica

Antoine Soulard, surveyor general of Upper Louisiana, provided Lewis with population estimates of colored slaves, Americans, French and Spanish in the area which were sent to Jefferson.

Lewis and Clark wanted to camp in St. Louis, but the Spanish governor would not give his permission, so they camped in Illinois. Louisiana Territory was given to Spain at the end of the Revolutionary War. After Napoleon conquered much of Europe and put his brother on the throne of Spain, the land reverted back to France in 1800. Napoleon was strapped for cash so he sold it to the U.S. in 1803 for about $15 million, roughly three cents an acre. The future state of Missouri would be part of our nation's first territorial acquisition.

Clark noted in January that the Missouri River was filled with blocks of ice **while the Mississippi had frozen over nine inches thick.**

The Spanish flag was lowered March 8, 1804, and replaced by the French ensign. Captain Lewis signed as a witness to the documents in the transfer ceremony of March 9. In deference to the numerous French citizens in St. Louis, the tri-color flag was allowed to fly one day and then the fifteen star American flag replaced the French one on March 10. Forty-five men on the expedition left to explore Louisiana Territory on May 14, 1804. Their fifty-five foot long keelboat, armed with a small cannon and two swivel guns, had twenty-two oars and a sail. They would keep a journal, chart and map the territory, collect plant and animal specimens and look for the fabled Northwest Passage. They reached **St. Charles**, a village of about 450, in two and a half days.

On May 23, the expedition reached the Femme Osage River, the area where **Daniel Boone** lived, although they do not mention seeing him. At **St. Albans** they noted Indian petroglyphs on the rocks. Lewis climbed the bluff, slipped and nearly fell off the cliff into the river, but saved himself by thrusting his knife into the ground. The crew nearly lost the boat at a dangerous stretch of the river called the Devil's Raceground. On May 25, they arrived at the small French settlement of La Charette, near present-day **Marthasville**.

On May 27, they reached the mouth of the Gasconade River where they took note of its latitude and longitude. On June 7, they passed Big Moniteau Bluffs where Clark sketched and described Indian pictographs. Next they encountered the brackish waters of Salt Creek. Occasionally they encountered French fur traders coming downstream after exchanging goods with the Sioux. The expedition camped at the mouth of the Grand River, near present-day **Brunswick**. Lewis and Clark also camped at the confluence of the Osage and Missouri rivers. Bonnots Mill was at this site; it was **the first and oldest French trading post in America.** On June 26 they reached the mouth of the Kansas River, the future site of **Kansas City**. It was here that the group saw their first shaggy-coated bison or buffalo. By July 9, they were at the future site of **St. Joseph**. Six days later, they reached the northern boundary of Missouri.

After traveling 1,600 miles, they stopped and built Fort Mandan in North Dakota. It was here that they hired a French Canadian named Toussaint Charbonneau who **won his wife Sacajawea in a card game**. The "bird woman," burdened with a new born child, proved invaluable on the expedition acting as the group's interpreter. At the Idaho/Montana border, they were the first U.S. citizens to cross the continental divide. During a difficult 11 day trek through the Bitterroot Mountains, the group killed their horses for food. They reached the Pacific Ocean November 7, 1805.

The expedition arrived back at St. Louis on September 23, 1806. Most people in St. Louis had given up on the expedition, thinking they were all dead. The expedition was deemed a huge success as the group brought back journals and specimens and maps of what they had explored.

Lewis was made governor of Upper Louisiana. He returned to his native Virginia, conversed with Jefferson, and came back to St. Louis a year later. Lewis was killed in November of 1809 in Tennessee while traveling to Washington. Most historians believe he committed suicide. Legend has it that his dog, Seaman, overcome with grief, died on his master's grave.

William Clark became the territory's agent for Indian affairs. In 1808, accompanied by Nathan Boone and a group of military dragoons, Clark built Fort Osage, located on a high cliff above the Osage River near present-day **Independence**. For 20 years, it was America's most western military outpost. A reconstructed Fort Osage stands on the present site.

In 1813, Clark became governor of Missouri Territory, a position he held until statehood. After that, he once again became the government agent for Indian affairs. Clark's St. Louis residence was at Main and Vine, now part of the Jefferson National Expansion Memorial grounds. He had a large room where he kept Indian artifacts that were given to him. It is considered the **first museum west of the Mississippi**. The room was visited by Lafayette during his 1825 visit.

One of the men on the Corps of Discovery was **John Colter**. During the return trip he was given permission to leave and join two trappers headed west. During his explorations, he became the **first white man to see Yellowstone Park and its geysers**. He was captured by the Blackfeet, stripped of his clothing, set free, and hunted like an animal. He outran all his pursuers but one, whom he killed with the warrior's own spear. He spent the remaining days of his life as a Missouri farmer near LaCharette and **New Haven**.

York, a slave, was the only black man on the Lewis and Clark expedition. He did not gain his freedom until long after the conclusion of the expedition.

The statue dedicated to Lewis and Clark's expedition is located on the St. Louis river front near the Eads Bridge.

A fabulous new Lewis and Clark Visitor/Interpretive Center was recently built on Route 3 at **Hartford**, Illinois. It is not far from the I-270 Chain of Rocks Bridge. The site of Camp Dubois was probably farther north but the exact location on Wood River (not to be confused with the town of Wood River) is not known due to changes in the river channel from floods. A life-size replica of the fort was built for the 200th anniversary celebration in 2004.

GREATEST PUBLISHING MISTAKE OF ALL TIME

One of the most famous historical photographs of all time was taken in 1948. It is a picture of President Harry Truman holding up a copy of the *Chicago Tribune* with the embarrassing headline: DEWEY DEFEATS TRUMAN. The mistake was made because the newspaper was under a printing deadline and nearly all of the polls had predicted a Dewey win. A last minute check with the paper's Washington D.C. correspondent validated that assumption. Truman, of course, with his famous "whistle-stop campaign," snatched victory from the jaws of defeat in one of the greatest upsets in history. The picture was taken in front of the Elms Hotel in **Excelsior Springs**, where Truman had gone to await the outcome of the election.

Steamboat J.M. White

MISSISSIPPI AND MISSOURI RIVER LORE

Introduction: Not many states in the union are blessed with riparian access as much as Missouri. It is bisected by the Missouri River and is bounded on the east by the Mississippi River. St. Louis is still a river city as it extends for nineteen miles along the Mississippi River.

When settlers first came to the state they usually settled along the banks of the rivers due to the commerce. In dozens of ways, the lives of these people were affected by the actions of Mother Nature and the rivers. Rivers ate away embankments and, by changing their course, sometimes placed a town along the banks in another state. Occasionally whole towns were washed downstream.

Farmers near rivers set their clocks by the punctual passing of boats and sleepy little villages were awakened from their lethargy with cries of "S-t-e-a-m-boat-a-comin'! " Upscale homes built along the Missouri or Mississippi often had a widow's walk or a cupola from which people could watch the comings and goings on the river. Many a steamboat bell found itself sitting inside a church bell tower after the ship was retired.

Most people along the river took trips on the excursion boats at some point in their life. This author has seen several old time melodramas performed on the refurbished *Goldenrod.* And I have fond teen memories of the arcade section on the bottom deck of the Streckfus steamer *Admiral*.

According to folklore artist S.S. Prentiss, when God made the world, He had a large amount of surplus water which He turned loose and told it to go where it pleased; it has been going where it pleases ever since, and that is the Mississippi River.

Missourians have long had an argument with the Mississippi River. They claim the Missouri River is the longest in the world and insist that the Mississippi empties into the Missouri. They also suggest a more appropriate name would be "Missour-issippi."

Railroads replaced steamboats as a major source of travel around 1872.

The section of Mississippi River between St. Louis and **Cairo**, in the 1850's, was called the "Graveyard" because more than 300 steamboats sank on that dangerous stretch by 1867.

When Hungarian revolutionary leader Louis Kossuth steamboated on the Mississippi (1851), he had a famous question. He wanted to know why the people who lived along its banks didn't filter the water before drinking it. An equally famous reply: "Because we are such go-ahead people we don't have time to filter our water."

A similar reply was made to a female traveler who asked a question about drinking unfiltered Missouri River water. "Because it (sand and mud) scours out your bowels."

Mike Fink, that notorious *habitué* of St. Louis saloons**,** had some interesting things to say about aquatic life and the food chain in the Mississippi. "I've seen trout swallow a perch, and a cat would come along and swallow the trout, and . . . the alligators use up the cat . . ." He also said there was so much dirt and dust in the Mississippi that you could occasionally see a catfish come up to the surface to sneeze.

Mississippi Queen- St. Louis riverfront – sank at moorings

Writer George Fitch once gave an interesting description of a steamboat. "A steamboat is an engine on a raft, with $11,000 worth of jig-saw work around it."

The Wiggins Ferry Company had a powerful monopoly on the ferry business between St. Louis and East St. Louis. The company purchased Bloody Island from the Illinois legislature, once it was attached to the Illinois shore.

The Mississippi, called "**the crookedest river in the world**" by Mark Twain, originally was narrow and deep. The port at St. Louis was once 100 feet deep. The river widened as trees were cut down and banks kept falling into the river. Today it is wide and shallow. In the days of the early French, the river was narrow enough for a man in **Cahokia** to yell over to the other side that he needed the ferry to come over and take him across.

The gradient drop of the river is an average of about half a foot a mile along the Illinois and Missouri borders. The river begins to widen significantly when it reaches **Cape Girardeau.**

The Golden Eagle Steamboat Museum was at Beetree Park in south St. Louis County. The two story mansion museum closed a few years ago. It was run by aged volunteers who slowly died off. Most of the stuff was shipped to Southeast Missouri State at Cape Girardeau for display at their museum on campus.

How a river lock works

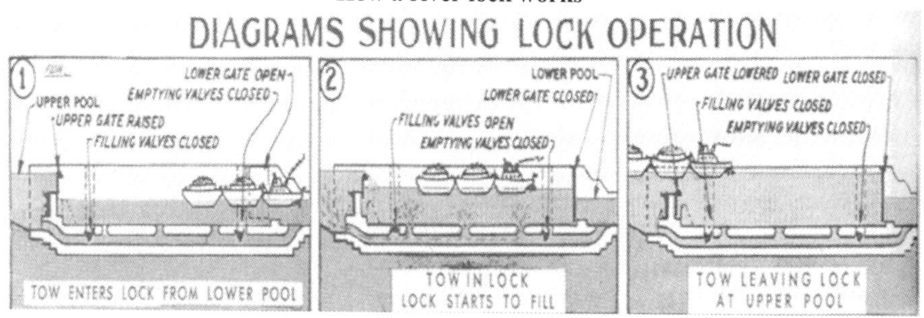

If it weren't for the locks and dams on the river, the Mississippi above St. Louis would be usable only about six months out of the year. The last dam or lock on the Mississippi is at **Granite City** – # 27.

Some area residents think the Army Corps of Engineers dumped rocks in the river at the Chain of Rocks. They didn't – those are naturally occurring rocks and boats could go over them only in high water. The Army Corps of Engineers built a canal to go around the rocks. There is only a lock at Granite City. The existing rocks form the dam.

Did you know there are holes in the Mississippi? The river wasn't formed over perfectly flat ground. Some of these deep spots, called pools, are 50 to 100 feet deep. The lower Mississippi has more deep spots than the upper.

In the past, it was sometimes possible to gain extra river bottom land without paying a cent for it. A group of men once owned some river bottom land near **Cape Girardeau**. It probably wasn't much good for farming, but it made a handsome site for a factory or a warehouse. They were offered a princely sum for it but refused to sell. One day they noticed the strip was getting emaciated. A surveyor's tape found that half of it had been washed away. Now the men wanted to sell but the market was sluggish. The next year the river ate so vigorously that only a narrow ribbon of ground was left, leaving the men much depressed. Suddenly the land began to increase. The Mississippi chose this site to deposit a 40-acre farm upon which it had foreclosed farther up the river. The men now sold the land and made a handsome profit.

A minimum depth or draft of water was necessary for steamboats to travel up shallow Missouri rivers. Some packet steamboats drew only three feet of water. A hackneyed expression said that steamboats on Western waters were built so they could run over a field after a heavy dew.

It was the job of the leadsman on a boat to take soundings of the river to make sure the water was deep enough. He was called a "leadsman" because the chain that was used had a weighted lead pipe at the end of it. There were leather strips tied to the chain at certain intervals so measurements could be made at night.

It was the roustabout who unloaded bales of cotton or barrels of molasses from steamboats. African-Americans were often used for this hard labor. It was the roustabouts who paved the way for jazz music on river steamboats. Roustabouts often played guitars for diversion, but their quarters were always on the lower decks. When upper deck passengers went down to lower decks to listen to them, this gave packet owners the idea of hiring jazz musicians.

When "St. Louis Blues" was recorded by W.C. Handy, "East St. Louis Blues" was on the flip side of that most famous record. I know because I have a copy of that record.

The beautiful, meandering Missouri River originates in the northern Rockies of Western Montana and is joined by the Kansas River at Kansas City. At 2,714 miles, it is the longest in America.

Here is another of this author's favorite tall tales about the Missouri River. A cook on board a steamboat decided to go fishing. He used as bait the carcass of a hog that had died on board. He attached the carcass to the stern by means of a meat hook. This type of line was usually left in the water overnight. When passengers awoke the next morning they were startled to find the boat going in the wrong direction. An enormous catfish had swallowed the bait and was now hurrying home, towing the steamship behind him. The captain, being used to such emergencies, got out his big bore buffalo rifle and shot the fish.

Mark Twain

Here's another. There was one steamboat that got stuck on a sandbar while taking on fuel at **Cape Girardeau** in southern Missouri. The captain tried to get the ship unstuck but to no avail. He remembered that below the deck was a boatload of turkeys for delivery. He had the men take the turkeys out of their cages and bring them up to the deck. Then the ship's carpenter fastened the turkeys' down with staples over their feet. The captain blew the whistle and had everyone on board wave rags at the turkeys and yell, Shoo! Shoo! The startled turkeys flew up and lifted the boat back into deep water.

Did you know early Illinoisans were referred to as "suckers?" It goes back to the early lead mines at **Galena**. Many Illinoisans, in 1830, went up the river to work the mines in the spring, stayed all summer, and came back to their homes in late fall. This was similar to the migratory habits of the sucker fish, so Missourians started calling their Illinois cousins suckers.

An alternate theory is that the lower part of the state was settled by emigrants from the South where tobacco was grown. These poor people were sometimes seen as a drain on the state, much like offshoots called suckers on a tobacco plant that have to be removed or they detract from the main growth.

It didn't take long for Illinoisans to retaliate and call Missourians "pukes." It had been Missourians at the **Galena** lead mines that gave Illinoisans the derogatory name "suckers." These Missourians were themselves rowdy, uncouth ruffians so Illinoisans retaliated from spite and called them "pukes." According to the story, Missourians ate so many of the sucker fish it made them ill and they regurgitated. These terms "Suckers" and "Pukes" remained common for about a hundred years but aren't used much in the current vernacular. Currently, the town of **Nixa** has a Sucker Day where schools close and the town's population swells to 15,000. There is a big feast on the bottom-feeding fish that nearly everyone else despises.

Murray Schumach tells the tale of a man fishing along the banks of a slough in the backwaters of the Mississippi near **New Madrid**. He heard that frogs made irresistible bait for catfish but he couldn't find any. Suddenly he spotted a water moccasin with a frog in his mouth. He tried to pull the frog away but the snake doggedly hung on to its meal. In desperation, the man reached down and pulled a bottle of whiskey from his boot and poured it down the snake's mouth. The snake let go and slithered away. A few minutes later, as the man was preparing to cast his line, he felt a tap on his boot. He looked down and there was the snake again with another frog in its mouth, looking for another drink.

James Audubon, the famous naturalist, visited southern Missouri in 1810 and came up with a tongue-in-cheek description of an unusual Mississippi fish. "It's called the Devil Jack Diamond fish and it's about ten feet long and weighs 400 pounds. It lies sometimes asleep or motionless on the surface of the water and may be mistaken for a log or snag. The whole body is covered with scales impervious to musket ball."

There once was a riverboat named ***Arabia***. It sank in the Missouri River and officials dug much of it out of a farmer's field in the late 1980s (the river had since shifted) and reconstructed it. The boat, and much of its cargo, now sits in a fantastic **Kansas City** Museum at 400 Grand Boulevard. 816-471-1856

Old-timers believed in a myth about taking a fish out of the Missouri and placing it into the Mississippi. They reasoned that it would die as quickly as if you had pierced it with a bullet.

There are places in Missouri along the Mississippi that are lined with fifty-foot high levees. What was the purpose of "walking the levee" in times of high water? It originated from a fear that Illinoisans on the other side of the river would come over and dynamite the levee to relieve pressure on their side. Levee walkers had orders to "shoot to kill."

Shoot the bear at the *Admiral's* first floor arcade – courtesy of Marilyn Kinsella of Fairview Heights

Levee boils were weak spots in the levee at the base on the dry side. Those who walked the levee were on constant lookout for boils – small geysers where the river had found a soft spot in the levee. Levee breaks usually came from boils enlarging themselves and not from the river running over the top. Once a boil was spotted it was quickly sandbagged.

Many of the old steamboats had torch baskets in lieu of searchlights. These were 18-inch diameter iron kettles that were hung out over the river from the forward deck so as to allow burning embers to fall into the river and not the deck.

Many newer steamboats had a calliope. They were keyboard instruments (much like steam operated organs) that did not become popular until about 1895.

Some captains devised innovative methods for plugging a steamboat leak. One captain felt a bump and went down to the hold of the ship to make sure everything was all right. He heard a terrible gurgling sound and saw a hole as big as a man in the prow where it had hit a piling. He yelled to his men and then jumped square into the breach to stop the leak. His men gave him cigars to smoke and whiskey to keep him warm. It took about an hour to ground the ship and when they pulled the captain out, he popped - like a cork in a champagne bottle.

According to Missouri fishing lore, it is useless to fish after a night with a full moon. Why? The fish gorge themselves feeding in the light of the moon and will not bite the next day.

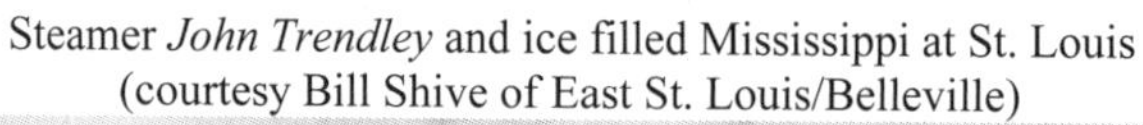

Steamer *John Trendley* and ice filled Mississippi at St. Louis (courtesy Bill Shive of East St. Louis/Belleville)

The Indians had their own version of how Reelfoot Lake was formed after the 1811 New Madrid earthquake. There was a Chickasaw Indian boy who was born with a deformity on one foot, and others in the tribe began calling him Reelfoot. The boy overcame this deformity and became a great warrior. However, because of his clubfoot, no maiden wished to marry him. He decided that he would steal a wife from the Choctaw tribe. When he informed the Sachem (medicine man) of his intent, the wise one warned that the Manitou (Great Spirit) would be angry because it was against his law to steal another man's wife.

Reelfoot ignored the warning and, with a war party, snatched a princess of the neighboring tribe. A great feast was prepared to celebrate the wedding, but as the people began to sing the wind started making its own music. Thunder began to roll and the earth rolled with it. Big cypress trees snapped like twigs. The Great Spirit was mad. He stamped his foot and the ground sank for miles around. He called to the Mississippi and it heard him and ran upstream till sundown. When the Great Spirit's anger was over, beautiful blue water covered the land once inhabited by Reelfoot's people.

River towns in Missouri are notorious for flood stories. Here is one from the 1993 flood. For a number of days, rescuers were trying to reach a stranded family, sure that food provisions were about to give out. When they found the family, up in the attic, they were hungry and exhausted. Rescuers noticed that the flood had brought in a half dozen fish that were swimming about in the shallow water that covered the attic. The rescuers asked why they hadn't captured the fish and eaten them. A gaunt survivor replied, "We couldn't eat them fish. They were fighting for their lives, same as us."

Samuel Clemens spent many a day navigating the Mississippi in Missouri waters. His name, Mark Twain, means two fathoms of water or 12 feet – very safe waters for steamboats.

The word *bushwhacking* was used by men traveling *upstream* in small boats to make progress. They would grab hold of over-hanging bushes to pull themselves forward.

In the 1940s, a **Collinsville** man named George Hopper swam the Mississippi River between St. Louis and **East St. Louis** every Fourth of July.

There is a difference between a flatboat and a keelboat. A flatboat is smooth on the bottom while a keelboat has a long narrow keel underneath, running most of the length of the boat for easier steering. The period from 1790-1820 is referred to as the Golden Age of Flatboating.

There were "snag boats" operating in Western Waters. The *Heliopolis* – designed in 1829 - had a twin hull and a winch for pulling half-sunken trees and other snags out of the Mississippi that were hazardous to navigation. Snag boats had drawbacks. They were expensive to operate; they were heavier than ordinary steamboats so they could not operate when water stages were low; at high water they could not reach the snags.

John Banvard painted the Mississippi River in 1847 with what was the **longest painting in the world** at the time. He first concocted the idea at age 15 when he floated down the river with his father. His panoramic canvas, three miles in length, was on rollers and depicted the Mississippi from **St. Louis** to New Orleans. The opening night of his exhibition was rainy and not one person came to see it. Undaunted, he gave free tickets to riverboat men who then spread the word about its beauty and authenticity.

Although Mike Fink was a real person, the stories about him are mostly tall tales. What was one of Fink's favorite drinking games? After guzzling down several cups of grog, Mike would have a friend of his stand about twenty paces away and he would aim his rifle and shoot the container off the man's head.

Steamboat *Robert E. Lee*

What were some of Fink's alleged exploits? It was said he could bite the head off of a live rattlesnake and drown a wild wolf with his bare hands. There was also the time he went to the doctor, complaining of stomach pain. After an examination, the man told Fink that he had ruined the lining of his stomach by drinking so much hard liquor over the years. Sadly, there was nothing he could do for him. Fink went away and pondered his problem. Then he went out and wrestled a bear, strangling him to death. He then skinned the bear, swallowed it, fur and all, and the new lining for his stomach enabled him to continue his hard drinking.

A legendary feat was accomplished by Mike Fink. He has title to the **longest jump on record**. He once boasted that he could jump across the Mississippi. When put to the test, he saw that he was going to fall short by about ten feet, so he changed course in midair and landed safely back at his starting point.

Mike Fink met an untimely death. His days of carousing, drinking and womanizing were ended by a bullet from an angry husband.

Jim Bowie, who invented the **bowie knife** and died with Davy Crockett defending the Alamo, was an expert riverboat gambler and was the most celebrated duelist of his day. There is a noteworthy story about Bowie saving a bridegroom from committing suicide. The young man and his wife were traveling on a steamboat going from St Louis to Natchez. He became involved in a card game and lost a sum of $30,000 in a crooked poker game. Jim Bowie was on board and talked the man out of killing himself. Bowie sat in on the next game, caught the men cheating and took back the money. He gave three-fourths of the money back to the man and kept the rest as spoils of war. Bowie made the man promise that he would never gamble again.

The most **famous steamboat race** in the annals of history took place in 1870. The *Robert E. Lee* and the *Natchez* tried to set a new record in an upstream trip from New Orleans to St. Louis. The old record was a little more than three days and twenty-three hours. It was originally conceived as part of a 4th of July celebration in St. Louis. There were so many people who bet on the outcome of the race that estimates ran as high as a total of a billion dollars in wagers. The *Natchez* was favored, because for years its captain had held the record. Huge crowds lined the river for miles at the starting point. As the boats slowed down and took on more wood and coal at places like Vicksburg and Memphis, crowds along the banks cheered themselves hoarse, rooting for their favorite. Telegraphers were on hand in each town to relay the progress to news-papers all over the country.

A pistol shot started the race, and the *Robert E. Lee* pulled ahead of the *Natchez* before the crowd lost sight of the boats. Engine troubles kept the *Natchez* in second place the entire race. The *Robert E. Lee* stopped at **Cairo** to prematurely celebrate an obvious victory and then disaster; it got stuck in the mud. The captain pulled it free just as the *Natchez* came into view.

At **Jefferson Barracks**, several miles south of St. Louis, the military there fired a cannon salute as each boat raced by. Jefferson Barracks is currently the third largest military cemetery in the U.S. The *Robert E. Lee* won the race and made the trip in record time – three days, eighteen hours and fourteen minutes. This was more than an hour less than the old record. The race was immortalized in song and a Currier and Ives print.

Several Missouri towns were brought into prominence by the Golden Age of Steamboats, including **Hannibal, St. Louis and Cape Girardeau**. Most river towns became notorious for being lawless, wicked and immoral (reputations richly deserved).

A code of rules existed for steamboats meeting each other going different directions on the Mississippi. The right of way always went to the descending boat moving downstream. The ascending craft was expected to blow its whistle first to announce its intent. One whistle blast meant the right direction was going to be taken; two blasts indicated the left. Orders to the crew were given by a simple set of bells that were rung.

Dance floor of S.S. Admiral – author's collection

Ever wonder how keelboats were pulled upstream? They had a long line nearly a thousand feet long called a *cordelle*. It was fastened to a thirty-foot tall mast in the center of the boat. The boat was pulled upstream with this line by men on shore. The line was connected to the bow by means of a "bridle," a short line fastened to a loop on the bow and to a ring through which the cordelle passed. The bridle prevented the boat from swinging under the force of the wind or current when the speed was not great enough to accomplish this purpose by means of a rudder.

Keelboats were typically about 60-feet long and most were made in Pittsburgh at a cost of about $3,000 each. Most keelboats had sails, but they were only useful in the case of an aft (rear) wind. Other terms used to describe the front and rear of a ship include fore and aft, stem and stern. How did the terms *starboard* and *port* come to be used for right and left sides of a ship? Ships pull into ports or wharves on their left or port side. On the open seas, captains used a sextant on the right side of the ship to "shoot the stars" and determine their position.

The term "packet" means that the steamboat was a passenger boat rather one that hauled freight.

What was the advantage of a side wheel steamboat over a stern-wheeler? They could turn and maneuver better in the river.

By 1820, seventy boats were regularly plying Missouri waters. In 1828, about 4,000 steamboats docked at **St. Louis.**

These riverboats consumed huge quantities of wood, necessitating frequent stops for cordage. One can only imagine the damage done to the environment by this massive cutting.

Bass Pro Shop near 5th Street/I-70 in St. Charles

Steamboats grew longer and taller and were either side-wheelers or sternwheelers. Many were huge floating palaces two or three stories high and a city block long. They provided passengers with every comfort imaginable including deep pile carpeting, crystal chandeliers and rich oak paneling. Some of the trips lasted for over a week and drinking and gambling became popular pastimes.

Larger steamboats often stopped at St. Louis where cargoes were transferred to smaller boats to continue up the shallower and narrower upper Mississippi and Illinois Rivers. The major destination at this time was often **Galena** which, because of its lead deposits, became the **nation's first mining boomtown.**

Early river commerce (Missouri Historical S)

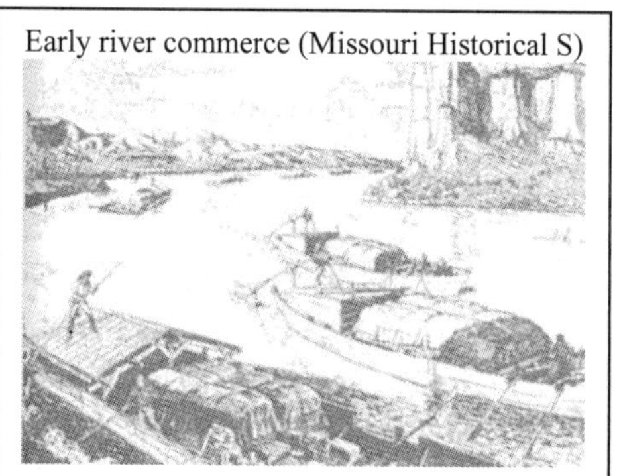

Boys back then dreamed of becoming riverboat pilots the same way they think about becoming airline pilots today. Samuel Clemens was one of the most famous pilots back then. He took the name Mark Twain, which is a nautical expression. Twain, who later became a famous writer and lecturer, once said that in the early days of steamboatin' **he could have bought the entire town of St. Louis for six million dollars**.

River travel was dangerous. Sometimes the boiler blew up, killing dozens of people. There were other boats, bridge piers, rocky shoals and submerged logs to look out for. In flood times, there were huge tree branches floating in the water. When the water was low, the boat could get stuck on a sandbar. Beginning in 1872, some of the hazards on the Mississippi and Missouri rivers were eliminated with the construction of dams and locks. When boats entered a lock from downstream, water is pumped in to raise it to the level of the water behind the dam. Coming the opposite direction, the water is drained to lower the boat.

Missouri rivers are not deserted as steamboats have been replaced by barges. Barges generally carry high bulk items such as coal, iron ore, sand, gravel, or rock salt. During high water in the spring, towboats are sometimes kept off the water so that their wakes will not damage the water-logged earthen levees. Barge workers generally earn good pay and work for 30 days straight and then have 30 days off.

Water is a very important resource. Fortunately, Missouri is the leading state in the nation when it comes to miles of rivers, lakes and streams, compared to total number of acres. Fresh water is needed by farms, homes, industries and cities. The average household uses over 100 gallons of water a day. It takes 65,000 gallons of water to make one ton of steel. Rivers produce about 19 percent of Missouri's electricity. The streams accommodate fish and waterfowl. The Mississippi and Missouri rivers are heavily used for barge traffic.

Missouri has over 11,000 miles of streams that flow all year. About 560 of those miles consist of the Mississippi River on the eastern border. Significant rivers include the White, Gasconade, Black, Current, Osage, Meramec, Chariton, Grand, Current, Platte, Salt, Fabius, Cuivre and St. Francis. Most of the larger rivers flow into the Missouri River, but practically all of them eventually empty into the Mississippi. About half the people in the state get their drinking water directly from the streams and rivers. These waters are more desirable than ground-water as a source because it has less mineral content. It is easier to settle, filter and chlorinate water than it is to remove the mineral content.

When it rains, most of the ground water sinks into the soil by gravity, with most of it remaining within a mile or two of the surface. This is called the **water table**.

The word Mississippi is an Ojibwa word -"Messi-Sipi meaning "Big River."

The Army Corps of Engineers is responsible for maintaining a channel a minimum of nine feet deep in the river as it meanders past the state of Missouri.

Abe Lincoln called the Mississippi River the "Backbone of the Rebellion."

BIG MUDDY - THE MISSOURI RIVER

Who were the first whites to see the mouth of the Missouri River? Father Marquette and Louis Joliet in June of 1673

What was their first impression of the river? It was almost terrifying because it emptied into the Mississippi in an agitated state and it was full of perilous floating trees and branches.

What happened to Cow Island, on the Kansas side of the Missouri River? In 1881, the river suddenly changed its course, throwing the island over to the Missouri side. Charles Keane had a saloon on the island and by Missouri law his sales were now illegal. The matter was taken to court where it was ruled that since the channel had shifted so suddenly, it would be patently unfair to penalize the man. Thirsty Missourians were delighted.

What is the old proverb about traveling up the Missouri River? The problem with going up the Missouri River in a boat is that half the time you have to carry the boat with you.

Since many parts of the Missouri were too shallow for flatboats, what boat was a more common sight? The Mackinaw, similar to a flatboat but with a pointed prow

What was the famous quote about the river being cantankerous? "The Missouri was like a cussed stubborn mule. No other river was so determined not to be navigated. It's the only stream in America that travels sideways." When pioneers were asked which side of the river they lived on they replied, "When I left home in the morning it was on the east side . . . this late in the afternoon I'm not too sure."

What is the old quote about the river's voracious appetite? "It's the hungriest river ever created. It's eating all the time – 80 acres at a mouthful, and then it picks its teeth with the timbers of a red barn that once stood on its banks."

Who is called the **Father of Navigation** on the Missouri? Spanish fur trader Manuel Lisa who was the first to navigate it with a specially-built keelboat in 1811

What was a bullboat? It was a light boat made with the frame of young striplings and covered with the hide of a male buffalo, fur outward. It wasn't very durable but was quite useful for a short trip.

What were sawyers? These were treacherous snags on the river that could tear out the bottom of a boat and send her to the bottom.

What was a typical meal on an 1811 keelboat? Mush with a pound of tallow (fat) in it

How difficult was it to go up the Missouri? On a bad day, progress could be as little as two miles.

What was unusual about **Fort Osage** on the Missouri, built by William Clark? It was triangular so occupants only had to defend three walls instead of four; it was the first outpost of the Louisiana Purchase. 816-650-3278

Where was the beginning of the Upper Missouri? The mouth of the Platte River; at this point the woodlands gave way to the grassy plain. Prairie dogs, horned frogs and magpies began to appear.

Steamboat *Columbia* (Library of Congress)

Men traveling on steamboats up the Missouri often whiled away the time by playing cards, chewing tobacco and spat into cuspidors, sometimes called spittoon.

Where, in most cases, did steamboat accidents occur on the Missouri? On bends in the river

What were the most common river hazards? Fire, boiler explosions, snags, sand-bars, collisions, bridge piers, rocks, ice

What was grass-hoppering? Steamboats carried long spars (beams) and when a boat ran aground the spars were jammed into the bottom of the river in front of the boat. A tackle block was rigged so that one end was fastened to the gunwale of the ship and the other end wound around the capstan. As the capstan turned and the paddlewheel revolved, the boat was thus lifted and pushed forward. Automobiles at the turn of the century used a similar method to pull themselves out of the mud.

Steamboats occasionally ran into difficulty making progress against a swift current. What dangerous trick did captains sometimes use to get past the rapids? A keg of nails was placed against the safety valve, allowing more pressure to build up in the boiler, thus giving the boat more power. This sometimes caused the boilers to explode. The steamboat *Saluda* was blown to glory in this manner near **Lexington**.

There is a story of an old woman who had heard numerous frightful tales about accidents on the river. She asked the captain if it was true that a great many men had drowned in the Missouri. He reassured her: "Madam, I have yet to meet a man who has drowned in this river."

What is the famous story about the Missouri river pilot who went blind? His blindness wouldn't stop him, he boasted. "I can smell my way up and down that river." He said the Missouri River was **too thick to drink and too thin to plow**.

Why did Missouri pilots look with disdain upon those who piloted the Mississippi? They thought the Mississippi River was much easier to navigate and claimed it took a real man with hair on his chest to navigate the Missouri.

Missouri was originally rat free. How did they arrive in the state? They were brought up from New Orleans in the hold of ships.

What method of rat and mouse control was used by Missourians on river boats? Mousers in the form of tomcats and tabbies

What unique comment did George Fitch make about boats

trying to navigate the Missouri? "A steamer that cannot, on occasion, climb a steep clay bank, go across a cornfield and corner a river that is trying to get away, has little excuse for trying to navigate the Missouri."

What was the first steamboat to navigate the Missouri? The *Independence* huffed and puffed its way 200 miles up the stubborn stream to **Franklin** in 13 days in 1819.

Who organized an expedition of four boats, in 1819, to travel up the Missouri and find the pass in the Rockies where the Columbia River supposedly was only five miles away? Major Stephen Long who, in effect, was still looking for the fabled **Northwest Passage**; he set out from St. Louis to make scientific observations.

Schultz Harley Davidson in St. Charles at I-70 Cave Springs exit

Numerous towns were built along the banks of the river and then abandoned. Why then are there no ghost towns for tourists to visit. As soon as the towns were abandoned, the wood was used as fuel for steamboats going up and down the river.

What was the main Indian tribe that lived along the banks of the Missouri? Sioux

What delicacy was served for meals on steamboats? Beaver tail

RIVERS AND STEAMBOATS
(Thanks to Bob Lockhart of Chester, Illinois)

Robert Fulton once tried to explain to Napoleon the concept of boats powered by steam boilers. The emperor replied, "**What, sir, you would make a ship sail against the wind by lighting a bonfire under her decks**? I pray you excuse me. I have no time for such nonsense."

Wiggins' Ferry at St. Louis/East St. Louis

Robert Fulton of New York, inventor of the *Clermont* steamboat, built another one called the *New Orleans*. It was the first steamboat in western waters and in 1812 it made a trip from **Cairo** to St. Louis. A brilliant comet streaked across the sky as the boat docked and blew its shrill whistle. Hundreds of startled people on both sides of the shore came down to the banks **to see if the comet had fallen into the Mississippi River**.

Five years later a new innovation allowed steamboats to travel on shallower waters. The boiler was now placed on the first deck instead of deep in the cargo hold. This reduced the draft to only three feet of water instead of the previous five that was required. With this improvement steamboat travel grew exponentially. By 1820, seventy boats were regularly plying Illinois waters. In 1828, more than 3,700 steamboats docked at **St. Louis**. The golden age of steam boating was in full swing.

One of the more interesting creatures seen by steamboat passengers on the river was the mayfly. Born by the millions along the river, **they live for only a day**. In the larval stage, when they are worms, they feed on green plants and algae on the river's bottom. When the worm floats to the surface and becomes a fly, it has wings and six legs but no mouth. It mates in mid air with the female while flying upside down.

Steamboats grew longer and taller and were either side-wheelers or stern-wheelers. Many were huge floating palaces two or three stories high and a city block long. They provided passengers with every comfort imaginable including deep pile carpeting, crystal chandeliers and rich oak paneling. Some of the trips lasted for over a week and drinking and gambling became popular pastimes.

Larger steamboats often stopped at St. Louis where cargoes were transferred to smaller boats to travel up the shallower upper Mississippi and Illinois Rivers.

River travel was dangerous. Sometimes the boiler blew up, killing dozens of people. There were other boats, bridge piers, rocky shoals and submerged logs that wreaked havoc. In flood times there were huge tree branches floating in the water. When the water was low, the boat could get stuck on a sandbar. The average life span of a steamboat was less than four years, shortened by exploding boilers, fires, snags, storms, ice and logjams. James Eads, of later bridge building fame, earned a fortune by salvaging sunken wrecks. **He did this by inventing a diving bell that enabled him to walk on the bottom of the Mississippi River**.

Charles Dickens and other notables were dumbstruck by the **lack of table manners** exhibited by travelers in western waters. Here is an 1844 vivid description by one such man.

"When the supper bell rang, with a rush, one grand race, and woe to the luckless wight who should stop in his course, he might well expect to be crushed to death – and then such a clatter of tableware, such screaming for waiters, such appeals to Tom, Bill, Jack, and such exhibitions of muscle and nerve as men entered with all their power into the game of knife and fork. It was worse than a second Babel . . ."

What are the decks of a steamboat? The lower or main deck contains boilers, engines and freight. The next level was called the boiler deck because it was over the boilers. It was the main deck for passengers. The third was called the hurricane deck because it was open to the wind. The 4th was the Texas deck because it became popular around the time Texas became a state. It contained the pilot house.

What was the job of the purser? He kept records,

assigned passengers to their rooms, handled complaints and collected fares and freight charges.

Where did it become popular to place the name on a steamboat? As side-wheelers began to dominate the name was placed on the enclosed outside of the side wheel.

What were steamboat boarding ramps called? Gangways

What were the first dams like on the Mississippi - 1907? Built by the Army Corps of Engineers to keep river levels high during low water level periods, wing dams were built by sinking barges that were loaded with rocks.

When did the Corps of Engineers start building the present system of dams and locks? 1930

For years, what was the most popular use of Mississippi clams? They never quite caught on (compared to salt water clams) as food but their **shells were used for making pearl buttons.** The clam meat was fed to hogs and chickens.

How many barges can fit through a typical lock at one time? Nine – with a maximum of three abreast

How long were kerosene beacon lights used on the Mississippi as navigation aids? From 1875-1960 when they switched over to battery powered lights. Since 1980 they have been lit by solar panels.

How many steamboats burned at St. Louis wharf in the tragic 1849 fire? Twenty-three with 254 lives lost. The fire was started by a boiler explosion.

What was the *Saluda* incident of 1852? The steamer *Saluda*, laden with Mormons, was destined for Utah. The captain, impatient with delays, ordered more fuel for the boiler fire to build up steam. When the boat reached **Lexington**, boilers exploded, causing the ship to sink immediately. Eighty-three persons were buried from the wreck. The iron safe, weighing about 550 pounds, was blown over the warehouses on the shore and half way up the bluff.

When did the Corps of Engineers construct a rock-fill dam below the Chain of Rocks to insure adequate river depth in North St. Louis? 1953 - the goal was to maintain a minimum channel depth of 9 ft.

What happened at the St. Louis wharf in 1860? There was another conflagration that took 299 steamboats with the loss of 254 lives.

What are the largest bulk items sent in current Mississippi River barges? Petroleum products; coal and grain come next, followed by scrap iron, sulfur, fertilizer and cement

Buttons from Mississippi clam shells

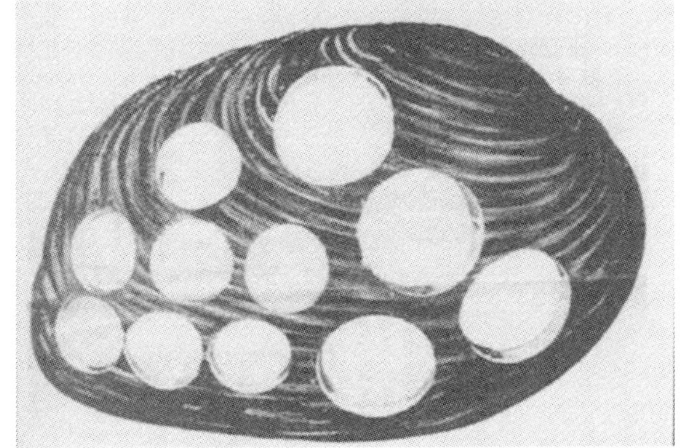

THE GREAT FLOOD OF 1993

When I was six years old (1945) my family moved from 7th Street in **East St. Louis** to 4901 Lincoln Avenue in the Washington Park section of East St. Louis. About a year after we purchased the property, a drenching rain began to fall. It rained all day and night for about three days in a row. Our house was at the bottom of a hill and situated on very flat land. The ditches and storm sewers couldn't handle the volume so the water began to rise.

I was barely seven years old at the time and had great fun sliding on the wet linoleum as the water started coming in through our doors. Our house sat on three rows of cinder blocks and we had a half basement underneath that housed a coal bin and a large coal furnace. My sister and I were evacuated by a neighbor who owned a jon boat. We stayed for about three or four weeks with an aunt and uncle who lived in the **Gompers Apartments**, near downtown. This part of East St. Louis did not flood because it had been raised about ten feet with fill dirt back around 1890.

Mom and dad stayed behind trying to put as many things as they could in the attic while stacking remaining things on the kitchen table. The water inside the house crested at three feet deep. Most of our furniture was ruined. After the floodwaters receded, cleanup and repainting was messy and tedious. I may have been too young to fully comprehend the heartbreak of a flood, but the experience was enough to cause me to have great sympathy for those who were devastated by the 1993 flood.

The Mississippi River, with all its tributaries, drains about half of the continental United States. Flooding is merely a natural cycle that occurs on a regular basis. Unfortunately, we humans just happened to be in the way of what was described as the 100 year flood – one that occurs only about every century.

Meteorologists tell us that this particular event occurred because the jet stream, which normally stays up north in Canada during the summer, inexplicably looped down into the Midwest and stayed put. Cool air met moisture-laden warm air from the Gulf and it water poured from the sky as it did in the old Liz Taylor movie, *The Rains of Ranchipur*.

As the rain continued to fall, the ground became so saturated that instead of soaking it up, the water became runoff into storm sewers and streams. That excess water went into already engorged rivers such as the Illinois, Missouri, Meramec, and Mississippi. At **Jefferson City**, the floodwaters of the Missouri cut highway traffic between the Capital and the northern half of the state.

By April, the river had risen high enough to make Leonor K. Sullivan Boulevard, the main riverfront street at St. Louis, impassable. There were several instances where flooded cemeteries had dozens of caskets pop out of the ground and float downstream. Illinois towns such as **Grafton, Alton, Valmeyer, and Chester** were flooded.

Farmers along the flood-plain suffered crop loss, damage to barns and homes and had pets and livestock that drowned. St. Charles County, Portage des Sioux, Kaskaskia Island, West Alton (Missouri), **Clarksville, Cape Girardeau**, and **Ste. Genevieve** were especially hit hard. Smartt Field and Spirit of St. Louis Airport (Chesterfield) both flooded.

Many of these low areas had been hit by floods in 1973 and in 1986. The damage to crops alone was estimated at over $2 billion.

Perhaps the best thing to come out of the flood was the thousands and thousands of volunteers who braved stifling heat, sunburn, mosquitoes and hours and hours of backbreaking work while filling and stacking sandbags. They did this without pay and their only rewards were smiles, handshakes and backslaps from those they helped. The American spirit of volunteerism and neighbor helping neighbor was brought to the forefront by this crisis.

Sandbags were stacked along the banks of River Des Peres, knowing full well that the swollen Mississippi would begin to back up along that venue. It was a losing battle as over 1,000 South St. Louis residents were eventually told to evacuate.

The flooding continued into May, June and July before it began to abate in August. The Missouri National Guard was called upon to rescue stranded citizens. Rubbernecking gawkers soon became traffic hazards on the highways.

One of the more disheartening episodes was the failure of the levees which had held back previous floodwaters. Swollen rivers can defeat levees in several ways. Sometimes they merely rise high enough to go over them. Often the levee becomes so saturated that it loses its strength and gives way. Finally, the water is sometimes able to eat away at the loose sand and gravel beneath the levee and breaks through on the other side.

For those of you who live near the aforementioned rivers and find statistics interesting, take note. Every year there is one chance out of a hundred that it will happen again.

There is a plaque on one of the 54 steps of the grand staircase on the Arch park grounds. It indicates the high water mark of the 1993 flood.

BURMA SHAVE SIGNS IN MISSOURI

This writer's wife was born in East St. Louis, but she still had plenty of relatives in rural Missouri. Her family usually drove from East St. Louis to visit with **Sullivan** relatives two or three times a year.

Part of the fun of going west was the car trip itself. After everyone piled into the car, her mother always made sure that she had changed into clean underwear. In case of a wreck, she didn't want the embarrassment of her daughter being taken to the hospital with dirty under-clothes. (This was an obsession with my mother as well.)

During the trip Lorna's mother often played various word games associated with car license plates, advertisements on the radio, and billboards. My sister (Jackie) and I did the same thing when we took trips to visit relatives in Kentucky.

Sometimes the boredom of the trip caused my sister and I to quarrel. "Mom, Jackie's giving me the evil stare!" Or, "Mom, Jackie's breathing my air!"

"Mom, this brat back here is making faces at me," she retaliated. It was probably the boredom of the long trip that caused these sibling spats.

One of the things we, as a family, enjoyed on these trips was looking for Burma Shave signs – those wonderful verses along the side of the road. Back in 1925 a liniment salesman from Wisconsin by the name of Clinton O'Dell decided to try and market a brushless shaving cream. Some of the oils for the secret formula came from the Far East, hence the name Burma Shave. The set of serial signs on the highway consisted of narrow thirty-six inch boards that were hand painted with brass stencils.

The first red and white signs didn't have jingles – just prose. SHAVE THE MODERN WAY/ FINE FOR THE SKIN/ DRUGGISTS HAVE IT/ BURMA SHAVE.

Sales were steady, but the essential spirit of what made Illinoisans and Missourians cherish the jaunty little signs was, of course, their light hearted spirit. Along came the Depression and humor was a scarce commodity. It was so scarce as to be virtually a trace element in advertising. Instead of the lapel-grabbing hard sell, O'Dell introduced Americans to an endearing brand of folksy, ironic humor.

When we spotted the first set of signs everyone in the car would read them out loud in unison. ARE YOUR WHISKERS/ WHEN YOU WAKE/ TOUGHER THAN/ A TWO-BIT STEAK?/ TRY BURMA SHAVE.

Once my family realized that the sign recipe followed a jingling cadence, frosted with a topping of humor, we became addicted. SUBSTITUTES CAN/ LET YOU DOWN/ QUICKER THAN/ A STRAPLESS GOWN/ BURMA SHAVE.

Another element that added to the fun was the controlled reading pace that O'Dell established by placing the signs about a city block apart. This heightened the suspense and anticipation. Our prying eyes could not race ahead and spoil the effect as we might have done on a printed page of advertising copy. HENRY THE EIGHTH/ SURE HAD TROUBLE/ SHORT TERM WIVES/ LONG TERM STUBBLE/ BURMA SHAVE.

After years of traveling the roads we began to spot patterns. One was the "accept no substitutes theme." For most advertisers, the idea of a customer wandering into a store and having a clerk sell him a rival brand was akin to a plot from a Greek tragedy. Even here, O'Dell contrived a note of gaiety. THE GAME LAWS/ OUGHT TO/ LET YOU SHOOT/ THE BIRD WHO HANDS YOU/ A SUBSTITUTE/ BURMA SHAVE. Over the years, we read so many signs we could just about predict the punch line ending. My sister and I guessed the ending to this one that read: IT GAVE/ MCDONALD/ THAT NEEDED CHARM/ HELLO HOLLYWOOD/ "**GOOD-BYE FARM**" we screamed at the top of our lungs.

Some were tougher. Mom was the only one who figured out the end to this one. It contained an oft-used theme and played on the eternal fear that a man might lose his loved one to a rival. BROKEN ROMANCE/ STATED FULLY/ SHE WENT WILD/ WHEN HE/ WENT WOOLY/ BURMA SHAVE.

In the early Sixties, the Burma Shave Company sold out to Phillip Morris Inc., and a corporate decision was made to replace the beloved signs with new advertising. Work crews quickly dismantled the old markers and a beloved bit of history slipped into memory.

Some years ago, my wife and I drove to visit her relatives in **Richland**. Somehow, a rustic set of signs had miraculously been overlooked and survived. I could barely decipher the faded lettering. It was one of my favorites. IF YOU/ DON'T KNOW/ WHOSE SIGNS/ THESE ARE/ YOU CAN'T/ HAVE DRIVEN/ VERY FAR/ BURMA SHAVE!

MISSOURI TROLLEYS

I grew up in East St. Louis during the 1940s and 1950s. By then the trolleys in that town had been replaced by buses, but I frequently visited relatives in St. Louis and streetcars were still in service there, so I have great memories from a bygone era.

One of the most interesting aspects of trolley cars was that when they reached the end of the line there was often no turn around. Passengers climbing aboard faced the uneasy prospect of riding in a car that would be going backwards. Vera Niemann (German) of **Fairview Heights**, Illinois wrote a memoir in which she described what happened next.

"Presto! The car stopped. The motorman picked up his detachable seat and moved to the rear, which now became the front of the car. The passengers stood up and flipped over the backs of the seats, which now faced the opposite direction. The entire process took only about two minutes. Streetcars were designed so that the front and rear of the car were identical."

Most St. Louis streetcars did not have this feature. Loops were built as turn-arounds at the end of the line. The most famous loop was at the end of Washington Avenue near the Eads Bridge. The earliest St. Louis streetcars had no loops so there were poles that could be attached to either end for horse hookup.

Although streetcars were often built by the same companies that made coaches pulled by steam engines, the ride was decidedly different. Instead of a chuffing sound of the engine and a jerking noise being made by knuckle couplers as the train lurched forward, trolley riders heard only the strange low roar of the electric motor revving up with a hum that progressively grew higher in pitch, but leveled off as the car attained its top speed. There was also that distinctive and unforgettable metallic groaning sound as the metal wheels crushed down on the ribbons of steel rails.

Milles Fountains at Union Station in St. Louis

St. Louis streetcars were built to broad gauge specifications of four feet ten inches. Standard gauge of railroads and trolleys was 4 feet, eight and ½ inches. According to tradition, this width was arrived at by engineers because **it was said to be the same width as the distance between the wheels on a Roman chariot**.

Streetcars were subject to pranks, especially on Halloween. Sometimes there was a steep grade that streetcars had to negotiate. Puckish youths sometimes obtained some grease from a local restaurant and smeared it on the tracks. The first car to hit the slick spot would stall and ten minutes later the next eastbound car came along and interurbans would back up until the grease was cleaned off.

Another common prank was committed when a trolley car made a stop to pick up a passenger. A mischievous youth would run up to the car and disconnect the overhead trolley mechanism from the power cable with a long clothes prop. The motorman, in his natty navy blue uniform, cheered on by the passengers, had to go outside and reattach the mechanism to restore power.

St. Louis Car Company, located just east of Broadway near the **Baden** area, made streetcars. They even made the special cars used to take people to the 1965 New York World's Fair. This author and his wife rode on one of those cars when we attended the Fair.

American Car and Foundry made coach cars for passenger trains in **St. Charles**. Another plant, near the Busch brewery, produced freight cars for trains. Their **Madison**, Illinois, plant made gondola cars for trains.

MAKING RAILROAD TIES IN MISSOURI

As more and more railroads crisscrossed the state, the demand for close-fibered hard-wood, resistant to decay and rot, increased exponentially. Factories sprung up at various places throughout the state to process wooden railroad ties. Many of these plants also processed telephone poles and pilings for wooden bridges.

Timber from the Missouri Ozarks provided most of the material. Two man crews, using cross-cut saws, felled the trees – usually red or white oak. The trees were then stripped of limbs and sawed into 8-foot lengths. The log was split into 8-inch square sections and rounded edges were squared off at a sawmill. Local farmers were able to supplement their incomes during the winter by chopping down trees and hacking out railroad ties. They earned ten cents in 1908 for each tie produced. The farmer, now known as a hacker, used a broad double-edged ax and steel wedges to split the lumber and square it into shape. The hacker had to be quite adept for the job required his standing on top of the tie while hacking away the edges in order to square it off.

The ties were then shipped to treatment plants where they were bored for spikes and loaded on trams that were pushed around by narrow gauge steam engines. The trams, carrying as many as 800 ties, were pushed into long metal cylinders that were closed and made airtight. Creosote, a preservative, was then pumped into the chamber and the ties were pressure treated. These cylinders were capable of withstanding pressures of up to 200 pounds per square inch.

After the correct penetration had been reached, the cylinder was blown clear of excess creosote which was sent to a holding tank. A vacuum removed excess creosote from the timbers. Pieces of metal S iron were driven into the ends of the ties to prevent splitting. The ties were then branded with a processing date and shipped to the site where railroads were being built.

AMAZING FACT: Untreated wood lasts about 6 years. Creosote treated ties gave from 20-40 years of service.

RAILROAD TRIVIA

What is the most distinguishing feature about Union Station's architecture? Its huge barrel vaulted ceilings inside and Tiffany stained glass windows

From what walled city in France did the designers borrow ideas for Union Station architecture? Carcassone

When was Union Station in St. Louis built? 1894 with 10,000 people attending the opening ceremonies

What distinction was held by Union Station in 1900? It was the largest and busiest in the world.

What is the **Whispering Arch** at Union Station? It is a forty foot archway over the main Market Street entrance to the grand hall. A person on one side can whisper something that can be heard by another person standing on the other side of the arch.

How was mail picked up and delivered from trains in whistle stop towns? Mail was thrown from the train to the depot in a leather pouch and a similar pouch was used for outgoing mail which was hung on a pole and grabbed by a hook as the train went by.

Before Standard Time for railroads was adopted in 1883, how did people with pocket watches know if their timepiece was slow or fast? Each town dropped a large "time ball" at noon from a tower or the roof of a prominent building.

When Sears started its catalog business, how did Missouri customers receive their mail order purchases? They picked them up at the local railroad depot.

What were "milk stops" for trains? Trains picked up milk cans from small towns every morning for fast delivery to larger cities.

Where does the Rock Island Railroad cross the Gasconade River? At **Freeburg**, on Route 63, a great spot to begin a float trip

Why did the metal rails used to build the Illinois Central in the 1850's have to be reheated and reshaped? Our nation's iron and steel industry was in its infancy, so many of the rails were shipped from England. To better fit in the hold of a ship, they came here in a U-shape.

Dave Sinclair on South Lindbergh near I-55 (courtesy Dave Sinclair)

What is the purpose of round domes that are seen perched on top of the old steam engines? These domes often contained sand that was placed on rails when additional traction was needed.

The old steam engines had no speedometers. Engineers made a guesstimate of speed by counting the amount of time it took to go from one mile marker to the next, or from one telephone pole to the tenth one down the line.

Approximately how many telephone poles along a railroad track equal a mile in Missouri? Forty

What railroad linked the town of **Cassville** to the Frisco Line? The Cassville & Exeter Railroad

What was notable about the railroad? It was billed as the "**shortest broad gauge railroad in the U.S.**" – 4.8 miles

Why were torpedoes placed on the tracks before the arrival of an approaching train? As the engine passed over the torpedo it would explode and let officials know that another train was coming in. Torpedoes had lead straps on them so they could be wrapped around a rail so as not to fall off. Railroad officials often carried them in empty Bull Durham sacks or in their coat pockets.

What was rule G? In the early days of railroading there were no rules about employees drinking alcohol on the job. Rule G, forbidding alcohol use while working, was implemented around 1910.

What was the "crane with the broken neck?" It was a subtle device used by railroad owners to "black-list" workers who had been active in union organizing. When such workers quit or were fired, they were given a letter with their service record on it. What they didn't know was that if their record was clean, the letter had a watermark on it that depicted a crane. For undesirables, their letter had a watermark of a crane with a broken neck. Watermarks can be seen by holding the paper up to a light.

Why were railroad "bulls" or policemen so hard on hoboes and tramps who endeavored to ride the rails for free? Because regular police weren't interested, and the scavengers sometimes turned into thieves. Railroad bulls put fear into the hearts of the vagrants by beating them, shooting them or by tossing them off the train while it was moving.

How did the old steam trains improve on their time by eliminating frequent stops for water? When passenger trains went long distances time was important. A unique system was devised to eliminate the need to stop for water. The tender had a scoop mechanism that picked up water in metal troughs below the tracks at designated points. Trains secured the water on the fly, eliminating the need for stopping.

Picking up water that way made a big splash. On one occasion there was a hobo catching a free ride on a freight train that secured water in this manner. He was drenched to the bone by the spatter. It happened in the dead of winter and, by the time the train arrived at its destination, **he was frozen stiff as a board.**

How much water did it take for a typical steam engine to travel 15 miles in 1869? When filling the tender it took and astounding 1,000 gallons of water.

Where did hoboes hide and hitch rides on passenger trains? In the oblong battery boxes that hung beneath passenger coaches midway of the car length. The batteries were needed to furnish power for the lighting system of the train. Hoboes could usually find one box that was empty.

Did vagrants and migrant workers try to hitch rides on the cow catcher? Not often, but here is Glen Mullen's account of an 1890 ride. "I hops on the cow catcher and nobody saw me, and when the engine snorted out, there was yours truly smilin' like a basket o' chips. But I didn't smile long. That was a passenger engine and it kicked up an awful wind. Open yer mouth and she'd blow you wrong side out, and so cold she felt like an icicle laid against your eyeballs. The headlight attracted all the bugs in Kansas. My mouth, eyes, and shirt got full of 'em. One bloaty hoptoad jumped up from between the rails ahead of me and hit me smack between the eyes."

What is the origin of the expression "trolley car?" The trolley is the mechanism on an electric streetcar that reaches up and connects with the overhead wires.

Did railroad detectives have nicknames for tramps? Yes – a *Timber* disguised his begging by selling pencils; a *Wangy* disguised begging by selling shoestrings; an *Alkee Stiff* was a drunkard; a *Shine* was a colored vagabond; a *Hay Bag* was a female vagrant; a *Blinkey* was a train rider who lost one eye.

What famous female railroad hitchhiker wrote a book called *Sister Of The Road*? "Boxcar" Bertha

What name did the Indians give to trains? Iron Horse

What are some examples of railroad jargon? Pike = rail line; hog = engine; reefer = refrigerator car; hotshot = fast train; drag = slow freight; Yardmaster = man who assembles trains in the yards; Hoghead = engineer; roundhouse = garage for storing and repairing engine; turn-table = motorized platform, often at the roundhouse, that turned the engines around; car toads = car repairers; glory wagon = caboose; ground hogs = brakemen; lizard scorchers = cooks; monkeys = bridge workers; monkey suit = trainman's uniform; mud hops = yard clerks

When did engineers ring the locomotive bell? As they pulled into stations and at crossings

What was the railroad man's prayer? "Now that I have flagged Thee, lift up my feet from the road of life and plant them safely on the deck of the train of salvation. Let me use the safety lamp of prudence, make all couplings with the link of love, let my hand-lamp be the Bible, and keep all switches closed that lead off the main line into the sidings with blind ends. Have every semaphore white along the line of hope, that I may make the run of life without stopping. Give me the Ten Commandments as a working card, and when I have finished the run on schedule time and pulled into the terminal, may Thou, superintendent of the universe, say, 'well done, good and faithful servant; come into the general office to sign the pay roll and receive your check for happiness.' "

What is a frog? It is a rail device permitting the wheels on one rail of track to cross an intersecting rail.

Were trains ever wrecked on purpose as an exhibition? Yes – back in 1896, W.G. Crush, of the MKT line in Texas, decided to stage a head on collision between locomotives as a promotion. A place with a natural amphitheater was chosen as the site and with heavy advertising, a city of 30,000 people existed for one day. Newspapers labeled it Crush City. Engineers backed the locomotives up until they were two miles apart. The two trains charged down the tracks with whistles shrieking at one another. The crowd gasped in horror, realizing the two engineers were going to be killed. At the last second, both men slammed on the brakes and the behemoths shuddered to a stop, their cow catchers clanging together. A roar went up from the crowd as they now perceived how spectacular the real thing was going to be. Both trains returned to the starting positions. Once more the whistles let out a yell – this time a death scream. The engineers got the trains rolling and then set the throttles on wide open before they jumped. The two trains came together in a mighty crash. A spectacular boiler explosion followed. Clouds of smoke and dust leapt skyward.

Then tragedy struck. A man who had climbed a tree for a better view was hit in the head and killed by a piece of flying iron. And a piece of chain flew through the air and struck a girl, killing her instantly.

What were some odd laws passed concerning railroads? A Kansas law said: "When two trains approach each other at a crossing, they shall both come to a full stop and neither shall start up until the other has gone." In South Dakota it was illegal to set firecrackers on a rail, "especially if you touch a match unto it." In Montana it was illegal to show the movie, *The Great Train Robbery*. Alabama's citizens were not allowed to wave a red flag at a train if there was no danger present.

What is the **legend of John Henry**? John Henry was a steel driver, the man who hammers steel into a rock to bore a hole for explosives. When the steam drill was invented, he was offended and challenged it to a race – man against machine. For 35 minutes the great Negro, with a 20-pound hammer in each hand, slung them down on the steel, driving them into the rock. When the contest was over, Henry, who worked for the Chesapeake & Ohio, had drilled two holes, each seven feet deep. The steam drill had but one hole, nine feet deep. According to the legend, the effort ostensibly killed John Henry as he died from a stroke later that evening.

Why did railroad men use flares? They were dropped from a moving train to protect the rear. When an engineer comes across one he is supposed to halt his train until the flare burns out. Flares burn for about a ten-minute span.

What was the biggest railroad in the world? Paul Bunyan had a brother named Cal who built the biggest railroad. Each rail tie was made from a giant redwood tree. Boulders were used for ballast. The rivets for the engine boiler were 24 inches in diameter, and the boiler-makers drove them in place by firing cannons at them. The engine was so large that the fireman's scoop shovel held two tons. The gigantic train could haul 700 huge cars at a time. On its first run, the **friction** burned up the rails and the train went so fast it defied the laws of gravity and flew off into outer space and was forever lost.

How did people get killed walking on railroad bridges? Rail bridges were usually wide enough to only accommodate the width of the train. People walking on the bridges were sometimes caught by surprise and couldn't make it to the other end before the train caught up with them. Sometimes sections of planking were removed from bridges to discourage pedestrian use.

When was the famous ballad "Casey Jones" popular in this country? Between 1906 and 1917, long after Illinois Central engineer Jones was killed in 1900

When Casey Jones was killed, how fast was Casey Jones going before he realized that four cars from another train were sticking out from a siding onto the main line? Seventy miles an hour in an effort to be on time; Jones' fireman wasn't killed in the crash because he jumped.

Why was Jones considered a hero in this crash? When they found his body, his lifeless hand was clutching the brake control.

What caused Missouri railroads to start installing sand boxes on their engines? There was a **plague of locusts** in 1836 and, at first, workers tried to clear the tracks with brooms, but to no avail. The liquid from the crushed bodies made the rails slippery. Someone finally hit upon the idea of a mechanism that sprinkled sand on the tracks ahead of the wheels for traction.

Early railroads south of Missouri had a tendency to lay tracks using broad gauge. How wide are most broad gauge tracks? Five feet

Why were narrow gauge tracks often used in mountainous regions out west? Narrow gauge allows for sharper curves.

What were gandy dancers? Irishmen employed to lay track - they often sang and did a little jig while performing their task.

Besides the *Green Diamond*, what other two Illinois Central passenger trains ran daily from St. Louis to Chicago (1936-58)? *Daylight* and *Night Diamond* (with sleeping cars)

What Chicago & Alton passenger trains ran daily from Chicago to St. Louis? *Alton Limited, Abraham Lincoln, Ann Rutledge, Midnight Special*

What two passenger trains did the Chicago & Eastern Illinois run daily from Chicago to St. Louis? *Zipper* and *Silent Knight*

Were *Blue Bird* and *Banner Blue*, the Wabash passenger trains from Chicago to St. Louis, painted blue? Yes

How many stops did the *Green Diamond* make between Chicago and St. Louis? Nine

How long did it take for the *Green Diamond* to make its 294 mile run from Chicago to St. Louis? About five hours

What irritants did passengers on early Missouri trains have to endure? The soot from the engine blackened their faces, and the sparks stuck to their clothing and ruined it.

What was the biggest disadvantage of early strap iron rails? These were wood rails with iron fastened on top of them. They fell into disuse because of their tendency to curl up and stab the cars – and sometimes the passengers.

Were wooden rails ever used on railroads? Yes. The 1834 line in **East St. Louis** that carried coal from the bluffs down to the Mississippi riverfront had wood rails at first. The cars were originally pulled by horses and mules instead of a steam engine.

What is a unit train? A train that carries only one commodity such as coal

What are the cities referred to in the Big Four Railroad? Cleveland, Cincinnati, Chicago, and St. Louis

Warren truss bridges for railroads can be found all over the state of Missouri. What feature is true of a Warren truss bridge? The diagonals are composed of equilateral triangles.

What were railroad detectives called back in 1950? "Cinder dicks" – police at that time were called "bulls," "flatfoots," "coppers," "dicks," etc.

In railroad parlance, what was featherbedding? When railroads switched from coal and steam power to diesel, the job of the fireman was no longer necessary. Powerful unions pressured the railroads into keeping these men on the job, although they were no longer needed.

What eliminated the need for cabooses? Technology – a device called the ETD – it has an antenna on top and it tells the engineer if any part of the train comes uncoupled.

Whose job did the ETD eliminate? The rear brakeman was no longer needed. There used to be five men on a train crew. Now there are only two, the engineer and conductor.

Who is in charge of the train, the engineer or conductor? The engineer follows the orders of the conductor.

What were "end of the line" amusement parks? These were amusement parks built at the end of a streetcar line to encourage ridership. Admission to the park was often included in the streetcar fare.

What did these "end of the line" parks often include? Croquet grounds, band concerts, peacocks, dance pavilions, small roller coasters, high wire acts, horseshoe throwing pits, vaudeville acts, swimming pools, walking trails and floral gardens

How was the caboose invented? It was difficult for the official at the end of a long train to see what was going on up front. One enterprising railroader took a boxcar and refitted it with an observation cupola.

Why did companies that mass-produced railroad ties pound an S-shaped piece of metal into the ends of each tie? These metal pieces were dated, and the procedure helped prevent the wood from checking or splitting. Today they use flat plates that seem to work better than the metal S.

What kind of crushed rock was the most frequently used as Illinois railroad ballast? Limestone

How did diesel engines get the nickname "Geeps?" The letters GP preceded number designations such as a GP 20

What did the letters GP signify? General Purpose

Whose job is it to take care of the paperwork and unhook boxcars? The conductor

Are railroad jobs in Missouri on the increase or decrease? Increase – there is now a school just west of Kansas City that offers an associate degree in railroading.

What did numerous Missouri railroads start doing around 1970 to eliminate the old clickety-clack sound of metal wheels on the rail joints? The rails were welded together

For many old railroads the tracks have been torn up and the roadbed paved over for bike trails. Yet the right of way along these roadbeds is being used for another high tech purpose. What is it? Fiber optics cables are being laid for communication and broad band internet purposes.

What engine type had two pilot wheels and eight driver wheels? Consolidated – known as a 2-8-0; a 2-8-2 engine type is called a Mikado; the designated name for a 4-6-2 wheel alignment is Pacific

Approximately how many tons of freight are still carried each year by Missouri railroads? 400 million tons

OLD MISSOURI SUPERSTITIONS

A story goes that the poet Oliver Wendell Holmes, of rare good humor, was once asked if he believed in ghosts. His prompt answer was, "No, I do not believe in ghosts," to which he added in a softer voice, "but I'd be afraid of one."

Many persons would reply in a similar manner if they were asked about superstitions. They definitely would deny being superstitious, yet they repeat and pass along many strange and baseless beliefs concerning almost everything from accidents to the zodiac.

Jefferson Hotel in St. Louis (David Lossos collection)

As a youngster in the 1950s, I knew from listening to Harry Caray's radio broadcasts that baseball players had their superstitions. It was considered bad luck to talk about the fact that a pitcher had a no hitter going. A certain pitcher was always careful not to step on foul lines going to and from the mound. If a player had a good day at the plate with a certain bat, that shillelagh became his "lucky bat."

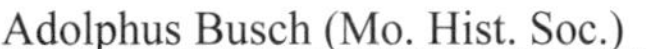
Adolphus Busch (Mo. Hist. Soc.)

My mother had a number of siblings and cousins who lived in St. Louis. When visiting them, I remember being "all ears" when their conversation drifted to superstitions. When playing with other kids, we knew the adage as we walked on a sidewalk, "step on a crack, break your mom's back." A broken mirror was sure to bring seven years of bad luck. Finding a four leaf clover brought good fortune. A man's hat on a bed meant that a friend of the family would die soon. When a prospective bride opened presents at a wedding shower, the number of bows that she broke was a sure indication of how many children she was going to bear. A black cat crossing your path was an ill omen, and nobody ever walked under a ladder.

That foods come in for their share of strange sayings was illustrated by the turn of conversation at the dinner table on New Year's Day when I was a mere youth of eight years. Cabbage was served; whether by design or coincidence is not known. A small head had been cut into eight sections and cooked. Knowing full well that eating one portion of a cabbage so prepared would bring good luck for the entire year, each ate accordingly.

The group was able to assemble a number of queer and hoary superstitions, many of which, evidently, were once firm beliefs. I learned that eating one of several foods on the first day of the year would equally well have warranted good fortune. Had cabbage not been available, kraut would have been just as effective. So would either black-eyed peas or white beans with pork. Even a dried herring would have done. In addition, fish was considered good brain food, but no better than cherries. Eating carrots was said to be good for the eyes. My adolescent brain decided that belief came from the fact that rabbits were never known to have need for glasses.

It was also learned that good-tasting food would spot a garment when spilled on it and that ill tasting food did not do so. Spilling salt foretells bad luck unless some of the spilled salt is picked up and tossed over the left shoulder. Spilling sugar also foretells ill fortune. Unfortunately, all at the table nodded in agreement; no measure to counter it.

Bread came in for its stock of strange beliefs. If a piece of bread is held in the mouth, one can peel onions without shedding tears. Even a bit of bread attached to the end of the knife will assure dry eyes. Eating bread crust was warranted to give one the ability to whistle; if crusts are eaten, cheeks will be rosy. I silently decided that this was simply a ploy by parents to get children to eat food they might otherwise object to. Boys were encouraged to eat certain foods with the homily that it would help them grow into manhood by "putting hair on their chest." "Eat your spinach, Sonny, and it will make you strong, like Popeye."

One was supposed to eat a slice of bread when it was whole, for to break it into crumbs would surely invite poverty somewhere along the road. Two persons were not supposed to hold a piece of bread to break it. If bread fell from the table butter down, and it generally did, someone hungry was coming for a visit. Ill fortune awaits the one who took the last piece of bread from a plate. If that last piece be a biscuit, the diner must always kiss the cook. A woman who cuts thick slices of bread would be a good stepmother. Whether in thick or thin slices, bread is not to be cut while the loaf is hot. A loaf that breaks while being cut bodes ill.

The foregoing superstitions about bread were old ones. A newer one held that an Easter hot cross bun, soaked in water, thoroughly dried and carefully wrapped, assured abiding good luck. It has been entirely forgotten that a piece of dry bread, laid on the lid of the pot used in cooking the cabbage, will suppress any odor in the kitchen.

It seemed that the bite of superstition had no end. I learned that drinking well water would make one tall, just as eating bananas would. If hands are crossed by two persons as they reach for food, they will end up in a quarrel. If tea leaves float, company is coming. Cream in hot tea will sicken you. Drinking tomato juice sobers a drunk. Drinking water rapidly will make you fat, but you can reduce by eating rhubarb and lemon. Food likewise is not so fattening when pineapple is eaten for desert. A listing of the effects of an expectant mother's craving for particular foods upon the offspring was legendary. If the mother craved pickles the newborn was likely to be a boy. If she hungered for strawberries, the offspring would be a girl. The list went on and on.

I often wonder how many of these myths are still alive and well in households today. Do children still tug on the turkey's breastbone (wishbone) after Thanksgiving dinner? Remember, it's only the one who gets the long piece whose wish will come true. And, does anyone out there still think that finding a penny, heads up, will bring good luck?

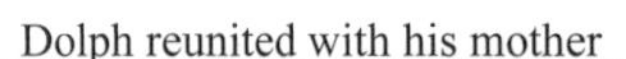
Gussie Busch with sons Adolphus and Peter

BUSCH BEER BARONS

There have been many prominent families whose names are woven into the fabric of St. Louis history. But none can match the 160 year history of a family with hops, malt and barley in its DNA – the Busch dynasty.

It was a saga that started in a town in the Rhine Valley, the very heart of Germany's wine country. Adolphus Busch was next to youngest of twenty-two children born to Ulrich Busch and his wife. Adolphus came to St. Louis in 1857 at the age of seventeen. He followed three brothers who previously had migrated to St. Louis due to poor harvests and failed social revolutions in their native land.

Dolph reunited with his mother

Young Adolphus quickly grew a beard to enhance his age. He worked for a while as a clerk on the river levee. Then he went into business with a partner and their firm sold brewing supplies to the forty different brewers that made St. Louis beer. Lagerbier was all the rage at the time. It was cool, golden light and topped with a white foam. It was either John Wagner or Adam Lemp (both St. Louisans) who **made the nation's first lager** (bottom fermented) beer, probably in the late 1830s. The key to Busch lager's success lay in its extra brewing time and the special imported hops from Bavaria.

St. Louis was teeming with immigrants and most of them found solace in life's struggle by drinking beer. The lone exception seemed to be the Irish who preferred whiskey. There were good profits in beer, which could be made for a dollar a barrel and sold for $8. Brewer Adam Lemp was already a rich man by the time Adolphus arrived in St. Louis.

Eberhard Anheuser was another German immigrant who had migrated to St. Louis. He made his fortune in the soap business and then gained control of Bavarian Brewery, on Carondelet, between Lynch and Dorcas streets, in 1860. Adolphus Busch had two connections to Anheuser. He sold supplies to his company and was courting his daughter Lilly in earnest. Older brother Ulrich was already courting another Anheuser daughter named Anna. In 1861, the brothers were married in a beautiful double wedding ceremony.

After the fall of Fort Sumter, in April of that year, Adolphus, Ulrich and their father-in-law patriotically joined the Federal Home Guard in an effort to keep Missouri in the Union. The two brothers were part of the force that surrounded and captured 900 secessionists who were plotting to seize the arsenal at St. Louis. Neither man volunteered to become part of the regular Federal Army. They were far too busy with beer making and promoting the brewery business.

Adolphus began working as a salesman for his father-in- law in 1864. He was one of those adept salesmen who could have sold blocks of ice to Eskimos. Thanks to his promotional schemes, their beer was soon selling almost as well as Lemp's. This was back in the days when saloons didn't have spittoons. Instead, they had wooden boxes filled with sawdust.

By 1870, Busch and Anheuser secured a loan, expanded the plant, and by the end of the decade there was a work force of 600 men. Busch also made numerous trips back to the fatherland to keep up with the latest innovations and developments in the brewing industry. He read Louis Pasteur's book about how bacteria affected the taste of beer and E. Anheuser & Co. became **the first in the nation to sell pasteurized (heat treated) beer**. This meant that bottled beer could be shipped long distances without fear of spoilage, and Busch saw to it that his beer was the first to go national by shipping it to faraway Texas and to Colorado mining camps.

A. Busch had 13 children and when Edward died of peritonitis while at **Kemper Military School** (near **Boonville**), son August Anheuser Busch became the heir apparent. Due to the rising importance of Adolphus Busch, the company name was changed to Anheuser-Busch in 1879. Papa Anheuser died of throat cancer in 1880. His stock was split among his four children. Son William was now running a soap company in San Francisco. Son Adolph died of liver problems in 1886. Adolphus Busch was quickly named company president. He began buying back stock from other members of the Anheuser family.

In the mid-1870s, Busch collaborated with his good friend, Carl Conrad, a St. Louis wine merchant and restaurant owner, to develop a new brand of beer that would be acceptable to all tastes. It used a secondary brewing process called Krausening. **This new brand, called Budweiser, after the Czech town of Budweis, was introduced in 1876**.

In 1894, Ernest Borchert of Pabst Brewing Co., proposed that five Western brewers, including Anheuser-Busch, form a loose combination for protective reasons. Adolphus supported the idea, as railroad, tobacco and oil had found similar policies profitable. Cooperation was short lived, as, by the end of the year, a price war had heated up in Texas. Such actions were eventually outlawed by the Sherman Act.

By 1877, Busch's lager beer could be bought in faraway places such as London, Paris and Singapore. He built a new office and hired two telegraphers to keep him in touch with the rest of the world. His workers were laboring fourteen hours, six days a week, and were paid $14 every Friday. In 1889, the Maltsters Union won a new contract that lowered working hours and promised free beer during the work day. Most of the workers at the brewery were Germans.

World's largest bottling plant at Busch Brewery (circa 1935)

Busch's mansion was built next to the brewery on a large tract of land called Busch Park. He also had large homes in Pasadena, Cooperstown, NY and in Germany. The family soon began spending their winters in Pasadena. At his St. Louis home, he entertained dignitaries such as Theodore Roosevelt, William H. Taft, Sarah Bernhardt, and Enrico Caruso. A huge stable was built to house coaches, beer wagons and about 30 horses. The compound was surrounded by an impressive wrought iron fence.

Trudy Busch – wife of August III

As Adolphus grew older, his silhouette became more portly. He usually dined at Tony Faust's Restaurant on the cobblestoned corner of Broadway and Elm. Faust had been a friend and drinking buddy of E. Anheuser's. Faust's son Edward became engaged to Anna, one of Busch's daughters. The gala wedding was held in 1897. The ostentatious affair reportedly cost $100,000.

Busch gained additional fame through advertising. In 1888, he acquired rights to a painting by Cassilly Adams titled ***Custer's Last Fight***. The company name was added to the bottom and lithographs were sent to saloons all over America to be prominently displayed behind the bar. Another advertising coup was a print of the bare-breasted Lorelei, that sea-dwelling nymph, discovering the Anheuser-Busch Brewery.

August A. Busch Sr. learned to run the business by starting as a brewer's apprentice and then working his way up. His father put him in charge when he went away on business trips. August married Alice Zeisemann in 1890. They were the parents of August A. "Gussie" Busch Jr., born 1899.

Adolphus Busch Jr. was also trained in the business and the two brothers became rivals. Adolphus died in 1898 from peritonitis, probably caused by a ruptured appendix. Peter, the other brother, went off to the Klondike to search for gold. Peter died in 1903 from complications caused by appendicitis.

Adolphus grew alarmed at the rising sentiment toward prohibition and temperance. Due to the influence of women such as Carrie Nation and Frances Willard, states such as Illinois and Missouri passed laws that allowed each county to decide whether to remain "wet" or go "dry." Bond County, home to **Greenville**, was one such dry Illinois entity. Adolphus responded by claiming to be responsible for turning America away from hard liquor – a positive good. Sadly, his friend Tony Faust died in 1906. Adolphus Busch also contributed heavily to political campaigns of "wet" or neutral politicians.

Unfortunately, Busch's efforts were like that old woman pushing a broom to keep the sea from coming to shore. The rising tide of reform was in the air. The Progressive Movement was gathering steam. Illinoisan William Jennings Bryan made speeches linking saloons with gambling, prostitution, liver disease and political corruption.

In 1911, Adolphus and Lilly celebrated their 50th wedding anniversary, along with 13,000 guests at the Coliseum who were given free food and drink. To mark the event, the children all received mansions from their doting parents. Daughter Anna and husband Ed Faust now lived at fashionable Portland Place. August A. built his beautiful home on Grant's Farm, located on 215 acres.

Adolphus died in 1913 from heart disease. His funeral was, perhaps, the most extravagant in St. Louis history. Over 100 rooms at the Planters and Jefferson hotels were reserved for out of town mourners. Roughly 30,000 people came to view the body. Musicians from the St. Louis symphony were hired to play at the funeral. At 2 P.M., the time of the funeral, all business activity in the city stopped for five minutes. Power to the city was shut down for the same length of time. The route to the burial at Bellefontaine Cemetery was lined with an unbroken assembly of people.

August A. Busch now took control of the company and its bottling plants. About $210,000 from the estate of Adolphus was willed to charity. A trust was established to maintain company wealth. There was a plan to name an elementary school after Adolphus, but it was squelched by the WCTU, headquartered in **Evanston**.

When war broke out in Europe, in August of 1914, Lilly Busch was visiting her beautiful villa in Germany. Lilly made the error of staying rather than coming back to America. Like many German-Americans, the Busch family also made the early mistake of seemingly showing sympathy with the Kaiser.

There was more bad news as five more states went dry and Canadians and Australians boycotted Busch beer because of its German name, When America declared war on Germany in 1917, the Busch family made plans to bring Lilly back to America. Lilly had two daughters (with German husbands) still living in Germany. The girls wanted their mother to stay. However, an aged Lilly decided to make the arduous trip to neutral Switzerland, and from there to neutral Spain where she could disembark on a liner. Once home, she reclaimed her assets which had been impounded by the government's Alien Property Department.

Prohibition went into effect January 16, 1920. August Busch tried to stay afloat by developing a non-alcoholic beverage called Bevo. The name was a derivative of a Bohemian word for beer. The product was legal since it was less than one percent alcohol. A new bottling plant was constructed for it on brewery grounds. At first the product did quite well, but it took a nosedive when the public took more of a liking to bathtub gin, home brew and illegal rotgut.

Eberhart Anheuser

In 1917, Busch built **Bevo Mill Café** on Gravois, near Grant's Farm, where Bevo was served in large quantities. The brewery stayed open during the Dry Decade by producing legal near beer, but a scofflaw public had access to the real thing at speakeasies.

August Busch spent most of the 1920s decade living on his huge Grant's Farm estate. To sate his appetite for duck hunting, he bought 437 marshy acres near **St. Peters,** Missouri. The place was even stocked with wild hogs from South America to give delight to his frequent hunting guests.

August Busch III

He acquired large numbers of wild animals and donated some of them to the St. Louis Zoo (including a pair of tigers), which he frequently visited.

Most of the Busch family, including husbands, wives, nieces and nephews, enjoyed elegant lifestyles. Balls, parties, castle-like houses, the latest fashions, expensive cars and gaudy jewelry, were all part of the trappings of the Busch family lifestyle. In fairness, this manner of living was the earmark of nearly all rich family dynasties.

As the gloom of Prohibition went longer than expected, a generous August Busch was forced to cut back on charitable giving and his huge Christmas parties for orphanages. According to an old family story, August Busch once sent son Gussie to meet with Al Capone at his Palm Island estate in Florida. Capone wanted brewery devices used to tap beer kegs. In return, Capone promised to make sure there would be plenty of demand for the company's legal yeast and malt products. Gussie agreed to the deal and Capone kept his word. Capone died from advanced syphilis at his Palm Island, Florida, estate in 1947.

Gussie always insisted it was the real estate business that saved the company during Prohibition. The company survived by selling off outdated assets such as warehouses and corner saloons. Gasoline companies paid top dollar for saloons and converted the property into filling stations.

In 1930, August A's 13 year old grandson Dolph, a student at **Country Day School**, was kidnapped by a masked gunman. The family was in panic, but the next day a man called and told them the kidnapper might be his son, and indicated where Dolph could be found. Dolph was discovered safe and unharmed near a house in **Webster Groves**. The kidnapper was tracked down by a sheriff and Harry Brundidge, a reporter for the *St. Louis Star*. Charles Abernathy, a black man, served eight years of a fifteen year sentence for the crime.

August A. Busch Sr. died in February of 1934. He was in failing health suffering from gout, dropsy and heart disease. Family members still owned most of the stock and the company was now being run by the two brothers, Adolphus III and Gussie. The quieter Adolphus tended to the yeast business while Gussie ran the brewery. The man who made Gussie's job easier was brewmaster Frank Schwaiger, an expert at the brewer's art who saw to it for decades that the quality of Budweiser was maintained.

Gussie Busch would revolutionize the beer business. Gussie once described himself as the original Peck's Bad Boy. A man with little formal education, he worked hard to build up the business. Gussie's second love was to ride horses, partially because his father and friends had founded the Bridlespur Hunt Club (in the 1920s) for the country club riding crowd.

Gussie married Marie Church in 1918 and the newlyweds moved into a stone mansion on Lindell Boulevard, across from Forest Park. Her ancestry was tied to William Clark of the Lewis and Clark expedition. The marriage, which produced two daughters, ended in 1930 when Marie caught cold and died from pneumonia. Lilly, Gussie's mother, died in 1928.

Prohibition of beer was repealed in April of 1933, and beer barons all over the country were back in business. To celebrate the return of 3.2 beer the company came up with a tour de force of advertising genius – the Clydesdale six horse hitch. A beer wagon was refurbished and painted bright red. The wheel spokes were bright yellow. Sixteen large horses were purchased from the Kansas City Stockyards. Within nine months, the Twenty-first Amendment, repealing the Eighteenth, became law. As a result, Gussie quickly became a supporter of FDR and the Democrats.

Gussie had four different wives. He fathered two daughters with his first wife, Marie Church. She died in 1930, and then he married Elizabeth Dozier who bore him a son and a daughter before they divorced in 1952. His third wife, Trudy Buholzer, gave him seven children. They were divorced in 1978 and next he married Margaret Snyder.

When World War II began, Gussie joined the Army and was assigned to the Pentagon where he oversaw arms production. By 1945, the best dressed man in the army (tailored uniforms) rose to the rank of full colonel. He was awarded the Legion of Merit ribbon. Meanwhile, a few daughters of the Busch blood line were living in Germany, married to Teutonic men, one of which became a German officer. Interestingly, Wilhelmina Busch Borchardt's castle was occupied by Americans and used as a hospital.

Adolphus III died in 1946, leaving brother Gussie in full control of the brewery's destiny. He was the highest paid chief executive in St. Louis with an annual salary of $132,222. He renovated Grant's Farm and restored the herds that had been sold off by his father during the lean Prohibition years.

After three daughters, Gussie didn't get his male heir until his second wife bore him a son (August III) in 1937. August attended Country Day and graduated from **Ladue High** in 1956. His classmates voted him "Most Likely to Succeed."

Anheuser Busch Brewery today (photo by Lorna Nunes)

In 1953, Gussie acquired the Cardinals baseball team. It became a public relations coup as the team quickly became identified with the brewery. Previous owner Fred Saigh got in trouble with the IRS and was sentenced to fifteen months in jail. The former real estate developer said he sold the team "for the good of baseball." Gussie wanted to rename the Sportsman's Park stadium Budweiser Park, but Commissioner Ford Frick nixed the idea. It was renamed Busch Stadium. Anheuser-Busch quickly spent $2.5 million to renovate the aging structure. Ownership of the team also gave Gussie a kind of celebrity status.

Gussie wanted a World Series championship, but he would have to wait 11 years for that to happen. He was also anxious to integrate the team because he knew the Cardinals had a strong following in the Deep South, thanks to powerful KMOX radio broadcasts.

Roy Rogers and George "Gabby" Hayes

By the early Sixties, Anheuser-Busch employed 8-10 thousand workers. August III started out as a playboy but quickly became a shrewd, efficient and dedicated worker. An experienced pilot, he took to flying to his office every day in a helicopter. By 1963, he was vice-president of marketing. Having dropped out of college, he hired a tutor to teach him principles of business administration. He was devoted to his work and became a taste expert, learning the subtle differences in beer taste.

August III met an attractive blond in L.A. on one of his frequent business trips. Susan Hornibrook was a former model, and they were married in 1963. They first lived in **Ladue**, then moved to the 1,200 acre Waldmeister Farm estate in **St. Peters**. After three children, they divorced in 1969, probably due to his penchant for long working hours. He married Virginia Wiley in 1974, and she bore him a son and a daughter. She earned a law degree at Washington University and went to work for the Public Defender's office in **St. Charles County**.

In 1967, Falstaff, owned by Joe Griesedieck, was the number one selling beer in St. Louis. Budweiser became king of the city when Falstaff went out of business.

Gussie had long been a Democrat and contributed heavily to the campaigns of FDR, Truman, Kennedy and Johnson. But after McGovern dropped St. Louisan **Tom Eagleton** as his running mate, he switched support to the Republicans. Eagleton's father was a lawyer for the brewery.

Gussie was close friends with Harry Caray and ballplayer Curt Flood. They spent a lot of time together drinking, card playing and chumming around. Harry Carabina grew up in the Irish-Syrian neighborhood in St. Louis. He changed his last name and became the Cardinal announcer in 1944. Harry's alleged penchant for skirt chasing and drunken shouting matches at taverns finally got him fired in 1969.

Gussie had his moments with Cardinal players. He made Stan Musial the highest paid player in baseball. In 1968, he doled out baseball's first million dollar payroll. When Roger Maris helped the Cardinals win another world championship in 1967, he was given a beer distributorship in Florida. The next year Curt Flood demanded a huge raise, despite a 30 point drop in his batting average. He was quickly traded. When Steve Carlton stubbornly insisted on a $5,000 raise, he was shipped off to Philadelphia.

Gussie built the business to become number one through expansion of plants to different cities and shrewd advertising. **Frank Sinatra** was hired to promote the beer on his television specials. Gussie also turned Grant's Farm into a tourist attraction. He converted the brewery grounds at Tampa, Florida into a tropical paradise for visitors. **Busch Gardens** became Florida's second largest attraction.

Gussie turned Catholic when he married Trudy, his third wife. Over the years he donated large sums to St. Louis University in the form of cash and stocks. He built a private chapel for his wife at Grant's Farm and had it blessed by **Cardinal Ritter**.

In 1971, Gussie, at age 72, promoted Dick Meyer to president of the company. August III became executive vice-president, and Gussie was CEO.

August A. Busch III was elected President of Anheuser Busch Inc. on February 27, 1974, and on May 8, 1975, he succeeded his father as Chief Executive Officer. He became the fourth generation of the family to lead Anheuser-Busch. August III continued many of his father's ideas by building four additional breweries and expanding the family entertainment business.

After the lackluster Cardinals stumbled through the 1970s, Gussie hired Whitey Herzog, who took the Cards to three World Series, winning in 1982 against Milwaukee.

Gussie's young son Peter eventually went to work for the brewery, but after marrying a nurse, he obtained a distributorship and moved to Fort Pierce, Florida. He is happily married with three children.

Beginning in 1980, August III took the company into the international marketplace where it became a major force brewing its beers in eleven countries and selling them in over sixty. To match the dynamic that light beer brought to brewing, August III introduced Bud Light in 1981. The comprehensive and expensive campaign was aimed at blue collar workers who consumed 80 percent of the nation's beer. "For all you do, this Bud's for you," became the tag line. Next, he took the company into sports advertising as he realized that cable television was making sports stars bigger than movie stars. We're talking hundreds of millions of dollars worth of advertising here.

McDonnell-Douglas/Boeing Company (Lorna Nunes photo)

August is also a Republican. He believes the Democrats are always taking pot shots at the business community – especially big business.

The company's Crown Prince is eldest son August IV, a dark haired energetic young man. He graduated from **Parkway West High School** in 1982 and attended the University of Arizona and St. Louis University. He earned a business degree with a major in finance.

Also in 1982, the U.S. government reported drunk-driving fatalities for the first time and, as a result, the public became much more aware of the severity of the problem. August Busch III recognized that as the industry leader, the company could, and should, play a significant role in helping fight drunk driving.

Mayor Vince Schoemehl (courtesy Wes Bokal)

It was then that the company launched its "Know When to Say When" campaign and in 1985, was the first in the industry to bring responsibility messages to network television. That evolved in 1989, when August III established the Consumer Awareness & Education Department dedicated solely to promoting responsible drinking among legal-age adults and preventing alcohol abuse.

Anti-alcohol groups began to target alcohol advertising. In 1989, all alcohol products were required by law to carry warning labels. Anheuser-Busch strongly defended its ads and their placement on programming and in publications with adult audiences. The company continued investing in responsibility campaigns, and now touts that it and the 600 wholesalers have invested more than a half billion dollars on these efforts since 1982.

Statistics showed that deaths from drunken driving accidents were steadily decreasing.

In 1981, Gussie Busch, at age 82, married for a fourth time. He tied the knot with sixty-four year old Margaret Snyder, his former secretary. He was frequently seen at Cardinal ball games wearing a red jacket and a red cowboy hat. Margaret died in 1988 from complications following surgery. Gussie died in September of 1989, about six months after his ninetieth birthday. His estimated worth at the time was about $1.5 billion.

On the American landscape, the Busch family ranks just below the Fords, Rockefellers and Kennedys. Roughly half of the beer sold in America comes from their breweries. The family has given huge sums to charity. Thousands and thousands of St. Louis area workers have been employed by them over the last 160 years. Both Gussie and August III have been given St. Louis "Man of the Year" awards. They are an American dynasty and any book about St. Louis would be incomplete without their story.

Anheuser Busch was the first brewery to ship their beer in refrigerated rail cars. They were also the first to put a "born on" date on their beer. They take pride in the fact that they take an extra step in the Budweiser lagering process through beechwood aging.

In recent years the company has diversified with barbeque sauce, pancake syrup, and Eagle brand snacks. Two of author Bill Nunes' friends work for the company – John Kauffman in security and daughter Meggan in the gift shop.

THE BILLIE BOYKINS AFFAIR

(From *Post-Dispatch* articles)

In the spring of 1989, Republican State Auditor Margaret Kelly issued a report on city offices that she had audited the previous winter. Her findings praised Virvis Jones and Ronald Leggett for their professionalism as Assessor and Collector of Revenue, **but cited License Collector Billie Boykins for gross mismanagement**. Kelly charged that Boykins had failed to collect millions of dollars in fees and had used city funds for speculative investments that lost money. Exact numbers were impossible to determine, said Kelly, since record keeping in the office was so abysmal.

Boykins responded by charging that the allegations were pure politics, but then switched to the race card after **Mayor Vince Schoemehl** publicly denounced her and Circuit Attorney George Peach filed suit to oust her.

Boykins maintained that most of the problems cited in the audit had already been corrected and that a larger issue was at stake. Despite the city's population being nearly split between Blacks and whites, Blacks were vastly under-represented in citywide offices.

In June, the Board of Aldermen voted to reduce Boykins' staff from fifty-three to two. Most of her duties were turned over to Comptroller Virvis Jones. Locks and keys were changed. Armed guards oversaw the barricading of hallways that led to Boykins office. Boykins was forced to vacate a suite of offices off the main hallway and move to a small room in the corner of City Hall.

"It's Billie Boykins today, who's it going to be tomorrow," said **Freeman Bosley**, who controlled 200 patronage jobs in the Circuit Court. (In 1993, Bosley became the first African-American Mayor of St. Louis - 1993-1997. Boykins was finally removed from her City Hall job in the early 1990s.

Billie's daughter, **Amber Boykins**, was elected to the state legislature in 1998. Since Billie also served in the legislature from 1978-1982, they became the **first mother-daughter combination to serve in the House of Reps**.

HOME REMEDIES AND QUACK CURES

"Feeling under the weather? Run to the nearest drug-store and get a 25-cent package of Schoenfeld Kidney and Liver Tea." "Grip left you with an achy back? Doan's Kidney Pills will cure it for 60 cents a box." "Squelch a cold . . . take Hill's Bromide."

These ads appeared in Missouri newspapers during the fall of 1918, near the close of the Great War. Thousands of Missourians were killed in World War I, but the real threat of the day was the Spanish flu. **The pandemic would kill 20 million people world-wide, twice the number of people who died in the war.**

What follows are some interesting examples of our Missouri forefathers (and foremothers) and their efforts to seek remedies for aches and pains, as well as their experiences with diseases for which there was no known cure at the time.

The infamous Edsel

The early French were a superstitious lot and often relied on someone in town who was said to have a "gift" for healing. They usually tried to heal with herbs, spices and incantations. For sprained ankles or wrists, a string with eleven knots was tied around it and healing took place in three days. Babies with teething problems had a rattlesnake vertebra tied around their necks. To raise a fallen palate, the hair on the top of the head was pulled tight and drawn into a knot. For sunstroke, the patient was bathed in a lotion of river water and salt.

Madstones were popular after the Civil War. **The use of a "madstone" back then was quite common as a home remedy for bites from insects, snakes and rabid animals.** When Louis Pasteur discovered a real cure for rabies, madstones quickly fell out of favor.

Ozark folklore said that the splitting of a persimmon seed would foretell in a general sense the coming winter weather. If the seeds reveal "spoons" that foretells the shoveling of winter snow. If they reveal "knives" that is indicative of cold cutting winds. And "forks" portend light snow.

Hotels sprang up near mineral springs. People would go there seeking relief from rheumatism, arthritis, sore joints, digestive problems and all manner of illnesses.

Apothecaries (drug stores) often sold a remedy called **Missouri Anodyne**, its formula supposedly taken from hieroglyphics on the walls of Egyptian tombs. Diseases back then were treated with a variety of ineffectual home remedies that included powdered castor seeds, camphor, snake root tea, grapevine smoked and inhaled into the lungs, and odd combinations of alcoholic spirits sprinkled with mustard seed.

Annie Turnbo Malone, of **Metropolis** (born in 1869), became fascinated by an aunt who practiced herbal medicine. At the age of 14, she moved to **Peoria** to live with her sister. In high school, she excelled at chemistry. Disdaining work as a domestic, or in the factory, or in the field, she developed herbal balms and became a hairdresser. She mixed a concoction and tried it on a stray cat suffering from the mange. Her mixture improved the cat's skin. Human experimentation produced satisfactory results. Knowing white women wouldn't trust her home made nostrum, she moved to **Brooklyn**, Illinois, an all-black community. She went door-to-door, selling her product as a hair straightener and restorer. Her product quickly caught on and she started hiring other women to promote sales. She expanded her product line to include face powder, cleanser and a cream for the treatment of tetter (skin disease). She moved to **St. Louis** to take advantage of sales opportunities offered by the 1904 World's Fair. **Annie's Wonderful Hair Grower** became so popular that she soon had hundreds of associates, set up on a model similar to Avon products. She undertook an impressive advertising campaign and by the 1920s, her estimated worth was $14 million.

IT LOOKED LIKE AN OLDSMOBILE SUCKING A LEMON

When British historian Robert Payne visited America in 1948, he was astonished to see a thriving nation on wheels that had achieved the world's highest standard of living. Not only did most working class Americans own cars, quite often the teenage son worked part-time at the drug store or filling station and, for about $50 bucks, purchased an old 1930s car that he converted into a hot rod. A teen's car was often "customized" and could be identified by the throaty roar heard through its Glaspac mufflers and a squirrel tail flying from its antenna.

Americans have long had a love affair with their automobiles. Many of the cars of earlier times had quite unique features. It was not unusual to see owners rocking their car back and forth (sideways) to disengage a Bendix starter gear that became stuck. The 1949 Ford was notorious for "vapor lock." Ingenious Americans overcame this by using a spring clothes pin to clamp a piece of tin foil onto the fuel line to dissipate the heat build up.

Automobile Club of Missouri, with big thermometer, on Lindell

Edwardsville resident Bruce Brubaker told me his 1940 Nash Statesman had a rear seat that folded out and converted into a bed. The front seat slid forward and the upright portion folded flat. One's lower extremities extended all the way into the car's trunk.

The Thunderbird had a radio whose volume automatically increased with the speed of the car to overcome road noise.

Kids my age, in the 1950s, took pride in the fact that they could identify just about every make and year that was on the road. The only thing to differentiate between the 1953 Chevy and 1954 model was that the former had round parking lights on the front while the latter's were rectangular. Model designs were changed nearly every year to plant a restless mood in consumers which would lead to more frequent new car purchases. Speed and power were highly desired qualities and car pedal-to-the-metal speedometers registered a cool 120 mph. The 1950 Mercury was billed as "big and powerful . . . with the kind of engine that ate asphalt." Since gasoline was a mere 18 cents a gallon (even cheaper when filling stations had gas wars), who cared if the chrome-laden, 8 cylinder behemoth got only sixteen miles per gallon.

Youth in the 1950s customized their cars with fender skirts, plastic white wall rings, blue dot tail lights, spotlights, steering wheel spinner knobs (now illegal), Ahh-Oogaaa horns, mechanical Bermuda Bells (Ding, Dong), souped-up engines, curb feelers, and a host of other products available through J.C. Whitney's catalog. (The inset of the spinner knob often featured a Vargas pin-up picture.)

One of my buddies put a spark plug in his tailpipe and operated it with a toggle switch on the dash. When he wanted to impress someone, he flipped the switch and flames shot out his tailpipe. Most were content to merely paint these flames on the sides of their fenders. Another guy I knew said he put mothballs in his gas tank to up the octane.

Many of these cars had metal sun visors over the windshields so it took a special periscope device on the dash to enable the driver to see when the stoplight turned green.

A few expensive cars of the era had triangular Conelrad markings on the radio dial. Drivers were supposed to dial in these places on the radio for instructions in case of nuclear attack (assuming the blast didn't vaporize them).

My parent's 1948 Chevy sedan didn't start up when you inserted and turned the key. You had to depress a starter mechanism on the floorboard with your left foot. Some of the Studebakers of the 1950s had a feature called a "hillholder." If you were parked uphill on a steep slope, you could depress the clutch in a certain manner that would keep the car from rolling backwards. One of the fancy Cadillacs had the gas tank access hidden behind one of the tail lights. The 1955 Crown Victoria had the option of a green Plexiglas roof panel. Ford's 1957 Fairlane Skyliner had a metal convertible top that folded back into the trunk. The front end of a 1951 Studebaker Champion had a pointed nose similar to that of the P-51 Mustang airplane. Buick introduced the LeSaber with a smooth Dynaflow transmission and futuristic design based on an F86 Saber Jet.

Thanks to the success of the T-Bird sports car, Ford executives had extra money to play with so they decided to produce a new car. It would be named for Edsel Ford, one of Henry's progeny. They decided on a new strategy that had never been tried before. People were surveyed and asked what qualities they liked in a car (such as self-adjusting brakes, a wrap-around front windshield and a Teletouch transmission shifting system in the center of the steering wheel). The suggestions that appeared the most were then incorporated into the features and design of the car. It wasn't a bad looking car except for one major flaw. A large, incongruous vertical grill was inserted into the horizontal front end design. One automotive reviewer's commentary was devastating. He said that "it looked like an Oldsmobile sucking a lemon." The Edsel, which lasted from 1958-1960, is usually singled out as the most spectacular failure in the history of the automotive business. Ford sales plummeted and the company did not recover until the mid-1960s when it came out with the Mustang.

PRESIDENT HARRY S TRUMAN

Truman was born in 1884 at **Lamar**, Missouri, of Scots-Irish parentage. His middle initial didn't stand for anything. As a young boy his main interests were reading and history. He got up at five every morning to practice the piano.

Truman graduated from Independence High School in 1901. As a young man he worked as a timekeeper on the Santa Fe Railroad, sleeping in hobo camps near the rail yards.

In 1917, he entered the military. Poor eyesight prevented

him from applying to West Point. He passed the army physical by memorizing the eye chart. During the war Truman was a Captain in the 129th Field Artillery. During one particular battle, his unit started to lose their nerve. Truman saved the day by ordering them back to their positions **using profanities that he had learned while working on the railroad**. After being discharged, he asked Bess Wallace to marry him. She had turned him down in 1911, but this time she accepted. Truman later rose to the rank of Colonel in the National Guard. His outstanding war record made possible his political career.

During the early years of marriage, Truman and a Jewish fellow named Jacobson opened a haberdashery shop in Kansas City. Jacobson's views on Zionism influenced Truman to make America the first nation to recognize the state of Israel when it was created after World War II. Daughter Margaret was born to the couple in 1924.

Rocky Marciano – undefeated heavyweight champ in the 1950s (died in '69 plane crash)

Truman began his relationship with Democratic boss Tom Pendergast when the party machine helped get him elected as an administrative judge. He then oversaw a ten year redevelopment plan for Kansas City's municipal buildings, done with Pendergast Ready Mixed concrete. In 1933, Truman was given a federal CWA job as payback to Pendergast for delivering the Kansas City vote for Franklin Roosevelt.

Pendergast backed Truman for Missouri U.S. senator in the 1934 election. Four people were killed at the polls, prompting an investigation into KC election practices. After Lloyd Stark won the governorship in 1936, Maurice Milligan successfully prosecuted 259 people involved in voter fraud. Pendergast later went to Leavenworth for 15 months due to income tax evasion.

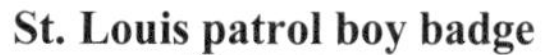

St. Louis patrol boy badge

Truman won hard fought re-election in 1940 and shortly after, was elected Grand Master of the Missouri Grand Lodge of Freemasonry.

After Hitler invaded Russia, Truman told reporters that if the Russians started winning, we ought to help Germany. This was roughly the same thing that George Patton would say at war's end, resulting in his demotion.

Despite numerous off the cuff faux pas remarks to reporters, Truman gained fame and respect during the war by investigating waste and fraud in defense contracts.

As the 1944 election approached, Democratic leaders mulled over the choice of FDR's running mate. Vice-president Henry Wallace was deemed too liberal, and James Byrnes was thought too conservative. Truman was chosen as a middle of the road compromise candidate. When Roosevelt died of a cerebral hemorrhage, Truman became president.

Truman was out of the loop concerning the secret Manhattan Project and had to be briefed on its existence. He authorized the atomic bomb's use at Hiroshima and Nagasaki.

The immediate post war years were marked by strikes and runaway inflation. Truman seized control of the railroads and threatened to draft striking workers. This bold action cost him support among organized labor.

Truman approved the **Marshall Plan** of economic assistance, which helped save Western Europe from communism. His **Truman Doctrine** sent aid to Greece and Turkey, helping save them from Communist takeovers. Truman also issued an executive order to desegregate the armed forces. The CIA and National Security Council were created under his auspices.

Truman won labor over when he vetoed the Taft-Hartley Act, authorizing federal injunctions in prolonged labor disputes. Congress passed the law over his veto.

In June of 1948, the Soviets blocked access to the western sectors of Berlin. Although Berlin was divided into a Soviet Zone and Western Zones, it was completely within the borders of East Germany. Instead of confrontation, Truman chose the **Berlin Airlift**, supplying the city by air until the blockade was lifted 11 months later.

Truman drastically cut defense spending. Many of our ships were either scrapped or sold to other countries. **Truman even tried to eliminate the Marines**, but a fierce letter writing campaign saved that part of the military. These actions left the U.S. quite vulnerable when we decided to intervene in Korea, in what would be termed a 1950-53 "police action." After Red China entered the conflict, General MacArthur wanted to bomb their supply bases near the Yalu River. Fearing it would widen the conflict, Truman denied permission. When MacArthur went public with his criticism, Truman fired him, resulting in another low mark in his popularity with the public. The *Chicago Tribune* called for his impeachment. When Truman lost the New Hampshire primary to Senator Kefauver, he canceled his plans to run for reelection in 1952.

In the spring of 1948, Truman's approval rating (36 percent) stood close to that of current President Bush. Most pundits thought he would lose to Republican nominee, Thomas E. Dewey of New York. Because of Truman's civil rights program, Southern Democrats bolted from the party and nominated Strom Thurmond on the Dixiecrat ticket. Truman countered by working hard with a 22,000 mile "whistle stop" campaign, giving speeches from the back of a train, snatching victory from the jaws of defeat.

During Truman's second term, NATO was formed in 1949, the Communists took control of China (that same year) and he used executive orders to launch a huge probe of government employees that led to hundreds of Communist sympathizers being removed from office. Julius and Ethel Rosenberg were executed as spies. Their treasonous activities enabled the Soviet Union to develop its own atomic bomb. Despite obvious attempts at communist subversion, Truman opposed Republican Joe McCarthy and his House Committee on Un-American Activities, saying that the man was trying to create hysteria.

In November of 1950, two Puerto Rican nationalists tried to assassinate Truman who was living at the Blair House at the time of the attack. The White House was declared structurally unsafe and was being renovated at the time. One of the assassins was killed and the other captured. He was given a death sentence which Truman commuted to life in prison.

Before Truman left office, a senate investigating committee discovered widespread corruption in his administration, mostly by his appointees and associates. When he left office in 1952, his popularity rating was at 22 percent, two points lower than Nixon's after the Watergate scandal.

Truman died in 1972. In recent years, historians have rehabilitated Truman's image to the point where he is now considered one of our best presidents. President Bush is banking on a similar vindication over his Iraq policy.

AMAZING FACTS: In 1922, Truman gave a friend $10 so he could join the KKK. Truman later asked for his money back and was never initiated into the Klan. Truman, at times, expressed anger in his diaries toward Jews and occasionally used the word "nigger."

In 1923, Harry Truman was elected administrative Judge of Jackson County. Two years later he failed to win re-election but found work with the American Automobile Association, selling memberships in the Kansas City area.

BIBLIOGRAPHY/SOURCES

Various programs on the city of St. Louis produced by Channel 9 Television
AAA Missouri: A Century of Service
***High and Mighty* booklet by *St. Louis Post Dispatch* (1993)**
The Library of Congress archives
***Missouri Life* magazine**
***Missouri Conservation* magazine**
1950 St. Louis cartoon map by Anheuser-Busch/Chuck Flachmann
Wikipedia – the free encyclopedia
St. Louis Memories books by Lonnie Tettaton
1939 *WPA Guide to Missouri*. Federal Writers Project
Missouri Film Commission (Univ. of Missouri) 573-882-1046
Missouri Highway Patrol History 1931-2000

Atchison, Michael. *True Sons: A Century of Missouri Basketball*, 2006
Auble, John. *A History of St. Louis Gangsters*, 2001.
Bartels, Carolyn. *Civil War Stories of Missouri*, 1995.
Beveridge, Thomas. *Geologic Wonders and Curiosities of Missouri*, 1980
Boyd, Castro, Early and Fields. *Seeking St. Louis: 1670-2000*
Branson, Edward. *The Geology of Missouri*, U of M, 1944.
Burnett, Betty. *St. Louis in World War II*, 1987.
Burns, Robert. *Big Red*, 1975.
Compton and Fry. *Pictorial Atlas of St. Louis* – 1875.
Corbett, Katherine. *In Her Place: A Guide to St. Louis Women's History*, U of M Press, 1999.
Curtiss, Skip. *Why'd They Name it That*? 1992.
Curtiss, Skip. *The Missouri U.S. 66 Tour Book*, 1994
DeLano, Patty and Johnson, Cathy. *Missouri: Off the Beaten Path*
Dyer, Alvin. *Refiner's Fire: Mormon History in Missouri, 1969.*
Earngey, Bill. *Missouri Roadsides*, 1995.
Ehrlich, Walter. *Zion in the Valley: St. Louis Jewish Community*, 1997
Elz, Ron. *1001 St. Louis Trivia Questions*, 1998.
Faherty, William. *Centuries of St. Louis*, 2007.
Faherty, William. *St. Louis German Catholics*, 1998.
Faherty, William. *St. Louis Irish*, 2001.
Faherty, William. *A Concise History of St. Louis*, 2004.
Fisher, John. *Catfish, Fiddles, Mules, and More: Missouri's State Symbols*, 2003
Fox, Tim and Sandweiss, Eric. *Where we Live: A Guide to St. Louis Communities*, 1995.
Garner, Doug. *The Forest Park Highlands*, 2007.
Goforth, Alan. *Tales From the Missouri Tigers*, 2003.
Graham, Shellee. *Tales From the Coral Court*, 2000.
Hannon, Robert. *St. Louis: It's Neighborhoods and Neighbors*, 1986.
Horgan, James. *City of Flight*: St. Louis Aviation, 1984.
Horrigan, Kevin. *White Rat*, 1987.
Hotchner, A.E. *King of the Hill: Boyhood memories of St. Louis*
Humphrey, Loren. *Quinine and Quarantine: Missouri Medical History* 2000
Kirschten, Ernest. *Catfish and Crystal*, (St. Louis history) 1960.
Kuban, Bob. *My Side of the Bandstand*, 2006
Larson, Captain Ron. *Upper Mississippi River History*, 1998
Larsen, Lawrence. *History of Missouri 1953-2003*, U of M
Lossos, David. *Irish St. Louis*, 2004
Lossos, David. *Now and Then* – St. Louis, 2005
Lossos, David. *St. Louis Casa Loma Ballroom*. 2005
MacLean, Harry. *In Broad Daylight* (Skidmore murder), 1988.
Magnan, William and Marcella. *Streets of St. Louis*, 1994.
Maracek, Greg. *Full Court* (St. Louis Hawks) 2006.
Matysik, Larry. *Wrestling at the Chase*, 2005.
McClure, Clarence and Potter, Marguerite. *Missouri: its Geography, History, Government*, 1949.
McReynolds, Edwin. *Missouri: A History of the Crossroads State*
Montesi, Albert and Deposki, Richard, *Union Station*, 2002.
Moore, John C. *Confederate Military History of Missouri*
Nagel, Paul. *Missouri: A History*, 1988.
Offutt, Jason. *Haunted Missouri*, 2000.
O'Neil, Tim and Curzon, Julian. *The Great Cyclone*, 1997.
Parrish, William, et al. *Missouri: Heart of the Nation*, 2005
Priesmeyer, Scottie. *The Cheaters: The Walter Scott Murder*, 1997
Priddy, *The Wide Missouri*: 3 volumes
Primm, James. *Lion of the Valley*, 1990.
Rains, Sally and Rob. *The Mighty 'MOX*, 2000.
Ramsey, Robert. *Our Storehouse of Missouri Place Names*. 1973
Rennie, Ross. *St. Louis Blues*, 1990.
Rogers, Ann. *Lewis and Clark in Missouri*, 2002.
Rother, Hubert and Charlotte, *Lost Caves of St. Louis*, 2004.
Scharf, Thomas. *History of St. Louis City and County*, 1883.
Scott, Quinta and Howard Miller. *The Eads Bridge*, U of M Press, 1999.
Spencer, Thomas. *The Other Missouri*. 2005.
Spencer, Thomas. *St. Louis Veiled Prophet Celebration: 1877-1995*, U of M Press, 2000.
Taylor, Troy. (Bill Nunes' Decatur, Illinois, friend) *Haunted St. Louis*, 2002.
Tettaton, Lonnie. *The Great St. Louis Adventure*. 2006.
Unklesbay, A.G. and Vineyard. *Missouri Geology*, 1992.
Viets, Elaine and Scott, Quinta. *Home on the River*, 1995.
Viets, Elaine. *Urban Affairs*, 1988.
Viles, Jonas. *A History of Missouri*, 1933.
Waugh, Daniel. *The Egan Rats*, 2007.
Wayman, Norbury. *St. Louis: Its Neighborhoods*, 1978.
Weiss, William. *St. Louis: Past, Present, Future*, 2005
Williams, Walter, *Missouri History*: 5 volumes
Williams, Walter, *The State of Missouri in 1904*, 1904.
Young, Josh. *Missouri Curiosities*, 2006.